MW00809374

My Daily Bible Blessings

comfort from

From

the Scriptures

to Recall

My Daily Bible Reading

Yvonne Waite

August - 2014

By
Yvonne S. Waite

Edited By
Pastor D. A. Waite, Th.D., Ph.D.
Director, THE BIBLE FOR TODAY, INCORPORATED

900 Park Ave.
Collingswood, N.J., 08108
U.S.A.

ISBN 978-1-56848-079-4

Published By
THE BIBLE FOR TODAY PRESS
900 Park Avenue
Collingswood, New Jersey 08108
USA

Church Phone: 856-854-4747
BFT Phone: 856-854-4452
Orders: 1-800-John 10:9
e-mail: BFT@BibleForToday.org
Website: www.BibleForToday.org.
Fax: 856-854-2464

BFT #4009

Cover Photograph, Cover, and Format by **TOP**:
The **O**ld **P**aths Publications, Inc.
Directors: H. D. & Patricia Williams
142 Gold Flume Way
Cleveland, GA 30528
Web: www.theoldpathspublications.com
Email: TOP@theoldpathspublications.com
Jeremiah 6:16

1.0

THE FOREWORD

The Method. In this book, *My Daily Bible Blessings*, Yvonne Sanborn Waite has taken time, as she read through the Bible, from Genesis through Revelation (at the rate of 85 verses per day) to select a few verses that blessed her soul. She then wrote down her thoughts about these verses to share them with others.

The Purpose. At first, Mrs. Waite just wanted to write down her blessings so that she could look back on them at the end of the year and see what the Lord had given her. There was no thought about making these into a book. That was suggested by a dear friend who saw great value in her words and thought others should also read them.

The Audience. The book has been written for her children, so that when she goes Home to be with the Lord, they will have something to remember her by. Certainly, women of all ages can profit from her work. She does not believe in women preachers. This is a woman to woman book. She believes that mothers, grandmothers, great-grandmothers, aunts, sisters, daughters and ladies of all ages and backgrounds might like to share in the blessings that the Lord gave to her as she read His Words faithfully every day of the year.

The Writer. This writer is a godly Christian lady, now 84 years of age, who has walked, step-by-step, with her Saviour, the Lord Jesus Christ since she was 10. By no means was she just born "yesterday." She is a woman of experience in the Words and ways of the Lord. As of this writing, she has been married since 1948 to one husband. She is the mother of five children– four sons and one daughter. She is the grandmother of eight grandchildren. She is the great-grandmother of eleven great-grandchildren. As you can read in her book, she has many ups and downs in her Christian life. Because of this, she has been made aware of the many joys and sorrows that other Christians endure. She adds, as she writes, touches of good humor as well.

The Writing. Though we have tried our best to be Biblically accurate, and to conform to proper spelling and punctuation throughout the book (having been helped by many who are named elsewhere), as in any book that is printed, there might be some things that we did not see that need changing. If you see some, please let us know, and we can make the corrections in our next edition.

Sincerely yours for God's Words,

D. A. Waite

Pastor D. A. Waite, Th.D., Ph.D.
(Mrs. Waite's husband since August, 1948)

DAW/w

i

THE AUTHOR'S DEDICATION

I dedicate this book to my *"life's work,"*
My children–all five of them,
Don Jr., David, Dick, Dianne, & Daniel,
They, along with their father, are the most precious people in my life,
together with my dear grandchildren and precious great grands.
May something that I have written be used to help them
have a closer walk with the Lord Jesus Christ.

"THEN I SAW HIM"
by Yvonne S. Waite

Then I saw him
Walking in beauty and bright,
Walking in beauty and splendor,
Walking in Heavenly Light.

Tall and dressed in kindness,
Dressed in glory and grace,
Dressed overwhelmingly happy,
Dressed magnificently faced.

Heaven his Home for the ages,
Heaven his place in the sky,
Heaven secure and protected,
Heaven protected and high.

Then I saw him
My son, vibrant and cured,
Mature and secure in his manner
With Jesus, his Saviour and Lord.

(I wrote this poem first at the death of Pastor Bob Steward a few years ago.
When David died, I thought of our son as I read the words again. They were true
for David, too. They were a comfort for me. How good for all pain and imperfection
to dissolve when death took him to Glory and its perfect perfection.)

THE AUTHOR'S PREFACE

"BLESS THE LORD, O MY SOUL:
AND ALL THAT IS WITHIN ME,
BLESS HIS HOLY NAME.
Bless the LORD, O my soul, and forget not all his benefits:
Bless the LORD, all his works in all places of his dominion:
Bless the LORD, O my soul."
(Psalm 103:1-2, 22)

BLESS THE LORD, O MY SOUL!

Recently I had some minor surgery. Because it had been my practice to quote a Scripture verse prior to being put to sleep for a procedure, I searched my heart for a Bible verse to take with me into the operating room. All that came to mind was *"BLESS THE LORD, O MY SOUL, AND ALL THAT IS WITHIN ME, BLESS HIS HOLY NAME!"* At the time, I thought it was a strange verse to meditate upon prior, during, and after surgery. BUT IT WAS MY VERSE; THE VERSE GOD GAVE ME FOR THAT TIME PERIOD OF MY LIFE!

MY GRANDMOTHER'S FAVORITE PSALM

Psalm 103 had been my grandmother's favorite psalm in her old age. She pondered it. She memorized it. That was the passage her pastor used at her memorial service. I wondered why the Lord brought it to my mind on the morning of my surgery. Of all the Bible verses that I knew, why would that particular one be mine that day?

WRITING "MY *DAILY BIBLE BLESSINGS*"

As the days went by, I remembered that all that year, and the year before, I had been writing down my own personal *DAILY BLESSING.* Those *"Blessings"* had come from my very soul! They were based upon my own, personal daily Bible reading! Indeed, *God had blessed my soul all my days while writing "MY DAILY BIBLE BLESSINGS."* Yes, He has blessed my soul!

"YEARLY BIBLE READING IN ACTION"

Years ago, as a college student, my husband-to-be, D. A. Waite, formulated a daily Bible reading plan that would help the Bible reader to read the Bible in one year. He called this plan *"YEARLY BIBLE READING IN ACTION."* If a person would read eighty-five verses a day, that person could read his or her Bible in one year–no problem!

v

Hundreds of Bible readers have worked this plan to their spiritual benefit. **The Yearly Bible Reader would start the New Year with the book of *Genesis* and end, that same year, finishing his Bible by reading the book of *Revelation*.** I have done this for more years than I can remember.

MY BIBLE READING BECAME A *"FORM"*

About three years ago, the thought came to me with such conviction that my DAILY BIBLE READING was becoming a *"form,"* or a personal requirement, without much meaning or spiritual benefit to my soul (II Timothy 3:5). I was bothered by this. So, I decided—as I read my eighty-five verses a day—that I would ask the Lord to give me *one special, personal "blessing"* each day. As I *daily* found that *"blessing,"* I would go to my computer, study the verse or verses, type them, and print them out on paper. That way I would know what my *"Daily Bible Blessing"* was, and I would be able to see some *personal benefit* from reading my Bible every day for that year.

GATHERING A PERSONAL *DAILY BLESSING*

This gathering of a *"personal blessing"* was no easy task. Like Ruth of old, I would "glean" from my Bible some daily spiritual food (Ruth 2:2)! Some days, the passage was very difficult. I had to study to understand it. Sometimes I would discuss the verses with my husband. Other days, the Lord would bring to mind experiences in my own life to illuminate the Bible to me in a very personal way. I must say, it truly became *A DAILY BIBLE BLESSING FROM MY DAILY BIBLE READING.*

I NEEDED COMFORT FOR MY SOUL

I had no idea that I was writing a book! It was not my intention at all! At first, *"My Daily Bible Blessing"* was a selfish one. *It was for me only.* I needed God to speak to me daily. Our second-born son had died suddenly the previous year. I missed him. I needed God to comfort my soul. Then I thought that I could daily read aloud, *"My Daily Bible Blessing"* on a CD, to help other women, who would call upon God with a personal need, such as I had. I knew in my heart that other women, like the wives of the Patriarchs of old, needed God's grace, strength, peace, and comfort poured into their lives, too.

MY MOTHER'S LITTLE RED BOOK

The year before I wrote *MY DAILY BIBLE BLESSINGS*, I rediscovered a little red book. It was filled with sayings, thoughts, and Biblical blessings from my mother's dedicated pen. It was in her own handwriting! Her name is Gertrude G. Sanborn (1904-1988). You may remember her. **She is referred to in *MY DAILY BLESSINGS* as *"ggs."*** I began reading her *little red book* at the beginning of the year 2008. I read one devotional comment every day of that year. What a blessing they were, to my soul! What a comfort! You see, it was in April of the year 2008 that our second-born son, David William Waite, went *"home"* to be *"with the Lord."* Though he had many medical problems, his death was sudden and unexpected! Mother's words comforted me daily all year! WHAT A DAILY BLESSING!

THE "GGS" WORDS COMFORT AND ENRICH MY SOUL!

It is not unusual for Gertrude G. Sanborn's (ggs) words to comfort and enrich my soul! During her lifetime, she wrote over three hundred poems. They are based on her life-experiences with the Lord Jesus Christ. **Several years ago, my husband and I, and our family, compiled her (ggs') poems in a beautifully bound book titled *"WITH TEARS IN MY HEART."*** Perhaps you have one of those books on your coffee table. Mother knew her Bible! In the stresses and disappointments of life, she wrote poems. From my early childhood, her writings have ministered to me in all circumstances. Mother's poems reflected her daily walk with the Lord Jesus Christ. *Praise God for such a mother!*

THANK YOU, MOTHER, FOR BLESSING ME

I kept reading my mother's *little red book*. It continued to bless my heart. Her words on death and life from the Words of God bathed my mind. She understood my loss! She, too, had an adult child die—my sister. She had disappointments in people, in life, in family, and in circumstances, too. She found comfort and peace from God's book and wrote about it. As I read from her *little red book*, it was as if my mother were speaking to me face to face. Her words, from her Bible, came from her heart to mine. My, how I needed them! So why should not I share *the blessings* from her *little red book* with you? That is why a meditation from "ggs" is found at the end of every one of *"MY DAILY BIBLE BLESSINGS."* Now you, too, can be enriched! *"She being dead yet speaketh"* (Hebrews 11:4). **THANK YOU, MOTHER, FOR BLESSING MY SOUL ONCE AGAIN! MAY YOU READERS BE BLESSED ALSO!**

MY "BLESSINGS" E-MAILED AROUND THE WORLD

With much determination and dedication in response to my request, our son, Daniel Stephen Waite, e-mailed *"MY DAILY BIBLE BLESSINGS"* to all my BIBLE FOR TODAY E-MAIL FRIENDS. This he did for the whole year of 2010. I have thanked him privately for doing this, but want to thank him publicly today for such an endeavor! It was a sacrifice of his time and talents to do so. He sent *"MY DAILY BIBLE BLESSINGS"* into the homes of hundreds of people—especially women. ***THANK YOU, DAN!***

AN UNEXPECTED BLESSING

The *"BLESSINGS"* **multiplied into others' lives in ways that I had no idea or understanding.** Though many wanted to be dropped from the list, others found *"blessings"* from my words. One man from Singapore sent me $500 to support these devotional *blessings.* ***THANK YOU, MR. B!*** (I had no idea what to do with that money, <u>but was thankful</u>, and put it aside. Later it was plain to me that God had provided some of the printing fees for my future-published book that I did not realize I was writing.)

THE FIRST PROOFREADER

JULIE MONAGHAN, from Pennsylvania, was the first to proofread *"My Daily Bible Blessings."* She looked up verses, and found factual and spelling errors. **THANK YOU, JULIE.** It was time consuming for her. It was such a task! A labor of love! I was grateful! It was from that corrected copy that our son e-mailed *"THE DAILY BIBLE BLESSINGS"* around the world. At that time, several friends said the *"Blessings"* should be put in a book. I paid no heed.

"MY DAILY BIBLE BLESSINGS" # IN A BOOK FORMAT

Then **PROOFREADER AND BOOK EDITOR, PATRICIA WILLIAMS, of "THE OLD PATHS PUBLICATIONS," in Cleveland, Georgia, encouraged me to put** *"My Daily Bible Blessings"* **into a book.** I thought to myself, *"Maybe!"* There was no *"maybe"* in her vocabulary! She formatted my hundreds of words into a book! She spent hours with my mother's (ggs) daily meditations, arranging them in poetic order at the end of each *"BLESSING."* It was then, that I came to the realization, *I really* **had** *written a book* without knowing it! Immediately proofreading went into full orbit! *THANK YOU, PAT!*

WRITING MAKES AN EXACT WOMAN

ANNE MARIE NOYLE, from Ontario, Canada, has been a gift from God. Tirelessly, she has read and reread, with a *figurative fine-tooth-comb*, finding mistakes on every page with every reading. Errors were discovered! More errors were found! Mistakes unendingly kept showing up! It was not an easy assignment! Sir Francis Bacon (1561-1626) was correct when he wrote, back in the sixteen-hundreds, *"Reading maketh a full man, conference a ready man, and WRITINGS AN EXACT MAN."* **THANK YOU, ANNE MARIE.**

MY HUSBAND PROOFREAD, TOO

An added blessing to me, *personally,* **is that my husband, PASTOR D. A. WAITE, Th.D., Ph.D., proofread my words, as well as inserting the plethora of corrections into the body of the book itself.** <u>I was touched that he would put aside</u>

<u>his own work to edit mine</u>. He could see that I was becoming overcome with correcting! His help was an overwhelming asset! Just to have him care enough to actually take hours and days to painstakingly look over the thousands of my words blessed my heart! **THANK YOU, DEAR HUSBAND FOR EDITING! THANK YOU FOR CARING! I THANK ALL THESE PROOF READERS AND EDITORS COLLECTIVELY AS WELL AS INDIVIDUALLY.** Without their help, my words would be a jumbled mess!

DEAR READER, I THANK GOD FOR YOU!

THEN YOU, DEAR READER—I THANK THE LORD FOR YOU! Your encouragement to me has been more than I ever expected. Mostly I have written "MY DAILY BIBLE BLESSINGS" for me and then for other spiritually needy women. At the start of this venture, I had no idea that anyone else would want to read these *"BLESSINGS"*–let alone to read them from a **real book**!

BLESS THE LORD, O MY SOUL!

Let me tell you another thing! My Grandmother Barker's verse has helped me in many ways since the day I took it as my own. When I've been distressed, I have whispered, *"Bless the Lord, O my soul; and all that is within me, bless His holy name!"* On the days that I have forgotten to let my soul *be "blessed"* by Him, life was harder for me, and the cares of this world overtook me. I must remember not to forget to permit my soul to be blessed by Him! **I WANT TO TAKE THIS TIME NOW TO PERSONALLY THANK OUR DAUGHTER, AUDREY DIANNE COSBY**, FOR HER LISTENING EAR AND SPIRITUAL COUNSEL DURING THE DIFFICULT EDITING PROCESS OF PUTTING THS BOOK TOGETHER. Some of my problems will still be with me—that is true—but my soul will be blessed in spite of those problems as long as I keep my eyes fixed on Jesus and *"lean not unto mine own understanding"* (Proverbs 3:5)! **THANK YOU, DIANNE!**

"Blessed are they which do hunger and thirst after righteousness: for they shall be filled."
(Matthew 5:6)
"Bless ye the LORD, all ye his hosts;
ye ministers of his, that do his pleasure.
Bless the LORD, all his works
in all places of his dominion:
Bless the LORD, O my soul.
Bless the LORD, O my soul.
O LORD my God,
Thou art very great; thou art clothed
with honour and majesty" . . .
(Psalm 103: 21-22, Psalm 104:1)

"TEARS"

By Yvonne S. Waite

O, Father, thank you for them,
For the depths of deeds
Which drew them to our eyes;
For the balm of soul their dampness brought us.
For that anguish sore they materialized.

For by those tears
We knew our hearts were human,
Not made of stone, insensitive to pain,
Not pumping ice in veins just mortal;
But instruments revealing our domain--
of care, regret, of love, or longing,
of loneliness and grief, of soul, of mind, or loss,
of indispensable need for relief.

For, in those tears, O LORD, we found THEE
Closer than a human hand,
Closer than a friend unfaithful,
Closer than an insincere command
To care for us--

Who could do it?
To comfort and caress with grace,
To touch with tenderness our feelings,
To transform that hopeless empty space?

Only Thee, a faithful FATHER,
Only Thee, the God of years unknown.
Only Thee, holding tomorrow's promise,
Only Thee, ETERNAL on the THRONE.

Thank Thee, Father, for them--
Those tears of grief and deep despair,
Thank Thee for Thy hand that wipes them
And the peace left by Thy perfect care.

Genesis 1:1—Genesis 4:5

THE BREATH OF LIFE

Genesis 2:7

"And the LORD God . . . breathed into his nostrils the breath of life . . . "

How lightly we take our daily breath. How little do we think of it. How many times do we breathe a day? An hour? A minute? We do not count the breaths. We do not notice our breathing—UNTIL. Then when our breathing becomes difficult and spasmodic, we gasp and wonder if we will take another. The truth is we are one breath away from dying. We are one moment away from the grave. It all has to do with that mighty *"breath"* from God that He breathed into Adam that day when *"man became a living soul."*

"In whose hand is the soul of every living thing, and the breath of all mankind" (Job 12:10).

"Let every thing that hath breath praise the LORD. Praise ye the LORD" (Psalm 150:6).

"Neither is worshipped with men's hands, as though he needed any thing, seeing he giveth to all life, and breath, and all things" . . . (Acts 17:25).

"A TABLE PREPARED"
(Psalm 23:5)

What grace, that as this new year dawns, we have before us, a *"table prepared"* by our Saviour and Provider for this year and the entire earthly journey of life. It is a Table of Fellowship and portions from God's Words. There is spiritual strength and wonderful benefits for the days before us. It is a *prepared provision* for a *prepared path* for all our needs and hunger. (ggs)

Genesis 4:6—Genesis 7:10

MISUNDERSTOOD CONVERSATION

Genesis 4:8

"And Cain talked with Abel his brother . . . "

Did you ever wonder what Cain and Abel talked about? The Bible does not tell us. I wonder why? Perhaps because some *"talks"* are private between the conversationalists. We can surmise that the words were about God's recent rejection of Cain's offering. It was not a blood sacrifice. It was one from Cain's good works. Cain was angry. The Bible says that he was very wroth! Then we read that angry Cain had a little talk with his sibling.

We do not read that Cain yelled at his brother. We do not read that Cain cursed at his brother. Nor do we read that Cain threatened his brother. It is not recorded as to exactly what the brothers talked about. But we do read that one day when they both were in the field, Cain got up from whatever he was doing and killed his brother!

Sometimes kind-sounding words can cover up an evil deed. Sometimes life's disappointments cause us to react in un-Christ-like manner. Some become angry with things like computers that fail or unkind drivers on the highway. If we are not careful, during such times, we may say or do things that do not edify. We could injure someone or a person's property in our anger. Then, sad to say, we have to pay for those words and following actions all the rest of our lives!

Poor Cain—his whole life was ruined because of jealousy and resentment that expressed itself in anger. The Bible says *"And Cain went out from the presence of the LORD, and dwelt in the land of Nod on the east of Eden"* (Genesis 4:16). Such a sad ending to a misunderstood conversation!

"A TABLE PREPARED"
(Psalm 23:5)
There are wonderful things on that TABLE BEFORE ME! Especially for those who feast at *"that Table."* How freely God has given us all things in Christ to feed upon *for all our needs and hunger.* I WILL NOT FEAR TOMORROW! It is all before me once more, as I step out upon a NEW YEAR and press on toward *the things* before me (Philippians 3:14). (ggs)

Today's Bible Blessing   *January 3*

Genesis 7:11—Genesis 10:20

GOD REMEMBERED NOAH

Genesis 8:1-2

"And God remembered Noah . . . and the rain from heaven was restrained;"

Have you ever been in a life situation when the rains of adversity or pain have fallen upon you? Have you ever felt that you could not stand it anymore? Have you cried out to God for relief and none came? I wonder about Noah and his family. I wonder what it was like for them to bear forty days and forty nights of rain and storm. That wave of water was not only the normal-type storms that we know about such as hurricanes and flooding—oh no! We read in the Bible that the *"fountains of the deep"* gushed up upon the weeping world.

Yet, a time came in that distress that God **"REMEMBERED NOAH."** It isn't that He actually forgot Noah—no. He cared for the *"just"* man. Had not he made a way for Noah and his family to be spared? Yes—but during the storms and trials of the forty-days-plus on that rocking boat, it may have seemed to the passengers that God had forgotten them. BUT *GOD REMEMBERED NOAH!* Let us, who know Jesus Christ as our Saviour, be comforted for such infinite memory. When we are in the storms of confusion and pain, let us not forget that God remembers His own and will open a window of relief in His time.

"SET YOUR HEART TO CHRIST AS YOU SET YOUR CLOCK TO THE SUN!" (ggs) (Colossians 3:2)

Today's Bible Blessing   *January 4*

Genesis 10:21—Genesis 14:3
NEVER TO BE FORGOTTEN

Genesis 11:11

"And Shem lived after he begat Arphaxad five hundred years, and begat sons and daughters."

The older I become, the more I am impressed with the many genealogies found in the Bible. Perhaps you wonder why. As I read them—and some of the names are unpronounceable—I realize that every one of those people mentioned in the verses before my eyes were people—human beings—with lives just like mine. Their mothers bore them with labor pains just like I had when I bore my children. They cared about their offspring and wanted them to have the best that life could offer. They taught them the skills of life such as hunting, fishing, cooking, and sewing.

They instructed their children in proper etiquette and manners to get by socially in the world about them. They cared! They cried! They loved! They laughed! And they died! Just because they had funny names and lived so long ago did not make the men in Genesis, chapter 11, less men because we have no pictures of them or any of their birth certificates or their voting records.

Now that my husband and I are getting older and making our way up to the dying position in our life's

journeys, I think about these names—*Salah, Eber, Peleg, Reu, Serug, Nahor, Terah, Abram, Sarai.* They were people. We know where some of them are buried. When they died, their loved ones cared and cried. Their children told their grandchildren about them. Better still, they are mentioned on the pages of Scripture, never to be forgotten. Praise the Lord for genealogies and the lives of people important enough to God to be written down for our learning and admonition to give us living people *"hope."*

"GOD IS FOR US"
(Job 23:16)
God is for us, though it may seem we are forsaken.
The Sovereign Lord of the universe is for us.
The first cause of everything–
It is He who is for us!
The Holy Spirit is within us, our Teacher and Comforter.
I sometimes feel that no one is for me
And nobody cares for me.
But God is for me!
So I press on and on—comforted and strengthened. (ggs)

Today's Bible Blessing   *January 5*

Genesis 14:4—Genesis 17:27
SUCCUMBING TO A SUGGESTION

Genesis 16:1

"Sarai Abram's wife bare him no children: and she had an handmaid . . ."

Sometimes we think that we know more than God. This is a dangerous mental attitude. First of all—it is not true. Second of all—it gets our human reasoning powers out of whack. How could beautiful Sarai be so stupid? Here she had a husband who adored her. He didn't even have a concubine. Abram acquired those in his later life after his beloved wife's death.

Because she wanted a child so very much, she came up with an evil plan. She decided to give her husband her handmaiden, a girl they had picked up during a faith lapse in Egypt a few years before. Now—Hagar was older, and of child-bearing age, an ideal female for Abraham to be with. This way Sarah could have a child!

Perhaps we should give Sarai the benefit of the doubt. It was to Abram that the promises were given, not to his wife. She may not have had the *"faith"*, at that time, to believe God. But what about Abram? It was his faith in the true God that had caused them to move

4

from their homeland of Ur to an unknown land. Why did he succumb to Sarai's suggestion?

Taking Hagar was not a step of faith. It was all of the flesh, and, as we know, deeds done in the flesh produce nothing but trouble and heartache. So—the birth of Ishmael has brought nothing but sorrow to the people of Israel from the day that Sarai gave Hagar to her husband. Therefore, the whole world is suffering today with Islam's false religion because of Sarai's bad advice and Abram listening to such drivel.

"HE LEADETH ME IN THE PATHS OF RIGHTEOUSNESS . . ."
Psalm 23:3)

"If we would just trust that God's way is the best way, we would be spared much anxicty!" (ggs)

Today's Bible Blessing   *January 6*

Genesis 18:1—Genesis 20:14
IN THE TENT

Genesis 18:9

"Where is Sarah thy wife? And he said, Behold, in the tent."

This verse has meant much to me since 1948, when Dr. D. A. Waite and I were married. Along with other Scriptures, I have come to admire Abraham's wife. She was a woman who learned to call her husband *"lord."* This showed him the *"respect"* due to his position as a husband. Doing this is not always easy.

We also have observed that Sarah learned to be happy in her tent. This, too, was something to be learned. That's where she was when the angels came and declared that she would be having a child in nine months. Though she laughed inwardly, she still showed *"respect,"* keeping behind her TENT DOOR listening.

So many women today do not believe that their primary function, as a wife, is to be the *"keeper"* of her home. It is her responsibility to guard that house, not only against thieves and people who would contaminate her children with worldliness, but also it is her responsibility to keep sexually pure for her husband and to protect him from women who would draw him away from her. This being *"a keeper of the house"* is a full time job!

> ### *"STRENGTH AND HONOR ARE HER CLOTHING!"*
> As Christian women, we should strive always to be what and where
> God wants us to be. This takes care of our attitude and action.
> Why should it be difficult to find virtuous women among us? (ggs)
> (Proverbs 31:25)

Today's Bible Blessing   *January 7*

Genesis 20:15—Genesis 24:3
SHE'S MY SISTER

Genesis 20:16b

"Behold, he is to thee a covering of the eyes, unto all . . . with thee . . ."

This verse has always been a blessing to me. It speaks of a husband's responsibility to protect his wife by being a faithful sexual protector of her. Years ago, when Abraham married his half-sister, Sarah, they bargained together that when a question arose as to her relationship to Abraham, she would always say he was her brother. Now this was half-true but not the whole truth; therefore, a lie.

I am not sure if she was veiled or not veiled; but whatever, the Bible tells us she was fair. Because she was beautiful, men noticed her. Abraham was not always that brave man that we have come to know. He was afraid.

In those days, if a powerful king wanted a beautiful woman, it did not matter if she were married or not. He would capture her and kill her husband. Abraham feared such a death. So, if it became known that Sarah was a "sister," Abraham had no danger that way.

In time, Abraham journeyed to Gerar. Of course, Sarah was with him there. The king of the land had eyes for Sarah. He was told that she was Abraham's sister. In this passage, the Bible says that *"God came to Abimelech in a dream by night."* God told the king that he was as good as dead. Do you wonder why?

Remember that the LORD had come to Sarah just recently and proclaimed that she was going to be *"with child"* and Isaac, the promised seed, would be soon born. If Abimelech had dared touch Sarah, he would have been a dead man. Also all the wombs of the women in his harem were closed as long as Sarah was on the premises. Perhaps Abimelech had become impotent. No wonder the women were sterile! I believe it was because of this physical embarrassment to the powerful king, that he reproved Sarah severely! The king told her to stay with Abraham for he gave her *"cover"* and *"protection."* What a shame that an ungodly potentate had to reprove a follower of the true God in this manner. You and I have much to learn from this account, don't we?

"HIS TRUTH IS OUR SHIELD"
(Psalm 91:4)
His truth shall be the protection when Satan attacks
The mind and heart with fears.
"Thou shalt not be afraid!"
Is this a commandment or a statement of fact?
When all seems hopeless, and we are helpless,
We have a shield against the *arrows of terror* by night
And the *sickness and destructions* of this life.
IIIS TRUTH IS OUR SHIELD!
Hide behind it! "Thus saith the Lord!" (ggs)

Today's Bible Blessing   *January 8*

Genesis 24:4—Genesis 25:21
WHOM TO MARRY

Genesis 24:4

"Thou shalt go unto my country . . . and take a wife unto my son Isaac."

Whom to marry is an important decision in a person's life. Perhaps it is the most important. We cannot help who our parents are. That was settled nine months before we were born. We cannot control how many children we have—though some feel they do with modern methods of birth control. We cannot choose the hour and place where we will die. But, we can control whom we marry! That is, if we think about it and do not let our emotions run away with our reason.

Abraham was concerned that his son Isaac would marry one of the Canaanite women. Canaan was where the father and son lived. It was the land to which God had led Abram and Sarai many years ago. It was the only land that Isaac knew. It was where father and son had friends and business acquaintances. Yet, Abraham knew that all those about him—except for a very few within his own household—were heathen people. They did not believe in the True God—the God with whom Abraham had a personal relationship.

The father's greatest fear was that his son would marry into a race and religion that was not proper. Many parents have this fear. Many sons and daughters have been taught by their parents to be careful to whom they marry. I am sure Isaac heard about it all his life. So, it was not a surprise to him that his elderly father would send a trusted servant to Abraham's far-away home town to search out the proper bride for his son.

We read later that forty-year-old Isaac married young Rebecca. He was a happy groom and she a trusting bride. The Bible tells us that Isaac loved Rebecca. What good words to read! Marriage should mean *"love"* as well as *"reason."* Let us encourage carefulness in marriage because the wrong decision can corrupt a life and ruin a future.

"GLORY AND HONOUR ARE IN HIS PRESENCE"
(I Chronicles 16:27)
A most beautiful verse! He is with us in the hardest strait!
If it is His place for me, I will be strong though I am weak.
I may be glad, though I may weep,
If I do my service as in His presence.
Glory and Honor unto him!
(ggs, partially copied)

Today's Bible Blessing   *January 9*

Genesis 25:22—Genesis 27:37
DECEIT & DESPAIR

Genesis 27:1

"And it came to pass, that when Isaac was old, and his eyes were dim . . . he called Esau his eldest son . . . and said . . . I am old . . ."

In a fast review of Isaac's life, we see how he respected his father, Abraham, loved Rebecca, and favored Esau above all others. Why he favored his oldest son, we don't know. This favoritism has been argued down through the times of Biblical history. In his old age, Isaac favored Esau more than ever. He enjoyed hearing of his son's hunting escapades and desired to eat the cooked catch of such adventures.

Being blind, there wasn't much enjoyment left in the old man's life except Esau and his food. Such a sad commentary on life that all we care about is food. Because of Isaac's appetite, as well as pure deceit by his wife and younger son, the last days of Isaac were days of family squabbles and deceit. How sad. LET US LEARN FROM SUCH DESPAIR TO MAKE THE CLOSING DAYS OF THOSE WE LOVE PLEASANT AND FILLED WITH HONESTY AS WELL AS CHRISTIAN KINDNESS.

> ## "GOD IS THE STRENGTH OF MY HEART!"
> It seemed I have had many hard and perplexing things happen to me and mine. These were too great for me to cope with. But God gave me this verse during a time of utter exhaustion. It has been mine ever since!
>
> *"MY STRENGTH AND MY HEART FAILETH:*
> *BUT GOD IS THE STRENGTH OF MY HEART*
> *AND MY PORTION FOREVER."*
> (Psalm 73:26)
> (ggs)

Today's Bible Blessing   *January 10*

Genesis 27:38—Genesis 30:19
PILLOW TALK

Genesis 28:16

"And Jacob awaked . . . and he said, Surely the LORD is in this place; and I knew it not."

In some ways, we can view Jacob as a coward. His mother had spoiled him. He was a *"mamma's boy."* He ran away from all the confusion he caused by *pretending* to be Esau. Therefore, he received his father's blessing—a blessing that belonged to his brother. His mother's advice was dishonest. It was based on pretense and deceit. Yet, God used it. Escaping from angry Esau, Jacob ran back to the land of his mother's nativity.

On his way to Uncle Laban's tent, he had an experience with the true God—something that his father, Isaac, and especially his grandfather Abraham, often had. There on the hard cold ground, with only a stone for a pillow, Jacob met the True God. He was promised to own the very land upon which he slept; and was told that he would have myriads of descendants to carry on his name. Besides all that, God told Jacob that He would be with Jacob and keep him no matter where he journeyed.

Strange that in the morning, unbelieving Jacob made a conditional dedication, of a sort, to the True God. He said, *"If God will be with me . . ."* Had not God just promised, *"I am with thee"*? Yes, he had. How like Jacob are we! We read in the Word of God, God's promises to us; and we immediately put a condition upon our belief!

"OURS ONLY BY ASKING"

GOD HAS CERTAIN BLESSINGS AND PROVISIONS THAT ARE OURS ONLY BY ASKING IN PRAYER. APART FROM THE FACT THAT GOD HAS TOLD US TO "ASK," THERE IS A SWEET SUBMISSION AND EXPECTANCY IN ASKING A SOVEREIGN GOD TO GRANT OUR REQUESTS.

"Ask largely that our joy may be full!
Let your requests be made known
And peace will guard your heart." (ggs)

$\mathcal{T}oday's\ \mathcal{B}ible\ \mathcal{B}lessing$ $\mathcal{J}anuary\ 11$

Genesis 30:20–Genesis 32:6

SCHEMING, DECEIT & MISTRUST

Genesis 31:36

"And Jacob was wroth, and chode with Laban: and Jacob answered and said to Laban, What is my trespass?"

It is noteworthy to notice that the **scheming and deceitful behavior inbred within all the relatives of Jacob continued throughout their whole lives.** It began when Isaac loved Esau more. It continued with the twins' mother, Rebecca, favoring Jacob who was more to her than life itself. It reflected back to the homeland when Uncle Laban schemed to keep Jacob in his employ by marrying him off to Leah, the wrong bride, making him stay longer for Rachel's hand in marriage, and changing the working rules with the multiplying of sheep and cattle.

Then when Jacob, the husband, left Laban, he sneaked off in the middle of the night. His favorite wife stole her father's *"gods"* and lied about doing so. The whole family had learned deceit well and practiced it daily. Even when Joseph and Benjamin were in Jacob's family, the brothers sold bragging Joseph as a slave to a band of cutthroats who passed by out in the sheep pastures. What a mess of a family!

Yet, God chose to use this family. It was from out of one of Jacob's sons that Jesus was born. In time—and it took time—Jacob became a staunch follower of the true God without conditions. Now we read about him in the Bible. Now it is profitable for our admonition and learning. Also, it encourages us when we see some of our faults and unbelief. God is still working with us and our families. He isn't finished with us yet! There is hope!

"JOY COMETH IN THE MORNING"
(Psalm 30:5)
There is something wonderful
About morning with its freshness.
No matter the night, the morning cometh
With its anticipation and faith
For the unknown and untried paths.
Let us praise Him for the morning
And his mercies ever new! (ggs)

Today's Bible Blessing   *January 12*

Genesis 32:7—Genesis 35:8

WRESTLING IN PRAYER

Genesis 32:30

"Jacob called the name of the place Peniel: for I have seen God face to face . . ."

The last time Jacob had a meeting with God, he vacillated, in my opinion, in his belief. He bargained with God: *"If God will be with me . . ."* He conjectured, for he was not fully walking by faith! We know how that is. After the all-night-wrestling-match with a *"man"* who was undoubtedly Jesus Christ (*a Christophany*), Jacob's perspective on Deity had improved. He said, *"I have seen God face to face, and my life is preserved."*

Previously in fear, Jacob had left his two wives, his two women servants, and his eleven sons at the brook *"over the ford Jabbok."* He was frightened out of his skin. So he decided he was going to pray. How like the rest of us—when in danger, we pray. The next day Jacob was scheduled to meet his brother, Esau. It had been years since their last face to face encounter. The former time, seeing him, was one of betrayal and deceit on Jacob's part and red-hot anger for Esau.

Jacob had lied—at his mother's suggestion—to his father and allowed the old man to bless him instead of his twin. Jacob had not only stolen Esau's birthright, but he had schemed away his brother's rightful *firstborn* blessing. By every law in the book, Esau had every right to destroy his brother and capture his wives, children, and cattle.

Something happened that evening in Peniel. The brothers called a truce and spoke as friends instead of enemies. Jacob had a meeting with God that changed his whole life and freed him from the fear of the unknown.

> ## *"EVEN TO YOUR OLD AGE, WILL I CARRY YOU!"*
> (Isaiah 46:4)
> This is a comforting verse as your years mount up!
> It implies He has carried us all of our years and will continue even
> in and unto OLD AGE!
> ### OUR HEAVENLY FATHER IS ALSO
> ### A TENDER SHEPHERD.
> He knows about the weariness and limitations of old age–and will
> help us.
> ### HE KNOWETH OUR FRAME. (ggs)

Today's Bible Blessing   *January 13*

Genesis 35:9—Genesis 37:21

DEATH IN THE LABOR ROOM

Genesis 35:16-17

*"And Rachel travailed, and she had hard labour. And it came
to pass, . . . the midwife said unto her, Fear not . . ."*

  It seemed to be soon after Jacob's revival at Bethel,
that Rachel went into *"hard labor."* Remember that was the
place where she and others gave up all their strange gods, as well as
their idol earrings. Those were the kinds of idols that previously
Rachel had stolen from her father. Perhaps some of them were the very
ones that were taken. That was when they left the farm to return to the
Canaan land. The giving away of her idols spoke of her dedication to
the true God, as well as to her obedience to her husband.

  **Prior to her pregnancies, Rachel's constant mantra
was, *"God, give me a baby!"*** Otherwise, things would have been
fine between Rachel and her husband. The jealousy she felt for her
sister Leah had been snuffed out with her first pregnancy.

  **It seemed that soon after the altar at Bethel, and all
that spiritual renewal, her new baby would arrive—a second
boy child!** Joy would come in the morning for Rachel! It should
have. Only it did not.

  Rachel would die in childbirth. In those days, many
people died in child birth because the medicines we have today were
unknown in that day. It is good to read that during her endless labor,
her midwife tried to comfort Rachel, *"Fear not, thou shalt have this
son also."* Could the midwife see a partially born child to discern such
news? Or was she just saying this? I don't know. Nor do we know why
Rachel died. Was it a breach birth? Was the baby turned the wrong

way in the womb? Did she lose too much blood? Did some childbirth disease overtake her?

Why did the baby live and Rachel die? If it had been today, perhaps there would have been a cesarean procedure—thus sparing the baby as well as the mother. Did she have *"childbed"* fever? Was the birth too much for her heart? All we know is what the Bible says, *"And it came to pass, as her soul was departing . . . that she called his name Benoni,"* which means *"son of my sorrow."*

We can well-imagine the sorrow Jacob had as he buried his sweetheart on the way to Bethlehem. The tears must have flowed uncontrollably. I wonder what Leah thought. She knew Jacob's love was toward her sister and not herself. This was no secret. But because Rachel was Leah's sister, she had grief, too. It must have been triple grief for Leah—grief for her sister, grief for her sister's motherless children, and grief that it would be impossible to comfort Jacob. How he loved Rachel!

No wonder young Joseph and little Benjamin were special to their father! They were all he had left of their mother—except for a pillar upon her grave that marked where Rachel's body lay. When we were in Israel a few years ago, I remember that some of our group saw Rachel's grave. Little did I know the significance of that place. I wish I had gone, too—but it is too late now.

"SO TODAY–BE STILL!"
Do not murmur. Do not ask. Do not weep.
BUT SIMPLY–BE STILL!
"HE RESTORETH MY SOUL!"
It is beside the still waters of His Words that He restoreth my soul!
(Psalm 43:5; Psalm 23:3)
(ggs)

Today's Bible Blessing   *January 14*

Genesis 37:22—Genesis 40:17

ALL COCKINESS GONE

Genesis 37:24

"And they took him, and cast him into a pit: and the pit was empty . . ."

I can't help but compare these two young men—**Joseph and Er.** We all know the story of Joseph and his coat of many colors. It was covered with the blood of a dead animal. That was the ruse the brothers used to deceive their father, to make him think his beloved son was dead.

Er was Judah's first born. Er was wicked. We don't know what the wickedness was but it was severe enough for God to kill him. We reflect on the sudden deaths of men in Scripture like Hophni and Phinehas, Eli's sons, or Uzza, the man who wrongfully touched the ark. Er's father, Judah, was one of Jacob's sons by Leah. He was her fourth born—a half-brother of Joseph.

It would be from Judah's line that the Lord Jesus would come. It was Judah's idea to sell his young brother to the Ishmaelites as they passed by the well in which they had thrown Joseph. It was better than killing him. Joseph lived. Er died. That was the end of him.

Joseph was as good as dead to his father. But it was not the end of him. He was noble and upright. It was not his time to die. I'm sure all that imprisonment knocked out his cockiness and braggadocio that had surfaced when he explained his teenage dreams to his family.

But in God's time, those dreams proved to be true and Joseph was vindicated. His father, Jacob, had the joy before he died, to hold and kiss his lost son again. But Judah never could hold his son again.

Death has a way of separating fathers and sons. It also is a leveling agent. Naked we came into the world and naked we go out. The only part of a person that lives on is his soul and spirit. It either lives in eternal Hell or eternal bliss. What do you think the end was of these two brothers?

"PERHAPS YOU HAVE THOUGHT"

THAT YOUR DOCTOR WAS KEEPING YOU WELL. Or perhaps, you thought your church was, or your husband, or even yourself! But No!

"THE LORD IS THY KEEPER!
HE WILL NOT SUFFER THY FOOT TO BE MOVED!"
Never for a moment will He cease to hold you fast!
He never slumbers nor loses His hold!
He keepeth thee through the day's heat and evening chill!
He will keep thy goings and comings now and evermore." (ggs)
(Psalm 121:3-5)

Genesis 40:18–Genesis 42:22

GRACE IN FORGETTING

Genesis 41:51b

"God hath made me forget all my toil, and all my father's house."

    Today in Genesis, we read that Joseph rose from prison to praise. He married Asenath, the daughter of the Egyptian priest of On. They had a son whom he named MANASSEH which means *"God hath made me forget all my toil and all my father's house."* When I reflect upon Joseph, I realize that he had much to forget and forgive. I think of the events and people in my life that I must forgive and forget.

    I marvel at Joseph who was sold and abandoned by his own family. Contemplate all he had to adjust to, all he had to put out of his mind, as he had to live in "adversity" and "advantage."

    I think of the hurts in our lives that keep returning to us. I don't want them, but they return. Regrets come! Fear that the situation will return in some form or another.

    Joseph never knew when he would be rejected again. He never really knew if his Pharaoh would turn on him as his brothers and Potiphar had done in the past. Those whom he had trusted and served had turned on him. He had come to realize that his only surety was his God!

"THE LORD YOUR GOD GOETH BEFORE YOU
AND WILL FIGHT FOR YOU!"
(Deuteronomy 1:30)
Believe it—and trust Him in the impasse and the impossible. (ggs)

Genesis 42:23—Genesis 45:1

THE HELPLESSNESS OF FAILURE

Genesis 42:28b

"What is this that God hath done unto us?"

    Often, because of our own misdeeds and failures, we human beings blame God for our troubles. It is hard for us to admit the failures that have come into our lives. Often these failures are a result of our own foolishness and lack of discernment. OFTEN WE RUSH AHEAD WITHOUT LEANING ON GODLY WISDOM! We want our own way! We want our own things! We want our own wisdom! We tend to reject spiritual leadership from our Heavenly Shepherd.

Catastrophes, unwise friendships, and unhealthy situations often come into our lives because we fail to keep close to Jesus. Then we cry out, *"All these things are against me."*

"IN HER TONGUE IS THE LAW OF KINDNESS"
(Proverbs 31:26)

Let this "law" govern my way in my life before the family and others.

Let it control my speaking, and let me grieve when I break this Heavenly law. (ggs)

Today's Bible Blessing   *January 17*

Genesis 45:2—Genesis 47:24

A BROTHER'S LOSS BRINGS GRIEF

GENESIS 45:14

"And he fell upon his brother Benjamin's neck, and wept . . ."

Joseph was overwhelmed with sorrow and joy! These must have been his feelings when he saw his youngest brother, Benjamin. They had the same mother. They were from the same womb. But years of separation were between them. They were strangers.

Benjamin had thought Joseph was dead. Joseph had heard not one word from Benjamin or any of his family since he was seventeen years old. Now Joseph was thirty and a ruler in Egypt. What a change from that dirty teenage youth that had been pulled from the mud pit.

I remember when I saw my younger sister, Beverly, after many months of absence. We were adults. She was moved to see me—and I her. She did not want to let me go! Beverly was brain-damaged from birth. I was not sure she really cared about me. In truth, I was all she had left of our family, and she for me. Our parents and other sister had long-ago died. We were from the same womb.

As I read of Joseph and his meeting with Benjamin that long-ago day in Egypt, I thought about Beverly. I reflected on Joseph's mixed emotions as he hugged Benjamin to his heart. There is a bond between siblings which cannot be explained.

> ## "WATER BY THE WAY OF EDOM"
> (II Kings 3:8-22)
> God can send help from unlikely sources!
> We are to expect help, and make ready for the blessing!
> He will send water from a desert, if necessary.
> The way He answers our prayers is often a mystery.
> The thousands and thousands of prayers that ascend
> Have as many kinds of answers, as the prayers that are prayed.
> (ggs)

Today's Bible Blessing   *January 18*

Genesis 47:25–Genesis 50:23

NO ESCAPE IN DEATH

Genesis 47:29

"And the time drew nigh that Israel must die . . ."

The older we become, the more we realize that God's Word is true when it says that *it is appointed unto man that he or she must die.* It is the final event in everyone's life. We cannot escape it. We cannot practice for it. There can be no dress rehearsal. **May I be so close to the Lord, that when my death comes, I will slip to the other side in peace.** I do not want to make a scene. But we cannot know what death does to us, or how we will behave.

From all I have been told by those who were there, I believe David, our son, though in pain, went HOME quickly, bravely, and welcoming his final end. His breath was taken from him—that holy *"life-breath"* that had been passed down to him from Adam's day to us in this century. My mother had a failing end with days of departing—not month upon month and years. My father died instantly in his wheelchair in his yard.

May God be gracious to you and me in death. It is all part of that *"unknown future."* We wonder what Heaven is like. *Not my will, but Thine be done!*

> ### *"I AM HELPED"*
> (Psalm 28:7)
> *The Lord is my strength and my shield.*
> *My heart trusted in Him and I am helped.*
> *Therefore, my heart greatly rejoiceth, and with*
> *my song will I praise Him.*
>
> Since He is our shield and defense in this life,
> and our strength for the day's battle,
> we grieve the heart of God when we try to
> defend and sustain our self.
>
> Rejoicing and song come only from a heart which is helped
> by trusting in Him. (ggs)

Today's Bible Blessing   *January 19*

Genesis 50: 24–Exodus 4:13

A CHILD'S BIRTH MEMORIES

Exodus 2:22

"I have been a stranger in a strange land."

I think of the loneliness of Moses. There he was in a *"strange land,"* married to a woman very unlike the women of Egypt whom he knew, or even like his birth-mother. There he was a father for the first time in a strange land. His whole life had taken on a new persona. He no longer had the status of the adopted child of a princess or even the birth-son of a slave. He was a shepherd out in the sun, away from the pleasures of Egypt.

As Moses gazed at his baby son, little Gershom, he was overcome with his circumstances. It was then that he cried, *"I have been a stranger in a strange land."* How many of us, like Moses, have journeyed far from our place of birth. We are literally in a *"strange land."* Now we are adjusting to the present and pushing away from our past. May God use us as He did Moses in such circumstances. Soon we will not be *"strangers"* in a *"strange land."* **We will be at *"HOME!"***

18

> ## *"OUR LIFE IS A VAPOR"*
> (James 4:14)
> Has there been a death of someone near and dear?
> What is the lesson in this for me?
> This loss should jolt us to take stock of our life.
> Is it pleasing to the Lord?
> Are we ready to meet Him?
> How is the ledger of my life if He should suddenly call my name?
> What have I done?
> The death of a dear one should teach us to do what we can
> to please and help others while they are here,
> so there will be no regrets when they go. (ggs)

Today's Bible Blessing   *January 20*

Exodus 4:14—Exodus 7:14

A WIFE IS A WIFE
NO MATTER WHAT

Exodus 4:20

"And Moses took his wife and his sons . . . to . . . Egypt . . ."

I think of Zipporah as a woman of the wilderness. She was a shepherdess. Her skin was wind-blown and sun-scorched. Though she was a queen of a woman, she was no pampered palace princess. Some feel Moses' spouse was a black woman. Others have a contrary opinion. Moses brought her and their son *"home"* to Egypt, a place she had never been.

It was there that she saw, firsthand, her husband's mission. It was to deliver his people from bondage. For Moses, it was not a return to *"pomp and glory,"* but a return to rejection and ridicule. I do not know if Zipporah knew the difficulty that would be her husband's job.

Many a wife has had to endure the rebuffs that come when her husband chooses the right path. She should not be surprised when she marries a man with strong, unpopular convictions, that she is rejected along with her husband. We should take a fresh look at this wife of the meekest man on earth and learn from her.

"IN BAR IN THE MIDST"

They made the middle crossbar run along the entire length of each side and rear of the Tent. It was set halfway up the frames." "He also made two boards for the two back corners of the tabernacle."
(Taken from Exodus 26:28; 36:33)

For some reason I have never seen this type explained,
but for some reason, this passage blesses me.
Christ is *in the midst* of two or three.
He is *in the midst* of the church in Revelation.
Christ dwells *in our hearts.*
"Blessed Bar" *in the midst* of the boards of the building.
He it is that holds us and sustains us.
In the midst of life's trials, He is THE BAR *in the midst.*
He is the support, the Sustainer! (ggs)

Today's Bible Blessings   *January 21*

Exodus 7:15–Exodus 10:7

DIVISIONS BRING COURAGE

Exodus 8:23a

"And I will put a division between my people and thy people"

God has a way of dividing people from one another and from things, as well as from groups and organizations. It was of interest to me this morning to see that He divided the Israeli slaves, bound in Egypt, from the powerful Egyptian Pharaoh and his people. Moses was assigned by God, with the help of Aaron his brother, to lead Israel out of Egypt.

How was he to do this? I am sure Moses wondered, too. God had a way! He always does. He drove hardhearted Pharaoh to scream out at Moses, *"Be gone!"* All the awful plagues found in these chapters and following, ended in the death of every firstborn of man or animal in the land. *"GO! GO! GO!"* cried the king!

But, did you notice in verse 32b of chapter 12, that Pharaoh implored Moses, "Bless me!" How like those who criticize us. Often in their need, they come to us for help!

"CIRCUMCISION OF THE HEART"
(Joshua 5:3, 8)
It is a type of *"separation."*
To be *"separated"* means to walk alone.
Each person must have it personally, and bear its pain.
It was commanded by God at that time
after they crossed over the Jordan River.
A sharp knife is used.
THE WORD OF GOD IS A SHARP KNIFE!
It hurts our pride. It costs us friends.
It makes *"separated Christians"* a marked people.
The wounds of separation exchange the reproach of Egypt
(*the world*) for the reproach of Christ! (ggs)

Today's Bible Blessing   *January 22*

Exodus 10:8—Exodus 13:2

MOSES REMEMBERED
BY HIS PEERS

Exodus 11:3b

"Moses was very great in the land of Egypt, in the sight of Pharaoh's servants, and in the sight of the people."

Perhaps you would not choose this verse as important because, in future chapters, we will read of the death of all the firstborn of every house, barn, and field in the land of Egypt. Only those who applied the blood of a lamb would be spared.

I was impressed with the fact that Moses, with one more plague in the wings, was well thought of in that land of soon-coming death and tears. The Egyptian people must have remembered him when he was a youth. They remembered him when he lived in the previous Pharaoh's palace. For some reason they liked him.

The children and young people of Moses' former days had now grown up into adults. They had matured as Moses grew in grace, laboring with sheep, and buffeted by wind there in the area of his burning bush experience. They remembered him. How could they forget the story of the baby pulled from the Nile by the Princess?

Even then, God was grooming the leader who would deliver his oppressed people! Perhaps they did not accept the message of a soon-coming DESTROYER. But they knew Moses! They may not have understood their nation's approaching, unexplainable

21

grief, but the common people saw Moses as a *"great"* man. No wonder their women showered the *Deliverer of Israel* with jewelry of silver and gold!

"SAFETY"
(Psalm 4:8)
I will both lay me down in peace and sleep
For thou, LORD, only makest me dwell in safety!
To be able to go to bed at night
Knowing that we are under the blood
Justified and declared righteous
Should give us peace and rest and relaxation.
HE ONLY MAKES ME DWELL SAFELY!
(ggs)

𝒯oday's 𝐵ible 𝐵lessing   𝒥anuary 23

Exodus 13:3—Exodus 16:7

MEMORIAL STONES ARE GOOD

Exodus 13:14

"When thy son asketh thee in time to come, saying, What is this?"

Children are curious people. They want to know why? So when the Israelites observed the Passover every year, it was only natural for a child to ask, *"WHY?"*

What a story the parents had to tell them! The little ones would learn of the *"Passover lamb"* and the death of all the firstborn where the blood of that lamb was not applied. Then the children would learn of the flight from Egypt by their relatives. They would learn of the parting of the Red Sea, of Moses' strength and faith, of the Pharaoh's hard heart and his armies, of chariots pursuing and drowning, of the sea's waters opening and closing. They would learn of the exuberance and adoration of the people as their prime enemies were dead.

Then the parents, if they were truthful, would tell of the complaining people, the very ones whom God had protected. They would learn how their forefathers decided life in Egypt was better than the unknown wilderness. The little ones would learn of the complaining—the lack of water, the fear, the ungrateful disbelief! The children would learn their relatives' faith in God was spasmodic. They would hear of the Israelites murmuring against Moses and Aaron, and would wonder at the ungratefulness of their great-grandparents.

But you and I are no different. We have wonderful spiritual journeys. We see our needs supplied. We find comfort and solace in the arms of God. But then, we begin to complain over some minor lack, or some slight from another person toward us. We complain! How sad and how human are we mortals!

Let us determine to be different and do all things without murmurings and complaining. Then we will discover, if we do not know it already, that we are just as human as those Israelites long ago who wanted to return to worldly Egypt. **Let's try not to be like them!**

"THE WALK WITHIN MY HOME"
(Psalm 101:2)
*"I will behave myself wisely in a perfect way . . .
I will walk within my house with a perfect heart!"*
What a lovely and timely motto for a Christian woman
to have before her.
To "BE LIKE JESUS ALL DAY LONG
IN THE HOME AND IN THE THRONG"
is not as easy to do as to sing.
*"Oh, Lord Jesus, teach me to behave myself wisely
within my house!* (ggs)

Today's Bible Blessing   *January 24*

Exodus 16:8–Exodus 19:13

ISRAEL & AMALEK: ENEMIES TODAY

Exodus 17:13

"And Joshua discomfited Amalek and his people with the edge of the sword."

Brave Joshua raged a battle against Israel's enemy, the people called the Amalekites. If you remember, it was during that war that Moses held his hands up as he stood high on a hill above the fray. As long as they were stretched toward the sky, Israel would win. But when weariness hit his body, Moses' hands dropped. Then the Amalekites would gain the advantage.

This seesaw battle went on and on. Seeing the problem, Aaron and Hur rushed to Moses' side. They found a stone upon which their tired leader could sit. Then they held his hands high for victory.

Amelek was an awful people. Many feel that enemy was descended from Esau, Isaac's son. Others feel that clan was in the land

23

during the days of Abraham. Amalek is a name given to the Amorites and the Canaanites, as well as to the Hyksos.

If you recall, Saul spared Agag, the king of the Amalekites. That was a sin! That heathen group kidnapped David's wives and others at Ziklag. It was an Amalekite who slew King Saul and took the fallen leader's crown to David.

In the book of Esther we learn that Haman was an Agagite. To win the battle with Amalek, *"in the days of Moses in the wilderness"* was a step in a good direction. God wanted them destroyed. It was such a glorious, newsworthy victory that God told Moses to write the results of that wilderness war in a book.

In gratitude, Moses built an altar and called it *JEHOVAH NISSI* (the Lord my banner). It was a war monument. *"I will utterly put out the remembrance of Amalek from under heaven"* was God's promise. The children of Israel and Amalek would be enemies forever.

In later years, some euphemistically speaking of Hitler, called him an Amalekite; and Rabbi Israel Hess claimed that the Palestinians were Amalekites. Israeli President Itzhak Ben-Zvi, in refusing mercy to Adolf Eichmann, repeated Samuel's words to Agag (I Samuel 15:33): *"As thy sword hath made women childless, so shall thy mother be childless among women."*

> **"IT IS GOD THAT GIRDETH ME WITH STRENGTH AND MAKETH MY WAY PERFECT!"**
> I have no strength, He girdeth me.
> My way is hard, He girdeth me.
> Some days
> it seems I cannot put forth any energy.
> I have learned that God is not necessarily glorified
> by our energies–
> UNLESS HE IS OUR STRENGTH IN THEM!" (ggs)
> (Psalm 18:32)

Today's Bible Blessing   *January 25*

Exodus 19:14—Exodus 22:11
CARE DON'T SWEAR

Exodus 20:7, 19

"Thou shalt not take the name of the LORD thy God in vain, for the LORD will not hold him guiltless . . ."

How very common it is today to hear the Name of the **LORD God taken in vain.** In the store or on the playground, we hear children from toddlers to teens say *"My God!"* for any infraction in their plans. They use the Name of GOD as a part of punctuation in common conversation, never knowing that they are defaming their Creator.

Where do our little ones learn such blaspheming and cursing? From the older generation who think nothing of peppering their daily talk with obscenities. Even some, who call themselves *"Christians,"* abuse the Name of God. Some curse, using Jesus' Name—the Name given by the Angel to Mary at the pronouncement of His birth.

GOD is damned daily—sometimes hourly, or more often by many. Jesus Christ is called out in curses for their slightest exclamation. Don't these people know that God commanded, *"Thou shalt not take the name of the LORD . . . in vain?"* How very crass and uncaring—as well as ignorant and uncouth!

In the Old Testament, we read that anyone who cursed his father or mother would be put to death. Cursing today is as common as water. People *"damn"* this one or that one without a thought as to what they are saying. Even television and radio commentators use foul language calling on body excrement to cover people, or casting condemnations on one another's *"hinder parts."*

Uncouth and corrupt speech is not becoming to anyone, let alone to those who claim Christ as Saviour. Let us determine not to curse, use foul language, or express our anger or disapproval of things or people with common curse words, unclean language, or the taking of God's Name in vain.

"SET YOUR HEART TO CHRIST"
Today deliberately take your heart devotion and desire from everything and set your heart affection on things above, Where Christ sitteth on the right hand of God. (ggs)

Today's Bible Blessing   *January 26*
Exodus 22:12—Exodus 25:14
BE NEIGHBORLY ANYHOW

Exodus 23:4

"If thou meet thine enemy's ox . . . going astray, thou shalt surely bring it back to him again."

When I look at this verse, I do not think of the *"enemy"* like the enemies associated with war. No—I think of neighbors and acquaintances and former friends who are no longer as close to us as they used to be.

If we lived on a farm—and many do—we could envision a cow or a horse going astray. The proper thing to do is to corral that animal and take it back to the owner, even if that owner is an *"enemy."* Or at least, we should phone the owner.

One time one of our sons saw a thief on a neighbor's porch stealing a bicycle. Immediately, I called the neighbor. The neighbor was nonchalant about it. In fact, he did not seem to care. Maybe he did not believe me. The next day he called me and asked what I knew about the thief on his porch. The bike had been stolen! I had done my job. I had been a good neighbor.

We live in the suburbs and do not have farm animals. I have never seen a stray sheep or pig walk by our house here in Collingswood. But, upon occasion, I have seen a dog or a cat, or a raccoon, rabbit, or possum. (The other night a coyote was spied by some friends.) If I knew the dog or cat was lost—and I knew the owner, I would contact him or her, even if that person was not a *"friend"* to me.

A month or so ago, we received a flier from a desperate dog owner. I did not know the dog or the owner. The dog had gone astray. I kept the flyer. I was concerned. I called the owner. She said the dog had returned. I wanted to find out more about the dog and make a friend of the owner. She was most impolite! She did not care that I cared. I had done my part.

So as I look at this verse, I believe the verse means that there are certain kindnesses and amenities that a follower of the Lord Jesus Christ should perform toward others, even if there is a division of some kind between the owner of the animal and the Christian. You may or may not make a friend—but that is not the point. We should be kind and concerned.

The next verse instructs the children of Israel that even if one of them sees a burdened-down donkey of an owner who hates them, the Israelite should help the beast. This is just common courtesy and friendship even to those who dislike us—even if we receive no recognition for our good deed. God keeps the records!

"SPEAK THE TRUTH IN LOVE"
There is so much truth to speak!
There is also much "love" to give.
Speak with a loving heart.
Someone has said that it is hard to exhort and be gracious at the same time, for self gets in the way.
Why should a Christian have to be thus exhorted? (ggs)
(Ephesians 4:15)

Today's Bible Blessing   *January 27*

Exodus 25:15–Exodus 28:1
THE MERCY SEAT
CAN WE FATHOM IT?

Exodus 25:17

"And thou shalt make a mercy seat of pure gold . . ."

The *"mercy seat"*—the beautiful mercy seat!—that was the *"place"* in the wilderness tabernacle where God, in full holiness and majesty, met man! The *"mercy seat"* was a work of art. It was placed on top of the ARK OF THE COVENANT where *"the Testimony,"* Aaron's rod, and some manna were kept. The *"mercy seat"* was crafted from one piece of gold, according to God's specifications.

Upon this forty-five-inch by twenty-seven-inch symbolic golden plane was the throne of God, in picture form. It was there where the Old Testament saints, in the person of their high priest, met God once a year.

Between the golden cherubim on the *mercy seat*, animal blood was sprinkled. It was for the *"atonement"* of all Israel. It was a forward look to Calvary. It was there the *"holy, sinless blood"* of Jesus was shed on the cross. The *"mercy seat"*! Can we ever fathom it? Can we really understand what Jesus did for us at Calvary?

Until the cross, the temple vail protected the *mercy seat.* It kept the common people away from the ark. When Christ died, the vail was torn in two from top to bottom. God did that! It was on the cross that Jesus Christ poured out His blood. He forgave the sin of the world for those who now believe. Because of Jesus' sacrifice, we, who are born-again, are told that we can have forgiveness of sin. We now *"have boldness to enter into the holiest by the blood of Jesus"* (Hebrews 10:19). Jesus paid it all so we could have access to the Heavenly Father.

It is there, to the *mercy seat* in Heaven, that the believer can come to God in prayer. It is there that we can plead the blood of Christ for our forgiveness and blessings.

H. Stowell has written this *"truth"* in beautiful words,

"From every stormy wind that blows, from every swelling tide of woes, there is a calm, a sure retreat; 'tis found beneath the mercy seat. There is a place where Jesus sheds the oil of gladness on our heads, a place than all beside more sweet; it is the blood-bought mercy seat. Ah! Whither could we flee for aid, when tempted, desolate, and dismayed; or how the host of hell defeat, had suffering saints no mercy seat?"

"GOD HAD TO CRIPPLE JACOB
TO GET HIM TO SURRENDER."
Many a wound brings us to great gain.
Our weaknesses make us hold to Him.
It seems, when we are well and healthy,
we go on our merry way
Unmindful of the Lord and His claim on our lives.
He has to *"cripple us"* to get us to slow down
and depend on Him! (ggs)
(Genesis 32:31)

Today's Bible Blessing   *January 28*

Exodus 28:2—Exodus 29:43

DRESS FOR GOD'S GLORY

Exodus 28:2, 42

"And thou shalt make holy garments for Aaron thy brother for glory and for beauty . . . to cover their nakedness . . ."

God is interested in the way we dress. Remember how He clothed Adam and Eve after they had sinned!

In this passage of Scripture, we see that God was interested in the way Aaron dressed from his head covering to his undergarments. So many dress details were given. Why? The High Priest had a holy position to maintain. People were watching him all the time. One thing the public would notice was how he dressed.

We, who are Christians, are called *"priests"* in the New Testament. Should we, who love Jesus Christ, not care what people see as they observe our dress? Should we not want to stand before the world dressed in a manner that would glorify God?

When people passed by, and saw Aaron, they knew he was a priest. His clothes gave him away. People see us every day. Can they tell by the way we dress that we are *"priests"*? As *believer-priests*, we have a duty to glorify God in every manner of our lives. That includes the way we dress. Modesty is part of *"glory"* and *"beauty."*

"UNTO HIM"
OUR SEPARATION IS UNTO HIM!
HE WOULD HAVE US HOLY AS HE IS HOLY!
The Lord was Holy, harmless, undefiled, and separate from sinners.
There are times when we must bear the reproach
which comes from being "without" the camp.
The *"separated life"* is more than living
separated from apostasy and the world.
It is living a life *unto Him.*
ALL OUR HEART'S YEARNING *"UNTO HIM"*! (ggs)
(Hebrews 13:13)

Today's Bible Blessing   *January 29*

Exodus 29:44–Exodus 32:26
A PLACE OF PRAYER

Exodus 30:1

"And thou shalt make an altar to burn incense upon: of shittim wood shalt thou make it."

Why did God command the Israelites to use wood from the *shittim wood tree* to be used in the making of the wilderness tabernacle and its furniture? What was there about that wood that it is mentioned so often in our Bible?

This hard, closed-grained wood, from the acacia tree, was common in the Arabian Desert. It was of orange-brown color. Even today, wood from the Acacia tree is used in furniture and hardwood floors. There is a site on the computer where one can buy *shittim wood* from a tree in Israel for one's own personal craftsmanship.

Some of the pictures of the wood show that there are thorns and waffles on the branches. All of those imperfections would have to be removed before the wood could be used to make anything—especially the *altar of incense.* Then, and only then, would gold be molded upon it.

That *altar of incense* was the place of prayer for the priests. It was a holy place of communion with God.

Oh, that we Christians could be like *shittim wood.* Oh, that we could be hard-core and steadfast in our convictions so that our lives would be used for God's service as a foundation for truth and righteousness. Oh, that our whole person would be a place of prayer in the service of God's work here on earth!

> ### *"OVERWHELMED"*
> *"When my heart is overwhelmed, attend unto my cry.*
> *Lead me to the Rock that is higher than I!"*
> How often are the cares and affairs of this life overwhelming,
> Causing us to become spiritual cowards!
> But praise God,
> there is a place to run that is HIGHER than any care.
> And to Him, we cry out in need.
> Many times each day we must run unto that Rock
> for shelter and strength.
> He must take us there.
> Yes, lead us there to that High Tower and our Rock! (ggs)
> (Psalm 61:1-4)

Today's Bible Blessing　　　　　　　　*January 30*

Exodus 32:27—Exodus 35:18
THE BOOK OF LIFE

Exodus 32:32-33

". . . if not, blot me . . . out of thy book which thou has written. And the LORD said unto Moses, Whosoever hath sinned against me, him will I blot out of my book."

Under Aaron's leadership, the children of Israel committed a terrible sin. They were a *"chosen people"*—the ones promised to Abraham many years ago. Foolish, compromising Aaron made a golden calf, like the kind that was worshipped in Egypt. It all happened while Moses was on Mount Sinai receiving the *Law of God*.

Now, Moses had advanced warning of the idolatry and immoral behavior. JEHOVAH knew what was going on in the camp. The LORD informed the leader that His people had turned away quickly from the pure worship of the true God. It was sickeningly true.

What would the LORD do? He, in His righteous fury, would kill every last one of them! He already had the Levites slay three thousand men—not including the women and children. Imagine the frightful sight at the ashes of that golden idol.

The LORD said He would begin a new nation whose descendants would be from Moses. Moses was horrified. What would Egypt think? He pleaded with JEHOVAH! Yes, the people had sinned! It was then that Moses implored, *"Blot out my name from thy BOOK instead of the people, O LORD."* I feel that the *BOOK* spoken of here was the *BOOK* spoken of in the *Revelation of Jesus Christ* (Revelation 20:12, 15; 22:19).

It was given to the Apostle John on Patmos Island. I personally feel that somewhere in God's care, there is a *"BOOK"* filled with the names of everyone who has ever, or will ever live. The Apostle Paul wrote of those whose names were written in the *"BOOK OF LIFE."* And near those names, and the others who are there, are written all the *"works"*—good or bad—that they did while alive. (Even in that book are included the natural or unnatural aborted babies as well as all the stillborn children of the world.)

The psalmist has written: *"Thou tellest my wanderings . . . are they not in THY BOOK?"* (See Psalm 56:8.) *". . . and in THY BOOK all my members are written . . ."* (Psalm 139:16). I believe **the BOOK** referred to here and in other passages is **the BOOK** mentioned in the New Testament Scripture as **THE BOOK OF LIFE!** (See Revelation 3:5; 13:8; 17:8.)

It seems to me that these verses teach that everyone's name is written in *The BOOK OF LIFE*—Christ died for all (Philippians 4:3). Those who reject his free salvation, *already paid for at Calvary*, will have his or her name blotted out of *THE BOOK*. It will be as if the person never had his or her name written there at all. WHAT DO YOU THINK?

"A NEW AND DELUDED MEANING"
(Jeremiah 23:30)
"Behold, I am against the prophets, saith the Lord, that steal my words . . ."
This is what cults, neo-liberation, and neo-evangelicalism have done. The Scriptural words and doctrines are given new and diluted meaning.
"THEY USE OUR VOCABULARY, BUT NOT OUR DICTIONARY."
(ggs)

Today's Bible Blessing   *January 31*

Exodus 35:19—Exodus 38:1

IS PUTTING STAMPS ON ENVELOPES THE LORD'S WORK?

Exodus 36:1

"Then wrought (worked) Bezaleel and Aholiab, and every wise hearted man, in whom the LORD put wisdom and understanding . . . for the service of the sanctuary . . ."

Sometimes we think that there is only one way to serve the LORD. We postulate that pulpit-preaching, Bible-teaching, and solo-singing are the exclusive methods of serving God. How wrong we are! **I remember a little boy who went with his mother to her church to do** *"the Lord's work."* They put stamps on envelopes! The puzzled boy looked at the stamps. Then he looked at his mother and said, *"Is putting stamps on envelopes the Lord's work?"*

Reflect on BEZALEEL. If you recall, his father's name was URI and his grandfather was a man named **HUR.** Remember Hur was the man, along with Aaron, who held up Moses' hands during the battle with the Amalekites.

BEZALEEL, with AHOLIAB, were skilled craftsmen! It makes us wonder what their relatives crafted, besides bricks, in the land of Egypt during the four-hundred-year-captivity. Weren't the pyramids overlaid with gold? To fashion something in gold was no problem for them! They knew how to work with their minds and hands to create furniture, not only for function, but also for beauty.

All their skill and talent was used by God in building the tabernacle and its contents. God had a plan. These men, along with other gifted men and women, followed God's pattern to build a place for sacrifice and worship. As we read about these talented artists, carpenters, and seamstresses, we can see that our service to God may come in many different packages. **Let us not forget to use those gifts for Him!**

"HE THAT IS MASTERED BY CHRIST IS THE MASTER OF EVERY CIRCUMSTANCE"

Does the circumstance press hard against you?
It is the Potter's hand! Do not push it away!
It is shaping you into a vessel of beauty and usefulness for Eternity. Your mastery will come, not by arresting its progress, but by enduring its discipline.

(Psalm 4:6; Psalm 27:5; Psalm 50:15)
(ggs–original author unknown)

Today's Bible Blessing   *February 1*

Exodus 38:2—Exodus 40:12

BRASS THE ENDURING METAL

Exodus 38:29

"And the brass of the offering was seventy talents, and two thousand and four hundred shekels."

Of all the metals mentioned that were used in the building of the wilderness tabernacle or its furnishings, the most durable, in my opinion, was the metal called *"brass."* There must be a reason. Evidently *brass* is able to stand the stress and strain of hard use and abuse.

We have some light fixtures in our house that are made of brass. I really never noticed them until my mother, who appreciated lovely things, pointed them out to me. Our house numbers at the front door are of brass. None of these brass beauties are ever polished by me. They are serviceable and strong. They have stood in their place for over eighty years as a part of our house.

Brass is a functional metal. It is strong and can stand the strains of life about it. *Brass was the substance of which the grate of the altar was made.* Upon that grate, heavy animals would be placed and burned for the sin of the Israelites.

If the grate could talk, it might cry out in pain—but grates don't talk. If the grate could see, if would have seen flesh and blood, fat and bones placed upon it for sacrifice.

All those sacrifices looked forward to the death of Jesus Christ for the atonement of people's sin. I think of the brasen serpent and how it was held high before the snake-bitten Israelites. That was a picture of the Lord Jesus Christ lifted high on the cross for the sin of the world.

The brasen altar spoke to the people, too. It spoke of the terrible death and the shedding of Christ's blood on the cross. He was judged for the unsaved souls. I am so glad that He became sin for us, aren't you? He bore the judgment so I would not have to do so.

"LORD IS IT I?"
Help me, *myself* to see—while I am looking at others,
Thou Lord, art looking at me? (ggs)

Today's Bible Blessing   *February 2*

Exodus 40:13–Leviticus 4:9

THE TABERNACLE WAS COMPLETED

Exodus 40:33

"And he reared up the court round about the tabernacle and the altar . . . So Moses finished the work."

Try to think about the wonder of the day—the day that Moses' Tabernacle was completed! All the hangings were in place that surrounded the area. Within that compound was placed every piece of furniture according to God's specifications. All was ready for worship: the BRASEN ALTAR for sacrifices, the LAVER for washing, the LAMP for illumination, the ALTAR OF INCENSE for prayer, the HOLY VAIL for separating the HOLY PLACE from the HOLY OF HOLIES, and the ARK OF THE COVENANT covered by the MERCY SEAT for communion, forgiveness, and acceptance by God. What an exciting and humble day!

Think of all the work that the wilderness-wandering people did to bring that tabernacle to completeness. Remember all the hours of building, sewing, painting, and working with fine metals. The skill and patience worked together in it all!

Have you ever been to a church building dedication? Recall with me, the financial and personal sacrifice that went into that project! Think about it! Such a glorious day! The actual completion of the building and seeing the beautiful sanctuary come to pass was overwhelming. Remember? So, too, we can put ourselves back in the book of Exodus. We can feel the excitement and euphoria of the Israelites on that day. As they viewed the beauty of their work and saw it all in place, they knew that Moses had finished the work! **It was then, and only then, that** *"THE CLOUD covered the tent of the congregation, and the glory of the LORD filled the tabernacle."*

"MY STRENGTH"
"BLESSED BE THE LORD MY STRENGTH"
(Psalm 144:1)
Many days I begin with no human energy for the hard tasks ahead.
What shall I do?
I must go on and on!
At the end of the day, I look back and I see
that He has performed that which concerneth me.
He has been My Strength and My Song.
He not only strengthened me,
but He is personally my energy and strength. (ggs)

𝒯oday's 𝒷ible 𝒷lessing   𝒯ebruary 3

Leviticus 4:10—Leviticus 7:10

CURSING NOT TOLERATED

Leviticus 5:1

"And if a soul sin, and hear the voice of swearing, and is a witness, whether he hath seen or known of it; if he do not utter it, then he shall bear his iniquity."

34

In today's world, a person cannot go out into that world without hearing the Lord's Name taken in vain. It is sad that people have become so corrupt in their thought and talk life! Have you noticed that *cursing* and *swearing* has become the *"norm"* today?

Today's little children say, *"O, my God!"* for any excitement or infraction large or small. The television is full of cursing and swearing. Some news commentators use gutter language as if it were pure. They cannot express a thought politely. Somehow they feel bad language gets their points across better. Does it?

People on buses, in the stores, and on the street have dirty mouths. Parents teach their children filthy talk by their bad examples. Bad words punctuate every conversation. **Jesus' name is maligned**. Hell is cursed on most anyone or thing. The *"f"* word is as common to some as rain falling on a rainy day. People's body parts are verbally thrown around with no care of offense.

Folk from other countries, who are learning English in America, punctuate their words with God's Name. They and our children know no better. It is what they hear. They learn by the examples of those around them and on the radio and TV.

In this verse, a soul who *heard* a swear word was as guilty as the person cursing. The hearer was defiled by the word. He became guilty of a trespass and had to go to the tabernacle to offer a sacrifice on the burnt altar. Can you imagine today, if we were under the law, the crowd of trespassers that would gather daily for such forgiveness?

Oh, that people in our generation would have such tender ears that cursing would not be tolerated by them or around them.

"HE THAT REFRAINETH HIS LIPS IS WISE"
(Proverbs 10:19; 11:13; 13:3)
These verses charge and rebuke me
after I have spoken unwisely or in haste.
"In the multitude of words, there is sin" (verse 10: 19)
Review your recent conversation and you will see it is so.
"Idle words" are worthless words.
We could say in fewer and better words what it is we have to say.
(ggs)

Leviticus 7:11—Leviticus 9:21

THE PRIESTHOOD: A BLOODY JOB

Leviticus 9:18

"He slew also the bullock and the ram . . . which was for the people: and Aaron's sons presented unto him the blood, which he sprinkled upon the altar round about,"

Most of us don't like to deal with blood or have anything to do with blood. A little child will cry and run to his mother if there is any blood on his wounds. Women have to deal with blood all their lives in one way or another. It is repulsive to us. It denotes sickness. It spreads diseases. It stains clothing. It is difficult to remove.

So it is, with some personal repulsion that we read about the blood that was shed for sin here in the book of Leviticus. Aaron, the High Priest, and his sons dealt with blood and death in some form or another daily. They killed animals as if they worked in a slaughter house, draining the animals of their blood and dissecting their inward parts. Some of this blood was offered and burned and poured at the base of the altar.

There were various types of offerings—the burnt, the peace, the trespass, the meat, and the sweet savour. Some involved blood, some meal, and some oil. God watched from Heaven.

All of these sacrificial ceremonies were pictures of the Lamb of God who would come some day and shed his holy, sinless blood at Calvary. God hid His face that day. All that blood poured out at the bottom of the altar looked forward to the final sacrifice for sin. All the sprinkling of the blood here and there looked forward to the final sacrifice of the Son of God.

I marvel at the priests down through the ages of the Israelites' history. They did not volunteer for such a job. They were born into it. Some of them did not care for their position. They degraded it by drinking and by unholy living, and were judged by God. Others took their ministry as a holy obligation to serve the Living God.

"THE BLOOD OF HIS CROSS"

The Blood of His cross—O how precious and holy!
It covers the sin of the lost guilty one.
It avails for the souls of our innocent children
And those who are sick and weak and undone.
The Blood of the Cross—that blest cleansing flow
We are, by His blood, made whiter than snow.
It availeth forever, its power will abide
That life-stream from Calvary that flowed from His side.
(ggs)   (From page 81, *With Tears in My Heart*)

Today's Bible Blessing   *February 5*

Leviticus 9:22—Leviticus 13:7

TWO DIE BY FIRE

Leviticus 10:12

"And Moses spake unto Aaron, and unto Eleazar and unto Ithamar, his sons that were left . . ."

It was a terrible experience!—that day when fire went out from the LORD and devoured Nadab and Abihu. They were the sons of High Priest Aaron. The truth was that he had four sons. They offered strange fire. Perhaps these two young priests were intoxicated as they performed their priestly duty in the newly dedicated Tabernacle (vs. 8-11). It reminds us of Eli's sons.

If you recall, God had specific instructions for everything concerning the Tabernacle—especially *the form* of worship and *the way* sacrifices and prayers were to be offered. It seems, from reading Leviticus 16:1, that these deceased priests may have been right by the altar of incense when they offered their "strange" fire.

The Bible says the men were disobedient. Those disobedient priests had mixed *"strange"* fire into their censers, combining it with the specially blended incense that represented prayers to the LORD. Whatever they did or wherever in the Tabernacle they were, it sorely displeased the LORD.

Without explanation or apology, the LORD devoured Nadab and Abihu with Holy Fire! What a dreadful sight for Aaron, their father to see.

My husband and I had a son burned in a fire over 31% of his body. Although the actual fire never touched his body, the heat from the fire roasted him, as if he had been in an oven. Perhaps that is what happened to these young priests, for their bodies could be picked up easily in the very clothes they were wearing.

Two of Aaron's nephews, Mishael and Elzaphan were called to remove their dead cousins. The Bible says, *"They went near, and carried them in their coats out of the camp."*

So much could be said about that disobedient defiant action of these sons. Had Aaron instructed his sons properly? Had he looked the other way as they imbibed intoxicating drink?

Later in this same chapter of Leviticus (10:16) there was another incident of disobedience. We read that the goat of the sin offering was burned. The priests, the living sons of Aaron— Eleazar and Ithamar, had not followed directions either. Was that family ever going to learn? They should have eaten the sacrifice, not burned it. Why?

Because the blood of the sacrifice had not been brought into the Holy Place. What was wrong with those brothers? Is it difficult to follow instructions? Had their parents never taught their children to obey?

Aaron made an excuse, as he was prone to do always. I am sure he feared more death by Holy Fire. He tried to rectify the error. Moses accepted the excuse. Life would go on for them, sad to say, to disobey once more.

"DEATH'S LESSON"

Has there been a death of someone near and dear?
What is the lesson in this for us?
This loss should jolt us to take stock of our life.
Is it pleasing to the Lord?
Are we ready to meet Him?
How is the ledger of my life if He should suddenly call my name?
What have I not done?
The death of a dear one should teach us to do what we can
to please and help others.
While they are here . . .
Then there will be no regrets when they go. (ggs)

Leviticus 13:8—Leviticus 14:33

PRIESTS AS MEDICAL EXPERTS

Leviticus 13:13

"Then the priest shall consider: and, behold . . . have covered all his flesh . . . he shall pronounce him clean that hath the plague . . ."

I marvel at the job description for the Old Testament priests, don't you? Not only were they the spiritual leaders of the Israelite camp, but also, they were skilled warriors in confrontation and battle.

Remember when the Levites (that's Aaron's tribe) felled three thousand men after the sordid worship of the golden calf in Exodus 32:28? Here we see that the priest had to be familiar with diseases such as the dreaded leprosy. The priests were somewhat like doctors in their day. All the leprosy symptoms were given in today's reading.

The diagnosis was put in the hands of the priests. What an awesome responsibility! It is no different, in some aspects, today. We look to our spiritual leaders for counsel and advice—even diagnosis of our health concerns.

Sad to say, many in church leadership let us down. It was no different in Aaron's day than today.

"SERVE THE LORD WITH FEAR"
"Rejoice with Trembling!"
(Psalm 2:11)
What a great and majestic God is our Lord God Almighty.
We should have all our service unto Him with reverence.
Even our praise should be with thanksgiving
and honor and awe.
When we consider Whom we serve,
we are humbled that He accepts our service
so small, so frail, and so faulty. (ggs)

Leviticus 14:34—Leviticus 16:28

WALKING INTO THE PRESENCE OF GOD

Leviticus 16:17

"And there shall be no man in the tabernacle of the congregation when he goeth in to make an atonement in the holy place, until he come out . . ."

As I read this passage, I am struck with the fact that **no one else but I can confess my sin and failures to God for His forgiveness.** So it was with Aaron. He must go alone to make atonement for sins. It was a great responsibility for Aaron and every high priest from then on to go alone, with the blood, into the Holy of Holies to make atonement for his sins and the sins of the people.

Can you imagine the fear Aaron had? Had not his own sons been killed in the Holy Place because they took upon themselves the place and the manner where they were going to minister? We read that Aaron was alone when he offered an atonement in the Most Holy Place. That's what the Bible says.

It must have been exceedingly quiet there that day. The people outside the tabernacle waited and listened. They heard and were comforted by the tinkling of the bells on the hem of Aaron's robe as he walked. Other than that, the only sound was the echo of his work as he took a bowl of blood from the young bull. They could hear as he passed the burnt altar, passed the laver, passed the candlestick, passed the shewbread, and passed the altar of incense as he entered the Holy of Holies.

I wonder how Aaron felt as he pushed the beautiful vail aside to walk into the very presence of God!

"LET ME HEAR THY VOICE"
(Song of Solomon 2:14)

"Teach me to Pray." There is a yearning to pray in all believers.
How can it be that a pleading word from my heart
can move God's hand?
He calls us to prayer. He wants us to tell Him.
"Prayer" and "supplication" brings *"peace"* and *"calm."*
The answer, itself, does not necessarily bring peace–
Just letting God know your requests does.
Leaving it all to Him brings peace.
*"Let your requests be made known unto God and the peace . . .
shall keep your hearts."* (Philippians 4:6-7)
"Let not your heart be troubled."
Whatever the answer, know it is the right answer for you! (ggs)

Today's Bible Blessing   *February 8*

Leviticus 16:29–Leviticus 19:33

DEVIL WORSHIP OUTSIDE THE CAMP

Leviticus 17:3-4

"What man . . . of the house of Israel, that killeth an ox, or lamb, or goat, in the camp . . . or out of the camp, and bringeth it not unto the door of the tabernacle . . . to offer an offering unto the LORD before the tabernacle . . . blood shall be imputed unto that man . . . that man shall be cut off from among his people:"

Evidently some of the Israelites were secretly offering an ox, a lamb, or a goat to idols, heathen deities, away from the proper God-approved place of offerings at the Tabernacle. This verse implies that it was happening on a regular basis. Behind the backs of the faithful, blood sacrifices were made *"in the camp"* and *"out of the camp"* to idols and false deities. The influence of the gods of Egypt and the ways of the heathen had rubbed off on some of the people whom God looked upon as His chosen.

Verse 7 implies that those disobedient Israelites were sacrificing unto devils to which they had spiritually prostituted themselves. Some had cut and tattooed themselves for the dead. They had cut their beards in heathen styles. They had sought after *"peeping wizards."* They had looked to enchantments and observed times. They were mean to strangers within their midst. They had cheated in business dealings with weights and measures. They had sacrificed their children to Molech, committed adultery with their neighbors' mates, and participated in homosexual and bestial sexual activities.

I believe they even drank the blood of their sacrifices as many heathen do today. All this spiritual unfaithfulness was abominable to the LORD! **God said that the life of the flesh was in the blood** (Leviticus 17:11, 14). These people were degrading the blood of the animals as they degraded themselves in heathen worship.

They did not see the big picture that someday in the future the Lamb of God, Jesus Christ, would sacrifice His holy, sinless blood to redeem their souls. All such animal sacrifices were to be brought to the door of the tabernacle. If they refused to do so, they would be cut off from among God's people.

You and I sit back and think *"How could they do such evil? How could they disregard the words of the LORD?"* They appeared to have no fear of Him! The answer lies within you and me. Some of us are the very same. We have His Words in our Scripture; yet we, too, often ignore what we read. We go our merry way and think no one knows what we are doing outside the camp of believers and away from those who walk godly.

"GOD IS GREATER THAN ANY MAN"
(Job 33:13)
"Why dost thou strive against Him?
For He giveth not account of any of His matters."
Why doth the clay say to the Potter, "WHY"?
A Sovereign God does not need to explain
though He often does. (ggs)

Today's Bible Blessing   *February 9*

Leviticus 19:34—Leviticus 22:30

WHY SUCH WORLDLINESS?

Leviticus 20:24b, 26a

". . . I am the LORD your God, which have separated you from other people . . . And ye shall be holy unto me; for I the LORD am holy . . ."

A reader of Scripture cannot help but notice that the LORD wanted His people to be exclusively His. He did not want them wandering after false deities or dabbling in sinful activities. He wanted them completely shut in to Him.

The LORD did not choose Israel because they were a **perfect people.** He chose Israel because He wanted them for a specific job. It would be through this people that the Messiah would be born. He was to be the sin-bearer for the whole world. So God, through various means, was pruning His children for that wonderful job!

He wanted to bless His people abundantly. He gave them the Ten Commandments to purify them. He gave them the law full of health and living rules to keep them free from diseases and disgusting habits. His goal was for a Holy people to live Holy lives and worship Him, the Holy God. He said in the last half of verse 26 that the purpose for such *"holiness"* was that they would be His exclusively.

As we read more and more of the history of the Israelites, we realize the depth of their failure. Even today for those of us who are redeemed by the precious blood of the Lord Jesus Christ, God wants us to be a separated people unto Himself (II Corinthians 6:14-20). He is still the GOD who separates!

Why are we so like the early Israelites? Why do we want to ape the world in dress and behavior? Why are we afraid to stand apart from such worldliness? Why? Why? Why?

"IT IS WELL WITH THE RIGHTEOUS ALWAYS"
(Isaiah 3:10)
The Word of God says so!
From the beginning of the year to the end of the year,
From the first gathering of evening shadows until the day star
in all conditions, and under all circumstances,
it shall be well with the righteous!
Even if you cannot see it, let the word of God stand instead of sight!
IT IS WELL WITH MY SOUL! (ggs)
(Isaiah 48:18)

Today's Bible Blessing   *February 10*

Leviticus 22:31—Leviticus 25:15

REMEMBER PEARL HARBOR

Leviticus 23:44

"And Moses declared unto the children of Israel the feasts of the LORD."

There are many events in the life of a nation that must **be remembered.** Here in the United States we have slogans that jump our memories to past battles or historic events such as *"Remember Pearl Harbor"* and *"Remember the Alamo."* **Most** recently it is three simple numbers: "9-11"! I am sure if we thought about it, we could come up with many more of them.

So it is with no surprise that God wanted His people never to forget certain events of their national life. We know that many of the happenings in their wilderness journey were traumatic—starting with the Passover experience. Who could forget that? But some would.

Those who were born in the wilderness and in future years would only have the accounts of such experiences told and retold to them by their parents and grandparents. They would not have firsthand knowledge. Even though some children may think it is boring for grandparents to retell their lives and how it was in *"the olden days,"* it is important for children to listen and remember.

That is why in today's reading, we see that the Israelites were to be instructed to observe seven memorial feasts every year. They were the following:
The Feast of the Passover
The Feast of Unleavened Bread
The Feast of First fruits
The Feast of Pentecost
The Feast of Trumpets
The Feast of Atonement
The Feast of Tabernacles

With every feast there were sacrifices for sin and praise. Reread this day's reading and ponder all of those meanings and instructions.

"THE FAINT"
(Isaiah 40:29)
"He giveth power to the faint;
and to them that have no might, he increaseth strength."
What a marvelous specific promise for such as I,
who am pressed above measure
and have little might, even for daily tasks.
I have experienced His strength
as His strength is exchanged for my weakness. (ggs)

Today's Bible Blessing　　　　　　　　　　*February 11*

Leviticus 25:16–Leviticus 26:45

ISRAEL'S FAILURE TO CARE

Leviticus 26:3

"If ye walk in my statutes, and keep my commandments, and do them;"

What a wonderful promise from the God of Israel who promised peace, as well as many other blessings, for devotion and obedience to Him. The LORD their God not only promised *"peace"* to Israel, but also, that their enemies would be slain by the sword. He would love Israel, and He would set his Tabernacle among them. He would be their God—the very One who brought them out of the land of Egypt, freeing them from unjust slavery.

What did the Israelites do instead? They despised God's statues (rules) and broke His commandments. Because of their rebellion, God sent terrors, consumption, and fevers. Their pride was broken. Their strength spent. Wild beasts roamed their area. Pestilence would come. All this and more was the lot of Israel when the Northern ten tribes were captured and dispersed into Assyria for many years. The Southern tribes were captured by Babylon for seventy years. How awful—faintness of heart for prosperity and blessing.

Are we not like these ungrateful Israelites? The LORD God has promised so much in this age of grace to us who have been *"redeemed"* by the *"precious blood"* of the Lord Jesus Christ. Yet, many of us neglect Him, worship idols of our hearts, and thumb our nose at His commandments. WHY?

"I WILL LOVE THEE, OH LORD!"
(Psalm 18:2)

1. my STRENGTH–for *every weakness*
2. my ROCK–in *any situation*
3. my FORTRESS–*protection always*
4. my DELIVERER–from *fear* or *foe* in *death* or in *life*
5. my GOD–my *CREATOR* and *SUSTAINER*
6. my BUCKLER–in *warfare*
7. my HORN–of *SALVATION* and *GRACE*
8. my HIGH TOWER–my *RECOURSE* and *REFUGE*

THERE IS NOTHING THAT I NEED
AS I WALK LIFE'S WAY
THAT MY LORD DOES NOT PROVIDE OR BE,
AS HIS WORD SAYS. (ggs)

Today's Bible Blessing   *February 12*

Leviticus 26:46–Numbers 1:50

FOR ME AND MY HOUSE

Leviticus 27:14

". . . When a man shall sanctify his house to be holy unto the LORD."

I remember very well being in a home in Maine. The husband was a deacon. His wife was devoted to him and to the church's ministry, as well as to the LORD. I enjoyed them very much. Sitting at their dining room table, the wife commented, *"This house is the LORD'S house! It belongs to Him."* She meant every room, every nook and cranny. It was an absolutely beautiful home. She spent much time and effort making it a show place from attic to basement. I was impressed! There were no children there.

To be truthful, I don't ever remember telling anyone that my house was the LORD's—even though I believed it was. There were times in the early BIBLE FOR TODAY days that I didn't want shipping boxes in the front hall all the time. How could one make a *"Home"* with stuff all about that had nothing whatsoever to do with *"homemaking"*?

I must confess, at the time that woman declared her house the LORD'S; I did not want just anyone wandering about our rooms and seeing all my mess. (I still feel that way. Oh, I didn't care if God saw it, for He knows my heart.)

Sometimes, or maybe often, during the Old Testament times—a person who loved the LORD with all his heart and mind would give his house to the LORD. (This of course, would mean the priests and Levites would have the house.) It would be like giving your house to your church. This is very interesting to me.

Giving of one's substance to the cause of Christ is a good work. It is a wonderful thing. But then later, in *verse 15*, it seemed that the *giver* could ask for his house back. If so, he paid the priests the original price of the property, plus one-fifth more. I am not sure if that meant the property owner's dedication had waned, or if this was a normal thing in those days.

I remember when a man in one of my husband's churches gave my husband beautiful office furniture. It was lovely. We have never had anything like it since. The man got mad at my husband and took all the furniture back. That didn't seem like a *"normal"* giving to me. It was for that giver.

One day I was telling another woman, who had a lovely house and no children, about the woman in Maine. I had forgotten that she, too—some months before—had said the same thing to me about her house belonging to the LORD. I told her that I had never said this about my house to anyone, but I guess I had given mine to Him without any big statement!

It sounds all glorious to say and hear, but it's another thing to actually turn your house over to God. *We have church in our living room.* Our dining room has become a parlor with the dining room furniture stored and scattered here and there. It is nothing to have it filled with recording equipment. Our sun room, or family room, is an office full of old desks, books, tapes, equipment, and people helping our ministry. Our basement is crowded with computers and stock for people to order, as well as a man down there filling orders. One bedroom is my husband's office and another is mine.

The UPS truck comes at least once a day, if not more, picking up and leaving packages. The third floor is a spare office and a storage place for books, tapes and videos. People come at any hour of the day, dropping in for Bibles, books, or counsel. Workers in our ministry work in our house during the day and into the early evenings.

The phone rings for everyone but for me most of the time. Our garage is full of books and storage for the ministry. Big semi-trucks back into our driveway delivering books and Bibles. Yet, I never made a big deal to people that I've given my house to the LORD. We just did it!

Often I've wondered about those women and others who have said, *"This is the Lord's house."* What would they do if God took them at their word and actually took their house for His work and His purposes? Would they take it back from God again? What would they really do? *"But as for me and my house, we will serve the LORD"* (Joshua 24:15).

"TRUST IS THE ANSWER TO FEAR"
(Psalm 56:3-4)
"What time I am afraid, I will trust in thee."
If we allow our old nature to govern our thoughts,
we will constantly fear;
for daily there are fearful things in our lives.
But, our attitude is stated in Psalm 56:10-12
"In God will I praise his word: in the LORD will I praise his word.
In God have I put my trust:
I will not be afraid what man can do unto me.
Thy vows are upon me, O God: I will render praises unto thee."
I WILL TRUST!
Praise keeps the heart singing.
Reading His word keep us believing. (ggs)

Today's Bible Blessing   *February 13*

Numbers 1:51–Numbers 3:47

WHAT BANNER ARE YOU FLYING?

Numbers 2:34

"And the children of Israel did according to all that the LORD commanded Moses: so they pitched by their standards . . . after their families, according to the house of their fathers."

A few years ago we visited Queen Elizabeth's palace. We went to England for our fiftieth wedding anniversary. We were told while there, that always, whenever she was in her London home, her royal banner waved over her roof. Anyone and everyone who looked in that direction knew that Queen Elizabeth was home.

So in today's *"blessing"* we learned that each tribe had a banner signifying who they were and where their tent was pitched. There was no doubt who lived there or what their names were.

I am sure you remember when the United States landed on the moon several decades ago. One of our national notable memories was the planting of *Old Glory* on the moon's crust. Anyone and everyone who saw that flag on the moon knew the USA had been there.

How about you and me? Do we fly our banner, of being a Christian, high above our house? Do we fly our testimony like a family flag for people around us to know that we belong to Jesus Christ? Just asking, that's all.

"STANDING IN THE STANCE OF FAITH"
(II Timothy 4:16-17; Ephesians 6:11-17)

"alone . . . together"
Daniel alone purposed not to defile himself.
Daniel alone prayed,
Yet, it is just as important to STAND TOGETHER
as it is to stand alone!
The three Hebrew children STOOD TOGETHER
and would not bow down.
Paul wrote that "no man stood with me"—
but "the LORD STOOD with me."
"STAND!"
Put your armour on!
WITHSTAND! and STAND!
STAND THEREFORE! (ggs)

Today's Bible Blessing   *February 14*

Numbers 3:48–Numbers 6:1
THE LAW OF JEALOUSY

Numbers 5:29

"This is the law of jealousies, when a wife goeth aside to another instead of her husband, and is defiled . . ."

Perhaps if we had such a *law of jealously* **today, there would be less** *adultery* **and** *fornication* **in the world.** Jealousy is a terrible fire. Often the imagination runs away in the mind of the jealous person. Yet, often there is a foundation for such jealousy.

Strange as it may seem to us, there was adultery in the wilderness. One would think with the very presence of God between the Cherubim at the Mercy Seat, the Israelites would want to live holy lives. This was the LORD'S desire for them. But, no—there was *adultery*. In today's reading, we become aware of this sin. It was practiced in the midst of the camp.

As I hear of all the *"living together"* **that is so popular today by celebrities and regular people, I reflect on what it must have been like in the days of Noah.** Sin must have been absolutely rampant! It was so horrendous that God destroyed the whole earth with a flood. Only THE NOAHS and their birds and animals were spared.

In our own century, there are murders, hating of parents, disowning of children, abortions, thieveries, lying, cursing, sodomies, as well as adulteries! How could there have been more sin in Noah's day?

Jealousy is a burning fire in the breast of the jealous person. It is difficult to put it out! All jealously is not bad. God said He was a *Jealous God*. When a person is married, that person is the exclusive emotional and sexual partner of the one to whom he or she is married. When that holy union is betrayed and broken between husband and wife, the fire of jealously flames.

If a man, in Moses' days, suspected that his wife had been with another man in a sexual way, Moses had a way of testing the faithfulness of the wife. He had a way of discovering if it were all in the husband's mind, or if the jealously had a foundation. It was sort-of a *wilderness lie detector test*.

The woman would be brought before the LORD in the tabernacle. She would be given a bitter drink, concocted from some of the tabernacle's dedicated water, mixed with dirt off the tabernacle floor. If her stomach swelled and her thigh rotted, the conclusion was that the wife was an *adulteress*. If she did not manifest either of those two symptoms, she was innocent, and her husband was just the jealous type. This procedure was called "THE LAW OF JEALOUSY."

If everyone today, who had a jealous husband or wife, would have the spouse take *a lie detector test*, much *adultery* and *fornication* would stop. In our day, such sexual unfaithfulness seems to be *"in vogue"* and publicized as the thing to do. Sad to say, 'living together' instead of marriage is becoming the *"norm"* today.

Many who practice such *adultery* and *fornication* do not consider they are living in sin. There are a few of us left today who would fear such publication of any unfaithful doings. There are still some of us left who believe in *"the sanctity of marriage"*! That's a good thing!

"BEFORE I WAS AFFLICTED I WENT ASTRAY"
(Psalm 119:67; Psalm 91:3)
Many have been spared a useless ruined life
by their sorrows and sicknesses.
Our troubles have been the means of our delivery
from a far greater evil.
SURELY HE SHALL DELIVER ME
FROM THE SNARE OF THE FOWLER.
I'm thinking of our precious grandson, David.
Perhaps God put him in the hospital to spare him
from evil men and Satan's snares. (ggs)

Today's Bible Blessing   *February 15*

Numbers 6:2–Numbers 7:59
THE AARONIC BLESSING

Numbers 6:26

"The LORD lift up his countenance upon thee, and give thee peace."
     When I was a child, our pastor always gave a closing benediction at the end of the morning church service. After the last hymn was sung, he would go to the back of the church, raise his hand in our direction, and give a benediction.

Different pastors gave different benedictions. I remember Jude 1:24-25 was often quoted, as well as Ephesians 3:20-21. Often I heard the Aaronic benediction. It is found in today's Bible reading. I do not know when Aaron spoke those words. All I know is that soon, we children who heard the same words Sunday after Sunday, learned them by heart.

In the same chapter, we read of the Nazarite vows that women or men would pledge as a sign of their pure separation to the LORD. Perhaps after the cutting of the Nazarite's hair and the burning of it upon the brasen altar, Aaron raised his hand and said *"THE LORD BLESS THEE, AND KEEP THEE . . ."* How wonderful to be *blessed* by the LORD!

My husband reminded me that this blessing was given to individual people—not a crowd of them. Aaron said, *"BLESS THEE!"* As you may remember, one of the beauties of the *King James Bible* is that its pronouns let us know how many people are being spoken to or about. Most of the modern versions do not do this. They just say *"YOU."* Here we see that High Priest, Aaron, is speaking to an individual. *"Thee" is a singular pronoun!! "Thee" is a personal pronoun!*

The benediction continued: "THE LORD MAKE HIS FACE SHINE UPON THEE . . ." Remember when Moses came down from THE MOUNT? He had been face-to-face with God. The great leader's face shone like the sun. Oh, if only we could have some of that *"glory"* and brightness reflected in our faces from being with Jesus. A Christian should look different.

"AND BE GRACIOUS UNTO THEE . . ." Has not God poured out His *grace* to the believer in the Person of HIS SON? *"For by grace are ye saved . . ."* Have we not experienced the *sufficient grace* of God in our lives in times of sickness and trial? I am sure that you must remember the times of personal fear and frustration when God swooped into your life with *sustaining grace*. It is there for the Christian in time of need. How gracious He has been to us!

"THE LORD LIFT UP HIS COUNTENANCE UPON THEE . . ." Picture with me our Heavenly Father looking up from His work and gazing into our eyes. Picture the smile of our Saviour, the Lord Jesus Christ, setting his eyes on our face. That look of understanding and love is special to the Christian. It shows that HE cares. What more does a child want from a father?

"AND GIVE THEE PEACE." *Peace!*—that is what the whole world is looking for. They fight wars and battles and long for them to stop. They want *peace*. Families have disagreements but really desire *"peace."* The truth is that the soul is restless without such *peace*.

Jesus promised His own that He would leave them *"PEACE"*! It is part of the fruit of the Spirit. The struggles of life are met with that *"peace."* Jesus' *"peace"* is the only place of rest for the Christian soldier. Sometimes our lives are in shambles. We have hurts, we have pain, and we have death. Yet, within our souls is the quiet comfort that only comes from that *peace* from God.

"THE LORD YOUR GOD WHICH GOETH BEFORE YOU, HE SHALL FIGHT FOR YOU"
(Deuteronomy 1:30)
There is no situation that he cannot straighten out.
Yes, even if He must do battle to make a way through,
There is no barrier He cannot remove
No enemies He cannot overcome.
Furthermore He goes in advance to perform this. (ggs)

Today's Bible Blessing   *February 16*

Numbers 7:60–Numbers 10:6

GOD'S CLOUD

Numbers 9:18

". . . as long as the cloud abode upon the tabernacle they rested in their tents."

I suppose if there were any verses in the Bible that expressed my husband and me better than most other verses, it is this verse. *"At the commandment of the LORD the children of Israel journeyed, and at the commandment of the LORD they pitched . . ."* For years we moved. For the first five years of our marriage, my husband was a student. Those five years, we spent in a twenty-six foot trailer which was parked behind Dallas Theological Seminary. No bathroom! No car! Had a bicycle. That was the beginning of the early years of learning to be married. Marriage is a learning process.

We arrived in Dallas as newlyweds and left parenting two young children with the third on his way. We moved to Cedarville, Ohio. We lived there for a brief year at a new Baptist college. Next we moved to Indiana and Purdue University where Dr. Waite was a graduate teaching assistant, who both taught and studied as a graduate student. Then he was a Navy chaplain on active duty for five years.

Next we found ourselves in the military, enjoying the warmth of Miami, Florida. During that time, my husband spent one year in Okinawa apart from the children and me. I was in Florida by myself with four children. It was a long year! Our next move was into a rented home in beautiful Mahwah, New Jersey, when my husband was on military sea transportation service (MSTS).

Soon we were sent to the tumbleweed of Corpus Christi, Texas and the Naval Air station there. The next stop was to Newton, Massachusetts, pastoring two churches, learning hard

52

lessons. And since 1965, we Waites have *rested in our tent* here in Collingswood, New Jersey. **The cloud has quivered a few times.** Yes, it has! A seminary in San Francisco wanted my husband to come and be their Greek teacher; as well as one in Northern Pennsylvania. They put out feelers. **The cloud never moved.** Wisely my husband did not feel God's blowing it in any other direction than Collingswood, New Jersey. How wise to be *"in tune"* to the moving of God's Spirit.

I remember when my husband spoke at a Christian college in the middle of the USA North Country. He was enamored with the whole set-up there. God was blowing on the cloud. It began to quiver. I started to save boxes for the move. Our back shed was filling up with the cardboard containers—waiting. But the door slammed. **The cloud stopped stirring.** I am so glad. If we would have moved, we would have dropped ourselves into much trouble and confusion. Everything that looks and smells like roses is not roses!

Another time a church in Canada called Dr. Waite to be their pastor. I wanted to go. I wanted the cloud to move. I was not very happy where I was. I was sick at the time. I told my husband, *"You get alone with God and you decide. It is your choice."* Then I went to bed ill. He concluded, after weighing this and that, that God did not want us to move. I was personally disappointed. We praised God for a cloud *standing still* over our heads.

I have always felt that the LORD leads me through my husband. I can give my input. I can give my druthers. But in the long run, it is my husband who makes the final decisions where we are to live. If we had moved any of those times, the tenor of my husband's ministry would have been directed in a completely different area. We would never have had **THE BIBLE FOR TODAY MINISTRY** as it is today, not alone **THE DEAN BURGON SOCIETY.**

Because we stayed and did not push the cloud, Dr. Waite's life and ministry has taken a direction he never would have had. He now is one of the foremost authorities and defenders of the Hebrew, Aramaic, and Greek Words that underlie the King James Version. He would never have written all those books in such defense, and I probably would not be writing these devotionals for your and my edification. Yes, we have learned to *"rest in our tent,"* have you? Be patient. God is not in a hurry! So why should we be?

"MY CAUSE"
(Job 5:8-9)
*"I would seek unto God,
and unto God would I commit my cause:
Which doeth great things and unsearchable;
marvellous things without number . . ."*
To know that He knows all about it.
He has permitted the very troubles which refine me.
It is good to meditate often on the attributes of the God
with whom we have to do—
Sovereign, Omnipotent, Omniscient!
FEAR GOD! (ggs)

Today's Bible Blessing   *February 17*

Numbers 10:7–Numbers 13:4

MOSES AT WIT'S END

Numbers 11:11

"And Moses said unto the LORD, Wherefore hast thou afflicted thy servant? . . . that thou layest the burden of all this people upon me?"

Moses had *"had it"*! Here he was, the leader of a bunch of people that did not want to be led. To top it off, Moses had not wanted the job to begin with. He had been perfectly happy out there in the desert with Zipporah and the sheep.

So he followed the Lord. So he made a fool of himself in front of Pharaoh who very well may have been his step-brother. So he commanded the Israelites, in a mighty band, marching out of Egypt. He obeyed God. He took command of an indifferent people. He had faith. He had met God in the burning bush. His people had not!

He'd been to the mountain for the giving of the Law. He'd disciplined his followers and his brother after the golden calf debacle. The tabernacle had been built. All was ready for a forward march, and now Moses hears complaining from the very ones he is trying to help. Food complaints are often heard—even in our day. These wilderness wanderers were no different. The mixed multitude within their midst had stirred them up. The food of Egypt was what they were used to. They wanted flesh to eat. They wanted fish and leeks and cucumbers. Their mouths watered for the melons, irrigated by the Nile River. They longed for the onions and garlic they used to store in their kitchens.

Moses needed help. He had begged Hobab, his father-in-law, to stay with him. The man was a Midianite who knew the territory like the back of his hand. He was a leader in his own right. But the man did not want to stay. He had his own life and his own family. (Each of us has to know our place in life.)

Every man cried and complained in his own tent. The camp was upset, to say the least. After the umpteenth time of hearing the people weep, the Bible says, in verse 10, *"the anger of the LORD was kindled greatly."* Moses was upset, too! He too began to cry out to the LORD, *"Why have you afflicted me, LORD? WHY have I not found favor in Thy sight?"* Moses was at *"wit's end"*! He could not understand WHY God had laid such a burden on him. The burden was the ungrateful, complaining people!

Have you ever been in such a predicament? Have you ever felt that your *"cup"* was too full of trouble? Have you ever run to your room and said to God, *"I QUIT! This work you have called me to do is just too much!"* Have you ever felt unappreciated no matter how hard you try to do right? I know you have. I have, and you are no different than I. So the LORD in his compassionate heart helped Moses.

Seventy men were gathered to help their depressed leader. Seventy men, who could prophesy, were appointed to draw alongside of Moses and to be his helpers on life's journey. **Take heart, dear Christian.** When things are rough and you are at the end of your rope, have a little talk with God in Jesus' Name. You'll be surprised what help can come to you.

"IT IS NOT FOR YOU TO KNOW THE TIMES OR THE SEASONS"
(Acts 1:7)

Many things we do not know in this world.
In fact most of our path is a hidden one.
But we do not need to know what lies ahead to be content,
for our omniscient God knows.
We simply follow the plan He hath laid out.
"One step ahead, I take. He goes before me.
One day at a time l live, He's always there.
The year ahead I see, but keep on trusting
For it is enough to know, I'm in His care." (ggs)

Today's Bible Blessing   *February 18*

Numbers 13:5–Numbers 15:11

THE MURMURERS' MADNESS

Numbers 14:10

"But all the congregation bade stone them with stones . . ."

Do you know of whom the wilderness wanderers were speaking? Do you know whom they wanted to put to death? It was none other than their future captain, Joshua, and that adventurous mountain-climber, Caleb.

Perhaps, as they spoke, the murmurers were gathering rocks to throw at God's point men. I can hear the crowd now—their jeering, their demanding, their running to and fro. I call it *murmurers' madness.* They could not think straight. Maybe they were grabbing at the clothes of the *"good reporters."* The murmurers demanded death! Maybe they were heading for the pit of execution as they screamed. It was the place where adulterers and disobedient children were stoned. It would be a pit from which Joshua and Caleb could not have escaped. I don't know.

All I do know is that the LORD was provoked! He said to Moses, *"How long will this people provoke me?"* You remember the account. The children of Israel were right at the entrance of their destination—the Promised Land—for which they all longed. God had told Moses to send one man from every tribe to spy out the land. This he did. Ten came back afraid of their own shadow. Two returned with a positive attitude. They were from the tribes of Judah and Ephraim. They believed the LORD.

Confidently, Caleb declared *"We are well able to overcome it."* They knew that the LORD would win the land for them. Yes, there were giants! Yes, there were walled cities! Yes, the people were strong. So what? Had not God promised to provoke and be with them?

Once again we see the anger of the LORD! Once again He wanted to destroy the whole kit and caboodle! He'd had it! Once again Moses interceded! This time Moses plead—not for the people. No—this time his intercession was for the testimony of the LORD himself. All these men and women who had seen God's glory in the wilderness continued to provoke Him by their unbelief.

Ten times they had complained. This time was the last straw. The LORD knew such murmuring and complaining was a pattern. It would continue and continue on and on and on. So He cursed the people whom He loved. He said, *"Your carcasses shall fall in this wilderness."* Every last adult soul who had crossed the Red Sea with Moses would die in the desert! Only their children would cross into the Promised Land.

What can you and I take away from this story? One lesson is to look at ourselves and see how we complain about the silliest things—like our computers, like our cars, like our employers, like our co-workers, like our husbands or wives, like our finances, like our churches, like our pastors and our pastors' wives. If we did not live in this wonderful age of GRACE, I dread to think how the LORD would kill us because of our incessant murmuring. No wonder the Apostle Paul enjoins us to *do all things without murmuring.* Why? So we can shine as lights for Jesus in this present evil world!

A MURMURING PERSON IS NOT A LIGHT!

"BE OF GOOD COURAGE!"
(Joshua 1:9)
"Be strong and of a good courage" is a command!
BE NOT AFRAID, NEITHER BE THOU DISMAYED
(Isaiah 41:10).
The Lord, thy God is with thee withersoever thou goest.
It is a promise. (ggs)

Today's Bible Blessing   *February* 19

Numbers 15:12—Numbers 17:5

SUDDEN DEATH

Numbers 16:48

"And he stood between the dead and the living; and the plague was stayed."

Who is the man that stood between the dead and the living? His name was Aaron. But Moses was the leader of Israel—the one to whom the people had complained. The complainers were *Korah, Dathan,* and *Abiram.* They figured they were as good as Moses and Aaron in leading the wanderers in the wilderness. So they said to Moses, *"Why do you take too much upon you?"* They and another two hundred fifty renowned men who felt that they were just as holy as their leaders were. Those grumblers were more than upset!

Moses, too, was distraught with them. He commanded the upstarts to fill their censors with incense and come before the tabernacle. Moses had had it! Were not these rebels satisfied with the holy authority they were given? It was their job to care for the tabernacle's holy things. Let God decide who would be the leader and who would be the high priest.

The LORD was minded to destroy the whole camp. Once again, Moses interceded. He commanded all the other Israelites to separate from the offenders. He stated that God was going to do a new thing. His action would prove that Moses was doing God's bidding. Moses said that the LORD would swallow up all those who were with Korah. No one had ever witnessed such a destruction of this type before.

As Moses was speaking, the earth quaked. The earth opened up right before all eyes. It swallowed Korah and all who were with him. It was a dreadful sight! In reality—God meant business! No question about it—Moses was the leader! Aaron was the High Priest!

Then THE PLAGUE began. I do not know what kind of plague it was; but whatever the infestation, it smote the people. It was plain awful! People fell over dead! Others screamed and died! Some crawled on the ground to escape. They could not! The truth was that no one could avoid the plague until Aaron stood between the dead and the living.

Have you ever rebelled against the leadership in your life? Perhaps it was one of your parents. Perhaps it was your husband or wife. Perhaps it was your pastor, your boss, your teacher, your town authority. Examine your heart.

Perhaps you are presently rebelling before the LORD God as to your eternal salvation. If so, consider that because of your unbelief, some kind of plague could come into your life. It could descend upon you like a blanket of grief, or illness, or death. Whatever it may be, ask the Saviour to stand between you and *"sudden death."* Receive Him into your heart as Saviour. He tasted death so you do not have to taste Hell.

"Satan"
(Ephesians 6:11-18)
SATAN IS TO BE FEARED AS A LION.
More to be dreaded as a serpent.
Even more to be alerted to than an "angel of light."
HAS HE CONFRONTED YOU TODAY?
We are not to be ignorant of his wiles and devices.
We have the armor for each attack!
Satan hates the Lord Jesus.
He hates the very peace that God gives.
Satan is jealous when he sees a yielded saint.
He hates the *"blessed book."* (ggs)

Today's Bible Blessing   *February 20*

Numbers 17:6–Numbers 20:23
NO FREE RIDE FOR THE LEVITES
Numbers 18:26

"Thus speak unto the Levites, and say unto them, When ye take of . . . the tithes . . . offer up . . . for the LORD, even a tenth part of the tithe."

It is of interest to me that not only were the people of the congregation to offer tithes to the Levites, but also, the Levites were to take a tenth of that tithe and give it to the LORD. I believe that their tithe was given to the Priests. *The chosen tribe of holy service to the LORD* got no "free ride."

When it comes to giving a gift to God from one's substance, no one is immune. I am afraid that many who claim the Name of Christ forget this. Just because one has bills to pay, just because a new baby and following expenses have come, or just because a job is lost, that is no excuse not to give a gift to God.

Today, we have no wilderness tabernacle. You and I can't lead a bull or a goat to the slaughtering place to be burned on the burnt altar. No. Today, we put money in an offering plate where ever we worship on Sunday, and we mail a contribution to the place where God has burdened our hearts to give. It is to that church of believers, or to the ministry that is proclaiming the truth, that you and I should contribute our financial gifts to God.

I am learning two truths from this passage in Numbers. First, that the general people—the ones from all the other tribes—were to give willingly a tenth of their substance to the Levites. This giving to those in the service at the Holy Tabernacle was the method God used to keep the Levites going financially. The Levites received goods and food in this manner.

Mostly it is to the local church that funds are given. Then it is from those funds that the pastor is paid, that the church expenses are met, and that the missionaries receive their monthly checks.

Sad to say, in the past, some who attended our church grew tired of our church and left. We missed them. To my surprise, in some instances, there was no significant financial loss to the ministry. (This was not true of everyone who had left, but of many.) The absence of their personal presence was a loss, but their financial absence was not evident. It must have meant that their giving was so small, that the absence of that giving was not felt at all. (I am not trying to demean a person with little to no income, but I am trying to emphasize that some who could contribute to the ministry were not.

It was not that important to them.) Personally, I think that this is a disgrace to the Name of the LORD.

Then there are others who had to move away from our fellowship for one reason or another. Their loss was not only felt by the loss of their personal presence with us, but their absence was very evident by the loss of their financial support to the ministry. If you dropped out of your church, would there be a financial loss to that church?

The other thing I learned from today's verse is that *it was required of the Levites to give a tithe* **of their substance to the LORD.** If you recall, the Levites included the priests and all those who transported the tabernacle here and there during the forty years of wilderness wanderings. Remember? They had a sacred duty to fulfill the LORD's commands given to them by Moses in regard to the care of all the holy things. They could not pocket all the offerings given to them and forget their duty to God. They could not conjecture that they were above *tithing*. So they gave.

I am afraid that some ministries and missionaries have this frame of mind, as well as many parishioners. Think of all that God could do if everyone–pastors and saved layman–gave a tenth of his income to the LORD'S work. What shame some will have when they stand before Him at the Judgment Seat of Christ and see how little they gave from their substance to the LORD while here on earth. Shame on some of us!

"DAILY BIBLE READING"
(II Timothy 2:15)
We should read our Bible every day. It is God speaking!
It is God's Words to us and for us.
If we miss a day, we miss His Words for us that day.
We do not have a guarantee of many days to read His Word.
The Bible is for us to read and study and obey on earth now!
One day we will be required to give an account
of this privilege and responsibility.
He may ask, "HAVE YOU READ MY WORDS?" (ggs)

Today's Bible Blessing   *February 21*

Numbers 20:24–Numbers 23:3

THE DEATH OF AARON
ON THE MOUNT

Numbers 20:28-29

"And Moses stripped Aaron of his garments . . . and Aaron died there in the top of the mount: and Moses and Eleazar came down from the mount. And . . . the congregation . . . mourned for Aaron thirty days."

Death is final. It is the last act of any person who has lived or who will ever die. One minute there is life and breath. The next minute, that life is gone. Death can be a time of extreme pain. It can come at a time of sleep. Or it can be in a sudden accident such as a fall.

No matter the person, the method, or the time, death is the same for all. No one alive today, can tell us about it. Some say they have *"out of body"* experiences and know all about it. Death is the ending of one's earthly life. But it is not the ending of *"life."* A born-again person leaves his body and enters into the PRESENCE of the LORD. Some say they have died and been to Heaven. How can this be? The Apostle Paul experienced it. He wrote about it. *For the born-again Christian, death is a glorious transformation from earth to the arms of Jesus.* But we, who are alive, watching death up close, often do not see all that glory.

Aaron did not appear ill. But he knew. Moses knew. The runner-up High Priest, Eleazar (Aaron's son), knew. They knew that death was only a mountain-climb away. The Bible reads that God said, *"Go to Mount Hor and strip Aaron of his priestly garb."* This mountain was on the eastern side of the Valley of Arabah. It was the highest of the whole range of Sandstone Mountains in Edom, on the eastern side of the ancient city of Petra. Aaron was to die there.

We do not read that Aaron tried to run away. We do not read that Aaron cried out to God to spare his life. He knew why he was going to die. We observe that Aaron, in obedience to the LORD's command, climbed the mount and let Moses strip him of his holy garments. He watched Moses take his robes and put them on Eleazar. Then Aaron died! Right there on the mountain–he died! Right there with Moses and the newly robed High Priest. They watched him die.

I never have been with a loved one when he or she died, have you? My absences were not by choice. My sister died at age twenty. I was not there. My mother died at age 83. I was not there. My father died at age 84. I was not there. Recently our second-born

61

son died at age 56. I was not there. We were called to his side. There we were told of his death. When we saw him, he was gone!

There is a look to a dead person that is different to one living and breathing. It must be *the look of death*. We don't know why many people die. But we do know that Aaron had disobeyed God at the *Water of Meribah*. He and Moses were only to *"speak"* to that Rock. Instead, in anger at the people, they hit the *"previously smitten"* Rock two times instead of no times. Water gushed out–but God was not pleased.

I wonder what would happen to some of us disobedient Christians today if we lived in those Old Testament times. I think the mountains would be filled with dead disobedient Christians who claimed to love the Lord, but did not obey His Words.

> ### *"DEATH: IT'S LESSON"*
> (James 4:14)
> Has there been a death of someone near and dear?
> What is the lesson in this for us?
> The loss should jolt us to take stock of our life.
> Is it pleasing to the Lord? Are we ready to meet Him?
> How is the ledger of my life
> if He should suddenly call my name?
> What have I not done?
> The death of a dear one should teach us to do what we can to please
> and help others while they are here
> So there will be no regrets when they go. (ggs)

Today's Bible Blessing   *February 22*
Numbers 23:4–Numbers 26:15
A SILVER TONGUE SILENCED
Numbers 24:25

"And Balaam rose up, and went and returned to his place: and Balak also went his way."

As we consider the life of Balaam, we see a man who is confused in many ways. He was a *"diviner of spirits"* and a user of charms and wizardry; yet God used him in an unusual way. Though Balaam wanted to curse Israel, he could not. He said, *"If Balak would give me his house full of silver and gold, I cannot go beyond the commandment of the LORD . . ."* He spoke prophetic words that we quote today–yet he did not believe them. Remember Numbers 23:19: *"God is not a man, that he should lie, neither the son of man, that he should repent: hath he said, and shall he not do it? or hath he spoken,* *and shall he not make it good?"* They were absolutely beautiful truths spoken as a Shakespearean actor.

It was from this chapter that the portrait painter, Samuel F. B. Morse, quoted when he exclaimed, *"What hath God wrought!"* Morse was the inventor of the Morse code, using that Scripture at the suggestion of a friend's daughter named Annie Ellsworth. The code was greatly used by President Lincoln during his tenure as commander in chief.

Instead of taking sides with the True God of Israel, Balaam returned to Midian. We know this for we read in Numbers 31:8 that Balaam, the son of Beor, was slain in the Midianite battle with Israel. It was to that battle that God called his people to arms when He declared, *"Avenge the children of Israel of the Midianites . . ."* (Numbers 31:2). One thousand of every Israelite tribe, along with Phinehas, the son of the high priest, went to war at the sounding of the trumpets. All the males were killed at God's command, including the kings of Midian and Balaam.

Such a sad commentary. A silver tongue was silenced! The day that this prophet went home to his *"place"* was the day he headed for death and destruction. So many of us today go our merry way—back to our sinful lives. With that doomed journey downward, some fall into destruction and sure death. May it not be you or I!!

"THE BACKSLIDDEN PROPHET OF BETHEL"
(I Kings 13:14-15)
The man of God knew what he was doing
when he tempted the prophet of God
to disobey God's command to sin.
God will judge him for putting a stumbling block in his way.
Let us hope that the death of the prophet from Judah
gave a warning, and was the means of restoring him
to his right state before God.
How sad to see a backslidden preacher attempt to influence others.
How much sadder to see that the Prophet from Judah
had a firm clear command.
Yet, he wondered and listened to a false word! (ggs)

Today's Bible Blessing   *February 23*

Numbers 26:16–Numbers 28:12

AN INHERITANCE FOR DAUGHTERS TOO

Numbers 27:1-3

"Then came the daughters of Zelophehad . . . and they stood before Moses, and before Eleazar the priest . . . saying, Our father died in the wilderness, and he was not in the company of . . . Korah; but died in his own sin, and had no sons.

Personally, I can understand Zelophehad's daughters, can't you? I am one of three daughters myself. My mother always told me that my father never grieved that he did not have sons. He was glad for us girls and we were glad for him as our *"Daddy."* We loved him. And he loved us! I am sure that *Mahlah, Noah, Hoglah, Milcah,* and *Tirzah* loved their father too.

Like my father, their father was a good man. How do I know this? One thing—because the girls said their Dad was not one of the rebellious ones who died in Korah's band. He was of the tribe of Manasseh whose father was Joseph. Remember him? Perhaps *MR. Z.* was wise and caring—just like his forefather. I do not know—but choose to think so.

Yes, the girls did say that their dad died in his own sin. Now what do you think that means? Because of Adam's sin, sin was passed on to all; therefore *"all have sinned and come short of the glory of God"* (Romans 3:23). I feel that their father offered all the sacrifices and burnt offerings, required by Mosaic Law, don't you? I think it was his time to die—and so he died.

There must have been much sadness at his death. Think of all the death in the camp out there in the wilderness! Besides the plagues put upon the wanderers, because of their rebellion and disbelief and murmuring, I am sure there were natural deaths, too.

We know for sure that there were no boys in the family. Should these daughters suffer deprivation of an inheritance just because they had no brother? Should their father's property and goods go to an uncle or a distant cousin because they were women instead of men? Moses took their case before the *LORD.* This was not one to be settled by *"THE SEVENTY."*

By the way, the Name *"LORD"* written here in all capital letters is the Name *"JEHOVAH"* in the Hebrew language. It is my belief that *JEHOVAH* in the Old Testament represents the Name of *"Jesus"* in the New Testament. *(Jesus means Saviour!)* All along in these chapters we see the capital letters for

"LORD"; therefore, we learn that it is the *LORD JESUS CHRIST* revealed and caring for His children from the time they left Egypt until they were in the Promised Land and onward. Let us never forget this.

Getting on with the narrative: What did the LORD say? It blesses my heart to tell you. He declared, *"If a man die, and have no son, then ye shall cause his inheritance to pass unto his daughter. And if he have no daughter, then ye shall give his inheritance unto his brethren, etc. etc."* Read about this in the rest of chapter 27. It blesses this daughter-heart of mine to read this. How about you?

"THE WALK WITHIN MY HOUSE"
(Psalm 101:2)
*"I WILL BEHAVE MYSELF WISELY IN A PERFECT WAY . . .
I WILL WALK WITHIN MY HOUSE WITH A PERFECT HEART!"*
What a lovely and timely motto
for a Christian woman to have before her!
To "be like Jesus all day long. In the home and in the throng"
Is not as easy to do as to sing!
Oh Lord Jesus, teach me to behave myself wisely
within my house! (ggs)

Today's Bible Blessing   *February 24*

Numbers 28:13–Numbers 31:10

TO VOW OR NOT TO VOW

Numbers 30: 13

"Every vow, and every binding oath to afflict the soul, her husband may establish it, or her husband may make it void."

Sometimes, in those days, a woman made a vow to the Lord. It was a vow of some kind concerning her life. If she be unmarried, her father could say to her, *"I don't think this is a good idea. I am going to disavow that vow."* So whether the woman wanted her vow voided or not, it was. Now if the father said nothing, she was obliged to keep that vow.

The same thing was true of a wife. If the husband heard with his own ears her vow made with her own lips and said nothing about it, her vow had to be kept. But if he did not approve of such a promise or pledge, he could disallow that vow. The Bible says in verse 13 that *"every vow, and every binding oath to afflict the soul, her husband may establish it, or her husband may make it void."*

Until I looked up this word, *"afflict"* in my Webster's dictionary, I had an altogether different idea what this verse

meant. I used to think that if a woman made some kind of commitment about something such as purchasing a product at a store, or promising a friend she would do a special deed, or if she were angry at someone and condemned them in some way, that she was committed to follow through with her word. But if her husband (or father) heard her, he could disavow that commitment. Maybe that is what it means.

Now that I have looked up the word, I am beginning to see the verse in a different light. The obsolete meaning of the word, *"afflict"* is *"to strike down, to overthrow."* The next definition was *"to inflict some great injury or hurt upon, causing continued pain or mental distress; to trouble grievously."* The synonym is *"distress, harass, torment, chasten."*

Now I am seeing the wisdom of the LORD in giving this rule concerning the vows that their women were publicly making. The husband, once again, was to be the protection to his wife. The husband was to be the buffer between a woman's unkind words and promises and God.

The next verse (vs. 14) says *"But if her husband altogether hold his peace at her from day to day, then he* establishes *all her vows, or all her bonds which are upon her: he confirmeth them, because he held his peace at her in the day that he heard them."* So there were some vows that were made within earshot of her husband that must have been approved by him. Those vows—whether good or vindictive—were to be kept. The statute was commanded by the LORD through Moses.

What is your opinion of these verses?

"DAILY FOLLOW HIM"
(Luke 9:23)
"Take up thy cross daily and follow me."
Every day we must pick up that portion of care
with which God has entrusted us.
It is part of the discipline of life to daily follow.
Though we are not aware of it,
the weight is helping to shape our stature.
For He is the one we follow. (ggs)

Today's Bible Blessing   *February 25*

Numbers 31:11—Numbers 32:41
STAYING ON THE WILDERNESS SIDE

Numbers 32:7

". . . Wherefore discourage ye the heart of the children of Israel from going over into the land which the LORD hath given them?"

How easy it is for one group of people to discourage the hearts of another group of people. I'm sure you have been at a church business meeting when one group had a brilliant idea for a church project and another group voted it down. Or maybe you had a keen idea for a summer vacation–even saving money for such fun–when your mate threw cold water on the whole thing and you ended up staying home.

In this passage we see that the children of Israel had finally come to the border of the Promised Land. They were getting ready to put their feet on the soil of the holy land promised to them through Father Abraham. How excited everyone was. Well, almost everyone! Suddenly the Reubenites began complaining. (Only the trained ear would pick up their words as *"complaining"*–in fact, almost *"murmuring."*) You see right there at the site where the whole group had camped—and there were thousands—there was plenteous grass for their sheep and cattle. *"We want to stay here!"* That's what the Reubenites were thinking, as well as the Gadites, and the half-tribe of Manasseh.

So they approached Moses. By this time, Moses was not surprised at anything! Forty years of wilderness wandering was a long time! He had been through so much! It was almost time for him to die! He asked them, *"Shall your brethren go to war, and shall ye sit here?"* As in past conquests the Israelite had to take the land by force. The nationals who lived there all those years were not going to just move over and give them the land!

Moses was distressed. He reminded those who wanted to stay on the wrong side of Jordan, of the discouragement that came into the camp back when the ten spies delivered discouraging news about NOT going into the land forty years ago. The people became so rebellious then. As a body, they refused to march into the land. Joshua and Caleb would have led them to victory. Instead, they refused and God sent a plague. Many died.

Also God said that none of the people, who had come from Egypt, except the faithful spies, would enter The

Promised Land. It was their unbelief that did it! Only the children, who were nineteen years of age or under, when they arrived at the entrance to The Land, would get into The Land.

This time, at the edge of conquering the land, the Reubenites tried to reassure Moses and said, "Oh no, we want to go in and fight with you to conquer Canaan. We wouldn't think of not helping in the war. We will set up housekeeping here on this side of the river and after our families are settled, we will strap on our swords and fight with you side by side for possession of the land. Then afterwards, we will return to our wives and children and cattle and settle down."

Do you know what Moses told those who wanted to stay on the wilderness side? He said to them, *"But if ye will not do so, behold ye have sinned against the LORD: and be sure your sin will find you out."* **How like some of us today.** We have grandiose plans to help fellow Christians or even our families. We say we will be there and we don't show up. We claim that we love them and stab them in the back when they are not looking. We promise financial support and fail to give one penny. Moses' words are good for those slackers. Let me repeat them here for you right now.

"BE SURE YOUR SIN WILL FIND YOU OUT!"

"ENDURANCE"
(2 Tim. 2:3) (1 Cor. 16:13)
Endure trials.
"Endure hardness as a good soldier."
"Quit you like men." "Be strong!"
Endure chastening.
"There is something about a soldier
that makes him want to win." (copied)
EXCELSIOR!
NO RESERVE! NO RETREAT! NO REGRETS!
I must go on,
I must continue,
Even if I can't.
God has a crown for those who endure! (ggs)

Today's Bible Blessing   *February 26*

Numbers 32:42–Numbers 34:28

AN EXTRA-LONG CAMPING TRIP

Numbers 33:3, 49

"And they departed from Rameses in the first month, on the fifteenth day . . . in the sight of all the Egyptians. And they pitched by Jordan . . . in the plains of Moab."

Have you ever done much traveling? I don't mean the kind where you go to a supreme vacation spot where all your needs are cared for and where money is no problem. I'm talking about the kind of traveling where you drive for several hours, stop at a camp site, and put up your tent about midnight. For a few years, when our children were younger and in their early teens (one son was already in college), we went camping in the state of Maryland. It was a beautiful spot with a lake and friends.

The camping part was very hard. We had to pitch a tent. Something we had never done before. We cooked outside, we ate outside, we roamed outside, and we had to walk to the bath house. It was rugged! It was on the verge of primitive. It was fun—but not something I would want to do my whole married life without a regular house to come home to. How about you?

Picture with me the children of Israel and their camping trip. It lasted forty years! True, it would have been shorter if they had not complained. It's easy to complain in primitive conditions. It's easy to complain when the rains and winds come and you are in a tent. It's easy to complain when death and sickness surround you and there is no help. It's easy to complain when a baby is being born as you trudge along the path to the next camp site. But complaining costs something. It cost the Israelites their lives. The LORD punished them.

Those who came out of Egypt and saw the Egyptians burying their dead firstborn were not able to enter the Promised Land. Are you surprised? Only those who were the young people—those we call teenagers today—could cross the Jordan River. It was at the time of the disbelief that God had had enough of their complaining and not believing His will for them. Only the young people would cross the Jordan River and set foot on the shores near Jericho. Those aged 20 and above who doubted Joshua & Caleb's good report, could cross over Jordan. None among them except Joshua and Caleb could cross over.

Aaron died on Mount Hor in the fortieth year of their journey. Soon Moses would die, never to set foot in the new land. Eleazar, the priest and son of Aaron, must have been under twenty at the time that *THE UNBELIEF* overtook the Israelites forty years earlier. He crossed over with the others who were nineteen years or under at the time. We read in Joshua 24:33 that Eleazar died in the *"Promised Land"* and was buried in a hill on Mount Ephraim.

What a long, unending trudge for those women and children. Yet, the Glory of God was among them. His very presence hovered over the tabernacle as a pillar of fire by night and a cloud of protection by day.

I wonder what you and I would have been like if we'd been on that journey. Probably we would have complained like all the other adults who died in the wilderness. We like to think we would be different. But would we be? All this *'camping,'* complaining, and judgment, as well as the hope of new life in the *"Promised Land,"* was written for our learning that we through the patience and comfort of the Scriptures might have hope (Romans 15:4). Did you know that?

"LET US SING!"
(Psalm 95:1; Psalm 96:1-2)
God put a "new song" in our hearts and it is supposed to be sung!
When we awake in the morning,
When we can't sleep at night,
When it's easier to cry,
When we can't pray,
LET US SING!
The Words of the grand hymns have a sweet healing and soothing balm as our hearts hear them sung, even with faltering melody.
Sometimes heard only in our hearts—inaudible to others. (ggs)
LET US SING!
PSALMS, HYMNS, SPIRITUAL SONGS!
I recall my mother and father, old and worn, yet singing hymns of the faith and praise.
LET US SING! (ggs)

Today's Bible Blessing   *February 27*

Numbers 34:29–Deuteronomy 1:37
DISCOURAGEMENT IS A FUNNY ANIMAL

Deuteronomy 1:28

"Our brethren have discouraged our heart . . ."

Discouragement is a funny animal. You can go along in life and do the job set before you without a whine or whimper. You can go forward, in spite of all odds; yet along comes a friend, and with one word of criticism, you become discouraged like you have never been in your whole life. Why is this? Suddenly, your courage is gone. Your spirit is emptied of purpose and cheer. Why is this? I suppose it depends on who is belittling you and on who is criticizing you. You try to please those you love. You long for their approval. With one word, they make you feel like life is too difficult and not worthwhile.

This must have been some of the emotional let-down that the children of Israel had when the ten spies returned to the camp with the disappointing conclusion that the Canaanites would be impossible to defeat. Instead of looking on the bright side of life, the wanderers cowered at the thought of meeting a giant or conquering a walled city. They forgot that the LORD was on their side. How quickly they forgot His power. Just about eleven days (Deuteronomy 1:2) previously, God had pushed the Red Sea aside and let all of them pass over to the other shore without a drop of sea water in their pockets.

Yet, what they considered *"bad news"* stilled them. They became discouraged. They refused to cross over Jordan at the proper time. So they had to wander back and forth and up and down for forty years until all the adults died off—even Moses and Aaron. Only the new generation, unstained by doubt and unbelief, would go into the new land. Shame on those who planted doubt into the eager Israelites. Shame on those who discouraged them in the way.

Are you a discourager? Or an encourager? Think about that today. Have your words soured your husband, your wife, your parents, your children from doing more in life because you said it was an impossible goal? If so, change your ways before it is too late or the one you love may become bogged down in a life unfulfilled of purpose and joy.

"THE JOY OF THE LORD"
(Nehemiah 8:10)
"Neither be ye sorry,
for the joy of the LORD is your strength!"
Why should we grieve when there is joy in the Lord?
He can cause the bitterest tear to glisten.
So let not your heart be troubled. (ggs)

Today's Bible Blessing   *February 28*

Deuteronomy 1:38–Deuteronomy 4:10

THE DAY GOD PUT HIS FOOT DOWN!

Deuteronomy 3:26b

"Let it suffice thee, speak no more unto me of this matter."

I'm sure you, as a parent, have had the experience of *"putting your foot down"* on a certain subject with your **children.** They have begged for a toy, they have pressed for a trip, they have wanted a favor, and you have said, *"NO!"* How they continue to harass you for that certain something that seems to mean more to them than anything in their life! They whine! They cajole! They yearn! But, you as a parent come down hard on them with a negative answer. Finally after minutes—perhaps hours or days of harassment, you look at them in full face and say, *"Speak no more unto me of this matter!"* You have had it!

You, as a parent, feel it is not wise for your child to have what he wants. Perhaps there is nothing really wrong with what he wants, but it is wrong for him at this time. Perhaps the child is being punished and his punishment is to not be given his desire. His disobedience has brought this denial on your part.

So it was with Moses and God! Moses was so disgusted with the children of Israel in their complaining about having no water, that he *"hit"* the Rock. God had told him to *"speak"* to the Rock. We think of Moses as being almost perfect, don't we? We think of him as meek and obedient in his relationship to the LORD. But here in this passage of Scripture, we see him in the flesh disobeying God. Because of this disobedience, he was not permitted to set a foot on the *"Promised Land."* (Aaron, too, disobeyed the LORD at the Rock.)

To you and me, it might not seem fair. It probably didn't seem fair to Moses either. For here in this verse, we read how Moses had asked God, *"Let me go over and see the good land . . ."* That is when God emphatically put his foot down and said, *"Speak no more unto me of this matter."*

I can't help but remember the Apostle Paul. He had some kind of ailment that he called *"a thorn in the flesh."* Whatever it was, it disturbed Paul. Satan used it to buffet (slap or hit) him. It made life more difficult than what it already was. He wrote in 2 Corinthians 12:8-10: *"For this thing I besought the Lord thrice, that it might depart from me."* We would think that such a man of prayer and such a faithful follower of the Lord Jesus Christ would have his health problems taken care of by God immediately. We would think that the

One, who called Paul to suffer so for Him, would answer his prayer, wouldn't you? But no! God's answer to Paul was just like his answer to Moses years before, *"Speak no more unto me of this matter."*

The exact words are found in 2 Corinthians: *"My grace is sufficient for thee . . ."* So when the time came, Moses climbed that mountain called PISGAH. He looked all around and saw with his own eyes the *"Good Land"* that he and Joshua fought so hard and faithfully to conquer. Yet, Moses accepted God's will in that most difficult situation.

So with Paul, he, too, climbed the mountain of *"sufficient grace"* **and looked over to the land of** *"supernatural strength."* In his *"weakness,"* Paul worked for Jesus Christ. All the while, he was *"glorying in his infirmities"*—infirmities that God would not remove from his life.

Do you have such infirmities? DO YOU HAVE SUCH WEAKNESSES? Do you have lands and projects that someone else must complete because of your disobedience? I don't know. I just know about me and my life. God must speak to each of us in His own way for each of our illnesses and disobedient acts. May we use Moses and Paul as our examples? They taught us how to live in spite of our distresses and disappointments. They taught us how to receive the grace of God and let it spill into our lives!

"THE PATHS OF RIGHTEOUSNESS"
(Psalm 23:3; Psalm 25:10)
"He leadeth me in the paths of righteousness"
THE PATHS: PARTICULAR SERVICES!
"All the paths of the Lord are mercy and truth unto such as keep his covenant and His testimonies."
ALL PATHS: OF ALL OF LIFE!
"For His Name's sake."
WHY? And REASONS!
If we would just trust that God's way is the best way, we would be spared much anxiety.
"Help me to stay on course today!"
HIS COURSE! HIS PATH! FOR HIS NAME'S SAKE.
(ggs)

Today's Bible Blessing   *March 1*

Deuteronomy 4:11–Deuteronomy 6:13

THAT IT MIGHT BE WELL WITH YOU

Deuteronomy 5:29

"O that there were such an heart in them, that they would fear me, and keep all my commandments always . . ."

As we remember, the book of Deuteronomy is a review of the forty years of the wilderness wanderings. I can feel the heart-cry of Moses as he reviewed the events of those long, sad years. He yearned that his children—and he did look upon the Israelites as his children—would not forget all that happened to them. He feared they would. And as time went on, they did forget much.

In this particular chapter, Moses reviewed *The Ten Commandments* to his people. He repeated every one of them. We find them first written down in full in Exodus 20. If you recall, Moses spent forty days with the LORD God on Mount Sinai receiving those rules. God wrote them with His own finger on a stone tablet. Now the senior leader is repeating them to the group prior to their march into Canaan, and prior to his soon-coming death on Mount Nebo. I think it is a dramatic reading, don't you? *"HEAR, O ISRAEL!"* was Moses' salutation.

Today, let's look again at these commandments (summarized) so we can see what *sin* is in the sight of GOD. How frightening it is to realize that most of the world breaks every one of them every day! All but one is repeated in the New Testament.

(1) Thou shalt have no other gods before me.
(2) Thou shalt not make any graven image or likeness or bow down and worship them.
(3) Thou shalt not take the Name of the LORD in vain.
(4) Keep the Sabbath day to sanctify it.
(5) Honour thy father and thy mother.
(6) Thou shalt not kill.
(7) Neither shalt thou commit adultery.
(8) Neither shalt thou steal.
(9) Neither shalt thou bear false witness.
(10) Neither shalt thou desire thy neighbor's wife, or anything that belongs to thy neighbor!

In our verse today, the LORD cried out, *"O that . . . they would keep all my commandments always."* WHY?– *"that it might be well with them, and with their children for ever!"* If we know the Lord Jesus Christ as our Saviour, we are His children. He wants it to be well with us, too.

74

> ## *"DO NOT FRET AGAINST THE LORD"*
> (Psalm 37:1, 7, 8; Proverbs 19:3)
> *FRET NOT THYSELF*
> *because of evil doers.*
> *FRET NOT THYSELF*
> *because of him who prospereth in his way.*
> *FRET NOT THYSELF*
> *in any wise to do evil.* (ggs)

Today's Bible Blessing   *March 2*

Deuteronomy 6:14–Deuteronomy 9:27

NO UNHOLY UNIONS

Deuteronomy 7:3

"Neither shalt thou make marriages with them; thy daughter thou shalt not give unto his son, nor his daughter shalt thou take unto thy son."

God's chosen people were called out from all nations to be a separate and distinct people. This was God's choice! Being a jealous God, He did not want His chosen people mingled with those who worshipped other gods. He wanted His people to be wholly for Him. They were to be *HOLY*–separated to Him.

When mixed marriages would occur, the Hebrew line would become contaminated. Not only would the race change, but the religion would change. We see this clearly, as time went on, with Solomon and his many marriages bringing about political alliances with heathen countries. God did not want this!

Moses instructed the people *"Do not make marriages with the people in the land."* One of the reasons God wanted the Canaanites destroyed was their filthy heathen ways. They were morally like animals, and spiritually, they were abusive and vile. The children of Israel were to be a peculiar, separated people in word and deed—and especially in marriage. This was God's will!

Today we see mixed marriages all about–not only in interracial unions but in inter-religious unions. This is a most difficult phenomenon causing much division in families, as well as heartache for the children who will be born to such unions.

> ## "EVERY MORNING DRAW THE SWORD"
> So "Christian" in *Pilgrim's Progress*, being refreshed,
> addressed himself to his journey with sword drawn in his hand"
> (*Pilgrim's Progress*, chapter 4, page 59)
> **Every morning, being refreshed,
> we should start our days walk
> with the drawn sword of the Word of God,
> ready for the enemy who is waiting for us to falter.** (ggs)

Today's Bible Blessing   *March 3*

Deuteronomy 9:28–Deuteronomy 12:29

A PREPARED PLACE

Deuteronomy 12:11

"Then there shall be a place which the LORD your God shall choose to cause his name to dwell there . . ."

A few weeks before our son, David, died, he said, *"Mom, I want my own place!"* He was tired of living in the boarding-group-home where he had to stay. He had a mental illness that made it impossible for him to care for himself. We had tried it, and it did not work out. He was not mentally retarded. He had a good brain. But he had a hurt mind. Previously, he had made friends with evil people who cared nothing about him, but only what they could steal from him. One of those people set his Christmas tree on fire. The result of that deed was that David was burned on 31½ per cent of his body.

It is put into the heart of a human being to want his own *"place."* I suppose that is why, when God created Adam, he prepared for Adam a *"place"* to live. It was a beautiful *"place"* called Eden.

Even street people claim their *"place"* over a heat vent on a city street. That is why it is sad when a person loses his house. Even though he may be in a trailer or an apartment or in a home shelter, he feels a deep loss, for he has lost his own *"place."*

The verse today is very special to me. Moses is reviewing his life as the leader of God's *Chosen People*. He is reminiscing. That is what old people do. They review events of their lives. They tell their children and grandchildren about the old days. Moses was no different.

He reminded the Wilderness Wanderers that over the Jordan River was their *"PLACE."* It was a *"place"* of the LORD their God's choosing. It was the *"place"* where God has put His Name!

Take time to observe the many times the word, *"place"* is used in chapter 12. It is comforting to me. The Land of Canaan would be a *"PLACE"* where God's Name would dwell forever. That *"place"* is called ISRAEL today. That *"PLACE"* is still a *"place"* of rejoicing for God's CHOSEN. Sadly, most of them do not know the God of Israel or recognize the Lord Jesus Christ as their Messiah.

You don't know how much these verses about the chosen *"place"* have comforted my heart today. Of course, I think of that conversation with our son. After he died, I remembered it. He longed for his own *"place"*! It was then that Jesus' words came to me. **"I go to prepare a *'PLACE'* for you."** My heart was comforted. Now David, who knew the Lord Jesus Christ as His Saviour, has his own *"PLACE."* What a comfort that brings to this Mother's heart!

"IF I HAVE FOUND GRACE IN THY SIGHT,
SHEW ME THY WAY, THAT I MAY KNOW THEE."
That I may know HIM . . .
To know Him better is the longing of every submissive heart.
We learn of Him in the Bible in things written aforetime.
The Holy Spirit shows us.
We learn of Him in affliction for He is so nigh. (ggs)

Today's Bible Blessing   *March 4*

Deuteronomy 12:30–Deuteronomy 16:12

TATTOOING & CUTTING FORBIDDEN

Deuteronomy 14:1

"Ye are the children of the LORD your GOD: ye shall not cut yourselves, nor make any baldness between your eyes for the dead."

In this day and age, it is becoming more difficult to find a person who has not had a tattoo of some kind on his person. Sometimes one can observe a man covered with colored pictures of all stripes on his body. It is not unusual for a woman to have many tattoos wherever she feels they should be gazed upon. Years ago, the only people who wore such markings were sailors. And when a sailor got saved, he apologized for the markings that marred his body. Now the biker-world is known for such tattoos—some with demonic pictures covering their arms and hands.

Nowadays it is becoming more the "norm" for Christians to be tattooed and think nothing of it. Piercing and cutting were common in heathen countries, but now they are seen wherever one might walk. There is no country immune from such cuttings.

When we were in West Africa, we saw some young Christian men with cuttings on their faces. They were tribal markings. They always apologized to me that those markings were put on their face when they were children before they were Christians.

O that the Christians in this country would be as sensitive to the heathenism that fosters such markings! Instead, many Christians are proud of their tattoos. They are proud of the long dangling earrings hanging from their ears. Many mothers pierce their babies' earlobes before the child can voice any opinion pro or con.

People want to be in style. Christians who claim the Name of Christ have forgotten that their bodies "*are the Temple of the Living God*" (2 Corinthians 6:16)! "*What agreement hath the temple of God with idols?*" For years the children of Israel lived in Egypt, probably becoming like the heathen around them, and wore their "gods" dangling from their ears.

The LORD God did not want His people to become like the Canaanites. He forbade the heathen cutting and godless practices that had been practiced in that land all those years. It repelled Him. Why? Because all that cutting, tattooing, and piercing, as well as a certain kind of unnatural baldness, represented false gods and false ways. God said in this passage: "*Ye are the children of the LORD . . . an holy people . . . the LORD hath chosen thee to be peculiar people unto himself.*" The children of Israel were to be a "one-of-a-kind nation," committed to the True God and His commandments.

How are you doing in your separation from such worldliness? Do you look just like the world? Are you considering getting a tattoo? Are you thinking about cuttings or piercing? If so, reconsider! DARE TO BE DIFFERENT!

"THE MYSTERY OF THE WORK OF GOD'S WORD"

How amazing that words on a page (God's Words)
Can comfort, instruct, rebuke, direct, and feed.
Sitting down with your Bible,
And reading what God wrote for your learning,
And submitting to the lesson,
Brings a precious effect of calm. (ggs)

Today's Bible Blessing **March 5**

Deuteronomy 16:13–Deuteronomy 20:12
WIZARDS ARE WRONG

Deuteronomy 18:10–12

"There shall not be found among you any one that maketh his son or his daughter to pass through the fire, or that useth divination, or an observer of times, or an enchanter, or a witch, Or a charmer, or a consulter with familiar spirits, or a wizard, or a necromancer. For all that do these things are an abomination unto the LORD . . ."

In this day and age when young people, as well as their parents, are seeking after a *"new thing"* with new experiences and different views that are contrary to the Scriptures, it is wise to warn them not to seek after those that have familiar spirits and from wizards that peep and mutter (Isaiah 8:19). The LORD God warned His people earlier of the damage that such associations could bring into the heart and minds of young people.

We see such a warning in today's meditation. Moses warned of devilish associations! The children of Israel would see such Satanic manifestations as they came into the Canaan Land. That was another reason for the young people not to marry those nationals who had lived in the land all those years—another reason to be Holy as God was Holy. (*"Holy"* means separate.)

Have you consulted a palm reader? Do you look at the daily horoscope and follow that advice? Do you use a divining rod? Do you use a Ouija Board? Are you reading books about wizards and vampires? How about playing cards that tell the future? Whatever— you are tampering with *"familiar spirits"* or *"fortune telling."* **Stop it!** It is more dangerous than you can ever imagine!

> ## "BEFORE ME"
> (Psalm 23; Philippians 3:13; Romans 8:32)
> **I reach for these things in anticipation.**
> **THERE IS A TABLE BEFORE ME!**
> Wonderful things are in prospect for the Christian
> who feasts at His Table.
> How freely He has given us all things in Christ
> to feast and feed upon.
> **I WILL NOT FEAR TOMORROW**
> It is all before me once more, as I step out upon a new year and
> press on toward the *things*.
> 1. Things before me in readiness,
>   as stated in God's Word.
> 2. Things before me in readiness,
>   ours at our new birth.
> 3. Things before me in a prepared love,
>   as in Song of Solomon 4:4.
> 4. Things before me in a personal way,
>   just for me.
> Before me FOR TODAY–
> every hour and for all my tomorrow. (ggs)

Today's Bible Blessing   *March 6*

Deuteronomy 20:13–Deuteronomy 23:24

OUTSIDE THE CAMP

Deuteronomy 21:22–23

"And if a man have committed a sin worthy of death . . . and thou hang him on a tree: His body shall not remain all night upon the tree, but thou shalt . . . bury him that day; (for he that is hanged is accursed of God) . . ."

When I read this passage, I immediately thought of my Saviour, the Lord Jesus Christ, who hung on the cross. What had He done to deserve the *"electric chair"* of His day? Absolutely nothing!

Crucifixions were done outside the camp or city. No one wanted such criminal punishment to go on within eye-view or ear-shot of the common people of the day. Watching someone die in such an agonizing death is far from pleasant. Each breath is pain personified. Each heartbeat longs for it to be the last. There was and is nothing humane about a crucifixion. It's excruciating!

The Lord Jesus Christ suffered such pain for you and me. *"For He hath made Him to be sin for us, Who knew no sin;"* (2 Corinthians 5:21). Can we fathom what *"being made sin"* must have been like? He was sinless! He had never had one unkind thought or done an evil deed—ever! He had never tasted the scum of sin in His life. But He did that day!

After an unjust trial, Jesus was dragged away, beaten, made to carry a heavy cross, and endured the humiliation reserved for murders and sinners. His only desire was to *"take away the sin of the world"* (John 1:29b). Yet, He was looked upon like the most awful person in the country that day. The sins placed upon His being and soul were so intense that the Heavenly Father could not look upon His Son. This had never happened before—ever.

All of this disgrace was born *"outside the camp."* Only a few stood there and stared. Some cried. Some couldn't wait until the death was over so they could get home to their families and have supper. Crucifying Jesus was just another day's work for the soldiers.

The only problem the soldiers had that day was the *"darkness"* **(Luke 23:44).** For some reason, darkness had fallen upon the sky. We know why, but the soldiers did not. The *"darkness"* occurred as the Lord Jesus Christ was in the dying process, bearing the sins of the world on the cross. The reason--so you and I could have eternal life.

"'Man of Sorrows!'
What a Name for the Son of God who came.
Ruined sinners to reclaim!
Hallelujah! What a Saviour!" (P. P. Bliss)

"WITHOUT THE CAMP"
(Hebrews 13:13)
As Christians, we must take our position without the camp!
1. BECAUSE HE DID SO.
2. BECAUSE IT IS OUR PLACE.
3. BECAUSE "THERE" IS WHERE WE WITNESS.
4. BECAUSE WE MAY NOT REMAIN "WITHIN."
To remain within the camp is religious apostasy.
"Within the camp" is no place for us to be–
We who yearn to be like Him and we who carry,
as a standard, the whole word of God
which is the LAMP and LIGHT for our path! (ggs)

Today's Bible Blessing　　　　　　　　　　*March 7*

Deuteronomy 23:25–Deuteronomy 27:24

LIVING WITHIN OUR CIRCUMSTANCES

Deuteronomy 26:7, 15a

"And when we cried unto the LORD God of our fathers, the LORD heard our voice, and looked on our affliction, and our labour, and our oppression . . . Look down from thy holy habitation, from heaven, and bless . . ."

The children of Israel were going to make a mighty move from Egypt to the Promised Land. So they prayed. They prayed to the LORD God of their fathers. I believe that many of them did not know Him. Many had never prayed to the True God.

They had been living in Egypt with heathen gods and ungodly ways all of their lives. A few kept to the LORD's standards. Joseph and his family were dead. No one to whom God had spoken was alive. THEN CAME MOSES! God spoke to Moses and instructed him to carry the Israelites out of the land.

Much prayer was offered. There was much anguish of mind. Much turmoil. God delivered them out of the land and they crossed the Red Sea without a drop of water touching their person.

Now let us think about ourselves for a moment. Often we have found ourselves in circumstances beyond our control. We prayed to escape. But there we were, in the midst of turmoil and heartache. Always, always, we strive to leave our present distress.

We pray fervently. We cry out like the Israelites, *"Look down from thy holy habitation . . . and bless!"* But all that we have before us is a wilderness of confusion and disappointment. Has God forgotten us? We have received His Son as our Saviour! Yet, life seems bleak!

I have come to the conclusion, in times like these, that we are trying to avoid our circumstances. That is the trouble! We cannot live above them. They are there. We cannot live beneath them for we are not there.

You and I must learn to live WITHIN our circumstances. That is where Jesus has promised the Christian, *"I will never leave thee or forsake thee."* It is WITHIN our circumstances that God blesses! It was IN THE WILDERNESS, that God performed miracles!

Yes, our Heavenly Father hears our voice. He looks on our affliction. He will be there WITHIN our circumstances holding our hand. Trust Him.

"THE JOY OF THE LORD IS YOUR STRENGTH"
(Psalm 105:4; Nehemiah 8:10b)
How we need His strength to go on and on and on!
It is one of His mercies which are new every morning
to those who seek His face.
"SEEK THE LORD AND HIS STRENGTH:
SEEK HIS FACE EVERMORE."
"Strength for today!"
"Bright hope for tomorrow!"
"Great is Thy faithfulness!"
(ggs)

Today's Bible Blessing   *March 8*

Deuteronomy 27:25–Deuteronomy 29:15
CANNIBALISM

Deuteronomy 28:53

"And thou shalt eat the fruit of thine own body, the flesh of thy sons and of thy daughters, which the LORD thy God hath given thee . . ."

This is an awful verse to contemplate. What can we learn from it? Cannibalism was a fact of life during the period when the children of Israel were in rebellion against their God, especially during the sieges of Jerusalem by both Assyria and Babylon. The hunger was so intense that they ate their own people! It is repulsive to us as we think of it. Who has ever been that hungry that they ate their own?

We all remember the Donner Party. A man by the name of George Donner, with his brother Jacob, headed-up a train of twenty wagons traveling on a new route to California. It was in April of 1846. Because of difficulties, they were not able to leave their camp by a lake in the eastern Sierras. It was October 31st. Snow came. The pass was blocked. Donner's group camped at Alder Creek. Seven made it across the Sierra on snow shoes. Needless to say, 40 of the 87 people survived. How? Starvation and death had been averted because of cannibalism.

I have other stories of cannibalism. Who can forget *Jeffrey Dahmer*, the serial killer who beguiled his male victims, murdering them, and eating their body parts? I recall in my recent lifetime of hearing of an airplane crash. Can't remember where— perhaps in Brazil. Some died in the crash. Others lived. When rescued, the living were in excellent health. Finally they confessed that they ate the frozen flesh of their dead. What would we have done?

It has been said that some people in some countries feel that eating their dead means that the deceased person lives on. Many feel such "eating" is a way to honor their dead. Some kings ate their sons so their own lives and thrones would be protected.

During the time of Columbus, it was discovered that Indian tribes called the Carib, in the West Indies, ate other human beings. In fact, the word *"cannibal"* comes from the mispronunciation of their name, *"Carib."* Ancient historians, along with Marco Polo in the 1200's, spoke of man-eating people who lived northeast of the Caspian Sea. That area is now called RUSSIA.

Sometimes the American Indians ate their prisoners of war. *The heart of a brave man was considered a delicacy.* The Aztecs of Mexico consumed parts of human victims who had been sacrificed to their war god. Eastern South America, western and central Africa, New Guinea, the Fiji Islands, Australia, and New Zealand prevailed with cannibalism during a time in history. Mostly this practice was a religious rite.

I read in the *Courier-Post* (June 4, 2007), that the rebels who followed Liberian leader and former president, Charles Taylor *"were known for eating the hearts of their slain enemies. They decorated check-points with human entrails,"* etc., etc.

All of this cannibalism, found among the Israelites, was a result of their disbelief and their disobedience to the true God. In this same Chapter 28, Moses told them of God's blessings to come IF they obeyed Him. Verse 4 says: *"BLESSED SHALL BE THE FRUIT OF THY BODY . . ."* but if they did not follow the LORD God, His curses that were proclaimed in that same chapter would be upon them: *"CURSED SHALL BE THE FRUIT OF THY BODY . . ."* (verse 18).

Let us learn from the unbelief of the Israelites!

"A TOUCH FROM GOD"
"A touch from God is not always a caress.
It may take a blow to cause us to yield.
Though God deals in love,
His dealings are often strenuous."
(source unknown, ggs)

Today's Bible Blessing   *March 9*

Deuteronomy 29:16–Deuteronomy 32:21

CHOOSE LIFE

Deuteronomy 30:19

"I call heaven and earth to record this day against you, that I have set before you life and death, blessing and cursing: therefore choose life, that both thou and thy seed may live:"

This verse affects me today in a very personal way. I have written in my Bible above this verse in blue pen, *"Our David and his smoking!"* Sad to say our second-born son became a chain-smoker. He learned to smoke cigarettes when he was in the mental hospital. It seems that was what all the patients did. Something about smoking must have helped them temporarily.

Then when they were no longer in the hospital, they continued to smoke. It didn't matter how expensive the cigarettes were, they managed to find the money someplace to buy them. They were hooked on *the weed.* David was no different. There seemed to be a pleasure in such smoking.

Then the next year when I read my Bible, I saw the same verse. Again it reminded me of our son. I wrote with a red pen this time: **MARCH 2008!** That meant the same was true in 2008 as it had been in 2007. *HE DIED IN APRIL OF THAT YEAR!*

Whenever we spoke to him about this habit, he would tell us, *"It will not be the smoking that kills me. It will be my medicine."* David had to take much medicine for his sicknesses. They were strong, mind-altering drugs. They wore out his body. They damaged him, along with the constant smoking.

I begged him, "CHOOSE LIFE!"

One day, without warning, God scooped David from the Land of the Living. It was very sudden. I am not sure what caused his death. The doctor said it was *a deep thrombosis* in his leg. It very well could have been. All I know is that he is now with Jesus in a *safe place.* He no longer needs medicine. He no longer has pain. He no longer needs to be cared for. He can breathe freely. **But I miss him.**

"MY THOUGHTS WITHIN"
(Psalm 94:19; Psalm 104:33)
*IN THE MULTITUDES OF MY THOUGHTS "WITHIN" ME,
THY COMFORTS DELIGHT MY SOUL!*
No condition or circumstances can interfere, day or night, with
meditation upon the things of Christ. We may exercise his
marvelous privilege of "thinking" thoughts given by the Spirit of
God—unheard and unknown by anyone except God and our inner
most self.
WHAT COMFORT AMID LIFE'S CONFUSION! (ggs)

Today's Bible Blessing   *March 10*

Deuteronomy 32:22–Joshua 1:13

THE FAITHFUL EVERLASTING ARMS

Deuteronomy 33:27

*"The eternal God is thy refuge, and underneath are the
everlasting arms . . ."*

This verse became real to me during a time of surgery.
Immediately after the operation, I was in extreme pain. The illness had
been taken care of, but the patient was suffering. I remember "coming
to" in the recovery room and saying, *"I feel like someone cut my
stomach with a knife."* The nurse agreed. She said, *"Someone has."*

**The following days were days of pain and counting the
hours before the next medication.** Then, deciding that the pain
was better than the dreams the medicine gave me, my doctor took the
medication away. I WAS GLAD! The worst was over.

**Sadly, in that frail condition, I discovered that I could
not pray!** I had never had this experience before. Though I am
neither a "Praying Elijah" nor a "Steadfast Paul," I do pray. I
discovered that it was then that others prayed for me. It was such a
comfort knowing this!

**I was too sick. I was too tired. All I could do was lie in
my hospital bed and *"lean."*** As I did this, I had a strange peace
and comfort flood my soul. I realized that *I was leaning on the
Everlasting Arms of my wise Heavenly Father.* The ETERNAL GOD
was my *'refuge."* His arms were *"underneath me."* They were sup-
porting me. They were strong. They were always there!

**Now look with me at the rest of today's verse. It is a
call to war!** It says that *HE*—the LORD God—WILL THRUST OUT

86

THE ENEMY BEFORE THE CHILDREN OF ISRAEL. Under the leadership of Joshua, God was pushing them into battle. Life is a battle!

Anything worth having is gained by a price. *"The Promised Land"* was not given to Israel on a silver platter. They had to fight for every inch of it. They had to push out the people who had taken over the land in their 430 years of absence in Egypt. God said, *"Destroy them!"*

In verse 25, the Israelites were reminded that *"As thy days so shall thy strength be."* Notice that the pronoun is singular. Moses was talking to each individual person—each one who would take a sword and conquer Canaan. What a reassurance for each individual to know that his or her strength would be renewed every day. They could depend on the LORD God. THE EVERLASTING ARMS WOULD NOT FAIL!

BEVERLY'S MINISTRY CONTINUED
(*Beverly was brain injured at birth.)
Beverly had serious surgery today. (1977)
She was near death several times.
GOD SPARED HER!
Our pastor said that God had a ministry for her to do here on earth.
I had not realized that she had a ministry. (ggs)

Today's Bible Blessing   *March 11*

Joshua 1:14–Joshua 5:15
RAHAB'S REFUGE

Joshua 2:18

"Behold, when we come into the land, thou shalt bind this line of scarlet thread in the window . . . and thou shalt bring thy father, and thy mother, and thy brethren, and all thy father's household, home unto thee."

I am moved almost to tears as I remember Rahab's reunion with her family. Rahab, that Jericho woman who protected the two Israelite spies, was a prostitute. The Bible calls her a *Harlot!* Even so, she is listed in the genealogy of the Lord Jesus Christ in Matthew 1:5. This shows the "open arms" of Jesus when He says to all, *"Come unto me, all ye . . .!"* (See Matthew 11:28.)

The King of Jericho knew the spies had come. He knew they had entered the house built upon the wall. It was *the harlot's house.* His men sought the intruders. The town was searched until darkness fell. Rahab lied! The town-gate was fastened. The spies had disappeared.

The truth was that Rahab had hidden her gentlemen callers in the flax-stalk roof. The men had buried themselves in the dry, bug infested roof refuge. But they were safe! Rahab had a plan. She grabbed a strong red cord. She fastened it to a window. The men plummeted down the rope. They took to the mountains and sneaked back to Joshua.

Before they left Rahab's premises, the two spies instructed her, "KEEP THE RED CORD IN THE WINDOW!" In the future, when the Israelites would conquer her city, they would watch for the red rope. It would protect the house and all who were within its walls.

Why did tears come to my eyes? Let me tell you. They came when I thought of the reconciliation between Rahab and her family. She had to approach her father. It may have been years since they talked. I think he was ashamed of her work. She had to go to her mother and beg her forgiveness, bringing the older woman to safety. Rahab had to find her brothers and sisters. She had to plead with them to accept her, to trust her, and to come live with her. Also, she would bring her aunts and uncles, the servants, and any who would live in her dwelling. They knew, along with their king, that the LORD God had done wonderful things for the children of Israel.

Praise God for the faith of this woman of the night. Her life was changed by her one act of kindness. Her house would be the only one left standing when the judgment fell. Someday, she would marry, have a regular home, and become the mother of Boaz who would later marry Ruth, the Moabitess, the great-great-grandmother of King David whose throne would be established forever and ever.

Has your life changed by meeting the LORD God? If so, you, too, have been protected in the major storms of your life!

"ASK OF ME, THE LORD!"
(Isaiah 45:11; Philippians 4:6-7)

God has certain blessings and promises that are ours only by asking in prayer! Apart from the fact that God has told us to "ask," there is a sweet submission and expectancy in asking a sovereign God to grant our requests.

ASK LARGELY THAT YOUR JOY MAY BE FULL!
LET YOUR REQUESTS BE MADE KNOWN
AND PEACE WILL GUARD YOUR HEART! (ggs)

Today's Bible Blessing   *March 12*

Joshua 6:1–Joshua 8:32
KEEP ON WALKING

Joshua 6:3-5

"And ye shall compass the city . . . and go round about the city once. Thus shalt thou do six days. And seven priests shall bear before the ark . . . the seventh day ye shall compass the city seven times . . . and the wall of the city shall fall down flat . . ."

As I was reading this passage, I noticed something about perseverance. The men of war were instructed by Joshua to march. The LORD's command was to compass the city. It was time to take Jericho. Go around the beautiful green city of Jericho one time for six days! That was the order. Just follow!

That seems easy enough. Even though the marchers were brave men, there must have been some trepidation. Would Jericho's soldiers shoot arrows at them? Would they throw large rocks as they passed? Would the Jericho army catapult stones and destroy them? In spite of fears, they marched. God told them to. Six days with one foot in front of the other! They persevered!

How close they were to the walls of Jericho, I do not know; but they were close enough to compass the city as a conquering army. In front of the marching men were seven priests bearing the Ark of the Covenant on their shoulders. Six days! Walking, bearing, and trusting.

I think of you and me on our life's walk. Every day, every month, every year—following God's commands in our lives. Keep walking, girl! Keep walking! Just do what I have told you to do. Some days the walk is dreary. Some days the walk is easy. Often we stumble. Often we cry out. Often we cry tears. Often we have no hope. Often we tire at the knees. But we keep on walking.

The warriors in this Scripture had followed the LORD God before—so have you and I. Fresh in their memories was the walk through the RED SEA. Fresh in our minds is His help in our time of need. They had followed the ARK before. We have, too. God's presence was before them. It has been before us, too. Six days and nothing happened. We know the feeling!

Every time they passed the wall where Rahab lived, they saw the red rope dangling from the window. They remembered her bravery. They, too, were brave. They remembered her FAITH and HOPE. They, too, had FAITH. They, too, had HOPE. We remember ours.

Then the seventh day came. They walked seven times around that city. Their feet may have been tired. The priests' arms may have become weary. They kept going. Seven times they walked 'round and 'round that city. The ark! The rams' horn-trumpets! The shouts! And THE WALL FELL!

HELP US, LORD, not to give up, but to keep walking until our walls fall down, too!

"EVEN IN OLD AGE WILL I CARRY YOU"
(Isaiah 46:4)

This is a comforting verse as the years mount up. It implies He has carried us all of our years, and will continue even unto old age—and in it!

OUR HEAVENLY FATHER IS ALSO A TENDER SHEPHERD.
He knows about the weariness and limitations of old age.
HE WILL HELP US.
HE KNOWETH OUR FRAME. (ggs)

Today's Bible Blessing   *March 13*

Joshua 8:33–Joshua 11:12

THE DECEPTION OF A MOTLEY CREW

Joshua 9:14-15

"And the men (the Gibeonites) took of their victuals (food) and asked not counsel at the mouth of the LORD. And Joshua made peace with them, and made a league with them . . . "

How very careful we must be when we make a "league" with anyone. We read in the New Testament that a Christian should not be *"unequally yoked together with unbelievers"* (2 Corinthians 6:14a). But we forget to pray about a matter. Sometimes we forget to consult God's Words and jump right into a situation that seemed so good, so right. When all along it is very wrong.

Sad to say, Joshua and the Princes of Israel forgot to consult the LORD in the matter of the Gibeonites. They were crafty. They had a scheme. They thought, *"All we have to do is act like we had traveled from afar."*

This motley crew had heard of the slaughters in Jericho and Ai. They were afraid to death. They feared that their whole clan would be killed by Joshua's army. So they devised a plan. They dressed in worn-out shoes and clothes. They brought moldy bread, etc. Joshua assumed the worn-out Gibeonites had traveled from afar. What deception! Yet, it worked! Joshua was fooled. He did not realize that those men with holes in their shoes were close neighbors.

The result of such wrong thinking was bleak! For all of their lives, the Gibeonites would be protected by Israel. The deceivers became Israel's servants. That was *"the league"*! The Gibeonites would be wood-choppers and water-haulers for life. I am sure Joshua was embarrassed. The common people were angry with him and angrier with the princes. Who wouldn't complain? And to make matters worse, five nearby kings decided to band together and kill the Gibeonites. They were angry that the Gibeonites were so afraid. Those kings were angry that Joshua had promised to protect them. **War was declared!**

Now Joshua and his men had to protect the Gibeonites. There was a big battle. Thousands were killed by the sword and more thousands were killed by God's hail stones! The battle was fierce. Night was upon them. In desperation, Joshua cried out to God, and said in the sight of Israel, ***"Sun stand thou still upon Gibeon, and thou, Moon, in the valley of Ajalon."*** Everyone everywhere, within earshot, heard him.

What do we learn from this account? First: **BE VERY CAREFUL ABOUT YOUR DECISIONS AND ALLIANCES!** Marriages, schools, houses, friends, jobs, are all important to the direction of our lives. For some reason, many people jump into situations without prayer or thought. Yet, God is faithful—in spite of our impulsiveness! **He may not make the sun stand still for you and me, but He has a way of answering our prayers and directing our lives in spite of our careless willfulness.**

"IF BY ANY MEANS"
(Romans 1:9-10)

How often we desire to perform a "good thing." We have the inward urge to act; yet we consider Paul's prayer,

"Making request, if by any means . . ."

Paul subordinated his own longings and impulses to the will of God. "Paul did not consider what many would regard as the Spirit's prompting as sufficient warrant" (copied)

HE MUST FIRST PRAY AND BE ASSURED

THAT IT WAS GOD'S WILL.

So should we! (ggs)

Joshua 11:13–Joshua 15:2

MORE MOUNTAINS TO CLIMB

Joshua 13:1

"Now Joshua was old . . . and the LORD said unto him, Thou art old and stricken in years, and there remaineth yet very much land to be possessed."

Have you ever come to a place in your life when you thought you were finished with a certain task, only to find that there was more work to be done on it? It could be discouraging. You are tired out from the work you already did, and here in front of you was more!

I think of grandparents who raised their children, expecting "time-off" and some enjoyment for themselves. When, all of a sudden, due to certain circumstances, their grandchildren are thrust into their care. They must start all over being *"parents"* again. They may be old. They may be tired, but they have a sacred responsibility to raise those grand-kids.

Perhaps that is the way JOSHUA felt when the LORD said, *"This is the land that yet remaineth: all the borders of the Philistines, and all Geshuri . . ."* (Verse 2) Other properties are mentioned. The border of Egypt was a goal, as well as the Southland of the Canaanites to the borders of the Amorites. All Lebanon and the hill country were also included. The Sidonian property is talked about as well as Gilead and the King of Og and King of the Amorites.

In Chapter 11, we read that Joshua left nothing undone of all that the LORD commanded Moses. But in today's verse, it sounded to me that God had a bigger plan. One that He had not mentioned to Moses (I am not sure). He put another war assignment on the shoulders of His commander.

As Christians, our life's work is not over until it is *"over."* There is no retirement for the BELIEVER! Some people who name the Name of the LORD think they can rest on their laurels and coast to Heaven. Oh no!

In Chapter 14, we meet CALEB again. Though he was eighty-five years old, he was set for the challenge of conquering a mountain. How encouraging to us! Caleb would not stop wholly following the LORD! Had not he and Joshua been faithful to HIM? Had not they told the truth about the land they were now invading? Had he not fought side by side with Joshua until now? He said that his physical strength and emotional stamina were strong! In what we today would call *"old age,"* his battle cry was *"GIVE ME THIS MOUNTAIN"* (Joshua 14:11-12)!

When I remember Caleb, I think of my husband and his work for the LORD in THE BIBLE FOR TODAY MINISTRY. All those nineteen years that he taught public school to support his family and the ministry. All those nights of studying and writing—and the children and me being alone! (The books he has written do not come by osmosis, you know.) He had many mountains to climb and many scoffers snarled at his ascent. His work is never done, for he sees another mountain before him! **I am comforted by God's words to Joshua. They ring in my husband's ears, too!** *"THERE REMAINETH YET VERY MUCH LAND TO BE POSSESSED!"*

"LET ME HEAR THY VOICE"
(Song of Solomon 2:14)
1. THE MASTERY OF PRAYER
"Teach us to pray!"
There is a yearning to pray in all believers.
2. THE MYSTERY OF PRAYER
How can it be that a pleading word from my heart
can move God's hand? He calls us to prayer.
"Let me hear thy voice."
He wants me to tell Him (ggs)

Today's Bible Blessing   *March 15*

Joshua 15:3–Joshua 17:14

A SPRING OF BLESSING

Joshua 15:18-19

". . . And Caleb said unto her, What wouldest thou?. . . (She answered) *Give me a blessing . . . give me also springs of water . . . And he gave her the upper springs . . ."*

In conquering his mountain, Caleb declared, *"I will give my daughter to be the wife of the man who takes Kirjathsepher."* If you recall, Caleb was going to claim a mountain for his own. Caleb needed help! He declared that the man who captured Kirjathsepher would have his daughter to wife. A brave man by the name of Othniel did the job. He happened to be the son of Caleb's brother. I suppose the prospective groom *"eyed"* Achsah, the intended bride, for many years. That was why, in my opinion, he was willing to fight so hard to capture that territory for Caleb. Love works wonders!

So this couple was married. In looking over their new property, Othniel had noticed a piece of land that had *"springs"* on it. He prevailed upon his new wife to ask her father to give her that prize field. One day when visiting her father, Achsah reminded him that he had given her the southland. Remembering her husband's request, she said, *"Daddy, could you please give us the Upper Springs and the Lower Springs adjacent to our property?"* How happy the newlyweds were when Caleb bestowed the *"blessing"* on them of springs of water. Most fathers who love their daughters do all they can to help them. Fathers love their daughters. There is a bond between them that only fathers and daughters understand.

We read in Joshua, chapter 17, verse 3 about another father, Zelophehad. He had no sons. Some men do not have sons. God blesses them with daughters instead. My father had three girls. Mother told me that he never regretted that he had no sons. I never heard any such talk of no sons when I was in his home.

So with Mr. Zelophehad. When his five girls reminded their Dad that they had no inheritance, the father did something about it. They spoke to Joshua and Eleazar, the high priest. They reminded their superiors that Moses had promised the girls an inheritance. That was it! The girls received their inheritance!

Let us not forget to listen to our children, especially our daughters. It is the goal of parents to keep the door of communication and care open. Yet, parents should strive not to interfere. Often the best of intentions can be construed as interference. Just because a daughter has married a husband does not mean that a father should forget to help his daughter when needed. This *"helping"* is a touchy situation, at times—especially if the daughter's husband does not want such help. As time goes on, the husband will have learned to love his in-laws, and then the husband will accept such help. There is something special about *"families."*

Let us be very careful not to damage such a relationship. Often hurt feelings come when only good intentions were given. When misunderstandings come, it often takes years for them to be overcome—perhaps never forgotten.

"THE NOURISHING WORDS OF GOD"
(Job 23:12)
THY WORDS ARE MORE THAN NECESSARY FOOD.
WE MUST EAT PROPER FOOD.
WE MUST EAT ON TIME.
WE MUST EAT FOR STRENGTH
B-U-T
MORE AND MORE NECESSARY
IS THE READING AND STUDYING DAILY GOD'S WORDS!
As food builds and sustains our bodies, so the Words of God
build and nourish our inner man. (ggs)

Today's Bible Blessing   *March 16*

Joshua 17:15–Joshua 20:2
AM I A CHRISTIAN SLACKER?

Joshua 18:3

"And Joshua said . . . How long are ye slack to go to possess the land, which the LORD God of your fathers hath given you?"

What a good question! If you remember the children of Israel were in *"the land"* that God had promised them. They had been claiming that property through military force a little at a time. First there was the Jordan River, then Jericho, then Ai, then Libnah, Lachish, Hebron, Debir, Bashan, etc., etc. (not necessarily in this order) The point here is that in their first enthusiasm, the Israelites pressed forward and took much land and possessed it.

Now in today's reading, we see that there were still seven more tribes that needed their promised territory. Evidently there was a real slow-down in enthusiasm. The men were tired. The women were complaining. The children were crying. Perhaps they saw no point in the whole thing. We are not told if there were, or how many Israelite deaths occurred because of the constant battles. There must have been hundreds of Canaanites killed as the PROMISED LAND was taken over by Joshua and his band.

The destroying of the Canaanites, who had taken over the land, was of God. It was His way of cleansing the land from all wickedness and perversion! God did not want His people exposed to such sin! He wanted His people separate from sin. That is His goal today for born-again Christians, too!

All we know is that Joshua was disturbed with his people. He was calling them *"slackers."* Why? Because they yet had to claim the rest of the territory!! Benjamin needed land! Simeon needed land! Zebulun needed land! Issachar needed land! Asher needed land! Naphtali needed land! And Dan needed land! (See Joshua 18.)

I can't help but think of you and me—our lives—our walk with the LORD. Our daily disappointments make us weak in body and spirit. We just want to roll over and go back to sleep every morning! People have disappointed us. Churches have become so "modern," trying to keep up with the latest fads of the world. Our hearts are heavy. We used to witness for our Saviour more. But, now we sit home and sulk. We nurse our spiritual wounds. We complain that life is hard. We do not to want to fight THE GOOD FIGHT of THE FAITH anymore!!

LET US SNAP OUT OF IT! God is still on THE THRONE! We must remember our HEAVENLY STATE. If we are born-again, we have been given PEACE. We have DIRECT ACCESS TO GOD through prayer. We have been RECONCILED TO GOD by the Cross. God's RICH MERCY has been poured upon us. His KINDNESS through Jesus Christ is ours. CHRIST DWELLS WITHIN OUR HEARTS! Because of His love, we can be FILLED WITH THE FULNESS OF GOD. One HOPE is ours, GRACE IS OURS—ours according to the measure of the gift of Christ. (Read Ephesians!) **No longer are we alienated from God.** HOW GOOD TO BE BORN-AGAIN! How could we so soon forget? **Let us determine not to be "slack" in our Christian walk. Let us possess the Land of the Living as a Christian should! Don't let anyone dare call us Christian "slackers"!!**

"STAND"
(Ephesians 6:13)
"PUT ON THE ARMOUR, NOT TO MARCH BUT TO STAND AND WITHSTAND" (copied)
Stand fast in Faith: I Corinthians 16:13
Stand fast in Liberty: Galatians 5:1
Stand fast in one Spirit: Philippians 1:27
Stand fast in the Lord: I Thessalonians 3:8
HAVING DONE ALL—STAND: Ephesians 6:13
There are times to march and there are times to stand! In this text, it is to stand and withstand. (ggs)

Today's Bible Blessing   *March 17*

Joshua 20:3–Joshua 22:33

WRONG ALTARS IN WRONG PLACES

Joshua 22:29

"God forbid that we should rebel against the LORD, and turn this day from following the LORD, to build an altar . . . for sacrifices, beside the altar of the LORD our God that is before his tabernacle."

If you remember, that 2 ½ TRIBES (Reuben, Gad, & the half tribe of Manasseh) thought so much of the pasture-land found prior to their crossing over the Jordan River that they wanted to make that territory their home-base. At first Joshua and the leaders were disturbed. But the three tribes

REASSURED their leaders that they would leave their families on this side of Jordan. Then they would the cross the river and help the rest of the tribes to conquer their land. This they did. All seemed well and good.

I am not sure how many years it took Joshua to lead the people in capturing THE PROMISED LAND. We know that Caleb was forty when he spied out the land. So we presume Joshua was about that age. Caleb was eighty-five when he began to claim his mountain. So Joshua, we assume, may have been around the same age. Joshua died at one hundred and ten (Joshua 24:29). I think that for almost all those years from 85 to 110, Joshua fought in some way or another for possession of Canaan. For many of those years, the 2 ½ tribes kept their word and fought with Joshua. Perhaps they returned home at times to see their families and cattle. I don't know–but I presume so.

So after DAYS AND DAYS of fighting for the land, Joshua instructed those who settled on "this side of Jordan" to go home. (Joshua said *"many days"* in Joshua 22:3). He proclaimed, *"Ye have kept all that Moses . . . commanded you . . . Ye have not left your brethren these many days . . . the LORD your God hath given rest unto your brethren . . . therefore now return . . . take diligent heed to do the commandment and the law . . . and to walk in all his (GOD's) ways"* (Joshua 22:2-5).

But what happened as soon as the 2 ½ tribes crossed back to their land? THEY SET UP AN ALTAR! It was right by the Jordan River. (I've seen big monuments by river banks, haven't you?) This *"altar"* greatly disturbed the rest of the children of Israel. It disturbed Joshua. It disturbed Phinehas the Priest, for he had the responsibility to keep the Israelites spiritually in tune. So he and ten tribal heads jumped into a boat to confront the two and a half tribes who had built such an altar. What were they doing?

Had not those altar-builders remembered the iniquity of Peor? If you recall it was the silver-tongued false prophet, Balaam, who mingled himself and his doctrines among the Israelites, teaching them *"to eat things sacrificed to idols, and to commit fornication"* (Revelation. 2:14). At the time, God had sent a plague upon Israel and hundreds died. Phinehas was concerned, even in his present day, that some of that poisonous teaching was still among them.

The people who had settled on the wrong side of Jordan explained. They said, "Oh, no! We have not built this altar upon which to sacrifice! Oh no. We have put it here by the Jordan River as a memorial stone. We want our children and their children to see it and remember how we are a part of those who crossed over the river. We want this altar as a WITNESS. We want our children to remember the True God, etc., etc." PRIEST, PHINEHAS, believed them.

My opinion is that the 2 ½ tribes meant what they said at the time. They wanted it for a witness. But, as I read the Scripture, I feel it was very wrong. It was a step toward apostasy. They had already prepared an altar for a future sacrifice at the wrong place. They had made a provision for the flesh. So many of us Christians today make such provision. And before we know it, we are trapped in wrong doctrine, listening to wrong preaching, reading from wrong Bibles, and desiring wrong friends. We find our daughters marrying unbelievers and our sons doing the same. All this compromise is the result of wrong altars built in wrong places. BEWARE LEST ANY MAN DECEIVE YOU!

"ANY BITTER ROOT–BEWARE!"
(Hebrews 12:15)
"Looking diligently . . . lest any root of bitterness springing up trouble you, and thereby many be defiled."
This "bitter root" may spring up any time, any place.
Suddenly!
There must be a "seed" before there is a root
Some little "falling away." Some little hurt.
Some little slight. A lie!
Some little act which was not forgotten.
It grew into a root from which a tree grew
and affected others adversely.
Look diligently lest we fail of the grace of God in this matter.
Keep alert! Beware lest! (ggs)

Today's Bible Blessing   *March 18*

Joshua 22:34–Judges 1:35
AND JOSHUA DIED

Joshua 24:29-30

"And it came to pass . . . that Joshua . . . the servant of the LORD, died, being an hundred and ten years old. And they buried him in the border of his inheritance in Timnathserah, which is in mount Ephraim . . ."

"It is appointed unto men once to die" (Hebrews 9:27). This is a fact! Because of Adam's sin, death has passed upon all. SO WITH JOSHUA, HE DIED!

I tend to think that this beloved captain of the Israelite army was worn out. Verse one of chapter twenty-three says, *"Joshua WAXED old and stricken in age."* He grew old! Some people age faster than others. I personally feel that Joshua was one

98

who came to be *"older"* quicker than some. For instance, Caleb said he was as strong as when he was a young man. My mother was a woman who looked years younger than her chronological age. Yet, we can name those who look ten, fifteen, twenty years older than their age. Joshua recognized his aging. He said, *"I am old and stricken in age!"* It is good, for us who are getting older, to acknowledge this and not to act foolishly as if we were "spring chickens."

The word "COURAGE" or "COURAGEOUS" is often used in the book of Joshua. It is synonymous with the man, Joshua. I believe he faced life with COURAGE. In his everyday life, he had COURAGE. In battle he was COURAGEOUS. In death, he was no different. He said, *"Behold, this day I am going the way of all the earth."*

Three men of God, and their deaths, are spoken of in this chapter–Joshua, Joseph, & Eleazar, the high priest. First, we read of Joshua's demise. His obituary was given in today's verse. It is not flowery. It is simple. It said that his father's name was Nun, that he was the servant of the LORD, that he died at one hundred & ten years of age, and that he was buried on the border of his inheritance on Mount Ephraim.

His influence was great. He was a strong commander. We note that Israel served the LORD all of Joshua's days. We are told precisely where his grave is. It is on the land he conquered for himself and his tribe there in Timnathserah on the North side of Gaash. What a man of faith he was!

Recently I heard of a woman, only 64 years of age, who died in her sleep. It was a shock! As far as I know there was no illness. She just died. Yesterday a famous actress fell on a snowy hill. At first, she was fine, but then she had a headache and rushed was to a hospital. Then we were told that she was "brain dead." Neither woman expected to die—but they did. Unless Jesus comes in our lifetime, we must die. *"It is appointed once unto men and women that they must die!"* **Are we ready?**

"OUR DEAD IN CHRIST"
(Psalm 17:15)
Our dead in Christ are not asleep,
Only their bodies.
They are awake in His likeness.
Eternally alive!
Beholding His face.
Satisfied in His presence.
Our dead in Christ are not lost.
We know where they are.
We who are "left," feel "lost" without them. (ggs)

Today's Bible Blessing   *March* 19
Judges 1:36–Judges 5:6
WEEPING ALL THE WAY
Judges 2:1, 5

"And an angel of the LORD came up from to Gilgal to Bochim . . . And they called the name of that place Bochim: and they sacrificed there unto the LORD."

This is a most interesting passage of Scripture. The people tramped from Gilgal to Bochim weeping all the way. What was there to cry about? All the greed of Gibeon and all the disobedience of Joshua and his leaders had come to light! The *"Angel of the LORD"* was there!

It was in Gilgal that the children of Israel pitched their tents. They had miraculously crossed the Jordan River. I can imagine the excitement of that time, can't you? It was in Gilgal that all the men and boys had to be circumcised. This rite had been forgotten! God told them that cutting *"rolled away the reproach of Egypt."* I am not sure but, I imagine, *"the reproach"* means the ungodly influences of the Egyptian gods and customs, along with the years of slavery they suffered after the death of Joseph.

It was in Gilgal, as they camped there, that the manna stopped. It ceased to appear on the ground like the morning dew. It ceased as quickly as it showed itself that first day forty years ago. The Hebrews began eating of the corn of the land! The Passover was kept for the first time in the new land. What a fellowship! They remembered the *"death angel."* They remembered the redemption that was their parents' as they escaped Egypt. It was a picture of the Lamb of God, the Lord Jesus Christ, Who someday would take away the sin of the world!

It was in Gilgal that the sneaking Gibeonites obtained a treaty of protection from Joshua and the leaders of the twelve tribes. And because of such an unwise promise, Joshua protected Gibeon from the five kings who swooped down to get them. Israel captured the king of Dor and other kings. We are reminded that Caleb was in Gilgal when he came to Joshua asking for a certain mountain to be his. Gilgal is full of past memories and future ones to come.

Today, we see that the *"Angel of the LORD"* came up from Gilgal to BOCHIM. Remember why the Name, LORD, is in full capital letters? It means Jehovah. That is the Old Testament Name for the Lord Jesus Christ Who is revealed in the New Testament.

I believe this "angel" was a *"CHRISTOPHANY"*–the appearance of the Lord Jesus Christ before His incarnation.

We see this several times in the Old Testament. (Remember Joshua and the Captain of the Host?) To have the Lord Jesus Christ appear in a body was a fearful sight! In this account, He came to reprove Joshua because of the treaty he had made with Gibeon. It was absolutely against the command of the LORD!

No wonder they were crying! No wonder they were in deep distress! As they moved from Gilgal to another place they named "Bochim"–*there was great sorrow within their midst.* The Cloud stood still. They camped for a while. The place was named *"Bochim."* It means *"WEEPING."*

Have you ever disobeyed God? Have you ever been deceived by someone who led you in the wrong path? Remember how it was when you discovered your sin? There was *"weeping"*! Tears of regret. Tears of disappointment. Tears of unbelief. Yet, for the rest of your life, you have had to live with the results of such disobedience. Yes, God forgives. All disobedience comes with a price. And with such self-disappointment, there is weeping!

"A WORD FROM HIM CAN CALM"
(Matthew 8:24-26)
When the night is darkest and the tempest is coming on,
our Heavenly Captain is always closest to the crew.
Why do we fear the great Tempest, when a word from Him can
bring a calm as great as the tempest? (ggs)

Today's Bible Blessing   *March 20*

Judges 5:7–Judges 7:20
A WOMAN WHO BECAME A JUDGE

Judges 5:12

"Awake, awake, Deborah: awake, awake, utter a song: arise, Barak, and lead thy captivity captive . . ."

Who is this DEBORAH? Why is she told to *"awake"*? If you recall after Joshua died and before Israel demanded a king to rule over them, the people did what was right in their own eyes. Because this never works, God ordained that *judges* would rule His people. Two of those fourteen judges were Samuel and Gideon. Today we have discovered that a woman has become a judge. She was so revered that people called her *"a mother in Israel"*! What an honor! What an awesome responsibility!

Please notice that four women are mentioned in Judges 5. It is most interesting. Two are followers of the LORD God and two are not. Remember *Jael?* She was brave. Barak, Deborah's captain, was in pursuit of Sisera. He, who led nine hundred men driving nine hundred iron chariots, was frightened to death! He must escape Deborah and Barak's pursuit. Sisera rushed into Jael's tent. It was then—after a cup of warm milk, followed by sleep—that a woman named *Jael* took a hammer and a nail. She *"smote the nail into his temple."* What a brave woman! Israel was saved that day! No wonder Deborah sang!

Sisera had a mother. We read that she waited and waited for the homecoming of her son. She was so proud of him! All day, she peered out her window saying, *"Where is my son? Why is he so long in coming home?"* We can't help but feel compassion for the woman. No matter our religion or our ethnicity, mothers are the same. They love their sons.

The mother of Sisera had "wise ladies" as friends with her. They too, were listening for the sound of Sisera's chariot wheels. Personally I think they suspected bad news but tried to encourage the worried mother. They contemplated for her sake that Sisera was taking care of business. Of course, he wasn't, for he had died by the hand of Jael. He never would ride up in victory to his mother's window again.

Deborah was married to a man named Lapidoth. She was not only a judge and a prophetess; she also accompanied her army leader, Barak, in battle. He appeared to be afraid of Sisera and his iron chariots. Who wouldn't be? He needed Deborah to leave her judgment seat under her palm tree. He froze at the thought of going to war without her. Perhaps it was his fear that brought women to do the job he was afraid to do.

It is a shame that some men are afraid to follow the LORD. They are not like Joshua or Caleb. They have trembling knees. Because of this, God may use a woman to do a man's work today. It is sad but true. As we read the Bible, we become aware that God chose very few women to lead His people. We should be very, very careful in this day and age, not to usurp the authority of a *God-called* man. A woman should not fill the gap when a man is there to do it. **There are very few "Deborahs" in the land!** Let us be very careful about thinking that we are one.

"JOY"
NEITHER BE YE SORRY
(Nehemiah 8:10)
"Neither be ye sorry; for the joy of the LORD is your strength"
Although in *"former"* days you were stronger,
don't mourn for yesterday.
WHAT DO WE MEAN BY THE JOY OF THE LORD?
Is it only the fruit of the Spirit?
Compare Hebrews 12:2 *"the joy set before Him."*
FOR IS *HE* MY JOY? (ggs)

Today's Bible Blessing   March 21

Judges 7:21–Judges 9:45
FROM VICTORY TO DEFEAT

Judges 8:24-27

"And Gideon said unto them, I would desire a request of you, that ye would give me every man the earrings of his prey. . . And they answered, We will willingly give them . . . And the weight of the golden earrings . . . was a thousand and seven hundred shekels of gold . . . And Gideon made an ephod . . ."

What a glorious victory was Gideon's. He instructed THE THREE HUNDRED brave warriors to compass the camp of the Midianites. With the precision of a general, Gideon divided his men into three companies of one hundred each. In each man's hand was a pitcher. In the pitchers were lighted lanterns, and in their hearts was a determination to capture the enemy for the LORD God.

Gideon's voice could be heard above all others. It rang in certainty and in confidence. Such shouting frightened the people. How they ran. Their Gideon's battle cry was *"THE SWORD OF THE LORD AND OF GIDEON!"* How the enemy fled! How confused they became! In that confusion they began to kill one another. God gave a triumphant victory that night for Israel!

The victorious captain held the lives of all his conquest in his hands. The men of Israel wanted Gideon to rule over them. In the process of gathering the battle's spoil, the Israelites gave their earrings. Those earrings were worth thousands of dollars! If you were Gideon, what would you have done with all that gold?

With sadness we read that this brave man, who previously had destroyed his own father's idol, took all the gold, ornaments, and beautiful cloth making it into an *"ephod."* An *"ephod"* is an embroidered outer vestment such as a cape or mantle. In time, this *"ephod"* became an idol. How do we know? We read that *"All Israel went thither a whoring after it."* That beautiful garment turned into an ugly thing in Gideon's later life. It became a *"snare"* and a trap to him. His spiritual walk with the TRUE GOD was stunted because of it. His testimony was marred.

Why is it that those who stand for the truth often trip over some small thing in their lives? That small thing has a way of growing into a publicly known stumbling block for other Christians. It shatters one's testimony for Jesus Christ. The Apostle Paul feared that he would become a *"castaway."* He feared that after preaching Christ Jesus for all his years, some *"EPHOD"* could destroy his testimony. It is good that we fear such a fall, too. Every day we must be

103

careful what we do with the spoils that abound around us in our life's battles.

Often, it is after great victory that the Devil gets a foothold in our lives. Such backsliding causes much grief to our families, to us, and to the testimony of Jesus Christ Himself.

"SERVE WITH GLADNESS"
(Psalm 100:2; Psalm 4:7)
Serve the Lord with gladness. Come singing!
Dear busy Martha!
What a faithful server!
Yet, she did not serve with gladness.
She came before His presence "cumbered."
−not with gladness and song!
Should we not be as Nehemiah,
to not be sad in the King's presence?
How little gladness there is in my service, Lord! (ggs)

Today's Bible Blessing   *March 22*

Judges 9:46–Judges 12:15
A RIGHT MAN–A WRONG VOW

Judges 11:29

"Then the Spirit of the LORD came upon Jephthah, and he passed over Gilead . . ."

The ministry of the Holy Spirit is different in Old Testament times compared to His ministry in the New Testament. When a person accepts the Lord Jesus Christ as personal Saviour, the Spirit takes abode within the believer's person. He never leaves. He can be grieved by the sin in the Christian's life, but He will never leave. He is a permanent part of the one who is *"born-again."* He is called THE COMFORTER.

The Spirit's job in the Old Testament was different. If you remember, the Holy Spirit did not indwell many people that we read about in the OLD TESTAMENT. Instead, the Holy Spirit came upon people for a certain period of time and then left. I'm sure you remember Saul, when the Spirit rested upon him. There were men such as Samson and David, and of course, there were the prophets and others when they *"spake as they were moved by the Holy Ghost"* to write the Scriptures.

So in this case, we see the HOLY SPIRIT rested upon Jephthah. Who was Jephthah? We know that his mother was a prostitute and that the other wives of his father Gilead

put him out of the house. That eviction happened when Jephthah grew up to be a man. He fled for his life and lived in a place called TOB. It was there that sinful men were drawn to Jephthah. He must have had a drawing personality that made him a natural leader.

It came to pass that Ammon's children made war with Israel. The Israelites were in a dither. They had no war hero to lead them in these battles. So what did they do? They called on the bastard Jephthah, the very one with whom they wanted nothing to do.

Perhaps, because he was so excited and wanted to be used, he became over-confident in his rejoicing. Somewhere around that time, he vowed a dangerous vow to the LORD. He said, *"Whatsoever comes out of the doors of my house, I will offer it up to the LORD."* Why would he say such a thing?

After a time of battle, the LORD delivered the Ammonites into Jephthah's hand. The LORD smote twenty cities, as well as the plains and vineyards. What a victory! How excited Jephthah was as he approached his house in Mizpeh. I don't know whom he was expecting to come out of the house to greet him. It was sad. As most little girls do, they wait for their daddies to come home. They watch from the windows with their nose flat against the window pane watching and waiting. Then at the first sight of their father, they dash out into his arms. This little girl was no different. At that moment, the sorrow that pierced Jephthah's heart had never before been experienced. Immediately, he remembered his vow to God. What was he supposed to do?

It seems to me that sometimes—even when we are serving the Lord with our whole hearts—that we, in our exuberance, make wrong decisions. Even the Apostle Paul in his great yearning for Israel's salvation made an unwise, unscriptural vow. Peter made a terrible vow when he said he would never deny the LORD JESUS—and turned right around and pretended not to even know Jesus at all. Perhaps you can think of others.

Jephthah paid dearly for his quick speaking tongue. His precious daughter probably had to pay with her life because of it. Some feel the little girl remained a virgin all her life as a kind of *"offering."* Others felt that she was a death sacrifice—giving her life to fulfill her father's unwise vow. Let us be very careful what and when we vow before the LORD. Do not speak before you think. And do not think wrong thoughts or make unwise promises!

"GLADNESS IN MY HEART"
(Psalm 4:7)
"Thou hast put gladness in my heart!"
ONLY THE LORD CAN DO THIS!
No event, no possession, no performance
can give joy in the heart unless He puts it there.
WE cannot manufacture *gladness.*
IT COMES FROM HIM!
A surrendered heart is the vehicle.
There is a difference between the gladness of the Lord
And the silly "ha ha" of today's fun! (ggs)

Today's Bible Blessings   *March 23*

Judges 13:1–Judges 16:20

THOU BAREST NOT

Judges 13:2-3a

"And there was a certain man of Zorah, of the family of the Danites, whose name was Manoah; and his wife was barren, and bare not. And the angel of THE LORD appeared unto the woman . . ."

Have you ever met a woman who wanted a baby but could not conceive? I have. It is most sad. How she and her husband yearn for a child! She tries every possible way she can think of to get pregnant, to no avail. There are tears of grief. There is unbelief that their hearts-desire to be parents is unfulfilled. THIS IS HOW IT WAS WITH MANOAH'S WIFE.

One day the barren woman, in our verse today was going about doing her daily duties when the angel of the LORD appeared unto her. His appearance was like an *"angel of God."* I do not know how she knew he was "of God."—except many times in the Bible when an *"angel"* appeared, the people seeing the *"angel"* recognized Him for who He was. Her descriptive word for this *"angel"* was *"TERRIBLE!"*

Right there before her was a CHRISTOPHANY. The Lord Jesus Christ had manifested Himself to her with a message. His Name was *"SECRET." SECRET in Hebrew means* "WONDERFUL!" And as you probably know, *"Wonderful"* is one of the Names for Jesus Christ that we read about in Isaiah 9:6-7. The message is that important!

What a shock, it must have been, to have an angel come to her side and speak to her! Perhaps more shocking were the words that *"the angel"* spoke. She seemed to be more shocked at His words than at His appearing. The message was that she would have a baby. What good news! How could this be? She and her husband had tried and tried to have a baby with no success. How do I know this? I think the words *"thou art barren, and barest not."* To me the *"barest not"* shows they tried and tried.

The exciting news of a future child came with special instructions. This child would be named SAMSON, and he was to be a NAZARITE. His hair was never to be cut, and he was never to drink of the fruit of the vine. In fact, she was not to drink wine or strong drink during the time she was carrying her baby. This is good advice for anyone who is pregnant.

What a joy was this news to Manoah's wife! Her child would become a judge and die a horrible death; but all of this future grief was unknown to this mother-to-be. This nameless woman and her baby were very important to the plan of God for Israel. His name would be *SAMSON*.

So, the same for you and me. We do not know the future. We only know today. It behooves us to live godly and follow the will of Him *"with whom we have to do"* (Hebrews 4:13). Perhaps some wonderful future work is forthcoming because we are willing to let the LORD use us in our daily walk with Him today.

"OUR SPEECH"
(Colossians 4:6)
"LET YOUR SPEECH BE ALWAY WITH GRACE, SEASONED WITH SALT . . ."
GRACE, GRACIOUS, UNMERITED KINDNESS (perhaps)!
Yet, *never compromise on doctrine*
Only a truly spiritual Christian's speech is always with grace—yet seasoned with salt.
THE LORD JESUS HAD GRACIOUS WORDS;
YET ALWAYS TRUE.
(ggs)

Today's Bible Blessing   *March 24*

Judges 16:21–19:30
SAMSON'S VINDICATION

Judges 16:28-30

"And Samson called unto the LORD, and said, O Lord GOD, remember me, I pray thee, and strengthen me . . . Let me die with the Philistines . . ."

We don't usually think of Samson as a man of prayer. But we read one of his most important prayers and see how the Lord GOD answered him. I think of Jonah's prayer in the belly of the whale; and there was Peter's cry, as he suddenly stopped walking on water. Prayer does not have to be fancy or long. It just has to be real and from the heart.

For some reason God chose Samson to mix-in with the Philistines. From the time he spied the beautiful woman of Timnath to the day he asked the young lad to place his hands on the pillars of Dagon's temple. Samson was a man who never tasted wine, mingled with the ungodly Philistines, and was chosen by God for God's work.

Why Samson was enticed by so many women such as Delilah, we don't know. It is written that he loved her. What a selfish woman who would use his love to betray him! Then he found a harlot in Judges 16:1—to say nothing of his failed marriage. How many other women he had, we do not know. Yet, the LORD used Samson to be a Judge of Israel in spite of his immoral behavior.

SAMSON'S VINDICATION IS GLORIOUS! It is written that more died with Samson, as he brought the house down upon them that infamous day, than in all the others he had slaughtered as God's champion. He was buried with his father, Manoah, and, I suppose, near his mother's grave also.

We are not told any more about his mother since his birth, but I choose to believe that she followed his career wondering so many *"whys"*—yet loving her son always, not understanding God's ways. How true that is of many mothers today. They often watch their adult children from afar and silently wonder what is going on.

"LORD, IS IT I?"
(Matthew 26:22)
"Lord, is it I?"
Help me, myself to see—
for while I am looking at others,
Thou Lord, are looking at me!
Today, as I read the account of the *"last supper,"*
I heard the disciples ask, *"Lord, is it I?"*
I, too, wondered about my fickle heart
and feared lest, while looking at others,
I might also deny my Lord.
If we women would look first to our own motives and desires,
we would look less at others in criticism. (ggs)

Today's Bible Blessing   *March 25*

Judges 20:1–Ruth 1:12

PHINEHAS: SON OF ELEAZAR

Judges 20:18, 27-28

"And the children of Israel arose, and went up to the house of God, and asked counsel of God . . . (for the ark of the covenant of God was there in those days, And Phinehas . . . stood before it . . .)"

Have you been impressed with Phinehas? I have. He was the grandson of Aaron, the High Priest. (Do not confuse him with Eli's wicked son by the same name.) His father was *Eleazar*, the High Priest. His uncles, *Nadab* and *Abihu* (Leviticus 10:1-2), were killed by the LORD when they offered strange fire to HIM. The Bible says the LORD's fire *"devoured"* them. Immediately after that *"just judgment,"* we read that Phinehas' Uncle Ithamar (another brother of Eleazar) had the anointing of the LORD upon them (Leviticus 10:7). I believe that Eleazar was the third-born son of Aaron, and the Bible tells us that he was the High Priest after his father Aaron died. What a responsibility! What an example for young Phinehas, his son.

In our verse today, we see that Phinehas stood before the Ark of the Covenant. As he stood there, he sought the LORD's direction asking, *"Shall I yet again go out to battle against the children of Benjamin my brother . . .?"* There was dreadful sin in Benjamin's tribe. It was the sin of sodomy. God wanted it judged! Young Phinehas was the man to lead that judgment! The LORD said, *"Go up, for tomorrow I will deliver them into thine hand."* This he did!!

I have been interested in this bold man named *Phinehas* ever since I learned of his bravery in the matter of *Zimri* and the adulterous woman, *Cozbi* (Numbers 25:14-15). How proud his father must have been of him! Phinehas took a javelin and thrust it through the woman. Twenty-four thousand died in the plague that followed. It was the judgment of God!

Phinehas turned away the LORD'S wrath from the children of Israel in Numbers 25:11. In Numbers 31:6, Phinehas, with 12,000 Israelites, warred against the Midianites using the holy instruments and trumpets! It was in that battle that Balaam, the son of Beor was slain with the sword. We were proud of Phinehas as he rushed back over the Jordan River to find out the truth about the altar of witness that Reuben erected in Joshua 22:10.

Sadly, the High Priest, Eleazar died. He was buried in a hill that belonged to his son, Phinehas, there in Mount Ephraim (Joshua 24:33). What a bold priest was Phinehas! If only we had more such men like him today!

"OUR FINGERS TO FIGHT"
(Psalm 144:1)
Teach our hands to war and our fingers to fight!
As a good solder, I must have my hands on my sword
ready to use it.
My hands should be ready to serve
and ready to hold forth His banner.
My hands: to write.
to proclaim.
to expose.
to explain.
to encourage.
OUR HANDS MAY HOLD THE BIBLE,
AND OUR FINGERS MAY POINT TO THE TEXT.
(ggs)

Today's Bible Blessing   March 26

Ruth 1:13–I Samuel 1:12

HOPE IN OUR ARMS SOMEDAY

Ruth 4:16

"And Naomi took the child, and laid it in her bosom, and became nurse unto it."

It's about time something went right for Naomi—after all she had been through. And here she sat holding her precious grandchild—the child with rosy cheeks and chubby hands. She held him close to her breast. This child was named *OBED*. That little boy would someday be the grandfather to King David. But she did not know this.

Of course, Naomi did not know it. She only knew that he took the place of her dead sons. For a mother to have a son die is an awful thing; but to have two boys die is a dreadful thing to a mother. No matter the faith of the mother, the death of a son is not pleasant. Burying a son was no different for Naomi.

In our town, there was a family. In fact, they lived on our street. Two of their sons were on a baseball team with one of our sons. This was years ago. One night, on the way home from a baseball game, the car these brothers were in skidded into a telephone pole. The boys died instantly! What a shock to their family. What a shock to all of us! Their mother wrote years later, *"Now I know bad things happen to good people."* I thought of Naomi. She was a good woman, too.

Naomi, her husband, and two sons went to the land of Moab. Their hometown of Bethlehem was in famine. The sons married Moabitish woman. That was sad. One was Orpah. The other was Ruth. Ruth stayed with Naomi as a daughter would stay with her own mother. Orpah left. Sometimes it is better to stay in the problem than escape it only to discover the present dilemma is worse than the famine in the other land.

After returning with Ruth to Bethlehem, the women of the community comforted Naomi. Ruth worked in the fields of Boaz. He married the Moabitess. They had a son, a grandson for Naomi. Life turned from *bitterness* to *sweetness* for the woman who once only had known tears of grief. This gives hope to us who have buried a son or a daughter—or even a husband. We, too, can find *hope* in our arms someday!

"LOANED TO US"

"A child in God's hands is better than a child in your hands if that is where the Lord wants him." (Copied)

This has been a comforting thought in regard to Beverly and all that befalls her. Our dear ones are loaned to us, and are His to reclaim whenever it is His blessed will. (ggs)

Today's Bible Blessing   *March 27*

I Samuel 1:13–I Samuel 4:12

IN PRAYER AND ACTIONS

I Samuel 1:15, 27

"I am a woman of a sorrowful spirit: I . . . have poured out my soul before the LORD. For this child I prayed . . ."

Have you ever been in a situation where there was no place to go for help but to God? You have felt as if your very life was being sucked out of you. Your grief was so great that you could not breathe. Your heart was broken. The pain of such heartbreak was unbearable! I think this is exactly how Hannah felt that day, as she was praying. She could not speak. She could not stand. She could not be comprehended by anyone but the LORD. In fact, Eli, the priest at Shiloh, thought she was intoxicated.

For what petition was Hannah pouring her soul out before the LORD? Her heart's desire was for a child. Though she was her husband's favorite wife–he had two–she could not conceive. The other wife was prolific, often taunting Hannah for her barrenness. All of her husband's words of consolation and actions of love could not comfort Hannah's empty arms.

BUT GOD ANSWERED HANNAH'S PRAYER! Samuel was born. After he was weaned, she took the young child to Shiloh. She reminded the priest of her prayer a few years earlier. That was the day she gave the LORD her son! I can feel the tug at her heart as she put her baby's hand into the hand of Eli that day. What a gift! I do not know if Hannah knew the sinful life of Eli's sons when she turned little Samuel over to GOD that day. I wonder if Eli took the child with some trepidation, wondering if he would do a better job of raising Hannah's son than he had done with his permissiveness in training his own boys. I do not know. All I know is that Samuel lived with Eli until he was old enough to step out as a prophet and priest on his own.

God honored Hannah. He gave her five more children. We never hear about them—how they lived and if they served the LORD. But we do read of Samuel, of his boldness and dedication to the words of God. He was an answer to his mother's prayer—just like many of our children are answers to our prayers. We never read about Hannah again in the Bible. But like any mother, she must have watched her son from afar, marveling at God's grace in both of their lives.

What does this true account mean to you and me? What can we learn from the life of Hannah? I think we learn that women have hurts that husbands do not completely understand. Women grieve in a way that men do not. WE LEARN ALSO THAT A WOMAN CAN PRAY! A woman can pour her heart out to the LORD

God in such a way that she touches Heaven. WE LEARNED THAT A WOMAN'S PRAYERS CAN BE HEARD. God hears our prayers, too. God hears the prayers of those who are born-again and come to Him in Jesus' Name. What a comfort! We learned that when the answer to our prayers is given, we must do our part to carry out what God has started. What if Hannah had reneged on giving the boy to God? What kind of mother would she have been?

What kind of mothers are we? Have we kept our word with God in regard to our children? When they were born, we dedicated them to God; but did we forget, and raise them contrary to His way and Word? It is not too late to change our ways and determine to be a *"Hannah"* in prayer and actions. Then trust God to do the rest! That's what Hannah did.

"HIS WORDS HEALED ME"
(Psalm 107:20)
He sent His Words and healed me!
There is a balm in the cleansing by the Word!
Our hurts and griefs can be healed by no other than the Lord.
If friends are able to help, it is because they use
the Words of God to comfort us.
He gives particular and especial portions to heal in our grief.
Simple phases are profound, when our Father points them out.
(ggs)

Today's Bible Blessing   *March 28*

I Samuel 4:13–I Samuel 9:3

OUR OWN CHILDREN FIRST?

I Samuel 8:1-3

". . . When Samuel was old . . . he made his sons judges over Israel . . . and his sons walked not in his ways, but turned aside after lucre, and took bribes, and perverted judgment."

One of the saddest things in a Christian parent's life is to have children who do not walk with the LORD. You and I have seen this often. We have noticed preachers or evangelists, or even great Bible teachers who have children who besmirch the Name of the Lord Jesus Christ. Their lifestyles cancel out everything their godly fathers have said.

I think of D. L. Moody, the famous evangelist of yesteryear. He preached all over the place in the United States and in England, etc., etc. Thousands of lost souls were brought to salvation through the Lord Jesus Christ because of his ministry. He founded

Moody Bible Institute where thousands more studied the Bible and won the unsaved to the Lord Jesus Christ. Yet, Mr. Moody's sons did not follow their father in the ways of the LORD. *It is a sad story!*

There was Billy Sunday. Those who study great evangelists know of him and his wife Ma Sunday. His evangelistic fervor was known throughout the land. Thousands accepted Jesus Christ as Saviour because of Billy Sunday's fiery messages. When I was in Bible school, I went with fellow-students to the Pacific Garden Mission where the Sundays preached. Yet, Billy & Ma Sunday had a least one son who drank himself drunk and did not follow the LORD. *It is a sad story!*

In our reading today, we are brought up short seeing the ungodly behavior of Samuel's sons. Their names were *Joel* and *Abiah*. (We have already seen the ungodly behavior of the sons of Eli in previous chapters.) Samuel had an active life for God. His mother prayed for his birth. God answered. She gave him to the LORD and to Eli to raise. Eli was the obese high priest at Shiloh who ministered in the Tabernacle of God. In spite of the fact that Eli's sons were unrighteous, drunken, immoral priests, Samuel grew in grace.

When Samuel became a man, the LORD God promoted him to be a judge, a prophet, and do priestly deeds. Yet, in all his godly endeavors, Samuel did not teach his sons to practice good and true judgments. His boys succumbed to the *"love of money."* They were dishonest priests. They judged unrighteous judgments based on *filthy lucre*. Their judicial decisions were based upon dishonorable and illicit findings which were twisted unrighteously by the bribes of those they judged. *It is the saddest story!*

This behooves you and me, as we parent our children, to teach them, not only by words but by deeds, to be honest and upright people. DO OUR OWN CHILDREN KNOW JESUS CHRIST AS SAVIOUR? We can have a Sunday school class full of well-taught children, but to lose our own children to the Devil is sinful. Our examples and our time should be devoted to the salvation and godly living of our own offspring FIRST. Let us rethink our Christian walk and work. What are our priorities for the LORD? In our enthusiasm to win the world, have we forgotten our homes and our own children who live in those homes?

"OUR MEMBER–OUR TONGUE"
(James 3:5-6)
TEACH ME AND I WILL WITHHOLD MY TONGUE.
In her tongue is the law of kindness.
Be kindly affectionate one to another.
Speak kindly.
So is the tongue among our members
that it defileth the whole body.
Set on fire–the course of nature.
A whisperer separates friends
In a mysterious way, it stirs up the old nature.
(Proverbs 16:27-28; 17:28)
James 1:19 says we should be *"swift to hear"*
and *"slow to speak,"* and *"slow to wrath."*
DEDICATE YOUR TONGUE TO THE LORD
AS YOU WOULD YOUR HANDS, FEET, OR TALENTS.
In the multitude of words there wanteth not sin.
(Proverbs 10:19)
He that shutteth his lips is esteemed a man of understanding.
(Proverbs 17:28) (ggs)

Today's Bible Blessing   *March 29*

I Samuel 9:4–I Samuel 12:19

A NEEDED WORD FROM GOD

I Samuel 9:27

"And as they were going down to the end of the city, Samuel said to Saul . . . stand thou still a while, that I may shew thee the word of God."

It broke Samuel's heart that the children of Israel wanted a king. They wanted to be like the rest of the heathen about them. It was not God's plan. So many times in our own lives, we take a turn that is not God's perfect plan for our lives. Once that turn is taken, we cannot reverse it. We must continue on. We must make the best of it. So with Samuel. So with Saul.

Saul was a handsome man. He was tall and goodly in all ways. Samuel could see that with his human eye. The LORD chose Saul for the job. He spoke into Samuel's ear and said, *"Tomorrow . . . I will send thee a man . . . and thou shalt anoint him to be captain over my people."* (I Samuel 9:16)

The fact is that Saul was not hunting for a kingdom; he was searching for his father's lost burros. Because he could not find them, he sought for a *"seer"* who could tell him where the animals had gone. That is when Samuel and Saul met each other. It was not a *"chance"* meeting. It was ordained of the LORD.

It was on the housetop, the flat roof of the dwelling in his city, that the Prophet Samuel fellowshipped with the future King of Israel. It was early morning. They had been visiting, eating, and getting acquainted. Suddenly Samuel looked at Saul and exclaimed: *"STAND THOU STILL A WHILE, THAT I MAY SHEW THEE THE WORD OF GOD!"*

Have you ever been visiting with a friend when all of a sudden, she or he would speak to you in a loving authoritative tone and say, *"Stop what you are doing, I want to read the Scriptures to you right now?"* I don't think this happens too often in this busy work-a-day world. There is so much hustle. There is so much bustle. There is so much scheduling that life has become a whirlwind of activity. We have not made room for the *"peace of God"* to comfort our hearts. Oh, for the good old days of our grandparents when we could sit on the front porch, sip lemonade, and just enjoy one another. Our lives are so caught up in the daily news, the car trips, the yard work, our calendars, and making a living wage that we do not sit down together with the *bread of life* and eat of it together.

Samuel knew that Saul would have a mission from God. Saul did not know it. Saul needed a few quiet words from the prophet. He did not know it. Soon Saul would be the anointed king. He would be thrust into a ministry that he knew not of. Soon he would journey to a Philistine city, meet a company of prophets, and *the Spirit of the LORD* would give him *"another heart."* And with that new heart for God, Saul's ministry would begin. How would this son of Kish handle the new responsibility of prophesying and becoming the King? That is a question we could ask ourselves as we step out today on a new endeavor in our own life's journey!

"GOD OPENS THE HEART TO RECEIVE"
(Acts 14:27)
God opened the door of faith to the Gentiles.
God opened the door to Lydia's heart.
Paul's message of the Gospel reached and was received by an open heart.
*"OF HIS OWN WILL BEGAT HE US
WITH THE WORD OF TRUTH."*
(James 1:18)
God sets before churches *"an open door."*
(ggs)

116

Today's Bible Blessing   *March 30*

I Samuel 12:20–I Samuel 15:4

KEEP PRAYING IN SPITE OF IT

I Samuel 12:23

"Moreover as for me, God forbid that I should sin against the LORD in ceasing to pray for you . . ."

Do we think of Samuel as a man of prayer? This is today's question. As I ponder this, I am reminded of his mother, Hannah. It was to her answered prayer that the LORD caused the baby Samuel to be born. In spite of all the difficulties to conceive, Hannah gave birth to this future prophet, priest, and judge of Israel. What a testimony to a woman of *prayer*! What a prayer-example for Samuel!

Samuel's continual communication to the LORD God is evident as we read of his life. Since he was a child in the tabernacle, God spoke to Samuel. In fact, He spoke to him at such a young age, that Samuel did not realize it was the LORD HIMSELF. From that time on, Samuel prayed. God answered. Samuel obeyed.

Here in this verse, Judge Samuel declared that it would be a sin for him if he did not pray for the Israelites. Have you ever considered it a sin if you did not pray for those you love? Sometimes we become so busy in our own world of rush and bustle, that we forget to pray for those we love. Other days, we are overburdened for a loved one so we can't accomplish much of anything else.

Perhaps we should use Samuel as a model for our prayer life. He was a bold man. He may not have been in the natural, but God gave him boldness about which most of us know nothing. In the preceding chapter, Samuel reviewed Israel's history to the faithfulness of God from the time of Moses and Aaron, to Sisera and Jerubbaal (Gideon), and Jephthah. He then reminded the people that it was they who wanted a king–not God. In spite of this, God would be faithful to them as long as they were faithful to God!

In answer to Samuel's prayer, God sent thunder and rain. It caused Israel to see the power of God in their midst. (It reminds us of Elijah—yet to be born.) The people were deathly afraid! Samuel prayed. They regretted their desire for a King. It was then that Samuel assured them that the LORD would not forsake them as long as they honored Him.

Sad to say, soon Saul would take matters into his own hands and make a sacrifice on an altar that he had built for the occasion. This displeased God. Samuel was angry. As we learn more about this new king, it appears that Saul was a man of the flesh. He seemed to be a willful man, an impatient man, an impulsive man, and an angry man.

When it came to King Saul, it is evident that Samuel had his prayer-life cut out for him. Some of us pray for our children who fail miserably in their Christian walk. But we pray on in spite of it. Sometimes they make ungodly and unwise decisions like Saul when he ruled that no one should eat until evening. I personally think it was unwise and wrong for Saul to bring the *Ark of God* into the battle (Chapter 14). *Yet, in spite of all this foolishness, Samuel still prayed and God still answered.*

"SONGS OF DELIVERANCE"
(Psalm 32:7c)
"Thou shalt compass me about with songs of deliverance."
Have you ever found yourself singing a certain hymn
as you moved about your daily task?
Or has a song been "singing" in your mind all night long?
Be thankful; for this is of the Lord,
and according to His Word.
He hides us in Himself.
His preserves us by His power
and gives release by "songs of deliverance." (ggs)

Today's Bible Blessing   *March 31*

I Samuel 15:5–I Samuel 17:31

TEARS OF SORROW & UNBELIEF

I Samuel 15:11b

"And it grieved Samuel; and he cried unto the LORD all night."
Have you ever cried unto the LORD all night? Have you ever been so disturbed that you could do NOTHING BUT CRY? This is what it was like for the old man, Samuel. His heart was broken. He'd put so much effort and prayer into King Saul's life—but to no avail. Saul had deliberately disobeyed the LORD's command. He was supposed to completely destroy all that Amalek had and kill every person and every beast. The Lord was very specific in His commands to King Saul.

What we see here in this account was Saul practicing *"partial obedience."* He was not, and would not be, the only one who would ever practice such a thing! After winning the battle with the Amalekites, Saul smote all of them—well almost all of them. *He let King Agag live!* Think of that! The ruler of the greatest enemy Israel ever had was kept alive. Then in practicing *"partial obedience"* Saul destroyed all that was vile and worthless. Wasn't that something? *But he kept the best of the animals.* In other words, he spared all that was good and killed all that was worthless. When Samuel confronted this disobedience, King Saul claimed his people wanted it so.

It was then that Samuel realized that the LORD was sorry that He had made Saul king. So the next day when King Saul lied to Samuel and claimed that he had wholly followed the LORD, Samuel spoke those famous words: *"BEHOLD, TO OBEY IS BETTER THAN SACRIFICE, AND TO HEARKEN THAN THE FAT OF RAMS."* From then on, the blessing of the LORD God was not upon Saul. Even though Saul cried out *"I have sinned,"* it was too late. The damage had been done! No wonder Samuel cried!

I'll ask you the question again, "Have you ever cried unto the LORD all night?" I have. I remember one night. It was after I learned that my sister had Hodgkin's disease. (That is a cancer of the lymph glands.) I couldn't believe it. She had just graduated from high school. She was beautiful and vivacious, as well as talented—and she was my sister. No one in the house, where I was staying that night, seemed to care. I suppose they did, but they could sleep. I went down to the living room and tried to read—anything to fill the time and my mind—but I cried. Our emotions and feelings are funny things. We are never quite sure how we will react to certain news.

It must not have been easy for Samuel to carry on, like the prophet he was, after that night of tears, but he had to. He had a job to do. He had to be the forth-teller for God the next day. He had to tell off the king. That would not be easy. So it is with you and me. Even though we may spend the night in prayer and tears, we must go on the next day and carry on the work that God has given us to do. We may have cried over a death, a broken marriage, a failed job, or a sick child, but God would have us continue on in obedience to Him. Tears come. Yes, they do. But life must be lived.

We read in verse 35, that Samuel mourned for Saul. The Prophet came no more to see the King. Such sad words! Such sorrow!

"HE HATH SET ME FOR HIS MARK"
(Job 16:12)
*"I was at ease, but He hath broken me asunder:
he hath also taken me by my neck, and shaken me to pieces,
and set me up for his mark."*
God deals with us sternly that we may be conformed
to the image of His Son.
If He did not use such stern measures,
we would remain at ease in our unloveliness.
How much He cares that He deals especially with me.
(ggs)

Today's Bible Blessing   *April 1*

I Samuel 17:32–I Samuel 20:4

WHOSE SON ART THOU?

I Samuel 17:46

"This day will the LORD deliver thee . . . I will smite thee, (GOLIATH), and take thine head from thee, "

In yesterday's reading, I was taken aback by the **demeaning remarks of David's oldest brother. His name was Eliab.** If you recall, Samuel went to Bethlehem to visit Jesse's house. When the town's elders saw him coming, they were upset. They need not have feared for God had told Samuel to anoint a new king for Israel there.

The first one to be seen by the prophet was Eliab, Jesse's firstborn. He was not chosen. You know the story. None of the seven older brothers passed inspection either. Samuel was alarmed. It was then that he learned there was one more son. His name was David. He was in the pasture caring for the sheep. It was not a position of grandeur.

On that eventful day, God chose David to be the future king of Israel. Notice in I Samuel 16:13 that Samuel *took the horn of oil, and anointed David* with all his brothers there. We conclude that Eliab was among them. So he must have seen the prophet pour the oil on his baby brother's head. The Bible says *THAT THE SPIRIT OF THE LORD CAME UPON DAVID FROM THAT DAY FORWARD.*

In today's reading, we noticed that it came to pass that Goliath of Gath was parading himself before the frightened Israelites. His hugeness made them tremble. If someone could *"down"* the giant, the people of the winning warrior would be counted as victorious in the battle. No one dared take on the mighty Philistine! David had come to deliver his brothers' lunches. He could not understand why the giant was such a challenge. Was not their God able?

When Eliab saw David, he was disturbed. Maybe he was old enough to be the boy's father. Complaining, and in anger, Eliab mocked, *"Hey Davie, what are you doing here?"* Then he chided, *"With whom have you left those few sheep in the wilderness?"* The *"few sheep"* innuendo was a belittling statement. It inferred that David could not handle anything bigger than the lowly sheep. Mother had always spoiled him.

The elder son of Jesse knew David well. He knew of his pride. He knew that often David did mischievous deeds. Yet, how could Eliab forget that day when Samuel anointed David with oil to be king? Perhaps the oldest brother did not comprehend that David would be the head of Israel. Certainly the elder must have noticed that

David was a different person after that anointing day. The Bible says that the *Spirit of God* came upon David. Sometimes brothers and sisters do not see their siblings as productive persons.

We all know the true account of the defeat of the Philistines that eventful day. We all know that young David did what he knew how to do. He chose five stones out of the nearby brook and said to laughing Goliath, *"Today I will smite thee and take thine head from thee . . ."* Had not he slain a bear and a lion in the same manner while protecting the lambs in the wilderness? In full confidence, David ran toward the enemy. He flung a stone at Goliath! Dazed, the giant fell. Then David stood on top of the creature, killed him, and cut off his head. Next he dragged that bleeding head to Jerusalem and presented it to King Saul who asked, *"Whose son art thou?"*

We do not read what big brother Eliab thought or said after that victory, but knowing big brothers, I think he was very proud of his brother, the Giant killer. Probably Eliab bragged about Davie's prowess for the rest of his life. We know also that God was pleased, for this true story is recorded in the Scriptures for all of us to read. From that day until now millions have read how David trusted God in spite of criticism and against all odds.

"WAIT AND KEEP HIS WAYS"
(Psalm 37:34)
*"Wait on the LORD, and keep His way,
and he shall exalt thee to inherit the land."*
TO BE TRUSTING AND WAITING ON GOD
TO ANSWER OUR PRAYERS IS GOOD.
BUT ALSO, WE MUST KEEP HIS WAY DAILY
WHILE WE ARE WAITING ON HIM TO WORK FOR US.
We must not lay aside our Christian service and hide away
while He "seems so long" in answering.
To keep His way is as important as the exhortation to wait.
Lord, that I may keep on while "all things work together."
THIS IS TRUSTING. (ggs)

Today's Bible Blessing   *April 2*

I Samuel 20:5–I Samuel 23:9
A JONATHAN/DAVID FRIENDSHIP

I Samuel 20:18

"Then Jonathan said to David, Tomorrow is the new moon: and thou shalt be missed, because thy seat will be empty."

The friendship between Jonathan and David has always been of interest to me. (Perhaps because I had such a friend.) I don't remember when the young men first met, do you? Perhaps it was when David was playing the harp for Jonathan's father, King Saul. Between the soothing melodies to quiet the depressed king, the two young men met. Perhaps it was then they talked and discovered their kindred spirit no matter where they met or why they met. The fact was that they soon became very good friends.

It was also a sad fact that King Saul was exceedingly jealous of David. If you remember, after David had slain the Giant, the people of the land compared David's triumphs with the King's. They rejoiced in song that David had killed ten thousand to Saul's one thousand. This jubilation did not go over well with the Monarch. Later, Saul promised David his daughter Michal, if the young man could bring Saul proof that David had killed one hundred Philistines. That David did. We could number other instances, time and again, when David outdid Saul. Quickly Saul became disgusted and jealous of this David. The King wanted him dead!

The incessant jealousy of King Saul was not without a cause. David was to be the future king of Israel! God had chosen him. In spite of such knowledge, Jonathan, the king's son, loved David with all his heart. (There has come a rumor in modern-day false Bible interpretation that the relationship between these two men was not pure, but homosexual. This is absolutely wrong! It is trumped-up conjecturing!) Because of their deep friendship, Jonathan protected his friend from the rage of Saul, his father. In today's Bible narrative, Saul observed that David was not at his place at the dining room table. Such an absence was not unnoticed.

After two days of absence, it became apparent to the sovereign that something was amiss. Jonathan made excuses for his friend. The king could not understand this. Why would the heir to *The Throne* be so loyal to the one who would someday take *The Throne* away from him? In his anger, Saul damned Jonathan's mother for rearing such a son. He began calling her names. He hollered out that she was a perverse and rebellious woman. In his rage, he threw a javelin at his own son and missed.

Have you ever had a *"Jonathan/David"* friendship? I have. Her name was *Rose*. We had a bond between us like I have not had before or after—except with my husband. I loved *Rose* as a sister. She was a dear person to me. Yes, I had other friends but none that stuck closer than a brother.

We came from the same church. We attended Bible school together. We shared secrets and hopes as young girls do. We were in each other's weddings. We went with our husbands as they enrolled and graduated from seminaries. We moved thousands of miles away from each other. We bore children.

Then one day *Rose* died. She was a beloved wife. She was a young mother of teenage children. She was a sister, a daughter, an aunt. And she was my friend. It was cancer. Such a sad, sad day for me. I have never had another friend like her. So, I can relate to the *David/Jonathan friendship* in today's reading. There is something about a dear, true friend that only true friends understand.

How good to have a friend in Jesus. He is better than any earthly friend or brother. The older we become, the more we, who know the Lord Jesus Christ, appreciate Him. He promised never to leave nor forsake us! (See Hebrews 13:5). What more do we want?

"SHOWING HIMSELF THROUGH THE LATTICE"
(Song of Solomon 2:9)
The intricate circumstances of life are all known to Him—
the workings of our daily life,
the varied interwoven trials, tests, and joys.
He sees it all and *"looketh in."*
His eye is over the righteous
showing Himself *"through the lattice."*
He is standing behind our wall. His presence is felt.
In all circumstances, He is there watching over us.
He is attending somewhere in the shadows, keeping watch.
I am cheered for I know He is there. (ggs)

Today's Bible Blessing   *April 3*

I Samuel 23:10–I Samuel 25:43
A HORRIBLE CHURCH SPLIT

I Samuel 24:10c

"I will not put forth mine hand against my lord, for he is the LORD'S anointed."

As a young girl and a young Christian, I remember this verse being used in the church where I was a member.

There was an *"internal division"* within the church brought on by a disagreement over some minor thing. But that minor thing was the cause of a *"power struggle"* between the pastor and those who agreed with him and leaders of the church who disagreed with the pastor. Those leaders were the deacons, the trustees, and all the *"important"* people of the flock. For me, as a young Christian, it was puzzling. I lost most of my girlfriends with that *church in-fighting*!

In all of this church fighting, today's verse came to my attention, *"Do not touch the LORD'S ANOINTED."* I heard it quoted over and over again. In that case—of what became a horrible church split—*the LORD'S ANOINTED* was my pastor. The *"power people"* decided they were going to starve out the pastor. It seems to me that the pastor received $5.00 a week. But I must be wrong. It must have been $25.00 a week. (I recall that my Uncle rented a farm house for $5.00 a month.) This must have been around 1935 or 1936. I was probably nine—maybe ten. It was during the time of the *great depression* or soon after, I suppose.

Being a child, I knew nothing about *the depression.* President Roosevelt was my president for more years than I can remember. My parents did not discuss their financial matters in front of us children. I do remember that we could get a pound of hamburger for twenty-five cents. I also remember that my father bartered his merchandise for an upright piano so I could take piano lessons. My dad was a door-to-door salesman at the time. Though he could understand why some men had to stand in *a bread line*, he never did.

As a little girl, I did not know anything about David's vow not to kill King Saul, but learned of it as I read the Bible. David had every right, I suppose, to destroy King Saul. God had given up on Israel's disobedient leader. Remember when he did not follow the LORD in regard to *King Agag*? As we read in today's reading, it is very evident that Saul had a different slant on killing David. Saul wanted David out of the way. As long as the younger man was alive, Saul's throne was in danger. It is a sad circumstance to watch jealousy and envying occur between two of God's servants.

If you remember, Saul went into a cave for personal reasons. David and his men saw him. Evidently Saul put his cloak down away from his view for a few minutes. It was then that David took a sharp knife and cut off some of Saul's kingly robe. It was then that David had every opportunity to kill his enemy, but he did not.

David's men wondered why. That is when David bowed himself to the ground, shouting to the king, *"Behold, this day thine eyes have seen how that the LORD had delivered thee to day into mine hand in the cave . . ."* He reminded the stunned Sovereign that many wanted David to kill Saul, but he determined, *"I will not put forth mine hand against my Lord; for he is the LORD'S anointed."*

Maybe we Christians should consider carefully our attitude and behavior when we "touch" those whom the LORD has called into His service. Yes, some pastors and missionaries do wrong, but is not God able to take care of their faults and failures without our help? I am just wondering, that's all.

"A GREAT MAN FALLS"
To Compromise is Sin!
(I Kings 13)
Judgment on the man of God was turned aside to fellowship with a lying, apostate preacher. (vs. 18)
A LESSON FOR US TODAY

A lone preacher was sent to cry against a false altar—verse 1.

A remarkable prophecy concerning Josiah—verse 2.

The sign: the rent altar immediately fulfilled—verse 3.

The king urges compromising friendship, offering a reward by inviting the prophet to go home with him—verse 7.

The charge from the Lord not to fellowship with the apostate king—verses 8-9.

The man of God deceived by an old prophet—verse 14.

The lone prophet invited to go home with the old prophet—verse 15. (Sometimes old preachers are deceived.)

The prophet understood God's command well—verse 16.

There is no excuse to sin—verse 17.

This was a sin unto death. The prophet was killed by a lion—verses 18-30.

The man of God believed something that was contrary to God's Words—verse 19. (ggs)

Today's Bible Blessing   *April 4*

I Samuel 25:44–I Samuel 30:11

DABBLING IN THE SATANIC WORLD

I Samuel 28:3

"Now Samuel was dead . . . and buried him . . . And Saul had put away those that had familiar spirits, and the wizards, out of the land."

If you remember, Israel wanted to be like the other nations about her. She wanted to have a king. Though it grieved the LORD God, He gave Israel her way. He chose Saul for the job. Even though Saul was an outstanding physical specimen of a human being, he was a humble person. The Spirit of God rested on him. He had a future as King!

As time went on, Saul became self-centered and self-willed. Samuel had many disappointing moments with Saul. The last straw was when Saul disobeyed the LORD and saved Agag as well as the goodly spoil from the battle with the dreaded Amalekites. After that, Samuel said that he would never visit King Saul again.

As time went on, Saul missed Samuel's counsel. After the prophet died, Saul needed help desperately. The Philistine army had gathered against Israel. What was Saul to do? He dashed for the *Urim* and asked the LORD's advice. No help there. He tried to discover the answer by *"dreams."* No help there either. Nothing was working! In a frantic effort to seek advice, he sought a person of *"familiar spirits."*

So desperate, backslidden Saul disguised himself, seeking the Witch of Endor. What a foolish move! At first the woman did not recognize the King. Still—she was somewhat afraid, not because she knew who he was. She was afraid because King Saul had ruled that no one was to practice wizardry any more in the land.

At Saul's request the woman of Endor did whatever witches do. She brought up Samuel. Almost frightened beyond words, she screeched, *"I saw gods ascending out of the earth!"* Yes, she actually saw *Samuel.* That is what the Bible says. It was then that she realized that her client was actually the King of Israel in disguise! *"Why hast thou deceived me?"* she cried in fright, *"Thou art Saul!"*

As the Witch stood amazed at what she had *"brought up,"* she quivered, *"He is an old man covered with a mantle!"* That was when King Saul knew for sure, it was Samuel. Immediately Saul fell to the ground and bowed himself. Samuel was not pleased at all that Saul had *"brought him up."* Distressed, Saul explained his situation, *"God is departed from me."* It was then that Samuel explained the situation to the God-forsaken king. Samuel advised that the LORD had violently ripped the kingdom from Saul's hands. HOW AWFUL! There was more bad news! Samuel declared, *"Tomorrow you and your sons will die.* He continued, *"Israel will be delivered into the hands of the Philistines!"*

Today the most popular books for young people are about wizards and witches. Children gobble up the *HARRY POTTER* books like candy. They are subconsciously learning the ways of witchcraft. Many, who are not spiritually grounded, will dabble into witchcraft on their own. *TWILIGHT,* one of a recent series of books about *vampires,* is high on the reading lists of young people today. The *vampire* in this story is said to be a *good vampire,* just as the *wizard* in Harry Potter is said to be a *good wizard.* Instead of being bewitched by such vampire ways and wizard words, we should tremble. Dabbling into the Satanic-spirit-world is dangerous indeed! It should be forbidden!

"IN THE BEGINNING GOD"
(Genesis 1:1)
What a profound statement!
If we believe this, we will believe and trust
the entire Words of God.
He was always!
He is always!
He will always be!
Compare Matthew 28:20 when Jesus said,
LO, I AM WITH YOU ALWAYS.
(ggs)

Today's Bible Blessing   *April 5*

I Samuel 30:12–II Samuel 2:25
STAYING HOME WITH THE STUFF
I Samuel 30:24

". . . As his part is that goeth down to the battle, so shall his part be that tarrieth by the stuff: they shall part alike."

When I was a young bride and then a mother, I had to stay home much of the time. My husband would go places. I stayed home. He went to Oklahoma. I stayed home. He went to Mexico. I stayed home. He went to Okinawa. I stayed home. He went to Europe. I stayed home. He would drive a car for miles with other people. I stayed home. It didn't seem fair to me. Off my husband would go—*"serving the Lord"* hither and yon, and everywhere.

What was I doing? I was changing diapers, nursing babies, contending with children, washing dishes, cleaning the house, doing yard work—worn out—and crying! It just didn't seem fair. Had not I given my life to the LORD to be used where He wanted to send me? Yes, I had prepared in Bible School. I thought, *"Certainly God could use me in some special way!"* Why was I always stuck *"staying home with the stuff?"* Question: *"Could my home be my work for the LORD"*?

Here in today's Bible reading, we noticed that the Amalekites, the continual enemy of God's people, had invaded Ziklag. Besides burning the city with fire, they captured the women. Two of those women were wives of David. (Don't ask me why the men in the Old Testament were permitted more than one wife at a time. I don't get it either!) David's own people were angry with him because of it. They wanted to stone David. During this disturbing development, *David encouraged himself in the LORD his God.*

127

After enquiring of the LORD, David, with six hundred men, pursued the enemy. That was at *Besor Brook.* Two hundred of those brave warriors were faint and tired. War can tire out a soldier, you know. David told those men to stay home and rest. Then they found a lone, weary, and hungry Egyptian man. David refreshed the man with food and water. It turned out that the man had been a servant to an Amalekite master who left him behind sick. With the help of this cast-off servant, David and his men smote the Amalekites. They fought fiercely from morning to night. David recaptured all that the Amalekites had taken from Israel, including his own wives and the wives of the other men. That day was a great day of victory!

After the battle, David came back to the two hundred weary men that he had left behind at the Brook Besor, It was then that the unbelievers—men of Belial, who had fought with David and his men—concocted a plan, *"We will not give those who stayed home any of the battle's spoil!"* This idea did not go well with David. He said that it was the wrong plan. After all, the LORD had preserved them and delivered the enemy into their hands, hadn't He?

David questioned the other men, *"Who is going to listen to this weird idea?"* He contended that those who stayed home with the stuff had as much right to the battle's spoil as those who fought in the war. David declared, *"As his part is that goeth down to the battle, so shall his part be that tarrieth by the stuff."*

What a comfort that verse became to me in my early marriage when our children were small. My husband was a Navy chaplain for five years on active duty. For one of those years, he was overseas in Okinawa with the Marines. After that, my husband had sea duty. I was not with him. I was all by myself with my little family. For every soul Chaplain Waite led to the Lord, for every marine he comforted, for every sermon he preached, my reward was as great as my husband's! That's what that verse said to me. When I realized this truth, staying *"home with the stuff"* became more appealing to me. How about you? Do you have to stand on the side lines while others get the *"glory"*? David's words to the homebound are for you, too!! Take heart. The more you *"stay with the stuff,"* the greater will be your reward.

"WRITTEN FOR OUR LEARNING"
(II Chronicles 32:31; Romans 14:4)
"God left him, to try him,
that he might know all that was in his heart."
This was spoken about King Hezekiah.
We wonder why we are alone and unnoticed in our problems.
God, as it were, seems to stand aside. So we can "go it alone."
So we may judge ourselves as to cause.
Job came forth in the end as pure gold (Job 23:10).
Also Job accepted the righteous judgment of our Holy God.
If God would look away for a second, we would fall and fail.
(ggs)

Today's Bible Blessing   *April 6*

II Samuel 2:26–II Samuel 6:2

TWO SENSELESS MURDERS

II Samuel 3:38

"Know ye not that there is a prince and a great man fallen this day in Israel?"

Yes, David was a *"bloody"* man! We can observe that. Though God anointed David to be the KING of ISRAEL, David was not able to slip into that job slot without difficulty. KING SAUL did not give up his throne for David easily. Then ISHBOSHETH, Saul's son, who was next in line, accused ABNER, his strong man, of immorality with one of Saul's concubines. This upset ABNER and he transferred his loyalty to David.

Testing him, David demanded that Abner get MICHAL for him. David wanted his original wife back in his harem. Abner brought Saul's daughter, David's first wife *"home."* Of course, this was very sad for the man who had been Michal's recent husband. It seemed that ABNER, as well as ISHBOSHETH, was involved in this venture.

Immediately ABNER began his campaign to install DAVID as KING. He said that it would be by David's hand that Israel would be saved from the Philistines. Abner whispered this news in the ears of the Benjamites, as well as the citizens of Hebron. So, when Abner and twenty other men were in Hebron, David made a great feast. They were making plans. There was good rapport among them. Abner went away in *peace.* All was fine between the two men.

Alas! JOAB had other ideas. When he discovered that David and Abner had made *peace* with each other, JOAB was livid and screamed at David, *"Abner has deceived you! He just wants to find out your plan and destroy you!!"* I don't know if this was true or not, but I tend to think David was a good judge of men, and he knew that ABNER was now on his side. BUT TOO LATE!!

As soon as ABNER returned to Hebron, JOAB met him at the gate and killed him. This was a revenge killing. WHY?–because ABNER had killed JOAB'S brother, ASAHEL. Look at II Samuel 2:23. This killing of ABNER upset David immensely! He cried out, *"Know ye not that there is a prince and a great man fallen this day in Israel?"* It exhausted him emotionally. Sadly he declared, *"I am weak . . . though anointed king . . ."*

Learning of the senseless death of ABNER, David instructed all that were with him, "Tear your clothes! Put on sackcloth and ashes!!" They mourned the death of the dead man. In grief, David followed the bier. He watched the deceased be buried in the ground. He wept. All the people cried. It was a sad day for David. He could not eat. He felt that this death was useless! He lamented, *"ABNER DIED AS A FOOL!"*

Immediately KING ISBOSHETH was shaking in his boots. When he heard that ABNER was dead, he was afraid! He had reason to be, for he was sitting on Saul's throne, the throne designated for David. His fear was great. He had to go to bed, staying there until noon the next day. It was in this feeble condition that the two sons of Rimmon surprised him. They killed him!!

Once again, we see what kind of man David was. In great distress, he reviewed how displeased he was to learn of Saul's death. The man who said he finished-off Saul thought David would be happy. That was wrong. David had that man put to death. Now with ISBOSHETH's senseless murder, he was angrier. He said that a righteous man had been killed for no cause at all. The sons of Rimmon were killed. ISBOSHETH's head was buried in Abner's sepulcher. No wonder David was called *"a bloody man."*

"HE UPBRAIDETH NOT"
(James 1:5)
"If any of you lack wisdom, let him ask of God, that giveth to all men liberally, and upbraideth not; and it shall be given him."
THIS IS A PROMISE!
We are so unlearned and so lacking when it comes to making decisions. Yet, here we have a marvelous invitation to get wisdom from the Omniscient God.
He will not scold or belittle us for showing our ignorance; but UPBRAIDETH NOT.
What confidence we derive from this wonderful Scripture and promise. (ggs)

Today's Bible Blessing   *April 7*

II Samuel 6:3–II Samuel 10:4
A RIGHT WAY AND A WRONG WAY
II Samuel 6:12b

"So David went and brought up the ark of God from the house of Obed-edom into the city of David with gladness."

If you recall, the ark of God was brought from Shiloh by Eli's sons way back in I Samuel 4:4-5. During the fighting, Hophni and Phinehas, the aforementioned sons, brought THE ARK of God into battle. Sadly the Philistines prevailed, won the conflict, and took the Ark. This was tragic, indeed. Remember how the news was so alarming that Phinehas' wife went into early labor and died. As she gave birth to her son, she named him ICHABOD (*THE GLORY IS DEPARTED.*)

Previously, after seven months of being with the PHILISTINES, we discovered THE ARK in Joshua's field in BETH-SHEMESH. The men of that community feared and questioned, *"Who is able to stand before this holy God?"* They asked the inhabitants of KIRJATH-JEARIM to come get the ark. This they did, bringing the ARK to ABINADAB'S house. They set apart his son, ELEAZAR, *"to keep the ark."* It rested there for twenty long years. During this time, the Israelites put away their false gods.

After the death of ISHBOSHETH, the elders of Israel anointed David their king. He was thirty years old. We discovered, as we learned more and more about this new king, that he had compassion and kindness for the infirm and oppressed. He also grew great, and the LORD God of hosts was with him.

After establishing his house in Hebron, and fighting fierce battles with the PHILISTINES, DAVID felt it was time to bring THE ARK OF GOD to the HOLY CITY. His men set the ark upon a new cart bringing it out of the house of ABINADAB in GIBEAH. I suppose they thought using a cart that had never before been used was a good thing. Abinadab's sons, UZZAH and AHIO, helped out with this venture, driving the cart. I picture them walking, one on each side of the oxen, keeping them moving, etc. All of a sudden, the cart must have hit a bump and the ARK wobbled. Attempting to steady it, UZZAH put out his hand, touching THE ARK. All this happened near the house of OBEDEDOM.

Immediately, the LORD'S anger was seen. UZZAH died, right there on the spot, without provocation or warning! It must have been a horrible sight. Sudden death is never pleasant! It leaves those who are alive and standing by in shock! They look at the dead man, and then at each other, wondering how that death happened. David was shocked, too. He was displeased that the LORD had made a *"breach"* on Uzzah! He called that death scene *"PEREZUZZAH"* (a breach upon Uzzah)! David feared. He wondered how he could ever get THE ARK home.

After three months, David heard how blessed OBEDEDOM's family was. He decided to bring the ARK back. He had investigated what the proper procedure was to move the ark. It was not to be put on a cart at all. It was to be covered properly and carried on two golden poles on the shoulders of two priests from the family of Aaron.

The Bible tells us that, after the men bearing the ark walked about thirty feet, everyone stopped and sacrificed oxen and fatlings to the LORD. It was then that DAVID danced with all his might before the LORD. He was dressed in a linen ephod—not his usual kingly garb, I suppose. MICHAL, one of David's many wives—a sad situation—observed his behavior and was embarrassed beyond words. Having been a daughter of a King, she felt her husband's behavior and dress was most unconventional for his position of royalty.

What can we learn from this account? First, God had a proper order for moving *THE ARK OF GOD.* So today, He has a proper order for the believer's worshipping Him, as well as their daily life-styles. Also, we see that others observe the way believers dress and behave, though they may think they are behaving and dressing to glorify God.

BE CAREFUL. You and I may be stumbling those by what we wear and how we act! Others are watching us!

"MY STRENGTH–MY PORTION FOREVER"
(Psalm 73:26)
"My flesh and my heart faileth:
but God is the strength of my heart,
and my portion for ever."
HOW TIRED I BECOME!
So many heavy duties connected with Beverly.
(She is so brain damaged.)
My flesh would fail, but for God who is my strength.
(My very energy!)
How I praise Him, that since I am His child,
HE IS MY PORTION FOREVER.
Truly my heart would fail and falter
BUT GOD!
I DESERVE NOTHING, BUT GOD IS MY PORTION!
(ggs's "very own" verse)

Today's Bible Blessing   *April 8*

II Samuel 10:5–II Samuel 13:12

AND DAVID WALKED UPON THE ROOF

II Samuel 11:1c-2

". . . But David tarried still at Jerusalem . . . And it came to pass in an eveningtide, that David . . . walked upon the roof of the king's house . . ."

When we visited London, we were told that no matter where the Queen of England was, her banner waved over her palace. That way, people would know that the Queen was home. So, whenever I read today's verse, I think of the banner that must have been flying over KING DAVID'S palace. If this be true, everyone in the surrounding areas, including the beautiful BATHSHEBA, knew that their KING was home.

There is always the question: Should David have been home? NEPHEW JOAB, the main general and trusted confidant of David, had returned to battle with the entire KING'S fighting force of Israel at his command. There was a season for such battles. Good battle conditions would be under good weather conditions. In those days, the KING went to war with his army.

For some reason, David stayed in his house. He could not sleep. Perhaps he couldn't because he wondered about his men. Perhaps he was ailing. Perhaps he was tired of such strife and wanted some peace. We do not know. But we do know that he walked on the roof of his house. Was he pacing? Was he meditating? We do not know. We do know he looked around. What did he see beside the evening sky? He saw *BEAUTIFUL BATHSHEBA* sponge bathing. In theory, he should have looked away. If the temptation to stay on the roof was overtaking him, he should have left the roof in search of one of his many wives. But no! He thought himself more able to bear such a temptation. But, he was like most powerful men. The temptation was too great, as it is for many men. He succumbed. He *wanted* BATHSHEBA. Being the powerful KING, he could have anything he wanted. So he sent for her.

Now let's think about BATHSHEBA. We know five things right off. We know that her name means *"daughter of an oath."* Some say it may not be clear in Hebrew, and may be from a Hittite derivative and/or from a Canaanite/Indo-European language. We know her father's name was ELIAM (AMMIEL) and some say her grandfather was David's counselor, AHITHOPHEL. Also, we know she was married to a Hittite named URIAH, one of David's mighty men.

We know that she was beautiful. I would say she had no previous children. A woman who has had children may be beautiful, but not as beautiful in body as a woman who has not borne children. Childbirth changes a woman in many ways. Also we know that she took a bath in plain view of anyone who wanted to look upon her. She did not prevent such voyeurism. We also know that she did not hurry in her bathing, nor did she put up a screen or a curtain to prevent prying eyes from seeing her.

We also know that her husband, *Uriah*, was out with General Joab and his army. We know that *her husband was one of David's mighty men,* as well as a man of integrity. That was a virtue that BATHSHEBA did not have. We know after the death of her husband, her child with David died also. She also was the mother (with David) of SHIMEA, SHOBAB, NATHAN and SOLOMON, who became king.

I do not excuse David for his adulterous eyes. Nor do I excuse BATHSHEBA, either, for her seductive bathing within plain sight of the King whose banner may have been floating on the very roof on which he stood. Yes, BATHSHEBA was lonely. Many women whose husbands are at war are lonely. They have sexual yearnings that are unfulfilled. But that does not mean they should seduce a man to whom they are not married–let alone the king of the land. In our own United States of America, we had a beautiful raven-haired woman seduce our president. Indirectly, his untoward sexual actions with her caused a ruckus in our country.

The long and the short of the whole affair, in Bathsheba's case, is that a child was born. Then a brave, moral husband was killed in battle. David tried to make an *"honest woman"* out of a *"dishonest"* one. Yes, the child of that adulterous affair died. According to Moses' Law, BATHSHEBA should have been stoned! The child's death was a grief to David. I am glad that he wept. Also, I think David truly loved the woman. Besides the baby that died, she bore four other sons to David. My personal opinion is that David tried to make-up for the loss of URIAH and their adulterous liaison of years ago, by promising BATHSHEBA that SOLOMON would be the next king. We read of BATHSHEBA in future chapters of the Bible where she made sure that Solomon reigned in her husband's stead.

What do we learn from this true story of passion, of sin, and of forgiveness? We learn that sin may be forgiven, but not necessarily out of mind. We learn that to *cover-up* sin, death may happen. We also learn that David's adultery—though forgiven—will be remembered always. I think the saddest summary of this is found in the *COLOPHON* to Psalm 51. *"To the chief Musician, a Psalm of David, when Nathan the prophet came unto him, after he had gone in to Bathsheba."* IT SAYS IT ALL!

"SHADOW OF HIS WINGS"
(Psalm 57:1; Psalm 91:1-4)
"For my soul trusteth in thee:
yea, in the shadow of thy wings
will I make my refuge, until these calamities be overpast."
THE SHADOW OF HIS WINGS–Psalm 91:1
MY REFUGE–Psalm 91:2
It is under His wings we find the TRUTH,
a SHIELD, and a BUCKLER.
IF EVEN THE "SHADOW" is a refuge,
WHAT OF THE VERY WINGS! (ggs)

Today's Bible Blessing   *April 9*

II Samuel 13:13–II Samuel 15:25

MISDIRECTED LOVE

II Samuel 13:1

". . . ABSALOM the son of David had a fair sister, whose name was TAMAR; and AMNON the son of David loved her."

This account of unbridled passion and jealousy is very **sad.** AMNON and ABSALOM were half-brothers. They had the same father who happened to be the king of Israel. His name was DAVID. Absalom had a beautiful sister. It is not a surprise to us that she was such a beauty, as Absalom, himself was most handsome. I can picture them now on the cover of some magazine for people to *"swoon"* over.

Before I go further in this true account, let us reflect upon KING DAVID. He started out married to *MICHAL*, the second daughter of Saul, if you remember. Then he acquired the concubines and wives of the former king whose name was ISHBOSHETH. He was the king that JOAB had killed as he was resting in bed. ABIGAIL and AHINOAM became wives of David around the time of Nabal's death. Then there was BATHSHEBA whom David stole from one of his mighty men. I do not understand this *"harem"* business, or why God permitted such marriage behavior to come about; but it is there in the Bible for us to see. I go into all of this marriage farce and sexual prowess of KING DAVID to help us understand the confusion of many marriages found in the royal family at the time of this account.

If DAVID had been paying attention to his adult sons, he would have noticed the undue attention that AMNON was paying to his beautiful half-sister, TAMAR, Absalom's sister. Instead, David became aware of this incest too late. Tamar tickled Amnon's fancy, and he pretended to be sick so she would come near

135

him. She made food for him and nursed him in his feigned illness. That was when they were all alone,

It was at that "alone time" that *"lovesick"* Amnon made his move. He humbled his sister in a cruel way. Then after being in bed with her, he decided he did not like her. Evidently the *"chase"* was more satisfying than the actual togetherness. Tamar was mortified! No longer was she a virgin! She tore off her colored robe that signified virginity and hung her head in shame. This reckless behavior toward Tamar by Amnon angered ABSALOM! But Absalom did nothing at the time. Just because a person does not retaliate does not mean that he is not upset with the situation.

In time—in fact two years—a situation came about where the two half-brothers had a sheep-shearing adventure with all the sons of David. I have no idea, at this time, how many there were. While there, ABSALOM commanded his staff to kill his half-brother. This was revenge to the tenth degree! When all the king's sons realized what had happened, they mounted their mules and fled the scene. Quickly news came to David's ears. He thought all of his sons were killed. What grief! But soon he was told that it was only AMNON. David rejoiced that all of his sons were not killed but he mourned for Absalom every day of the three years that Absalom had found refuge in Geshur.

The moral of this true account comes to me. The sin of adultery and fornication was practiced by the father. His sons observed this. Children know their dad well. One wife after another was David's nightly habit, I am sure. There probably were favorite ones. I tend to believe that Bathsheba was one of them. So Amnon's desire for his sister and his attack upon her virginity was something he had learned firsthand from his father. That's my opinion.

Then, for Absalom to wait for the proper time to get even with his half-brother must have been a pattern. He had observed Joab's actions and his own father's killing-off people who got in his way. Let us not be like these brothers. They were selfish to the detriment of the whole family.

"THE PATH OF LIFE"
(Psalm 16:11)
"Thou wilt shew me the path of life:
in thy presence is fulness of joy;
at thy right hand there are pleasures for evermore."

I have taught thee in the way of wisdom;
I have led thee in right paths. (Proverbs 4:11)

But the path of the just is as the shining light,
that shineth more and more unto the perfect day. (Pr. 4:18)

He restoreth my soul:
he leadeth me in the paths of righteousness
for his Name's sake. (Psalm 23:3)

Yea, though I walk through the valley
of the shadow of death,
I will fear no evil. (Psalm 23: 4)

Then shalt thou understand righteousness, and judgment,
and equity; yea, every good path. (Proverbs 2:9)

All the paths of the LORD are mercy and truth
unto such as keep his covenant
and his testimonies. (Psalm 25:10)
THERE IS FULNESS OF JOY FOR EVERMORE.

Today's Bible Blessing   *April 10*

II Samuel 15:26—II Samuel 18:21

SIBLING RIVALRY BRINGS COMPLICATIONS

II Samuel 17:19

"And the woman . . . spread a covering over the well's mouth, and spread ground corn thereon; and the thing was not known."

It is of interest that unnamed people are used of the Lord. Just because we are not privy to all the names of people in Scripture does not mean that God does not know who they are, or that they were not used of the LORD for a specific duty.

137

In the reading today, we see many names of people who had a definite part in returning David to His throne. This division was during the time that ABSALOM was usurping his father's throne. It was a sad time for both men! Such a divide between David and his handsome son! Personally, I believe it all began when AMNON lured his half-sister, TAMAR, into his bedroom. As you remember, ABSALOM was the full brother of his wounded sister. In time he killed AMNON. It was a revenge killing! That was when ABSALOM fled out of the presence of his father, the King.

It must be remembered that David never stopped loving his son. He never wanted any harm to come to him. Perhaps he would have been willing to lose his THRONE to spare ABSALOM sorrow.

In the process of all this running from and chasing after one another, many people were involved. Some took the side of the son. Some took the side of the King. It must be remembered that David was in serious danger of losing his throne to ABSALOM for Absalom had won the hearts of thousands of Israelites.

AHITHOPHEL'S sage advice was known in the land. At his council, ABSALOM set up a tent on the KING'S ROOF and had sexual relations with his father's concubines. This degrading action toward his father's most private area of life signified that ABSALOM meant business. He was determined to be KING!

DAVID sent HUSHAI, his trusted friend to ABSALOM'S side. HUSHAI pretended to be on the usurper's side. For some reason, Hushai's advice was followed. This humiliated wise AHITHOPHEL to such an extent that he put his affairs in order and unwisely killed himself. Through the priests, HUSHAI—still loyal to David—warned DAVID not to stay in the wilderness that night.

It is now we see that two of the priest's sons were in on the plan. Their names were JONATHAN and AHIMAAZ. They found refuge at a woman's house. A little girl relayed this information to King David. The lady of the house let the priest's sons climb down into a hole in the ground. In order to protect the men, she covered the hole over with a cloth and spread corn thereupon. It turned out to be excellent camouflage.

A young nameless lad told ABSALOM he'd seen the men go to the woman's house. The woman was as cool as a cucumber in this touchy situation. She told the men, that David's men had long-gone. It was then that David was satisfied that AHITHOPHEL'S advice had not been taken. So DAVID and all his people passed over the JORDAN. He detoured to MAHANAIM while ABSALOM and his men passed over Jordan, too—pitching their tents in Gilead. At this time ABSALOM made AMASA captain of the army of Israel instead of JOAB. This did not go over well with Joab. In fact we learn later that JOAB killed AMASA surreptitiously.

All in all, we see that sibling rivalry brings serious complications within a family!

> ### "MY HEART STANDETH IN AWE OF THY WORD"
> (Psalm 119:161b)
> How often in reading the Scriptures
> certain words of admonition comfort.
> Challenges leap out from the page
> stirring us to rest in Him,
> to hold fast, or to press on.
> Just the very words we need—just the encouragement for that day.
> Precious Words of God!
> Truly my heart standeth in awe of the Word! (ggs)

Today's Bible Blessing   *April 11*

II Samuel 18:22–21:4
AN UNBEARABLE DEATH

II Samuel 18:33

"And the king was much moved . . . and wept . . . O my son Absalom, my son, my son Absalom! would God I had died for thee, O Absalom, my son, my son!"

How King David loved his son Absalom! He had other sons, but this one seemed extra special. Perhaps Absalom reminded David of himself. Maybe Absalom's physical strength and dogged determination to take the kingdom made David proud! It could be that David loved Absalom's mother more than his other wives. Maybe David had a semi-guilty conscience because he had not protected Absalom's beautiful sister, Tamar, from being raped by her half-brother. I really don't know. It very well could be that DAVID had a strong love for all of his children. We know that when the first child that he and Bathsheba had, died, he grieved in the depths of his soul. We will never really know the *"why"* of David's grief. But, we do know that David, the father, did not want his son to die! To lose a son is most difficult to bear.

Had not David specifically instructed his generals, *"Deal gently for my sake with the young man . . . Absalom?"* That was said immediately after David divided his army into three commands. One group was under JOAB. Another under ABISHAI. (Both of those men were David's nephews.) And the third division was put under ITTAI the Gittite. After these assignments were given, David determined to go to battle himself. But, the people were frightened and persuaded David to stay with them to protect them from the enemy. So David stood by the gate as all the armies marched by.

It was then that the king commanded his three generals to deal gently with his son, Absalom. It must be concluded that David not only did not want to lose the Kingdom, but also, he did not want to lose a son in the battle either. The Bible tells us that all the people heard him give this charge!

Therefore, it was a shock to be told that ABSALOM had died. How did this happen? For some reason as ABSALOM rode his mule under a tree, his beautiful head was caught in a tree limb. Perhaps he was resting on his mule and the wind blew his locks into the air and became entangled in a branch, pulling his head into the tree. Whatever—he was caught in a branch. It is hard for us to fathom such an accident. Perhaps he was vain, when it came to his locks, and he let them flow down upon his shoulders instead of tying up his hair during battle. Whatever—his head was caught in the tree branches. **David's son was not dead. He had been stopped in his tracks—hanging in mid-air.** Along came one of David's men. He saw ABSALOM dangling there. The mule had ridden off without him, but the man laid not a finger on the helpless man. He remembered the king's words. David did not want ABSALOM hurt! JOAB had another idea. He threw three darts at the helpless man's heart. Then the men who bore JOAB'S armour surrounded the hanging body of the beautiful son of David and finished him off. ABSALOM WAS DEAD! Who would tell the King?

When King DAVID learned of the fate of his son, he wept. When a son dies, a father cries. A parent does not expect to out-live a son. A father's tears come without warning. They fall down the cheeks—at first slowly, then in gushes of wetness. The grieving man went to his room above the gate. He did not care that his men had won the battle. He cared about nothing but the fact that his beautiful son was dead. The loss of a son brings sorrow that cannot be explained nor put into words. Absalom had no children—just a monument. This passage of Scripture is one of the saddest in the Bible.

"I LIE DOWN AND SLEPT"
(Psalm 3:5; Psalm 127:2)
"I laid me down and slept; I awaked; for the LORD sustained me. "
How marvelous, after we have whispered our good nights
and after we have prayed with thanksgiving
to simply go to sleep–
To commit all our cares and unsolved problems
to Him who knows all the answers–
and who "ever liveth" to manage our affairs.
"He giveth His beloved sleep."
We know this from His Words—
that when I awaken, it is because the Lord sustained me. (ggs)

Today's Bible Blessing   *April 12*

II Samuel 21:5–II Samuel 23:16
DELIVERANCE IN DISTRESS

II Samuel 22:7

"In my distress I called upon the LORD, and cried to my God: and he did hear my voice out of his temple, and my cry did enter into his ears."

So much had happened to David since we first met him. That meeting came about at the time the PROPHET SAMUEL anointed David to be king. He was a shepherd boy–the youngest son of Jesse's family. We watched him kill GOLIATH as he had the bear and the lion out in the sheep fields. We saw him play his harp for the spiritual soul-hunger of KING SAUL. We noted his close friendship with Saul's son, JONATHAN. We were amazed how he felled scores of Philistines as an exchange to be wed to Saul's daughter.

We couldn't help but notice how the Israelites favored him to be their king. David's victories in battles were numerous. His bravery was great. We sorrowed when he committed adultery with BATHSHEBA and had her husband killed in battle. We saw the downfall of morals within his own family. The rivalry between the brothers was fierce. ABSALOM killed a brother to pay back the dead man's rape of his sister, TAMAR. The fellowship between father and son was never the same. Absalom politicked and won the hearts of his father's subjects—almost taking the kingdom from his Dad. We grieved with David as tears flowed like a fountain at Absalom's untimely death.

We saw the rivalry within his camp between some of his followers and David's main general, Joab. Joab killed as easily as most men breathe. We noticed that David did not always approve. We saw David's kindness to Jonathan's crippled son, MEPHIBOSHETH. We observed his patience with aged BARZILLAI, his tolerance of SHIMEI'S cursing, his wisdom in dealing with SHEBA who wanted to be king. We saw his dealing during the three year famine, his kindness to RIZPAH concerning the bones of Jonathan and Saul—as well as the battle at Gath when Goliath's brothers were killed by David's nephew. His life was dotted with wars, unhappiness, and alone-time with God.

Now today we are blessed with David's devotional thoughts. It was like old times for him. He remembered his youthful years out with the sheep when the LORD spoke to him mouth to heart. If we did not have chapter 22 of II Samuel, we would have forgotten that King David spent quiet time with God. We would have forgotten that David loved the LORD, his *Shepherd*, his *Rock*, his *Fortress*, and his *Deliverer*. David's words concerning his LORD were military terms such as *"shield," "horn," "high tower," "refuge,"* and *"violence."*

It is good to know—even comforting—to realize that David *"called on the LORD"* when he was surrounded by his enemies. He wrote: *"When the waves of death compassed me, the floods of ungodly men made me afraid."* All around him, it was like Hell. Many who have been in battle say that *"war is hell."* David experienced that torture! Every place he looked, while in battle, was death! It was before him, behind him, and on each side of him. Even some of his sons wanted him dead!

Where did David go in his discomfort? He tells us in today's verse. *HE CALLED UPON THE LORD, AND CRIED TO HIS GOD!* Oh, that you and I would learn this truth. There is only one place to go! That place is to GOD! Even though we are in the midst of floods and earthquakes, as well as strong enemies, and personality battles, the LORD can deliver us from such *strong distress!*

"WATER BY WAY OF EDOM"
(Isaiah 43:19)
"Behold, I will do a new thing; now it shall spring forth;
shall ye not know it?
I will even make a way in the wilderness,
and rivers in the desert."
There is nothing impossible with Him.
No matter how barren is our desert,
He will make a way where there is an impasse
and a river where the well runs dry.
The most bleak circumstance is refreshed by His Presence.
(ggs)

Today's Bible Blessing   *April 13*

II Samuel 23:17–I Kings 1:37
I HAVE SINNED!

II Samuel 24:10

"And David's heart smote him . . . and David said . . . I have sinned greatly . . ."

I think that sometimes rulers get carried away with their own power. Somehow this may have been the case with King David in today's Bible reading. All of us who have read the Bible are familiar with the fact that God did not want his people *"numbered."* Certain kings were punished by such numbering. Now, don't get me wrong. When it was God's idea to *"number,"* it was all right.

In our passage today, there was *"the anger of the LORD"* manifested against Israel—see II Samuel 24:1. *"The anger of the Lord"* which manifested itself against Israel *was combined with Satan's provoking* David to number Israel. (I Chronicles 21:1) This action was a sin. It was a *"testing,"* permitted by God, of the King. David's failure to pass the test brought much confusion to the land. Though Joab knew it was wrong, he followed the King's orders and numbered Israel from DAN to BEERSHEBA. In other words, David wanted to know how many men were in his kingdom from North to South—the whole land. Now those in leadership knew this was a wrong thing to do. Even GENERAL JOAB questioned the King David. He asked, *"Why doth my lord the king delight in this thing?"*

Because the KING was KING, his words prevailed and JOAB, being a loyal subject and captain of the army did as he was commanded to do. At the end of nine months and twenty days the job was completed. There were 13 million men in the land. If we would guess the number of women and children we would have many more million people counted that year.

Guess how David felt after the *"numbering"*? He was most miserable. The Bible says that *DAVID'S HEART WAS SMITTEN.* As soon as he learned the number, his conscience bothered him. He knew it was wrong. I do not know why he could not have had such sorrow sooner. He could have stopped the *numbering* at any time; but he let JOAB do the whole land. He cried out, *"I HAVE SINNED!"*

I have been struck with the fact that several men in the Bible have said those same three words when they were confronted with their sin. We read that PHARAOH said this to Moses (Exodus 9:27, 10:16). BALAAM confessed to the angel of the LORD, *"I have sinned!"* (See Numbers 22:34.) ACHAN told Joshua, *"Indeed I have sinned"* (Joshua 7:20). SAUL said the same thing to Samuel (I Samuel 15:24). He repeated the words (I Samuel 26:21) in regard to his actions toward David.

DAVID confessed to Nathan concerning the Bathsheba affair, *"I have sinned against the LORD"* (II Samuel 12:13). SHIMEI said to David, *"I have sinned"* (II Samuel 19:20). In the incident of *numbering* the people DAVID confessed *"I have sinned"* in three passages of Scripture. (II Samuel 24:10; II Samuel 24:17; & I Chronicles 21:8). DAVID cried out to the LORD in Psalm 41:4, *"I have sinned against thee."* JOB confessed, *"I have sinned"* in Job 7:20 while others who perverted that which was right said, *"I have sinned!"* also (Job 33:27). MICAH, in bearing the indignation of the LORD, cried out *"I have sinned!'* JUDAS, when he realized Jesus was going to be crucified, said, *"I have sinned . . ."* (Matthew 27:4). THE PRODIGAL SON decided to return to his father after he said *"I have sinned"* (Luke 15:18). He repeated this confession to his father in person in Luke 15:21.

How like some of us when we have set our mind to do something. An inner voice may tell us that it is wrong; but the stronger pull of our flesh keeps us in the sin. How well I remember the stir that was caused when a leading television evangelist was discovered in an adulterous/fornicator situation. He cried on camera and called out, *"I HAVE SINNED!"*

But WHY did not an inner voice tell him not to begin such error in the first place? I am reminded of JAMES 1:14-15. *"But every man is tempted, when he is drawn away of his own lust, and enticed. Then when lust hath conceived, it bringeth forth sin: and sin, when it is finished, bringeth forth death."*

"OVER A WALL"
(Psalm 18:29)
"For by thee I have run through a troop;
and by my God have I leaped over a wall."
A wall of circumstances
A wall is no barrier to God;
but it is impassable apart from God! (ggs)

𝒯oday's 𝓑ible 𝓑lessing   𝒜pril 14

I Kings 1:38—I Kings 3:23

GOD SAVE THE KING!

I Kings 1:39

"And Zadok the priest took an horn of oil out of the tabernacle, and anointed Solomon. And they blew the trumpet, and all the people said, God save King Solomon."

It was a great day of rejoicing! His ascension to the throne did not come easily. Even though David had promised Solomon's mother, Bathsheba, that their son would be king, ADONIJAH had other ideas. He was already parading around as the ruler of the land with ABIATHAR the priest and JOAB, David's Captain of the host, aiding and abetting his rise to the Throne. If you remember, his mother was HAGGITH, and his brother was the slain ABSALOM—the handsome son for whom David had grieved. In some ways we cannot blame ADONIJAH, as his father had never called him on such an assumption (I Kings 1:5-7). Perhaps in his old age and failing health, David did not comprehend what was going on in his kingdom.

When NATHAN realized that ADONIJAH was proceeding with his inaugural celebrations, he approached BATHSHEBA in alarm. He informed Solomon's mother about the formal proceedings, telling her that *"David our lord knoweth it not!"* So Bathsheba came to David's sick room. She reminded her husband that he had promised her years ago that their son SOLOMON would be king after David. Yes, David remembered! Soon Nathan entered the room, explaining the situation. Then David commanded, *"Let Zadok, the priest, and Nathan the prophet anoint Solomon king over Israel. Blow the trumpet and say GOD SAVE THE KING!"*

"OUR GOD FOREVER"
(Psalm 48:12-14)

Walk around Zion.
Go round about her.
Tell the tower thereof.
Mark well her bulwarks.
Consider her palaces (to tell).
This God is our God forever.
He will be our guide even unto death.
A study of types and shadows speak of Heaven.
It also speaks of the Glorious Church.
THIS IS OUR GOD FOREVER!
It is a sustaining statement. (ggs)

Today's Bible Blessing   *April* 15

I Kings 3:24–I Kings 6:28

SOLOMON'S UNDERSTANDING HEART

I Kings 4:29

"And God gave Solomon wisdom and understanding exceeding much, and largeness of heart, even as the sand that is on the sea shore."

Solomon asked God for an understanding heart. God answered that prayer and added *"wisdom"* unto him, also. What a blessing! We first see this wisdom when he discerned the lying of the mother who had traded her dead child for her friend's living one. Over and over his wisdom was seen. People flocked to his side to hear his wisdom! He made Benaiah, one of David's mighty men, to be his captain of the armies. Zadok and Abiathar were the priests. Good men!

Solomon reigned from the river unto the land of the Philistines, unto Egypt's borders. Judah and Israel were safe under his care from Dan to Beersheba all of Solomon's days. *His wisdom excelled the wisdom of all the children of the east country and* *the wisdom of Egypt.* He spoke in 3,000 proverbs and sang 1,005 songs! What a gifted man!–so much like his father, David. Solomon was a man of peace not of war.

King Hiram of Tyre cared for David. They were friends. It was to Hiram that Solomon confessed that David was not permitted to build the temple. Why? David was a man of war. Solomon was a man of peace. King Hiram provided wonderful fir trees to build the house of the LORD. What a wonderful gift! Solomon had great stones brought to Jerusalem for the foundation.

In the four hundred and eightieth year, after the children of Israel had come out of Egypt, the TEMPLE of the LORD was begun to be built. That was in Solomon's fourth year as king. It was the month of Zif. All the stones for the temple were prepared away from the temple site. No hammer or axe or any tool was heard as the building was put together. It must have been an awesome experience to see such an edifice erected without a sound!

Every man is gifted in his own area of expertise. David knew how to wield the sword and conquer land and people for his country. Solomon's expertise was in diplomacy. He made friends with all nations, married many wives, and got along with most everyone. Each of us has a field of work suited to our own personalities and gifts. We cannot be a *"Solomon"* if we are a *"David"*; nor a *"David"* if we are a *"Solomon."* It is up to us to discover what God has for us in our life's work, do it, and be happy that He has led us in that direction.

"STAND THEREFORE"
"A man is known by the company he avoids." (Spurgeon)
LISTEN FOR THE "ABSENT NOTE" in preaching.
Note what the preacher does not say!
(ggs)

Today's Bible Blessing   *April 16*

I Kings 6:29–I Kings 8:24

A SON'S PRIDE

I Kings 8:17

"And it was in the heart of David my father to build an house for the name of the LORD God of Israel."

As I read this passage of Scripture, I am struck with the many times Solomon mentioned the name of his father, David, when Solomon dedicated the temple. It warmed my heart! How proud he was of his father! How deep was his love for the man! It is my personal opinion that King David spent much time with Solomon to teach him how to be a king. Had not his father, David, promised Solomon's mother that her son would be the one to sit on the throne after his demise? Therefore, Solomon wanted to fulfill his father's wishes to build a house of the LORD God! He knew how important that project was to his Dad.

Over and over again the new king of Israel and Judah spoke with pride of his parent! It did my heart good to see these references. It was the seventh month! The king and all the heads of Israel gathered at the *feast of Ethanim*. The priests were there, too. They brought *the Ark of the Covenant* to the *Holy Place* between the cherubim. It was a momentous, sacred moment! It was a holy day! No one had ever seen another like it.

As the priests retreated from the Holy Place, the cloud filled the house of the LORD. Solomon blessed the people. He reminded them that the LORD God of Israel spake with his mouth to his father David (I Kings 8:15). He said, *"It was in the heart of David his father to build an house for the Name of the LORD God of Israel* (I Kings 8:17). He reflected that the LORD God said it was well that his father wanted to build a house (I Kings 8:18). But David knew that Solomon was a man of peace and would build the *Temple in Jerusalem.*

Solomon rejoiced that he was risen up in place of his father (I Kings 8:20) to sit on the throne. He announced that God had fulfilled His word. *The Temple was built!* He also proclaimed God's truth that *"There shall not fail thee a man in my sight to sit on the throne of Israel . . ."* What a comfort for the new King to see the LORD God's promise begin to be fulfilled in him. God's word was being *verified*—the very words that were promised to David his father had come to pass.

Some sons are not proud of their fathers. Even if the father is some renowned person, the sons shy away from acknowledging that man is their Dad. Solomon was not like that. Sometimes sons are slightly ashamed. They may not agree with their Dad. They cannot bear the reproach some of their father's ideas may bring. Solomon was not like that. Some sons may not understand how their father can be loved and respected by others. They do not see their father in such a light. Solomon was not like that! Other sons are extremely proud of their father's accomplishments. Solomon could not stop praising his Dad! He was very happy to carry on his father's work!

We had one son who always introduced his father with such pride. As I reflect on that pride, it warms my heart that our son wanted people to know he had an important and good father. Now that he has passed on to Glory, it warms his father's heart to know that his son was proud of him, like Solomon was proud of his father, David.

"LIFE'S LOYALTIES"
I am not bound to win,
but I am bound to be true.
I am not bound to succeed,
but I am bound to live by the light I have.
I must stand with anybody that stands right.
Stand with him while he is right
and part with him when he goes wrong.
(by Abraham Lincoln) (ggs)

Today's Bible Blessing   *April 17*

I Kings 8:25–I Kings 10:15

HEAVEN IS A PLACE

I Kings 8:30b

"Hear thou in heaven thy dwelling place: and when thou hearest, forgive."

Picture with me King Solomon standing in front of the altar of the LORD! See his arms held high. Notice the palms of his hands upward and opened to the God of Heaven. What a prayer he prayed that day! It is one of the longest prayers recorded in the Bible. The Spirit of God moved Solomon's tender heart to petition and praise! I wonder what it was like. Could everyone hear him? Or did only his body language convey his heart cry?

Yesterday we saw how Solomon spoke so reverently about his father. Today, we hear him speak to his Heavenly Father. It is a blessing to realize the reverence David's son had at that time for the LORD of Heaven. That Heaven was the dwelling place of the LORD God, Solomon knew. He said in our verse today, "HEAR THOU IN HEAVEN THY DWELLING PLACE."

In Chapter Eight, we learned that Solomon's LORD, his God, would "do" and "judge" Israel from Heaven. He would *"forgive the sins of Israel and bring them unto the land"* if they stayed true in future years. Solomon realized the LORD knew the hearts of His children. Because of this, He would *"give to every man according to each man's ways."* What a trembling thought! God knows our hearts better than we know them ourselves! Solomon's prayer was that the LORD would hear from Heaven so all the people on earth would know His Name, and that God would maintain their cause.

When the average person thinks of Heaven, his mind goes "Up"! But I ask you how HIGH is *"UP"*? As you and I look up into the sky, we see the ATMOSPHERIC HEAVEN. We know that

148

HEAVEN very well. It is where we see the sunrises and sunsets of our lives. It is where the birds fly and from where the rain falls.

Then high above where the birds fly is the SIDEREAL HEAVEN. That is where the stars and planets stay. That is the STARRY HEAVEN! Now with rockets and space ships, man has punctured that canopy. Sometimes, on our television sets, we see pictures from planets many light years away. They have always been there—but we never saw them before.

Yet there is another HEAVEN. It is the "HEAVEN" where Solomon was pointing us to in his prayer. It is where the LORD God dwells. It is what theologians refer to as THE HEAVEN. Yes, THAT IS WHERE GOD DWELLS! It is also where the soul that has genuinely trusted the Lord Jesus Christ as personal Saviour goes at death. This *"Heaven"* holds more mystery for us. For no one that we know of today has ever been there and returned.

We read that the Apostle Paul in the Bible had been there. He saw glorious sights which he could not really explain. It made him not fear death. We have loved ones there, yet it is a *"place"* we do not fully understand. It is a *"place"* Christians sing about and look forward to being in, but do everything to keep from going there when they are sick. They sing about HEAVEN. It brings much comfort to know about HEAVEN at funerals—but we cry when our loved ones go there and leave us. Jesus knows our frailties of faith. He comforts us with the thought of HEAVEN and encourages us not to be troubled.

Isaiah, the prophet, gave us an insight into that HEAVEN when he said *"I saw the LORD sitting upon a throne, high and lifted up, and his train filled the temple."* Jesus spoke of Heaven. It is comforting to read in Matthew 5:34 that HEAVEN is GOD'S THRONE! In teaching His disciples to pray, Jesus instructed them to address their HEAVENLY FATHER by praying, *"OUR FATHER WHICH ART IN HEAVEN!"*

It is good to remember that HEAVEN is a "PLACE"! It is a *"place"* where God dwells. It is a *"place"* where prayer is heard. It is a *"place"* where Jesus sits next to His Father. It is a *"place"* where Jesus has *"PREPARED"* for the redeemed of the LORD. And it is a *"place"* where we who know the Lord Jesus Christ as Saviour, will dwell forever with Him.

"FAR BETTER"
(Philippians 1:23)
A dear Christian friend died yesterday.
Suddenly God called his name
and he left this world and his tired, weak frame,
and went instantly into the *Glorious Presence.*
His works have preceded him, and his reward awaits him.
He is absent from us but present with the Lord,
beholding His face.
Indeed this is gain, and far better for him.
"We are not far from "HOME." A moment will bring us there.
If this would be *that moment*, am I ready?" (ggs)

Today's Bible Blessing　　　　　　　　*April 18*

I Kings 10:16–I Kings 12:28

KING SOLOMON'S SAD DEMISE

I Kings 11:4

"For it came to pass, when Solomon was old, that his wives turned away his heart after other gods: and his heart was not perfect with the LORD his GOD, as was the heart of David his father."

In my opinion, this is one of the saddest verses in the Bible. In our last two *"Blessings"* we are drawn to Solomon for two reasons. One is his great respect for his father, David. It warmed our hearts to see a son's love for his Dad. The second reason we were drawn to Solomon was because he was a man of prayer who called upon the God of Heaven believing that the LORD God heard and answered prayer.

So with sadness beyond words, we find Solomon turning to the gods of his many wives and concubines. It has been evident that he was a man of peace. But at what a price! Marrying Pharaoh's daughter was a political move to keep on good terms with Egypt. Perhaps we could understand that. But, woman after woman came into his life. He married most of them–700 to be exact. (This did not count his 300 concubines–and who knows how many *"flings"* the King had.) Yes, he probably barely knew some of them. They were a part of his harem; but no one can be deceived that he did not *"know"* many of them. Each wife drew him farther from the God of his father! The Bible says in verse five of chapter eleven that *Solomon went after ASHTORETH and MILCOM.* With this religious compromise, he built a high place for CHEMOSH and MOLECH.

ASHTORETH was the female counterpart of BAAL and his consort, as well as a moon goddess. She was the queen of Canaan. Had not God commanded the children of Israel to have nothing whatsoever to do with the gods of the land? Though this cultist Babylonian goddess was androgynous in origin, the Semitic people thought of her solely as female–with a faint memory of her masculine side. She had equal footing with male divinities. On the MOABITE STONE, ISHTAR is identified with CHEMOSH (another one of Solomon's favorites) as a *"god."*

There were many ASHTORETHS. They represented various forms under which the goddess was worshipped in different localities (Judges 10:6; I Samuel 7:4; 12:10, etc.). Sometimes she was called Naamah, or Astor-nos, or the mother of Ashman, or the moon-goddess. Often she was symbolized by the horns of a cow or a woman with the tail of a fish. The immoral rites connected with her worship were called upon by God for Israel to extirpate.

As for MOLOCH–he was probably the "baal" worshiped by AHAB. He was the god of the Ammonites. It has been traditionally defined in the context of *"passing children through fire"*. This was understood to mean burning children alive unto their god, *Moloch*. Children were sacrificed with the Assyrian/Babylonia *Malik* and with another god called *"Lord"* (*Baal or Bel*), the Ammonites' sun god. *Baal Moloch,* known as the *Sacred Bull,* was conceived under the form of a calf, or an ox, or depicted as a man with the head of a bull. *Milton*, the poet, wrote that *Moloch* was a frightening and terrible demon covered with mothers' tears and children's blood.

Legend says Moloch was a huge brass statue with the head of a bull. In its hollow belly, burned a glowing red fire. Children were placed in the statue's hands which were raised to its mouth as if eating. Then the children fell into the fire. The people gathered before the Moloch dancing to the sound of flutes and drums. This way, the screams of the burning children could not be heard.

How could Solomon who knew the true God, fall into such degradation? No wonder the LORD tore the kingdom from his hands and gave it to his servant! *"THOU HAST NOT KEPT MY COVENANT AND MY STATUES!"*

"DISPLAY THE BANNER"
(Song of Solomon 2:4)
Thou hast given an honor to them that fear thee
that it may be displayed because of the truth.
The Words of God are His banner and ensign.
IT ONLY IS TRUTH!
THE LORD OUR BANNER
"Me and My Words!"
"His banner over me is love." (ggs)

Today's Bible Blessings   *April 19*

I Kings 12:29–15:15

WHAT KIND OF MOTHER ARE YOU?

I Kings 15:2, 10

"Three years reigned he (Abijam) in Jerusalem. And his mother's name was Maachah, the daughter of Abishalom. And forty and one years reigned he (Asa) . . . his mother's name was MAACHAH . . ."

Often, when we read about a king in the Bible, immediately after his name is mentioned, comes the name of his mother. I ALWAYS WONDER what kind of mother she was. If the king turned out to be a good king, I silently praise his mother. I think how she taught him the proper ways of life and how to walk with the LORD God. I reflect on her pride that her son was such a good man and ruler. But when the king turned out to be a bad king I assumed his mother would be ashamed by her son's evil ways. I pondered that she would hide her head when she would hear that he did not walk with the LORD, that he would blaspheme His Holy Name, and that he worshipped the wrong gods in the high places.

In our verses today we learn about a mother named MAACHAH. Much to my surprise I've discovered that she was not only the mother of ABIJAM, an evil king of Judah, but also the *"mother"* of good KING ASA. No doubt, she was actually the *"grandmother"* of ASA. In both references we are told that her father's name was ABISHALOM. Sad to say, ABIJAM'S heart was not *"perfect"* as the heart of King David. There was always war and discord between ABIJAM and JEROBOAM

Now ASA was ABIJAM'S son according to I Kings 15:8. Perhaps his mother died, as we only read about his evil grandmother. (For ten years, during Asa's reign of forty-one years, there were no wars.) He did that which was right in the sight of the LORD. For instance, he removed all the sodomites as well as burning the idols. This was a brave thing to do. Not only that, but he took his GRANDMOTHER MAACHAH off the throne and destroyed her idol. It takes a man of convictions to take such a stand with his *"grandmother,"* but right is right and wrong is wrong. For this we must praise God for ASA! His heart was *"perfect"* with the LORD all his days. That is more than can be said for Solomon whose heart was turned against the LORD in his old age.

While thinking about GRANDMOTHER MAACHAH, I scanned the Bible for more information and discovered interesting facts about her or those who bore her name. It was an eye opener. A boy by that name was the son of Nachor, Abraham's brother.

Manasseh's son, Machir, had a wife by that name. Caleb had a concubine with that name. David's wife, the daughter of the King of Geshur, had that name. She was the mother of Absalom and Tamar. Also a King of Gath, to whose son Shimei's servant fled during Solomon's reign, had the name.

MAACHAH was the wife of KING REHOBOAM, king of Judah, and mother of Abijam. She is called the daughter or granddaughter of Abishalom in I Kings 15 but of Absalom in II Chronicles 11. She was the great-granddaughter of five. This is the MAACAH whom ASA removed from the position of *"queen mother."* In I Chronicles 9, we see a woman by that name as the wife of Jehiel. Two fathers are recorded—one the father of Hanan in David's army and the other the father of Shephatiah, an office man in David's time.

The point of pondering MAACHAH and those she *"mothered"* is that she was an evil woman. It is evident that she had influence with her own son, ABIJAM. I'm beginning to think that the reason ASA turned out like he did was that he had a *good mother*, though unnamed, and that *good mother* had a mighty influence in his life. Perhaps she died young. No matter what, the result was, ASA turned out godly. I choose to believe it was his mother's influence that pointed him in the right direction for the rest of his life. **It behooves mothers of sons to teach their sons to be *men of God*, to be *fearless for the truth*, and *to stand strong for the Lord Jesus Christ* in adversity. WHAT KIND OF MOTHER OR GRANDMOTHER ARE YOU?**

"OVER A WALL"
(Psalm 18:29)
"For by thee I have run through a troop;
and by my God have I leaped over a wall."
By Thee I have run through a "troop"—"forces" against me.
I leaped over a "wall"—a "wall" of circumstances.
A "wall" is no barrier to God,
but it is impossible without Him! (ggs)

Today's Bible Blessing   *April 20*

I Kings 15:16–I Kings 18:8
GO HIDE YOURSELF

I Kings 17:2-3

"And the word of the LORD came unto him (ELIJAH), saying, Get thee hence, and turn thee eastward, and hide thyself by the brook Cherith, that is before Jordan."

Bold Elijah, came before the powerful, king of Israel declaring in no uncertain terms that there would be no rain in Israel for three years. Not only no rain, but no dew! This was a dreadful proclamation. How long can a people exist without rain or dew?

An evil king, named Ahab lived in Samaria, ruling over the land for twenty-two years. In his day, the foundation of Jericho was laid. AHAB'S father's name was OMRI—another evil ruler. AHAB was *"a chip off the old block"*! He married the dreaded JEZEBEL, the daughter of the king of Zidonia. They worshipped BAAL together. He built an altar in the House of Baal for his filthy god. Perhaps that was the altar that the heathen priests used to call down their gods in I Kings 18:26. The Bible says that AHAB provoked the LORD God of Israel more than any other king before him.

It was a bold move, on ELIJAH's part, to face this king with the news of *NO RAIN*! Have you ever had to confront a strong person whose ideas and values differed from yours? Have you ever stood alone when no one in the room agreed with you? Have you ever declared unwelcome news to a man who could assassinate you? This is what Elijah did. He stood face to face with the worst heathen in the land and said, *"It is not going to rain for three years!"*

After the delivery of such a message, the PROPHET ELIJAH was spent. All of his energy was sapped from his body. He felt limp and weary. God knew this. He knows man's frame. So the word of the LORD came to Elijah and said, *"Get thee from this place and go EAST."* The instructions continued, *"Go hide yourself!"* God gave specific instructions. Hide out by the BROOK CHERITH. That was near the Jordan River. I believe Elijah was well-aware of the territory. God even informed the exhausted prophet that ravens would feed him.

The Bible says *"So Elijah went and did according unto the word of the LORD . . ."* Those are comforting words to me as a Christian. Elijah obeyed. I don't suppose he ever hid out like that before with no food or a known-place to sleep. But he obeyed. He went. He slept. He rested. He ate bread twice a day and drank water whenever thirsty.

Have you ever been in a place where you were more than *"tired?"* You had worked hard. You had taken a stand for the LORD JESUS CHRIST. You had defended His Words. You had given of yourself so that there was little life left in you. You went to your room and lay down on your bed completely spent for God. You got in your car and drove to the shore for a day or two of recuperation. How good to be alone with God—away from the pressures of life. No one knew you were there. You could rest. You ate simple foods. You walked the beaches. God was renewing your mind.

If you have been in such a place in your life, you know how ELIJAH felt. You know, too, how needed was *your rest* at the

BROOK CHERITH. You thought, *"I could stay here forever."* That is how ELIJAH felt. He never wanted to leave Cherith. The water was sweet. The bread was delicious. He hoped it would go on forever! But ELIJAH had work to do that he knew not of. BUT GOD KNEW IT! The brook dried up. (Remember–there had been no rain.) The LORD moved Elijah on. The woman in Zarephath needed him. So with you and me. We must arise from our rest. Someone around the corner is waiting for us to help them. Don't miss the opportunity to fill a barrel with meal and a cruise with oil.

"I WILL CRY UNTO GOD"
(Psalm 57:2)
"I will cry unto God . . . that performeth all things for me"
Lord, to whom else shall we go?
Only Thou performeth for me!
"No one understands like Jesus"
Dear ones care, but do not really comprehend. (ggs)

Today's Bible Blessing   *April 21*

I Kings 18:9–I Kings 20:26
A LITTLE BIT OF NOTHING

I Kings 18:43

"And he went up, and looked, and said, 'There is nothing.'"

If you recall, there had not been rain in the land for at least three years. I am not sure the purpose of this dearth–but it was *"of God."* When would it rain again? I suppose everyone around the area wondered, too.

It seemed rather humorous to me to discover the time and place that the rain would fall again. Remember the two altars on top of Mount Carmel? One was tended to by four hundred and fifty priests who ate at Jezebel's table. Baal had made spectacles of them that day. They screamed to their *"god,"* imploring him to send fire down upon their heathen altar. It was an embarrassing, emotional frenzy. Perhaps brought on by drink and drugs and sexual immorality– they begged their deaf god to send fire upon their wood. Of course, he did nothing! He was just a statue made by man's hands.

Then Elijah, full of faith, called upon the TRUE GOD. It was the time of the evening sacrifice. In answer to the prophet's prayer, fire fell from Heaven, licking up the water surrounding the altar that night. It was a humiliating day for Baal and a hallowed one for the LORD God.

155

It was then–after such victory–that Elijah put his hand to his ear and proclaimed to AHAB, *"Get thee up, eat and drink; for there is a sound of abundance of rain!"* No one could hear the *"sound."* Perhaps even Elijah did not hear it as most men hear; but with his *"ear of faith,"* he heard rain.

We read in the New Testament in the book of James (5:17-18) that ELIJAH was a man just like the men we know today. He had similar feelings as we do today. He was a man of earnest prayer. He implored the LORD God that it would not rain. And it did not for three years and six months–exactly. All those years it did not rain. All those years AHAB and JEZEBEL were angry with ELIJAH. All those years, as the people thirsted and walked on their parched ground, they cursed the prophet for his praying.

Then Elijah prayed again. Perhaps that prayer for rain to return began to be prayed as he called down fire from Heaven that afternoon on Mount Carmel. We know that he went up to Mount Carmel again. Up there, he got down on the ground with his head between his knees. I don't know if he was in a sitting position or if he was curled up on all fours. All I know is that he prayed–probably like he had never prayed before. He pleaded with God to send the rain.

After earnest prayer, he called his servant. *"Go look,"* he said, *"and see if there is a cloud in the sky."* Word came back, *"THERE IS NOTHING!"* Have you ever prayed? Have you ever moaned and cried out to your Heavenly Father? You pleaded with Him. Your heart had a need. You begged for an affirmative answer. As you arose from your knees and looked at the sky, you saw *"NOTHING!"* After seeing no cloud–just a lot of *"nothing"* in the sky, Elijah commanded his servant, *"Go back seven times! And let me know!"* Elijah did not give up on God. Sometimes we give up! God was not trying to discourage Elijah with a *"nothing"* cloud. That was his answer at the time.

But that little bit of "nothing" was enough for Elijah. He told AHAB, "Get your chariot ready and get going back to your palace before the rain stops your trip!" James tells us that "ELIJAH PRAYED AGAIN AND THE HEAVEN GAVE RAIN, AND THE EARTH BROUGHT FORTH HER FRUIT!"

The answer came. *"There ariseth a little cloud out of the sea, like a man's hand."* How we should praise God for the *little cloud* answers to our *big cloud* prayers. It is not up to us how God answers. Remember this: It is up to us to pray and for God to give us the answer He sees fit to bestow! When will we ever learn?

"HIGHER THAN I"
(Psalm 61:2)
"WHEN MY HEART IS OVERWHELMED:
LEAD ME TO THE ROCK THAT IS HIGHER THAN I."
How high is our rock for the lowest estate?
El Elton–THE HIGHEST
There is nothing overwhelming, but what the Rock is higher!
(ggs)

Today's Bible Blessing   *April 22*

I Kings 20:27–I Kings 22:39
COVETING DOES NOT PAY

I Kings 21:4

"And Ahab came into his house . . . displeased because . . . Naboth . . . had said, I will not give thee the inheritance of my fathers. And he (Ahab) laid . . . upon his bed, and turned away his face, and would eat no bread."

Most all of us are familiar with the account of King Ahab's coveting his neighbor's vineyard. I'm sure it was a well-kept vineyard, but that was not the reason AHAB wanted the land. He wanted to plant a garden of herbs there. It would have been very handy to the palace. If he had that land, he could go out at any time to pick herbs to spice-up his daily meals. Also, it would have been a convenient place in which to sit and watch the birds, read, or entertain friends.

The only problem with the king's plan was that the owner of the vineyard, Mr. Naboth, did not want to sell. His reasons were excellent reasons. The land was a part of his family inheritance. Naboth did not want to mar that inheritance. But, King Ahab was in no mood to care about family pride and inheritances. He wanted that land!

As the word *"NO!'* was heard in AHAB's royal ears, depression struck his person. He went home! He went to bed! He sulked! He refused to eat! It seemed to me he accepted the refusal with his mental faculties, but his emotional side could not. That is when his wife, the heathen JEZEBEL, observed her husband's behavior of carrying on in an *"unkingly"* manner. She reminded him that he was king and that he could have anything he wanted.

In a scheming fashion, she worked it out that NABOTH would be a guest of honor at a banquet. How Naboth enjoyed the attention! Sad to say, he would be remembered for something other than honor. Wicked men—part of Jezebel's religious conclave—who were paid off by the Queen, lied about Naboth. They said he blasphemed his God and the King. This was untrue, but that did not matter to the Jezebels in the room. They stoned Naboth!

Immediately the KING took possession of the neighboring land for his own. Now, prophet ELIJAH the Tishbite, got wind of this dastardly deed and unnecessary death. Swiftly, he paid a visit on the greedy king who happened to be sitting in the deceased's garden. The king greeted the prophet by calling out, *"O my enemy!"* Elijah proclaimed the word directly from the LORD God that day. He said, *"I will bring evil upon thee."* He also told AHAB that no male heirs of his would be left in Israel alive. God was angry! Ahab would die a horrible death! Dogs would lick up his blood in the exact place where Naboth's blood was shed. It was most distressing news. Ahab had a repentant response. He tore his clothes. He fasted, wore sackcloth, and tiptoed around the palace. His whole attitude changed. God noticed this humility and postponed the predicted evil to his family until after AHAB's death.

I am reminded of a true account told me awhile back. There was a small assembly of believers that met several times a week in a small, humble church-type building. They enjoyed their Christian fellowship and breaking of bread together. They did not seek an updated, pretentious building. They were satisfied. Next to them was a well-financed company—I will not give the name. That company wanted the little Christian group to sell their property to them. I do not know why. Perhaps they did not like the little group being there.

In the passage of time, a very sad thing happened to that small congregation. The building caught on fire. It was completely destroyed. No longer could the humble group meet together in that place and sing hymns, read the Word of God, or break bread together. What were they to do? I do not know if they could afford to rebuild. But all I know is that they sold the land to that bigger company, and as far as I know, that was the end of the little group and their Bible fellowship. When I heard this true account, I remembered AHAB and how he coveted Naboth's vineyard. The Bible tells us plainly, *"THOU SHALT NOT COVET!"* It does not pay. Ask AHAB!

"THE RIGHT TO CHOOSE"
(Mark 10:17-22)
The rich young ruler really wanted Jesus.
He came running and knelt at His feet.
The rich young ruler had the right to choose,
but he had the responsibility to choose right.
He turned his back on the LORD.
He would not turn to God from his riches.
The one thing he lacked was the right choice.
He chose possessions instead of Jesus.
He knew the commandment mentioned in verse 19.
He was not ignorant. But He would not put God first
He would not choose the treasures of Heaven'
For he desired the possessions of earth. (ggs)

Today's Bible Blessing   *April 23*

I Kings 22:40–II Kings 4:1

THE WHIRLWIND & CHARIOT OF FIRE

II Kings 2:11

"And it came to pass . . . there appeared a chariot of fire, and horses of fire . . . and Elijah went up by a whirlwind into heaven."

Here in this verse we are a witness to the rapture of Elijah from this earth to Heaven. ELISHA was a witness to the astounding sight! This event happened by the RIVER JORDAN like so many other amazing events in Scripture. In II Kings 2:7, we read that fifty other men stood afar to view the circumstances concerning ELIJAH'S last moments on earth.

Some of us have seen chariots in museums. We have imagined them pulled by beautiful horses in the time of early Egypt or Israel. Today we are wondering what a *"chariot of fire"* would look like. Evidently this *"chariot"* was not like any other ever seen before. It was not made of metal or wood. It did not have wheels or a seat carved from a tree. The BIBLE says it was *"of fire."* When we think of fire, we think of purification. The works of a Christian are going to be tried by *"fire"* to see what sort they are. God will provide that fire! We recall the furnace of *"fire"* that Daniel's three friends had to endure. It did not necessarily purify them—although they were never the same after the experience. If we think about it, that fire, in many ways, protected them from death because the LORD was with them in that rage.

So what exactly was the *"fire"* that composed ELIJAH'S chariot? We don't know. But we do know that it was a frightening sight! Death is not pleasant for those who watch. It is not always pleasant for those who are dying. It is like a *"fire"* of passage from one life to another. When death comes there is nothing left! Nothing—but a *dead body*.

On this date in 2008, my husband and I, as well as our living children, stood by a casket in a church. In that flower-draped box lay the body of our second-born son. He was dead. But his soul and spirit were with Jesus. We had not expected him to die. But an unexpected pain, brought on by a blood clot, stabbed him. No longer could he breathe. He was dead. There was no *"chariot of fire"* around his deathbed when we got there. It had come. It was gone. We stood there, like the *"fifty,"* not understanding the sight before our eyes. But we trusted God and His way in our son's life! Our son, like ELIJAH, was ready to go. And we, like ELISHA, stood there holding his garment.

In ELIJAH'S case, a *whirlwind* came. It came with unexpected swiftness. It came boldly—out of the *"blue."* It was startling! It was frightening! ELISHA, who was standing close by, may not have fully comprehended the movement of the air about him. The surprise. The rush. He may have been knocked off his feet. The wind swooped down! With one mighty gust, that moving air swiftly swirled the *living* ELIJAH up, in its blowing arms, out of the sight of any who watched. ELIJAH WAS GONE! One moment, he was talking. One moment, he was walking. One moment, he was dividing the water with his cape. In the next, that same mantle lay lifeless on the ground. Look as he would, ELISHA saw the man he called his *"father"* no more. The young prophet, who over and over, vowed, *"I will never leave thee, Elijah!"* stood *"left" and alone* with nothing but the mantle of Elijah in his hand.

This is how it is when someone we love leaves us for realms on High. One minute, they are alive and laughing. The next moment they are gone! Only a shadow and a shell of them are left behind. But think of the GLORY that was ELIJAH'S! Think of the joy that came upon him! Think of the rewards of Heaven. We know that Elijah is still alive—not on earth but in GLORY. Did not he appear with Jesus in Matthew 17 at the *MOUNT OF TRANSFIGURATION?* There he was, with Moses and Jesus and the three disciples, talking and praising God together! What better proof of the life hereafter to those of us who genuinely trust in the Lord Jesus Christ.

Today's Bible Blessing　　　　　　　　　　　*April 24*

II Kings 4:2–II Kings 6:15

A SICK & PROUD MAN

II Kings 5:11

"But Naaman was wroth, and went away, and said, Behold, I thought, He will surely come out to me, and stand, and call on the name of the LORD his God, and strike his hand over the place, and recover the leper."

Here we find a very proud man! I suppose as far as *"pride"* is concerned, CAPTAIN NAAMAN had every reason in the world to be proud. Had not he been the victorious champion for the king of Syria? But we are told in verse 1 of chapter 5 that Naaman was a *"great"* man. To be great in one's own country is a worthwhile tribute of praise for anyone.

The only problem with this warrior was he had a serious chronic disorder called *"leprosy."* This was a terrible disease and most dreaded. We do not know how long he was so afflicted. I assume it was new to him. The reason I say this is, if he were like KING UZZIAH (II Kings 15:5-6), he would have been living in a separate house, and not even be able to lead the Syrian armies.

Today this disease is called *HANSEN'S DISEASE.* Medical men feel that much of the *leprosy* of former days really was undiagnosed syphilis—as syphilis has similar symptoms. That wrong diagnosis could have been the cause of people associating leprosy with the skin and parts of the body changing. Thankfully some medicines have been developed since 1930 (DAPSONE), and in 1980 *multidrug therapies* began to be used which have been very helpful. Leprosy is caused by bacteria and brings permanent damage to the skin, nerves, limbs, and eyes. The incubation period for this disease is from two to ten years. In the Old Testament, a leper was required to put a rag in front of his mouth and cry out *"Unclean! Unclean!"* wherever he went. They had to live outside the camp away from the uninfected.

It was in this sad condition that NAAMAN found himself. So it was with great anticipation that he followed the suggestion of his wife's young Israelite maid, and contacted the PROPHET ELISHA. So with great aplomb, the mighty Naaman rode up to Elisha's humble house. I can picture him now–dressed in military array, standing in the best chariot of his land with high bred horses sniffing the air and pawing the dust. Instead of the prophet rushing to this mighty man's side, Elisha sent his servant. How humiliating this action was to Captain Naaman. He was used to people fawning all over him. After all he was Naaman!

The message that came to the captain's ears was more humiliating than having a servant sent to his side. *"Wash in the JORDAN RIVER seven times!"* Those were the instructions straight from the prophet's lips. Elisha also affirmed to Naaman, *"And thou shalt be clean!"* I am not sure Naaman heard those words. His anger rolled up in his body. He lashed out in cruel words, *"I thought he would come to me and call on the Name of the LORD in front of me. I thought he would lay his hands upon me. I thought I would be healed!"* Instead: *"Wash seven times in the Jordan River!"* How much this account of a proud–though sick—man makes me reflect on those who refuse to receive the Lord Jesus Christ as Saviour. Many unsaved people want to be *"saved."* They want to know their sins are forgiven. They want a home in Heaven–but they want to get there in their own way. Naaman said, in his self-righteous way, *"Are not the rivers of Damascus better?"* Or *"Is not my church better than yours?"* Why should he humble himself and dip in the dirty, Israelite Jordan River? Even though he was dreadfully ill, he still had his own ideas how to be healed. That's how many people are. Maybe you are one of them. You want *"eternal life."* You don't want to go to Hell! But you have your own way. *"I go to church!"* *"I do good works!"* *"I never beat my wife!"* All God says to you is *"Dip in the JORDAN!"* He says, *"Believe you are a sinner and that Jesus Christ died for your sins."* Eventually Naaman did the simple thing. He believed the prophet! He was healed!

"THREE MORE YEARS TO LIVE"

Suppose your health was not good,
and the doctor said you had only three more years.
What would you do?
When the Lord Jesus Christ was thirty years old,
He had three more years to live.
What did He do?
He preached. He taught.
He helped train others to carry on when He left.
He said, *"Go and make disciples."* (ggs)

II Kings 6:16–II Kings 9:18
JEHU: FURIOUS AND BRAVE

II Kings 9:3a

"Then take the box of oil, and pour it on his (Jehu's) head, and say, Thus saith the LORD, I have anointed thee king over Israel"

Jehu has always interested me. I am not sure why—perhaps it was because I used to hear preachers preach about Jehu's *furious* driving. Evidently this king drove his chariot in a manner that was peculiar to him (II Kings 9:20). It is too bad, today, if Christian leaders are known to be such fast drivers that they do not care if they keep within the speed limits of the law or not. I suppose that was one of Jehu's characteristics also.

Strange as it seemed to me, Jehu's bad chariot driving was all that I remembered about his life. So today, as I read in II Kings, chapter nine, I was surprised to be reminded that Jehu was a king, as I didn't think of him as one. His commission from the LORD seemed to be to get rid of Jezebel and all those of the house of Ahab. Of course, Ahab had died previously when a man drew a bow at random, and just happened to hit Israel's King Ahab–killing him.

There was nothing remarkable about the calling of Jehu or of his formal anointing. In fact, it was unremarkable. I remembered with what little aplomb David was anointed by Samuel. In this case, the Prophet Elisha sent one of the children of a prophet to find Jehu. His mission was to anoint Jehu king. When that young person found Jehu, he asked the Captain to go into a private room with him. There, a flask of oil was opened and the contents were poured on the head of Jehu, the son of JEHOSHAPHAT. *"Thus saith the LORD, I have anointed thee king over Israel,"* were the words spoken.

The commission of the newly anointed king-to-be was to avenge the house of AHAB for the deaths of all the prophets who had died at Jezebel's command, including Naboth's wrongful death. It was pointed out also that JEZEBEL would suffer a humiliating death. Dogs would eat her flesh and no one would be there to bury her. At this *"anointing,"* there was no pomp, no circumstances–just a proclamation that Jehu was king! Perhaps today, we make too much of a *"to-do"* as the reigns of government are transferred from one ruler or president to another. Sometimes the most important events in our lives come upon us with no *ruffles and flourishes* by others about us.

It seemed that the main goal of Jehu's rule was to rid Israel of Ahab's seed. God had told Ahab that this would happen after his death. This killing of Ahab's descendants was to vindicate

Naboth's death! Now we see this prediction coming to pass. It began to be fulfilled with the death of JORAM, Ahab's son. KING JORAM had been wounded in battle. He returned to his hometown of JEZREEL to recover. While on his sickbed, he learned that Jehu was coming to get him. He kept asking his men to inquire of JEHU, *"Are you coming in peace?"* Of course, he wasn't. Jehu determined to do away with the king of Israel.

As the account closed, we find KING JORAM of Israel and KING AHAZIAH of Judah were out in the field trying to figure out what JEHU was up to. To make a long story short, Jehu drove there in his chariot. With his full strength, he shot an arrow at Joram's heart. JORAM was dead! His body was thrown on the plot of land that had been NABOTH'S VINEYARD, the very land that his father had coveted! The LORD had predicted this to Ahab years ago. AHAZIAH fled on horseback. He could see that *"death"* was coming. Jehu's men pursued him, killed him, and buried him where his father had been buried. Personally, I am glad I am not called to do such a thing. It seemed that it was nothing to Jehu. He was a man of war and killing. God uses all kinds of people to do His will. JEHU was a prepared man for a certain task.

FOR WHAT HAS GOD PREPARED YOU?

> ### *"TODAY"*
> LIFE IS SO SHORT THAT NO MAN
> CAN AFFORD TO LOSE A DAY.
> Not only is TODAY the day of salvation,
> It is the day of service.
> Let us live and love and serve
> so that if He should call us up today,
> we will be glad we did what pleased Him. (ggs)

Today's Bible Blessing   *April 26*

II Kings 9:19–II Kings 12:9

JEZEBEL, ATHALIAH, & JEHOSHEBA

II Kings 9:30; 11:1-2

"And when Jehu was come to Jezreel, Jezebel heard of it, and she painted her face, and tired her head, and looked out at a window . . . when ATHALIAH, the mother of AHAZIAH, saw that her son was dead . . . she destroyed all the seed royal. But

JEHOSHEBA . . . took JOASH, the son of AHAZIAH . . . so that he was not slain."

In today's reading we have three women whom we should not forget. They are important to the history of the children of Israel. One woman is associated with bossiness and unsubmissiveness, as well as a leader of a false religion! The second is remembered as a selfish and murderous woman, a daughter of a king, who would stop at nothing to become the queen and ruler of the land. The last woman's name is less familiar, but her act of courage and dedication to the line of kings to the throne of David is spectacular. Mother's Day sermons should be made about her! Most of us do not know her name!

We all know about JEZEBEL. She reigned with AHAB, her depressed husband, and is best known for her dishonest dealings with Naboth and her emotional and financial support for her evil BAAL worship. Her home was in JEZREEL. Some say it is the land from Italy to Iran and from Greece to Egypt; but we, who read the Bible, think of Jezebel's home as mainly in Israel—the land on both sides of the Jordan River. It had very hot summers with plenty of rain. No wonder Jezebel was furious with Elijah who stopped the rain for three years!

Remember JEHU? He had been commissioned by the LORD to kill Jezebel. I am not sure she knew it. If she did, why would she paint her face, dress up in her finest, and look out the window for the arrival of JEHU? Her concern was for Zimri. I don't know why. Her question to JEHU was, *"Had Zimri peace, who slew his master?"* When JEHU looked up and saw her, he knew he had his *target* before him. How would he get to her with all her guards? Then it was his turn to ask a question. He called, *"Who is on my side?"* Two or three *men*, who must not have cared for the queen, grabbed her and threw her down to the ground below. The fall killed her! Perhaps, previously, she had made eunuchs of the men and they were more than glad to throw her out the window. As her body hit the ground, breaking her bones, her blood spattered on the wall. Then horses came by and trampled it. No one cared about the body of the dead queen. Dogs ate her flesh—just as Elijah had predicted. There was nothing left to bury. A sad fate for anyone.

According to some, ATHALIA ruled the kingdom for a period of time before her son was king. When he was killed by Jehu, she assumed the throne in full. There is a discussion if she were the daughter of Ahab by Jezebel (or another wife) or his sister. It is recorded that he and she had Omri as their father. If so, she would be Ahab's sister. No matter, she comes from a line of wicked BAAL worshippers bent on being queen. That is why at the death of her son, Ahaziah, she had the entire seed royal killed. At least *she thought she had them all destroyed.*

This is where JEHOSHEBA, King Joram's daughter, came into the picture. She took baby JOASH and hid him away from the wicked queen in her bedroom. The priest, JEHOIDA, and others who were for the plan, crowned the seven-year old boy king, standing him by the altar in the temple. They anointed him, put the *"testimony"* (Moses' writings) in his hands, and clapped their hands crying out, *"GOD SAVE THE KING!"* Then they sat him on the throne of the kings! What a glorious day. ATHALIAH was stunned! She cried out, "TREASON, TREASON!" She was killed by the king's house. Some say Jehu slew her.

"IT IS NOT FOR YOU TO KNOW"
(Acts 1:7)
Many things we do not know in this world,
In fact, most of our path is a hidden one.
But we do not need to know what lies ahead to be content
for our omniscient God knows,
and we simply follow the plan He has laid out. (ggs)

**"One step ahead, I take.
He goes before me.
One day at a time, I live.
He's always there.
The year behind I see
but keep on trusting,
for it is enough to know
I'm in His care."**
(ggs)

𝒯oday's 𝓑ible 𝓑lessing   𝒜pril 27

II Kings 12:10–II Kings 15:19
TEARS WEPT OVER HIS FACE

II Kings 13:14

"Now Elisha was fallen sick of his sickness whereof he died."

These are very sad words indeed. The beloved prophet of Israel would die. He must have had a long sickness. It is interesting that he who could heal others was not healed himself. This reminds me of the APOSTLE PAUL who helped so many sick people; yet he himself was not healed. Some people say that a Christian should never be sick. They infer that if the Christian is sick, the believer is not walking with the Lord—and some may infer that he is not *"saved."* So it is of interest that ELISHA had a sickness that ended in death for him.

Joash, the King of Israel, loved Elisha. He grieved that his prophet was *sick unto death.* The Bible says he *"wept over his face."* I think this means that tears ran down Joash's face like streams of water. Uncontrollable tears! I remember this has happened to me a few times. When overwhelming sadness has touched my soul, *tears have wept over my face.* Have you ever had *tears weep over your face?*

Joash cried out very interesting words. He wept, *"O my father, my father, the chariot of Israel, and the horsemen thereof."* Was he describing the man—as the *"chariot of Israel"?* If you recall, prior to ELIJAH being swooped up to Heaven in a whirlwind, there was a *"chariot of fire"* sighted. But in this passage, there is no mention of *"fire."* Why did the king call his beloved prophet a *"chariot"*–or did he?

A chariot is a horse-drawn, two-wheeled cart used in ancient times for war, racing, parades, etc. In what way was Elisha, the son of Shaphat a *"chariot"?* Could it be because he *"carried"* the word of the LORD like a mighty man of war? Could it be that he was decisive in his message. Could it be that he came into an area or room with great assurance like a chariot drives up to its destination? I don't know. Besides calling him a *"chariot,"* the king mentioned that the *"chariot"* was accompanied by *"horsemen."* Horsemen are skilled in managing and driving horses. If a man was not a horseman himself, he would have one or two with him in his chariot, as he sat on the seat being transported to and fro. This was Elisha! He had a message from God. He went to and fro with that message. Often others transported him, or that message for him, to various destinations. With his death, the chariot and horsemen would be silenced. The message would no longer come from the mouth of the Prophet Elisha. There would be stillness—a mammoth miss in the country with his death. That absence was felt by Joash! Tears flowed down his cheeks for such a loss.

There is no mention of *"fire"* in this passage, as there was with Elijah. And there is no mention of the horses here with ELISHA either–only the horsemen. But it could be that as Christians are comforted by the presence of *"Guardian Angels"* that such *"angels"* accompany the dying believer to Heaven. For a want of better words, these *"Angels"* are like a *"Chariot"* and *"horsemen."* Whatever–it is comforting to know that those who have trusted in Jesus Christ as personal Saviour are not alone in death. It may appear to be so for us who look at their dead body; but for the one who died, perhaps, he was swooped off to Glory accompanied by a *"chariot"* and *"horsemen"*

Elisha died. He was buried. Today there seems to be a rash of people, who claim the Name of the Lord Jesus Christ, who have decided not to be buried. Even though Jesus Christ gave us the example of being buried and not burned up and his ashes poured into a vase. Christians are doing this. They are desecrating what was the *"temple of the Holy Spirit"* by heathen cremation. Even if it is "cheaper" to **burn up** the body of a loved-one like the heathen do, what kind of a Christian testimony is that? Several years ago, I interviewed a few morticians about cremation. After they gave me their sales pitch on the subject, I asked every one of them, *"Will you be* cremated?" And to a man, their answer was *"NO!"* What would you have thought of Elisha's loved ones if they had burned his body like the heathen who denied the true God?

"DWELLING AMONG THE PLANTS AND HEDGES"
(I Chronicles 4:23)
"These were the potters,
and those that dwelt among plants and hedges.
There they dwelt with the king for his work."
Potters work with clay and in hard places.
PERHAPS THIS IS LIKE ME.
I dwell with the King among my plants (dear sick ones) and hedges.
(ggs)

Today's Bible Blessing   *April 28*

II Kings 15:20–II Kings 18:5

PRAISE GOD FOR KING HEZEKIAH

II Kings 18:1-3

"In the third year of Hoshea . . . Hezekiah . . . king of Judah began to reign . . . and he did that which was right in the sight of the LORD."

Why was it so remarkable that HEZEKIAH trusted in the LORD God? Should not that have been the religious flavor of every king of Judah and Israel? Sad to say, usually the kings had no dealings with the true God. Usually they served the gods of Baal or other false deities. This fact is to the shame of Israel and Judah. Kings died, kings were born, and new kings reigned. It makes my head spin to read of the unbelief and wickedness that prevailed continually. There was such jealousy and rivalry! Shamefully, it brought about murders and killings!

For instance in today's reading alone, we hear of MENAHEM who killed SHALLUM, the son of JABESH who reigned in Samaria. Previously we learned that ZACHARIAH did evil in the sight of the LORD. MENAHEM smote TIPHSAH, as well as all the pregnant women, ripping the unborn from their mother's bodies. Then Menahem became king of Israel, reigning for ten years. He departed not from his evil ways and continued worshipping the JEROBOAM calves.

KING PUL of Assyria came at Menahem's kingdom. To pacify him, Menahem gave PUL a thousand talents of silver. His mighty men of wealth gave silver to the Assyrian ruler. This saved his country. Menahem was the nineteenth king of Israel. His son

PEKAHIAH reigned in his stead. In the end, he was slain by PEKAH who rose to the Throne. He, too, was evil in the LORD'S sight. King Tiglathpileser of Assyria conquered many lands.

    The name of HOSHEA appeared in II Kings 15:30. He conspired against PEKAH and killed him. It was in Pekah's second year that UZZIAH'S son, JOTHAM, began to reign. He was the 11th king of JUDAH. His mother's name was JERUSHA. He did that which was right in the eyes of the LORD, except the high places were not removed. Jotham was buried in the city of David and AHAZ, his son, reigned in his stead.

    It is no surprise to learn that AHAZ walked NOT with the LORD. He made his son pass through the fire, according to the abominations of the heathen, and offered sacrifices in high places, on hills, and under every green tree. During the advancement against Israel, AHAZ stood strong and was not overcome by the king of Syria or by KING PEKAH of Israel. But AHAZ seemed to fear the KING TIGLATHPILESER of Assyria, telling him, *"I am thy servant,"* as well as giving him the temple's silver, gold, and precious things. Then Assyria's king killed KING REZIN of SYRIA.

    There was wrong altar-building and sacrifices were made. They were wrong sacrifices! Then the real altar from the Temple was brought to them and placed between the House of the LORD and the false altar—putting it on the north side of the false altar (the best I understand this). URIJAH seemed to be the priest here and did what KING AHAZ commanded. He took the Temple's laver off its base and proceeded to put it upon his own stones. They seemed to make this a place of worship—not according to the LORD's ways, but according to their own willfulness. AHAZ died, was buried in Jerusalem, and KING HEZEKIAH of Judah began his reign.

    We have another mention of HOSHEA (the 22ⁿᵈ king of JUDAH) in 17:1, who was evil—reigning nine years over Israel. Before his death he gave gifts to SHALMANESER, king of Assyria, becoming his servant. It was SHALMANESER who bound HOSHEA, casting him in prison, and carried Israel into Assyria! This captivity was the result of Israel's sin. They would not hear or believe in the LORD their God. It is very sad! **PRAISE GOD FOR THE COMING OF HEZEKIAH!**

> ## *"Alone"*
> (Isaiah 40:31; Luke 10:40)
> *"MOUNT UP WITH WINGS AS EAGLES"*
> LEARN TO WALK ALONE WITH GOD!
> Enoch walked *alone.*
> Abraham walked *alone.*
> Moses walked *alone.*
> Paul walked *alone.*
> The Lord Jesus walked *alone.*
> *"Eagles are solitary birds; yet, no weakling.*
> *It does not travel in a flock as boisterous geese."* (copied)
> It flies high.
> Martha did not know how to serve *alone.*
> She felt neglected and abused.
> Carest thou not that I serve *alone?*
> *"Dost thou not care that my sister hath left me*
> *to serve alone?"* (ggs)

Today's Bible Blessing   *April 29*

II Kings 18:6–II Kings 20:16

THE ASSYRIAN THREAT

II Kings 19:14

"And Hezekiah received the letter . . . and read it . . . and went up into the house of the LORD, and spread it before the LORD."

Of all the kings mentioned in today's reading, KING HEZEKIAH was the only one who served the LORD God. Refresh your memory here. (When we read the words LORD God in the OLD TESTAMENT, those words for *"deity"* refer to **JEHOVAH**, the Lord Jesus Christ.) **Evidently Assyria was a mighty nation. RABSHAKEH, who was bilingual, was her spokesman.**

When HEZEKIAH was twenty-five years old, he began to reign over JUDAH. That was in the third year of HOSHEA, the king of Israel's reign. During that time, HEZEKIAH removed all the High Places and smashed the images. He also destroyed the brasen serpent that Moses had made during a wilderness plague. They had kept it all these years making it an *"idol."* The Hebrews had been worshipping it, burning incense to it, and HEZEKIAH named it NEHUSHTAN. The Bible says of HEZEKIAH, *"He trusted in the LORD God of Israel, so that after him was none like him among all the kings of Judah, nor any that were before him for he clave to the LORD . . ."* (II Kings 18:5-6 & following.)

Because the King of Assyria was used to running rough shod over a country, capturing it, and taking its king and people to himself, he began the process of wearing down HEZEKIAH and his people for the kill. It began with putting Israel's KING HOSHEA in prison, and then setting up a blockade for three years. It must have been a terrible time for the people. Religiously–they were a mess, for they secretly set up images and groves, burning incense in high places as the heathen did. This behavior provoked the LORD to anger.

After years of pacifying the King of Assyria, with gold and silver taken from the holy temple, he sent RABSHAKEH and others to discuss with HEZEKIAH in Whom he was trusting. They met by the conduit—a place where water collected. My husband and I saw this while in Israel. Our guide called it *"HEZEKIAH'S FOUNTAIN"* (or *"conduit"* 2 Kings 18:17).

When KING HEZEKIAH heard that the Assyrians were going to get them, he put on sackcloth instead of his kingly garment and went into the House of the Lord, calling for the Prophet Isaiah. *"Be not afraid of the words which thou hast heard . . ."* was the Prophet's comforting message. Soon after this event, the Assyrian king sent a disturbing reply. He reiterated that all the *"gods"* of the many nations that he had captured did not deliver those people. He questioned why Hezekiah thought his God would be any different in saving them.

With great concern, HEZEKIAH read the letter. Quickly he entered the Temple. He spread the letter out before the LORD. Then he prayed! He reminded God that it was true the Assyrians had destroyed the nations and lands about them, and it was true they cast their captured gods into the fire. But, Hezekiah reminded God that HE was His God and the God of His people. He begged the LORD God to save them out of the Assyrian's hand.

The most wonderful assurance came from God by the mouth of Isaiah. The LORD God assured the king, *"I HAVE HEARD!"* What more could Hezekiah ask?

Today many of us are facing difficult situations with difficult people. They try to overpower us with their ways. We quake in their presence–yet we know they are wrong. We know they do not trust in the *True God* or believe in Jesus Christ as Saviour. It is at times like this, that we must spread our fears before the Lord and believe He has heard our cry!

> ## "PRAISE IS COMELY FOR THE UPRIGHT"
> (Psalm 33:1-2; Psalm 147:1)
> So often we complain.
> So quickly we murmur.
> So easily we weep.
> So continually we grumble.
> But people are watching the Christian.
> The unsaved murmuring can never be called "comely."
> BUT PRAISE IS COMELY FOR THE CHRISTIAN.
> *It is good and pleasant to sing praises unto our God.* (ggs)

Today's Bible Blessing   *April 30*

II Kings 20:17–II Kings 23:34

ONE GOOD KING AMONG SO MANY

II Kings 23:25

"And like unto him (Josiah) was there no king before him, that turned to the LORD with all his heart, and with all his soul . . ."

We are coming to a part in Scripture where we learn about one of the most, if not the most, wicked king that ever ruled in Judah. His name was *MANASSEH*, and he began his reign at age twelve. He dealt with *familiar spirits and wizards*, along with other evil worship practices. His father was one of the best kings ever. His name was *HEZEKIAH*! How this dichotomy of change from good to bad came to pass, I am not sure. Always I have had the feeling the *"goodness"* and *"badness"* of a son had to do with the *"mother."* If one had a godly mother, more than likely the child would become a godly person. This is not always so–but, more than often, it is. His mother's name was *HEPHZIBAH*! He reigned fifty-five years.

AMON was the son of MANASSEH. His mother's name was *MESHULLEMETH*. He was a wicked king! He did evil in the sight of the LORD–like his father. That meant he served his father's idols. In the events of his life, AMON was not the son-of-his-father chosen *"to pass through the fire."* One of his brothers gave his life for such religious corruption, as hundreds and hundreds of children have had to do. What horrendous slaughter comes when innocent children are killed! Later KING AMON was killed in his own house by his own servants. Both he and his father were buried in the Garden of UZZA.

Now comes a good king! His name was JOSIAH. His mother's name was JEDIDAH. He was only eight-years-old when he was crowned. The Bible says *"he did that which was right in the sight of the LORD."* Our verse today tells us that JOSIAH did that which no king like him ever, ever, ever did, when he turned to the LORD! What did JOSIAH do that gave him such an outstanding record with the LORD God?

First of all, he instigated major repairs to the Temple. Silver, timbers, and stones were brought to use in the restoration. Everyone trusted one another because all who worked were trustworthy workmen. This can't be said today in all church repair or building projects. This renovation happened in the eighteenth year of JOSIAH'S thirty-one year reign.

In the process of clearing-out the rubbish that had collected in the house of the LORD, remnants of Baal worship were discovered within its walls. Then the WORD OF GOD WAS FOUND!! It is amazing that God's Words were always in the Temple, but unread and unheeded. There was a *"grove"* in the midst of the rubble, as well as a sodomite house next door. Evil women hung around its doors wearing special seductive *"grove hangings,"*

JOSIAH was thrilled with the WORD OF GOD! It gave him great joy to obey it! He destroyed the altar at Bethel and the high places that JEROBOAM had made which caused Israel to sin. He stamped them to powder and killed the corrupted priests. With such revival, from hearing the Word of God, the PASSOVER was kept. Who knows when it was last observed? He did everything according to *THE BOOK*, killing the wizards and destroying the images and idols. Hilkiah, the high priest, fulfilled his GOD-GIVEN DUTY. So many priests had been unfaithful to God's commands. I am sure this good priest had a great influence on the King.

Trouble did not escape JOSIAH's reign. Just because he followed the BOOK OF THE LAW, did not mean that the sins of the former kings, and their followers, would go unpunished. King *PHARAOHNECHOH* of Egypt and the KING of ASSYRIA came to the Euphrates River. It was not good. They were *"after"* Judah. King Josiah went against them. HE WAS KILLED! It was at MEGIDDO! His servants transported his body in a chariot to Jerusalem. They buried him in his own sepulcher. His son, JEHOAHAZ became king. Time would tell if he would be good or evil.

"GOD KNOWS OUR WAY"
(Job 23:10; Psalm 103:14)
"HE KNOWETH THE WAY THAT I TAKE."
"HE KNOWETH OUR FRAME;
HE REMEMBERETH THAT WE ARE DUST."
We forget it and think we are strong.
(This was written on April 15th many years before this very date in 2008 that ggs's grandson, David, would be taken Home to Heaven.)

Today's Bible Blessing   *May 1*

II Kings 23:35–I Chronicles 1:32
FINALLY AN ACT OF KINDNESS

II Kings 25:27-28

"And it came to pass . . . Evilmerodach king of Babylon . . . did lift up . . . Jehoiachin king of Judah out of prison . . . and set his throne above the throne of the kings."

Over and over, we see that kings took the throne in JUDAH, and over and over we see that those kings did evil in the sight of the LORD. Some became king after the natural deaths of their fathers, while others took the throne after servants or relatives killed their fathers. Over and over, the king's mother's names were recorded.

Egypt's KING PHARAOHNECHOH seemed to favor one of JOSIAH's sons and gave him the name of JEHOIAKIM. In so doing–under Egypt's thumb, Josiah's son gave silver and gold to the Pharaoh. JEHOIAKIM'S reign of subservience was eleven years in Jerusalem. It was a shame of a kingship!

Suddenly we see the name of NEBUCHADNEZZAR. He is a king we have heard about since childhood. It was to NEBUCHADNEZZAR that JEHOIAKIM became a servant for three years with some rebellion. At his death, his eighteen-year-old son JEHOIACHIN became an evil king of JUDAH. At this time, the LORD sent bands of Chaldees, Syrians, Moabites, and Ammonites against Judah to destroy it. This was retaliation for the innocent blood that was shed during MANASSEH's reign. That bloodshed could refer to the thousands of babies killed in abortion and in sacrifices.

With the rise of NEBUCHADNEZZAR came the besieging of Jerusalem. What a hopeless time! Besides carrying away ten thousand captives, all the treasures of Solomon's Temple were scooped up—along with the craftsmen and the mighty men, as well as the princes of the land. JEHOIACHIN and his mother and wives were captives, too. Among those taken captive were Daniel and his friends–many of whom were made eunuchs to serve the Babylonian kings. Only the poorest of the poor and those with no skills or education were left. It was a sad, sad day! It was the day of which prophets had warned. It was a day of reckoning and rebuke from the hand of the LORD God!

Meanwhile back in the land of Judah, the mighty king of Babylon made twenty-one year-old ZEDEKIAH king of what was left of the homeland. His reign in Jerusalem was for eleven years. He was as evil as JEHOIAKIM! Somewhere at this time, ZEDEKIAH rebelled against Babylon. He tried to protect Jerusalem and hold on to his land. To no avail! In the ninth year of his reign, NEBUCHADNEZZAR surrounded Jerusalem for one year. The pursuit of ZEDEKIAH and his army ended in the plains of Jericho. He was taken captive and judged in Riblah. Right before ZEDEKIAH'S eyes his sons were murdered. Then Zedekiah's eyes were put out. He was taken to Babylon! Then Jerusalem was burned. Only the poor farmers were left to till the ground. The chief priest, his assistants, and the temple's door keepers were taken (they were killed in Riblah), along with all the brass and anything of value that was left in the temple. A man named GEDALIAH was left to rule the motley-few who remained. He, too, was killed with some Jews and Chaldees at Mizpah. Such a bloody mess!

Now KING EVILMERODACH of Babylon comes upon the scene. He is kind to KING JEHOIACHIN of Judah. He removes him from prison! He puts him on a throne in Babylon with other kings that, I suppose, he had captured. He removed his prison garb and dressed him in fine array, and gave him a kingly allowance for the rest of his life. For some reason, EVILMERODACH had a kindness and tender heart for those of royalty that had been captured by his predecessors—a good trait for any man.

What can we learn from all of this? One fact is that when God says he will punish for sin, he means it. Israel and Judah had all the opportunity in the world to do right—but they refused to worship only the true God!

"EACH DAY IS HOLY"
(Nehemiah 8:10)
"This day is holy unto our Lord: neither be ye sorry."
Take each day as from His sovereign hand.
Accept its joys and sorrows.
He has allowed all that comes this day,
And He knows beforehand all about our days! (ggs)

Today's Bible Blessing   *May 2*

I Chronicles 1:33–I Chronicles 3:8

EVERY NAME IS IMPORTANT TO GOD

I Chronicles 1:34, 43-50; 2:13-16

"And Abraham begat Isaac . . . Now these are the kings that reigned in the land of Edom . . . Jobab was dead . . . Husham was dead . . . Hadad was dead . . . Samlah was dead . . .

Shaul was dead . . . Baalhanan was dead . . . And Jesse begat . . . David . . . whose sisters were Zeruiah, and Abigail . . ."

At first reading of the genealogies in our passage today, we can't help but wonder what spiritual blessing could possibly come from a bunch of names. The truth is, the older I have become, the more precious are these genealogies. Just think what a privilege to be mentioned in Scripture—even if it is only recorded that you lived and died. Names of people, we would never have known, are written down for the ages to read. Not only people like ABRAHAM'S son, ISAAC and his sons ESAU and ISRAEL but folk like LOTAN and his sister, TIMNA. Would we ever have known about these siblings except for I CHRONICLES, chapter one?

Another interesting thing I discovered a few years ago when reading such lists of names was that people died. Of course, we know they die, but seeing them in black and white is like one grand obituary. Most of us have had loved ones pass from this earth to yonder shores. When I read these words soon after our son had died, I was struck with the sorrow such few words signified. Notice verses forty-four through fifty-five. *"Bela was dead. Jobab was dead. Husham was dead. Hadad was dead. Samlah was dead. Shaul was dead. Baalhanan was dead. And Hadad died also."* What sorrow is hidden behind every word in their eulogies. These deceased were the kings of Edom. That would be Esau's prodigy. How many wives were left alone holding their fatherless babies? How many mothers grieved with the brothers and sisters of the dead one? How many people were left in their cities alone without leadership, fearing for the future?

The more I looked at these names, the more I found out about the people who had passed on. Little tidbits of information, we would never have known if we did not have it written down before our eyes today. *ACHAR* was the *"troubler of Israel."* We'd never have known that! A man by the name of NAHSHON was a *"prince of the children of Judah."* How interesting! OBED'S son, JESSE'S oldest son was ELIAB and OBED'S youngest was DAVID, the eighth-born (I Samuel 16:10). David's sisters were ZERUIAH and ABIGAIL. Though we knew this, it was good to see it written down in one place, and to review that ZERUIAH'S sons were ABISHAI, JOAB, & ASAHEL. They were David's nephews. As we see their names again, their lives flash before our memories.

We noticed that there was another Caleb in the Bible. We have seen this before, but it was interesting that he had a son named *"HUR."* Perhaps he was named after the other *"HUR"* in the Bible. A man named *HEZRON* went into the daughter of *MACHIR* when he was sixty years old. In I Chronicles 2:21, we see she was his wife. A child came from that union named *SEGUB.* Then *SEGUB* begat *JAIR* who had twenty-three cities in the land of Gilead—where *MACHIR* was from. *ABIAH, HEZRON'S wife*, bare a son named *ASHUR.* He was born after *HEZRON*, the father, died. We can't help but wonder if *HEZRON* knew she was pregnant, and how sad it was for the new mother and fatherless child.

There was a man named OREN–similar to my father's name, REN. I wondered if my father ever noticed. There was *JETHER* who died without children. In those days that was very sad— not like today when couples choose to be childless. SHESHAN only had daughters. The scribe's families dwelt at Jabez. In chapter 3, we see a list of David's sons. Six were born in Hebron and nine in Jerusalem. The chapter ends with Solomon's son and the grandsons. He must have had more, but only REHOBOAM is listed. **All of this demonstrates that every soul is important to God.**

"I SERVE"
(Luke 10:40)
"*I serve*" should be the motto of all the Princes
of the royal family of Heaven.
Martha's fault was not that she served too much,
but that she grew cumbered, and forgot Him,
the object of her service.
We should surrender to our cause
which He has set before us and purpose!
"EVERY BUSH IS A BURNING BUSH"
(ggs)

Today's Bible Blessing　　　　　　　　　　*May 3*

I Chronicles 3:9–I Chronicles 5:26

MORE NAMES, MORE SINS, MORE TROUBLES

I Chronicles 4:33

"And all their villages that were round about the same cities, unto Baal. These were their habitations, and their genealogy."

It is of interest that God cared enough for these people to list their names in a chronology. Some were good people and some were bad. Occasionally a note concerning some accomplishment or disappointment is recorded. How good to see them, and to remember that there were people back in the times before and after the kings, that had lived, loved, and died. Every hair of their head was counted by God. So even today, every breath of those who walk this earth is noted. It is a comfort to realize that God has concern for us.

As we look at these verses, we observe that the line of David is clearly shown. We have SOLOMON–then REHOBOAM and ABIA, his son. Then ASA, JEHOSHAPHAT, and JORAM, his son. Then AHAZIAH, and JOASH, AMAZIAH, AZARIAH, and JOTHAM. There is AHAZ, HEZEKIAH, and MANASSEH. Then we noticed AMON and JOSIAH. From now on in Chapter Three of First Chronicles, more than one son is mentioned for the kings. We see the four sons of Josiah. One was ZEDEKIAH, who had his eyes poked out by the Babylonian ruler. These were the kings from the kingdom of Judah. Remember that all the kings of Israel were bad kings–not a good one in the bunch. Some of Judah's kings were good and some were bad. This is very evident as we read the Scripture.

In Chapter Four, the genealogies of Jacob's sons began. It started with JUDAH and his sons and grandsons. Of interest is HUR of which it says–*"the firstborn of EPHRATAH who became the father of BETHLEHEM."* Of course this *"rings a bell"* because Jesus, of the tribe of JUDAH was BORN in BETHLEHEM. In recent years, there were sermons and books written about one of COZ's sons. His name was JABEZ. Two verses are devoted to this man who gave his mother a hard time at birth. Many readers can identify with her. He called on God for a blessing. Then we see the names of OTHNIEL and OPHRAH and the craftsman named JOAB who lived in a valley (4:14).

SIMEON and five hundred men went to MOUNT SEIR. It was there they finished off the rest of the AMALEKITES–the ones who had previously escaped being captured. In chapter five, we see the sons of REUBEN, Jacob's firstborn. There is a mention of BEERAH who was captured by TILGATHPILNESER. BELA, who was related to a JOEL, dwelt eastward, unto the entering into the wilderness from the Euphrates River. It was in those days that Saul made war with the Hagarites in the land of Gilead. In the days of KING JOTHAM of Judah and the days of KING JEROBOAM of Israel, the kinfolk of ABIHAIL lived in Gilead and the suburbs of Sharon.

We see MERED, one of EZRA's many sons. He married Pharaoh's daughter. One of JUDAH'S grandsons was a weaver of fine linen. Men like JOKIM in Moab worked *"ancient things."* They were historians and museum curators. Also they were potters and gardeners who worked for the kings. Though SHIMEI had twenty-two children, his brothers had few. It is mentioned that *"they dwelt in Beersheba,"* as well as other areas (4:28). It is in this listing that we see the cities and villages associated with the reign of KING DAVID. It is sad to see the mention of BAAL.

Verse thirty-eight of chapter four tells us that those, listed by name here, were princes and their houses increased greatly. Their rich pastures went to the entrance of Gedor to the eastside of the valley. There is a mention of HAM's people—one of Noah's sons from olden times. During the days of HEZEKIAH, that particular land was cleared by some kind of destruction to make room for the sons of SHIPHI. Then REUBEN'S GROUP (5:18), skillful in war, trusted God. When they cried out to Him in battle, He answered! The children of MANASSEH sinned against their fathers' God. So KING PUL of ASSYRIA carried away the Reubenites, the Gadites, and the half of Manasseh. Such a tragic ending for such a gifted people!

"THAT HOLY THING"
CONSIDER HIM
For our meditation today, allow your mind to dwell
on the birth of the Lord Jesus Christ.
Forget about the "silly" pagan December festival.
He was called "The Son of The Highest"!
–A HOLY CHILD–
NO SIN NATURE!
Nothing in Him! Impossible to sin!
Even to respond to it.
He was born in a prepared body,
cradled in a prepared Virgin's womb,
Found and "fashioned" as a man.
Made in "likeness" (except for the sin nature),
Of human flesh
In "form as a servant"
Yes, HE IS GOD IN A HUMAN BODY.
THAT HOLY CHILD, JESUS.
THE INCARNATION! (ggs)

Today's Bible Blessing　　　　　　　　　　*May 4*

I Chronicles 6:1–I Chronicles 7:4

GOD'S WILL FOR MY LIFE

I Chronicles 6:31

"And these are they whom David set over the service of song in the house of the LORD . . ."

Have you ever walked in a cemetery to look for Bible verses on the tombstones? Usually more verses can be found in the old cemeteries. It seemed as if people in the *"olden days"* thought more about Bible words. I saw an interesting sentence on a tombstone the other day. It was not a Bible verse. It was a memory of time spent with that person. It said, *"Will miss our every-other Tuesdays."* It was signed by several single names. Perhaps they were siblings. Perhaps they were friends. Much can be read into those words. What happened every-other Tuesday? Was it a biweekly lunch together? Was it a meeting of old school mates? Was it a church Bible study? Only those who carved those words on that stone know. The rest of us are left wondering.

So it is with the obituary/genealogies in today's reading. Right off in I Chronicles 6:1, we are introduced to the sons of LEVI. All of us are familiar with him. He was one of Jacob's sons. It was from his tribe that Moses, Aaron, and Miriam came. LEVI was their great-grandfather. One of his three sons was KOHATH–their grandfather. Kohath's son was AMRAM who was Moses' father. We see that AMRAM had a boy named ELEAZAR who had a son named PHINEHAS. This priestly line is most interesting.

In verse 10, we see that AZARIAH was the priest who performed the priestly duty in the Jerusalem temple which Solomon built. Perhaps you remember him. We learned in verse 14 that another priest with the same name, AZARIAH, had a grandson named JEHOZADAK. He was part of the *"captivity"* that was taken by NEBUCHADNEZZAR. The wording of this verse is most interesting. It says *"JEHOZADAK went into captivity, when the LORD carried away Judah and Jerusalem by the hand of NEBUCHADNEZZAR.*

The next thing I want us to notice on these *"tomb-stones"* are verses 31-33. Here we noticed that KING DAVID put certain people in charge of the *"service of song"* in the LORD'S HOUSE. These appointments, according to this verse, were made after the ark rested. I suppose it is referring to the time David brought the ark the proper way to its proper place. Their assignment was to minister before the TABERNACLE with singing. When Solomon built the HOUSE in Jerusalem, they waited for orders if they were to sing or not. A list of names is given of those who waited. (It is important to learn how to *"wait"*!) We note that HEMAN (vs. 33) was a singer. I noticed the familiar name of ASAPH in verse 39. We have read his psalms many times. The psalms were songs the ISRAELITES sang.

Today I would like us just to think about those singers, as well as the priestly line from Levi. I wonder what they thought when they had such a *"family assignment."* Even today, we see sons who follow in their father's footsteps when it comes to their life's work. Sometimes a printer has a son who is a printer. Sometimes a doctor has a son who is a doctor. Sometimes a lineman has a son who is a lineman. *"Like father, like son"* is a saying we often hear. But in the case of the people in today's reading, they had no choice what so ever in their life's work. It not only was *"expected"* that a son would be what he was assigned to do, but it could be no other way. It was God's way!

To be thrust into a certain line of work is not always easy, I suppose. But when you, as the son or daughter know that it is a position appointed by God, how can you complain? God would not make a mistake in your life. It is up to you to accept it–to take it from His loving hand. When my husband was a Navy chaplain and he got *"orders,"* no matter where those *"orders"* took him—even if they took him away from me—I accepted them as God's will for my life. It was not always easy—but there was no doubt in my mind that *it was of the LORD!*

"SPIRITUAL ACTIVITY"
WATCHING–while praying
RUNNING–while looking
PRESSING–while reaching
SERVING–while waiting
God can do big things as easily as He can do small things!
(ggs)

Today's Bible Blessing   *May 5*

I Chronicles 7:5–I Chronicles 9:9

NAMES, PLACES, AND DUTIES

I Chronicles 9:1

"So all Israel were reckoned by genealogies; and . . . written in the book . . ."

Once again we are face to face with lists of names. If we look carefully, they are not death notices. Mostly we read of people who lived, their tribes, their father's name with an occasional mention of the mother's name, and their occupations. This information, though not in detail, was very important to God to be recorded; therefore, today's reading is very important for us to read.

Today one of Jacob's sons named ISSACHAR was first mentioned. His family was full of valiant men of might. There were 87,000 of them. Then comes along others of Jacob's sons. There are records of thousands of brave men of BENJAMIN. We see NAPHTALI in I Chronicles 7:13. MACHIR'S mother was a concubine of his father, MANASSEH, and an Aramitess.

We observed a father mourning at the death of his four sons (vs. 21-22). They were protecting their cattle from thieves when they were murdered. Their family came to comfort the grieving father. There is a difference between *"crying"* and *"mourning."* Only those who have *"mourned"* know what I mean. Don't be too harsh on those who do. Don't think you understand when you don't. Just listen and care or appear to care.

Interesting that MEGIDDO is a town connected with the children of MANASSEH. It plays an important part in the end-times. There is a mention of a *"sister"* to HEBER'S sons in verse 32. As the chapter closes, we are reminded that the men in ASHER's family were *"apt to war and battle."* It is needful for us to remember that the

Israelites were told by God to gain all the land of Canaan. To do so, they had to *"war"* often for protection, as well as possession. This reminds me of the Christian's continual spiritual warfare in this world—our Canaan land.

As chapter eight begins, we learn that BELA was BENJAMIN'S firstborn and ADDAR was BELA'S firstborn. A man named SHAHARAIM had children in the country of MOAB, *"and he sent them away."* One wonders why he sent his children away. Was it because of the sin in MOAB? Then in verse 13, two men drove away the inhabitants of GATH. They were BERIAH and SHEMA who lived in AIJALON. **It is fascinating to read about SAUL'S father, KISH.** KISH'S father was NER. So NER would be SAUL'S grandfather. It seemed as if the relatives—in the past—lived at GIBEON. The place was named after a man named GIBEON who was a relative of SAUL. We read in verse 33 that SAUL had a son named JONATHAN whose son was MERIBAAL. He had a child named MICAH. Micah's father's name has *"baal"* in it. It certainly must have something to do with the terrible *idol-god* of the land.

We read of the priests, JEDAIAH, JEHOIARIB, and JACHIM, etc. who were *"able men for the work of the service of the house of GOD!"* (vs. 13) How we need such men today! We read of the LEVITES who were *"porters"* and served at the king's gate. Then there were the sons of KORAH who were keepers of the tabernacle gates. The psalmist sang: *"I had rather be a doorkeeper in the house of my God, than to dwell in the tents of wickedness!"* There were LEVITES, called chief porters, who were over the rooms in God's house for the treasuries. What remarkable, trusted servants! There were singers, who were employed day and night. Over and over we read of people dedicated to the service of the LORD God. Not all were priests, but all had assignments. Without each one of them, the work of God would be stifled. So today—not all are pastors or officers in the church. Many have *"lesser duties"* in the eyes of man. Yet without them, the work of God would be incomplete!

"GOD LOVES US"
(Hebrews 12:6)
God loves us, though it may not look like it.
"For whom the Lord loveth he chasteneth"
The husbandman is never as close to the vine
as when He is pruning it. (John 15)
Our very trial is given to refine us!
He who holds the pruning knife is also
He who is transforming us. (ggs)

I Chronicles 9:10–I Chronicles 11:36

MIGHTY MEN STRENGTHEN ONE ANOTHER

I Chronicles 11:10

"These also are the chief of the mighty men whom David had, who strengthened themselves with him in his kingdom, and with all Israel, to make him king, according to the word of the LORD concerning Israel."

Now we are finishing up the chronologies of Judah and Israel before and after they were captured by Babylon. The reason they were carried away out of their land, that they worked so hard to gain, was because of their sin. It is sad but true. God told them of all the blessing they would have if they followed HIM; but instead they chose the opposite. He told them what would happen to them if they worshipped the local gods and not HIM. They rejected all that counsel and worshipped the gods of the land–gods made of wood and stone.

From now on, we will have a review of most of the doings of the children of Israel and Judah. We read about them in the Kings and maybe the Samuels. If you recall Saul died a horrible death. He was wounded, so asked his armor bearer to thrust through a sword. The young man refused, so Saul fell on his own sword. The Bible says in I Chronicles 10:13: *"So Saul died for his transgression which he committed against the LORD, even against the word of the LORD, which he kept not . . ."* That included his contact with familiar spirits. It is a very sad sight to see a man of God fall into sin! Even after confession, things are never the same.

After that, the men of Hebron and Israel came to David, made a covenant with him, and anointed him king. He chose Joab, his nephew, to be his *"chief"* because he smote the JEBUSITES first. They had a long military relationship until Joab betrayed David by siding-up with ABSALOM, David's handsome son. If you recall, Absalom wanted to be king in the worse way.

The Bible says in I Chronicles 11:9: *So David waxed greater and greater: for the LORD of hosts was with him."* With the help of the LORD of hosts, David gathered around him *"mighty men."* Often we read of these mighty men (verse 10) and how they *"strengthened themselves with him."* They helped him to be king. Then the Scriptures list the names of these men.

Let me name two. JASHOBEAM was a chief of the captains. He lifted his spear against three hundred at once. There was ELEAZAR who was one of the three mightiest. He fought for a barley field that the Philistines had taken. The people were frightened and ran, forsaking their field. It was delivered back to David's people for *"The LORD saved them!"*

Wouldn't you and I like to be numbered as God's *"mighty men and women"* **today?** Would not we like to be close enough to a leader of the Word of God to *strengthen ourselves* with him? Or we might be that leader ourselves to give spiritual and physical *"strength"* to those about us? If we trusted one another, as *together* we trusted the LORD of hosts, we could do so much for Him and our families *together*. Yet, we lay back.

We are afraid to serve Him. Or worse yet, the things of the world about us consume our thoughts and strength so there is nothing left with which to serve the LORD JESUS.

"NOW AND THEN"
(Mark 10:30)
ONE HUNDREDFOLD NOW
FOR FOLLOWING WITH PERSECUTION
1. **A hundred fold now**–a faithful missionary has many trophies, souls & brethren in faith & in persecution.
2. **Eternal Life in the world to come.** A faithful servant has more than one-hundredfold in the world to come.
RECOGNITION, PROMINENCE, & PREEMINENCE HERE
MAY BE RESERVED THERE
like Job would have what he lost,
and also what he gained
after his trial. (ggs)

Today's Bible Blessing   *May 7*

I Chronicles 11:37–I Chronicles 15:3

DOUBLE MINDED MEN
NEED NOT APPLY

I Chronicles 12:18

"Then the spirit came upon AMASAI, who was chief of the captains, and he said, Thine are we . . ."

Today I am impressed with David's charisma! People flocked to him! Brave men volunteered to defend him! Women were drawn to him! GOD BLESSED HIM! All Israel gathered together at HEBRON reminding him that he was bone of their bone and flesh of their flesh. He was one of them! Even when Saul was doing well on the

Throne, David helped Israel militarily. The LORD, David's God, said to him, *"Thou shalt feed my people Israel, and thou shalt be ruler over my people . . ."* (I Chronicles 11:2).

In yesterday's reading, David and all Israel went to Jerusalem, where the JEBUSITES were, and *"took the castle of ZION."* This became *"the city of David."* It was during this battle that JOAB, David's sister's son, became the military *"chief."*

There were many *"mighty men"* **in David's army besides the thousands who followed him and his cause–all wanted him to be the crowned king!** The men mentioned by name in chapter eleven stayed with him in ZIKLAG where David stayed close by because Saul was after him. He wanted to kill David. These men were skilled in *"hurling stones"* and *"shooting arrows."* Perhaps you know a man who can throw a baseball from the outfield to home base. I recall seeing one of our sons do this often. This was the gift that David's men had. Think of the golfers who can make a *"hole in one."* Imagine David's men doing such with a stick or a club.

The GADITES, who separated themselves to defend David, who were *"fit for war,"* **were experts in** *"shield and buckler."* It is written that their faces were frightening like those of lions (I Chronicles 12:8). ISSACHAR'S TRIBE were men that had *"understanding of the times"* to know what Israel was to do. ZEBULUN'S group *"could keep rank"* and were not *"double minded"* (James 1:8). These men of war came with *"a perfect heart"* to Hebron. They were dependable!

One day, men from the tribes of Benjamin and Judah came where DAVID was hiding out. They wanted to join the future king. He questioned their loyalty. AMASAI was their spokesman. He assured that they came in "peace," and said, *"THINE ARE WE, DAVID!"*

Have you ever been in a life situation where your motives have been questioned? Perhaps there was a good reason for such doubt. Perhaps your previous life was one of untruthfulness or betrayal of a friend. But into your life came SOMETHING or SOMEONE of what, or whom, you wanted to be a part. If so, you know that your loyalty had to be tested and proven.

It is sad that some people are not honest people! This applies to Christians, too. In little things some lie. Such as those who say, *"I'll be in church Sunday."* or *"Let me help you with that computer project."* Or, *"Pastor, you can count on me! I'll never leave the church!"* Soon the pastor knows that you do not do what you say you will do. So he does not expect it.

Sadder still, (and that is sad), is a parent who promises his child to go someplace or to give him something–and nothing happens. I watched a father look out the window with his teenage son, instructing him in detail what should be done in the yard the following day. I was impressed that the father took the time for such instruction; and I was impressed that the son stood there and listened to every detail. What happened the next day? Absolutely nothing! They had other things to do. The father forgot the yard work for other duties. The son didn't care. The grass was never cut!

DAVID COULD NOT HAVE DOUBLE MINDED MEN ON HIS STAFF, FOR THEY ARE UNSTABLE IN ALL THEIR WAYS!

"BE STILL MY SOUL"
(Psalm 4:4; 46:10)
Stand in awe, and sin not:
commune with your own heart upon your bed,
and be still.
A most difficult admonition, and one which we refuse to attempt.
Yet, to be still before our Great God
is to be at Worship and at attention.
It is in the stillness of Soul that He can speak to us,
and that we do hear His voice. (ggs)

Today's Bible Blessing   *May 8*

I Chronicles 15:4–I Chronicles 17:16
REJOICING AND REJECTION

I Chronicles 17:4

" . . . Thus saith the LORD, Thou shalt not build me an house to dwell in . . . "

There are so many thoughts that come to me today as I read our Bible reading. I want to write about the *beautiful music* that accompanied the *Ark of God* as it finally came to its proper resting place in Jerusalem. King David had researched the proper way to move that *HOLY* thing. Remember the fiasco in an earlier year when it was put on an ordinary cart?

I wish I could have been there to hear the sound of the trumpets as the *ARK OF THE COVENANT* moved through the countryside, finally resting in a *"tent."* Could that *"tent"* have been the one in which MOSES and AARON served those many years ago? We refer to that place of worship as *"the tabernacle in the wilderness"* I wish I could have been there to receive *"a loaf of bread"* and *"a good piece of flesh"* from King David's hand (I Chronicles 16:3).

Oh, to have heard ASAPH sound the *cymbals* and PRIESTS, BENAIAH and JAHAZIEL blow their *trumpets* as they stood before the *ARK OF THE COVENANT OF GOD* (vs.6)! To have heard HEMAN and JEDUTHUN give thanks to the

LORD with their trumpets and their *cymbals*, also, as well as other musical instruments of God (vs. 42). It must have been a spiritual experience! THE SOUND OF PRAISE FILLED THE AIR OF THE SOULS OF ALL STANDING THERE THAT DAY! And KING DAVID was moved beyond words. He danced and praised God! There he stood–playing an instrument, dressed in white linen, wearing a richly embroidered outer vestment called an ephod.

The Bible says "THEN ON THAT DAY DAVID DELIVERED FIRST THIS PSALM TO THANK THE LORD TO ASAPH AND HIS BRETHREN." Listen to those words! What a glorious psalm!

Give thanks! Sing unto Him! Sing psalms!
Talk ye of His wondrous works!
Glory ye in his HOLY NAME! Rejoice!
Seek the LORD and His strength!
Seek his face! Seek His face!
Remember!
Be mindful of His covenant, the word
which he commanded to a thousand generations!

In the flush of such praise, King David contemplated the difference between his palace and the house of curtains where the ark stood. Yes, the place to worship the LORD remained under curtains. David wanted to build a proper *temple* for God! Much to his surprise, NATHAN, the prophet, relayed the LORD's message. It was not God's plan for David's life! *(David thought it was.)* After DAVID'S DEATH, his son would build that house! Disappointment was not the word! But he understood and accepted the disappointment with thanksgiving.

Have you ever desired to do a special job for the LORD, and He did not permit this in your life? If so, be consoled by KING DAVID'S disappointment. Realize that HIS plan is best, and rejoice that someone else will do it better!

"A RENEWED MIND"
(Isaiah 26:3)
When we are weary,
our mind does not keep up with our heart.
How we should value and stand in awe
of our clear, sound mind.
God can slow down the windmill of our minds.
Compare NEBUCHADNEZZAR.
But for His grace and restraint, our minds would snap.
THOU WILT KEEP IN PERFECT PEACE OUR MINDS BECAUSE
HE TRUSTETH IN THEE.
(ggs)

I Chronicles 17:17–I Chronicles 21:30

THE CONSTANT HAND OF GOD

I Chronicles 18:6b

"Thus the LORD preserved David whithersoever he went."

What a glorious verse! I don't suppose that David realized in full the protective hand of his God. I'm sure he realized it in part, for his life had been spared in most difficult circumstances of war. Yes, David was a *"man of war"* (1 Chronicles 28:3). We will see, as we meditate further, that his son, Solomon, was a man of *"peace."* As I reflect upon this—it may not be good to have continual *"peace"* for it is the *"wars"* of our lives that give us strength and courage, as well as full dependence upon our God to keep us in those conflicts.

In today's reading we see the constant strife in David's life. Once again David smote the Philistines and took GATH. He smote the Moabites and they became his servants. He smote KING HADAREZER to establish dominion by the River Euphrates. It was then that he captured thousands of chariots and 7,000 horsemen. When the Syrians of Damascus swooped in to help Zobah's KING HADAREZER, he and his men killed 22,000 Syrians. He put garrisons in Syrian-Damascus making the Syrians his servants! It is in I Chronicles 18:6 that the Holy Spirit put our verse today. *"Thus the LORD preserved David whithersoever he went!"* It is absolutely amazing to read about the exploits of this man. Think about it! Think about the battles that he led and the death of men in those battles. Why wasn't David killed as many of the kings before him? Why did he die in his old age and not by the sword of a Philistine? It was The LORD God's protective and guiding hand!

It was the constant *hand of God* upon David—even when he was wrong and in sin—that pulled him back to the right path. For us, who know the Lord Jesus Christ as Saviour, it is that same *"hand"* upon us that pulls us to Himself when we are wrong, and that keeps us to Himself when we are right. *Truly, our times are in His hand!* What a comfort to us who are lonely and to us who wonder what is going on in our lives. In all the fury and unrest about us, in all the discordant chords heard by our tired ears, and in all the lack of being understood by those we love, we see that the LORD preserved us whithersoever we went!

> ## "COME FORTH–COME HITHER
>
> King Nebuchadnezzar had placed the bound, three Hebrew boys in a fiery furnace.
>
> Why? Because they refused to bow down to his image.
>
> When "LO"–the king beheld three men loosed and walking within the huge kiln-like furnace.
>
> With them was the FOURTH, like the Son of God!
> One day, like KING NEBUCHADNEZZAR,
> our ABSOLUTE MONARCH
> will call and say to us, who are in the fiery trial,
> "COME FORTH AND COME HITHER!"
> (ggs)

Today's Bible Blessing   *May 10*

I Chronicles 22:1–I Chronicles 25:3

GOD'S CHOICES FOR HIS OWN

I Chronicles 22:19

"Now set your heart and your soul to seek the LORD your God; arise therefore, and build . . ."

If anyone wanted to do something for the LORD more than David did, we would have a difficult time finding such a person. He desperately desired to build the TEMPLE! It was his life's dream. *BUT GOD!* The Bible says in I Chronicles 22:8 that *"the word of the LORD came"* to David. The LORD God made it very clear to King David that he could not build the house of the LORD. I am sure this was a disappointment to the king. It was his heart's desire. God made it clear that it would be SOLOMON who would be the builder of the place of worship for Israel. God said, *"He shall build an house for my name . . ."*

Sometimes we wonder if Solomon had such a desire. Did he have other plans for his life? After all, he was not the oldest son. After all, it was his mother who had humiliated herself by committing adultery with his father prior to their marriage. Yet, Solomon was chosen by God for a tremendous building project.

Reflect on your life. What are you doing now? Was your occupation today the dream of your youthful days? Perhaps it was. Maybe, what you do today has fulfilled every dream of your life. On the contrary, your youthful dream was dashed many years ago, and you sit today in a place you had no idea would be your lot in life. What are you doing with your *"TODAY"*? Are you being the very best of where you find yourself *TODAY*? Or are you, not like King David who accepted God's will for his life, GRUMBLING about what could have been? Think about it!

David's dream was to build the "house of the Lord." I don't suppose as a young shepherd boy, he thought to himself, "Someday, I am going to kill thousands of people!" Or, "Someday I will be the king of the Jews." Or, "Someday the Messiah will come from my family line." The circumstances of his life brought him to the position he held as warrior, king, and ancestor to the Lord Jesus Christ. But you and I know that "circumstances" are not just "happenstances"!

Solomon may have had other dreams. He may have enjoyed the fields like his father did in his youthful days. The beauty of the earth may have called his soul for appreciation and holiness. But, God put his hand upon Solomon. He declared concerning Solomon, *"I will give peace and quietness unto Israel in his days . . ."*

Why was this *"peace"* and *"quietness"* given to David's son when it was not given to David? It is very evident. There would have been no kingdom without David's skill in battle. We first noticed his determination and skill with the incident in regard to GOLIATH'S death.

In Solomon's case, his gift was *"peace."* It was so the land would be still from war. The huge TEMPLE PROJECT could never be accomplished otherwise. King David collected much of the precious metal, as well as the hewn stones for the building, the iron for the nails, and the brass; but more was needed. From Zidonia and Tyre, cedar wood came during David's lifetime. Yes, King David prepared abundantly for the Temple prior to his death, but it was SOLOMON, in the stillness of conciliation, that the bulk of the trees came, and that the TEMPLE was erected!

"SURELY"
(Psalm 23)
*"Surely goodness and mercy shall follow me
all the days of my life."*
Under God's care, we run no risks.
GOD SAID, "SURELY!"
*"SURELY"–"HE HAS BORN OUR GRIEFS
AND CARRIED OUR SORROWS"*
Sometimes, we forget that HE cares!
Sometimes we forget the Word says "SURELY"! (ggs)

Today's Bible Blessing   *May 11*

I Chronicles 25:4—I Chronicles 27:25
BENAIAH: A MIGHTY MAN

I Chronicles 27:5-6

"The third captain of the host . . . was BENAIAH the son of JEHOIADA, a chief priest . . . who was mighty among the thirty . . ."

I have been interested in BENAIAH ever since I studied the *"lions"* of the Bible. I was teaching about the Devil, who is like a roaring lion who seeks to devour Christians. His name is mentioned in the Bible forty-one times.

BENAIAH was the son of a chief priest in II Samuel 23:20-22. His father, JEHOIADA, was a *valiant man–"like father, like son."* They were from a place called KABZEEL. Another fact is that we know that BENAIAH was one of DAVID'S MIGHTY MEN! That was an accomplishment!

One day, he spied a lion in a pit. There was snow on the ground. Lions can be dangerous running around a community. BENAIAH jumped into that pit and killed that lion! Can you imagine that? If that was not enough, one day he saw two *"lion-like men."* Guess what he did? He killed them. I am sure he had a reason to destroy those men. Perhaps they were enemies of KING DAVID.

Another time, he came upon a goodly man who was an Egyptian. I think it meant the Egyptian was handsome for that is the term used for David when he was a young man in the time of Samuel. No matter–the good-looking man carried a spear. He was going to use it on BENAIAH. What did BENAIAH do? He grabbed that spear, armed only with a staff, and slew the handsome man. We are told that BENAIAH was more honorable than the thirty, but was not one of David's top mighty men. Neither was he one of the three who bravely brought water from Bethlehem's well to thirsty David.

In today's Scripture passage, the Holy Spirit wants us to know that BENAIAH was above *"the thirty"* mighty men that are mentioned in II Samuel 23:20-23–not *of the "thirty"*–but not one of the *"mightiest men."* All this ranking may not seem important to us, but it was very important to David in David's time. Being strong in the Lord and being strong in personal might is paramount when it comes to fighting battles. David had to have men he could depend upon to do the job necessary for that particular day's conflict. (I suppose we could say that God wants us to be *"mighty"* in strength and valor for our present day's life's battles.)

Another fact is found in I Chronicles 18:17. We read that DAVID reigned over Israel. JOAB was over the army. JEHOSHAPHAT was the son of the recorder. ZADOK and ABIMELECH were the priests.

SHAVSHA was the scribe. BENAIAH was over the CHERETHITES and the PELETHITES. The sons of David were chief above the king. I point out these responsibilities of these head men to you, because BENAIAH is listed among these influential leaders. If I remember, in the time of SOLOMON, BENAIAH became the head of the army.

In I Kings 2:24-25, new King Solomon sent BENAIAH to kill ADONIJAH. That half-brother of Solomon had asked a wrongful favor—an act of treason, if fulfilled. If the favor had been granted, it would have been a step for ADONIJAH to usurp the throne. Whom did Solomon trust to destroy the usurper? It was his trusted servant and one of his father's *mighty men*, BENAIAH. Joab had conspired with ADONIJAH for the throne. Joab fled for his life to the TABERNACLE. Solomon gave the command to BENAIAH, *"Fall on him!"* This he did. So King Solomon trusted BENAIAH so much that he promoted him to be the GENERAL of all his armies (I KINGS 2:35).

"IT IS WELL"
(Isaiah 3:10)
Say unto the righteous, *"It shall be well with him."*
We have a word of comfort to the righteous.
GOD'S WAY IS PERFECT!
Therefore, it shall always be well with the Christian. (ggs)

Today's Bible Blessing   *May 12*

I Chronicles 27:26—II Chronicles 2:8

CONSECRATED, LORD, TO THEE

I Chronicles 29:5b

"And who then is willing to consecrate his service this day unto the LORD?"

This is the verse that influenced FRANCES HAVERGAL to consecrate her life's service to the LORD. It was the verse, like an ever-ticking clock's beckoning call that caused her to yield her life to Jesus Christ for His service. As the months turned into years, she yielded more and more of her life to Him until *"all"* was consecrated to her KING. She begged him to take her *life*, her *hands*, her *feet*, her *voice*, her *lips*, her *silver* and *gold*, and her *love*. She wrote *"Take myself and I will be ever, only, all for Thee!"* The beauty of it all was that her KING accepted her consecration and used her for HIS GLORY! She became a well-known Christian poet and hymnist.

In today's reading, not only do we observe old King David anticipating the building of the Temple, but also we

view the coronation of his son as KING. For years DAVID had collected valuable treasures for such a construction. He told his people that his son, Solomon, was young and eager to fulfill his father's wishes in such a building project. David implored his people to consecrate their valuables—such as silver, gold, and jewels—to the project. His enthusiasm for such construction was catching. Many gave. Many donated to the treasury. How the people praised (I Chronicles 29:9)! David's heart overflowed with blessing to the LORD God! What a day of rejoicing it was!

David prayed: *"Thine, O LORD, is the greatness and the power, the glory, the victory, the majesty!"* He reminded God that the heaven and earth were His. In this day and age when space ships are swirling the Heavens and men are determining how to protect the *"green"* earth, it would do us well to agree with old King David that those places belong to God! He admitted, *"All things come of Thee, and of Thine own have we given Thee."* In other words, everything that is, belongs to God. When we give to Him, we are really giving back to Him what is His already.

Then the father of the new King prayed precious words. He did not ask for riches for his son. He did not ask for fame or prestige. DAVID begged God that his son would have *"a perfect heart."*

What does it mean to have a *"perfect"* heart? I suppose it means to be completely *"sold out to the LORD!"* To be for HIM 100%. That is the fruit of a *"perfect"* heart! And with that *"perfect"* heart, the father's prayer was that SOLOMON would keep God's commandments. He prayed that Solomon would obey God's testimonies and God's statutes.

That prayer was similar to FRANCES HAVERGAL'S consecration hymn when she prayed to her KING: *"Take my life and let it be consecrated, Lord to Thee."* This was Solomon's determination that coronation day. He was determined to serve the LORD, as his father had prayed. For many years, I believed Solomon was faithful to his consecration; but something happened in his old age. Let us learn from SOLOMON'S mistakes. Let us keep to the dedication of our lives to God—that life's dedication we made when we were young and fresh for God. May our feet be *"swift and beautiful"* for HIM. May our voices sing only His praise! May our hands move at *"the impulse of HIS love."* May our lips be filled with messages for the LORD! May our *"silver and our gold"* not be withheld from His use! There are so many lessons that we can learn from Solomon's life. May they not go unheeded!

"HIS GREAT POWER IN MY UNBELIEF"
(Job 23:6)
"WILL HE PLEAD AGAINST ME
WITH HIS GREAT POWER?
NO; BUT HE WOULD PUT STRENGTH IN ME!"
God is for us and will be entreated of us.
We may order our cause before Him
and He will solve our problems. (ggs)

Today's Bible Blessing   *May 13*

II Chronicles 2:9—II Chronicles 6:22

HIRAM–KING OF TYRE

II Chronicles 2:11

"Then Huram the king of Tyre answered in writing, which he sent to Solomon . . ."

What an exciting time for the children of Israel! What an awesome season for King Solomon! The house of the Lord was beginning to be built. Everyone was excited! Everyone wanted to help! People contributed the needed supplies from precious metals and jewels to timber and iron nails. How I would have liked to have been a little bird watching the whole procedure.

How grand must have been the cedar trees of Lebanon–the fir trees, the algum trees! I can imagine the joy the woodsmen had as they cried *"TIMBER"* and saw tall trees fall to the ground. Imagine the rush of adrenalin as the last cut was made–the one that loosed the tree from its stump. With a rush of wind the giant swayed–and fell! Can you imagine the *"rush"* as those giant tress were rolled onto huge rafts and drifted down the River to the HOLY LAND? These were *holy trees*! Trees to be used for God's glory in His House in Jerusalem.

HIRAM or HURAM–the spelling in our reading today–was a friend of David throughout his latter life. He was Solomon's friend, too. *Hiram was the King of Tyre!* Not only did he supply the trees for the Temple project, but also he gave men for the construction with those trees for the building of the worship place. Solomon repaid him with wheat and olive oil.

Jewish Rabbinical literature tells us that HIRAM lived a long life. Some believe he was living during the time of EZEKIEL. One reason HIRAM thought himself to be a *"god"* was because he survived David and Solomon, as well as twenty-one kings of Israel, twenty kings of Judah, ten prophets, and ten high priests. The friendly correspondence between Hiram and Solomon is mentioned in Scripture and preserved for centuries in the archives of Tyre.

NEBUCHADNEZZAR dethroned his stepfather, **HIRAM.** It is said that, at the end of his life, every day, a piece of Hiram's flesh was cut from his body. He was made to eat his own flesh, until he died from such punishment. How awful!

It was interesting to see what the Jewish historians had written about HIRAM. How much is true and how much is not true about him, I don't really know. But if a smidgen is true, it goes to show how pride in oneself and one's accomplishments can bring a person low in the eyes of God.

Let us be careful that we don't start out well for the LORD and end up cancelling out our testimony for Him by our evil ways in our old age. Paul wrote in I Corinthians 9:27 the following: *"Lest. . . when I have preached to others, I myself should be a castaway."* How frightening to be *disapproved* of God!

"I AM HIS"
(Romans 8:38)
"DANGERS ARE NIGH!—
AND FEAR!
My mind is shaking.
Hearts seem to dread what life may hold in store;
BUT I AM HIS.
I know the way that I am taking.
More blessed, still, He goeth on before"
(J. D. Smith)
This was enclosed in a missionary letter. It blessed and encouraged me.
(ggs)

Today's Bible Blessing   May 14

II Chronicles 6:23—II Chronicles 9:25

THE CURIOUS QUEEN

II Chronicles 9:1

"When the queen of Sheba heard of the fame of Solomon, she came to prove Solomon with hard questions at Jerusalem . . ."

Let us look at this QUEEN named SHEBA who came all the way from the ancient country of SHEBA to JERUSALEM to check out KING SOLOMON. What an inquisitive woman she was!

She did not sneak into the area unbeknownst. How could she? For accompanying the wealthy queen was a *great company* *of camels.* They were laden with goods such as spices, gold, and precious stones. Some say the weight of her gift of *"gold"* was 4.5 tons. It looked like she planned to stay for a while. She meant business! Her gifts signified that she was royalty and her questions revealed her inquisitive mind.

The country of SHEBA could have been parts of ERITREA, ETHIOPIA, and YEMEN as we know them today. Though Solomon called her *"Sheba,"* she was known as *MAKEDA* to the Ethiopian people. Josephus called her *NICAULE.* Some say she was born on January 5th in the 10ᵗʰ century BCE (*before the Christian era*).

When QUEEN SHEBA sat down with the king, she held nothing back. The Bible says that *she communed with him of all that was in her heart.* Are you a bit curious as to what was in her heart? I am. What had she heard about KING SOLOMON that she made such an effort to see him? Perhaps this was the usual thing for a country's royalty to do to another country's royalty. Whatever–she came and asked *"in-depth"* queries.

I think that SOLOMON was intrigued with SHEBA. He told her everything she wanted to know—and then some (II Chronicles 9:2). *FLABBERGASTED* was the word! It is the best one I can think of to describe the reaction of SHEBA to SOLOMON–just plain *FLABBER-GASTED!* She saw his wisdom firsthand. She tasted of his food at his table. She saw his gracious servants, his impressive cupbearers. She observed their beautiful attire. She was overwhelmed with the way Solomon walked into the HOUSE OF THE LORD–his poise, his reverence, his access to the LORD God! The grandeur of it all!

After seeing all of this, her truthful response to Solomon was *"It was a true report which I heard in mine own land of thine acts, and thy wisdom!"* She confessed that she would never have believed it, if she had not seen it with her own eyes. With true reverence, she said, *"Blessed be the LORD thy God, which delighted in thee to set thee on His throne . . . because thy God loved Israel . . ."* It is interesting to notice that SHEBA recognized that the KING'S THRONE was GOD'S THRONE not Solomon's!

SHEBA is mentioned two times in the New Testament (Matthew 12:42; Luke 11:31). When I discussed these passages with my husband he said that Solomon was visited by the Queen of Sheba. She was overwhelmed with his wisdom and learning. She received his message, and went home filled with wonderful truths. By contrast, in the New Testament, the Pharisees and unbelievers of His day heard Him not as *SHEBA heard SOLOMON.* There was a vast difference in the *"hearing."* The unbelievers did not accept Jesus' wisdom as SHEBA had accepted SOLOMON'S. In teaching this, Jesus told his hearers that He (JESUS) was greater than Solomon; and He was there in the midst of them. They didn't care!

John 1:11-12 states clearly, the unbelief of the people in Jesus' day. *"He came unto his own, and his own received him not. But as many as received him, to them gave he power to become the sons of God, even to them that believe on his name:"*

"MY HIDING PLACE"

"IN THE SHADOW OF THY WINGS WILL I MAKE MY REFUGE, UNTIL THESE CALAMITIES BE OVERPAST."
(Psalm 57:1)
MY SHIELD–
Protesting, preventing—His truth shall be my shield.
The armor of God–I hold His Word before me
as a shield against the enemy.
MY HOPE IS THY WORD
(Psalm 119:49, 81, 114)

Today's Bible Blessing   *May 15*

II Chronicles 9:26–II Chronicles 13:21

THE STORY OF THREE KINGS

II Chronicles 13:1-2

". . . ABIJAH . . . reigned three years in Jerusalem. "

Today there are many kings about whom I could write. There is *SOLOMON* who died and was buried in the city of David, his father. There was his son, *REHOBOAM,* who was made king in Shechem where all Israel went to crown him. Many were there, even Solomon's servant, *JEROBOAM,* who returned home from Egypt for the occasion. If you recall previously, he had fled, escaping *Solomon's wrath.* AHIJAH, the prophet, had predicted that Israel would be divided and that JEROBOAM would be the king (I Kings 11:40). Bad news for REHOBOAM!

Even though JEROBOAM was a rank unbeliever in the true LORD God, he was a skillful leader. He discouraged REHOBOAM from over-taxing his people. This was not only JEROBOAM'S sage advice; it was, also, the advice of the community elders. To no avail, KING REHOBOAM taxed the people so greatly that there arose a rebellion. Therefore, the kingdom split. Ten tribes went with Solomon's servant and two-and-a-half tribes stayed with Rehoboam. All this division happened because of the unbelief and idol worship within Israel and Judah's camps. It was predicted by God. There were constant wars between these two men and their countries. JEROBOAM was a wicked king. If you remember, he was the ruler who set up two calf-idols for worship—one in Dan and one in Bethel.

Also, he sent all the priests who lived in his territory back to Judah. He did not want anyone indoctrinated in the right ways of the TRUE GOD! One wonders if REHOBOAM ever regretted turning a deaf ear to Jeroboam's taxation advice!

REHOBOAM's mother's name was NAAMAH. She was an AMMONITESS! If you recall, AMMON was one of the sons born during Lot's incestuous relationship with one of his daughters. The truth was that REHOBOAM'S heart was not prepared to seek the LORD. At the age of fifty-eight, he died and was buried in the city of David. This is a sad commentary on Solomon's choice of a mother for the next king! One wonders if there was not one son, from all those wives and concubines he had that may have walked with the LORD! If so, why choose Rehoboam?

So now we come to KING ABIJAH. He was a good king as far as his battles were concerned, but spiritually he was disappointing (see I Kings 15:1-7). With 400,000 valiant men, he stood high on a mountain proclaiming to wicked JEROBOAM that GOD gave Israel to David forever! He reminded JEROBOAM that he had gathered worthless men around him, and reviewed the golden calves situation. He remembered that JEROBOAM had kicked out the priests of the LORD from his kingdom, replacing them with heathen ones. He also declared that he and his men had not forsaken the true GOD and that God HIMSELF was with them and not with JEROBOAM. What a brave and bold king!

GOD smote Jeroboam and all Israel before Abijah and Israel. They had prevailed because they *"relied upon the LORD God of their fathers."* Abijah became great and strong. Jeroboam never regained his strength while ABIJAH was living.

How proud MICHAIAH, his mother, was of ABIJAH. She was the daughter—perhaps the granddaughter—of URIEL of Gibeah. If he was the same URIEL, he was the LEVITE mentioned in I Chronicles 15:11, who helped bring the ARK to its place for King David. I think that MICHAIAH taught her son the deep things of the true God, and that he depended on HIM for daily guidance. It is too bad that his reign only lasted three years.

"SPIRITUAL MELODY"
(Ephesians 5:19; Colossians 3:16)

What an amazing privilege to commit ALL our affairs to our Heavenly Father, and find that HE gives us Songs and melodies in our heart.

Our body may be too heavy to audibly sing, but not our spirits.

SONGS IN THE NIGHT, IN THE DAY,
DIRECTED BY THE LORD JESUS.
Songs of His love, He brings to memory.
Giving me strength to live courageously
Restraining me, sustaining me. (ggs)

II Chronicles 13:22–II Chronicles 18:17
THE DEMISE OF A PROUD KING
II Chronicles 16:12

"And Asa . . . was diseased in his feet . . . yet . . . he sought not to the LORD . . ."

ASA, the KING OF JUDAH was a good king! He was the son of ABIJAH. In chapter 14:2, we read that *"ASA did that which was good and right in the eyes of the LORD his God."* Prior to Asa, Israel had been without a teaching-priest to teach them about the true God. When ASA heard the prophecy of ODED, he *took courage* and cleaned up the land of sin. In I Kings 15:12-15, we read that bold ASA removed the sodomites from his land, the idols, and the *queen mother* from the throne. He smote the Ethiopians, and cried out to the LORD. The Bible says that ASA's heart was perfect all his days (II Chronicles 15:17b).

So it is with some surprise that I read about ASA'S foot illness and his refusal to seek the Lord in it. Some have problems with their feet, but it does not take their lives. Other foot problems are so severe that the foot must be amputated to save the patient's life. What was ASA's disease? Was he a *diabetic*? Did he have a *blood clot*? Did he have *cancer*? Did he have *blood poisoning*?

When my husband was a little boy, his father had blood poisoning. It began in his foot. *Then the poison crept up his leg.* It was a frightening thing! HE WAS CLOSE TO DEATH! That was in the time when there were not all the medicines that we have today. I do not know the details; but my father in-law's life was spared.

Let us review some of the events in KING ASA's life before his sickness. In the 36th year of KING ASA'S reign, KING BAASHA of ISRAEL fought against JUDAH. He built *"RAMAH"* so no one could get to Judah–perhaps it was a wall, I don't know. ASA sent precious coins from the Temple's treasury, reminding KING BENHADAD of SYRIA that their two countries had an alliance. *"Break the league between Syria and Israel"* was Asa's request. This BENHADAD did! When BAASHA heard this, in fear, he ceased building *"RAMAH!"*

The PROPHET HANANI rebuked ASA. HANANI reminded powerful ASA concerning the *"RAMAH"* problem with KING BAASHA, that ASA had relied upon the KING of SYRIA in that situation rather than on the LORD. *"Had not the Ethiopians been defeated because of the LORD?"* That was the prophet's question. HANANI reminded the king that *"the eyes of the LORD run to and fro throughout the whole earth, to shew himself strong in the behalf of* *them whose heart is perfect toward him"* (II Chronicles 16:9). WHAT A REBUKE TO A PROUD KING! Guess what ASA did. He put the prophet in prison! Then he oppressed some of the people in his kingdom.

Now we return to ASA's *disease* and *death*. Personally, I believe it was *ASA's pride* that kept him from calling upon a prophet of God. The Bible says that *"he sought not to the LORD, but to the physicians."* Who were these *"physicians"*? Were they wizards?

There was HANANI rotting away in the dreaded prison. It appeared that KING ASA had backslidden to such an extent that he would not call upon that prophet ever again! Were there others in the land who could seek God for ASA? I think so. All I know is that ASA died in his forty-first year of his reign, being sick unto death for at least two years. What a sad demise—deliberately turning his face away from God.

ASA died. He had his own sepulcher there in Jerusalem. He was laid on a bed of flowers and spices. There was a great viewing for him with the pomp and circumstances due a king. And—I suppose HANANI was hearing it all from his dungeon somewhere in Jerusalem. I wonder if he ever got out of prison.

"LAW OF KINDNESS"
(Proverbs 31:26b)
"In her tongue is the law of kindness."
The tongue is a member of the body.
It needs to submit to the Lord and obey Him.
BE YE KIND ONE TO ANOTHER,
TENDER HEARTED, KINDLY AFFECTIONATE.
The Christian woman should obey the admonition to be kind,
as though it were one of the ten commandments.
She should be submissive to it in all areas of life. (ggs)

Today's Bible Blessing   *May 17*

II Chronicles 18:18–II Chronicles 21:20
GOD'S BATTLE—NOT YOURS

II Chronicles 20:15b

"Thus saith the LORD . . . Be not afraid nor dismayed . . . for the battle is not yours, but God's."

Have you ever been dismayed? Have you ever been terrified of a situation? Has the very spirit of *hope* and *courage* been drained from your very being? If so, you have somewhat of the emotional feeling that KING JEHOSHAPHAT felt when he learned that the AMMONITES and MOABITES—all in battle array—were coming to invade JUDAH. These were descendents of LOT, by his daughters. They were the people that GOD had forbidden the children of Israel to capture, when they were on the way to Canaan (Deuteronomy 2:19).

All JEHOSHAPHAT could do was fall on his face before the LORD begging for help. He prayed, *"We have no might against this great company . . . neither know we what to do."* (II Chronicles 20:12) He assured God that their eyes were upon HIM. Have you ever been in a circumstance of life where there was no place to turn? You fell on your knees in despair with no place to turn but to GOD! If so, you have something in common with Judah and their king today.

It was in this dire condition, with skilled warriors outnumbering them, that the PROPHET JAHAZIEL (verse 14) spoke assuring words to the KING. He said, by the direction of the HOLY SPIRIT, *"The battle is not yours, but God's!"*

I remember very well a time in my life, when all my human energy and strength was spent in the care for our son. No matter how hard I tried, things were not working out—at least not how I thought they should work out. He was a sick person, but in his sickness, he had a will to go in a different direction. I tried and tried to help him. One day in utter despair God spoke to me—as real as if he had a verbal voice in my ear, ***"BE NOT DISMAYED. . .THE BATTLE IS NOT YOURS, BUT GOD'S!"*** That was the day, I gave up trying. I recognized that I could not do a thing to help my son. I knew the only ONE who could help him fight his battle with mental illness was God. It is a long story that I have CONDENSED in today's *"blessing,"* but it is one that is worth repeating to you in case you are dismayed TODAY.

"HIS LEFT HAND"
(Song of Solomon 2:6; Job 23:9)
*"His left hand is under my head,
and his right hand doth embrace me "*
I am enclosed in HIS embrace.
What an amazing promise of protection, safety, and security.
His left hand—His "secret working" of Providence,
guiding me in the affairs of life.
He is secretly working things together.
Embraced by His arms, I am truly secure and comforted. (ggs)

Today's Bible Blessing   *May 18*

II Chronicles 22:1–II Chronicles 25:25

DO YOU GIVE AS THE LORD PROSPERS?

II Chronicles 24:8-9

". . . they made a chest . . . at the gate of the house of the LORD . . . to bring in to the LORD the collection . . ."

The beautiful Temple, the House of the LORD, was in disarray. During her life-time, wicked ATHALIAH had broken-up the Holy Place where the children of Israel had worshipped the True God. She had given the *"dedicated things"* within the Temple to BAALIM. If you remember, previously she had killed all the heirs to the throne wanting to promote herself to be the ruler. Little JOASH escaped and was under the tutoring of the priest, JEHOIDA who influenced the young king to repair the Temple.

As an aside: the priest supervised the young king to do godly deeds, but JEHOIDA did not teach JOASH to have personal convictions for the true God. We know this because after the priest died, the young king—who never made a decision without JEHOIDA—turned toward ungodly friends and sinful pursuits. This should be a lesson to us parents. We must do everything we can to teach our children to have *heart convictions* on spiritual matters.

Getting back to today's thought. How were the people of JUDAH to pay for such a temple restoration project? It would cost more than they had in their treasury. It was then that they remembered what MOSES had done (II Chronicles 24: 9). Someone made a chest for money offerings. It was placed outside the temple by the temple gate. With much rejoicing all the people and the princes cast coins into that box. Every time the chest was full, it was emptied and put back for more offerings. How happy they were at the prospect that their Temple would be restored!

Have you ever been in a church where people gave with great gusto for a project before them that needed funds? I have. Everyone was eager for a church building to be built. Or they were anticipating an addition to the church. Or they looked forward to sending one of their own members to the mission field. Or they gathered an offering to send to a Bible college student to aid him in his tuition. Yes, you probably have been a part of such a collection. *REMEMBER THE JOY?*

Often God blesses a Christian with funds so that the Christians, so blessed, can give to others. It is a warm, happy, silent joy that engulfs such giving. Have you ever experienced this joy? I have. It is not something we go around talking about; but it is something that God laid upon our hearts and we HAD to do it. It says in II Chronicles 24:11 *"Thus they did day by day, and gathered money in abundance!"*

Have you ever given abundantly to the LORD's work? Maybe you have helped build a building in some African village. Perhaps you have financed a student in school. Maybe you have given new carpet for the church sanctuary. Maybe you have seen a lonely woman and taken her out to dinner. Whatever your gift-giving was, it was done out of love for the LORD God. *"Inasmuch as ye did it not to one of the least of these, ye did it not to me" (Matthew 25:45).* **Don't you dare miss out on God's blessing by not giving as the LORD has prospered you!**

"THE FAINT"
(Isaiah 40:29)
"He giveth power to the faint; and to them that have no might he increaseth strength . . ."
What a marvelous specific promise for such as I,
who am pressed above measure and have little might,
even for daily tasks.
I have experienced His Strength in my weakness.
He has exchanged His strength for it. (ggs)

Today's Bible Blessing   *May 19*

II Chronicles 25:26—II Chronicles 29:23
THE KING WHO OVERSTEPPED HIS AUTHORITY

II Chronicles 26:16

". . .When he (UZZIAH) was strong, his heart was lifted up to his destruction: for he . . . went into the temple . . . to burn incense upon the altar of incense. "

For the most part UZZIAH was a good king. He was a king who did that which was right in the sight of the LORD. BUT! Often there is a *"BUT"* in the lives of Christians. They lead an exemplary life. They love the LORD JESUS with all their heart and soul. They are faithful husbands and good fathers–"BUT!" I don't know what it is exactly, but Satan seems to get a foothold in the lives of some upstanding men. I suppose it is because the Devil does not want a Christian man (or woman) to be a good testimony. So he *stumbles* that Christian in a way that only that particular *stumbling block* could make him fall. The truth is that there is always a *"stumbling block"* waiting for the Christian to fall over. It is up to the believer to be aware that Satan is like a roaring Lion seeking whom he may *devour*. He started this *devouring* in the garden of Eden with ADAM and EVE and has not stopped his pursuit of the Christian to fall ever since.

So it was with KING UZZIAH. He began to be king when he was sixteen years old. He reigned fifty-two years. That is a young age to bear the responsibilities of ruling a nation, but he did it. He did that which was right in the eyes of God–always seeking HIM. God helped UZZIAH in many a battle. It seemed as if the kings of Judah did nothing but fight battles. He was good at it. Even the dreaded AMMONITES gave him gifts. They must have feared him. Those in Egypt spoke well of him. UZZIAH built towers. From those towers skillful men would shoot arrows and hurl stones. The towers made the nation strong.

It was during this time of *"strength"* that KING UZZIAH's heart swelled with pride. It led to his destruction. He went into the TEMPLE–the beautiful Temple. What did he do there? He decided to burn *"incense."* The burning of *"incense"* signified *"prayer."* This was not the job of the king. It was the designated responsibility of the Priests. That was God's order. It must have been *"pride"* that had KING UZZIAH strut into the temple and presume that he could do that which was the priests' sole responsibility.

It was then that AZARIAH, the priest, observed the King's errant behavior. With eighty other priests by his side, AZARIAH warned the king. He told the king, who was standing before him with a censer in his hand, *"INCENSE BURNING DOES NOT PERTAIN TO YOU!"* AZARIAH informed the presumptuous king that it was the responsibility of the priests and the Levites, not the king's! I am sure the king knew this to begin with; but his pride went before his fall. UZZIAH was determined to *"worship"* God in his own way. It was the wrong way.

Anger arose in the King's heart. His face was red with rage. Who was this PRIEST AZARIAH to tell him, the mighty KING UZZIAH, what he could or could not do? With his rage, something else happened to the king. Suddenly, appearing on his forehead was the dreaded LEPROSY! Right there before the eyes of the priests, and right there in front of the ALTAR OF INCENSE, KING UZZIAH became LEPROUS! That was the leprosy that plagued him for the rest of his life!

BEWARE LEST WE BECOME OVERTAKEN WITH PRIDE AND WILLFULLY DISOBEY GOD'S WORDS!

> ### *"THE MIDST OF TROUBLE"*
> (Psalm 138:7-8)
> In the midst of trouble, the Lord will perfect
> that which concerneth me.
> HELP FROM ABOVE
> STRENGTH IMPARTED
> WISDOM BESTOWED
> INTERCESSION BY OTHERS
> LOVE DEMONSTRATED
> PRESENCE FELT
> He cares for me and is concerned with that which concerneth me.
> (ggs)

Today's Bible Blessing   *May 20*

II Chronicles 29:24—II Chronicles 32:24

A COMMAND TO CONSECRATION

II Chronicles 30:26-27

"So there was great joy in Jerusalem: for since the time of Solomon . . . the priests . . . prayer came up to . . . heaven. "

It is most disturbing to me to read about the continual backsliding of the nation of Israel. How could they be so fickle? How could they turn themselves from serving the LORD God to *idols*? In yesterday's DAILY READING, we saw king UZZIAH. Today, we see a good king named HEZEKIAH who was AHAZ's son. ABIJAH was his mother. HEZEKIAH trusted the true God! He reigned 29 years in Jerusalem.

When HEZEKIAH became king, one of the first deeds he did was to open the doors of the HOUSE of THE LORD. My questions are, *"Why were they shut?"* We can ask that question about many closed churches today. In Europe, beautiful buildings, that were churches of all kinds of denominations, are closed to worship. They have become market places, or tourist attractions. In the United States, we see church buildings turned into restaurants, or feed stores, or homes to live in. WHY?

HEZEKIAH decided to do something about the spiritual mess his people were in. He called all the priests together, as well as the Levites, and told them to get themselves right with God. He said, *"Sanctify yourselves and the house of the LORD!"* According to Scripture, the Temple was *filthy*! No wonder the wrath of God was upon JUDAH (II Chronicles 29:8-10)!!

205

It really is something else that the ruler of the land must command those who are to be standing the tallest for God to get right with Him. But that apparently is what transpired in chapter twenty-nine. The shame of it all: *incense* was not offered, nor *burnt offerings* for years. The TEMPLE LAMPS were snuffed out. The *doors* shut. The *holy place* ignored. Can you relate to such disorder?

When HEZEKIAH saw that the Temple had been cleansed and the RUBBISH thrown into the brook KIDRON, he declared they would observe THE PASSOVER. How many years this had not been done, I do not know. He demanded that the Levites and priests prepare themselves for the Passover. Six hundred oxen and three thousand sheep were part of this consecration. A sad report: there were not enough priests to flay the animals! What a spiritual decline had hit JUDAH! Things were in such disarray that the PASSOVER had to be observed in the second month, instead of the first.

The next thing the KING did was invite all of ISRAEL, as well as JUDAH to attend THE PASSOVER! A proclamation was sent throughout all Israel from Beersheba to Dan! The KING begged the people to *"YIELD YOURSELVES UNTO THE LORD."* The recipients of the proclamation MOCKED and LAUGHED! But THE TRIBES OF ASHER, MANASSEH, and ZEBULUN *humbled themselves* and came. What rejoicing!

We read in II Chronicles 30:15 that some of the LEVITES were *ashamed.* And well they should have been! Their backsliding was great! A great number of priests sanctified themselves. The people began to tithe again. The priests and Levites were no longer hungry–for they had been *neglected* because of the backslidden condition of the people. There had not been such joy in Jerusalem since the days of SOLOMON!

There is always joy when Christian people walk uprightly before the LORD. One of the FIRST manifestations of a Christian who is in right relationship with his LORD is what he does with his *pocket book.* No one has to tell *the restored Christian* to give of HIMSELF and of his FUNDS to the LORD. He just does it. (II Corinthians 9:7)!

What is your spiritual condition today?

"THE WORK OF RIGHTEOUSNESS–PEACE"
(Isaiah 32:17)
It takes real trial and tragedy to stop and examine one's faith.
The Lord gave me again one of His precious verses to comfort.
In November 1952, He gave this verse.
In March 1977, He gave it to my heart again with new emphasis.
THE WORK OF RIGHTEOUSNESS IS PEACE.
THE EFFECT OF RIGHTEOUSNESS IS
QUIETNESS AND ASSURANCE.
Blessed fruit of righteousness to comfort and sustain. (ggs)

Today's Bible Blessing   *May 21*

II Chronicles 32:25—II Chronicles 35:18

FROM BAD TO GOOD
IN ONE LIFETIME

II Chronicles 33:12

"And when he (MANASSEH) was in affliction, he besought the LORD his God"

We now come to the reign of MANASSEH. He was the son of HEZEKIAH—born during the bonus fifteen-year-period that God gave Hezekiah to live. Remember MANASSEH'S father was nigh unto death when he cried to the LORD to heal him. I ponder why such a good king as HEZEKIAH would not bring up his child in the ways of the true God. My conclusions are that, for the most part, it has to do with the *"mother"* of the child.

So MANASSEH was twelve years old when he became king. What can a king know to rule a land at twelve years of age? But—that was older than some of the other boy-kings! At such a young age, these *"child kings"* had to be influenced by their *"handlers."* The children were *"mouth pieces"* for them. I've seen children who wanted to be missionaries or preachers at young ages. They dedicated their lives to such Christian service, only to depart from all that *holy dedication* when they got out on their own, away from their parents. So was that desire to be in the LORD'S WORK only their parent's desire? A true *"call"* of God comes no matter if *"handlers"* are living or dead.

So MANASSEH built up the high places again. He seemed to reverse all the good his Dad, HEZEKIAH, had done—even constructing altars for Baalim. What a shame! MANASSEH passed his children through fire, as well as frequenting wizards. The man was just plain evil! It seemed like these wicked kings that we have been reading about felt they *had* to desecrate the *House of the LORD.* Perhaps that was to show their utter disregard for all that was *Holy.*

I remember a church my husband pastored in Massachusetts. It was supposed to be the *"leading"* church in that area. Turned out that it was very NEW EVANGELICAL! After we left there, the church completely disintegrated. There had been a horrible church split. It was a lesson in what Christian love is not.

We went back there about sixteen years ago just to look around. The building is now a GREEK ORTHODOX CHURCH with golden altars, etc. In the entrance of that church were bags of food, as well as fruits and vegetables all over the floor. Loaves of bread were piled nearby. It turned out to be the community food bank.

Some things never change. The woman *"in charge"* of the food bank, in that church, was a women we had known. Prior to our being there, she had lived through a previous church split. The first one was when the congregation came out of the American Baptist Convention. That was several years before my husband was its pastor. The woman had a strange loyalty to the building. No matter who the pastor was, no matter what his theological position, no matter the sin that caused such commotion to cause the splits, that woman stayed with that building! Instead of rising up and standing for the truth to return that church in that building to Jesus Christ and His Words, she went along with *whatever* and *whoever* was preaching or teaching in that building.

In thinking about MANASSEH and his degradation of the Temple, I remembered that Massachusetts church. It is no longer the LIGHTHOUSE, it used to be–*very sad to behold.*

But, I must say one more thing about MANASSEH. In later years, HE HAD A HEART CHANGE! He had an affliction. We are not told what it was, but it turned him around spiritually. He humbled himself. He sought the LORD. HE PRAYED TO THE LORD GOD. *God heard him.* MANASSEH TOOK AWAY THE STRANGE GODS. He repaired the altar of the LORD.

Yes, MANASSEH had a change of heart—but he could never repair the evil his children saw him do before his heart-change. His son, *AMON,* was an evil king and sacrificed to *carved images,* the very images his father had made previously. AMON was such an evil king that his own servants killed him!

"OUR FATHER IS THE HUSBANDMAN"
Christians are the branches. We are joined to the vine.
Some bear no fruit. Some bear some fruit.
He prunes for little or more fruit.
There is no life in the branches, but in the Vine.
We cannot bear fruit alone.
"Without Me–NOTHING"
The reason is to bring *glory* to God!
He knows how to prune branches.
He knows which instrument to use.
He knows *who* to prune.
He knows *where* to prune.
He knows the *right time* to prune.
He knows *how much* to prune.
He knows *WHY* He does it.
I'M GLAD THAT MY HEAVENLY FATHER IS THE HUSBANDMAN!
(ggs)

Today's Bible Blessing   *May 22*

II Chronicles 35:19—Ezra 2:42
"GO OR GIVE!"—SAID THE KING

Ezra 1:1

"In the first year of Cyrus . . . the LORD stirred up . . . the king . . ."

I wonder what PERSIA'S KING CYRUS thought as the LORD began to *"stir him up"*! Jeremiah's powerful words were to the point. Cyrus heard them. Even though he was a heathen king, Cyrus acted upon them. Oh, that those who claim the Name of Christ would let the Words of God stir them up to action! So many of us just sit back—take in the view, listen to pulpit platitudes and let the "praise songs" begin. But not Cyrus!

KING CYRUS MEANT BUSINESS! He made a proclamation. He stated that the LORD God of Heaven had given him all the kingdoms of the earth. My, he was a powerful king! God also charged CYRUS to build God a HOUSE in Jerusalem. It is interesting to me that the LORD God wanted a specific *"place"* where His children could know that it was His *"place."* The children of God like to gather together in a *"place"* where they can worship together. The *"place"* for God's house was JERUSALEM. No other *"place"* would do!

KING CYRUS WAS A QUESTIONER! Look at his question in Ezra 1:3. He asked, *"Who among all God's people will go back to Jerusalem and build God a house?"* That was a good question—a penetrating question. I think we must realize that the children of Israel had become comfortable as captives in a strange land. Often people adjust to their circumstances as long as they are somewhat comfortable.

Immediately, KING CYRUS, a heathen potentate, began organizing the Hebrew people to get going or get giving! He said, "If you don't want to go back to Jerusalem to build a HOUSE for your God, then help the project with your silver and gold, your goods, and your beasts to carry all the supplies back to your land." In other words, he said, "If you do not want to go, give!" Cyrus knew that nothing could be done for the LORD if there were no supplies to do the deeds.

Guess what? The head men of Judah and Benjamin, as well as their priests were excited about the project! They prepared to go do the job! That was really wonderful, wasn't it? The people, who were not going physically with them, *"strengthened their hands"* with willing offerings of money and goods. It was an exciting time! It always is when God moves in the midst of a group of people who love Him and want to do His will.

Why, CYRUS got into the act of "giving," too! Cyrus found the vessels of the LORD that Nebuchadnezzar had taken from the beautiful TEMPLE in Jerusalem when the Hebrews had been captured years before. Besides that, he persuaded his treasurer, a man named MITHREDATH, to donate huge containers—thirty gold ones and one thousand silver ones—as well as twenty-nine knives. In fact, these "gifts" were probably stolen from the Temple during the captivity also. But, what a gift from a heathen king!

How exciting! All the people, of the various provinces that went back to Jerusalem from the land of their captivity, settled in their own cities back in the land. It had been years and years and years since they had been *"home."* Can you feel their joy? People, who had not seen Elam for decades, were back. The same with those from Bethlehem, Ramah, Ai, Harim, Jericho, Pashur, and so many other *"home towns."* The old streets were vibrant once more. Feet of former captives walked there, joyfully skipping beside their stubborn donkeys once again.

"WE SHINE AS LIGHTS"
(Philippians 2:15)
Tonight, there was an eclipse of the moon.
When the moon was in the full shadow of the sun,
its light dimmed.
A small star called "Spica"—previously invisible—shone brightly!
It was arrestingly distinct.
I thought, as I looked at this phenomena,
that we were like this little star—
UNNOTICED UNTIL WE WERE IN A SHADOW OF A TRIAL.
Then our witness became visible to all.
A CHRISTIAN WOMAN IS A LIGHT IN A DARK PLACE. (ggs)

Today's Bible Blessing   *May 23*

Ezra 2:43–Ezra 6:3

THE ANCIENT MEN WEPT

Ezra 3:12-13

"Many of the . . . ancient men . . . wept with a loud voice."

This a very exciting, fast moving narrative in today's reading. *KING CYRUS* of the *Persian* kingdom encouraged and promoted those Jewish captives, who wanted to return to Jerusalem to rebuild the Temple. If you recall, the Jewish people were in CAPTIVITY in Babylon for *seventy years.* For some, *"seventy years"* is a very long time, but for others, *seventy years* is just a wink of the eye. It depends how old one is, to view *seventy years* as a long time, or a short time.

In our reading today, we catch up with the children of Israel back in their land. Now, you must remember that all of them did not leave Babylon to return *"home"* to rebuild the temple. In some ways, the ones who did were like missionaries returning to their home towns to reestablish a long, lost *"faith."* As we further read into the book of EZRA and NEHEMIAH, we will be persuaded that many people, who lived in the land during that *seventy-year captivity period*, were without the true God.

After being in THE LAND seven months, the Jews traveled to JERUSALEM to celebrate *THE FEAST OF TABERNACLES.* This was one of the seven feasts that the Israelites practiced every year. I think it was on October 15th. (Their first month was April.) The celebration lasted for seven days every year (Leviticus 23:34c). They offered one hundred, ninety-nine offerings during that week. What an exciting time!

The two main priests, JESHUA and ZERUBBABEL, encouraged such a gathering. What a glorious day! Over and over we read in the history of God's chosen people about the building of *altars.* The purpose of the *altars* was for animal blood sacrifices. Animals would be slain, flayed, and burned on the BRASEN ALTAR, which was rebuilt for the occasion. Blood shedding may sound gory to you and me–and it probably is. *The purpose of all the sacrifices, was looking forward to the shedding of Jesus' blood at the cross of Calvary, many centuries in the future.* The blood of bulls and goats only *"covered"* the sins of the people. Jesus' blood sacrifice removed the sin. Only those who *"receive HIM"* are "saved" (John 1:12).

That day there was much singing and praising. The foundation of the new House of God was laid. The people rejoiced. The priests stood in their priestly garments ministering to the people. A strange thing happened that day. *While the young people rejoiced, the older folk wept.*

The Bible tells us that the *"ancient men"* who had seen SOLOMON'S TEMPLE previously *wept in a loud voice.* Those old men had witnessed the grandeur of the first Temple. They remembered its beauty, its pillars, and gold. By looking at the new foundation that day, the *"ancient"* knew intuitively that the Temple would be only a *shadow* of its original splendor. Their hearts were broken! Memories of what used to be hurt! This is the way with older people. They have cherished memories of many things and events–people, relatives, special days, and buildings. They remember. It is good to remember, but sometimes we must move on and forget because *remembering hurts* too much.

The younger people who gathered that week in Jerusalem were rejoicing. They only knew the present foundation of the House of God. If they saw their elders weeping, they were mystified, *"Why were these old men crying?"* Yet, the young people's joy was great. They shouted praise with thanksgiving.

"THE NAME OF THE LORD"
(Proverbs 18:10)
"The name of the LORD is a strong tower:
the righteous runneth into it, and is safe."
SAY HIS NAME OVER AND OVER AGAIN
TO SOOTHE YOUR HEART.
"Precious name, Oh how sweet,
Hope of earth And JOY of Heaven."
NO OTHER NAME
Run to His dear name! Hide in the Precious Holy Name!
His name says all He is.
How often, I have hidden in the tender, beautiful Name
of the Lord Jesus Christ!
(ggs)

Today's Bible Blessing   *May 24*

Ezra 6:4–Ezra 9:2

BUILDING THE HOUSE
OF THE LORD

Ezra 6:15

"And this house was finished on the third day of the month ADAR, which was in the sixth year of the reign of Darius the king."

The way I see it, everyone in the land of Israel was not happy with the rebuilding of the temple. Well, almost everyone–but those complainers! They *pretended* to want to help the builders. The priests saw through this farce and forbade such help, continuing the work as KING CYRUS had commanded. Such subterfuge delayed the temple construction. Then, during the time of AHASUERUS, those upstarts wrote the ruler a letter of complaint. More letters were written in the days of ARTAXERTXES, complaining in the Syrian language. Men with names such as BISHLAM, MITHREDATH, TABEEL, SHIMSHAI, AND REHUM were the writers.

During the dormant years, other nations had set up shop in Samaria. They wanted nothing to do with the true GOD, His TEMPLE, or His worship. They dragged their feet as much as possible to delay progress. They lied to the KING back in Babylon, saying the Jews were building a rebellious city, and that they had no intention of paying taxes to the Babylonian king. Their letters stopped the Temple building. KING ARTAXERXES ordered all work to cease!

Think how disappointed the Jews in Jerusalem were. Two prophets named HAGGAI and ZECHARIAH ministered to the forlorn Jews. Probably you have read their prophesies in the Bible. Around that time, two men by the names of ZERUBBABEL and JESHUA began to build the *House of God* with the help of the PROPHETS OF GOD. I wonder what people thought! GOVERNOR TATNAI and others rushed right over and scolded, *"Who said you could build this House?"* It must have been some encounter!

So once again DARIUS received a letter from GOVERNOR TATNAI. This time it was from the JEWS who explained the whole scenario, going back to the time of NEBUCHADNEZZAR. They wrote of CYRUS' desire to rebuild the House of God. *"Yet,"* they cried, *"It is not finished!"* When KING DARIUS read the letter, he ordered that a search be made of all the records to see if the Jews were telling the truth. Yes they were! Right there before the king's eyes were Cyrus' words, *"LET THE HOUSE BE BUILT!"*

The order back to TATNAI was strong. *"Let the work of the House of God alone!"* The building of the HOUSE of GOD could commence once again! What joy! Finally! *"Finance them! Give them animals for sacrifice!"* he commanded. The King meant business. If anyone hindered the building, that person was to be hung from a scaffold made from the timbers of his own house.

When the news reached *"home,"* **the elders of the Jews, with the encouragement of Haggai and ZECHARIAH, built the TEMPLE.** *It was finished! It was dedicated! How they rejoiced!* Once again the priests and Levites served their *"courses"* according to *the Book of Moses!* They separated themselves from the filthiness of the heathen around them. They kept THE PASSOVER. *"The LORD had turned the heart of the king of Assyria unto them."*

What is the message for you today from this reading? God has a plan. Often that *plan* is thwarted. Sometimes there is great delay–often because of your own waywardness. Sometimes, the postponement comes because of a set of circumstances. Does this mean that you, who know what God wants you to do, should give up and go the way of the world? No, it does not! You must look for the *"ram in the bushes"* just as God provided for Abraham when he was about to offer his son as a sacrifice. It may not be a bush that holds the solution to your failure. It may not be a Babylonian king or an ungrateful friend. LOOK FOR THE ESCAPE! God still has *a plan* for you to fulfill!

> ## "GOD'S TIMING IS BEST"
> God's way is best.
> To have our way, and not be in His will,
> will not bring joy.
> We would not want our dear one to live, if it were not His will—
> No matter our loss.
> His will is best for our dear one, and for us, and for His glory.
> GOD'S TIMING IS BEST! (ggs)

Today's Bible Blessing   *May 25*

Ezra 9:3–Nehemiah 2:17
A MARRIAGE MIX-UP

Ezra 9:12

". . . give not your daughters unto their sons, neither take their daughters unto your sons, nor seek their peace or their wealth for ever: that ye may . . . eat the good of the land and leave it for an inheritance to your children forever."

Ezra was a scribe. The Bible says he was a *"ready scribe."* I suppose that means that he was *"ready"* for any writing of important documents at any time. EZRA had prepared his heart to learn to obey THE LAW, so he could teach THE LAW to the people of God in THE LAND. What a noble and worthy goal! How good to be as ready for the Lord's service as Ezra. Besides being a scribe, Ezra was a priest.

One day Ezra left Babylon for the *"home"* turf of Jerusalem. He had the blessings of the king to do so—as those who earlier had left Babylon with Cyrus's blessing to build the House of God. Ezra had a letter from KING ARTAXERXES that gave EZRA and his followers authority to go beyond THE RIVER. They were to contribute to the TEMPLE precious metals and jewels and any needful thing to aid in the worship of the LORD God.

In Ezra 8, we see EZRA, the scribe, busily recording the names of the people who were traveling with him from Babylon to Jerusalem. In so doing, he discovered that the sons of Levi were missing. Quickly he sent for some chief men and men of understanding to go to IDDO and bring some Levites to minister to them. Next Ezra proclaimed *a fast* for God's protection for them as they journeyed. How thankful they were to God for protection and safety as they entered *The Land* of their fathers.

When Ezra got to The Land, he was dumbfounded, discovering that the people had intermarried with the people of the land. Even the priests had done this. Why some of them had children with the non-Israelite women. This was not according to God's plan for them at all (Ezra 9:10-12). Ezra turned to God in prayer, *"O LORD God of Israel . . . we are before Thee in our trespasses . . ."* People in tears gathered about Ezra as he prayed before the House of God. They were dismayed. They were repentant. They made a covenant with God and put away their *"strange"* wives. It must not have been an easy thing to do; but they determined to get right with God and obey his words. Ezra mourned with tears and fasting for this great sin. It seemed to be the rainy season, but the men who had taken *strange wives* kept coming before chosen men and ridding themselves of their "strange" wives and their sin. It was an awful day, but it was a good day of confessing sin and obeying God.

The women the Israelite men were marrying, were heathen women. Probably they were a different hue than the Israelites. Not only that, but religiously they were downright unbelievers. It seemed strange that a group of people who left Babylon years before for the express purpose of worshipping the true God and building Him a proper house, would backslide so severely that they married outside the boundaries of their race and the precepts of their religion. Perhaps there were few Israelite women to marry. I do not know. But the Hebrews were expressly told by God not to do this.

Men and woman are no different today, for they do the same thing. A beautiful woman who does not love the Lord Jesus may look very attractive to a lonely man who does. Does a man (or a woman) really love Jesus Christ when he yokes up with a mate who does not? Marriage is difficult enough without having an unequal religious yoke. Many feel that yoking up with a mate of a different race makes added difficulties in marriage. What do you think?

"GOD IS WITH ME"
(Psalm 55:6-8)
I would hasten my escape from the windy storm and tempest.
"Oh, that I had wings like a dove!
for then I would fly away, and–rest."
I GET SO TIRED!
Some days the tempest rages and I call for Him to still the storms.
I forget He is in the tumult with me. (ggs)

Today's Bible Blessing   *May 26*

Nehemiah 2:18–Nehemiah 6:8
NEHEMIAH'S BURDEN FULFILLED

Nehemiah 4:9

"Nevertheless we made our prayer unto our God, and set a watch against them day and night . . ."

Nehemiah's father must have been proud of his son. HACHALIAH could brag about NEHEMIAH's job, for his son was a cup bearer to the great and mighty KING ARTAXERXES. Do you remember him? Being a cupbearer is an important job. Nehemiah was daily in the presence of the king, tasting his food as well as passing the time of day. After twelve years, the two became friends. So it was not unusual for the King to observe the downheartedness of his servant.

You see NEHEMIAH had been fasting and praying. He had learned from his friend, HANANI, that things were not going too well in Jerusalem. The wall was broken down and the gates had been burned. As the king inquired concerning NEHEMIAH'S sadness, Nehemiah asked a favor, *"Would you write a letter to the governors beyond the river and let me deliver it to them?"* The letter would request timber and building materials to rebuild the city's wall. This request disturbed some who were not in favor of such rebuilding.

Upon arriving in Jerusalem, NEHEMIAH observed the mess in which he found his city. It was a reproach to all those about it! Encouraging them, he said, *"Let us rise up and build!"* Discouragers like SANBALLAT, TOBIAH, and GESHEM the ARABIAN laughed at him. They believed to rebuild was rebelling against the king.

It was then that the HIGH PRIEST ELIASHIB took the lead and built the SHEEP GATE. The men of Jericho got in the act. The FISH GATE was built by HASSENAAH. The OLD GATE was repaired by JEHOIADA and MESHULLLAM. The GOLDSMITHS and the APOTHECARIES used their talents, too. The VALLEY GATE was fixed by HANUN, as well as the DUNG GATE. SHALLUN repaired the GATE of the FOUNTAIN and the POOL OF SILOAH by the king's garden. The area near the SEPULCHERS OF DAVID was improved, as well as the WATER GATE and its TOWER. The HORSE GATE, the EAST GATE, the SHEEP GATE, THE GATE MIPHKAD, and THE WALL leading to the HIGH PRIEST'S HOUSE were all repaired!

SANBALLAT'S GROUP hated this progress. They attempted to stop it by a war against Jerusalem. NEHEMIAH saw all of this. He encouraged his Jerusalem friends in God, *"Be not ye afraid of them: remember the LORD, which is great and terrible . . .!"* GOD WOULD FIGHT FOR THEM! NEHEMIAH and the workers continue wall-building with a trowel in one hand and a sword in the other. The trumpeter was stationed by NEHEMIAH'S side. Any change about them would be noted, and the trumpeter was alerted. The trumpet sound would inform the workers on the wall as to what they should do–to fight or work. Dedication to the task was great. The men did not change their clothes, except for washing them. The job was intense. It had to be done!

What lesson can we apply to our lives for today?

FIRST: God will supply in time of need. When all seems lost, pray and trust Him.

SECOND: When enemies make fun of us, keep on. Ignore their grimaces and discouraging words.

THIRD: Get the vision. Start one *"gate"* at a time. Be a leader in repairing the broken-down church, house, or even a person. Reach out to work faithfully and carefully.

FOURTH: Be ready to fight for the cause, as well as to fix the situation.

FIFTH: Don't be afraid to step out in faith and help a situation.

Remember NEHEMIAH. Remember how he left the luxurious palace to help his ruined city.

**THERE IS A GREAT NEED FOR SUCH BOLD HELP TODAY.
DO IT!**

"BUT THEN HE SPEAKS"
"But then, He speaks to me
And cares and clouds roll away.
I hear His voice so sweet.
And then, I hear Him say
Just lift thy heart to praise,
Trust me–I am Thy God.
I love thee, child of mine,
I know the path you've trod."
(Poem by ggs)

𝒯𝑜𝒹𝒶𝓎'𝓈 𝐵𝒾𝒷𝓁𝑒 𝐵𝓁𝑒𝓈𝓈𝒾𝓃𝑔   𝑀𝒶𝓎 27

Nehemiah 6:9–Nehemiah 8:1
O GOD, STRENGTHEN MY HANDS!
Nehemiah 6:15

"So the wall was finished in the twenty and fifth day of the month Elul, in fifty and two days."

    In yesterday's reading (chapter 5), we observed that there was a *dearth* in the land. Because of the lack of rain, there was a lack of food. The people borrowed money from the king's treasury and mortgaged their land to buy food. Soon they realized that they were slaves–so to speak–to their creditors. Some of their daughters were in bondage already, and their sons were servants.

NEHEMIAH was angry when he heard this! He was disturbed! He questioned the nobles and rulers, *"Why are you charging interest to your brethren?"* He pointed out that previously they had *"redeemed"* their Jewish brethren. The heathen around them had seen that kindness. Now they were enslaving their own people themselves. What a bad testimony before the world! He exhorted them to walk in the fear of GOD! NEHEMIAH, as Governor of Judah, had provided for their food when they were building the wall—not like the former governors. With the PRIESTS as witnesses, the repentant noblemen and rulers promised that they would give back the fields and vineyard to their down-trodden brethren.

In Nehemiah 6, we see the surprise of the antagonists, SANBALLAT, TOBIAH, and GESHEM. They did not realize the wall was almost completely finished—except for the doors and gates. They devised a plot against Nehemiah and his crew to hinder the completion. Four times they asked to meet with NEHEMIAH. Four times NEHEMIAH said, "NO!" The fifth time, a servant of SANBALLAT sent an open letter to the KING. They claimed that the Jews, who were building the wall, were doing it in order to have a fortress for a rebellious uprising against the KING.

Because of all these lies, NEHEMIAH'S life was threatened. He declared that he would not run to the Temple to save his life. Often men did this by holding on to the horns of the brasen altar. NEHEMIAH called out, *"O God, strengthen my hands!"* The trouble makers were trying to stop the work! Some of the men OF JUDAH sided with TOBIAH because he had married into an important family. TOBIAH sent more letters to NEHEMIAH. It brought nothing but confusion and jealousy. In spite of it, the wall was finished! It took fifty-two days.

When the wall was built, work assignments had to be made. HANANI (remember him from Nehemiah 1:2) and HANANIAH were put in charge over Jerusalem. What a responsibility! Not many houses had been built within the walls as of then. Important genealogies were found and noted. Gate instructions were given. They were very stringent! Life had begun anew in Jerusalem!

The *"in-fighting"* and *"opposition"* that Nehemiah experienced during his wall-building days, reminded me of the *"church fights"* I've seen in some churches where I was a member. Some of the disagreements became so strong that church splits occurred. It seemed such a shame. The *"fighting"* did not remain within the walls of the church. Oh, No! The whole community became aware that the Christians over there in that church could not get along.

In the *"church fighting,"* each side thought they were right. We know that NEHEMIAH was right for we have the Bible to show us the truth. Today in *"church fighting,"* each side thinks they are right. How does one tell which side is correct? What difference does it matter the color of the carpet? Or who is a deacon? Or why they don't follow the church constitution? Or worse yet, *"Why they ignore what the Bible says on the subject?"* Where was NEHEMIAH when those churches needed him?

"HOW OFTEN, WEARY AND TIRED, WE FEEL FORGOTTEN AND OFFENDED?"
Our cares seem greater than our strength,
and we do not act like "new creatures in Christ."
WE MURMUR!
But then, He speaks to our hearts
and the cares do not matter, as we hear His dear voice! (ggs)

Today's Bible Blessing   *May 28*

Nehemiah 8:2—Nehemiah 10:30
READING, WEEPING, REJOICING

Nehemiah 8:10b

". . . this day is holy unto our Lord: neither be ye sorry, for the joy of the LORD is your strength."

In chapter 8, we observe a very interesting thing. All the people gathered together before the Water Gate. They asked EZRA to bring the BOOK OF THE LAW and read from it to them. This was the law of Moses which God had given to ISRAEL. With great anticipation, the people listened. They wanted to hear what God had to say in HIS *BOOK*.

So Ezra stood on a wooden platform and read from the law from morning to midday. Thirteen important men of Judah stood to the left and right of him as he read. The Bible says that all the people were attentive to what the book said. If only people today who say they love the Bible would want to hear it read; and after hearing it read, would do what the Bible says. What a different world we would have today!

After reading the words from the *Holy Book*, EZRA explained what they had just read. The people said, *"Amen, A-men,"* which means "So be it!"! They understood what was being said. They bowed their heads and worshipped the LORD. I do not think they had chairs or benches to sit on. They just stood there listening, praying, and praising.

A few times in my life when the *Word of God* and the preaching from that Word had been proclaimed, there was

such a holy awe and reverence, that time stood still. The power of the MIGHTY GOD overshadowed us. The blessing was so great, that time had no meaning. Usually, people look at their watches, if the preacher goes a few minutes overtime.

Back there in EZRA and NEHEMIAH'S day, the listening people wept. They were very moved by the reading of the WORDS of God. Both NEHEMIAH and EZRA exhorted them to *"mourn not, or weep."* They reminded the people that the day was *"holy"*! It was a day *"separated unto the LORD God."*

As they left for the day, they ate delicious foods and took portions of it to those who had not been to the reading and were hungry. Perhaps the infirm could not attend, or the elderly, or the mothers with small children. Once again they were told not to be sorry, but to rejoice. Then the people were given sweet words—words that you and I often recite in times of weakness or troubles. *"THE JOY OF THE LORD IS YOUR STRENGTH!* (Nehemiah 8:10). What an encouragement. What a balm! What a truth!

As the people went home that day, the warmth of GOD'S WORDS washed their hearts with joy. They remembered the former difficult days of wall-building. They recalled the unexpected opposition. They thought about the long years they forgot the TRUE GOD. They regretted the wasted days they could have served Him, but did not. They remembered their weaknesses—of body and spirit. But deep inside their souls was an unexplained *"bubbling."*

At the core of their very being was a *strength* they did not understand. It was something they had never experienced before. Ezra said it! Nehemiah voiced it! It was *THE JOY OF THE LORD!* Have you ever felt that joy? If so, you know of its *strength*!

"PRAISE AND THANKSGIVING"
(Psalm 50:14, 23)
It is impossible to offer praise to God and complain.
Even though circumstances may seem hopeless,
continue to praise the Lord.
THANKSGIVING IS AN EXPRESSION OF APPRECIATION
FOR WHAT WE HAVE RECEIVED.
Of all our debts, we should give priority to the most important –
PAYING OUR VOWS TO GOD!
*"By Him, therefore, let us offer the sacrifice of praise
to God continually."*
(Hebrews 13:15)
(ggs)

Today's Bible Blessing   *May 29*

Nehemiah 10:31—Nehemiah 12:40
THE PEOPLE AND WALL DEDICATED

Nehemiah 12:27

". . . at the dedication of the wall of Jerusalem . . . with gladness . . . with thanksgiving . . . singing . . . cymbals, psalteries, and . . . harps."

On the twenty-fourth day of the month, the children of Israel assembled. They fasted! They wore sackcloth! They put dirt on their bodies and faces! They repented! They separated themselves from the *"strangers."* They confessed their sins and the sins of their forefathers. It was a time of introspection and confession.

Once again they listened to the Law of God being read. Once again their hearts burned with the realization they had been disobedient. Once again they confessed their sin and worshipped the LORD their God. *"Thou even Thou art LORD alone, Thou hast made heaven, the heaven of heavens . . . the earth . . . the seas . . ."* They recognized that He chose Abram. They remembered their affliction in Egypt. They reviewed the Red Sea miracle, etc. etc. Their history was read to them. Their hearts burned with the truth.

They saw the great mercies of God toward them in the wilderness. They lacked nothing! Their shoes never wore out—even with all that walking! Their feet never swelled! They saw their children multiply as the sand of the sea! They conquered the land! Took strong cities! They were filled! Yet, they disobeyed and rebelled against God. They slew His prophets for telling the truth! Yet, God's great mercies continued. Their princes and priests did not keep the Law! They did not turn from their wicked ways! Now they are servants in the *"promised land."*

That day, they asked the Levites to make a covenant that they could sign. Chapter Ten is full of the signature of those who signed their names that day. They entered into an oath to WALK IN GOD'S LAW! They would respect the SABBATH DAY! They would observe the SEVENTH YEAR! They would not forsake the HOUSE OF THEIR GOD! *What a glorious set of promises* I think they meant every word at the time.

One out of every ten persons said they would live in Jerusalem. The rest would go out into the land and replenish it. But first THE WALL WAS DEDICATED. The Levites came with gladness from wherever they were. The priests served. There was singing, thanksgiving, and gladness. Trumpets blew! Stringed instruments were heard! Cymbals rang! Harps sounded! What a wonderful, *HOLY DAY!* Nehemiah and Ezra had fulfilled their duty. Now it was up to the people.

"HOW WE LOVE HIM"
(Hebrews 1:3; Genesis 1:16)
"We have loved the stars too fondly to be afraid of the night."
(Quoted from source unknown.)
Ah, yes! How we love Him!
He who made the stars.
What time I am afraid, I will trust in Him
"Who upholdeth all things by the word of His power."
"LORD JESUS, I LOVE THEE I KNOW THOU ART MINE,
FOR THEE ALL THE FOLLIES OF SIN I RESIGN."

Today's Bible Blessing   *May 30*

Nehemiah 12:41–Esther 3:2
A BOLD REFUSAL

Esther 1:12

". . . the queen Vashti refused to come at the king's commandment . . . and his anger burned in him."

The book of Esther is an interesting book. Within its pages, the reader can see the *Hand of God* working behind the scenes. As it works, the will of God is fulfilled in the lives of the main characters of the book. Yet, His name is never mentioned. As we investigate the life of QUEEN ESTHER and her godly UNCLE MORDECAI we will be encouraged to live for the LORD JESUS CHRIST in a faithful, quiet, yet bold way.

The name of ESTHER is not mentioned in Chapter One. We see it for the first time in Chapter TWO. The setting is the magnificent palace called *"SHUSHAN."* AHASUERUS was king. His kingdom stretched from India to Ethiopia. He was Persia's and Media's *chief potentate*–one to be feared.

After reigning for three years, AHASUERUS welcomed every prominent man he could think of to his palace. After one hundred-and-eighty-days of displaying his kingdom's riches to his guests, he threw a banquet. Banquets in those days lasted for days. The room was magnificent. They drank from unique goblets of gold. The wine was plenteous. After drinking for seven days, AHASUERUS called for his favorite wife, QUEEN VASHTI. **It was not difficult to find VASHTI.** She was having a feast for the women in the royal house. Probably her guests were the wives of the prominent men drinking themselves into oblivion with the king.

Now the account becomes complicated. The reason the king wanted VASHTI to appear before his drunken friends was to show off her *"beauty."* Probably there were sexual connotations here. Many a husband who has a beautiful wife wants to show her off to some extent. He wants his friends to know what a good choice he made. But in verse 11, I do not think AHASUERUS only wanted to introduce his men friends to his wife, but he wanted to exploit her. He wanted them to *SEE* her beauty up close and personal.

Now I feel that VASHTI, a woman of beautiful body and face, was not properly dressed for the public eye that day—not alone a room full of drunken men. When women were together away from the eyes of men, they did not wear the many veils and robes that they do in public. Women, in such countries, only show themselves away from the public view. Yet, the boasting king beckoned her. Even in today's world, it seems that some husbands enjoy showing off their wives. I assume this by the way the wives dress. Today women expose themselves in embarrassing ways anywhere–even in church. So, some men today are no different than this king. We read in verse 12, that she refused his request.

Women in Vashti's time did not refuse their husband's requests! Was it because she knew he was intoxicated, and, if sober, would not ask her to come before his friends unveiled? Did she feel that after he sobered-up, he would regret such a request and be glad she did not obey? I do not know. Whatever her reason, she embarrassed him to the *"tenth degree."* Perhaps she thought her beauty would win her point with him later. After all, there were scores of women in his Harem, and he had chosen her only to be THE QUEEN. As you may or may not know, no one refuses such a powerful king. Vashti found this out the hard way!

The King's advisers said that if the kingdom learned that the Queen disobeyed the King, the women of the land would follow her example. If they did, there would be a female uprising in the land. AHASUERUS could not let that happen. So QUEEN VASHTI was banished from her husband's presence. We never heard from her again. No doubt she was beheaded!

"A VERY PRESENT HELP"
(Exodus 33:14; Psalm 46:1)
"My Presence shall go with thee, and I will give thee rest."
A very PRESENT help!
I am WITH THEE always.
It is not only on daring and brave endeavors
that we are promised His presence,
but in the ordinary, and sometimes trying duties of life,
He walks with us, and cheers us, encouraging us onward. (ggs)

Today's Bible Blessing   *May 31*

Esther 3:3–Esther 8:17
A MISSION TO FULFILL
Esther 4:16b

". . . so will I go in into the king . . . and if I perish, I perish."

What do you remember when you think of Queen
Esther? I suppose the first thing we remember is that she was
beautiful. She was more than beautiful. She had a special personality
that made her more accepted by KING AHASUERUS than any of the
other women in the king's harem. Her given name was HADASSAH,
but we know her as ESTHER. Then we remember that *she was an
orphan* who was raised by an older cousin named MORDECAI, whom
she looked upon as an "UNCLE." She was a Jewess–but the king did
not know.

After ESTHER became the favorite queen, she had a
special status in the royal line-up of those closest to the king;
yet, she could not barge into his presence without being called upon to
do so. AHASUERUS was a powerful potentate. When he wrote a law or
decree, nothing could change it. Even though Esther was his
"favorite," she could not step into his presence without being asked to,
and then, not without proper recognition.

Great tragedy was coming upon her people. The
wicked, scheming HAMAN hated the Jews. HAMAN was high up in the
cabinet of the king. This hatred led to fiery jealousy because of
MORDECAI, the JEW, who recently saved the life of the king.
MORDECAI had reported a death plot against the ruler. The king was
grateful. This infuriated HAMAN. Because of his hatred of MORDECAI
and THE JEWS, HAMAN influenced the KING. Because of this, the
Jews were to be killed.

Esther learned of this plight from her cousin. She was
frightened. What could she do? What should she do? UNCLE
MORDECAI reminded her that she had an influence with the king that
others did not have. She had to speak up! Esther was not used to
doing this. She had been raised to be a quiet, submissive woman. Also,
she had never revealed her Hebrew heritage to the king. She was
afraid! If she told him, what would he say? What would he do? She
knew that he had not called her to his side for over a month. She
remembered VASHTI. She knew that no one ever crossed the king and
survived. MORDECAI reminded his *"child"* that she may have come to
her position as the *favorite wife* of their MIGHTY MAJESTY for *"such
a time as this."*

After a period of *"fasting"* with her ladies-in-waiting,
**and with great dedication and determination, she dressed
herself in proper attire to appear before her husband, the**

KING of one-hundred-and-twenty-seven provinces. With every step toward his *Throne Room*, she knew that those steps might be her very last. In her head, she kept saying, *"If I perish, I perish!"*

As I write those words, I can't help thinking of you and me. What would we have done in such a crisis? If we had risen up from an ordinary lifestyle, an orphan raised by an older cousin, to become the favorite QUEEN of THE LAND, what would we have done? If we had been noticed among all the woman of the kingdom to be a part of the King's Harem, what emotions would that have engendered in our souls? What if the KING had loved me more than any woman in the land? Would I have wanted to destroy that love? She remembered VASHTI! Would I have *"chanced"* death for the sake of my countrymen? Would you?

I am sure ESTHER had many such thoughts. She knew the danger of approaching the king without first being called upon to do so. She knew of his recent decree to have the Jews slaughtered. Would he kill her on the spot? He had not called for her for thirty days. All of these fears ran rampant in the heart of the queen. Nevertheless, ESTHER stood in the outer court–waiting. She had a mission to fulfill. Do you?

"WE DON'T HAVE TO STAY ALIVE!"
We only have to be faithful to the Lord Jesus Christ.
It seems, all our life, we endeavor to stay alive.
This is to no avail unless we yearn to live for Him! (ggs)

Today's Bible Blessing　　　　　　　　　　*June 1*

Esther 9:1–Job 3:15
ALL WAS WELL IN THE LAND OF UZ

Job 1:1

"There was a man in the land of Uz, whose name was Job. . ."

We must remember, as we look at the BOOK OF JOB, that Job and his family and friends lived during the time of Genesis. He lived in UZ which was between DAMASCUS on the North and EDOM on the South. Some feel he lived during Solomon's time–but I go along with the Genesis period. For all we know, Job may have known Abraham personally or some of his children. It does help us to understand the people in this Bible book when we contemplate the world in the time of Genesis.

One of the highlights of this account is the certainty we feel that Job, though suffering, *"feared God"* and *abstained from evil.* He was very concerned about the spiritual welfare of himself, his wife, and his children. We know this for often he offered burnt sacrifices on his and their behalf. Oh, that we had more fathers and heads of families to care that much about the spiritual welfare of their sons and daughters.

Right off, we realized that Job was a successful man like Abraham was. Verse three of chapter one tells us that Job was the greatest of all men of the East. Job owned 7,000 sheep, 3,000 cattle, and 500 yoke of oxen. (I think that would be 1,000 oxen.) He and his wife had seven sons and three daughters, as well as household servants and hired hands. I take it that our man was a diligent, hard worker. From the contents of this first chapter, I see that he trained his sons well. They had homes and property and livestock, too. At first blush, it appeared that Job had everything for which to live. He was rich, had a faithful wife, and had godly children who got along with each other. He and his offspring had beautiful homes and they had an excellent standing in the community. He continually praised God for His goodness in his life. What more could he ask? Then life changed. It never was the same.

Sometimes we see people we know who appear to have no major problems in their lives. They earn money easily. They own houses, fancy cars, and boats–maybe even an airplane. Their lives go along merrily without a hitch. Many of these people have no time for God. That doesn't seem to affect them or their financial progress. They are healthy. They are robust. They play golf all the time.

Then there are others who have one physical ailment after the other. Medical bills swamp them. They can't walk. They can't work. They have crippled children. Mental retardation or illness hits them hard. They experience deaths in the family Some of these people love the Lord Jesus Christ. Yet, they suffer one upset after another. It is hard to fathom the differences between the two types of families. The family that disregards God prospers and the family that trusts in Him suffers.

For years Job was one of those men who had one of those families where tragedy never hit. All was right with the world at Job's house! I wonder if people noticed. But–*"someone"* did notice. He saw all the *"goodness"* and *"happiness"* at the Job household. That *"someone"* was SATAN! Having been one of the lead angels, an archangel, in the past, he was familiar with the Courts on High. One day he presented himself before God. He and God had a conversation about Job. It was then that God asked Satan, *"Have you noticed my servant Job?"* God said that Job was a *"perfect"* and *"upright"* man! What a compliment from the mouth of *The Almighty*!

That was the beginning of Job's troubles!

"THERE IS NONE WHO CARES BUT THE LORD"
(Psalm 73:25)
There is NONE upon the earth but Thee who careth for me!
None have I in Heaven but Thee,
This is enough, for He has said,
"THE LORD IS MY HELPER"
and *"He careth for you."*
Those dear friends who care, care only for an hour at the most,
for they, also, have cares.
But THOU, LORD, art my Portion forever—
today, and tomorrow.
(ggs)

Today's Bible Blessing   *June 2*

Job 3:16–Job 6:26
SUDDEN LOSSES

Job 1:21

"Naked came I out of my mother's womb, and naked shall I return . . . the LORD gave and the LORD hath taken away. blessed be the name of the LORD."

Yesterday we saw that God and Satan were having a conversation in the courts of Heaven concerning Job. Satan mentioned that God had built a *"protective hedge"* about the man making it impossible for trouble to touch Job. It may have been true, because God said that Satan could touch Job's property and children but not Job's person. It was comforting for me to read of this *"protective care"* that Job had directly from the hand of God. Think what some of the conflicts of life would be if the Christians did not have such protection. If we think we have problems now, what would it be like if God said to Satan concerning us, *"Go get her!"* Or *"Hurt that man over there!"*

Yet, some of the believer's sicknesses, deaths, troubles—such as flood and fires—may be directly due to Satan or his emissary's prodding in our lives, permitted from the hand of God for testing. Testing is not always fun. Sometimes there is no pain in the testing because of the strength of that being tested. A bridge tested by a heavy railroad engine passing over it, has no pain. The bridge was strong. It withstood the engine for it could bear the test without strain. But, other *"tests"* such as a tree in a storm can be strained and break branches. Or the tree may stand the test. Other *"tests"* tear the object or person to pieces causing lifelong harm. We see in Job 1:11-19 the greatest shock a father can imagine.

Now comes the beginning of Job's tests. We must keep in mind that God permitted them in Job's life, as He permits them in our lives, too. His oxen were captured by the Sabeans. Stunned, Job could barely comprehend. Suddenly another messenger came. He said all of Job's seven thousand sheep were burned to death. How could that happen? Perhaps Job sat down–dazed. Then someone announced that three bands of Chaldeans took his camels, slaying the camel-men in the process. All his servants were killed. He could barely comprehend. Shock upon shock!

Another messenger ran to Job's side. He gave the news that Job's children were dead! His sons and daughters were eating in one of the son's homes. Then the house fell upon them. All were killed. **I don't know where Mrs. Job was.** Had she been standing next to Job when the messengers arrived? I am sure that the news that *ALL* her children had died, knocked her off her feet. No matter when she heard it, nor how she heard it, the declaration must have collapsed her body on the spot. I can see her stooped to the ground in grief and utter disbelief! Perhaps she even fainted. It is bad enough to lose your possessions–but to lose all your children in death! ALL TEN GONE? How could it be?

Job tore his clothes and declared, *THE LORD GAVE, AND THE LORD HATH TAKEN AWAY–BLESSED BE THE NAME OF THE LORD* (Job 1: 21). How can a man make such a statement when his children lie dead at his feet and when every earthly possession had perished? I don't really know. Except there are some truths that we know and that we believe. One of them, for the believer in Jesus Christ, is that He is in charge. No matter what comes upon us, He is there. He cares even when we don't feel that He does. He would not let anything touch us that He does not permit. We see this clearly in the book of Job.

Later we read that SATAN smote Job with sores from the top of his head to the soles of his feet. God knew it was going to happen. He permitted it. Job's wife had "had it"! Life did not look all glorious anymore. Job wished he'd never been born. He did not want to hear one note of joy.

Job was in despair. Still he trusted God!

"MY TEARS"
(II Kings 20:5)
My tears? Are they not in Thy Book?
He keeps a record of my grief.
He is a *"man of sorrows"* and acquainted with grief,
Touched with the feelings of my infirmities.
God said to King Hezekiah, *"I have seen thy tears!"*
God gives us tears to wash away the pain and disappointments.
QUESTION: WHAT ARE YOU CRYING ABOUT TODAY?
(ggs)

Today's Bible Blessing   *June 3*
Job 6:27–Job 10:3
JOB'S FOOLISH, GRIEVING WIFE
Job 3:21

"Which long for death, but it cometh not, and dig for it more than for hid treasures."

Here we are again looking at the man named JOB whom God had watched and protected for many years. If you remember, Satan pointed out that JOB was such a godly man because God had put a *"hedge"* around him and his family. I remember when touring Northern Ireland's country-side—or was it England?—that we were shown strong hedges that circled a sheep pasture. I'm sorry I can't remember the name of those hedges. We were told that it was practically impossible for an animal or a person to penetrate that growth. Just think what it must have been like for JOB to be surrounded by *God's Guard* all of his adult life!

Perhaps that was why Job was flabbergasted that his life had been destroyed by God's granting Satan permission to touch Job. We read what happened when *"the hedge"* was removed. Satan's touch was awful and aggressive—not gentle as with Eve in the Garden. It seemed that JOB was covered with boils from head to toe. As I meditated upon that physical hardship, I wondered why Satan chose *"boils."* Why did he not choose a broken hip or arm? Why did he not doom the man with *tuberculosis*? It could have been a *skin cancer*. Was this disease like *smallpox,* or measles? Was it something like a *"staph infection"*? Does it creep to distraction all over the body and into the blood system? We do not know.

Perhaps God did not reveal the exact disease so that, when we are physically afflicted, we can think our sufferings are the same as JOB's. I believe that is why we are not told the exact illness of the Apostle Paul. He called it his *"thorn in the flesh"* (II Corinthians 12:7-8). Notice that Paul, too, attributed his incurable illness to the *"messenger of Satan."* He was not ill because of sin. He was ill because God permitted an *illness* to touch him. My friend, *rest assured*, that though you are ill and miserable, God knows! There are no surprises to Him.

JOB'S GRIEVING WIFE was beside herself. We can tell this is true by her advice to her ailing husband. She said, *"Curse God and die!"* (See Job 2:9.) Job understood his wife's concerns. I feel certain that she regretted her sharp tongue in future years. She watched her beloved husband suffer physically and emotionally. She had never seen a man so distraught. *They had buried ten children—remember?* Perhaps the burial plot was on their own property. *JOB rebuked his wife.* Even in his horrible pain, he took his husbandly responsibility to set her straight. JOB told his wife that she talked like the *"foolish women."* I'm sure that did not go over too well with her. There must have been many of those *"foolish women"* in their circle of friends. Mrs. Job knew who they were. She knew how they acted. We never heard of any more rebellion from her mouth for the rest of this book.

THE BOOK OF JOB IS A BOOK DEVOTED TO HUMAN SUFFERING and MENTAL PAIN. It changed Mrs. Job's whole life for the rest of her life. What do you think? **Job had wished he'd never been born! He longed for death. He cried, I *"long for death, but it cometh not, and dig for it more than for hid treasures."* Death did not come! Yet!**

"LIFE IS BUT A DAY TO GOD"
(Job 14:5)
The longest life is but a day to God!
A long life does not necessarily mean enjoyment.
A long life is not necessarily a profitable life.
Which is more beautiful? A rose bud or a full bloom rose?
Sometimes I think all life is short.
God knows the number of our days. (ggs)

Today's Bible Blessing   *June 4*

Job 10:4–Job 13:21
THE CRY OF A DEPRESSED MAN
Job 9:2b

" . . . how should a man be just with God?"

We notice as we read the BOOK OF JOB that much of the narrative is from conversations that Job had with his four friends. Their names are ELIPHAZ, the Temanite, BILDAD, the Shuhite, ZOPHAR, the Naamathite; and lastly the youngest was named ELIHU, the Buzite. We are not told too much about these men except they were friends of Job. Where they came from is interesting, as their lands were in proximity to the *Land of Uz* which Job called home. Perhaps Job met them when he was on business trips for **Job was an Uzzite. He and his friends lived in the Arabian Desert, west from Babylon and adjacent to Mt Seir.**

Job's friends thought themselves *"wise"* and *"all knowing."* We know this by the way they conducted themselves with Job. Perhaps they came to *"comfort"* Job as a duty and not out of sympathy and kindness. I don't know. Sometimes their advice was good and sometimes it was bad. They based their whole premise that sin caused Job's illness, as well as his previous catastrophes. They looked upon Job as a terrible sinner. To some extent, we can conclude that they came to *"comfort"* their friend with their minds already made up. It seemed as if they really did not listen to Job at all. They just wanted to talk.

How JOB'S FRIENDS learned about his sickness, I don't know. Perhaps Mrs. Job told them. I am sure that the whole area had heard of Job's financial losses, as well as the relentless deaths of his seven sons and three daughters. No matter how they learned of the tragedies, his four friends came to *"comfort"* Job. Sad to say, they came with a predetermined mindset that it was because of JOB'S SIN, and that, because of that SIN, God was *corrupting* Job's body.

Sometimes we, as friends, think we know it all. We think we know exactly what is going wrong in a friend's life. We spout off like *"know-it-alls,"* having a sure solution to the problem. None of this helped Job. He was discouraged already. Their talk discouraged him more. Some day Job would understand, but not yet!

Job called out, *"My soul is weary of my life!"* He was depressed. He said, *"I will complain in the bitterness of my soul"* (7:11b). Some say that Christians, who know Jesus Christ, are not to be *depressed.* How little those critics understand. His friend called him a hypocrite (8:13). Job cried out for a *DAYSMAN* (9:33)–a *MEDIATOR* between him and God. Christ Jesus, Who was yet to come to earth and die for Job's sin, is that *"DAYSMAN-Mediator."* Job admits that he is a burden to himself (7:20b). Job reflects upon his life–how it is speeding along. It is short. It is full of troubles and pains. He complained that his days were swifter than a weaver's shuttle (7:6). BILDAD agrees that man's days on earth are as a *"shadow"* (8:9). The two men refute one another–back and forth, repeatedly.

Then out of the blue, JOB asks an important, soul-searching question: HOW SHOULD A MAN BE JUST WITH GOD (Job 9:2)? Job was a man of *theology.* He was a man of *prayer.* Just because he was ill did not mean that Job's interest and dedication to spiritual things had passed. I don't think that his friends understood this fact about their friend. Job had half of his question answered in verse 20: *"If I justify myself, mine own mouth shall condemn me. If I say I am perfect it shall also prove me perverse."* The APOSTLE PAUL had the whole answer when he wrote in Romans 5:1 the following: *"Therefore being justified by faith, we have peace with God through our Lord Jesus Christ."* Only through Jesus Christ can one be justified. **HE IS THE PERFECT DAYSMAN!**

"A NEW MEANING TO ISAIAH 32:17"
And the work of righteousness shall be peace;
and the effect of righteousness quietness and assurance for ever.
QUIETNESS in face of tribulation!
ASSURANCE when there seems to be perplexity!
THE FRUIT OF RIGHTEOUSNESS IS PEACE
WHEN THERE IS NO PEACE.
"FOREVER IS A BEAUTIFUL WORD! (ggs)

Today's Bible Blessing   *June 5*
Job 13:22—Job 16:21
WHAT HAPPENS AFTER DEATH?
Job 14:14a
"If a man die, shall he live again?"

We find ourselves approaching the middle of the Book of Job. This is a true account of a genuine PATRIARCH, a man who hated evil and did good. As you remember, Mr. Job had sudden, perplexing tragedies in his life–one right after the other. Satan accused God of protecting the PATRIARCH. Would God remove *the hedge* of protection that had been placed around Job's life? Yes, He would! *THE HEDGE WAS TAKEN AWAY!*

There stood grieving Job and his broken-hearted wife, *alone.* All they had ever worked for was gone! They were *alone.* That is when Satan peppered Job with boils from head to foot. God permitted it. Though this was a terrible tragedy and an overwhelming test for God's servant, it is comforting for you and me who know Jesus Christ as personal Saviour. Why? We have observed that the plagues that came to JOB were from Satan's devices. God allowed such torture to prove Job. Job may have never known that what was happening to him was permitted by God. But, God knew. The same with us. It helps explain the trials we suffer.

My parents had a severe trial with each of their three daughters. I was sick as a child and hospitalized for three years. My sister, Audrey, died of Hodgkin's disease at age twenty. Beverly was brain-injured at birth. My parents knew what a *Job-like trial* was like. Could it be that God looked upon them as he looked upon Job? Could it be that Satan wanted to test them like he did Job? THAT'S WHY JOB'S LIFE IS COMFORTING TO ME! We may not know the reason on this EARTH, but we may BE THANKFUL that the trials are ours because God trusted us with such sorrow!

As we noticed in past readings, FRIENDS stopped by to see Job. As I think about this meeting, I wonder if it commenced at the CITY GATE! Also in the past, I assumed these visitors were age-contemporary with Job; except for ELIHU who, by his own admission, was younger than the earlier three. In Job 15:10, ELIPHAZ lets us in on an *"age secret."* He said—when speaking about himself and the others—*"With us are both the gray headed and very aged men, much elder than thy father."* I wonder if many *aged men* were in the group at THE GATE who did not speak. Perhaps—as important elders of the city, they sat at the gate. What are your thoughts on this? No matter—"THE FOUR" came, they said, *to comfort him.* But, it seemed, as we read, they mostly *condemned* him.

In yesterday's Scripture reading, we heard Job beg his *"comforters"* to leave him alone. Sometimes people say the most offhanded remarks in trying to comfort. People don't have the faintest idea what you are going through. Yet, they talk like *Mr. Experience* himself.

Job maintained his trust in God. He proclaimed, *"Though he slay me, yet will I trust in him . . ."* (Job 13:15). He wanted his *"friends"* to get away from him (13:21), but they did not go! He knew they would write bitter accounts concerning him (13:26). He did not want this. Job agreed that every man that is born into the world had days full of troubles. Those few days, like *a shadow,* are numbered by God. They cannot be added to or taken away from God's plan (14:1-5).

Job asks the age-old question, *"After man dies, where does he go?"* (Job 14:10). With a note of victory, he asked his friends, *"If a man die, shall he live again?"* He postulated about his *"appointed time"* when his *"change would come"* (Job 14:14). Job, like believers today, expected a "change" after death. He was going to live on in a *changed body.* What a man of faith.

Paul, the apostle, wrote that the last enemy to be destroyed was DEATH (I Corinthians 15:26). We read further in that chapter of *the resurrection of the dead.* The body is sown in *corruption* and raised in *incorruption.* It is sown in *dishonor.* It is raised in *glory.* It is sown in *weakness.* It is raised in *power.* It is sown a *natural body.* It is raised a *spiritual body.* What a condition to look forward to!

"Press on"
(Philippians 3:14)
Short is life's race,
Stern is God's pace,
But He is the Prize before our eyes.
Press on! Press on!
PRESS ON!
(ggs)

Today's Bible Blessing   *June 6*

Job 16:22–Job 20:18
A FAITH BEYOND SIGHT

Job 19:25-27

"For I know that my redeemer liveth . . . and though after my skin worms destroy this body, yet in my flesh shall I see God!"

As we meet Job in today's reading, we see a man heading for "death." His pain is great. His despair deep. There is nothing left, no *"hope,"* no *"purpose,"* no *"friends."* He declares, *"When a few years are come, then I shall go the way whence I shall not return"* (Job 16:22). His breath is corrupt. No one wants to stand near him. He is a complete physical mess. No one is left to flatter him, to honestly care for him. Even his wife wants him to die. He longs to rest in the *"shadow of death"* (vs. 16).

His friends afflict his soul with their vain platitudes. They have good answers, but their answers are to the wrong questions. They infer that Job is a sinner and that God is judging him because of his sin. In unbelief, Job calls his *"miserable comforters"* nothing but windbags! *"With friends like this,"* Job thinks, *"Who needs enemies?"*

The truth was that Job was in *"Satan's sieve"*! But Job did not know it. He cried out to God. God had deaf ears! He said that God had stripped him of his *"glory."* He had lost all *"hope."* Life was bleak and purposeless for Job. He felt the wrath of God falling upon him. When in reality it was Satan's darts. Even little children were afraid of him. These were the feelings of a decrepit, sick, and lonely man, *"Everyone has turned against me! No one pities me! God has forsaken me! No one cares for my soul!"* (See Job 19).

Job wishes that his words could be written down in a book (Job 19:23-24). He wishes that they could be kept forever for others to read. He wishes his suffering could be recorded for others to find benefit. He intuitively questioned his friend, BILDAD, *How long will you afflict my soul with words?* Job tells them that it is God who has captured him in a net (Job 19:6). Job's pain is no different. His friends still condemn him with poetic sayings, but Job saw beyond those hurtful words to a better *"hope"*!

Then we come to some of the most beautifully written words in Scripture found in Job 19: 25-27. Job concluded his suffering statements with a HOPE beyond his ability to understand or fathom. *"For I know that my redeemer liveth!"* With an eye of faith, Job knew that Jesus Christ was his REDEEMER. Prophetically, he saw His REDEEMER standing on the earth in the *"latter day."* (Probably the millennial reign of Christ.) Job's faith had not failed! Even though his body would be eaten by worms in death, Job still knew HE WOULD SEE GOD WITH HIS OWN EYES! Job projected that he, in his own flesh, would see his REDEEMER with his own eyes! Job believed in a bodily resurrection of the Saints! What a faith! What a hope! What a man!

You and I can benefit from Job's faith, as well as his suffering. We can be comforted that all illness is not due to sin. Some illnesses are, of course. If we misuse our bodies in any way, illnesses and death will follow. Yet, we learned from this study that God, in His wisdom, may permit the Devil, or his Demons, to touch our bodies with unexplainable sicknesses. Also we learn that a human being can withstand pain and torture beyond understanding. We see that a man, or a woman, can maintain FAITH in the LORD God in spite of pain, persecution, and betrayal. If Job had not had a strong faith in the LIVING GOD, he could not have withstood the Satanic pain or the taunting of his friends' words.

Today, and this year forward, we must strengthen our faith so we can withstand, if the day ever comes when we are persecuted like God's "SERVANT JOB."

"HE STANDETH IN THE SHADOW"
(Numbers 13:33; Song of Solomon 4:6)
A Christian's dark night is as bright as the world's day!
There are shadows.
There are dark hours.
There is overwhelming grief.
There are "giants"!
But for the Christian—He standeth in the shadows!
He is The Light in the dark hours.
He comforts in our grief.
He is greater than the "giants"!
(ggs)

Today's Bible Blessing   *June 7*

Job 20:19–Job 23:10
JOB'S JUDGMENTAL KNOW-IT-ALL FRIEND

Job 21:3
"Suffer me that I may speak; and after that I have spoken, mock on."

Job's friend, ZOPHAR, came at Job with fire and tongs. His judgment of Job is relentless. It is unfounded. It is like a knife in Job's back. It cut to the very heart! ZOPHAR can't wait to condemn (Job 20:2). He thinks he has the *"spirit of understanding."*

How like many of our friends, who sit in their Ivory Towers and judge our lives from their perspective–not God's. He declared that the *"joy of the hypocrite"* is for a moment. Zophar is confident that Job is a BIG HYPOCRITE! In other words, Job's wicked ways are catching up to him! Now Job must suffer the consequences for them!

Zophar chants more and more *"traditional proverbs"* to his friend. He has the right answers to the wrong questions:

"Ye shall perish as dung."
"Your bones are full of sin!"
"The gall of poisonous snakes is in him."
"Job will swallow riches and spit them up."
"Job has forsaken the poor."
"Every hand of the wicked will come upon him."
"God will cast the fury of his wrath upon him."
"A steel bow will strike him through."
"Job's children will forget him."

How does Job answer such folly? He put on his *verbal boxing gloves* and punches back, *"Permit me to say a few words, and after I have spoken, MOCK ON!"* He then orders his *false comforters*, in no uncertain terms, TO SHUT UP! My mother always instructed me to not use the words, *"shut up!"* It was unkind and *"ladies"* did not talk that way. Yet, Mother would agree with Job. It was time for Job to talk in language they could understand!

Job asks, *"Why do the wicked grow old and become powerful before they die?"* He notices that *"The 'rod of God' is not upon them."* This is an observance many who follow the Lord ask themselves today. They observe ungodly men prosper. Their cattle produce. Their little ones are happy. Their lying politicians are re-elected. Their music is uninterrupted. They live wealthy lives, and are buried in wealth and pomp. Job rightly observed that those ungodly, who appear to have no care, thumb their noses at God to their dying day.

Job asks, "How oft is the candle of the wicked put out? *"How oft cometh their destruction upon them? God distributeth sorrows in his anger . . ."* (Job 21:17). Many who ignore God seem "to have it all," Someday they will have their comeuppance! Their judgment time will come! Wait and see!

Then Job gives a brilliant soliloquy on *Death*! One dies in full strength! Another dies in bitterness of soul! One is wholly at ease and quiet. Another never had any pleasure. But, *"They shall lie down alike in the dust, and the worms shall cover them . . . They shall be brought to the same grave and remain in the tomb."*

I, too, have noticed the graveyards. Within the earth of such cemeteries lie men of all degrees–rich and poor. One can't help but read their pretentious memorial stones. Then some have small stones that must be searched out to be found. Within those graves are expensive mahogany caskets, decorated by skillful craftsmen. Within other graves, are caskets no better than a *pine box.* Yet all that are buried are *just as dead* as the other. *Death is a leveling agent.*

Dead is just as *dead* no matter the material loss or gain. Only those who know Jesus Christ as Saviour have HOPE!

"HE KNOWETH"
(Job 23:10)
"He knoweth the way that I take:
when HE hath tried me, I shall come forth as gold."
God's foreknowledge comforts me.
He will try me.
It is to change me into the likeness of His dear lovely, holy Son.
My Sorrows! His Promise!
"I shall come forth as gold–like unto His glorious beauty.
He tries me, not the world. (ggs)

Today's Bible Blessing   *June 8*
Job 23:11–Job 28:10
JOB'S NECESSARY FOOD
Job 23:12
"Neither have I gone back from the commandment of his lips . . ."
Sometimes when my husband, Dr. D. A. Waite, speaks in churches, people come up to him to sign their Bibles. I remember as a child seeing people do this. Some folk have scores of well-known Bible teachers' signatures written in their Bibles. So–when my husband signs a Bible, or some other book, he writes under his name today's *"blessing verses."* I suppose we could say that Job 23:10-12 are his life verses.

"But HE knoweth the way that I take: when he hath tried me, I shall come forth as gold." That's what Job said. Can you imagine someone who had suffered as much as Job suffered, saying in so many words, that God was *spinning gold* from his trials? All his *pain* and *suffering* was the stuff of which gold was made. Imagine with me, the brightness and glory of that spinning room!

I remember reading that FRANCES HAVERGAL, the well-known English poet and hymnist, suffered. We are never completely told what her weakness was, even though she spent months and sometimes years weak and infirm. She pondered to her friends, *"I wonder what God will do with all the gold that is brought forth?"*

Job continued, *"My foot hath held his steps, his way have I kept, and not declined."* At first blush, this seems a rather conceited statement. As we meditate, we can see it is the goal of Job's heart. It was *his dedication* to his God and his conviction to confess, not only his sin to Him, but the sins of his sons also. That kept his steps aright. Always–even with his body covered with pus-filled boils–his spiritual goal was to walk in the steps of the ALMIGHTY! How unfair it was of his self-righteous friends to judge Job's heart-dedication.

Look at the next statement from this man of God. He said, *"Neither have I gone back from the commandment of His lips; I have esteemed the words of His mouth more than my necessary food."* Think right now what "necessary food" you eat every day. The basic foods are what? Fruits! Vegetables! Whole grains! Milk! They say that if we eat these foods, plus water, exercise, and sleep, we will be healthy. There is no mention on the "necessary" food charts of candy or ice cream or soda pop! Nor is there mention of tea and coffee.

Probably up until his Satanic sickness, Job ate well and healthy. Yet, more important to him then, and during his illness, were the *words from God's mouth!* How did Job receive *"words"* from God's mouth? Did God speak to Job like He spoke to Adam in the Garden of Eden? Did God speak to Job as He did to Moses at the *burning bush?* Was it like the *"still small voice"* that Elijah heard after the whirlwind ceased? Did God speak to Job like He did when the Apostle Paul fell to the earth by the mighty voice of Jesus Christ calling in his ears? I don't know. Job may have been personal friends with Abraham and learned firsthand of the revelations that God had given his friend. *Whatever and whenever, the words of God's mouth were better to Job than his daily food!*

I don't know how Job knew what *the commandments of God's lips* were, but he did. Those *commandments* were not the TEN COMMANDMENTS, for they had not been given yet. Those *commandments* were special for him and from the *mouth of God.* You and I have *God's commandments* like Job had. We have them in the Scriptures—the Old Testament and the New Testament. Deep in the heart of those Holy pages are sweet morsels of holy food for our *admonition and learning.* How can we neglect such TRUTH?

If Job, wearied and worn from sickness and condemnations, could esteem God's words better than earthly food, why can't we just taste a bite or two from God's mouth in our mouths in our everyday living?

"COME WITH ME"
(Song of Solomon 4:8)
"Come with me from Lebanon, my spouse, with me from Lebanon: look from the top of Amana, from the top of Shenir and Hermon, from the lions' dens, from the mountains of the leopards."
He has invited us to leave the best heights this world has to offer, and to leave the trials and tests Satan puts to us, and go with Him to sweeter things of Lebanon and Hermon, and to go to safer places than the Mountains of Leopards. (ggs)

Today's Bible Blessing   *June 9*

Job 28:11–Job 31:11
AS A MAN THINKETH SO IS HE

Job 31:1

"I made a covenant with mine eyes; why then should I think upon a maid?"

It is evident that Job keeps searching his heart. Could it be that he had unknown sin in his life that would cause God to so chastise him? Sometimes we are not aware of the sin that so easily besets us. We become hardened to the ways of the world. We see things on television, on billboards, and even worldly people around us who stumble us. The way people dress. The street words they use. The ungodly manner, in which others conduct themselves, will become our way of life, if we don't watch out. If we are not careful, all of this worldly exposure that excites the flesh will get the better of our *flesh, our old natures. It* is with us every day of our lives. If we are not watchful, the arousal of the *"old nature"* within us will cause us to sin!

Let us use Job as an example. He writes that he made *"a covenant with his eyes."* This is very interesting. Prior to Satan's attacks upon his property, his children, his servants, and his person, Job was an extremely wealthy man. He was kind to widows and helped hungry children. He was a leading light in his community. He could have *"cheated"* on his wife and gotten away with it. Or he could have openly flaunted his sexual escapades, like many wealthy men do today in our society. But Job was different. He wanted to be sexually pure before God and man. He did not have a *"mistress"* hidden away in some house by the sea. You see, Job made a *"covenant with his eyes."* Oh, that all husbands (and wives, too) would make such a promise!

The "covenant" was that he would not have sexual relations with a young girl who was not his wife. That would have been a good *promise* for men to keep today. THE *"COVENANT"* JOB MADE WITH HIS EYES WAS THAT HE WOULD NOT **THINK** UPON A MAID!! Jesus said that a man commits adultery when he *"looks* upon a woman in his heart" (Matthew 5:28). Jesus was talking about the *"thought life."* Job, too, was thinking of his *"thought life."* He wanted to keep it pure. Job didn't *want* to *"think"* wrong thoughts when he saw a beautiful young woman pass by.

Women today are contributing more than ever to the corruption of men's thoughts. Have you noticed how risqué women's clothes are today? Often the hemlines are too short. The dresses are cut too low in front so the women are almost completely exposed. Dresses are too tight. Bathing suits are scandalous as they cover very little at all. Many women look exactly like *"street walkers"* used to look in former years. It behooves Christian women to dress godly. Often Christian men dress in ways that provoke the *thought life* of women and even other men. Oh, for more Jobs in the world today, who have made a covenant with their eyes!

Usually we do not picture our eyes as *"THINKING,"* do we? Eyes SEE! Eyes do not *HEAR*! Eyes do not *SPEAK*! Eyes do not *TASTE*! Eyes do not *SMELL*! JOB's eyes could *THINK*! Probably in his early life when he began to walk with God, he decided that *he would not let his eyes THINK* upon a woman who was not his wife. What a good world we would have today if husbands and wives would have their PURE THINKING CAPS on, every day of their lives! *As man thinks in his heart, so is he* (Proverbs 23:7). Remember this: **It is the "thought life" that precedes the good or sinful actions of a man or woman.**

"THOU SHALT NOT BE AFRAID"
(Psalm 74:16; Psalm 91:5)
"Thou shalt not be afraid of the terror by night . . ."
THE NIGHT IS THINE ALSO.
"ARROW BY NIGHT": perhaps Satan attacks boldly then.
"PESTILENCE": sickness that walks.
"DESTRUCTION": wastes–deterioration (old age)
In all theses terrors, God's Words to us are,
"THOU SHALT NOT BE AFRAID."
(ggs)

Today's Bible Blessing   *June 10*

Job 31:12–Job 34:1
THE CRY OF AN INNOCENT MAN
Job 33:9

"I am clean without transgression, I am innocent, neither is there iniquity in me."

Perhaps we should stop and look again at the sufferings of Job. His physical handicaps and pains are explained in today's reading. I think we should not pass by the symptoms found therein. **Today we will look at Job's trial through the eye of the youngest of the four friends.** He came to chastise Job under the guise of comforting him. ELIHU continued the haranguing of Job, as the older men had.

Because he was the youngest, ELIHU waited until the other men ceased speaking. I personally believe that all this talking back and forth lasted for a number of days. I may be wrong, but that is how I see it. So ELIHU, looking at Job, agreed. *"I have heard the voice of thy words."* Yes, he *heard*, but he was not *listening*.

Job declared, *"I am clean without transgression, I am innocent, neither is there iniquity in me."* It seemed to me that with each insult, he became more defensive of his spiritual condition. Perhaps I am like his *"friends"* but I can't help wondering how anyone could possibly be as *spiritual* and *sinless* as Job made himself out to be. Yet, as days went on, we saw his spiritual stamina keep him alive and mentally alert.

To Job, his condition was as torturous as having his feet in the stocks (Job 33:11). He could not escape from the *misery.* Think of the pain!*—the never-ending pain!* ELIHU concluded that Job was being chastened by God. It was ceaseless. Even upon his bed, there was *agony.* His bones hurt. I have known *"bone ache"* as a child. *It is a gnawing, unending, burning.* Poor JOB! He could not eat! The sight of food gagged him. *His skin was discolored and eaten away by the angry, poisonous, pus-filled boils.* His bones protruded out of his skin. In agony, he cried out. No one cared! In *anguish*, he rolled upon the ground. Every bone in his body screamed for relief! *Agony burned the very fiber of his soul.* In anguish, he prayed for relief. His body was close to death. The grave opened its mouth— waiting! The Destroyer stood by his side. Poor, pitiful Job! How much more could he endure?

In closing, let us turn to the New Testament and read James 5:10-11, 13 and see the end of the story.

> *"Take, my brethren, the prophets, who have spoken in the name of the Lord, for an example of SUFFERING AFFLICTION, and of patience. Behold, we count them happy which ENDURE. YE HAVE HEARD OF THE PATIENCE OF JOB, and have seen the end of the Lord; that the Lord is very pitiful, and of tender mercy . . . IS ANY AMONG YOU AFFLICTED? LET HIM PRAY. Is any merry, let him sing psalms. . ."*

By the time the book of Job is over, ELIHU will be hanging his head in shame for his presumptuous words to Job, his elder. I WONDER IF HE EVER APOLOGIZED!

"SWEET, SWEET CALM"
William Blaine
Oh, the joy of knowing all my sins are forgiven.
Oh, the blessedness of going "HOME" to Heaven.
Oh, the rest, the "rest" of giving all, Oh, Lord, to Thee.
Oh, the deep sweet calm of living for Eternity.
(THIS POEM WAS A BLESSING TO ME [1980]—ggs)

Today's Bible Blessing   *June 11*
Job 34:2–Job 36:33
WHAT INSOLENCE!

Job 34:36
"My desire is that Job may be tried unto the end because of his answers . . ."

Every time when I read ELIHU'S comments, I become disturbed. Here is this *young whippersnapper* who thinks he knows it all. I will say for him, that he waited until the older men spoke. He observed the customs of the time. It would be good, if young people respected their elders like they did in Job's time and like they do in the Chinese and other cultures today. Also, ELIHU did not interrupt any of their words of condemnation to Job.

I would like to interject a comment here. *More younger people should listen to their elders!* They would be surprised how much they can learn from a grandparent or other senior citizens. ELIHU waited his turn and bowed to the customs of his time. *Sad to say, he did not listen to Job's words–ever!*

If ELIHU had listened, he would have known that his condemnation of the senior citizen was completely wrong. *I think of the newly crowned KING REHOBOAM, son of SOLOMON. REHOBOAM gave a deaf ear to his father's older counselors, and listened to the younger counselors in his own age range. Heeding his contemporary's unwise words, in time, brought destruction to the new king!*

So ELIHU began *harping* on the fact that Job was a sinner, and that the sin in his life was the reason God was corrupting Job's body and mind with such an illness. All of his findings and those of BILDAD, ZOPHAR, and ELIPHAZ were off-base. These men honestly felt that the PATRIARCH JOB had a hidden sinful past.

Many of us today *"self-judge"* people. I am not immune. You are not immune. I remember vividly when my husband, Dr. Waite, had cancer a few decades ago. Some people in the ministry thought this disease was a judgment of God upon my husband. Why? Because Dr. Waite wrote a monthly paper which expressed many of his views and comments with which all people did not agree. So they thought that God agreed with them, the criticizers; and that God was giving Dr. Waite an illness which would lead to death as a judgment of God. I felt, as his wife, that those people really wanted my husband to die!

What motives were in ELIHU'S dissertations, I do not know; any more than we know why some people *pontificate* when they disagree with us. ELIHU said, *"The ear trieth words, as the mouth tasteth meat."* This is true. It takes a wise man to discern judgment–whether it be good or bad. He said that Job lapped up *scorning* like one who drank water. In other words, *he must have felt that JOB paid no heed to all the condemning advice* his friends had given. All their talk was in vain. So this much younger man decided it was his job to *grind down* JOB with his condemning words.

A few years ago, I had a similar "ELIHU" experience. Some young women, whom I dearly loved, criticized me. It was unmerciful! They gossiped about me. It was difficult to take because I was just coming out of the hospital. I had a kidney stone that required three in-house hospital procedures. Along, with the *"stone,"* I had *septic blood!* I was treated with special care and days of IV's. It was during the *"at home recovery time"* that the women decided to correct me. Prior to this, they told me of their love. *Then the "other shoe" dropped!* It was an emotional shock! So, I can understand, in a small way, what it was like for Job to be so criticized *in the Name of the Lord.*

ELIHU snarled, *"My desire is that Job may be tried unto the end because of his answer for wicked men. For he addeth rebellion into his sin, he clapped his hands among us, and multiplieth his words against God."*
WHAT INSOLENCE!!

"RECKON YOURSELVES DEAD"
(Romans 6:11, 13)
RECKON YOURSELVES ALSO TO BE DEAD INDEED UNTO SIN. YIELD YOURSELVES UNTO GOD AS INSTRUMENTS OF RIGHTEOUSNESS UNTO GOD.
As a child of God, we are responsible to reckon (accept as a fact)
that sin no longer is our master.
We are to be dead to the old nature.
This doesn't mean we are not able to sin,
but we are able NOT to sin.
Our freedom of choice is not destroyed;
but we have been given the power to make the right choice.
(ggs)

Today's Bible Blessing   *June 12*
Job 37:1–Job 39:20
THE LOCKED DOOR

Job 38:3
"Gird up now thy loins like a man; for I will demand of thee, and answer thou me."

Often we wonder what God would say to us if we could hear Him speak in our ears. Job had this experience in today's chapter, and following chapters. It is good to hear Him. It is good to see what He wants to tell Job face to face—or I should say *from God's mouth to Job's ears.*

Do you know *where* God spoke to Job? Job 38:1 reads that God spoke to Job *"out of the whirlwind."* This must have been frightening! This brings to mind Elijah, and how God spoke to him after the *whirlwind* was over. When the storm stopped, God whispered to the prophet in a still small voice (I Kings 19:12). We can conclude that God speaks to those he wants to speak to in the manner in which He chooses. He is GOD!

What form of speech did God use with JOB? He asked questions. In fact, according to my husband, Dr. D. A. Waite, GOD ASKED JOB SEVENTY QUESTIONS. One of the best ways to teach a class is the *"question & answer"* method. My husband uses this method in his teaching all the time. Questions get students to think! Not only did God ask questions, He expected Job to answer them. God said in verse three, *"I will demand of thee, and answer thou me!"*

1. Where wast thou when I laid the foundations of the earth?
2. Who hath laid the measures thereof?
3. Who hath stretched the line upon it?
4. Whereupon are the foundations thereof fastened?
5. Who laid the cornerstone thereof?
6. Or who hath shut up the sea with doors?
7. Hast thou entered into the springs of the sea?
8. Hast thou seen the doors of the *shadow of death*?
9. Hast thou perceived the breadth of the earth?
10. Where is the way where light dwelleth?
11. And for darkness where is the place thereof?
12. Hast thou entered into the treasures of the snow?
13. Hast thou seen the treasures of the hail?
14. By what way is the light parted?
15. Who hath divided a watercourse for the overflowing of waters, or . . . lightning . . .?

The plethora of questions go on and on. The answers are in HIM. GOD is the answer to all questions. JOB knew it!

One of the questions not listed above is found in JOB 38:17. God asked the all-important query. Job was interested. *He felt close to death.* His illness was more than he could bear. He had fever. He had pain. He had bones poking out of his flesh. He had the odor of a dying man upon him. Death was staring him in the face. So I am sure his ears pricked up when God asked, *"HAVE THE GATES OF DEATH BEEN OPENED UNTO THEE?"*

For Job, *THE DOORS OF THE SHADOW OF DEATH* were closed. Job did not know why. He felt as if he would be better off dead than alive. He would have sweet rest. (His wife would no longer have to worry over him.) The care of his person may have worn her out. His friends had done all they could for him. They had prodded him with deep questions—to no avail.

The fact was: It was not time for GOD to unlock Job's final door!

"I SLEEP, BUT MY HEART WAKETH!"
(Song of Solomon 5:2)
How dull we are—and inattentive to our Lord and Saviour
during the daily hum drum of life.
Yet, how our hearts are moved and stirred and quickened
at some special Scripture, or a lovely hymn of praise.
PRAISE THE LORD!
HE GAVE ME A NEW HEART–
ever awake unto Him.
Though I sleep, my spiritual heart is listening to His voice always.
(ggs)

Today's Bible Blessing   *June 13*
Job 39:21–Job 42:17
A CONVERSATION WITH GOD
Job 42:10
"The Lord turned the captivity of Job when he prayed for his friends . . ."

God continues his questions and answers to his servant Job in our reading today. He affirms who He is. He relates his *great power* and the *intricacies* of his creation. He tells of the beauty of the peacocks and the foolishness of the ostrich. They bury their eggs in the sand, forgetting them, and seemingly not caring if someone tramples on them. Today expectant mothers kill their babies in the womb, caring nothing about the death of human life either, just like the ostrich.

The LORD asks, "Shall he that contendeth with the ALMIGHTY instruct Him?" It was God who let Satan attack Job. It was Job's friends who *"contended"* the attacks were because of Job's sin. Job admitted he was *"vile."* How could he admit to anything less when talking mouth to mouth with God? If only we would see ourselves in the light of God's presence we would act differently. God asks Job, *"Can you speak with a voice of thunder as God speaks?"* Of course, the answer was *"NO!"* God instructed Job to throw off his rage and cause the proud to be humble. Perhaps Job was expressing anger because of his judgmental friends' attitudes. It must have been a humiliating thing to face God in a *"whirlwind!"* One could barely stand up at all. Perhaps the wind knocked Job to the ground. In that precarious position, God explained life to his servant. He blew words of great depth and understanding. Job could do nothing but try to maintain his equilibrium and listen.

Job admits that all God had shown him was too wonderful for him to understand. He was overwhelmed at *"seeing"* God—THE ALMIGHTY—about Whom, he had only heard. The more Job *heard* God, the more he abhorred himself. The LORD'S holiness is greater than all!

It is interesting that the LORD did not let Job's friends *"off the hook."* They had sinned greatly by their faulty judgments. They had to confess and forsake their unbelief. Job would pray for them, and offer burnt sacrifices for their sin. What a man of God was Job! The LORD HIMSELF would choose him to intercede for his mocking men. The LORD accepted Job's offerings; therefore, God forgave Job's friends.

The Bible says in Job 42:10 that *"the LORD turned the captivity of Job, when he prayed for his friends!"* This teaches us something about *"praying"* for others. It is a spiritual refreshment for the praying person, as it is a spiritual relief for the one who was prayed for. It is an act of worship! It is a selfless act for the care and nurturing of another.

Much of our praying today is for ourselves. It behooves the Christian to intercede for others instead of *"Me, Me, and Me"* all the time. It was as Job prayed for his friends, the ones who had so maligned him, that God released Job of his sickness. That's what I think that verse means. I may be wrong.

Remember—Job had lost everything—his property, his livestock, his servants, and his children. All he had of that *"old life"* was his wife. She had grieved over his illnesses. His family and friends came to his side and *sympathized* with Job over his losses. I suppose he had been suffering from his illness to such an extent that he himself had no time to *grieve.* People must have *"grieving"* time after death or destruction. The human spirit must be able to take it all in eventually. The unbelievable cannot always be believed—at first.

The LORD did a remarkable thing in the life of His servant, Job. He blessed his later years more than his former years prior to the tragedies. He lived to be one-hundred-and-forty years old. Seven sons and three beautiful daughters were born to him. I assume it was the same wife who was their mother. His cattle and property were doubled. God could not bless Job enough! When Job died, he died old and full of years. His children lived on for four generations. Who would have thought!

"BE READY"

(Ruth 3:18)

"The tests of character is what it will take to stop you"

FEAR OF RIDICULE

FEAR OF HEART

FRAILTY OF BODY

FERVOR GONE

Be ready for TOMORROW, Sanctify yourself TODAY

for what God will do!

To Ruth who wondered, Naomi said,

"Sit still my daughter—until!"

(ggs)

Today's Bible Blessing   *June 14*

Psalm 1:1–Psalm 9:3

CROWNED WITH GLORY & HONOR

Psalm 8:4-5

"What is man, that thou art mindful of him?"

The psalmist looked up at the Heavens and saw that they were the works of the fingers of God! High in the Heavens, the *moon* and the *stars* were ordained as lights in the darkened sky. The Name of the LORD was excellent in all the earth! His glory excelled in the Heavens! The wonder of it all! Then DAVID looked inward. He saw himself. He thought of his friends. He thought of his father, his brothers, his nephews, perhaps his sons. In great humility he asked, *"WHAT IS MAN?"* I do not know if it was a rhetorical question, or if he verbally addressed his Lord. All I know is that Psalm eight is a marvelous soliloquy on *"WHAT IS MAN?"*

We read in verse 5 that man was made a little lower than the angels. The angels were those magnificent beings created to worship and to praise the Lord, as well as carry out His bidding. Yet, man, who was lower than these beings, was crowned with *glory* and *honor*. What does it mean to wear *"glory"* and *"honor"* on one's head? I don't really know.

Adam was created in the "image of God." He had no sin. He was innocent. He wore no clothes.

My mother used to explain to me that Adam and Eve were not naked, as they became after they sinned. They were *clothed* in God's *"GLORY"–THE SHEKINAH GLORY OF GOD.* The *"presence of God"* covered them. This same *"glory"* and *"presence"* led and protected the children of Israel in the wilderness in the form of a *cloud* by day and a *pillar of fire* by night. It also was present on the

Mercy Seat.

When ADAM and EVE sinned, that *"GLORY"* faded from their persons. It was very sad. What did it mean to be clothed with *Honor*? I think of the verse in the New Testament where Christian children are instructed to Honor their fathers and mothers (Ephesians 6:2). What emotion within us is felt when we honor parents? I suppose the greatest is the feeling of *"respect."*

Some parents do not lend themselves to *"respect."* Does that mean we should not hold them in high esteem? We *honor* our country's flag. When the color guard walks by, we are hushed, stand tall, and often salute. That flag represents our country—the homeland we love. Some despise the American flag. They burn it. They trample upon it. They do not honor it.

Adam, not only was covered with *"GLORY,"* he was wearing God's *"Honor"* upon his head. Every time God walked with Adam in the Garden of Eden, God viewed his creation with great respect. That was before Adam sinned and ruined this wonderful relationship with his Creator!

In the Old Testament time, to make oneself right with God, burnt animal sacrifices were offered. The blood of animals was shed. Men like Job and Abraham looked forward to the *REDEEMER'S GREAT SACRIFICE AT CALVARY.* Though blood was shed for sin, sin *could not* be taken away. It could only be *"covered."*

The man who walked *not* in *the counsel of the ungodly* was like *a tree planted by the rivers of water* (Psalm 1). He was nourished by that river–the *WORDS OF GOD.* His *delight* was in *THE LAW day and* night. What a man of God! *"The foolish shall not stand in God's sight."* God hates iniquity. He destroys those who lie (Psalms 5:6). The LORD abhors the deceitful man. He who walks in *the counsel of the ungodly,* does not prosper. *The wicked shall be turned into Hell.* The man who does not *"fear"* (respect and honor) the LORD will not prevail. *He will be judged!*

When the Christians are in HEAVEN, sin will be a thing of the past. Those who are *"born-again"* will delight in the Lord! Heaven will ring again. *"Glory and Honor"* will be restored. What a day that will be!

> ### *"UNDER HIS SHADOW"*
> (Psalm 91; Psalm 119:148)
> Under His shadow–the shadow of the ALMIGHTY!
> There I can say
> HE IS MY REFUGE,
> MY FORTRESS, MY GOD!
> In Him I will trust!
> It is less difficult to praise and to pray when we are under His wing,
> sheltered and protected.
> Mine eyes prevent the night watches,
> that I might meditate in Thy Word.
> Often, He keeps us awake to pray or meditate. (ggs)

Today's Bible Blessing   *June 15*

Psalm 9:4–Psalm 17:6
GOD'S WORDS WILL NOT PASS AWAY

Psalm 12:6-7
"Thou shalt preserve them . . . for ever!"

Today is our second day to discover *"blessings"* in the book of Psalms. During the years when I had my children home with me, I found refuge in this book. It seemed as if the psalmist knew my heart, and wrote down in black and white my emotions. *In reality, it was my Heavenly Father listening to my heart cry and comforting me with His WORDS from this precious poetical book.* I remember telling this to a friend of ours. He asked me how the Psalms could speak to me with such distinct knowledge of my innermost feelings. It was hard to explain. It still is. I thought everyone felt the same way that I did about the Psalms. Now, I have the challenge to choose one or two thoughts from this wonderful book, to bless your heart and mine for many days. **I wonder, with you, what God is going to give us.**

Psalm 11:3 states: *"If the foundations be destroyed, what can the righteous do?* I can't tell you how many times I have heard my husband, Dr. D. A. Waite, use this verse to explain the necessity to have the RIGHT FOUNDATION for the Words of God. He explains the need for *the proper Hebrew, Aramaic, and Greek Words* to underlie our Bibles. If we do not have *the correct Hebrew, Aramaic, and Greek Words* from which to translate the Scriptures, we will have a faulty foundation. When a house is built upon a weak foundation, the house will tilt, be unsteady, and shake. Soon that house will collapse. Jesus knew this. He told of men who built on sand and how that house could not withstand the stress of the storm. It would fall down. So it is with the new MODERN BIBLE VERSIONS. Almost all of them are built on the wrong foundation. They do not have the TEXTUS RECEPTUS GREEK foundation. *THE KING JAMES BIBLE DOES!*

You have probably wondered why the various so-called BIBLE VERSIONS read differently from the *King James Bible.* Some words are completely different. Some are slightly changed. Those translations have a weak foundation. Another reason the "other" versions read differently is because of "dynamic equivalency."

What is *DYNAMIC EQUIVALENCY? Dynamic equivalency* **is when a translator decides on his own what the word should or shouldn't be.** He can take away words. He can add words. Or he can change them in any way he sees fit. It is a very dangerous kind of translation; yet this is the kind of translation work that is found in many of the *modern Bible versions.* BEWARE of DYNAMIC EQUIVALENCY! You could very well be reading a Bible that is not what God said at all. It could be filled with what the translator thought God said.

Two good verses concerning BIBLE PRESERVATION are found Psalm 12:6-7. This psalm is one of the *seventy-three psalms* that David wrote.

"The words of the LORD are pure words as silver tried in
a furnace of earth, purified seven times. Thou shalt keep
them, O LORD, Thou shalt preserve them from this
generation for ever."

The psalmist is teaching us that God's Words are preserved forever. Jesus Himself said that the word of God endures forever. *"Heaven and earth shall pass away, but my words shall not pass away"* (Matthew 24:35). Some people teach that the *exact words* of God are not important. They say what is important is only the *"thoughts"* of God, or *what He meant to say.* This kind of translation is DYNAMIC EQUIVALENCE gone awry.

If you noticed, when a leader of another nation speaks, the translator or interpreter of that speech must be exact. The interpretation must say EXACTLY what the speaker has said. If it is not correct, the world will be DECEIVED! **How much more should the Words of God** *be exact* **when translated!**

"A LIFE PURPOSE"
(Psalm 119:112; Psalm 91: 3-4, 11)
I have inclined mine heart to perform thy statutes alway,
even unto the end.
A LIFE-LONG PURPOSE!
He shall deliver me from the fowler (Satan).
He shall cover me with His feathers (closeness).
He shall give His angels charge over thee to keep thee. (ggs)

Today's Bible Blessing   *June 16*

Psalm 17:7–Psalm 21:3
IN HIS LIKENESS

Psalm 17:15
". . . I shall be satisfied, when I awake, with thy likeness."

David is praying in this psalm. We don't usually think of David as a *"praying"* man, do we? Perhaps, we would be surprised at those we know who are *praying* men and women. Some brag about their prayer lives. Others pray.

He cried to God, *"HEAR MY PRAYER!"* (Psalm 17:1). *God is a prayer-hearing God.* What comfort to our weary souls. David begged God to look at his doings. *"Measure them equal with other men!"* he prayed. GOD had proved David. He visited him in his sleepless night. Even in great despair, David purposed in his heart not to sin with his lips. Many today have loose lips. They curse, they swear, they use street language. Even Christians use *"minced oaths!"*

David kept himself out of the way of the Destroyer. *"Evil communications corrupt good manners"* (I Corinthians 15:33). David sought good men for friends. He prayed that his footsteps would not slip. There are many verses about *"feet"* in the Bible. When I was pregnant with my first child, I trusted God to keep me from falling.

David knew the LORD'S *"lovingkindness" (Psalm 17: 7)*. He could testify to it. God's *right-hand" of protection* had been on him in battle. David knew that the LORD had an *"eye"* fixed on him. Never was he out of God's sight. David was precious to God and David knew it. How blessed to be kept in the very center of God's eye! David's eye was protected from the beating sun of unpleasantness. He was found in the very shadow of God's wings. Like a baby bird, David had a refuge in the storms of life!

Enemies surrounded David. They were fat and loud-mouthed. They were like greedy lions lurking and spying. Death breathed down David's neck! He prayed fervently, *"Deliver my soul from the wicked!"* (See verse 13.) God's *"wicked"* were *GOD'S SWORD*. Often, the LORD used wicked men to carry out His purposes. Other nations or people would swoop down and destroy God's people with God's approval. David had seen this often. As bold lions, they killed God's own. They carried out God's will. David prayed to be delivered from such.

Now we come to today's verse. It is beautiful! It is meaningful! It was David's heart and hope! *"As for me, I will behold thy face in righteousness: I shall be satisfied, when I awake with thy likeness."* Just think about it—David was a man of war. Every day in every way, DEATH stalked him. In the morning the sound of the enemy was heard. At noonday, he could sense their hoof beats. At night the sword sought him. That was David's life! This was David's fear. It was David's daily fare. So—he prayed to God for protection.

BUT DAVID BELIEVED IN GOD. He knew when he died, he would come face to face with RIGHTEOUSNESS! When he would meet his Maker, he would be completely right with God. He would have no sin, no stain of Adam anymore. David relished the fact that to see God *face to face* would mean he would be pure and sinless. What a hope! David trusted in the HOPE of ISRAEL. He wrote of the joy. *"I SHALL BE SATISFIED, WHEN I AWAKE, WITH THY LIKENESS!"*

Think with David what that joy will be like. To die in pain and poverty and awaken rich and pain free. To be put in the grave still and dead and awaken alive again. And you, dear Christian—your soul and spirit will be free at last from its limited body and earthly ties. As you find yourself with the LORD OF CREATION, you will discover that you look like Jesus. You will be *"like"* Him! The Apostle John wrote, *"We shall be like him, for we shall see him as He is"* (I John 3:2).

I think of our son who died recently. I thrill for him, for after he died so suddenly, he found himself in Heaven. (He had received Jesus Christ as Saviour.) There before Him was his Saviour, and our son saw that he was the reflected image of His LORD—as David had predicted long ago.

"I HAD FAINTED UNLESS . . ."
(Psalm 27:13-14)

What a kindred spirit we have with the psalmist when he cried,
"I had fainted unless I had believed to see THE GOODNESS OF THE LORD in the land of the living."
LIFE IS HARD!
Too hard, unless we hope in Him!
Truly, we would have fainted many times
under its pressures and cares
unless we looked to THE GOODNESS OF THE LORD.
As long as we live, we must live expectantly,
knowing He shall strengthen and sustain. (ggs)

Today's Bible Blessing   *June 17*
Psalm 21:4–Psalm 26:6
THE GRACE OF GOD IN PSALM 23

Psalm 23:1
"The LORD is my shepherd, I shall not want."

In this portion of the PSALTER, we find THE TWENTY-THIRD PSALM. It is the most loved and best known psalm of all the one-hundred-and-fifty. Children lisp it at an early age. Mothers are comforted by it at the death of their children. Fathers find solace in its words as they plow their fields. Soldiers chant it in prayer before going into battle.

Think of the comfort the words were to David, the shepherd boy! All his life he remembered them–as he ruled the land, as he fought in wars, as he cried at deaths, and as he sought life's direction. THE TWENTY-THIRD PSALM! Probably you can repeat it from memory even now.

Fanny Crosby, the hymn writer, tells of a sermon she heard on the *"grace of God."* The minister used the 23rd Psalm as his text. Perhaps, we could look at it now and see God's *matchless grace* shining in its words like diamonds in the sunshine.

First let us define *"grace."* The old adage says *"GRACE IS UNMERITED FAVOR."* Another one is *"God's riches at Christ's expense."* These sayings are heard so much that they become trite and meaningless. **Grace is God giving us something we do not deserve.** *It is the "grace of God" that brings salvation.* *"FOR BY GRACE ARE YE SAVED!"* (See Ephesians 2:8-9.) It was because of *"grace"* that the Lord Jesus became *"poor"* so that you and I could be *"rich"* in His *"salvation"* (II Corinthians 8:9).

Another aspect of *"grace"* is the *"grace"* that Paul had as he suffered from his *"thorn"* in the flesh (II Corinthians 12:9). *"Grace came to him in his weakness."* It covered him in death. *Grace was his constant companion!* It was God's balm in Gilead for his tired soul!

Now, let's get to the Psalm. The born-again person is like a sheep to the LORD. We sheep are in His flock and we belong to Him. He watches and cares for us morning, noon, and night. What *grace* from God that *the LORD IS OUR SHEPHERD!* We are sheep–dumb sheep! We need a leader. He is JESUS CHRIST! He is our leader! He is the GOOD SHEPHERD! Because he tends to our needs, we shall not want. Notice this is a very personal psalm. It is written in the first person.

My Shepherd takes care of me, as if I am the only one important to Him. What grace! In times of fear, He makes me lie down. At first I don't want to do this. I have my own plans. But he makes me lie there in green pastures. It is a perfect spot. It is near water that is quiet. I am not afraid. He is there. His *grace* showers me with *care* and *peace*. He feeds me with food and pours oil on my wounds. My soul finds restoration. I confess my sin. His grace discovers righteous paths on which I can walk.

Even though the Death Valley frightens me, my Shepherd is by my side. He gives me *grace* and *courage* to walk there. Loved ones die. I see the Valley. I cry! It has fears for me. I must face them. I cannot shut my eyes. Then my Shepherd moves me quickly from the sorrow. He uses his rod and staff. Sometimes they hurt me. There is much *"hurt"* in the Valley–but my Shepherd knows how much I can bear. He feeds me when I do not want to eat. His grace has prepared my food. He puts it on a table right where my enemies are watching. He bathes my wounds with oil and fills my cup with grace until it runs over in praise to His Name.

We don't stay long in the VALLEY. He prods me on. We will find more pasture land. Another day is coming. I walk into the *"unknown."* It is not *"unknown"* to my Shepherd. He *knows* the way. I am not alone. Two friends follow me. They are GOODNESS and MERCY. What would I do without them? My Shepherd provides. They will follow me all of my life. With such *grace*, how can I help but stay in God's House forever?

"THE COMMAND OF THE LORD"
(Psalm 42:8)
Loving kindness in daytime–
In the night, His song shall be with me.
He is the God of my life.
He cares for me all day
and causes me to sing at night. (ggs)

Today's Bible Blessing   *June 18*

Psalm 26:7–Psalm 32:9
FIND A HIDING PLACE

Psalm 32:8

". . . I will guide thee with mine eye."

As we begin this *"blessing,"* we are struck with the fact that all of today's psalms are written by DAVID. What a song writer he was! The Jewish people were singers! They sang the psalms like you and I sing the hymns of the faith. In fact, for years even Christians sang psalms at home as well as in church. It may have been Isaac Watts who dared to put words to music which were different from the psalms for church worship.

We read what the LORD said to David concerning His instructions. Look in Psalm 32:8: *"I will instruct thee and teach thee in the way which thou shalt go: I will guide thee with mine eye."* Where do you and I receive such holy instruction? The answer is in the Words of God! The beauty of having the LORD as our instructor is that He *"follows up"* on his teaching. The Holy Spirit works in the believer's heart, teaching and pointing to the right path. **God's eye is upon us!** We cannot hide from Him. He knows everything we do or say. Sometimes we forget this.

We had a friend named Bob. He had a good father. When Bob did something wrong, his father would *"give him the eye."* That look was all Bob needed to *"shape up and do right."* One time Bob was misbehaving. His father came into the room. Bob looked at his dad and said, *"Don't 'eye' me Daddy!"* This is what our Heavenly Father does to us who know His Son as Saviour. When we are doing something bad, He *"eyes"* us!

Now look at Psalm 27, verse one: *"The LORD is my light and my salvation; whom shall I fear? The LORD is the STRENGTH of my life; of whom shall I be afraid?"* With the "eye" of the LORD "eyeing" us, why should we be afraid? The truth is that often we are. Jesus is the LIGHT OF THE WORLD! We should never be in the dark. When we stay in that LIGHT, we have fellowship with the Lord and with other believers. That LIGHT is our salvation! He is our STRENGTH! *"Wait on the LORD: BE OF GOOD COURAGE, AND HE SHALL STRENGTHEN THINE HEART: wait, I say, on the LORD"* (Psalm 27:14).

Sometimes we rush into things. We want things done NOW! We do not wait for the LIGHT to lead the way. We stumble in the darkness. God not only wants us to *"WAIT,"* but *"WAIT ON THE LORD!"* There is a big difference how, and for whom you wait. **WHILE WAITING, *"HAVE COURAGE"*** What is courage? *"Courage is not having the strength to go on; it is going on when you don't have the strength . . ."* (Teddy Roosevelt)

As we develop *"courage,"* we are strengthened. Psalm 28:7 tells us, concerning David, that the LORD was his strength. Often, as we read about the kings preparing for battle, they *"strengthened themselves IN THE LORD."* How do you suppose they did that? I imagine the same way we would do it. They probably meditated on the Law of the Lord. Perhaps they sought out a prophet. They prayed to the LORD God. Some spread out their prayers on the tabernacle floor. Some prayed publicly. Some wept, confessing their sins.

You and I can *"strengthen"* ourselves spiritually, in the same way. If you want to increase your arms strength, you exercise. Soon they become stronger. If you want to have stronger legs to climb the stairs, you don't take the elevator. You climb the stairs. Soon you have strong leg muscles, and stair climbing is easy. The world is in a rush. We are dashing about all the time. No wonder our *"courage"* is small. No wonder our spiritual strength is weak.

The LORD will give *strength* unto his people (Psalm 29:11). The Christian finds *strength* in the Words of God. He finds *courage* in prayer. He finds *comfort* in fellowshipping with other believers.

The Psalmist continues in Psalm 31:24: *BE OF GOOD COURAGE, AND HE SHALL STRENGTHEN YOUR HEART, all ye that HOPE in the LORD!*

Find a *HIDING PLACE* (vs. 7) and learn to sing!

"HIS EYES WERE OPENED"
(Psalm 55:17)
"Evening, and morning, and at noon, will I pray,
and cry aloud: and HE SHALL HEAR my voice."
What a comfort that He hears me.
THERE IS NO TIME THAT HIS EAR
IS NOT OPENED TO MY CRY!
He hears the unformed words of our grief!
His open EAR is as marvelous as His all-seeing eye! (ggs)

Today's Bible Blessing   *June 19*

Psalm 32:10—Psalm 36:11

DELIVERED FROM FEAR

Psalm 34:4

"I sought the LORD, and he heard me, and delivered me from all my fears."

The verse I've chosen for today's meditation is a very personal verse for me. It was the Scripture verse that *comforted my sister* when she had *Hodgkin's disease* way back in 1950-1952. I remember it as if it happened yesterday. My sister was lying in a hospital bed at the Community Hospital in our home town of Berea, Ohio. She had just had a biopsy on her neck. A lymph node had been removed. She was groggy—coming out of the anesthesia.

Our pastor had been with her before the surgery. They took her early. He knew hospitals, so he was there. We came on time and missed her. We were very concerned. *She was only eighteen.* She had graduated from high school at the end of that school year. She was tall and willowy, blonde and beautiful, very talented and a young woman who loved the Lord Jesus Christ as her personal Saviour. That was Audrey!

For a graduation gift, Uncle Clayton and Aunt Lucille took her home with them to Florida. It was an exciting time for Audrey. She swam in the sea, rested on the beach, and for the first time in her life, she got a suntan without sun burning. After a few weeks, it was time to come home. I don't remember how she got home. She must have taken a plane.

It was a Sunday morning. I was in church, in the children's department, playing the piano for the children. Without warning Audrey appeared. There she stood, looking at me over the old upright piano. I saw her. I did not notice her tanned face. I did not notice that her long blonde hair was cut. *I only saw her neck.* It was swollen. It was humped-out from a growth of some sort. What was it?

Immediately, the next day, Audrey was at the doctor's office. Without hesitation, she was in the hospital for a biopsy. It was so quick! It was so unexpected! We were told it was either Hodgkin's disease, Lymphoma, or a common cold. We had never heard of Hodgkin's and knew little about lymphoma. Yes, it was an uneasy time for the Sanborn family! A time of shock! A time of unbelief!

In a few days, the diagnosis was given. It was HODGKIN'S DISEASE! At that time there was no cure for that cancer of the lymph glands. Nothing but some *alternative remedies* that worked for some, but not for Audrey. There was only radiation. *But there was "prayer."*

I'll never forget the night I learned that my sister had cancer. She was five-and-a-half years younger than I. I could not sleep all night. I went down to the living room and read a book. It was a large room. There I sat in my in-law's beautiful parlor. *I was in shock.* Already my parents had my youngest sister who was brain damaged from a birth injury. They had me who previously had been hospitalized for a long three years with a bone disease. Now they had this—*their "perfect" child!* She was overtaken with a killer disease!

I was not in the room when Audrey learned of her illness. I did not see her face. I am sure she was stunned. Yet, when I saw her, and when others saw her, she whispered, *"I sought the LORD, and he heard me, and delivered me from all my fears!"*

"HIS TRUTH AND SHIELD"
(Psalm 91:4)
"His truth shall be thy shield and buckler."
Though we may not understand, yet His Word is true!
The trial is hard,
yet the promise is firm and sure and comforting.
When we cannot face life, His Word held forth as a shield,
protects us.
WE CANNOT FIGHT!
"THE TRUTH" HIMSELF HOLDS THE SHIELD.
HE IS THE BUCKLER.
It is not what we "think" is true,
but what the Bible says is TRUTH! (ggs)

Psalm 36:12—Psalm 40:9
DELIVERED FROM FEAR

Psalm 37:4-5

"Delight thyself also in the LORD; and He shall give thee the desires of thine heart."

Many of us have read these verses and have applied them to our own hearts and lives. We have seen the LORD use them. We have felt the Holy Spirit's direction in our lives because of them.

I remember as a young person I wanted to be a nurse. My early life was spent with nurses, for I lived in a hospital as a sick child for three years. Doctors and nurses were my heroes. They were my ideals. In high school, I took science courses with nursing as my goal. But there came a time in my young womanhood that the LORD dealt with me about nursing. I remember the battle well.

God did not want me to be a nurse. It was very plain. It was a struggle for me to give up that idea. *Then one day, He took the desire away from me and gave me a new desire.* It was like a miracle! I committed my life to HIM with *the new desire* and He brought my *new desire* to pass. I have never regretted yielding *"nursing"* to Him. I've seen the wisdom of God in my life in the matter. I would never have had the endurance to be a nurse, and God knew it. I didn't!

Another time in my life, my dear husband had cancer. *It was Hodgkin's disease,* the very same disease that took my sister. *It was déjà vu!* I was stunned! My husband had an illness that we both knew could be fatal. What was God doing in our lives? What was God doing in my husband's life? He faced death! I faced widowhood! He was fifty-six years old at the time! We prepared for the new direction of the will of God in our lives.

I had seen my parents endure great illnesses in their own lives, and in the lives of my sisters and me, as well as other members in our families. I saw how they took the *"blows"* as they *trusted God.* I had them as examples in great troubles. They had taught me how to *trust God in adversity!* We prayed! *We trusted God!*

One day a preacher-friend came to our house. *His name was Alex Morrison.* My husband, said, *"Alex, will you pray for me?"* Dr. Waite continued speaking, *"In Psalm 37: 4-5, we read God's words, and the Bible says that if we delight ourselves in the Lord, and commit our way unto Him, He will bring it to pass."* Then my husband confessed. *"It is my desire to live for the LORD. I believe He has work for me to do still. That is my "desire." Please pray that God will "bring it to pass."* Right then, where they were, they prayed. **So my husband trusted God "to bring it to pass."**

I remember that day. The men came upstairs from the basement where they had been working. I did not know they had been praying. They were talking about the *"desires of the heart."*

God reached down and healed my husband.

Many years before, when my sister died of Hodgkin's disease, there was no medical *"cure"* in sight. I remember a nurse scoffed at me when I asked for prayer for Audrey. She said, *"There is no use praying for your sister. There is no cure for Hodgkin's Disease!"* I thought she was unkind and very crude. Could not God heal her if He wanted to? Couldn't He?

That day in 1985, down in the basement of our house here in Collingswood, New Jersey, Alex prayed for my husband. God heard! He always does! His answers are not always the same for everyone. My husband had many chemotherapy treatments. Some non-traditional help as well. He chose not to have radiation. God used it all. He worked it *"together for good."*

My husband was healed! *GOD BROUGHT IT TO PASS!*

"PERHAPS THERE IS TIME"
(Joshua 13:1)
The Lord speaks to an old man and gives him a charge!
"Yet there is much land to be possessed!"
OLD AGE HAS ITS CHALLENGES!
Our work is not done. Much land must be taken.
ARE WE WHAT WE SHOULD BE?
Have we room for improvement?
Is there no flesh to conquer?
Have we possessed our possessions?
PERHAPS THERE IS TIME! (ggs)

Today's Bible Blessing   *June 21*

Psalm 40:10—Psalm 46:5
THE LORD BE MAGNIFIED

Psalm 40:16b
"Let all those that seek thee rejoice and be glad . . .The LORD be magnified. "

As I look over today's reading, I am pondering which of these verses, or sets of verses, I should consider for today's *"blessing."* I am struck with the despair in the heart of David, as he writes the 40th, 41st, & 42nd Psalm. He wrote *to himself,* *"Why art thou cast down, O my soul? Why art thou disquieted in me?"* (Psalm 42:5, 11; 43:5). These questions are like a refrain to a sad man's ballad.

He is very disturbed. He feels as if deep waves of water are rushing over him. I can picture him struggling–almost drowning in the turbulent sea of mental distress. His distress is an overwhelming emotion of self-pity. People have ganged-up against him. They seek him for no good. He feels trapped and unwanted. No one understands him.

What event transpired in David's life at this time, I do not know. I do know that in Psalm 40:1, he tells us that he waited patiently for the LORD. At that time, the LORD leaned down with his ear and listened to David's complaint. In so doing, *He heard David's cry!* The very fact that the LORD heard, listened, and cared, brought about change in David's attitude. The Psalmist said: *"He brought me up also out of an horrible pit, out of the miry clay . . . and established my goings"* (Psalm 40:2). His feet were put on safe, solid ground again. His way was established once more.

In review, David tells us that innumerable evils encircled him. Not only that, but his iniquities took hold of him. His sin made it impossible for him to look up to God. His heart was failing him. I don't think this meant that he was having a heart attack–although it could have meant that. I think it meant his convictions, his hope, and his goal, to live for the LORD was weak. *He cried out, in Psalm 40:13, to be delivered.* He prayed that those who perplexed him would be ashamed, and those that sought his soul to destroy it would be driven backward and be put to shame (Psalm 40:14). In the middle of all that mess, he found himself! GOD WOULD BE MAGNIFIED! (vs. 16).

Have you ever been in the middle of a mess? Have you ever been a *"Peter"* and denied the Lord Jesus? Have you ever been a *"Moses"* and wanted to quit the work God called you to? Have you ever been a *"Martha"* and got caught up in mundane daily tasks? If so, you can understand David's condition and the shame that followed.

Jesus Christ cannot be magnified in a life that is not living for the Lord. He cannot be magnified when the believer speaks evil words, or accomplishes evil actions. Yet, so many Christians want to do both. They sin and expect a blessing. They curse using God's Name in vain and expect His smile.

David finally made a statement: *"THE LORD BE MAGNIFIED!"* He wanted a huge magnifying glass placed over his life, so that all that could be seen would be the LORD God! If it were put over your life, would Jesus Christ be seen?

> ### *"TOMORROW"*
> Don't be afraid of tomorrow!
> It is all "NOW" to God!
> Yesterday, Today, & Tomorrow are viewed as a whole.
> Looking back? Has He not led us here?–even today?
> Doth He not provide?
> TOMORROW WILL HE CHANGE?
> No! He cannot change.
> DON'T BE AFRAID FOR WHAT IS IN THE MIND OF GOD
> FOR US! (ggs)

Today's Bible Blessing   *June 22*

Psalm 46:6—Psalm 51:13
BE STILL AND KNOW

Psalm 46:10a

"Be still, and know that I am God."

One time my husband and I attended the high school graduation of one of our granddaughters. We flew to the area, stayed in a nearby motel, and enjoyed the company of MRS. COSBY. She was our son-in-law's mother. She was from Richmond, Virginia. Her name was Eva.

Now we had known Eva for many years, perhaps twenty. Yet, we really did not *know* her until this time. We had such fun together. We ate breakfast at the motel. We drove back and forth together to our daughter's and her son's home. We sat by each other at the graduation and attended church on Sunday. I looked forward to another graduation and another time we could be together. But, that was the last time we saw Eva.

During our visit, we had some "in-depth" talks. At the time, I was disturbed about a certain situation. Eva gave me advice. It was what she did in times of distress. It was her formula from God to help her solve the problems of her life. The advice Eva gave me that day was found in Psalm 46:10–*"Be still and know that I am God ..."*

"BE STILL!" That was what Eva did in the storms of her life. Instead of fluttering around like a wet hen, *she sat quietly still.* She forced herself to be quiet. *She assumed the "still" stance.* She waited for God to do the work. She *stilled* her mind, her distresses, and her hurts in the presence of God. She practiced today's verse: **"BE STILL, AND KNOW THAT I AM GOD."**

The more I think about that verse, the more powerful it becomes to my soul. Who are we to think about in the *"stillness"*? The answer is GOD! **The GREAT *"I AM!"*** The *"I AM"* who spoke out of the *stillness* of the burning bush to Moses. The GREAT GOD who talked to Elijah in the *"stillness"* after the whirlwind. The *"I AM"*—the Lord JESUS CHRIST who said, *"I AM the way, the truth and the Life!"*

The one who said *"I AM"* the bread of Life. We are to find nourishment in Him. He is the One before Whom we should be *stilled.* The *"I AM,"* the Good Shepherd who cares for His sheep. He wants us to *"still"* ourselves in His green pastures. We need *THE PEACE.* We are to *be stilled* by the One who said, *"I AM THE VINE!"* As His branches, we must find our life in Him. Over and over again, *we must rest before Him,* quietly, for He is GOD!

I can't tell you how many times since that visit that I have thought of Eva and her advice to me that day as we sat at that breakfast table, "BE STILL!"

A few years ago, Eva died. No longer do we see her at family functions. No longer do we see her beautiful face and smile. She is missed.

I must confess that as the years have gone by, I had forgotten Eva's advice to me. I did not always *"rest"* in the *"STILLNESS"* of God's presence. I'd forgotten. So today, I am glad to think about this verse again, and remember the wise counsel of a woman who had learned to *Be still and know that God is God!*

"THOU SHALT NOT BE AFRAID"
(Psalm 91:5-6)

1. The terror by night
2. The arrow that flieth by day
3. The pestilence that walketh in darkness
4. The destruction that wasteth at noonday

WHATSOEVER OUR FEARS, HE IS GREATER THAN OUR FEAR!

The path of the just is as the shining light,
that shineth more and more unto the perfect day.

THE LIGHT KEEPS SHINING!
This has always been a good verse,
but in my late years (seventy-five),
it has a been a beautiful verse—
THE UNVEILING OF HIS DIRECTION FOR ME
AS LIFE MOVES UPWARD! (ggs)

Today's Bible Blessing   *June 23*

Psalm 51:14—Psalm 58:10
HIDE NOT THY FACE FROM MY SIN

Psalm 51:17

"The sacrifices of God are a broken spirit: a broken and a contrite heart, O God, thou wilt not despise."

In the Old Testament times, before God would accept burnt offerings upon the altar of burnt sacrifice, He expected the person offering the sacrifice to have searched his own heart for his own sin. Confession was to be made to God. The offering and the confession was as one breath from the man to His God for forgiveness. God told Saul that *"to obey was better than sacrifice"* (I Samuel 15:22). Because God is God, no one can fool Him. He knows the contrite heart. He knows the folly of that heart. He knows the guilt and desire to be forgiven of the act that brought about such rebellion, guilt, and soul destruction.

King David deliberately sinned. He saw Bathsheba. He was enticed by her beauty and he called for her to come to his bed chamber. It was no accident that David committed adultery. It was planned, contrived, and carried out.

How many men today, with wide open eyes, destroy their marriage vows and *"go after"* a woman who is not his wife? How many women fain interest and practice *caring ways* toward a man who is not her husband with the idea of capturing him sexually? The answer is more than you and I can number. What is that *"power"* that causes a good man to succumb to a bad woman's wiles?

I feel that any woman who *"sleeps"* with a married man is not a good woman. Any woman who plays with a man's emotions is a bad woman. Her aim is to take him to her bed. No matter how kind and beautiful she is, she is a *vile* woman. Any woman who draws a husband away from his wife is *"no good!"* Mark it down. She is *a deceiving Delilah* with no better intention than to get her own will with her wiles. BEWARE OF SUCH A WHORE! May the woman who reads this *"blessing"* never be numbered with that crowd! May the men, who may see these words, vow to stay away from the fire that can burn his very soul!

The Prophet Nathan pointed his finger at David's face and said, *"THOU ART THE MAN!"* David was the adulterer! How dare he presume he could fool God? He cried out for *"mercy—according to God's lovingkindness."* He confessed his sin! He begged that his transgression be blotted out! He agreed that his sin was against God and God only.

Do those who commit adultery realize that they are sinning again God? Perhaps, if they did, they would not do the

263

deed. God created man with an inward sexual yearning. When directed toward one's mate, it is good. When practiced out of wedlock, it is sin! The *"desire"* is so strong that a man, no matter how he has vowed he never would commit adultery, plunges into the act with gusto.

There are no words that can explain the hurt caused by adultery. There is no way the sorrow can be put into words. *"Hide thy face from my sins . . ."* David cried! Many a man has cried. He has ruined his marriage. Though the wife may forgive and take him back, the marriage will never be the same. The *"one-flesh"* union is marred when another person takes the wife's place in a bed! Time can dull the pain but it cannot take away the memory from the guilty one or from the innocent mate.

"O GOD," **cried David, as well as every adulterer and adulteress,** *"RENEW A RIGHT SPIRIT WITHIN ME!"* GOD DOES FORGIVE. A MATE CAN FORGIVE. Forgetting is more difficult. The solution to the whole problem is to be *"faithful until death parts."*

"URGENCY"
(Song of Solomon 2:8-9)
The voice of my "BELOVED"!
He cometh!
Behold! He stands behind our wall!
He looks forth at the window and observes me.
He shows himself through the lattice of circumstances
As Jesus showed his hands and feet to Thomas;
And like the form of "The Fourth" in the fiery furnace
showed Himself in the fires. (ggs)

𝒯𝑜𝑑𝑎𝑦'𝑠 𝐵𝑖𝑏𝑙𝑒 𝐵𝑙𝑒𝑠𝑠𝑖𝑛𝑔   𝒥𝑢𝑛𝑒 24

Psalm 58:11—Psalm 66:1
MY MOTHER'S HIGH TOWER

Psalm 61:3
"Thou hast been a shelter for me, and a strong tower from the enemy."

Some of you may know my mother or have read Mother's poems. Besides being a poet, Gertrude Sanborn (ggs) was a student of the Words of God. I believe that Mother got to know the Bible because of great need. God had permitted tragedies in her life in regard to her children. I was hospitalized for three years, I've told you about this before. My sister Audrey died at age twenty of a form of cancer called Hodgkin's Disease. My youngest sister was brain damaged at birth.

When God permitted Beverly, her youngest child, to be—what we called then—*"retarded,"* **it was a terrific blow to**

Mother. She couldn't believe it! She begged God to heal her. One day, she realized that God was not going to heal her daughter. Mother yielded to caring for Beverly all the rest of her life.

How did my mother manage to stay sane? To continue day after day with such a child? To trust the LORD in spite of her sorrow? Let me tell you. **She ran to *HER HIGH TOWER!*** (Psalm 61:3).

Though her house had no literal *"high tower,"* daily Gertrude found one in the Bible. She ran to it! She sought refuge in it! She found consolation in it! From the WORDS OF GOD she found help and hope for her daily walk. In times of stress, in days of despair, in hours of hopelessness, she found a consolation in the Bible. **It was her *HIGH TOWER!***

Jesus Christ was her *ROCK* and *SALVATION*. Just as the psalmist said in Psalm 62:2. She found Him to be her *DEFENSE!* Twice in this psalm, David confessed that God was his *Rock*, his *salvation*, and his *defense* (See Psalm 62:2, 6).

Gertrude Sanborn (ggs) wrote a little gospel chorus which said,

"Lead me to the Rock
That is higher than I.
Lead me to the Rock
Attend unto my cry.
When my soul is overwhelmed,
And my spirit wonders, "Why?"
Lead me to the Rock that is higher than I."

"Trust in him at all times; ye people. pour out your heart before him: God is a refuge for us. Selah. (Psalm 62:8). *O God, thou art my God, early will I seek thee: my soul thirsteth for thee, my flesh longeth for thee in a dry and thirsty land, where no water is"* (Psalm 63:1).

I watched my mother run to the Words of God–her *HIGH TOWER*. I observed what those *WORDS* did in her life. In spite of the trials that God permitted to be hers during her eighty-three years on this earth, they gave her *victory*.

Praise God for such a memory.
Praise God for such a mother!

"A PLACE OF REST"
(Song of Solomon 1:7)
"Tell me, O thou whom my soul loveth, where thou feedest,
where thou makest thy flock to rest at noon:
for why should I. . .turn aside. . ."
DRAW ME, TELL ME
AND WE WILL RUN AFTER THEE!
In the heat of the day, there is a place of rest!
In His Words
On His bosom
In prayer
In perfect trust. (ggs)

Today's Bible Blessing　　　　　　　　　*June 25*

Psalm 66:2—Psalm 69:24
NO LONGER LONELY

Psalm 68:6a

"God setteth the solitary in families . . ."

The psalms are a collection of songs or hymns. The ancient Hebrews called them "TEHILLIM" which means *"songs of praise."* These songs were sung in the Temple and synagogue worship. They were cherished by God's people.

Today I want us to look at Psalm 68:6 for a while. *"God sets the solitary in families."* There is nothing so precious to a person as his family. Families are the core of our life. Without a family, we have no heritage. We have no basis for being here–no purpose. No matter the trouble that may be in a family, that family is a personal group of people that *"belong."*

There is something special about *"belonging."* Have you ever been some place with a group of people all about you, yet you did not *"belong"* to that group? You were a misfit. You were not a part of them. When one has a *"family"* one has a place where one belongs. If there is a family picnic and you are not there, you are missed! The *"family"* is not complete without you! Your mother misses you when you are not there. She wonders where you are and how you are.

God wants a person to have a *"family"*! In the beginning when He created Adam and Eve, he told them to have children–to have a *"family."* When He promised Abraham that he and Sarah would have a child, God was promising them a *"family."* The same was true of almost all the people in the Bible. A man married a wife. They had children. This brought about a *"family."* Some have *large families* with many children. Some have *small families* with only one or two

266

children. No matter how many children, it is a *"family."*

Even Jesus, as the Son of Man, had a mother and an *"earthly"* father. Mary and Joseph had children, making brothers and sisters for Jesus. That was a *"family."*

God sets people in *"families"* so they would not be lonely. It is God's plan. This verse says He puts *lonely people* in families.

I had a good family. My father was a *"Sanborn."* My mother was a *"Barker."* They married. **When I was born, I was born into that *"family."*** Every day I slept in the bed in a house where MY family slept. I lived with MY family. I did my daily childhood chores for MY family. I may have had friends in other families, but I did not belong to my friend's families. I belonged to mine.

Other people did not love me like my family loved me. I did not love other families like I did mine. On special days, my family would gather with Uncles and Aunts and Cousins at our Grandparents' house. That was MY family! It was not yours or the one across the street. A family shows ownership!

Think about your family today. THANK GOD THAT HE CARED ENOUGH FOR YOU NOT TO BE LONELY. He put you in the family that was right for you. It may not be perfect—no family is. There may be great troubles in your family. But it is yours! BE THANKFUL THAT YOU "BELONG"!! No more are you lonely. You have a family and you are loved because of it!

I would be remiss, if I did not tell you about another *"family."* It is *"THE FAMILY OF GOD"*! When a person receives Jesus Christ as personal Saviour, that person has another *"family."* It is the *"family"* where GOD IS HIS FATHER. No longer is the newly *"saved"* child a child of the Devil. He is a child of the Heavenly Father. When you accept Jesus Christ as your Saviour, you have a Heavenly Family where everyone is washed in the blood of the Lord Jesus Christ and redeemed. **What kind of spiritual family do you have?**

"BUT GOD"
(Psalm 48:2; Psalm 75:6-7; Jeremiah 6:22)
For promotion cometh neither from the east,
nor from the west, nor from the south,
but God is the Judge!

Sometimes we forget that HE does hold the whole world in His hand, and we fret if we seem to be passed over when honors are bestowed.

BUT GOD IS IMPARTIAL,
AND SETTETH UP AND PUTTETH DOWN
ACCORDING TO HIS GREAT LOVE AND PURPOSE FOR US.
(ggs)

Today's Bible Blessing   *June 26*

Psalm 69:25—Psalm 73:24
TAUGHT BY GOD FROM CHILDHOOD

Psalm 71:9

"Cast me not off in the time of old age; forsake me not when my strength faileth.

When we think of the psalms, we think of *"music"*— music played on a string instrument. I suppose the instrument was like the *"harp"* that young David used to sooth Saul's melancholy. Today we have read a collection of devotional poetry found in the third division of the Hebrew canon. It is called *"the writings."*

There are several verses in today's reading that refer to *"old age."* The psalmist recalls in verse 5 that the LORD was his *HOPE* since his youth. The word *"hope"* means *"something in the future. It is something assured."* In other words, when we "HOPE," we can't see the *"NOW."* We look forward to the fulfillment of that which we are looking for or expecting.

We read in I Peter 1:3 that, according to the abundant mercy of God the Father, and the LORD JESUS CHRIST, we have been begotten (fathered) unto a lively (active) *HOPE.* We have that *HOPE* because of the resurrection of Jesus Christ. Because He rose from the dead, we who know Jesus Christ as personal Saviour, will be raised from the dead also. *That is a LIVING HOPE!*

The psalmist declared, *"Thou art my trust from my youth!"* He said that the Lord GOD was his *"REFUGE."* This "REFUGE" is the older man's *PLACE OF SAFETY!* God was a *place* to run to in great distress. How often we have done this, too! When life is overwhelming, we rush to our room and run to God in prayer. We seek assurance from His WORDS, don't we?

Now the man is old. He begs God, *"Cast me not off in the time of old age"* (vs. 9). Sometimes we have seen old men or women on the street. They are poor and hungry. They feel like castoffs. It is very sad. The psalmist must have had such a fear. His strength is waning. He can't do the things he used to do. He cried out to God, *"Forsake me not when my strength faileth."*

It is very sad to see a man who had been strong and virile, bent over in pain and weakness. Still he is proud! He said, *"Thou art my trust from my youth!"* He is determined to do what he can; yet he knows that he is weak. His soul cries out to his Maker, *"Do not forsake me now that I am weak."* Sometimes men are forsaken in their old age. They are not asked to do anything. Young men think they are no good.

I remember my Dad who was a friendly, outgoing man. He was in his late seventies or early eighties. It was his custom to stand at the church door and greet people. He did this for years. Then he lost his leg and was in a wheel chair. He still wanted to be at the door and welcome folks to the services. A new pastor came. He did not want my father there greeting visitors; yet, he would send a deacon to my father's house every week for his offering. Yes, the pastor would take my father's money, but he did not want my Dad out front shaking hands. I suppose it was bad for the church image. In reality, it was unkind! It hurt my daddy. My father was *"cast off"* in the time of his old age.

Like my father, God had taught the psalmist the things of God and His Words from his youth. What an honor to know Jesus Christ from an early age! What a privilege to read God's Holy Word daily from childhood! In verse 17, the writer declared God's wonderful works! He could not stop praising the LORD! Oh, that we would do that, too! He said, *"Thou art my trust from my youth!"*

Then, in our old age, we can know that we have been faithful to our Heavenly Father all the days of our lives.

"THE BIBLE"
(II Timothy 3:16)
What a blessed fact that our Bible—its sixty-six books—
in the original language is exempt from error.
INERRANT and INFALLIBLE
CERTAIN!
A miracle book!
God used fallible men born along by the Holy Spirit!
Every letter of every word in every part
VERBAL—PLENARY!
GIVEN FOR OUR LEARNING (ggs)

Today's Bible Blessing   *June 27*

Psalm 73:25—Psalm 78:16
MY STRENGTH & PORTION FOREVER

Psalm 73:26

"My flesh and my heart faileth: but God is the strength of my heart, and my portion for ever."

It is fitting that I look at this psalm again. What is the reason? This psalm was my mother's psalm! Today's verses are the verses that she signed on her letters. It was her heart cry! We engraved this Scripture on her burial place. If you knew Gertrude Sanborn (ggs), you would know that she was not a strong woman in the natural. Perhaps as a younger woman, full of life and the abundance of exuberance, she was stronger; but as a maturing woman her strength had to be renewed daily–sometimes hourly.

From the time that she learned that her daughter, Beverly, was *brain damaged*, Mother cared for her with all her heart and strength. That strength was not her own. Her own failed! *Her strength was of God.*

God was her "*portion.*" He was her daily *strength.* When a mother serves the food at dinner time, she *"portions-out"* the amount each child needs. This was God's grace in Gertrude's life. God served her just the amount of *"strength"* needed daily. He gave her extra *"strength"* for more difficult tasks and small strength for little needs. God was her portion forever! Yes, the *joy of the LORD* was my mother's strength. There was no doubt about it.

Gertrude would ask her LORD on the most difficult days, "*Whom have I in Heaven but Thee?*" With that fact settled, she would continue, *"Whom do I have on earth but Thee?"* The Psalmist agreed; *"There is none upon earth that I desire beside Thee."*

I've told you before about Mother's *HIGH TOWER* (Psalm 18:2). It was to that *STRONG TOWER* (Psalm 61:3) that Mother went. The *Tower* was *the Words of God* to which my mother fled. It was from the *"quick and powerful sword"* that she found solace, strength, protection, and determination to keep on keeping on.

God's counsel guided her. There was no other *"leader"* in the confusion of caring for Beverly. Yes, in her old age, God led my dear mother from earth to Glory. That was the day she left her tired, thin body. That was the day she *flew away* (Psalm 90:10).

Mother had seen others flee from Jesus. They did not want anything to do with Him! Some, who had problems, ran from God instead of running to Him, as she did (Psalm 73:27). The truth was that those fleeing from God would perish in Hell.

Mother would not perish. She had *"everlasting life"* (John 3:16-19). God would destroy all of those who prostituted themselves to false religions and gods. Mother knew that. Her plea for lost souls was *"be saved!"* Some came as she told them about Jesus. Some rejected Him.

My mother was a teacher. She was a woman of prayer. She cared for the sick and infirm. She had tenderness for the aged. Then one day she became *"old."* She had a stroke.

No longer could she care for Beverly, or even her husband, my father. She was never the same. Soon another stroke hit her body and mind. She passed on to the Golden Shore. I miss her. I miss her prayers for me. I miss her letters. I miss her–yes I do; but *she is with Jesus.*

In truth God was the "strength of her heart." He was and is her *"portion"* forever!

"THE PRAYERS OF THE SAINTS"
The Saints of Old had many secrets for their life of faith
in pleasing God. But their praying was their greatest.
Some examples of those who prayed:
CHRIST HIMSELF prayed and prays now.
ABRAHAM
JACOB
MOSES
ELIJAH
DANIEL
and others in the Old and New Testaments.
THE PRAYING CHRIST
IS THE SUPREME ARGUMENT FOR PRAYER. (ggs)

Today's Bible Blessing   June 28
Psalm 78:17—Psalm 80:16
THE WONDROUS WORKS OF GOD
Psalm 78:7
"That they might set their hope in God, and not forget the works of God, but keep his commandments."

Who was ASAPH, the writer of Psalm 78? He was a Levite of the family of GERSHOM. Because his musical ability was well known, David appointed him to be in charge of the sacred choir. Even after 1000 B.C. *"the sons of ASAPH"* are associated with the music of the Holy Temple. Twelve of the psalms bear his name or his son's names.

Today's blessing is most marvelous. It is a review of the journeys of the children of Israel before, during, and after their time as slaves in Egypt. The Israelites were to *"incline their ears"* to what ASAPH was singing. They were to pay attention to the words, that they might *"set their hope in God . . . and keep His commandments."* It was important! His words were to be remembered for four generations: (1) their fathers, (2) their children, (3) their grandchildren, and (4) their great grandchildren. How important for us today to tell our progeny the great things that God has done in our lives beginning with *"eternal life"* through Jesus Christ, our Lord–his miraculous birth, his sinless life, his death on the cross, and his bodily resurrection. Jesus was the great *"sin bearer."* It is only through Him that forgiveness of sin is possible.

WHAT WERE SOME OF THE WONDROUS WORKS OF GOD?

He divided the sea, causing them to pass through the waters.
He led them by a cloud in the day and fire by night.
He split the Rock and gave them water to drink in the wilderness.
He brought streams out of the Rock and water ran like a river.
He provided flesh and *"bread"* for his people.
He rained down *manna* to eat, called *angels'* food.
He was filled with compassion and forgave their iniquity.
He turned his anger away from them.
He turned the rivers of Egypt into blood.
He sent flies and frogs to discourage the Egyptians.
He killed their vines with hail, and their cattle with thunderbolts.
He smote all the Egyptians' firstborn.
He led the Israelites safely out of Egypt.
He brought them to the mountain; the border of His sanctuary.
He forsook The Tabernacle because of their unfaithfulness to Him.
He gave His people to the *"sword."* Fire consumed the young men.
He smote the enemies. He rescued Israel.
He chose Mount Zion and the Tribe of Judah.
He chose DAVID, His servant, taking him from the sheepfold.
He fed them according to the integrity of His heart.
He guided them by the skillfulness of His hands.

WHAT A GLORIOUS HERITAGE! WHAT A WONDERFUL GOD! WHAT A JOYOUS FUTURE!

"BEHOLD"
(Isaiah 54:16)
*"I have created the smith that bloweth the coals in the fire,
and that bringeth forth an instrument for His work."*
"The future is not yet over; Perhaps it never will be.
If it comes, it may come wholly different from what we have foreseen.
Let us shut our eyes then, to that which God hides from us
and keeps in reserve in the treasures of His deep counsel.
Let us worship without seeing."
(Copied by ggs)

Today's Bible Blessing   *June 29*

Psalm 80:17—Psalm 86:15
NO GOOD THING WITHHELD

Psalm 84:2

"My soul longeth, yea, even fainteth for the courts of the LORD."

It is of interest that this psalm was written for and sung by the *"sons of Korah."* Evidently some of his sons, if not all of them, were not destroyed when God opened up the earth back in Moses' day (Numbers 16:30). That was a dreadful time of rebellion. Yes, God judged Korah and his band!

So the singers and poets from Korah's seed lived to serve the Lord. How blessed they were to be alive! What praise they could utter because of it. They had seen firsthand how *HOLY* the God of Israel is Because they were spared *"the end"* that their father suffered, we conclude that they must have dwelt in separate tents from the tents of their father—having families of their own.

Now we see in Psalm 84 one of the most beloved psalms. Music has been set to the words. *"How amiable are thy tabernacles, O LORD of hosts!"* What beauty! What poetical praise! *"My soul longeth, yea, even fainteth for the courts of the LORD; my heart and my flesh crieth out for the living God."*

These words are all the more meaningful when we consider the rebellion of Korah. He wanted to be the leader instead of Moses. He wanted his way instead of God's way. How like many of us when *"push comes to shove."* We do not want to yield our wills to the will of the Almighty!

"The sparrow hath found an house, and the swallow a nest for herself . . ." Where were the birds nesting? They had found a perfect place on the ALTAR OF THE LORD! What better place of safety than that? You and I should find our contentment and safety on the altar of Calvary. That was where Jesus Christ, our sacrifice, was slain. We, who have trusted in His blood atonement, can rest like a birdling in its nest. No matter the activity around us, we are safe.

The man or woman who lives in the House of the Lord should praise God. This speaks to me of the fellowship that believers have with each other in a church fellowship. It is a sad state of affairs when there are church splits and fights! Verse 5 says that a man who finds his *"strength"* in the Lord is happy. The psalm says in verse 6, when such a person passes through the *VALLEY OF WEEPING (Baca)*, he will turn the tears into a well. I think this is very interesting.

Even though a person delights in the Lord, spends time in His House, and finds His strength in spiritual times with God, he will have sorrows, disappointments, and discouragement. These human frailties and hurts bring tears. But, the man who spends time with God, he will pour his tears into a well like rain falling into a pool. His tears will 🕅 not be wasted. They will be used of God to make the Believer stronger in THE FAITH and in the FIGHT for Him.

Each son of Korah reached out to his God, beseeching, *"O God, hear my prayer. Give ear to my plea. O God, OUR SHIELD!"* By calling God a *"shield,"* it is inferred that the Believer's life is one of battling the world, the flesh, and the Devil. It is a constant struggle to keep our eyes on HIM and not fall by the wayside like KORAH, the father of these sons, did in the days of old.

The psalmist could have had a more prestigious job, but he considered being a *doorkeeper* **in the Lord's House, a prize occupation.** It was so much better than living in the *"tents of the wicked."* In the past, their father had a beautiful tent–but what good did all that wealth do? It made him greedy for more power. It caused his downfall and death.

Then we have the conclusion of this wonderful psalm. *THE LORD (Jehovah) God (Elohim) WAS HIS SUN AND HIS SHIELD! NO GOOD THING WILL HE WITHHOLD FROM THEM THAT WALK UPRIGHTLY!*

"ONLY A PRAYER AWAY"
There is nothing to compare to the expanse of prayer.
If we can see the inner action of God behind the veil,
wc would see that **GOD IS ONLY A PRAYER AWAY**
from any one of us.
We would see how disposed God is to answer.
We would never doubt, never fear, never give up.
GOD HAS, SO TO SPEAK,
WIRED THE WHOLE UNIVERSE FOR PRAYER.
(Copied by ggs)

Today's Bible Blessing   *June 30*
Psalm 86:16—Psalm 90:6
NO GOOD THING WITHHELD
Psalm 88:3
"My soul is full of troubles: and my life draweth nigh unto the grave."
Tonight a woman asked my husband how many children we had. We had been talking about our oldest son who would be sixty in a few days. She asked, *"Do all your children live in Maryland?"* That is where our oldest lives, as well as our third-born. In the discussion, my husband told her that our second-born died last year. As far as we know, it was a blood clot of some sort. He stopped

breathing! It was sudden! Today's verse reminds me of our son, David. He was fifty-six.

As I am writing this, the world is grieving over the death of Michael Jackson. He was called *"The King of Pop."* From all the reports, his death was from the misuse of the anesthetic drug called *propofol*, also known as *Diprivan*. The morning of the day that he died, the beautiful Farrah Fawcett died, too. She had valiantly fought the cancer battle. The cancer won, as it often does. Others died this week also. *Their souls were full of troubles. Their life drew to the grave.*

I did not know Michael Jackson or Farrah Fawcett. If I'd seen them on the street, I would have recognized them; but I did not know them personally. I did know David. He was born to me when we lived in Dallas, Texas. I remember very well the minute of his birth. I remember the beautiful baby that God had given me. I knew David. I loved David. I miss him.

To the observer, our son had a different, difficult life; but it was his life. He had experiences that many never had, or would have. He had *ups* and *downs*. One thing he always said to his father and me, *"Don't you dare say that I am not born-again and saved!"* He knew Jesus Christ as his Saviour. He felt that he would die soon. I don't know why he had that suspicion. He knew his body better than I did. He knew he was failing. He seemed to know that his life was drawing nigh unto the grave. So, when God snuffed it out so unexpectedly, I, as his mother, had the assurance that he knew Jesus Christ as his Saviour. On his grave stone we carved, *"BORN-AGAIN AND SAVED!"* He would have liked that.

The Psalmist in Psalm 88:10 asks a question, "WILT THOU SHEW WONDERS TO THE DEAD?" You and I have that same question. He goes on with another question, *"SHALL THE DEAD ARISE AND PRAISE THEE?"* How very human was the writer. He was no different from you and me. I think of my son's body in the grave. I know that HE IS NOT THERE—but I wonder, *"Shall the dead arise?'* I know what the Bible says in I Thessalonians 4:16b: *"and the dead in Christ shall rise first."* I must believe it! David is *"in Christ."* So he will rise first! *"He will be caught up with Christ first!"*

The Bible says *"Then we which are alive and remain shall be caught up TOGETHER with them (that would be with our son, David, and other risen believers) *in the clouds, to meet the LORD in the air: and so shall we ever be with the Lord."*

But what about the others mentioned above? Were they "born-again"? I don't really know, but I had observed their life styles. I will not enumerate the things we who watched, heard, and saw. There didn't appear to be any evidence of *"New life in Christ."* There may have been. I was not in their hearts. All I know is that the question, *"Where will you spend eternity?"* must be asked and answered while a person's heart is still beating.

In Psalm 89:47-48, we are reminded how "short our time is." We are asked, *"What man is he that liveth, and shall not see death?"* Skip to Psalm 90:12, and agree with Moses when he exhorts, *"Teach us to number our days, that we may apply our hearts unto wisdom."* Seventy years is a full life. If one lives to be in the eighties, one's strength will turn to sorrow. When death comes, we are cut off and fly away!! **BE READY!**

"PRAYER"
(the disciples said, *"Teach us to pray."*)
God is only a prayer away from your burden now.
He is only a prayer away from your longing,
Your sigh, your tears, your problems,
your heartaches for your children.
From our inward rebellion.
***

The Bible is a revelation,
an unveiling of God in action in prayer.
The Scriptures reveal that the great people of the Bible
were praying people. (ggs)

Today's Bible Blessing   *July 1*

Psalm 90:7–Psalm 96:4
ABIDING UNDER A SHADOW

Psalm 91:2
"I will say of the LORD, He is my refuge and my fortress: my God."

It is of interest that the Psalms—all one hundred and fifty of them—are arranged in five books. Psalms 1, 42, 73, 90, & 107 begin each book. Many of the poetic songs are written in the style, form, and expression of the fourteenth century BC epic poetry from ancient Ugarit. Some of them would be considered *"pre-exilic."* In fact, some could be dated prior to the times of Solomon and David.

Today we are going to look at Psalm 91. It is beautiful poetry! Just reading it refreshes the soul. Just meditating upon it, strengthens the spirit. We do not know who wrote this psalm. Perhaps that is good. Imagine some person who might have written similar words. Perhaps we could think it was our mother, or our father, or an older brother. Perhaps it was by our pastor or our mate. No matter, the words are deep and colorful. They reach to our very hearts. They give us faith to believe that our LORD cares for us. He strengthens us. He protects us.

This psalm was read at our son's funeral. It was read by his brother, Richard. It was read with meaning. *"HE THAT*

DWELLETH IN THE SECRET PLACE OF THE MOST HIGH."
Where is that *"secret place"?* **What is that** *"secret place"?*
As we continue the verse we see that if we are in the *"secret*
place," **we will** *"abide"* **or** *"dwell"* **or** *"live"* under the *"shadow"*
of *THE ALMIGHTY*!   So we gather that the *"secret place"* is at the
foot of the LORD God's Throne. His *"place"* casts a shadow. We read
in James 1:17 that *THE FATHER OF LIGHTS* gives good and perfect
gifts. With him there is no change, nor even a *shadow of turning.* I
take it that the *"shadow"* that is cast near THE ALMIGHTY never
turns. He is always the same and His years never change Him.

   What a place to hide! What a fortress in war! What a
strength in weakness! Verse 2 says that the LORD is MY REFUGE!
I think of the refugees who have escaped persecution, war, and
ravaging. They flee from the enemy. They run and hide.

   I remember our Liberian friends from West Africa.
When the oppressing president sought to kill so many of his own
people, thousands *"ran"* to other countries. We visited the JOAHS in
their REFUGEE CAMP in Sierra Leone. They escaped with very little–
themselves and the clothes on their backs. They found a *refuge* in
another country on an old, mud-pocked airplane runway.

   To the believer, God is more than an airplane runway
in a foreign country. He is GOD! We can run to HIM with our
spiritual shoes and be safe. The second verse goes on to say that *"GOD*
IS MY FORTRESS." This is very interesting. A FORTRESS is much
different than a *"refuge."* Think about it. When you *"run"* to a
"refuge," you are not thinking about going to war or even defending
yourself from an enemy, you are thinking about *"safety"*–an escape, a
"hiding place."

   But when we contemplate what a "FORTRESS" is, we
think of war–at least preparation for war. When people protect
themselves from a pursuing enemy, they surround themselves with a
wall; a fort. In the olden days, the taller and thicker the wall, the
greater the protection. So when the enemy comes with darts and
arrows, with battering rams, and cannon balls, the wall is stronger than
they are. It is a FORTRESS against all evil. That is what the LORD was
to the writer of Psalm 91. That is what HE is to you and me, if we are
His child. Think about it!

   To top it off with an added protection, verse 11 says:
"HE SHALL GIVE HIS ANGELS CHARGE OVER THEE, TO
KEEP THEE IN ALL THY WAYS!" What more protection does the
child of God need?

"MY CHAIN"
(II Timothy 1:16)
Some were not ashamed of "my chain," my brain-injured daughter.
Often, she is an embarrassment to others.
Some would rather not have her around.
They want her "hidden."
Just a few are not ashamed of my poor little "chain."
I don't blame those who are.
I take the "hurt" to GOD.
They do not understand that "my chain" is "my blessing"!
(ggs)

Today's Bible Blessing   *July 2*
Psalm 96:5–Psalm 103:5
HOLY, HOLY, HOLY, LORD GOD ALMIGHTY

Psalm 96:9
"O worship the Lord in the beauty of holiness . . ."

In reading today's Bible reading, I was struck at the number of times that the word *"HOLY"* was used. Psalm 96:9 declares, *"O WORSHIP THE LORD IN THE BEAUTY OF HOLINESS."* I became curious. **What is the *"BEAUTY"* of HOLINESS?** In verse 6, we see that *"HONOR and MAJESTY are before Him."* Then the psalmist goes on to say that "STRENGTH and BEAUTY" are in His sanctuary. So we observe that *"beauty"* is in this psalm twice. What is this *"beauty"*? Whatever it is, *"beauty"* helps bring us to *"holiness"*! At least, that is a conclusion I am drawing. How about you?

My mind immediately runs to ISAIAH 6, doesn't yours? Here we see, through the prophet's eyes, that the LORD sits upon A THRONE. It is high and lifted up. The LORD has a train. It fills the temple. Now I don't know which temple this is, but I do not think it is on earth. I believe it is in Heaven. That is where God's throne is.

We read that situated above the Lord and His throne there are standing six-winged *seraphim*. The Lord is *MAJESTIC* and *BEAUTIFUL*, as well as *"holy,"* He is so very *HOLY* that these creatures stand above Him with their face and feet covered. They only use two wings to fly. They must use them to hover over THE THRONE.

These creatures can speak. They cry out to each other, declaring: ***"HOLY, HOLY, HOLY!"*** Some have said the three

278

Holies are statements concerning THE FATHER, THE SON, and THE HOLY SPIRIT. It seems logical to me, as God is three persons in one Entity. This call of the Seraphim helps me understand the Trinity better. How about you?

Besides declaring the obvious, concerning the LORD, that HE IS HOLY, the seraphim tell us that the whole earth is FULL of HIS GLORY. We wonder about this. Then we see, as Isaiah writes, that the door posts shook to some extent. They must be the door posts in the Temple. At the same time, the whole area was filled with smoke. I do not know if this smoke was like the incense that burned on the Altar of Incense, or if it was from another source. (Remember, Isaiah was seeing a *vision*. Visions show life, objects, and people in an unusual way.)

We do know that *incense* represented the prayers of the priests and the people to their Holy God. Now we continue with today's reading. We see that those who love the LORD hate evil. Also, we see that the Lord *"preserveth"* the souls of his saints (Psalm 97:10). What a blessed truth! He delivers the souls of the saints out of the hand of the wicked. This is a precious promise for those who die *"in the Lord."* Verse 12 reminds the righteous to remember GOD'S HOLINESS and give thanks for it!

What does *"holy"* mean? It means "no sin." God has no sin! *"Holy"* means to be *"separated"* from sin and evil. *God is separate from sin and evil.* If we know Jesus Christ as our Saviour, we should be like the *Seraphim* and realize how sinless and free from evil the LORD GOD is! He wants us to be *"holy,"* too. Psalm 98:1 tells us that His right hand and His HOLY ARM gives us *"HOLY VICTORY!"* We are to sing about that Holiness! Just think that in the battles of life, we can have *"victory"* because of the HOLINESS of GOD! But, if we do not keep our personal sins confessed, we cannot claim such victory. God cannot face unholiness! We must practice 1 JOHN 1:9 to keep us *"separated"* unto Him.

Psalm 99:3-5 tells us that God's Name is *TERRIBLE*. That means that it produces *"reverential fear."* I think that we forget how HOLY God really is! We run before Him like He is some school mate. We jump into His presence without thinking. We disrespect Him. That is sin! We are to worship at His feet. The psalmist says *"at His footstool"* (Psalm 99:5).

We must remember to take a lowly place–like Mary when she washed the feet of the LORD!

"MOUNT UP WITH WINGS AS EAGLES"
(Isaiah 40:31)
Here God speaks of Eagles!
An eagle is the only bird which goes high enough
to sustain its position.
Christians are seated in the heavenlies.
Yet, often, we do not mount up "spiritually" and live in the Spirit.
When we are "up," our view is His view.
Our circumstances are considered from God's side of the trial.
Therefore, our hearts are able to see
the whole and ultimate purpose.
When we live expectantly, we will be able to "mount up."
Having done so, we can run the race
And not be weary and walk our path without fainting. (ggs)

Today's Bible Blessing   *July 3*
Psalm 103:6–Psalm 105:33
BLESS THE LORD. O MY SOUL!
Psalm 103:1
"Bless the LORD, O my soul: and all that is within me, bless His holy name."

    Jenny Barker, my grandmother, lived to be ninety-one. She was a woman of THE WORD and PRAYER. I recall visiting my mother, while Grandma Barker was living with her. It was night. I could hear Grandma praying before she went to sleep. It was very dear–a wonderful memory. She prayed for her family. I could hear her pray the names of her children, grandchildren, and great grand-children. I heard my name. *It blessed my soul.* There is something special to a grandchild to know that her grandmother prays for her.

    While Grandma lived with my parents at the close of her life, she was becoming blind. Soon she could not read. Mother would read her books about the Lord or Christian novels of interest. It was a precious time for my mother, even though she was very busy caring for my brain damaged sister.

    It was during these days that Grandma wanted those within the household to memorize PSALM 103. My parents didn't necessarily want to memorize it, but Grandma did–so it became a habit to learn Psalm 103 daily at their dinner table. Soon it became a great blessing to them.

    "BLESS THE LORD, O MY SOUL!" This is how Psalm 103 begins. It commanded, *"SOUL, ADORE THE LORD!"* The psalmist required his soul to praise the Lord and to kneel before Him

in adoration. Such *"blessing"* is a happy, joyous emotion. It is one that some of us, who are very tired of our earthly work and ways, forget to do. No wonder we are unhappy. No wonder we allow the cares of life to overtake us.

"ALL THAT IS WITHIN ME, BLESS HIS HOLY NAME!" Let's face it. If we were *honestly praising* and *adoring* the LORD, we would not complain or be overwhelmed with our troubles. Such *adoration* would not mean that we would have no trials or tribulations. It would mean that we were walking so close to the LORD that we could bear them with true HOLY SPIRIT JOY!

Some of the reasons for such praise are that the LORD forgives iniquities. He heals diseases. He redeems life from destruction. He crowns us with loving kindness. He satisfies our mouths with good things. He renews our strength like he renews the strength of young eagles. He executes righteous judgments. What more can the Christian want?

The truth is we have sinned. But God has not dealt with us because of it like he could have. He had *mercy* on us. His *mercy* is as high as the Heavens. That is very high! He has removed our transgressions as far from us, like the distance between the East and the West. They never meet! The LORD is like a caring father. He pities us because we respect and fear Him.

God knows our frame. He remembers that we are basically *"dust."* The psalmist says that people are like *"grass"* or a *"flower."* The wind blows upon us and we are gone. Men spend so much time and money on their grass. They water it. They feed it. They want a beautiful lawn. In truth it is temporal. It can be destroyed by a strong wind and rain storm. So with man. He spends time on his outward health and appearances, but forgets to feed and to water his soul!

What is enduring in life is THE MERCY OF THE LORD. It is from EVERLASTING TO EVERLASTING upon those who *"adore"* Him. And to them that *"keep"* His covenant and *"do"* his commandments.

Bless the LORD, O my soul!!

"HE EVER LIVETH TO MAKE INTERCESSION"
"God's throne is where the action is.
The events that shape history, the destiny of the nations,
and the happenings in nature are governed at that Throne.
The astronauts landing on the moon was nothing compared to
the ascension of the Lord Jesus Christ,
and His sitting down at the right hand of that very Throne of God.
He is there interceding for you and for me,
Hearing and answering our prayers"
(Copied by ggs)

Today's Bible Blessing   *July 4*

Psalm 105:34–Psalm 107:25
GOD WAS THERE ALL THE TIME!

Psalm 107:8, 15, 21, 31

"Oh that men would praise the LORD for his goodness . . ."

If you recall, I've mentioned that the Psalms were songs. They were the Israelites' hymns—so to speak. Many of them were sung as they walked to Jerusalem for their yearly worship of the LORD God as they sacrificed their offerings. Probably singing the songs made the journey less boring. The melodies kept them together as a unit. They passed the time reviewing their histories in cadence. This particular psalm, as some of the others, has a refrain or chorus repeated at least four times over and over again. (See the *"blessing"* verses.) It must have been an interesting sight, seeing the many family groups merging together, as one unit, as they came closer and closer to Jerusalem singing the songs of Zion with joy.

Both the 106th and 107th Psalms, as well as Psalm 105, review the history of the children of Israel. Other psalms do the same reviewing, if you remember. These three are rather long psalms with forty-five verses (the 105th), forty-eight verses (the 106th) and forty-three verses (the 107th). We are going to look at the 107th, and also Psalm 105:37.

In that verse, I find encouragement, as an older woman, to learn, when the Israelites left Egypt, there was not one feeble person among their tribes. This means to me that all the walking and deprivation had to be endured by all, even the elderly. It seems that the older folk were not feeble with canes and walkers, or confused in mind. They were able to go forth into the wilderness, first crossing the Red Sea, with vigor. If you recall, Moses, *at age eighty,* was their leader. He was not feeble nor was his eye dim. I am encouraged to continue my life with such physical and emotional strength. How about you?

We are told again in Psalm 107:4 of the *"wilderness wanderings."* Of course, that was the result of Israel's unbelief. They were forced for forty years, to walk the *"solitary way"* with no continuing city. Sadly, like the children of Israel, much of our *"wandering"* is the result of our own fear and unbelief. As usual, they cried in their hunger and unbelief; and true to His character, God delivered them! How like us were they!

Those that were shackled in iron, sitting in *"darkness"* and in *"the shadow of death"* were delivered (verse 10). It seemed many of the Israelites were chained together—imprisoned in some way, perhaps for disobedience to their slave masters. I don't really know. I do know that verse 14 tells us that after crying out to the Lord, He brought them out of that dark place and near-death by breaking their bands in two. Much of Israel's suffering, as slaves, is not written down on the page. We do know that they lived in *"cruel bondage."* No wonder Moses cried, *"Let my people go!"*

In the storms of our lives, when the winds carry our frail crafts up and down on the waves of despair, we should find comfort in such tossing. For it is in the tempests of our turmoil—when we are at the end of our own *"wit"*—that we cry out to God. The psalmist writes in verses 23-28 of such an experience. We would never see God's *wonders*, if we had not boarded the *frightening frigate* that took us into the *"deep."* It is in the *depths* of that *"deep"* that our Heavenly Father hears our cries. It is in the troubled tossing of our lives that our helpless craft finds itself in the hollow of God's hand. The Christian's troubles, which melt our souls, are the lessons of life that we would never learn if we had stayed away from that boat. We staggered in our losses. We stumbled in our confusion. But God was there all the time.

As verse 28 says "THEN they cry unto the LORD in their trouble, and He bringeth them out of their distresses."

---

*"HE STAYED THE ROUGH WIND
IN THE DAY OF THE EAST WIND"*
(Isaiah 22:8)
Even the wind and the sea obey Him! (Matthew 8:27)
Even the winds and water, and they obey Him. (Luke 8:25)

Today's Bible Blessing   *July 5*

Psalm 107:26–Psalm 112:6
GRANDMA WAS WISE, ARE YOU?

Psalm 111:10

"The fear of the LORD is the beginning of wisdom: a good understanding have all they that do his commandments: His praise endureth for ever."

Often we are introduced in person, or via the media, to wise men and women. People are impressed with their wisdom. Sometimes these men—or women—are political leaders or professors in some prestigious institute of learning. We listen to what they say. They astound us with their knowledge which sometimes we confuse with *"wisdom."*

Other times, we meet a person—perhaps an elderly individual—who doesn't look like much of anything, as far as the fashion of the world is concerned. If only we would take time from our rushing about to sit with that ELDERLY SAINT, we might be very surprised. As she talks with us, we are dumbfounded at the *"wisdom"* that comes from her lips. The years of living have taught her much. A white-haired man, if given a chance, can bring forth from his long life of learning wisdom that baffles the hearer. Neither of these people is known beyond their own back yards; yet, as they talk about world affairs, we are in wonder at their knowledge and following wisdom.

The letter-writer named James talks about *"wisdom."* He wrote in his letter (James 1:5):

> *"If any of you lack wisdom, let him ask of God that giveth to all men liberally, and upbraideth not, and it shall be given him."*

Our verse today is a good one (Psalm 111:10). It answers the questions, *"How does one become "wise"?* And *"When does 'wisdom' begin?"* Wisdom begins by having a GOOD UNDERSTANDING of the Bible! A person, who claims to love the LORD GOD and is a born-again Christian, should get to know the Bible. It is a treasure of information to make one wise!

It is from the precious BOOK, we call THE BIBLE, that a *"believer"* discovers the *"fear of the LORD."* It is from that *"reverential fear of God,"* that *"wisdom"* comes! That is what today's Bible verse tells us: **THE FEAR OF THE LORD IS THE BEGINNING OF WISDOM!**

Without the Words of God, there is no wisdom and absolutely no BEGINNING of wisdom! People don't seem to understand this fact. I talk with many people in airports and on planes as I travel all over the place. I am really taken back when I discover they know nothing of God's Words! Nothing! And they claim to be educated individuals. Such a loss! Such a lack of *"wisdom that is from above"*!

I remember my Grandmother. She was not educated past a few grades in school—fourth or fifth, I suppose. Yet, she was a very bright woman. Anyone that knew Grandma would call her *"smart."* During the GREAT DEPRESSION YEARS of the 1930's, she made money for her family. She became *a seamstress* and *a baker.* She took the skills she had and applied them to her need. Also, Grandma studied her Bible. She knew the Word. She introduced people to the Lord Jesus as Saviour. Until the little, newly-formed church had a man who could be the treasurer, Grandma kept the books and wrote the checks. To talk with her, the wisdom of her years came out of her mouth. I am sure you know people like Grandma Barker. She was a woman who became *"WISE"* by keeping God's commandments.

How wise are you?

"HE IS MINE"
(Song of Solomon 2:16-17)
My BELOVED is mine–
Until the day break and the shadows flee.
This is one of the most beautiful confidences we may have.
Nothing else is truly mine—only loaned.
BUT HE IS MINE! (ggs)

Today's Bible Blessing　　　　　　　　　　　*July 6*

Psalm 112:7–Psalm 118:25

A JOYFUL MOTHER OF CHILDREN

Psalm 113:9

"He maketh the barren woman to keep house, and to be a joyful mother of children. Praise ye the LORD."

Every time I read this verse in Psalm 113:9, I think of one of my daughters-in-law. How she wanted children! For some reason, the Lord did not let her have babies. It was a great grief to her. All her friends were having children. This was extremely difficult for her to bear. *Certainly God would give her the desire of her heart.* But–he did not! Not then!

So–after several years of praying and waiting and waiting and praying, *she and our son adopted a child.* Adoption does not come cheap, you know. They saved their money so they could pay for such an acquisition.

One day they were called to the adoption agency. *Their baby was there.* Their *newborn* was ready to go *"home"* with them. *"Home"* was never the same from that day on. That was an exciting day—the day that BABY BETH was put in my daughter-in-law's arms. I was not there, but I can imagine the joy. All the hurtful waiting to be a mother was over. In her arms was the most beautiful baby she had ever seen! The baby was precious. She was round and cuddly. She nestled in her *"mother's"* arms. It was where the baby belonged. OUR GRANDDAUGHTER WAS *"HOME!!"*

Our son was happy. He, too, had wanted parenthood. He, too, felt the *sting* of no children. His heart bounded with joy! His face told the story. It beamed with delight. Their baby was here!

They took her home. They loved her. They nurtured her. They told her about the LORD JESUS CHRIST. They protected her from evil. They watched her mature. They watched her grow tall and beautiful. They hurt when she rebelled–but they loved her still. She nearly died from an automobile accident. Time stood still! She lingered between life and death. God spared her life. She was well again. She married. She has a good husband! She has a home of her own. She is the mother of children herself. What joy BABY BETH brought to us! We could not love her more if she had been born from her mother's womb!

Why do I tell you this true story? I am writing about this because the LORD made my *barren* daughter-in-law *to keep house*. SHE BECAME A JOYFUL MOTHER OF CHILDREN! And now grandchildren! God answered her prayer. He answered our son's prayer, too. Yes, she became a mother.

Some dear, young woman chose to carry her baby to *full term*. That young girl chose LIFE instead of DEATH. She took the *"sting"* of being *an unmarried mother* to give our granddaughter LIFE! I do not know who the birth-mother is. But I do know *THE MOTHER* who cared for that birth-mother's baby all these years. I do know *THE BABY* who grew up to be a lovely woman, wife, and mother. With the psalmist I say *PRAISE YE THE LORD!*

Look at Psalm 115:14 and rejoice! The psalmist wrote *"The LORD shall increase you more and more, you and your children."* Now my daughter-in-law is a grandmother. Now *BETH* has four babies of her own. It is fun to see the *"barren woman"* as a grandmother, loving the babies that her daughter has born.

PRAISE YE THE LORD! (Psalm 113:9)

"MY HEART WAKETH"
(Song of Solomon 5:2)
I sleep, but my heart waketh.
I am lazy, drowsy, lethargic, lazy in His service;
but I am saved.
I do love Him.
Yet, my heart sleepest oft.
Slothful in time of harvest. (Proverbs 24:30-31)
Sometimes I am weary in body, but my heart is awake
to the call of my Lord and fellow believers. (ggs)

Today's Bible Blessing   *July 7*

Psalm 118:26–Psalm 119:81
HOW TO KEEP CLEAN

Psalm 119:9-11
"Wherewithal shall a young man cleanse his way? By taking heed thereto according to thy word."

We now come to the longest psalm, as well as the longest chapter in the Bible. There are 176 verses in this psalm. None of the verses are very long. They are pithy and to the point. In fact, there are only eight verses in each of the twenty-two sections. Heading each one of the sections is a Hebrew letter, written out from the Hebrew alphabet. Of interest, each verse in each section begins with the letter of the Hebrew alphabet that heads those eight verses. Bibles have the letter written out, and some Bibles have the actual Hebrew symbol for that letter, too. This is an interesting feature of the psalm. Enjoy it as you read it.

Today our *"blessing"* begins with an important question. *"WHEREWITHAL SHALL A YOUNG MAN CLEANSE HIS WAY?"* In other words, *"How is a young fellow going to keep his life clean?"* The world is a filthy place! There are many temptations that can take a man in the wrong direction. He (or she) could be tempted sexually. He could fall into drunkenness. He could smoke pot or take drugs. He could fall into bad language and street talk.

We have all known dear little boys with much potential who grew up to be degenerate men. It is sad! Also, we know good, clean men who expose themselves to temptations, succumbing to a sinful lifestyle. Many a man comes from a good home, only to become—like the Prodigal son—seeking his fortune in the world. Once away from home, he dabbles in sin. It is then he finds himself in dire straits—ashamed—but caught in the trap of Satan.

How is a young man to cleanse His way? How? God does not let a question like that go unanswered. The answer is *"by taking heed thereto according to Thy word."* The Words of God tell a man how to live. *"Abstain from fleshly lusts which war against the soul" (I Peter 2:11). "Flee also youthful lusts!"* (See II Timothy 2:22.) *"Love not the world neither the things that are in the world!"* (See I John 2:15.) *"Trust in the LORD with all thine heart and lean not unto thine own understanding"* (Proverbs 3:5) and *"Abstain from fornication"* (I Thessalonians 4:3).

You and I could name talented men with much potential for the LORD who have succumbed to a woman's wiles. The same for some women! In so doing, they have ruined their marriages, their lives, their goals, and their testimonies for the Lord. Some are forgiven by their mates and families; but there is always a scar, no matter how much *"mercy"* was given. You have seen men take a drink of wine, and end up as a drunk on the street corner, begging for money. You have seen women drugged and staggering, prostituting their bodies for drug money. This was not what their mothers had in mind the day they gave birth. But this is what he or she has become because he or she did not *"take heed"* to what the Words of God told them to do and not to do.

"With my whole heart have I sought thee, O let me not wander from thy commandments!" (Psalm 119:10). This is the plea of the psalmist. *"God, do not let me wander from Thy Word!"* It is a heart-determination for a person to stay true to the verities of

Scripture. Don't think that you are so strong that you will not trip over a sin that will destroy your life. You are not strong! It is only God who is strong! Put blinders on your eyes and stuff your ears with the Words of God. Otherwise, you will be like one of those derelicts, too.

"Thy word have I hid in mine heart, that I might not sin against thee" (vs. 11). Please don't be like some I know who can quote Scripture till it comes out of their ears and read their Bibles daily; yet, they have found themselves in adulteress situations. The Bible must be in the HEART—not in the HEAD. No one is that strong that he can dabble in fire and not be burned! Please take today's *"blessing"* seriously.

Do not be found numbered with the transgressors. It is a long road back to home when this happens. Believe me!

"OUR SPEECH"
(Proverbs 25:11; Proverbs 15:23)
"You are the master of the unspoken word!
Once it is out of our mouth, you are a slave." (copied)
SPEAK THE TRUTH IN LOVE—always with grace.
"A word fitly spoken is like apples of gold in pictures of silver."
"A word spoken in season, how good it is!" (ggs)

Today's Bible Blessing   *July 8*
Psalm 119:82–Psalm 119:166
LIGHT FROM THE "FOREVER" WORD

Psalm 119: 89
"For ever, O LORD, thy word is settled in heaven."

There are several verses that I find interesting for today's *"Blessing."* Perhaps they stand out for you also. The first one is in the section that has the Hebrew letter *"LAMED"* at the beginning of its eight-verse-section. So that means Psalm 119:89 begins with the letter *"LAMED."* If I knew how to write the Hebrew alphabet, I would do so for you.

This is an important verse for the permanency of the Scriptures. The psalmist here calls it *"THY WORD."* The verse says, *"FOR EVER, O LORD, THY WORD IS SETTLED IN HEAVEN."* Think about this! If God's Word is settled in Heaven forever, it is permanent! It cannot be changed. Right? When the Holy Spirit moved upon the writers of Scripture, he was writing—through the pens of specially chosen men—to write words that were already written in Heaven.

I never really thought about this in such depth before. *"For ever"* is forever! *"For ever"* was always. There is only one conclusion that can be made. The original Hebrew and Greek Words (some Aramaic also) that the writers of the Words of Scripture wrote were from the mind of God. They were words that were always in eternity! Think about that! It gives me chills! The Words were from the *"breath of God"*! That is called *INSPIRATION*!

It is that very same *"forever"* WORD that the psalmist declares in verse 105: *THY WORD IS A LAMP UNTO MY FEET, AND A LIGHT UNTO MY PATH!* Think about it! The very WORD that was FOREVER settled in Heaven became a LAMP and a LIGHT to the psalmist. I wish that I knew the writer of this psalm. How good it would be to talk with him; but no name is associated with it.

Today in our BIBLE FOR TODAY THEOLOGY CLASS, the teacher, DANIEL WAITE, was talking about the olden days when there were no street lights—electric or oil. At night on a moonless night, it was extremely dark! A person could not see his hand in front of his face. Evil robbers would attack those who walked in such blackness. It was frightening. In those days, certain people were hired to be TORCH BEARERS. They held their fiery torches high so people could see the pathway. The torch bearers walked along with people in the darkened night. Their light was a comfort. It showed them the way. It protected them from marauders. It kept away the wild animals.

The *DAILY MEDITATIONS* from the WORD of God lit the writer's pathway (vs. 97). The TORCH of God's Words was held high above the psalmist's head. His way was made clear. The path ahead could be seen. His feet did not stumble in the dark. His road was revealed by the LIGHT from God!

You and I can have such a LIGHT BEARER, too. We can read the *FOREVER WORDS* and be helped. Our darkened life can be bright with His *"quickened (living) precepts"* (vs. 93). We, too, like the psalmist, can be made wiser than our enemies (vs. 98). It is *God's commandments* that give us wisdom. We will hate *every false way* because of God's Words (vs. 104).

Then we will agree with the psalmist as he penned Psalm 119:114. He declared to the LORD: *THOU ART MY HIDING PLACE AND MY SHIELD. I HOPE IN THY WORD!* Let's agree with him today and own that same *HOPE* now!

"YET I WILL REJOICE"
(Habakkuk 3:17-18)
Overwhelmed by the things of life,
the sins of this world,
the certain judgment of God,
say with this prophet
and rest in Him.
"Although the fig tree shall not blossom,
neither shall fruit be in the vines;
the labour of the olive shall fail,
and the fields shall yield no meat;
the flock shall be cut off from the fold,
and there shall be no herd in the stalls:
Yet I will rejoice in the LORD, I will joy in the God of my salvation.
The LORD God is my strength,
and he will make my feet like hinds' feet,
and he will make me to walk upon mine high places."
LIFT YOUR FAITH AND JOY IN GOD!
SAY TO YOUR HEART, "NO MATTER WHAT COMES,
I WILL REJOICE. I WILL JOY IN GOD!
THE LORD GOD IS MY STRENGTH!"
(ggs)

Today's Bible Blessing   *July 9*

Psalm 119:167—Psalm 131:1
THE HAPPY FATHER
IS A HAPPY MAN

Psalm 127: 3-5
"Lo, children are an heritage of the LORD . . ."

Today we are going to look into the psalms which are called *"THE SONGS OF DEGREES."* These songs (psalms) were sung as the Israelites traveled to Jerusalem. They are short and to the point and easily memorized and sung. I wish I could have been an "eye" and an "ear" during the assent to Jerusalem. If you remember Jesus, as a young lad of twelve, went to Jerusalem. Probably they walked. I am sure He sang these psalms with Mary and Joseph and the others looking forward to the Temple and their sacrifices.

We have chosen some dear verses today. They have to do with *children* and *families*. God has put people in *families* so they won't be lonely—so they have a purpose in life. What good are wealth, land, and possessions when there is no one with whom you can share them?

"Lo, children are an heritage of the LORD, and the fruit of the womb is His reward!" **(See Psalm 127:3.)** What is a heritage? Sometimes one thinks of "heritage" as an "inheritance." It is a tangible "something" such as money, land, a business, or a house– that a person receives after the death of a parent, or uncle, or a dear friend. Usually there is a monetary-worth associated with an inheritance. God has a different idea of what a heritage or inheritance is.

What do you think of when you see a mother and father and many children? Do you think, *"How rich Mrs. & Mrs. Parent of Many Children"* are? Or do you think, *"What in the world are those people thinking of to have so many children?"* Do you marvel at the good behavior of the children? Do you criticize the boys for running around, climbing trees, and crawling on top of the barn roof? Do you watch the little girls sitting at a table playing Barbie dolls?

Do you wonder at the medical bills, the school book bills, the shoes that wear out, and the food demands? Or do you think to yourself, "HOW RICH THOSE PARENTS ARE!" Do you praise the Lord that He has rewarded them with *"fruit"* called "children?" Are you slightly envious at the rich reward God has given them? I hope so.

The Bible goes on to tell us in Psalm 127:4, that children are like *"arrows"* in the hand of a skillful bowman. A good father is a *skillful father.* A young father knows his children. He knows how to handle each child for his or her specific purpose. He knows which child, like an arrow, to draw out of his quiver for his assigned purpose. In a family of many children, each child has a place and rank in the family for specific responsibilities. It is a joy to see well-disciplined children. It is a sorrow to see a child that never has been taught to obey.

The next verse (vs. 5) tells us that such a father is a happy man. The reasons for his happiness is that his *quiver*–the place where he keeps his arrows (his children)–is full. I was told one time that a full quiver contains five arrows. I do not know if this is true or not. I have five children. So I choose to think that my children's father, my husband, has a full quiver. Perhaps each family has a different size *"quiver"* suited for that family; and we should not criticize those who have less arrows or more arrows in their quiver.

The rest of that verse is interesting. *"They shall not be ashamed, but they shall speak with the enemies in the gate."* **At first, those words seem rather strange to me.** Who are the *"they"*? Perhaps it refers back to verse one which speaks of *"they"* that build a house.

The plain fact is IF the LORD does not build the family (the house), all the *plans* of the father and mother are vain plans. *"Children are an heritage of the LORD."* I have known couples who *"plan"* their families. *They* decide how many children *they* are going to have and when *they* are going to have them. Some of these *plans* work out. Often they do not. Some go childless with all their *planning*. Some have disobedient *planned* children. Some have sick *planned* children. Some *planned* children die. All of the *self-planning* is to no avail.

"Except the LORD build the house, they labour in vain . . ."

"UNDER HIS WINGS"
(Psalm 91:4; 57:1)
". . . under his wings shalt thou trust . . ."
HE IS MY REFUGE!
"In the shadow of thy wings will I make my refuge!"
WE SHOULD LEARN TO RUN TO HIM
IN EVERY TRIAL AND STORM.
Under His wings is safety.
But even in the shadow, I am sheltered. (ggs)

Today's Bible Blessing   *July 10*

Psalm 131:2—Psalm 138:3
THE BLESSING OF BRETHREN UNIFIED!

Psalm 133:1

"Behold, how good and how pleasant it is for brethren to dwell together . . ."

Besides the psalms containing beautiful poetry full of devotional meaning, several of them contain prophetic passages. *Psalm 2, Psalm 16, Psalm 22, Psalm 45, Psalm 72,* and *Psalm 110* are such passages. It has not been my purpose to go into prophecy for our daily *"Blessings,"* but I wanted you to be aware of these passages dealing with Jesus Christ and the future. Usually we do not think of the Psalms as prophecy, but some of them are.

Today is one of DAVID'S songs of degrees. It was sung as the people traveled to Jerusalem. Jerusalem was *"up."* Everyone had to climb *"up."* They progressed upward by degrees.

Look at Psalm 133! There are only three verses in this song. The first word out of David's mouth is *"BEHOLD!"* He is telling us to *"LOOK!"* Look everybody, at a pleasant phenomenon–*"brethren"* are together in one accord! Perhaps in those days living in *"unity"* was rare. There may have been much discord and division in households. I am not sure. All I know is that David marveled that relatives were getting along.

It could be that these congenial people were in a **gathering who met together for prayer.** Or they may have been in a committee who worked together on a joint project. They could have been a group that decided major decisions for a whole company of people. Whoever they were, they were of *one mind* and *one accord.*

David likened this *"oneness"* of *spirit* and *purpose* to the precious ointment that was put on Aaron's head. Aaron was the first High Priest. He was *wholly consecrated* to the LORD in every way and every day. He had an awesome responsibility to be true to God and His LAW. Aaron was the High priest who went into the Holy of Holies once a year, on the day of atonement. He was very important in the worship of the LORD God!

Look with me at Exodus 29:4-7. This is the reference that tells us about *the anointing oil* being poured on Aaron's head. **It is most interesting.**

> *"And Aaron and his sons thou shalt bring unto the door of the tabernacle . . . And thou shalt take the garments, and put upon Aaron the coat, and the robe of the ephod, and the ephod, and the breastplate, and gird him with the curious girdle of the ephod: And thou shalt put the mitre upon his head, and put the holy crown upon the mitre. THEN SHALT THOU TAKE THE ANOINTING OIL, AND POUR IT UPON HIS HEAD, AND ANOINT HIM."*

What a time of consecration for Aaron! Perfumed ointment was put upon his head. As he stood there, doing his priestly work, the heat from his body and the warmth of the air melted the ointment. It moved slowly down his face to his beard, melting and mellowing his flowing robes. As it slowly moved toward the ground, we observe a complete picture of *"unity."* The oil covered his whole being, blending it into one complete perfumed person. The ointment unified his person into one sweet odor. His whole being was dedicated and infused into a fragrance of sweet smell. Perfume was in the air wherever he walked!

This was a picture of "brethren" living and working in the oneness that unity brings. Such a blend of personality and purpose is rare today. **When it is seen, we can't help but praise God for such unity!**

"IT IS A GOOD THING TO GIVE THANKS"
(Psalm 91:1, 2; Job 35:10)
HE GIVETH SONGS IN THE NIGHT!
Anyone can sing in the daytime when the birds sing
and it is sunshine.
But no man can make his own song in the "night."
God gives that song! (ggs)

Today's Bible Blessing   *July 11*

Psalm 138:4—Psalm 144:14
THE CAVE OF DESPAIR

Psalm 142:2

"I poured out my complaint before him; I shewed . . . him my trouble."

Let us look at David's song of *contemplation*. At the beginning of Psalm 142 we find the words, "MASCHIL OF DAVID." "Maschil" means a poem of thoughtful observation or "contemplation." This is a prayer—a cry to the LORD. It was prayed when David was hiding from Saul.

David was crouched in a cave, not knowing what his end would be. He called out with a pleading voice, *"Thou art my refuge and my portion in the land of the living!"*

Review with me the times that we found David in such a predicament. One of his cave-dwelling periods happened after David's hunger episode.

Famished and afraid, David stopped at the Tabernacle. The priest, AHIMELECH, gave him the day-old hallowed bread to eat.

David had another need. He needed a weapon to defend himself against Saul. So the priest gave Goliath's sword to David. As you know, David was familiar with that sword!

Observing the whole thing was DOEG an EDOMITE. He cared for Saul's sheep. He was no friend of David. Nor did he care a *"hoot and a holler"* about the priests. This was bad news!

When David fled from the priest's place, the king of GATH recognized him. David was afraid. He pretended to be mentally ill. That behavior disturbed Gath's ruler. So he thought David a crazy man, and paid little attention to him—thinking he was harmless.

David was frightened. So he fled to a cave called ADULLAM. When his family and friends heard that David was in ADULLAM, they went to him. Many discontented and debt-ridden men gathered around David. He became their captain. Near this time he sought refuge for his parents with the King of Moab in Mizpeh. His parents were safe.

When David left the cave, he departed to the land of Judah. Saul was angered that David had a following. He was mad that the priests had helped his enemy. Therefore to please Saul, Doeg killed Ahimelch and all the priests!

Sadly, eighty-five priests were slain that day. It was a time of terrible slaughter.

These wicked killings grieved David. He knew that he

had caused this slaughter by going to the priest and requesting Goliath's sword.

It may have been these circumstances that brought forth the anguish we read in Psalm 142. *"I cried unto the LORD with my voice, with my voice unto the LORD did I make supplication"* WHERE ELSE COULD HE GO BUT TO GOD? *"I showed before Him my trouble!"* No one else understood. NO ONE ELSE COULD HEAR! No one else really cared!

He said his spirit was overwhelmed. Wherever he walked, someone laid a trap for him. He looked to the right and left and found no help! He concluded that *"NO MAN CARED FOR MY SOUL!"*

How about you? Do you feel as if you are in "prison" (vs. 7)? David did. He was at the end of his rope! He expected the LORD to bring him out of such despair. He looked forward to the soon-bountiful help from the LORD. We know the end of the story. David did have victory over Saul. He did become King. He did see God's care and protection. But in this psalm, he only has the *"hope"* of such a rescue.

May you and I find such *"hope"* today. My husband says that *"Hope"* is defined as *"something in the future that is assured."* Believe, as David did, even though you are in the CAVE OF ADULLAM (the *CAVE OF DESPAIR)* that God hears your prayer if you are His child. There is *"hope"* that a rescue is coming soon!

"I LEAPED OVER THE WALL"
(Psalm 18:29)
"For by thee I have run through a troop;
and by my God have I leaped over a wall."
"Things" have taken over to such an extent
that I cannot get "over" them.
Problems unsolved have become a wall,
and I am a captive enclosed.
BUT BY MY GOD, I HAVE RUN THRU A TROOP
AND BY MY GOD I LEAPED OVER THE WALL.
THRU the details and perplexities and OVER the problems.
As Song of Solomon 2:9 says
"HE STANDETH BEHIND OUR WALL!"
(ggs–partially copied)

Psalm 144:15—Proverbs 1:4
DAVID'S PSALM OF PRAISE

Psalm 145:1

"I will extol thee, my God, O king, and I will bless thy name for ever and ever."

Psalm 145 is a psalm of PRAISE! It is the last song of David. In my opinion, that makes it a very special psalm. It gives us twenty-four characteristics of God. I thought it would be a good way to close the book by numbering those characteristics. I wonder if I will find all twenty-four.

In extolling God, David says he will bless God's Name forever.

His greatness is unsearchable

A father will tell his children to praise God's Name.

God does terrible and mighty acts.

People will have a memory of His greatness.

The LORD is gracious and full of compassion.

He is slow to anger.

He has great mercy.

He is good to all.

His mercies are shown in all His works.

His works will praise Him.

The Saints will bless Him.

His kingdom is glorious.

People will talk of His great power.

His kingdom is glorious in majesty.

Men will see His mighty acts.

His kingdom is everlasting.

His dominion endures throughout all generations.

The Lord upholds all who fall.

He raises up those who are bowed down.

The eyes of all wait on Him.

He gives food in due season.

His hand is open to the desire of every living thing.

The LORD is righteous in all his ways.

He is holy in all His works.

The LORD is close to all who call upon Him in truth.

He will give those who fear Him their desire.

He hears their cry and saves them.

The LORD preserves them who love Him.

He will destroy the wicked.

He will save them.

I agree with the psalmist when he declared: *"MY MOUTH SHALL SPEAK THE PRAISE OF THE LORD! And all* *flesh bless His holy name for ever and ever."* Thank God for the psalms. They are a balm for our needs!

"COMFORT"
(Isaiah 43:1-2; Romans 15:4)
FEAR NOT!
I HAVE REDEEMED THEE
I HAVE CALLED THEE BY NAME
THOU ART MINE.
When in this world we Christians have troubles
and are passing through the waters,
we are not to be overwhelmed; God has promised to be with us.
The rivers will not overflow.
Nor shall flames kindle upon us.
For I AM THE LORD THY GOD, THY SAVIOUR! (ggs)

Today's Bible Blessing   July 13
Proverbs 1:5–Proverbs 3:34
KEEP CLOSE TO JESUS

Proverbs 1:10
"My son, if sinners entice thee, consent thou not."

Proverbs 1:10 is a verse that I have known all my life. I didn't really memorize it. It was a verse that I was told about. You see, I had an Uncle. His name was Richard Charles Barker. I do not remember him, but I have seen pictures of him. My mother told me about my Uncle. She loved him very much. He called her *"Gerch."* Her name was Gertrude. I have many post cards from him. He sent them to me when I was a little child in the hospital. He was in the Navy. That would have been in the late 1920's or the early 1930's. He was a Navy pilot.

My grandmother had many concerns for her son. He was a lady's man. He dabbled in worldly pursuits. She would whisper in his ear, *"Keep close to Jesus!"* I had forgotten all about that admonition, until this morning, when I read today's Scripture verse. "KEEP CLOSE TO JESUS!" What better advice could a mother give her son?

Grandma gave my Uncle another counsel. It was our verse today. *"MY SON, IF SINNERS ENTICE THEE, CONSENT THOU NOT!"* I wonder as he mingled with the world and its people and pleasures, if Grandma's words rang in his ears.

The reason I do not remember him is that he died when he was either twenty-three or twenty four-years of age. I have seen pictures of him. His memory to me is a precious one. He died of the *terrible tuberculosis* that many people died from in those days. That was before the wonderful medicines that we have today to help that disease.

As the disease took over his body, he could no longer pilot the planes. Perhaps you have seen pictures of those bi-planes. They are nothing like the big airplanes of today, or even the small private ones we see by private homes. Because he was ill, he could not fly the planes, but he had to work. He was still in the military. He was one of the men who would hold on to the plane wings and run with the plane to help the plane get off the ground. Then one day, he could no longer *"run"* with the planes. He began to cough up blood.

He found himself in bed, ill, and dying. It was a sad time. Grandma would visit Uncle Dick. (He signed his cards to me that way.) As she always did, she would whisper in his ear. *"KEEP CLOSE TO JESUS!"* Often she would quote Proverbs 1:10 to him. With tears in her voice she would say, *"My son, if sinners entice thee, consent thou not."*

To see your child suffer pain and struggling to breathe is horrible for a mother. To lose a son in death is shocking. A mother does not expect to have her child die. Grandma knew this pain. My mother loved her brother and the loss of him stayed with her all her life. He was buried in a cemetery in Cleveland, Ohio. His body was lowered down deep in the ground waiting the resurrection day. Above the ground—reaching for the sun—was the most beautiful tree. It was a weeping willow tree.

Day and night it stood over my uncle's grave "weeping" at the loss of my grandmother's son. His last words echoed in her ears. He had whispered her words back to her. From his parched lips she could hear the admonition she often gave to him, *"Mom, Keep Close to Jesus!"*

"MY CANDLE, MY DARKNESS"
(Psalm 18:28)
HOW GREAT IS OUR DARKNESS!
Some times in great distress and trial,
it seems we can see no way out.
The way looks dark ahead,
but here He promises to "light my candle"
or give me spiritual illumination for my darkness.
THE LORD WILL ENLIGHTEN ME.
THAT IS A PROMISE! (ggs)

Today's Bible Blessing   *July 14*

Proverbs 3:35–Proverbs 6:34
RAVISHED BY LOVE

Proverbs 5:18
"Let thy fountain be blessed: and rejoice with the wife of thy youth."

We find ourselves in the book of Proverbs. Many of us have had grandparents or parents who have quoted these pithy sentences of *deliberate thought* to us. Solomon is the author of most of this practical wisdom. Let us learn from all these words!

Today I want us to look at some very practical, as well as needful, verses. If every man and woman heeded them, there would be no unfaithful husbands and wives–certainly no divorces! But alas, people are human–too human and sinful.

The lust of the flesh is a strong desire that cannot be explained. Many a husband has ruined his marriage by yielding to the siren song of a *"strange woman"* with her *honeycomb lips* (Proverbs 5:3).

Many a woman has fallen into sexual guilt by drinking water from another man's cistern, turning from her husband's sweet well (Proverbs 5:15).

The question is asked of the reader, "Why wilt thou, my son, be ravished with a strange woman. . .?" (See verse 20.)

A man is encouraged to rejoice with the wife of his youth. No matter how long the marriage, the husband should be thrilled and happy with the *"bride"* he chose many years ago. Love is not something that grows when neglected. That is why many office romances bloom.

The girl in the office is more attentive than the wife in the kitchen. A man is flattered by the attention that a co-worker gives him. Everyone is all nice and pleasant at work, or at church, or at the local McDonalds! While at home, with the pressures that a family brings, a man can feel like he doesn't belong. The children are noisy and demanding attention. The wife is worn-out from childbirth and daily duties. How can love be nourished and fed under such straining circumstances?

Faithfulness to a mate is a matter of the mind. We must determine to be so. *"Let her be as the loving hind* (deer) *and pleasant roe* (young, red, female deer), *let her breasts satisfy thee at all times, and be thou ravished* (enraptured) *always with her love"* (vs. 19). Think about the "fun" a young female deer has, as she comes into "womanhood," finding her first mate, and bearing babies. This is how a wife should be toward her husband. This is what a husband wants from a wife–no matter her age. Her form and figure should "ravish" his heart.

Notice verses 19 and 20. There we find the word *"ravished"* in each verse. In verse 19—the *"ravishing"* is within holy marriage. In verse 20—the word *"ravished"* is used in regard to an adulterous/fornicating woman. The word actually means *"TRANSPORTED WITH JOY"*!

A man can be *"transported with joy"* by most any woman. It is a matter of his heart determination to be *"ravished"* ONLY by his own wife. There is nothing sweeter than seeing a couple married for fifty or more years who still are *"in love"* with one another!

Don't go to a strange woman or man for such ravishing! *"Drink waters out of thine own cistern, and running waters out of thine own well"* (vs. 15).

REJOICE WITH THE WIFE OF THY YOUTH!

"THY WORDS WERE HEARD"
(Daniel 10:12)
*"Fear not, Daniel: for from the first day that thou didst set thine heart to understand,
and to chasten thyself before thy God,
thy words were heard ..."*
God knows our prayers as our hearts first form the yearning.
Yea, He knows before this.
From our first cry, He hears and observes our need.
Though our willfulness may block the answers,
or Satan seeks to hinder the execution of it,
the answer will come,
for our words have been heard!
(ggs–source unknown)

Today's Bible Blessing   *July* 15

Proverbs 6:35–Proverbs 10:3

A SIMPLE MAN & AN IMPUDENT WOMAN

Proverbs 7:2, 5

"Keep my commandments . . . they may keep thee from the strange woman, from the stranger which flattereth with her words."

The first few verses of Proverbs 7 are instructions for a son to keep his father's words. Many times sons think their fathers do not know anything. Sometimes it takes years for a son to realize the wisdom of his Dad. In these early verses, the son is reminded to bind his fingers with the commandment of God, to write them on his heart, and to practice *wisdom*, and say to it, *"Thou art my sister."* He is to realize that *"understanding"* is like a close relative.

The reason this father tells his son to keep close to the precepts of God is to keep the son from the clutches of a scheming woman. The world is full of such fake, flattering females. They want to get their clutches into the heart and soul of a fine man to ruin him. *They pretend they care.* In truth, they only care for their own pleasure!

The father said that he could look out his window and see those awful women going after men–both young and old–who do not have the faintest idea what the women are doing to them until it is too late. The father told of a certain lurking woman on a certain city street. She was scantily dressed, leaving little to the imagination. In fact, she dressed like the town prostitutes. (Sad to say many women dress immodestly today who are not ladies of the night.) The woman in this chapter was crafty— planning how to *"get"* the man's son. She is loud and stubborn– knowing what she wanted. Her goal was to get that young man into her bed. She had plans.

Because the offensive woman's husband was out of town, she knew that no one would be in her house to see her wicked ways. She had the perfect plan.

As the boy passed her corner, she reached out her hand and touched him. Then she caught him. She threw her arms about his neck, kissing him shamelessly. Pretending a spirituality that she really did not possess, she talked of her *"peace offerings."* She knew he was a religious youth. She knew such *"God talk"* would weaken his guard.

She said, *"I came out here on the street to meet you."* (She had seen him before.) She wanted him in a sexual way. *"I have found you!"* How happy she was to have him close to her.

She told him that her bed was *"inviting"* with perfumes and spices. Certain odors invite intimacy. *"Come!"* she whispered, *"Let us make love until morning!"* How many young men could resist such an offer? She begged him for *"comfort,"* feigning fear of being alone.

Her sensuous words sounded like a soft breeze on a summer's night to the beguiled man. They were irresistible sounds to his ears.

He was falling into her trap–not really knowing it was such! All this sweet talk caused him to yield. Before he knew it, he was like an ox going to slaughter. He was like a foolish, drunken man pushed into a jail cell! No self-will or power to resist temptation!

It all seemed too good to be true. This woman wanted him! But after a night in her perfumed bed, she kicked him out. He had been as a bird flying into a trap–not knowing death was near. His manhood was gone. His shame was intense. He left her presence wounded. Something had died within his soul. Too late—he had learned that *"her house was the way to Hell."*

This was the illustration the wise father gave his innocent son. It was told to deter him from foolish women. The father desired to save the soul and purity of his son. I wonder if the youth heeded his father's advice, or did he run the way of the world and damn his own soul?

What is the lesson that Proverbs 7 has taught us today? It tells me that no matter the age of a man, he will be subject to the wiles of an impudent woman who is *"after"* him. No matter how young or old a man is, there is always a woman who wants to make him fall.

Woe be to that man! And cursed is that woman!

"ALL THE SUGAR IS IN THE BOTTOM OF THE CUP"
The last of life is what the first of life was made for.
Today is my mother's birthday.
JENNY BARKER'S DATES ARE JULY 8, 1883-1974.
The last of her life of ninety-one years was very hard.
She could not understand her being "old," nearly blind,
deaf, and weary.
She said, *"I thought all the sugar was in the bottom of the cup.
Here at the bottom of the cup,
there is nothing sweet about old age."*
I told her, *"Perhaps the sugar was in Heaven—
the bottom of the cup."*
**For me, her daughter, the lesson was
that I loved and appreciated her more in her last years
than all the other years of her life.** (ggs)

Today's Bible Blessing   *July 16*
Proverbs 10:4–Proverbs 12:25
THE TALE OF TWO STREET MEETINGS

Proverbs 9:8
"Reprove not a scorner . . . rebuke a wise man . . ."
"Reprove not a scorner, lest he hate thee:
rebuke a wise man, and he will love thee."
As I contemplate this truth, my mind goes back over sixty years ago to the city of Chicago. I was in Bible school then. Often, we students were assigned various *"practical Christian work"*

My Daily Bible Blessings

assignments. The one I want to tell you about was a *"street meeting"* assignment.

Do you know what a "street meeting" is? A *"street meeting"*—for most Christians—means that people, who know Jesus Christ as Saviour, get together and go to an agreed place. They gather together and sing songs about the LORD. They give testimonies. Usually one man preaches. Often they have a public address system that airs their words loudly to the surrounding areas. Sometimes someone is playing a portable organ. A portable organ is a small, *"piano-type,"* instrument that can be carried around like a large suitcase. The organ player sits on a small chair and pumps air into the box with her feet. Often there is a trumpet or trombone sounding from the group. Maybe today, there would be guitars. Now-a-days people need a permit to do this. Many times the community does not want such *"noise." It bothers the town!*

Our town here in South Jersey has *"street meetings"* of a sort. They are not religious. They have big doings on certain Saturday nights to attract customers to the stores and restaurants. As one drives down THE AVENUE, one can hear rock bands & singers of all sorts. Not one of them is singing gospel songs or hymns. (I wonder if they would permit them.)

I remember distinctly one day when I was a part of a street meeting. I cannot remember where it was in Chicago. Seems like it was in the Cicero section. Not sure. As we were singing and giving testimonies, a person came up to me and spit at me. I had never had anything like that happen to me before. It has left an indelible impression on my memory.

That person was a *"SCORNER."* Our words concerning the Lord Jesus Christ and His *"whosoever will"* salvation was contrary to her *"good works"* salvation. She believed that baptism and holy communion, as well as *"works"* could save her soul. How wrong! Our words at that street meeting reproved her. *They censored her religious beliefs!*

I remember another street meeting in our home town of Berea, Ohio. Our pastor—his name was George Nika—was *fresh* out of Bible School. He was eager to tell the town about Jesus Christ being the WAY to Heaven. Every Friday night, during a certain summer, we met at the *"triangle."* (Our town square was in the shape of a *"triangle"*). The gospel was preached. I remember giving my testimony.

Listening to the gospel, sitting on a bench, near the street meeting, was a young man in his early twenties. He had a great spiritual need. If I remember correctly, his father had just been sent to prison. This left him broken-hearted and empty. The words from the Bible that he heard Friday night after Friday night pricked his heart. Soon he realized that he was *"lost"* and on the way to Hell! He came to our pastor. He heard firsthand how much Jesus loved him.

303

Soon he received the Lord Jesus Christ as his Saviour. He was a *"wise"* man. Why? Because he heard the *"rebuke."* He received the truth that he was a sinner. He asked God to forgive him and he received Jesus Christ into his heart and life.

For many years, our church continued its street meetings at the triangle. We still proclaimed the gospel week after week for several years. The young man, who had heard the gospel there a few years before, attended those street meetings.

Now, he came as a new person in Christ. In fact, he brought his trumpet with him. The melody that he played from his golden horn could be heard all over the town.

It sounded forth the praise of one who had been "rebuked," but now was in love with the LORD who saved him. HE WAS A WISE MAN!

"EACH DAY–HIS WORDS"
READ GOD'S WORDS TODAY!
Tomorrow may deprive us of the privilege.
READ IT EVERY DAY, FOR EVERY DAY
GOD HAS A WORD FOR YOU.
If you miss one day, you miss His words for you for that day.
There is a wonder in the living breathing Scriptures.
They save. They build. They cheer. They guide.
OH BLESSED BOOK! (ggs)

Today's Bible Blessing   *July 17*
Proverbs 12:26–Proverbs 15:22
HOPE! WHAT DOES IT MEAN?
Proverbs 13:12
"Hope deferred maketh the heart sick . . ."

HOPE! **What does it mean?** My husband, Dr. D. A. Waite, gave an excellent definition of the word in a sermon recently. **He said that *HOPE MEANS SOMETHING IN THE FUTURE, BUT ASSURED.*** He was teaching I Peter 1:3. *"According to His abundant mercy,"* God the Father has begotten (fathered) us unto a lively HOPE. This HOPE comes to us because of the resurrection of Jesus Christ from the dead. The believer has the *"living hope"* that he or she will be resurrected from the dead because Jesus Christ was resurrected. This is a wondrous HOPE for Christians! Death does not have the *"sting"* it has for the unbeliever. *They die without HOPE! It is sad! We who know Jesus Christ die with HOPE!*

My husband gave me a dictionary when we were first married. That old dictionary says that *"HOPE"* defined is the

following:
>   (1) Desire with expectation of obtaining what is desired, or belief that it is obtainable;
>   (2) Trust, reliance;
>   (3) Ground or source of happy expectation; hence good promise; as, land of hope;
>   (4) That which is hoped for; an object of hope.

I must confess that there was a time in a certain situation of my life that I lost all hope! It was a very sad time for me. I do not speak about it much at all. It was a very real loss! I never felt *"hopeless"* before. I do not wish it on anyone. I had a great disappointment! It was a personal disappointment. Someone had let me down. It was from someone I trusted completely. How could this happen? How could this happen *TO ME*?

This sadness or hopelessness came to me in two waves. After the first shock, I rested in one fact. That was I HAD HOPE! I could look forward to that loss being over. I could see some future pleasure, some future satisfaction, and some future contentment. The past was over. I had HOPE of tomorrow. HOPE WAS THERE!

Then about a year later, I learned that I was mistaken about the glowing future—that HOPE. My world crashed. At that moment, I felt HOPE drain from my body. It seeped out of me as disappointment reigned. I couldn't believe it. How could such a thing happen to me? ALL HOPE WAS GONE!

Not many people knew about this emotional loss. People on the outside cannot see inside of another person's soul. I walked the same. I talked the same. I looked the same. But I felt like I was a *"shell"* of who I really was.

I asked people, *"Can you give some Bible verses about 'hope'"?* (I was too distressed to find them for myself.) I asked preachers–several of them. I asked lay people, too. All they gave me were verses about the *"hope"* of eternal life, or verses on *"the second coming,"* or the "resurrection hope." Nothing for me on the *"hope"* I had lost in my very person!

After a few years, "hope" returned. I learned that life is not all peaches and cream. It is full of pitfalls and hurts. People cannot be trusted completely. Their word is not full-truth. They are human and sinful–no matter how good they appear. We all have corruptness in our core. Even people who are *"born-again"* have the evil nature lurking inside their souls. That evil wants to break out! A person may be redeemed, but—unless properly nourished—the world, the flesh, and the devil will corrupt us. *Fleshly ooze* will erupt out of the heart when that person is left to the flesh's control.

After a passage of time-and the comfort of Scripture, I came out of that *"spiritual hodgepodge."* I rediscovered a verse in Romans 15:13. It was just what I needed. It was there all the time, but I—being lost in my hurt and hopelessness—didn't remember it. No one else remembered it either.

"Now THE GOD OF HOPE fill you with all joy and peace in believing that ye may ABOUND IN HOPE, through the power of the Holy Ghost!" God in HIS TIME, when I needed it, revealed the verse to me once again. It comforted me.

YES, I DID HAVE HOPE! I could abound in it once more!

"GLEAN AND BEAT OUT"
(Ruth 2:17)
"So she gleaned in the field until even,
and beat out that she had gleaned . . ."
It takes a life time to "glean" and "beat out," if we start early.
What a void if we never "glean."
What an absolute loss if we never "beat-out" in meditation
of the precious hunger-satisfying corn of the Scripture!
(Source unknown from ggs)

Today's Bible Blessing   *July 18*

Proverbs 15:23–Proverbs 18:13
THE TONGUES ANSWER

Proverbs 16:24
"Pleasant words are as an honeycomb, sweet to the soul . . ."

Let's look at chapter 16 of Proverbs, verses 1-3. I was impressed, as I read, about the *"preparation of a man's heart"* (vs. 1). If a man has a *prepared heart* from the LORD, his tongue will be clean and truthful. Today there are so many lying people, as well as so-called Christians who have *"dirty"* mouths.

I am amazed how many people who say they know Jesus Christ, who take GOD's Name in vain. The Bible says in Exodus 20:7: *"Thou shalt not take the Name of the LORD thy God in vain; for the LORD will not hold him guiltless that taketh his name in vain."*

No matter where we go, we hear people saying "Oh GOD!" or some similar swearing. If we would say to that person, *"Why are you swearing?"* she would claim that she was not swearing. Little children who can barely talk, say, *"Oh, God!"* They do not know what they are saying. Mothers think nothing of taking God's Name in vain in front of their children. **On television, it is common to hear God's Name defamed. Why is this?**

The LORD is the only ONE who can clean a man's mouth! Look at verse 2, *"All the ways of a man are clean in his own* *eyes."* How very true this proverb is. People do not see their own unclean ways! I am not sure why this is. Even Christians, who have the Holy Spirit dwelling within, do not (or will not) recognize their sin. They use all sorts of excuses for their deception.

That is how sin is. It is a huge deception mill! It grinds the soul to such an extent that the guilty see no sin within! The Bible says that *"There is a way that seemeth right unto a man, but the end thereof are the ways of death"* (Proverbs 16:25). Yes, *"the LORD weigheth the spirits!"* I never thought about our innermost heart being weighed, have you?

The handwriting on the wall in the book of Daniel speaks of weighing sin. That frightening finger wrote, *"Thou art weighed in the balances and art found wanting"!* (See Daniel 5:27.)

The thought life should be clean. This is very important, but difficult, for many who have been steeped in sin, prior to salvation.

God tells us in Proverbs 16:3 that a believer must "commit" his works unto the LORD. If we do this *"committing,"* our thoughts will be established.

One must do more than say, *"Oh, I am committing my thought-life to God"* and then go his merry way, bumping into the worldly ways all day long. The psalmist advised to each one of us: *"Commit thy way unto the LORD, trust also in Him . . ."* (Psalm 37:5).

When one goes sailing, one learns to "let the wind fill the sails!" No longer is the sailor trusting the motor to move the boat, or is he resorting to the oars to navigate his craft. It is the wind that does the work. The sailor hoists his sails. Then he lets the wind take charge.

This is exactly how a Christian should "commit" his life to the LORD. You should put yourself in the place of God's leading. Let Him do the work! You will be pleasantly surprised how your *"thoughts will be established."* and your words will be *sweet as a honeycomb* (Proverbs 16:24).

"BUILD NOT YOUR NEST ON ANY EARTHLY TREE"
FOR THE WHOLE FOREST IS DOOMED TO BE CUT DOWN.
Sometimes a person, a teacher, a leader says or does a foolish thing.
It hurts for we see how he has such earthy feet of clay.
Let his actions be a lesson to all not to do as he has done!
(ggs)

$\mathcal{T}oday's\ \mathcal{B}ible\ \mathcal{B}lessing$ $\mathcal{J}uly\ 19$

Proverbs 18:14–Proverbs 21:15
BEFORE IT IS TOO LATE

Proverbs 19:18

"Chasten thy son while there is hope . . ."

It is interesting to note that the Proverbs given to Israel were short, pithy statements of wisdom to be taken home in the pocket of one's life to be used when needed. At any time these *"condensed parables"* could be expanded to longer stories of wisdom for the benefit of the hearer. Let us keep this in mind as we look at today's *"blessing."*

Proverbs 19:18 gives timely, concise advice to all parents. It would do you well, if you have a young child, to heed such counsel! *"Chasten thy son WHILE THERE IS HOPE, and let not thy soul spare for his crying."* I think the important words in this verse are *"WHILE THERE IS HOPE!"*

Recently we looked at the word *"HOPE."* Let's review quickly the meaning. The dictionary defines the word *as "a desire with expectation of obtaining what is desired. Or a belief that it is obtainable."* Keep that in mind as we proceed.

What does *"chasten"* mean? Does it mean *"Sit in a naughty chair?"* Does it mean *"no television for a week"*? Does it mean *"Go to your* room?" I have news for you. *"Chasten"* means *"correct by punishing."* Now we have to figure out what *"punishing"* means.

Once again I turn to my dictionary. It says that punishment is *"a penalty inflicted upon an offender as a retribution, and incidently for reformation and prevention."* I gather from this definition that *"chastening"* is given to a child who has disobeyed, in some manner, what his parents or an authority has asked him to do or not do.

There seems to be a time limit to such *"chastening."* Notice the rest of the verse: *"WHILE THERE IS HOPE!"* **That is the time limit!** We discussed *"hope."* The idea of punishing a child for disobedience is that when the child grows up to be an adolescent, he will be obedient.

When he becomes an adult, he will be a law-abiding person with potential of fruitful opportunities. If the *"chastening"* or *"punishment"* is not given early (WHILE THERE IS *"HOPE"*) there is no sense trying to make a boy or girl obey anymore. IT IS TOO LATE! They are bent for disobedience and breaking the law. They will write graffiti on walls and tear down stop signs. They will rob stores for drug money, etc. etc. A *"child"* who has learned to obey will be law-abiding BECAUSE he learned to obey his parents!

Now go back a few chapters to Proverbs 13:24. *"HE THAT SPARETH HIS ROD HATETH HIS SON: BUT HE THAT LOVETH HIM CHASTENETH HIM BETIMES!"* "Betimes" means EARLY or PROMPTLY! A parent who does not discipline his child does not really love his son or daughter. Is that hard for you to hear?

Our verse in chapter 19 continues: *"AND LET NOT THY SOUL SPARE FOR HIS CRYING!"* No one wants to hear his child cry. But a parent cannot be swayed by tears when there has been disobedience. If a parent wavers in the discipline, the child will not shape up!

A child, who can manipulate his parent, will have a rude awakening when he tries such tactics in school and/or in the business world. Mother and Daddy are not able to come to the rescue when the police arrest the son or when the daughter has stolen from the local Walmart.

Now as to the "naughty chair." **It worked for my sister.** I remember her sitting on a chair when she had been disobedient. *"No Television for a week"* will work for a teenager who has learned to obey as a small child. When one of our sons was a young man, he had some kind of infraction of our rules. I do not remember what it was. He was a very good son. But I knew I had to punish him. He was way too old and big for spanking. So I took away a sports activity. That was a strong punishment for him. I felt bad. He obeyed. He did not sneak away and do it anyhow. He had learned to obey.

I remember seeing our adult son discipline his toddler when she misbehaved in church. It hurt me to see her taken out and spanked over and over again. I said nothing. Soon that little girl could sit in church without a peep! Her father had not *"spared for her crying."* I have seen other children very disruptive who were never taught as a small child to be quiet in church!

"THE LIGHT GROWS BRIGHTER"
(Proverbs 4:18)
"But the path of the just is as the shining light,
that shineth more and more unto the perfect day."
One of the reasons God allows us to get old is that we can know
the answers to the questions young people ask us.
Another reason:
We can tell of His faithfulness.
Old people have so much to tell about God.
It is true that the path of the just is as the shining light that leads on
shining more and more as we approach Heaven.
This verse has become very real to me this year. (ggs)

Proverbs 21:16–Proverbs 24:5
A GRANDFATHER'S INHERITANCE

Proverbs 22:1

"A good name is rather to be chosen than great riches, and loving favour rather than silver and gold."

This is an interesting verse. It is filled with wisdom and pathos. It speaks to the very heart of a man or woman. Her name! His name! The family name! We come into the world with very little. Just ourselves—our baby selves! We cry as we are born out from our mothers. It's a boy! It's a girl! Immediately, the mother looks her baby over. Is she all there? Does he have all his fingers and toes?

I remember holding my babies—each one. How very dear they were to me. I labored in childbirth as they were born. The pain was deep. It was strong. It was overwhelming. Yet, as I held that newborn in my arms, I did not remember the pain, or the unending pressure to give birth. I only knew the joy of holding that baby in my arms. That child was a part of my husband and me. He or she was a living open expression of our love. Yet, he had no name!

There is something precious and holy about husband/wife love. That love given to one another in marriage is an openness only for the two of them. There is a closeness, too. Private hours and personal pleasures are only for each other and each other alone. Their kisses are only for the mouths of each other. Their embraces are only for the arms of the other. The Apostle Paul was right when he wrote that marriage is honourable in all, and the marriage bed is "UNDEFILED"!

"MARRIAGE IS HONOURABLE IN ALL, AND THE (MARRIAGE) BED UNDEFILED . . ." (Hebrews 13:4).

So after the mother examines her baby, what does she do? She talks to the little ball of love and re-wraps her in her blanket again. She kisses her feet and holds her to herself. Soon she nurses the child as God intended a baby to be fed. The closeness between a mother and a nursing child cannot be explained or understood except by another mother who has done the same thing.

Then a serious time comes. A decision must be made as to what to name the baby. Often a name has been previously chosen. Other times, no thought has come to mind. It is then that both mother and father discuss the possibilities. Sometimes the previously chosen name does not fit the baby. The baby doesn't look like the name! Sometimes the mother chooses a name that the father does not like. Sometimes the father insists on a name that the mother does not like—but it is a family name! Soon the birth certificate is signed and the child is named! The decision has been made! There is much rejoicing!

Now the question comes to mind. WHAT IS THE CHILD GOING TO DO WITH THAT NAME? Is he going to wear it with pride? Or is he going to defame that name that was chosen with so much care and maybe prayer?

I remember being told of a conversation that our second born son had with his grandfather. I think we were at some family function at the time. David and his grandfather were sitting near each other. Grandpa Waite was an old man at the time–probably in his eighties. He was going blind with serious glaucoma. It was sad!

As they were talking, Grandpa told David that he (Grandpa) had given David a very valuable treasure. That treasure was worth more than any other inheritance that could ever be given to him. THAT TREASURE WAS A GOOD NAME! Grandpa explained that it was up to his grandson to keep that name well. He was not to tarnish that name with wrongful living or evil ways.

David never forgot that talk that day with his Grandpa. In fact, that good name was all the inheritance David received from Grandpa, but to David, that inheritance was far better than *"great riches, loving favour, or silver and gold!"*

I don't know if Grandpa Waite knew the verse in Proverbs 22:1 or not; but he certainly knew the meaning of every word that was written therein. His gift was better than any material gift of any kind. A good name will never lose its value unless we invest it in foolish and *riotous* living (Proverbs 28:7).

Whoso keepeth the law is a wise son: but he that is a companion of riotous men shameth his father.
A GOOD NAME IS RATHER TO BE CHOSEN THAN GREAT RICHES, AND LOVING FAVOUR RATHER THAN SILVER AND GOLD.

"WE CANNOT SUFFER TOO MUCH OR BE RELIEVED TOO LATE."
"He who hath fixed the bounds of our habitation,
hath also fixed the bounds of our tribulation."
He who makes no mistakes in balancing the clouds
and meeting out the heavens,
commits no error in measuring out the ingredients
which composes the medicine of souls.
We cannot suffer too much or be relieved too late."
(copied by ggs from Spurgeon's
MORNING & EVENING)

Proverbs 24:6–Proverbs 26:28

AN OBEDIENT EAR

Proverbs 25:11

"A word fitly spoken is like apples of gold in pictures of silver."

Let us look today at Proverbs 25:11, and learn the **practical wisdom found therein.** *"A word fitly spoken is like apples of gold in pictures of silver."* As I am writing these words down for you, I am realizing that I have misunderstood this verse all these years. The word is *"pictures"*–not *"pitchers."* Because I do not always *"hear"* the letters in certain words (many words, in fact) correctly and precisely, often I completely misunderstand the meaning or spelling of that word.

Here before me is an example of that! I always saw in my mind's eye the *"golden apples"*—made by a gifted craftsman–in a beautiful silver pitcher. I would think of the *"pitcher"* placed in the middle of a well-polished mahogany table. I suppose the table was mahogany because my mother's dining room table was of that wood. It was always a well-kept room—beautiful—and ready to be used for dinner guests.

But no! This verse is saying nothing about a "vessel"! *It is talking about an "image carved in relief."* I learned the definition by glancing down at the footnote in the DEFINED KING JAMES BIBLE. An image carved *"in relief"* means, in this case, golden apples carved or sculpted on a silver surface so that the apples stand out. They are projected out from the back of the picture. I've seen such carvings, haven't you? They are beautiful, intricate, unusual works of art! When one views such a sculpture, one stops in one's tracks. The artwork is lovely–so unusual. A person is compelled to pause and look.

So it is with a *"word fitly spoken."* Have you ever been in distress? Perhaps a great calamity had befallen you. Then someone came to you with a word of care and comfort. It was just what you needed. It was a balm to your wounded heart! That was *"a word fitly spoken."* Perhaps, as you are reading these words, you are reflecting on some words that were *"fitly spoken"* to you during a certain life's crisis. It may not have been in sorrow that you heard such words. It may have been during a financial decision that had to be made, or at the time of contemplating marriage to the wrong person. No matter—we all know when some caring person is brave enough to speak to us. It was like *"apples of gold in pictures of silver."*

Look at verses twelve & thirteen! It gives further commentary on *"FITLY SPOKEN WORDS."*

> *"As an earring of gold, and an ornament of fine gold, so is a wise reprover upon an obedient ear. As the cold of snow in the time of harvest, so is a faithful messenger to them that*

send him: for he refresheth the soul of his masters."

It is interesting–these words were spoken as *"reproving"* **words.** Surprise! Surprise! They were welcomed by the hearer. They were words of correction–perhaps of discipline. Yet, the words spoken in this case were like *golden jewels* to the *"obedient ear"* of the hearer. The words of *"reproof"* were welcomed.

The illustration given by Solomon was interesting. He thought of the hot days of harvest. He thought of the harvesters' need for cool relief. How they would have welcomed a wagon full of white, *cold snow*! The wise man wrote that *"snow"* on a hot day, would be like a *"fitly spoken word of correction"* to an *"obedient ear."*

I am thinking of our oldest son as I write these words. This is his birthday! He was an obedient son. He had an *"obedient ear."* He took correction like *"apples of gold in pictures of silver."* I am thankful for his *obedient ear*!

We must practice the art of listening to correction. We must determine to receive it and be willing to hear what is being said. It will refresh our souls and the souls of those who are doing the correcting.

But let us be careful in our *"correcting"* **to be sure it is needed and well founded, and not correction because of a personal vendetta.**

"ALL ALONG OUR PATH, WE HAVE A GUIDE"
(Psalm 48:14; Proverbs 4:18)
"He will be our guide, even unto death."
Sometimes we forget this truth,
as old age, weakness, and fear come to us.
Yet, we read in Proverbs
"The path of the just is as the shining light,
that shineth more and more unto the perfect day."
His smile is clearer and nearer.
THERE IS GLORY AT THE END OF THE PATH. (ggs)

𝒯𝑜𝑑𝑎𝑦'𝑠 𝐵𝑖𝑏𝑙𝑒 𝐵𝑙𝑒𝑠𝑠𝑖𝑛𝑔   𝒥𝑢𝑙𝑦 22
Proverbs 27:1–Proverbs 30:3
WHO IS A FRIEND?

Proverbs 27:6
"Faithful are the wounds of a friend; but the kisses of an enemy are deceitful."

As I quickly review Proverbs 27, I am struck with one of the subjects spoken therein. The theme is *"friends."* For instance verse six: *Faithful are the wounds of a friend; but the kisses of an enemy are deceitful.* The verse prior to that one, is Proverbs

27:5—*"Open rebuke is better than secret love."*

To me, a person who is a *"friend"* is a very special person, indeed. I have very few such *"special persons."* I am talking about real friends, the kind of *"friend"* who is like *"family"*—like a sister. Oh, I have *"friends"* who are casual, who are kind, and who are close for a season. Some of those have turned out to be *"fair weather friends."* Others have turned out to be dear people to me. In truth, in times of real distress or need, some *"friends"* are nowhere to be found.

Dinah Craik wrote about a true friend when she composed her poem called *"FRIENDSHIP."*
*"Oh, the comfort—the inexpressible comfort
of feeling safe with a person,
Having neither to weigh thoughts, nor measure words—
but pouring them all right out—just as they are—
Chaff and grain together—
Certain that a faithful hand will take and sift them—
Keep what is worth keeping—
And with the breath of kindness blow the rest away."*

It is during times of great distress and unrest that we humans discover who our real friends are. It is often surprising. Someone comes to us, whom we never expected, with kindness and comfort. That unexpected *"someone"* draws to our side and helps us. He or she may never have been that close before until now. She is by our side. She has a hand of help and a heart of understanding. We are surprised that she cares. Her very presence is a comfort. How we needed her! *Ointment and perfume rejoice the heart: so doth the sweetness of a man's friend by hearty counsel* (Proverbs 27:9).

There is another kind of friendship. It is not the kind during *death* or *illness*. It is the friendship that comes when two people have kindred thoughts on a specific matter. Separately each person has fought some battle. Individually they have paid a dear price because of soul and heart conviction. These two meet each other for the first time. Their souls are knit together because they agree on a certain matter. Or, they may disagree in a specific area of a matter. It is then that their friendship grows. Why? Because *Iron sharpeneth iron; so a man sharpeneth the countenance of his friend* (Proverbs 27:17). Each person becomes better if they have each other. *Open rebuke is better than secret love. Faithful are the wounds of a friend; but the kisses of an enemy are deceitful* (Proverbs 27:5-6).

Also, we learn a very important lesson in this chapter. What is that lesson? Give your friend some space.
"He that blesseth his friend with a loud voice, rising early in the morning, it shall be counted a curse to him. A continual dropping in a very rainy day and a contentious woman are alike" (Proverbs 27:14-16).
Familiarity breeds contempt! Friends must give their friends breathing room. Too much togetherness can lead to unhealthy relationships.

Everyone needs "alone" time. To keep a friendship healthy, don't smother your friend with your continual presence.

Allow her to have an opinion of her own. Make him glad to see you!

"UNDERSTANDING"
(Matthew 13:19)

"When any one heareth the word of the kingdom, and understandest it not, then cometh the wicked one, and catcheth away that which was sown in his heart. This is he which received seed by the way side."

HOW IMPORTANT THAT WE READ GOD'S HOLY WORDS
EXPECTANTLY, & INTELLIGENTLY, & REVERENTLY.
It is the LORD GOD ALMIGHTY who has spoken!
Faith and submission are requisite to understanding–
else Satan will interrupt and stop the work of the seed in our hearts.
This interrupts our witness and growth. (ggs)

Today's Bible Blessing　　　　　　*July 23*

Proverbs 30:4–Ecclesiastes 2:6
WHO CAN FIND A WOMAN OF VIRTUE?

Proverbs 31:10

"Who can find a virtuous woman? for her price is far above rubies.

Who is Lemuel? We don't really know. Some feel he was an insignificant Arabian prince. Some think the author here refers to Hezekiah; but many feel Solomon wrote chapter thirty. If it were Solomon, that would mean he is telling the things that his mother, *Bathsheba*, taught him about life, women, and marriage. If this be true, she must have missed a few lessons on multiplication of wives and worshipping idols, as well as the sin of adultery.

I choose to believe that *"Lemuel"* was someone by the name of *Lemuel*. The important thing, in this chapter, is not who penned it, but that God *"breathed out"* His Words in this portion of Scripture for our admonition and learning.

The first warning of a mother to her son was most important! *"Do not give your manly strength to a woman with whom you are not married."* Nor should a son practice *"ways"* that would damn his soul or destroy his kingdom! A king should not drink wine or strong drink. Such imbibing influences one's mental stability and judgment. A leader should have a clear head. He is to be the *"mouth"* for those who cannot speak, as well as *be good to the poor.*

315

With all this advice, the teaching-mother launched out with marital advice to her young son. Her wisdom was good! She instructed that the first rule for a wife is that she be *virtuous*! (Proverbs 31:10). She must be *chaste* and *morally pure*. No money can purchase such virtue. *Virtue is within the woman!* Because of her *moral excellence*, a wife's husband can trust her. *Trust is the most important virtue in marriage!* Because of her *chaste forthrightness*, a virtuous woman will do her husband good always.

This kind of woman is no slouch. She goes to the market and purchases *clothes* for her family to wear. She buys *food* for them to eat. She buys or makes *warm coats* for the cold days. They will never be cold in the winter! They will never be naked or hungry in summer or winter. She is sure that her vineyard and garden are cared for. If she cannot do this herself, she hires someone to do the job. Her husband and children never have to sit in the dark after sundown. She has provided light for the evenings. (Today, we would say that she pays her light bill on time.) Her needlework is a thing of beauty. Her hands are never idle. Her heart and hands reach out to the hungry and poor.

Her husband is one of the town dignitaries. She has taken the strain of running the household off of his shoulders, so he can tend to his business affairs.

Her moral strength and honor show! She is not only beautiful without, she is beautiful within. Her speech is wholesome! Curse words and street slang are not a part of her vocabulary. Her children love her. They respect her. They call her *"blessed!"*

Most of all—she is a woman who fears the Lord. *"Who can find a virtuous woman? for her price is far above rubies"* (Proverbs 31:10). In other words, she is priceless!

Now I am wondering about you who are reading today's Bible verses. Two questions come to mind—yea, three. Husband, did you marry a virtuous woman? Woman, are you a woman of virtue and strength in the LORD? Young person, what kind of husband (or wife) are you looking for? *"Favour is deceitful, and beauty is vain: but a woman that feareth the LORD, she shall be praised"* (Proverbs 31:30).

"ADONAI–LORD"
(Ephesians 5:17; Acts 9:6)
Master, Despot, Owner has to do with obedience to our Lord.
We are to understand what the will of ADONAI is.
The first words to fall from the lips of Paul, when converted, were,
"MASTER, ADONAI, what will Thou have me to do?" (ggs)

Today's Bible Blessing   *July 24*

Ecclesiastes 2:7–Ecclesiastes 6:7
WHAT ARE WE DOING WITH OUR "TIMES"?

Ecclesiastes 3:1

"To every thing there is . . . a time to every purpose . . ."

The book of Ecclesiastes was written by Solomon. It contains writings of an old man who has seen it all. He had tried every-thing that the world had to offer—every bauble, every building, every whim, good wine, and many women; only to find it all just plain *vanity!* In this book he is called the *"preacher."* He was one who addressed an assembly. **It is said that this *"roll"* (this book of Ecclesiastes) was read at the feast of *"Booths"* every year.**

He had seen everything that life had to offer. It was all emptiness and frustration! The sun rose every morning and set every night. So what? The wind blew continually. So? Man's eyes are never satisfied with seeing. *"There is no new thing under the sun!"* (Ecclesiastes 1:9b). *For in much wisdom is much grief: and he that increaseth knowledge increaseth sorrow* (vs. 18). In truth, Solomon sounded like someone who had *"had it"* with life! **Do you know anyone like that?**

In chapter three, Solomon discusses the *"times"* of life. See Ecclesiastes 3:1-11. After a man or woman has lived a few years, he has tasted life to its fullest, and has found disappointments. Solomon tells us that life has its *"seasons"*—just like the weather—spring, summer, autumn and winter. Each has its own peculiarities and advantages.

There is a time to be born and a time to die. How true. We have new great-grandchildren. They are darling with future potential. Then, there are people like my husband and me. We are moving to the slot where *"death"* will come soon. When it does—that will be *"our time."* Occasionally, a young person moves into the dying position. He leaves us unexpectedly, without warning. We must accept that was *his* or *her* *"time."*

We all know there is a time to plant and a time for harvest. But the "time" to kill is most unwelcome. I think of wars and floods and pestilence. That *time of "killing"* is painful. Then God, in His goodness, gives us *healing.* Yes, there is a time to *"heal."*

Oh, even a time to *"break down"* (Ecclesiastes 3:3). At first I thought of the *mental* and *emotional "break-downs"* that human beings are prone to have. Life and its burdens become more than the human mind can stand. The escape comes in what we call a *"break down."* The *"building up"* takes months of recovery and patience. Probably, Solomon did not mean that kind of *"break down."* He may have meant destroying an old house to build another, but I am comforted in the first meaning. How about you? Our human emotional system can only stand so much strain. It would be well with us if we remembered that when dealing with our loved ones. Too much harshness brings *heartbreak*. Too much *stress* brings *struggles*. We all are guilty of pushing those we love in a direction they cannot go. May God forgive us!

A time to weep, and a time to laugh; a time to mourn, and a time to dance! **THESE ARE ALL THE "TIMES" YOU AND I HAVE IN OUR LIVES.** *A time to cast away stones, and a time to gather stones together; a time to embrace, and a time to refrain from embracing.* **ARE YOU AND I TAKING ADVANTAGE OF THE MANY DAILY OPPORTUNITIES WE HAVE, OR ARE WE SOURED AND BITTER, LIKE SOLOMON, WITH THE VANITIES OF LIFE?**

Look at them—see the "times" you are throwing away because of sullenness or self-pity: *A time to get, and a time to lose; a time to keep, and a time to cast away; A time to rend, and a time to sew; a time to keep silence, and a time to speak; A time to love, and a time to hate; a time of war, and a time of peace.*

Solomon has covered the waterfront of life. He has laid it out in black and white. So many opportunities to serve the LORD JESUS daily. Yet, we mope and feel sorry for ourselves. **Let us get up out of our pity-party and take advantage of our *"times"* before we have none left!**

"HEAVEN"
WE ARE NOT FAR FROM HOME—
A MOMENT WILL BRING US THERE.
Let us determine not to waste one moment in murmuring,
or useless activities or crying for that which we may not have.
Let us live so that, if this were our last moment,
it would be pleasing to God. (ggs)

Today's Bible Blessing　　　　　　　　　　*July 25*
Ecclesiastes 6:8—Ecclesiastes 10:16
WHY IS SORROW
BETTER THAN LAUGHTER?

Ecclesiastes 7:3
". . . by the sadness of the countenance the heart is made better."
　　　In the book of Ecclesiastes there is an underlying theme. *It is the fact that there is more to "life" than what we see*

here. There is future–a *"BEYOND!"* Jesus tells us that *"beyond"* is with Him and the Heavenly Father in Heaven. He tells those, who have genuinely trusted Him, that He has prepared a *"place"* for them. The author of Ecclesiastes is Solomon. He had beautiful *"places"* while he was king. He had *all glory* and *splendor*; but his earthly realm was nothing like the *"fields of glory"* in the *Ivory Palaces of our Heavenly Home.*

There are so many random thoughts in Ecclesiastes. It seems that the writer scatters them on the page as he thought of them. Sometimes we write letters like that. We just write what we are thinking about at the time. Let us glance at chapter seven.

In verse one, we are challenged to keep *"our name"* clear of charges that would cast aspersions on it. I remember our son, David, telling me often that his Grandpa Waite challenged Him to keep his name clean. *He told his grandson that he had given his grandson a good name.*

A GOOD NAME IS BETTER THAN PRECIOUS OINTMENT! (vs. 1). **Solomon claimed that the day of one's death was better than the day of one's birth.** I wonder why he said that. He claimed that *it was better to go to a house of mourning than a house of feasting* (Ecclesiastes1:2). Let's think about that for a moment. When one goes to a party of people gathered for pleasure, there is laughter and gaiety—often silliness. But, when one attends a funeral, there is seriousness and sadness.

There is a quietness in the house where a loved one has died. People are pondering life and death thoughts. There is a seriousness, a soberness, a thoughtfulness that is not in the house of gaiety and silliness.

Then the writer embellishes that thought in verse three: *"SORROW IS BETTER THAN LAUGHTER . . ."* How is that possible? He goes on to explain: *"BY SADNESS OF THE COUNTENANCE, THE HEART IS MADE BETTER."* How can that be? It is a mystery. READ ON! *"The heart of the wise is in the house of mourning; but the heart of fools is in the house of mirth."* That says it all!

What do we learn from frivolous conversation? Nothing! It is empty wind. Oh, it is fun. We need to laugh once in a while; but the depth of a serious conversation from a person who has lived life gives us a depth of meaning to our everyday living that laughter cannot give. *It is better to hear the rebuke of the wise, than for a man to hear the song of fools* (vs. 5).

The need for some serious thought and talk is explained as we read on: *"For the crackling of thorns under a pot, so is the laughter of the fool: this also is vanity"* (vs. 6). Picture with me a campfire. The flames are licking a pot of water. They are wildly warming the edges of the vessel. The flame is intense. It heats the pot before it heats the water. The fire makes a spectacle of itself. Soon the water is boiling in excitement. The flames die out. The water gets cold. So it is with joking and silly banter coated with empty laughter. What was really learned from that warm fuzzy feeling of hilarity?

On my kitchen wall I've placed a saying that speaks volumes. (It is by Robert Browning)

> *I walked a mile with pleasure, she chattered all the way,*
> *And left me none the wiser for all she had to say.*
> *I walked a mile with sorrow, and not a word said she,*
> *But oh the things I learned from her when sorrow walked with me.*

"A SPARROW ALONE"
(Psalm 102:7)
"A sparrow alone on the house top."
Such eloquent words to set forth the aloneness of our dear Saviour!
Forsaken and despised
Alone he went to the cross for me.
Alone He died and bore my sin.
He was alone, so that believers could be together.
Christians can be so alone—even in a crowd.
Unkindness and high standards make us aware of it.
He knows it all! (ggs)

Today's Bible Blessing   *July 26*

Ecclesiastes 10:17–Song of Solomon 4:12
A FATHER'S ADMONITION TO HIS DAUGHTER

Ecclesiastes 12:1

"Remember now thy Creator in the days of thy youth . . ."

Now we are coming to the close of the Preacher's exhortation on life! He is winding down his words. He sounds discouraged. He talks to the *"youth"* in their exuberance to live a full life. He writes of *old age* and *its demise*. He declares: *"But if a man live many years, and rejoice in them all; yet let him remember the days of darkness; for they shall be many. All that cometh is vanity"* (Ecclesiastes 11:8).

It is a shame. It seems that Solomon is *"bad-mouthing"* life. It goes to show that riches and pleasures do not bring satisfaction. He looks back at it all and sees very little for which to rejoice. Then he seems to get a grip on himself. He reflects on youth. *"Rejoice, O young man!"* He tells the young to enjoy the years they have. *"Be of good cheer! Walk in the ways of your heart!"* *"But,"* he reminds them that if they do not walk in a godly manner, they will suffer God's judgment for their sin. This is good advice. He should know!

After encouraging young people to remove *sorrow* from their lives and to put evil from their flesh, he exhorts them to *REMEMBER NOW THEIR CREATOR!* (See Ecclesiastes 12:1).

Perhaps our writer is whistling in the dark. You and I know that young people are not immune to sickness or sorrow. Usually we think of the young as being carefree without a trouble in the world. That is not always true. Perhaps Solomon is trying to encourage the youth to look on the bright side of things. He wants them to remember the LORD God. He wants them to think on spiritual things while they can think.

He wants them to step out for the Creator of the Universe. Who is this *Creator*? He is the Lord Jesus Christ. Young people today should think about HIM. They need to be saved. There is so much futility and disappointment in this old world. Solomon knew this. *Seek ye first the Kingdom of God and His righteousness! Set your affection on things above.* This is what Solomon is teaching the young people of his day. This is what he is teaching us today.

There will come a time, we read in verse one of chapter twelve, when a person will have no pleasure in any day. As one grows older, one's health will deteriorate. There is nothing a person can do to deter it. The words are very plain in this chapter. Notice! His legs will weaken. He will be stooped, using a cane. His teeth will rot. His eyes will dim. His ears will not hear. He will not sleep well. His hair will turn white. His strength will go. He will be impotent. He will die. His heart will stop. His brain will die. He will be turned to dust. Then his spirit will return to the God who gave him life. He will go to Heaven if he is *"born-again,"* or he will go to Hell if he rejected Christ while living.

I must admit that all of this seems very depressing. Life is a continual cycle. There is birth. There is life. There is death. There is Heaven or Hell.

Let us hear the conclusion of the whole matter: *"Fear God, and keep his commandments: for this is the whole duty of man. For God shall bring every work into judgment, with every secret thing, whether it be good, or whether it be evil"* (Ecclesiastes 12:13-14).

When I was a young girl, my father gave me a Bible. It had a leather cover. Previously, I had a hard back Bible. I was thrilled to have *a real* Bible. (I still have that precious *Book* someplace in this big house.) He wrote two Scripture verses in the fly leaf of my new Bible. One was I John 2:15-17 exhorting me to *"Love not the world!"* I cherished those verses. They continue to be admonition from my dear father to me, even in my old age.

321

He must have known the following verses concerning *old age* and *death,* but he did not mention them. His whole prayer for me was that I would be a Christian woman who loved the LORD JESUS more than the world about me. **He was a good *DADDY*! And I loved him.**

"TODAY HEAR HIS VOICE"
Keep listening!
(Hebrews 4:7)
**LIFE IS SO BRIEF THAT NO MAN
CAN AFFORD TO LOSE A DAY.**
Oh Lord, that I may put such a value on each day,
Let me take each twenty-four hours, the minutes;
and yes, it's very breath of grace
as a gift of God to use for His Glory.
Forbid that I should take lightly the privilege of one day
to live and use for His Glory and Grace.
**EVERY MOMENT YOU ARE NOT USING YOUR LIFE,
YOU ARE LOSING YOUR LIFE!** (ggs)

Today's Bible Blessing   *July 27*
Song of Solomon 4:13–Isaiah 1:25
A "CANTICLE" OF LOVE

Song of Solomon 1:2
"Let him kiss me with the kisses of his mouth . . ."

We now come to a beautiful song written by Solomon. It is called a *"Canticle"* and one of five short songs that were sung at Jewish special occasions. *The New Unger's Dictionary* tells us that *Song of Solomon* was read at the greatest feast of the year, THE PASSOVER. It is interesting for me to learn this, because in church congregations today, this beautiful love story is not read. It is too embarrassing for many to hear in a mixed gathering. I recall being told that a former pastor was hindered from teaching this love story. Previously he had taught it in our church, but was forbidden to teach it to his new congregation.

My mother, Gertrude Sanborn (ggs), loved this book. She enjoyed teaching it to women. She saw the Lord Jesus Christ in every aspect of the narrative. I have some notes of hers on *Song of Solomon,* but sad to say, I cannot find them as I write.

I remember her studying this book—the allegory—that shows the Lord Jesus Christ's love and devotion to His Church. It is a beautiful teaching, but not everyone can see the teaching.

Most people see THE SONG OF SOLOMON as it stands. It is a true story of Solomon's first love. It is sweet. It is pure. It is a love that all lovers would desire to emulate. *"Let him kiss me with the kisses of his mouth: for thy love is better than wine."* The shepherdess compares her lover's kisses better than wine.

She was amazed that this wonderful man would love her—a shepherd girl. Her skin was *not* like those royal princesses' complexions. She was darkened from the sun—always being with her sheep in the field. She was ashamed, but he loved her as she was. How good for a man to love his bride for who she is and how she looks. This is what a woman wants to hear. May he not let his eyes wander away to another pasture and to another woman's personality and form. How easy for a man to be attracted to a new woman. It is a heart dedication and a sexual determination not to stray from the one to whom we have promised to love until death parts us.

The groom compares his lover to the horses that pull Pharaoh's chariots. What strength she had for child bearing! Her high cheek bones were a thing of beauty. Rows of jewels—perhaps were her lovely teeth. Her neck was firm and beautifully fashioned with a golden chain. She had style! Her eyes were only for him. She was ready for him. Her bed was perfumed. She longed to spend the night with him with his head resting on her breast. He, too, looked forward to such a union. What a picture of pure love and dedication!

Now let us look at this Song with "the eyes" of one who sees the intimate relationship between Christ and His Bride, the Church. I am going to quote from *The Scofield Reference Bible* so you can taste the beauty that many find in this lovely book. *"It is most comforting to see that all these tender thoughts of Christ are for His bride in her unperfected state. The varied exercises of her heart are part of that inner discipline suggested by Ephesians 5:25-27."*

> *"Husbands, love your wives, even as Christ also loved the church, and gave himself for it; That he might sanctify and cleanse it with the washing of water by the word, That he might present it to himself a glorious church, not having spot, or wrinkle, or any such thing; but that it should be holy and without blemish"* (Ephesians 5:25-27).

Notice Song of Solomon 2:14:

> *"O my dove, that art in the clefts of the rock, in the secret places of the stairs, let me see thy countenance, let me hear thy voice; for sweet is thy voice, and thy countenance is comely."*

When she thinks of herself, she sees her imperfections; but when he looks at her, she is "blameless and harmless" (Philippians 2:15). She always has access to Him by the stairs for He is her BELOVED.

"STAND FAST AND HOLD TO THE WRITING"
(II Thessalonians 2:15)
Hold to the writings—record—that God has given us.
Hold not to what men say.
HOLD TO THE WRITTEN WORD!
The WRITINGS are greater than the church creed.
The WRITINGS are God's inspired record!
The WRITINGS TELL OF THE LORD JESUS CHRIST!
(ggs)

Today's Bible Blessing   *July 28*

Isaiah 1:26–Isaiah 5:25
THE LORD'S DISAPPOINTMENT
Isaiah 1:18

"Though your sins be as scarlet, they shall be as white as snow . . ."

Isaiah was a very interesting man. *Many have referred to him as the evangelical prophet.* He dressed in dark clothes as if he were in constant mourning (Isaiah 20:2). Besides the fact that his father's name was *AMOZ* (Isaiah 1:1), and he and his prophetess wife had two sons with long, difficult names of *Mahershalalhashbaz* (8:3) and *Shearjashub* (7:3), we do not know too much about him.

We do know that he was used of God to pen beautiful, meaningful words of prophetic nature that have been passed down to all who read them as God's Holy Scriptures! It is said that this family lived near the TEMPLE in Jerusalem. It must have been an exciting life—but also, a life of being scorned and unbelieved by others. His message was not received well. It must have been difficult. For the most part, we do not think of Isaiah as a person who lived, walked, talked, ate, and slept like other men; but he was as human as any man we have ever known. He was called of God. We should be glad that he answered that call! He wrote during the reigns of several kings of Judah—UZZIAH, JOTHAM, AHAZ, and HEZEKIAH.

The first words from the mouth of Isaiah are words of disappointment and rebuke from the God of Israel: *"I have nourished and brought up children, and they have rebelled against me!"* (See Isaiah 1:2.) Does not your heart go out to God? I know what it is like to put *"my all"* into my children. I know what it is like for some to spurn my advice and go their own way. I know what it is like to be disappointed in their disobedience. And I am not anything like the Almighty God. Just think of the *"slap in the face"* to God after all He did for His chosen children. He did everything for His people and they *"thumbed their noses"* at Him. I can feel the exasperation of

His heart, the disappointment of His soul!

God points out that his people are not just a little bit sick, they are wholly sick. *"The whole head is sick, and the whole heart faint!"* (See Isaiah 1:5.) Their country was desolate. Their cities burned. Before their eyes, strangers came in and devoured their land. Beautiful Zion was left like a servant's hut out in the vineyard.

I have visited a Southern plantation in the New Orleans area. Out by the growing fields were rows of *"small cottages"* where the *Creoles* lived. A *"lodge"* or *"cottage* was the simile Isaiah used to show the great *"loss"* that Jerusalem suffered. They used to have magnificent dwellings. Now, little huts to hide in.

"Except the LORD of hosts had left unto us a very small remnant, we should have been as Sodom, and we should have been like unto Gomorrah" (Isaiah 1:9). As I write these words on this page, I can hear the pathos in the voice of Isaiah. He felt such sorrow over the great loss of face and property that Israel had in those days.

The LORD of hosts made a very astute statement. He asked, *"To what purpose is the multitude of your sacrifices unto me?"* (See verse 11.) It reminds me of the time He stated, through the Prophet Samuel, in I Samuel 15:22: *"Hath the LORD as great delight in burnt offerings and sacrifices, as in obeying the voice of the LORD? Behold, to obey is better than sacrifice, and to hearken than the fat of rams."*

Then God pleaded with His own through the prophet Isaiah,
> *"Come now, and let us reason together, saith the LORD; though your sins be as scarlet, they shall be as white as snow; though they be red like crimson, they shall be as wool"* (Isaiah 1:18).

This verse was one of the Bible verses that I learned in my early Christian life. The LORD continues to *"reason"* with sinners that they receive Jesus Christ as personal Saviour. Your sins and my sins were red like crimson—dark and unrighteous! Jesus made it possible that our sins can be washed away, and become like white wool. RECEIVE HIM TODAY! He is waiting.

He died that you could be forgiven of your unrighteousness.

"HEAVEN"
(Isaiah 33:17)
*"Thine eyes shall see the king in his beauty:
they shall behold the land that is very far off."*
Heaven is very "far off."
We see it dimly in a few Bible passages.
But it is there.
WITHIN THE GATES IS THE KING IN HIS BEAUTY!
Yes, our Saviour has gone into Heaven itself! (ggs)

Today's Bible Blessing   *July 29*

Isaiah 5:26–Isaiah 9:20
THE CALL OF ISAIAH THE PROPHET

Isaiah 6:8

"Whom shall I send, and who will go for us?"

Today let us make a quick review of the early chapters in the book of Isaiah that we have not mentioned so far. I think this is a good thing to do because there are important verses that we do not want to overlook at this time. I have a note in one of my Bibles that tells me to *"LOOK FOR THE MESSIAH IN EVERY VERSE."* This must be the *"secret"* in understanding the sixty-six chapters in this book.

Let us not forget that the PROPHET ISAIAH ministered from c. 740 B.C. to c. 700 B.C. or later. He was one of the first prophets to warn Israel of impending danger—unless there was *repentance.* Let us be encouraged with Isaiah 1:9.

We see that there will be *A REMNANT* of Jews who will believe and take heed to the prophecy. The *REMNANT* is like a holy seed (or a *spiritual kernel*) planted and growing to produce a believing people. What an encouragement for us today!

In Isaiah 2:8, 18, 20, we observe that the LORD'S PEOPLE were idolaters. The LORD'S HOUSE, THE TEMPLE, will be reestablished in Zion during the reign of the LORD JESUS CHRIST in the MILLENNIUM. There will be no more wars! Their swords will be made into plows and their spears into pruning tools. Everyone will *"walk in the light of the LORD!"* It is then that the *"haughtiness"* of men will be made low! There will be great fright. Everyone will try to flee from God; but it will not be possible.

Now look at Isaiah, CHAPTER THREE. Besides hunger, there will be *disrespect* for elders. The younger people will rule over the seniors. They will not care if their elders live or die. Anyone who has clothes and food is looked to for leadership. Jerusalem will be ruined. *The LORD will be provoked!* Open Sodomy will be accepted. No shame!

Haughty women become rulers! They walk provocatively, are unrestrained, and are sexually loose. The LORD will destroy with scabs their coiffeur and beauty. They will give forth an awful stench. Most men will die in war. Women will grab the same man just to have an association with one (4:1). During the millennium, some will remain in Zion, and will be called HOLY after the Lord judges and washes away the filth of Jerusalem.

God will remove His protective hedge from His people (Chapter 5). He calls them His *"vineyard."* **He pronounces six woes on His people.**

1-**Woe** to them that join one to another with no privacy.

2-**Woe** to them that drink strong drink early in the morning.

3-**Woe** to those that practice iniquity like it is nothing.

4-**Woe** to them that call *evil good* and *good evil.*

5-**Woe** to them that think they can do no wrong.

6-**Woe** to them that give their strength to strong drink and to those that justify the wicked for a reward.

NOW WE COME TO ONE OF THE BEST KNOWN AND LOVED CHAPTERS IN ISAIAH–chapter 6. The narrative began in the year that KING UZZIAH died. This king was one of the most successful kings of Judah–a runner-up to Solomon. At sixteen, he became co-regent with his father. He was good in battle–gaining victories with many of his father's enemies. Jerusalem's walls were reinforced by him. He was a patron of agriculture and always worshipped the TRUE GOD! But pride overtook him. Taking an *incense censor*, he was determined to burn it on God's altar. It was then that God smote him with dreaded leprosy, and he was a leper until the day of his death.

It was after UZZIAH's death, that ISAIAH received *his* "call" to the ministry. He saw the LORD sitting on a high throne with ministering Seraphim about Him. In utter fear for his life, Isaiah cried out, "WOE IS ME!" With such holiness surrounding him, he felt dirty and unworthy. God touched the lips of an ordinary man, and at the same time gave him the pen of a ready writer. When the call sounded forth, ***"WHOM SHALL I SEND?"*** Isaiah's heart responded, **"HERE AM I SEND ME!"** With those words of acceptance, God received Isaiah's dedication, sending him out to warn Judah of impending danger and gave him prophetic utterances that are sung to magnificent music today.

"GOD IS FAITHFUL"
(I Corinthians 10:13)
Build your life on the strong premise that only God is truly faithful!
Some are faithful for a while.
Some try to be;
BUT GOD IS FAITHFUL ALWAYS IN ALL THINGS. (ggs)

Today's Bible Blessing   *July 30*

Isaiah 9:21–Isaiah 14:6
WHOSE SON IS HE?

Isaiah 9:6a

"For unto us a child is born, unto us a son is given . . ."

Today I want us to look at the theologically correct verses found in ISAIAH 9:6-7. The absolute beauty of the words astounds us! *"For the prophecy came not in old time by the will of man: but holy men of God spake as they were moved by the Holy Ghost"* (II Peter 1:21).

"FOR UNTO US A CHILD IS BORN, UNTO US A SON IS GIVEN"! We reflect on Mary in the book of Luke. She was young, lovely in form, and attitude. Of all the girls in the world, she was chosen by God to be *the vessel* that would carry His Son into the world. There was no other way for Him to come to earth, become a man, and taste the death of the cross, except He come as any other man through a woman. In the wisdom of God, He made *"woman"* to be able to carry a child within her womb so that child could be born into the world as a perfect, sinless, person. How wonderful! How beautiful! This is what happened to Jesus. The only difference was there was no human father. The *"power of the HIGHEST overshadowed her."*

For you, who have been "mothers," you know that overwhelming feeling of being pregnant. It is a mystery–even though you are married. It still is a mystery of life. A husband and a wife come together in the God-planned manner to conceive a child. If it is amazing for a natural conception, how do you think a woman would feel if an angel suddenly swooped into her room and said she was pregnant with the Son of God?

I think of Mary and her wonder of it all. I think of Mary and her awe. I think of Mary as the angel startled her with such news that she was *"with child."* I think of Mary when she asked, *"How shall this be?"* (See Luke 1:34.) I don't know how old Mary was. Some think she was as young as thirteen or fourteen. I do not know. I never thought her to be that young–perhaps sixteen, or eighteen? She was old enough to know how babies came, for she said, *"I know not a man!"* No matter her age, she was a virgin. She knew that. God knew that! It was His plan that a child would be born to her *in the fullness of time. FOR UNTO US A CHILD IS BORN!* That was the incarnation–**GOD BECAME MAN!**

UNTO US A SON IS GIVEN! Whose Son was given? Was He Mary's son? No, He was God's son! From all eternity past to all eternity present there was *God the Son.* GOD THE FATHER and GOD THE SON and GOD THE HOLY SPIRIT were *forever.* *"IN THE BEGINNING GOD!"* THE SON that was *'given"* by THE FATHER. He was always the eternal Son of God! They were there at "creation!" *"In* the beginning was the WORD and the WORD was WITH GOD, and the WORD WAS GOD!" Jesus Christ is that eternal WORD! He always was. *God THE FATHER so loved the World that He gave His only begotten Son that whosoever believeth in Him should not perish but have everlasting life* (John 3:16). *"For God sent not His son into the world to condemn the world but that the world through Him might be saved"* (John 3:17).

> **For unto us a child is born, unto us a son is given: and the government shall be upon his shoulder: and his name shall be called Wonderful, Counsellor, The mighty God, The everlasting Father, The Prince of Peace. Of the increase of his government and peace there shall be no end. . . (Isaiah 9:6-7a).**

WHOSE SON IS HE?

"THIS IS THE DAY THE LORD HAS MADE!"
(Psalm 118:24)

Today the Lord gently led me into a "truth"
Though I had been acquainted with it,
I had not really apprehended it.
Each day, as I rise, I have been saying,
"Thank you for this day which is mine to use for Thee,
for myself, or for others."
BUT TODAY, GOD SPOKE TO ME AND SAID,
"NO, CHILD, THIS DAY IS NOT THINE. IT IS MINE!"
God said, "Today is mine! I am letting you use it!
The twenty-four hours are Mine, and each moment is Mine.
I have placed you in "MY" day.
It is your privilege to serve "ME."
During its hours, when you are submissive or rebellious,
you are not against the task, you are against "Me." (ggs)

Today's Bible Blessing   *July 31*
Isaiah 14:7–Isaiah 19:15
LUCIFER'S SLIDE FROM SPLENDOR

Isaiah 14:12a
"How art thou fallen from heaven, O Lucifer, son of the morning"

Today we will look at some startling verses. They speak of Lucifer. The prophet Isaiah called him, *"son of the morning"* (Isaiah 14:12). What a title! The morning sky is bright and beautiful. The rising of the sun from the evening's darkness is surprising in its splendor.

Suddenly out of darkness comes light! So with this being called LUCIFER! He was bright in appearance and magnificent in splendor! His beauty is indescribable!

Many believe that Lucifer, whose name means *brightness*, was an archangel, like MICHAEL. In fact, they feel he was the lead angel! Archangels were given the greater duties. See I Thessalonians 4:16 & Jude 9. They were *important heavenly beings* in God's realm. Lucifer's *"covering"* was laden with precious stones— sardius, topaz and the diamond, the beryl, the onyx, the jasper, the sapphire, the emerald, and a deep red stone called the carbuncle (Ezekiel 28:13).

I remember my mother teaching me about this being called LUCIFER and his early beauty. She reminded me that many human beings have beautiful voices. When some speak, it is like music to the ear. When some sing, the tone and range is wondrous. But, when Lucifer spoke, there was a vocal sound not heard in the human realm. When you or I speak or sing, there is a single tone sounded--beautiful or not. When Lucifer spoke or sang, he had a vocal sound of chords (or pipes) that could present music on two or more levels. His voice, before his *"fall"*—was like an organ of sound! The Bible says that the *"workmanship"* of Lucifer's *"tabrets"* (small drums) and *"pipes"* (flutes) was prepared **in** him the day he was created (Ezekiel 28:13). *"Thou wast perfect in thy ways from the day that thou wast created till iniquity was found in thee"* (28:15). **Yes, he was an awesome, powerful created being!**

Then somehow, somewhere, LUCIFER looked around at his sphere of influence and wanted more. Because he was so glorious and powerful, in pride, he reached beyond his territory of power. He must have forgotten that he was a created being. He must have forgotten that he was not a creator. He was only made to help the Creator.

One day in the archives of *"time,"* THIS *LUCIFER*, the *SON OF THE MORNING*, puffed-up himself with self-pride. He decided that he would dethrone God. Boldly, he exclaimed:

> *"I will ascend into heaven, I will exalt my throne above the stars of God: I will sit also upon the mount of the congregation, in the sides of the north: I will ascend above the heights of the clouds; I will be like the most High."*

This is called the *"FALL OF SATAN."* It is sad to relate that this powerful being influenced other lower angels with his prideful, self-willed importance. They, too, fell with their leader, formerly known as *Lucifer.*

Someday, with him, the former son of the morning will be cast into *The Lake of Fire!* (See Revelation 19:20.) In today's reading the prophet wrote of Satan, *"Yet thou shalt be brought down to hell, to the sides of the pit!"* (See Isaiah 14:15.)

The boastful pride of self-importance brought rebuke and condemnation from the *fallen angel's* CREATOR, the LORD God on HIGH. Lucifer was cast out of Heaven to roam. He became the *"prince of the power of the air"* (Ephesians 2:2). He became the *"spirit that now worketh in the children of disobedience."* What a low position for one who had been at the top of creation!

No longer was Lucifer well-thought-of by the Heavenly hosts. He lost his glory and name. Forever he will be known as SATAN or The DEVIL. His self-imposed assignment is to accuse those who know Jesus Christ as Saviour (Revelation 12:10). Christians can only overcome such accusations by the blood of the Lamb, and by the word of their testimony. We read of Satan's accusative finger in the book of Job. Watch out for that accusing finger pointing at you!

"STAND STILL"
(Exodus 14:13)
KEEP THE POSTURE!

These words contain God's command to the believer when he is reduced to great straights and brought into extraordinary difficulties.

He cannot retreat. He cannot go forward.
He is shut up on the right hand and on the left.
WHAT IS HE TO DO?
THE MASTER'S WORD TO HIM IS "STAND STILL!"
Despair whispers, "Lie down or die! Give up!"
Cowardice says "Retreat! Go back!"
Haste says "DO SOMETHING!"
Presumption boasts "Expect a miracle."
Faith says, "STAND STILL"
Keep the posture of an upright man ready for action.
Cheerfully and patiently awaiting the directing voice.
(Copied from Spurgeon by ggs)

Today's Bible Blessing   *August 1*

Isaiah 19:16—Isaiah 24:9
WATCHMAN, WHAT OF THE NIGHT?

Isaiah 21:6
"Go, set a watchman, let him declare what he seeth."

In reading Dr. Unger's dictionary, who by the way was my husband's Hebrew teacher at Dallas Seminary, I saw that

Isaiah appeared to have held a high rank in Jerusalem. The reason being that King Hezekiah, when sending a message to the prophet, sent a high ranking officer, as well as an older priest to do the job (II Kings 19:2). It very well could have been that Isaiah was the *"head man"* over all the prophets. That position was like the one that Elisha had in the school of the prophets, if you recall.

We could agree that Isaiah was a WATCHMAN! (Isaiah 21:5-6):

> *"Prepare the table, watch in the watchtower, eat, drink:*
> *arise, ye princes, and anoint the shield.*
> *For thus hath the Lord said unto me,*
> *Go, set a watchman, let him declare what he seeth."*

What does a *"watchman"* do? First of all, he must be a GUARD. His primary job is to "watch." The next question would be *"WHERE DOES HE WATCH?"* And *"WHAT DOES HE WATCH?"* As I think about these questions, I realize that a watchman must position himself in such a place that he can see everything.

My son-in-law is a hunter. Sometimes he climbs up in a high tree to watch the woods for deer. He observes everything that goes on in those woods, even things that you and I would not think very important. So with a military watchman. He observes everything.

A prophet is *to watch*, like a hunter *watches* for his prey, or like a military man who observes any unusual happening that would affect his men. Watchmen are very important in any warfare situation.

In some ways a mother is a "watchman." She tunes her ears and her eyes to anything unusual. When my children were small, I was a good *"watchman,"* but, I am afraid (as I learned later), that I was not always as good a *"watchman"* to some of my teenage children. I thought I was, but I did not always know the signs. Sometimes, some of them would sneak behind my back and do things that I did not know about. I learned this years later.

Isaiah had a duty to watch. He was not an ordinary watcher. He was ordained of God to do the job. A preacher is to *watch* over the souls of his church people (Hebrews 13:17):

> *"Obey them that have the rule over you, and submit yourselves: FOR THEY WATCH FOR YOUR SOULS, as they that must give account, that they may do it with joy, and not with grief: for that is unprofitable for you."*

Once, in chapter twenty-one, a chariot with horsemen approached. The watchman saw a chariot with donkeys and camels coming. The watchman saw. Then with a loud voice, the watchman called out, *"Chariots are coming!"* The town heard him and prepared for such arrivals. Another time a lion approached the town. The watchman was at his post, looking, seeing, and warning. Once the watchman called out *"Babylon is fallen and her graven images have fallen to the ground!"* He called out of Seir, *"Watchman, what of the night?"*

The Apostle Paul tells the men in Corinth, *"Watch ye, stand fast in the faith, quit you like men, be strong"* (I Corinthians 16:13). *"Continue in prayer, and watch in the same with thanksgiving"* In Colossians 4:2 were his instructions to those in Colossi. To the Thessalonians, he wrote, *"Therefore let us not sleep, as do others; but let us watch and be sober"* (I Thessalonians 5:6).

Are you carefully *"watching"* so you do not stumble into sin? IS THE ROARING LION STALKING YOU? In this day and age, with so much temptation to the flesh, we must be careful not to fall when tempted. Stand on a high place away from the crowd—as a watchman on the watchtower, and warn your soul of any evil that approaches you!

"CONFORMED TO HIS IMAGE"
Jesus has saved us and will have us serve Him
in the way He has laid out.
If we willfully resist and insist in walking according to the flesh,
we must be disciplined.
God loves the Christian, but will have us to be
conformed to the image of His Son.
WE CANNOT "FIGHT" GOD!
If we try, God pins us down at the site of our strength
until we know we cannot serve in our own energies.
God's blows are as holy and loving as His caresses.
Each has its purpose. (ggs)

Today's Bible Blessing   *August 2*

Isaiah 24:10—Isaiah 28:25

AN INFINITE CALM

Isaiah 26:3

"Thou wilt keep him in perfect peace, whose mind is stayed on thee: because he trusteth in thee."

What Christian has not come to today's verse with a need for *"peace"* and *"quiet,"* but most of all, for assurance that her LORD is near. The situation may be tense. The problem may be great. The heartache may be strong--BUT GOD! He comes in like a balm of wind and comforts our hearts.

I remember, in the recent past, that I was in the emergency ward at our local hospital. My doctor told me to go there. There was nothing wrong with me. Well, at least I didn't think there was. After a battery of tests, it was confirmed that my assessment was true. While there, a friend was rushed into the area where I had been placed. I recognized her. I was in the hall. She was put in a cubicle with a curtain between her and me. That meant that there was something seriously wrong. I could hear the confusion the nurses were having caring for my friend. It sounded very serious. Indeed it was.

After a while she was wheeled out into the hall next to my bed. *"Fancy meeting you here,"* I joked softly. It was not a time for hilarity. I knew it. It had been years since we had talked. Because I sensed her condition was serious, I was concerned. What could I do to comfort her? Here, I was a patient, too. So I shut my eyes and sang a song about *"peace."* If I recall, it was a hymn written by W. D. Cornell, called *"WONDERFUL PEACE."* You probably know it.

"Far away in the depths of my spirit tonight rolls a melody sweeter than psalm; In celestial-like strains it unceasingly falls O'er my soul like an infinite calm. Peace! Peace! Wonderful peace, Coming down from the Father above; Sweep over my spirit forever, I pray in fathomless billows of love."

A strange thing happened that day. Our souls were united in a common need for *peace* from our Heavenly Father. Soon my friend was wheeled out into another part of the hospital. She was a real emergency case! Off she went, with her concerned husband by her side.

"LORD, in trouble have they visited thee, they poured out a prayer when thy chastening was upon them. Like as a woman with child, that draweth near the time of her delivery, is in pain, and crieth out in her pangs; so have we been in thy sight, O LORD. We have been with child, we have been in pain. we have as it were brought forth wind; we have not wrought any deliverance in the earth; neither have the inhabitants of the world fallen" (Isaiah 26:17-18).

Another time, another woman, another problem! There was great heartache, great emotional pain. The agony was as if she were giving birth to anguish and sorrow. This same chapter of Isaiah gave me comfort. I passed the verse on to her. It was the twentieth verse of this twenty-sixth chapter.

"O Come, my people, enter thou into thy chambers, and shut thy doors about thee: hide thyself as it were for a little moment, until the indignation be overpast."

One does not have to be in a hospital bed to experience God's great hand of mercy in the depth of sorrow. Sometimes, He puts us in a chamber where we can shut the door (Isaiah 26:20). It is then that He soothes our hearts and lets us cry.

"Trust ye in the LORD for ever: for in the LORD JEHOVAH is everlasting strength: For He bringeth down them that dwell on high; the lofty city, He layeth it low; He layeth it low, even to the ground" . . . (Isaiah 26:4-5).

"WHEN GOD MET JACOB, THERE WAS A CHANGE"
(Genesis 32)
One dark and lonely night, the Lord dealt with Jacob.
God was there. Jacob was there.
In firm, stern measures, God stopped Jacob in his journey
and broke him.,
THE LORD WRESTLED WITH JACOB—
NOT JACOB WITH THE LORD.
1. God dealt with Jacob in the night time alone.
2. God smote him on the thigh, the site of his strength.
3. Jacob resisted a disabling blow to his body.
   It was necessary for God to subdue him.
4. Jacob smitten now realized his weakness and clings.
5. Broken at last, he is ready for the blessing.
       A touch from God is not always a caress.
       It may take a blow to cause him to yield.
Though God deals in love, His dealings are often strenuous.
ggs—copied in part)

Today's Bible Blessing   *August 3*
Isaiah 28:26—Isaiah 32:15
QUIETNESS RESTORES CONFIDENCE

Isaiah 30:15
"In quietness and in confidence shall be your strength . . ."

As I meditate in the lovely writings of the prophet, Isaiah, I find comfort. I am not trying to teach the prophecies. I could not, even if I wanted to. I am not a theologian—nor do I want to be. I am a woman, wife, a mother, a grandmother—even a great grandmother. Mostly people do not pay too much attention to what I think or write. But God has burdened my heart to write a *"blessing"* a day from our **DAILY BIBLE READINGS.** I long to receive just *that—A BLESSING.* And, if you are *blessed with me,* that is a double *blessing* for me!

Today, let us look at a beautiful admonition from Isaiah's pen. They are words directly from the LORD'S mouth: *"For thus saith the Lord GOD, the Holy One of Israel . . ."* (Isaiah 30:15). Let me tell you about the Name of God here, *THE LORD GOD.* It is called a **Tetragrammaton.** Those are the four consonants of the ancient Hebrew Name for God. It is variously transliterated *JHVH, IHVH, JHWH, YHVH, and YHWH.* This Name of God is considered

335

too sacred to be spoken aloud! The modem reconstructions are *Yahweh, or Jehovah. Jehovah* is the proper reconstruction rather than *Yahweh.*

This is so beautiful! The Name of *JEHOVAH* was so precious that the Hebrews were not supposed to pronounce it. They substituted other Names like *"LORD"* in its place. Jehovah's Name here was not pronounced. How HOLY is His Name! Yet today, the Name of the Lord is taken in vain on every doorstep. People think nothing of using His Name as if it were a punctuation mark in a sentence.

Just thinking about that HOLY NAME, brings an awe, a hush, a silence. Isaiah wrote *"in returning and rest shall ye be saved. . ."* The Israelites were floundering. They were in great distress. They did not want to hear the strong prophecies. They said, *"Prophesy not unto us right things, speak unto us smooth things. prophesy deceits"* (Isaiah 30:10). They did not want the straight truth!

How we human beings need times of *"quietness"!* Sometimes the hustle and bustle of life is too much! It wears us down. It wars against our souls. Sometimes our nervous system cannot stand anymore. We must come apart and rest, or we will fall apart without it! The human body can only take so much. We push ourselves or someone else pushes us until we break!

***"Quietness"* restores confidence.** As I write, I am remembering a time when my husband and I were in Michigan. We were visiting a certain pastor's home. Their home was humble, but there was a *"joy of family"* in that house! They had many children. Most were adults and out of the nest. There were two left at home that I remember. They were the last of the lot! How they were loved! I was in need of *"quietness."* So I found a little room in the attic welcoming me with *peace* and *silence.* I remember it well. The *"peace,"* the *"rest,"* the *"quietness."* I needed it so! All that *"quietness"* brought a sweet *"confidence"* to my weary soul!

The sad fact about these verses in Isaiah 30:15-16 is that Judah would not wait for the Lord GOD to work out their problem. They rushed ahead of Him and said, *"No, for we will flee upon horses . . ."*

Are you in a rush today? Do you have unrest in your soul? Are you turning a deaf ear to God's plea for you to wait on Him in *quietness?* If so, stop today! There is a voice behind you speaking. IT IS GOD'S VOICE! It is saying *"This is the way, walk ye in it!"* (See Isaiah 30:21.)

"IS HE REALLY FOR ME?"
(Job 23:6)
Will He plead against me with His great power?
No!
But He will put strength in me.
He cares when we are weary and overwhelmed.
Not only does He care, but He imparts strength.
Indeed He is my strength. (ggs)

Today's Bible Blessing   *August 4*
Isaiah 32:16—Isaiah 37:7
SAILING UNDER THE BRIDGE
Isaiah 32:20
"Blessed are ye that sow beside all waters . . ."

I have this Scripture verse on my cupboard door in my kitchen. It speaks to me. Let's meditate on these words today. When I dedicated my life to the LORD to be used where ever He wanted and whenever He wanted, I had no idea where I would end up. For some reason, I thought I would be an active Bible teacher with children and women. Perhaps I would be on some foreign shore. I'd taken Spanish and thought: "Perhaps God would have me be a missionary in a Spanish-speaking country." I did not know.

When I began dating my husband, whom I had known in high school, he went off to college to study medicine. I thought, *"Oh, I would be a medical doctor's wife in some foreign land."* Instead, when we were married, we drove to Dallas, Texas, where my husband spent five years studying the Bible, and Greek, and Hebrew. Where would God lead us to serve Him? We did not know.

After seminary, we were at a little Ohio college for a year. That was a learning experience. Then we were at Purdue University in Indiana where my husband was a *"graduate teaching assistant."* Soon he became a Navy chaplain and served five years on active duty both in the USA, on the sea, and overseas. After that, he was a pastor of a good-sized church in Massachusetts. (That was before the super aggressive churches.) Then after a church split, he pastored a smaller church in the area. Then we moved to Collingswood, New Jersey, in 1965. All the while, I followed where my husband went. He was my leader.

Now why am I telling you this? All of these places (and a few I left out) were *"waters"* of service for my husband and me. All of them were not pleasant. Some were. Some were not. The truth is that *all waters* are not pleasant either.

When we were dating, my husband and I sailed. I enjoy sailing. I loved to feel the wind take hold of the sails and send our boat scooting across the lake. Some days a storm would approach. We would hurry home. Some days the sea was calm. We could sail with ease and grace. Sometimes other crafts would be near. We had to be careful not to bump into them. My husband was a good sailor. He knew how to navigate on all waters.

I remember once a friend at the Jersey shore invited us to sail with him. He had a beautiful boat. We came to a bridge that we would have to sail under. Our host was going to start his auxiliary engine to motor us under that bridge. I asked, *"Why are you doing that?"* He told us it was tricky to sail under that bridge. He was afraid of the water there. He did not want to hit the sides. I looked at my husband and my husband looked at me. I said to our host, *"My husband can sail your boat under that bridge."* So our friend gave the *"con"* to Dr. Waite. My husband took the tiller and sailed under the bridge with ease. He had the skill. It was fun!

So with life—some places you and I find ourselves in are not much fun! The *"water"* is frightening and dirty. The *"water"* is deep. It is full of unpleasant objects floating around. Life is not good there. Other times we find ourselves in *delightful "water."* Everyone is nice to us there. Flowers are floating around us. The fish are beautiful. The stream is healthy. It is a joy to be there.

As we grow spiritually in the Lord, we find ourselves appreciating varied areas of service where the Lord has put us. All manner of people come to us. All kinds of opportunities open to our work. Who would have thought, in those early Seminary years, that today Dr. Waite would become an authority in the defense of the King James Bible and its underlying Hebrew, Aramaic, and Greek Words. If we had not sailed our lives in many waters, we would never have been able to sail under the difficult bridge of BIBLICAL DEFENSE that we find ourselves in today.

May you be encouraged as you sow beside all waters too. You'll be surprised how blessed you can be!

"MORE DEAR, MORE NEAR"
"Lord Jesus, make thyself to me
a living bright reality,
More present to faith's vision keen
Than any earthy object seen.
More dear, more intimately nigh
Than e'en the sweetest earthly tie."
(ggs copied this; author unknown)
This poem has helped me often. I heard it first quoted
by Pastor Eric Folsom at Calvary Baptist Church.

Isaiah 37:8—Isaiah 40:24
BE NOT AFRAID OF WORDS
Isaiah 35:4

"Be strong . . . your God will come with vengeance . . . and save."

Now we come to a very exciting narrative given by Isaiah, starting with chapter 36. If you remember, Assyria was a powerful nation. They had swooped in and taken Israel away from their homeland for at least one hundred years before the seventy years Babylonian captivity. Because of the Assyrians' military power, nations feared them and fell under their spell.

Assyria wanted to capture Jerusalem and all of Judah. In the natural, it would have been very easy. It seemed they wanted to take Judah without bloodshed. Their king, *Sennacherib*, a Napoleon-like figure, sent *Rabshakeh* from Lachish to Jerusalem, meeting *Eliakim* and *Joah* by "HEZEKIAH'S FOUNTAIN" (Isaiah 36:2). This water supply was shown to Dr. Waite and me when we were in Israel a few years ago. *Rabshakeh* insisted upon speaking in the Hebrew tongue so everyone within hearing range could understand their threats. *King Hezekiah* trusted *"his people"* completely. He had instructed them to listen, but say not a word.

The Assyrian threat conveyed the thought that Egypt was weak and would be no military help to Jerusalem at all. Also, they reminded *Eliakim and Joah* that Hezekiah had removed all of the *evil "high places,"* requiring His people to worship the TRUE GOD in Jerusalem only. Of course, this was the right thing for Hezekiah to do. In other words, it was inferred that Israel's God would be weak in battle! Sennacherib's plan was to give Judah 2,000 horses in exchange for gold pilfered from the temple. Weak Egypt could not match that offer! All within ear-shot heard the Assyrian's boisterous threat: *"Let not Hezekiah deceive you: for he shall not be able to deliver you!"* Those words *brought fear* to everyone who heard them!

Hezekiah's men held their peace. They said not a word. They tore their clothes in fear and ran to Hezekiah's doorstep. Hezekiah, too, tore his clothes, a sign of great distress. This was bad news indeed! Covered in sackcloth, the king went into the HOUSE OF THE LORD. It was then that Hezekiah sent for the PROPHET ISAIAH! The King knew where to go for spiritual and physical help! (Isaiah 37:2).

Isaiah's message to his king was the following:
"Thus saith the LORD, Be not afraid of the words that thou hast heard, wherewith the servants of the king of Assyria have blasphemed me. Behold, I will send a blast upon him, and he shall hear a rumour, and return to his own land; and I will cause him to fall by the sword in his own land."

When Rabshakeh returned to the king of Assyria, he found the Assyrian king warring against Libnah. King Sennacherib brazenly declared, in a message to King Hezekiah, that Hezekiah's God could do nothing to help Jerusalem. These were real threats! Hezekiah was reminded—if all the gods of the other nations could not protect them, how could Hezekiah's God help Jerusalem? All these words frightened Hezekiah more than ever.

King Hezekiah ran into the Temple, laid the message/letter out before the LORD, and prayed: *"O Lord of hosts."* Hezekiah cried, *"God of Israel, that dwellest between the cherubims . . . open thine eyes, O LORD, and see: and hear all the words of Sennacherib, which hath sent to reproach the living God"* (Isaiah 37: 16-17).

HEZEKIAH'S FAITH WAS RENEWED! ISAIAH'S PROPHECIES HELD TRUE! The LORD defended Jerusalem for His sake and for David's sake. The ANGEL of the LORD entered the Assyrian camp. He killed 185,000 in one night. Sennacherib fled to Nineveh for refuge. Afterwards, as he worshipped his god, his own sons killed him with a sword! HAVE YOU EVER BEEN AT THE END OF YOURSELF—NO PLACE TO GO—LIFE AT A STANDSTILL? Go to the LORD. Put your distress out before Him. Watch him send a *"blast"* to rescue and renew you!

"STOP! Arrest Your Heart!"
"In the house of thy Father, there are many places to sit.
(John 14:2)
STOP!
Arrest your heart!
Stop your heart that it has no fear.
I will bear you to the house of My Father"
(ggs. from the Congo translation--without endorsement)

Today's Bible Blessing   August 6
Isaiah 40:25—Isaiah 43:24
BE NOT DISMAYED

Isaiah 41:10
"Fear thou not for I am with thee: be not dismayed; for I am thy God:"

My mother had a plaque on her kitchen wall. It was the words of this beautiful verse in Isaiah 41. After she died, I took those words from her wall and put them on my wall. I look at them almost daily. The paper on which the words are printed is *water marked* and *old;* but the words are as living today as they were when mother put them on her wall. For that matter, they are as living today as they were the day that Isaiah put them down on some parchment.

Sometime last year, I thought to myself, "I *would like to write about this verse.* " I would like to ponder each word. I kept wondering what *"be not dismayed"* really meant. Those three words are couched between *"FEAR THOU NOT"* and "FOR I AM THY GOD!" I remembered that verse when our son David died very suddenly. God whispered in my ear, *"BE NOT DISMAYED!"*

It's almost like *the protection* a mother and father give to their small child as they walk down the street. Each of the child's hands is held by a parent, the mother on one side and the father on the other. She is *protected* between the two people who love her more than anyone in the whole world. There is no fear in such protection. There is no cause for alarm, for Mommie and Daddy are there. That's God's protection to me and to you, too, that is, if you know Jesus Christ as Saviour.

Let's look at the word, *"DISMAY."* I asked my husband what that word meant in the Hebrew language. He said it meant "to look," "to gaze," "to look about in anxiety." The King James Bible translators chose the word, "DISMAY" to convey such a meaning. "FEAR THOU NOT!! DON'T LOOK ABOUT YOUR CIRCUMSTANCES OF LIFE WITH SUCH ANXIETY! I AM THY GOD!"

How that speaks to me today! I must confess, at this writing, that I am going through terrific *stress, anxiousness,* and *alarm.* I don't want to be this way. My body is overwhelmed with such alarm. It seems that I have no control over the pain this *"DISMAY"* has brought.

How good of my Heavenly Father to give me this verse today just when I needed it! "FEAR THOU NOT, I AM THY GOD!" Yes, I know that He is God and that He is my God! I am *"born-again."* Yet the *"dismay"* has left me *"diminished of courage"* and *"intimidated."* Another word for it is *"daunt."*

I remind myself of Elijah on Mount Carmel when he faced Jezebel's false prophets. He thought he was the only one who dared such truthful separation! My, he was bold. He was fearless and brave! *"HOW LONG HALT YE BETWEEN TWO OPINIONS?"* His boldness could not be equaled. Yes, there have been brave men and women who have stood up for the truth. But none can surpass the brave boldness of the PROPHET ELIJAH!

Then Jezebel did her dastardly deed! How easily a bold Christian can become *discouraged* by an ill-advised *spoken word.* The Bible tells us in I Kings 19:1, *"Ahab told Jezebel all that Elijah had done."* The very fact that the *wicked woman* was *"on Elijah's case"* put *fear* into his heart.

Sometimes it doesn't take much to discourage a Christian—especially one who has been on the front lines of warfare as Elijah was. He had slain 450 prophets of Baal and 400 prophets of the groves (I Kings 18:19). He was exhausted. Then Jezebel threatened him. She cast a death-spell on Elijah (I Kings 19: 1-2). He crumbled in fear! He ran for his life into the wilderness and sat under a juniper tree wanting to die.

Then an angel came to Elijah and strengthened him. I like to think that God whispered in his ear, *"FEAR THOU NOT, FOR I AM WITH THEE. BE NOT DISMAYED. I AM THY GOD. I WILL STRENGTHEN THEE. I WILL HELP THEE."*

So I ask myself, "What more do I need to hear in the trials of my life than the "STILL SMALL VOICE OF GOD saying to me, "BE NOT DISMAYED!"

"STAND STILL & LISTEN"
(Exodus 14:13)
Sometimes God would have us "stand still"
in an overwhelming trial.
"Stand still and see the salvation of the LORD!"
DESPAIR says GIVE UP AND DIE!
COWARDS say RETREAT!
IMPATIENCE says DO SOMETHING!
PRESUMPTION says EXPECT A MIRACLE!
But FAITH says LISTEN TO GOD AND HEAR HIM SAY
STAND STILL & SEE!
(Copied by GGS from Spurgeon's Morning & Evening)

Today's Bible Blessing   *August 7*
Isaiah 43:25—Isaiah 47:15
I WILL BE WITH THEE

Isaiah 43:2
"When thou passest through the waters, I will be with thee . . ."
Isaiah was a bold prophet of the true God! He told Judah that it would be conquered and destroyed, except for a small remnant of the Jews. These were times of *"hope"* expressed by the prophet to give *"hope"* and assurance that someday the Messiah would come. He would come again after his *"first coming"* (the rapture) and establish a kingdom on the earth. This was very exciting prophecy! It was mostly not believed in Isaiah's day, or, for that matter–in our day.

> *"When thou passest through the waters, I will be with*
> *thee; and through the rivers, they shall not overflow*
> *thee: when thou walkest through the fire, thou shalt*
> *not be burned; neither shall the flame kindle upon thee.*
> *For I am the LORD thy God, the Holy One of Israel, thy*

Saviour. Since thou wast precious in my sight, thou hast been honourable, and I have loved thee: therefore will I give men for thee, and people for thy life. Fear not: for I am with thee: I will bring thy seed from the east, and gather thee from the west. . ." (Isaiah 43:2-5).

What a reassuring prophecy for the ears of the Jewish people. Yet, I am not sure they fully understood what Isaiah was saying. If the people would have reflected on God's mercy to them all of their lives, after escaping the bitter Egyptian Pharaoh, they would have seen His grace in their lives. Did not God lead them through the Red Sea? Did not Moses raise his rod and the waters stood in heaps on each side? Did not the thousands of Israelites walk on dry ground? The fiery cloud confused and blinded the Egyptian armies! When they rushed on the river bed, the heaps of water fell flat. The confused army drowned. Israel was safe! They had *"passed through the waters."* How could they ever forget? But they did.

Isaiah pressed forward in his prophecies. He saw the fiery furnace in Nebuchadnezzar's day. Into that inferno, the three Hebrew children were thrown. They would not bow to the idol of gold. After a night of horrid anticipation, the king looked in the furnace. There he saw them! Those Hebrew children were alive! Not a hair on their head was burned. Not a thread of clothes that covered them was charred. As the king peered into the furnace, he saw another *"man"* with the living Hebrew men. That *"man"* was the Son of God. *"When thou walkest through the fire, thou shalt not be burned . . ."* That prophecy would come to pass! God's word is true! It never fails!

One of my father's favorite songs speaks of this verse. My Dad knew tribulation. Almost every one of his loved ones had suffered an illness or poverty. One brother and his sister had tuberculosis. Another brother died of cancer. His daughters knew suffering. One died at twenty, one was birth injured, and another suffered a long illness. Then Mother knew pain in her old age. My father lost a leg suddenly—without warning. Daddy knew the gasping for breath when the waters of grief overwhelmed him. He knew the heat of pain when sorrow and death compassed his soul. Yet, like the patriarch, Job, REN O. SANBORN, my dad, never blamed God or cursed His Name.

My father's song was *GOD LEADS US ALONG*. The words are by G. A. Young who was born in 1903, which—by the way—is the same year of my father's birth. Listen to Mr. Young's words:

In shady green pastures so rich and so sweet,
God leads his dear children along;
Where the water's cool flow bathes the weary one's feet,
God leads His dear children along.
Some through the waters, Some through the flood,
Some through the fire, But all through the blood:
Some through great sorrow, But God gives a song
In the night season and all the day long.

"A PURPOSE"
(Psalm 101:2)
"I WILL WALK WITHIN MY HOUSE WITH A PERFECT HEART!"
A GOOD MOTTO!
A HARD SAYING!
"Be like Jesus all day long in the home and in the throng . . ."
Within my house and my circumstances,
I will purpose to walk uprightly! (ggs)

Today's Bible Blessing   *August 8*

Isaiah 48:1—Isaiah 52:3
WHAT ARE WE SAYING?

Isaiah 49:2

"And he hath made my mouth like a sharp sword . . ."

Chapter 49 is interesting to me. Isaiah is begging people of Judah to listen to him. He tells them that the LORD hath called him from his mother's womb. Yes, his mother knew he was going to be a man who would mention the Name of the LORD. She knew this long before he was born!

How wonderful to be called of God before you are born! This was true of the Lord Jesus Christ. Jesus' conception was different from any other man's. He was named before He was born. His work at Calvary was known before the foundation of the world.

A few other mothers knew the sex of their children, such as John the Baptist's mother and Isaac's mother. Now-a-days, with all our modern methods, mothers are told the sex of their children long before they are born. Often this is a sure way that a pregnant woman decides against or for abortion. That *"thing"* inside of her is not just a lump of nothing, but it is *a real, living person* who, when born, can run and talk and love and cry.

Look at verse two: Isaiah's mouth was the mouth of a prophet! *God would make his words sharp and to the point.* When he was a young boy, Isaiah was set aside—in the shadow of God's hand. The boy had been hidden away, waiting his "time" to prophesy. His life was full of many things to do. He had work. He had friends. He had goals. So with Jesus, His ministry did not begin until He was thirty.

Then one day Isaiah saw God. That was the time Isaiah saw Him *"high and lifted up."* God's train filled the Temple! *Seraphim were there! Words that spoke of God's holiness were heard!* That was the day Isaiah answered God's call: *"WHO WILL GO FOR US?"* (Notice the *"us"* which speaks of *the Triune God*.)

It was then that Isaiah came to realize that God was *"preparing & polishing him"* for His service all those years. It was then that Isaiah discovered that God was *"protecting & pruning him,"* so he could be God's special servant. Yes, Isaiah's writings would cause many to glorify God!

So with the Lord Jesus Christ–His mouth was like a sharp sword. We read about His mouth in the book of *Revelation.* JESUS WOULD SAY PROFOUND THINGS! He would know of everything there was to know. He would know the past and the future. For He would be the Son of God!

> *"And to the angel of the church in Pergamos write; These things saith he which hath the sharp sword with two edges; (Revelation 2: 12). And out of his mouth goeth a sharp sword, that with it he should smite the nations: and he shall rule them with a rod of iron: and he treadeth the winepress of the fierceness and wrath of Almighty God" (Revelation 19: 15).*

We know that LOGOS—the living WORD. The Apostle John tells us the following in John 1:1-3:

> *"In the beginning was the Word, and the Word was with God, and the Word was God. The same was in the beginning with God. We also know that the WRITTEN WORD OF GOD is quick, and powerful, and sharper than any two-edged sword, piercing even to the dividing asunder of soul and spirit, and of the joints and marrow, and is a discerner of the thoughts and intents of the heart."*

The prophet's mouth spoke words that were sharp and biting. Jesus, THE WORD MADE FLESH, had a mouth like a cutting blade that spoke truth concerning life and death!

What are you and I doing with our mouths? Are we speaking words of discernment based on Biblical wisdom and knowledge? Or are we cursing with our mouths, taking God's Name in vain, or denying the Lord that bought us by our complaining words and bitter spirit? Can we not learn something from Isaiah? Should we not get a fresh look at the Holiness of God and clean up our mouths to praise His Holy Name?

THOU ART MY SERVANT, O ISRAEL, IN WHOM I WILL BE GLORIFIED! (Isaiah 49:3).

"FOR THIS CHILD I PRAYED"
(I Samuel 1:27)
"Take this child away and nurse it for me . . ." (Exodus 2:9)
". . . and when he is old, he will not depart from it."
(Proverbs 22:6)
To TRAIN UP A CHILD IS NOT FOR A YEAR,
BUT ALL HIS YEARS
BY PRECEPT AND SCRIPTURE AND LIFE!
If a child learns to walk in The WAY,
he will remain in THE WAY into mature life.
Proverbs 22:6 may be a statement of faith, not a promise.
To "train" a child early is to assure "a pattern" for maturity!
(ggs)

Today's Bible Blessing   *August 9*

Isaiah 52:4—Isaiah 57:19
THE SUFFERING MESSIAH

Isaiah 53:6b
". . . The LORD hath laid on him the iniquity of us all . . ."

Today, we come to some of the most beautiful words in the Bible: ISAIAH 53! The Holy Spirit moved Isaiah to pen classic words of beauty! It is the prophecy of the suffering Messiah. God's people, the Jews, have no excuse! In their own Scriptures, they can find Him for Whom they long to see!

Sad to say, many of the Jewish people are ignorant of the *"words"* in the Old Testament. The very oracles of God that they preserved and guarded are like mysterious words to them. Worse yet, many Jewish people do not know the simplest Biblical accounts of their historic ancestors.

Many people know these *"words"* by heart, not realizing they know Scripture. The gifted musician/composer, named Handel, wrote glorious music with these *"words"* taken verbatim from this Bible passage.

Who is the "He," and the "Him" referred to in Psalm 53? It is none other than the Lord Jesus Christ, the very *Messiah* for Whom the Jews longed. They did not recognize Him when He came. Some believed. Most in authority did not!

This Psalm predicted the crucifixion of Jesus. Pilate asked, "What shall I do then with Jesus which is called *Christ?"* (See Matthew 27:22.) The answer came roaring back to his ears, *"CRUCIFY HIM!"*

When I was in my high school chorus, we sang *HANDEL'S MESSIAH.* Every year Mr. Hilty led the high school in this glorious music. The freshmen would learn it from the upper classmen. When they became seniors, they taught it to the new ones coming into the group. All those students sang, *"Surely HE hath borne our griefs, and carried our sorrows . . ."* I can hear it now in my mind's musical ear.

Softly and slowly, with pathos and clarity, we sang *"HE WAS WOUNDED FOR OUR TRANSGRESSIONS!"* Then suddenly, the singers would awaken! We would sing–almost in *tears– "THE CHASTISEMENT OF OUR PEACE WAS UPON HIM."* Then the sorrowful words were pronounced, *"AND WITH HIS STRIPES, AND WITH HIS STRIPES, WE ARE HEALED."* How can anyone read this passage and not see Jesus, the Messiah?

> *"And when they were come to the place, which is called Calvary, there they crucified him, and the malefactors, one on the right hand, and the other on the left. Then said Jesus, Father, forgive them; for they know not what they do. And they parted his raiment, and cast lots. And the people stood beholding. And the rulers also with them derided him, saying, He saved others; let him save himself, if he be Christ, the chosen of God. And the soldiers also mocked him, coming to him, and offering him vinegar, And saying, If thou be the king of the Jews, save thyself. And a superscription also was written over him in letters of Greek, and Latin, and Hebrew, THIS IS THE KING OF THE JEWS"* (Luke 23:33-38).

YOU AND I ARE LIKE DUMB SHEEP. It is not very flattering. But–sin is not pretty! We have gone *"astray"*! We have turned to our own sinful way! So what did GOD THE FATHER DO?

John the Baptist exclaimed of Jesus, *"BEHOLD THE LAMB OF GOD THAT TAKETH AWAY THE SIN OF THE WORLD!" (See John* 1:29.) That is exactly what Isaiah predicted in Isaiah 53. God the Father laid on Jesus the *"iniquity"* (sin) of us all! As a dumb sheep, Jesus who took YOUR place and MY place at Calvary.

> *"All we like sheep have gone astray; we have turned everyone to HIS own way; and the LORD hath laid on HIM the iniquity of us all"* (Isaiah 53:6).

What have you done with Jesus, who is called the Christ? THINK ABOUT IT!

347

> **"THE SHEPHERD OF MY SOUL"**
> (I Peter 2:25)
> *"'The Lord is MY Shepherd!'"*
> By day He gently leads. By night He is The DOOR.
> He protects from the very real perils that are round about us.
> Our Shepherd knows us individually.
> He knows each particular need, our weaknesses, our peculiarities,
> and tendencies to stray.
> When we are sorely tired, He will gently lead on.
> When we are weary and wounded,
> He will anoint our heads and heal our wounds.
> He refreshes us with his tender touch and care.
> We know that whatever the trial of the day,
> His goodness and loving kindness follow."
> (copied by ggs, probably from Morning & Evening; not sure.)
> [I changed it some before I knew it was a quote]

Today's Bible Blessing   *August 10*

Isaiah 57:20—Isaiah 63:3
"CHRISTIAN LYING"

Isaiah 59:14
". . . truth is fallen in the street . . ."

What is truth? That is the question Pilate asked of Jesus, prior to His crucifixion, at the judgment hall (John 18:38). It was Jesus' statement concerning *"truth"* that brought Pilate to such a question. See verse thirty-seven! Pilate's first question of Jesus was *"ART THOU THE KING OF THE JEWS?"* (See John 18:33, 37.) Then Jesus claimed that His kingdom was not of this world. If it were, Jesus said that His servants would fight for him. Then Jesus made a startling statement. He said that He was born into this world to bear witness to *THE TRUTH.*

It was then that a confused Pilate asked Jesus, *"What is truth?"* *"Was Jesus a king?"* was another question. Jesus' response was, *"To this end was I born, and for this cause came I into the world."* The rest of that sentence is extremely interesting. Jesus said he came into the world that He should bear witness unto *THE TRUTH.* It was after Pilate asked this question about *"truth,"* that he announced to the Jews. *"I find in him no fault at all."*

Now look at our Isaiah 59:13-15 passage. THE PROPHET SAID THAT THE PEOPLE WERE LYING AGAINST THE LORD! They were uttering FALSEHOOD from their heart right in front of Him! I've heard of some who cannot speak the truth, apparently. They have lied so much that they don't even know what the truth is. Their mouths are full of lies! What a condition to be in! *Satan is the "father" of lies.* John 8:44 says so.

TRUTH FAILETH! Sometimes *lying* **becomes such a habit that there is no truth found in the mouth of the liar.** Nothing can be believed! He has become a *"forger"* of lies, a *"refuge"* of lies. His life bears the *"fruit"* of his lies. In fact, he has become a *"teacher"* of lies.

> *"Truth forever on the scaffold,*
> *Wrong forever on the throne—*
> *Yet that scaffold sways the future,*
> *And, behind the dim unknown,*
> *Standeth God within the shadow,*
> *Keeping watch above his own."*
> *(James Russell Lowell)*

Today there is so much *casual lying.* **Have you noticed?** People will say, *"I'll be in church!"* And they are not there. They say, *"I'll help you with the church address directory!"* But they do not do it. They say, *"Oh, I will proofread for you, Pastor."* But they never do. Some say, *"Come to the gathering and I'll take you home!"* You come to the gathering, and no one takes you home.

Far worse are the lies that Christians tell their Lord and Saviour. *"I'll go where you want me to go, dear Lord,"* they sing. Some even go to Bible school or college. Yet, when the time comes, they skip the mission field and decide to make money in a secular job. They don't even *"go"* to church faithfully. *"Take my silver and my gold,"* they sing. Yet, they seldom put a coin in the offering box.

Many Christians marry, promising faithfulness and love to their mates for life. Soon the love dies, the heart grows cold, and they find another who makes them feel better than the mate they married. Often Christian parents dedicate their baby to the Lord. They promise to teach him the Bible and bring him to church. They promise to live before the child with a dedicated heart and life and be a Christian example. Soon their commitment is forgotten and the child seldom hears a Bible story or goes to Sunday School. ALL THIS IS CALLED *"CHRISTIAN LYING"*!

God says concerning lying "None calleth for justice, nor any pleadeth for truth: they trust in vanity, and speak lies; they conceive mischief, and bring forth iniquity" (Isaiah 59:4).

Do you remember who Jesus is? Never forget—He is *THE TRUTH!* If you are His, you should be TRUTH, too! Never forget the words of John the Beloved when he said, *"I have no greater joy than to hear that my children walk in truth"* (III John 4).
WHERE HAVE YOU BEEN WALKING LATELY?

"READ THE BOOK"
(I Peter 4:12)
"In order to get the answers to your prayers,
you must be reading The Book,
So God, by His Spirit, can put His spotlight on a verse."
A PROMISE! AN ANSWER! A HELP!
We may think no one ever had such a need, or care as we;
But ever since man first began to pray, he has had the same "cry."
And His Word has the same answers!
Not a prayer is unheard, when heeded.
He is "touched" by our sorrows.
(ggs: copied in part. Source unknown)

Today's Bible Blessing   *August 11*
Isaiah 63:4—Jeremiah 1:8
WHAT THE EYE CANNOT SEE
Isaiah 64:4
"Neither hath the eye seen . . . what He hath prepared . . ."

This will be our last "blessing" from the prophet
Isaiah's work. I will quote from **THE NEW UNGER'S BIBLE
DICTIONARY**: "Isaiah in his ministry emphasized the spiritual and
the social. He struck at the root of the nation's trouble in its apostasy
and idolatry and sought to save Judah from its moral and political and
social corruption. He failed, however, to turn the nation Godward. His
divine commission carried the warning that this would be the case
(Isaiah 6:9-12). Thereupon he boldly declared the inevitable crash of
Judah and the preservation of a small godly remnant (6:13). However,
gleams of hope radiate throughout this prophecy."

**One of the loveliest passages in Scripture is found in I
Corinthians 2:9.** I'm sure you remember these words:

"But as it is written, Eye hath not seen, nor ear heard,
neither have entered into the heart of man, the things which
God hath prepared for them that love him."

**This verse is a reflection of today's verse in ISAIAH
64:4.** It is thrilling for me, personally, to see Paul take Isaiah and
explain it to the Christians at Corinth—and by extension to us. Look at
the Isaiah passage with me.

"For since the beginning of the world men have not heard, nor
perceived by the ear, neither hath the eye seen, O God, beside
thee, what he hath prepared for him that waiteth for him."

**When I was a young Christian, I heard the passage in
I Corinthians taught as the believer looking forward to the**

unknown wonders of Heaven. It is true that our eyes have not seen Heaven, and our ears have not heard the *"Holy, Holy, Holy"* of the Seraphim like Isaiah saw and heard in the sixth chapter, BUT THIS IS NOT WHAT PAUL WAS TALKING ABOUT.

Paul was talking about the full revelation of the Words of God to mankind! Man could not fathom God's revelation—His Words—written for our learning and admonition. Paul saw it. It had been revealed to him on the backside of the desert. For three years the Lord Jesus taught the apostle, who was called out of *"due time."* He learned truths never before revealed. He heard about the body of Christ—the *"church."* He learned other *"mysteries"* and truth for the edification of us believers!

If the *"princes of this world"* had known, they would not have killed the Lord of glory. That's what I Corinthians 2: 8 says. This wonderful Saviour, His *"salvation,"* and the *"Church"* which is His body were a *"hidden mystery."* Even though it was ordained before the world began, the *"church"* was unknown—except through the prophesies. It was the Apostle Paul's duty to tell us about this *"mystery."* I am glad that he obeyed his high and holy calling, aren't you?

I Corinthians 2:10 tells us that God *"revealed"* this hidden *"mystery . . . unto us . . . by His Spirit."* The "us" would be Paul, the Corinthians, and you and me by extension. It was the Holy Spirit who superintended the writing of Scripture. *"Holy men of God spake as they were moved by the Holy Ghost . . ."* (II Peter 1:21).

What a treasure we have in God's WORDS! We do not have them from man's wisdom. It is the Holy Spirit who teaches us to compare spiritual truths with spiritual truths. None of *"truth"* can come from any other place but the Words of God. It is from those *"words"* that we discover that *"our righteousnesses are as filthy rags"* and that *"our iniquities, like the wind have taken us away"* (Isaiah 64:6). It is from those words that we learn of a *Saviour* and *"The Way"* to have our sins washed away and ETERNAL LIFE!

"THE MINISTRY OF HYMNS"

In mansions of Glory and Endless Delight.
I'll ever adore Thee in Heaven so bright.
And I'll sing with the glittering crown on my brow,
If ever I loved Thee,
Lord Jesus, 'tis now!
"My Jesus I love Thee" is a precious hymn to me.
I sing it in my heart to myself often in the night.
The words are by William R. Featherstone
set to A. J. Gordon's music. (ggs)
This was sung in full at my mother's funeral.
It was a hymn (every stanza) she taught her children.

Today's Bible Blessing   *August 12*

Jeremiah 1:9—Jeremiah 4:12

THE FOUNTAIN OF LIVING WATER FORSAKEN

Jeremiah 2:13

"My people have committed two evils . . ."

When I was in Bible School in the city of Chicago, I had the privilege of attending Moody Memorial Church. HARRY IRONSIDE was the esteemed pastor and Bible teacher! It was a privilege to sit under his ministry! If I did not have a Christian work assignment, which I often had that took me to another part of the Chicago area, I would take a streetcar and attend his church. It was the biggest church I had ever been in at the time. I would sit up front, so I could see Dr. Ironside as close as I could. To my left, high in the balcony, was his secretary. She had a stenographer's pad and would take shorthand, writing every word he spoke. This is how he was able to write so many books.

One of my delights, in those days, was to slip into his Sunday School class before the morning service. I remember well that he was teaching the book of Jeremiah. Only thing is that I don't remember too much of what he taught. I am sure many of his words are in my subconscious waiting to come out. Perhaps they will come to me as we discover *"blessings"* in Jeremiah together.

The prophet Jeremiah was the second greatest prophet mentioned in the Bible. He began his ministry as a young person. He called himself a *"child"* (Jeremiah 1:7). It is interesting to me that most of the prophets felt they were not worthy and said they could not speak. It shows me that God does not always call the eloquent. He takes who we are, and what we have, and uses it. This shows that God is the *"power"* behind the man and not the man's self-talent.

Jeremiah's ministry was to the remnant of the people of Judah who stayed in the land after the Babylonians took the cream of the crop into captivity. Later, he went to Egypt (Jeremiah 43:7-8). He was the son of a priest named Hilkiah in the land of Benjamin. His father may or may not have been the high priest mentioned in II Kings 22:8.

Jeremiah wrote, in chapter 2:13, that the LORD's people had (1) forsaken Him who was the fountain of living waters. (2) They had dug out cisterns which were broken that could not hold any water. They were a pathetic people! Their land was ruined and laid waste. Roaring lions roamed their area. It was frightening! Their dignity was brought low by the people of Noph and Tahapanes. In all this distress, they did not turn to the LORD.

Instead, they forsook Him!

Always, Jeremiah's job was to encourage God's people to return to Him and love Him as they should. *"Return, thou backsliding Israel,"* said the LORD through Jeremiah's voice. *"I will not keep anger for ever!"* (3:12). If only they would acknowledge their iniquity and their transgressions against the LORD their God! They had not obeyed HIS VOICE! Why not?

"Turn O backsliding children. I am married unto you. *I will take you and bring you from the city and from your family and bring you to Zion,"* is what the LORD pleaded. We can feel the pathos of God's heart as He pleads. Read Jeremiah 3:20-21 and feel His broken heart weeping:

> *"Surely as a wife treacherously departeth from her husband, so have ye dealt treacherously with me, O house of Israel, saith the LORD. A voice was heard upon the high places, weeping and supplications of the children of Israel: for they have perverted their way, and they have forgotten the LORD their God. Return, ye backsliding children, and I will heal your backslidings. Behold, we come unto thee; for thou art the LORD our God."*

Let us reflect upon our lives today. As we condemn the people to whom Jeremiah warned, let us look at ourselves. Are we any different than they were? We have so much. We are blessed with spiritual blessings in every area of our lives; yet we are indifferent to the sin that so easily besets us (Hebrews 12: 1). We ignore *it or pamper it.*
Let us run with patience the race that is set before us, LOOKING UNTO JESUS, the author and finisher of our faith!

"GOD'S PERFECT WILL"
(Romans 12:2)
IN THE CRISES OF LIFE, JUST LET GOD LEAD!
The will of God takes you through problems, heartaches, sorrows, and tests.
HIS WILL AND HIS WAY ARE PERFECT.
IF YOU WILL SIMPLY REVERENTLY TRUST HIM,
YOU MAY FIND IT "ACCEPTABLE"!
Surrender to what God allows in your life.
(ggs: in part from a sermon by Dr. Hopewell)

Today's Bible Blessing   *August 13*

Jeremiah 4:13—Jeremiah 7:5
THE ALARM OF WAR

Jeremiah 4:19

"I cannot hold my peace . . . O my soul, the sound of the trumpet . . . "

About sixty years after Isaiah died, Jeremiah began his ministry. It was in the thirteenth year of the reign of King Josiah. During his lifetime, the kingdom of Judah was swallowed up by Babylon. The best of the best was taken, leaving a small ragamuffin remnant. When the Remnant fled to Egypt, Jeremiah was captured and taken there with them. Zephaniah and Habakkuk were Jeremiah's early contemporaries, as well as Daniel during Jeremiah's later years of ministry. Jeremiah lived long years and died during the seventy year Babylonian captivity.

I find myself having a difficult time choosing the verses to meditate upon today. There are so many! Jeremiah 4: 19 is a powerful verse. JOHN WILLIAM BURGON USED IT TO EXPRESS THE FIRE IN HIS SOUL!

He could not do anything else but defend the Greek Words underlying the *Authorized King James Bible*. As Jeremiah saw the future destruction of Judah and the city of Jerusalem, Burgon saw the utter despair at the destroying of the Words of God. That is why Burgon cried out with Jeremiah:

> *"I am pained at my very heart; my heart maketh*
> *a noise in me; I cannot hold my peace, because*
> *thou hast heard, O my soul, the sound of the*
> *trumpet, the alarm of war"* (Jeremiah 4:19).

John Burgon saw the utter butchering of the Words of God in the *ENGLISH REVISED VERSION* of 1881. It pained his soul to see the beautiful, accurate words of his English Bible twisted and changed in the new translation. The *English Revised Version of 1881 was* influenced by the *corrupted Gnostic Critical Greek Text* of Westcott and Hort. Words and phrases had been changed. Meanings were different. The beautiful soul of the Bible was pierced by the penknife of mistranslation. The very utterances of the LORD were changed before his eyes!

Burgon cried from the depths of his soul, *"SOUND THE TRUMPET!"* The Dean of Chichester called for war! And war there was! He was a battler! Someone had to do it! His stand cost him! He was never promoted! He never made professor or became a canon or church bishop—or even the head of a college! Oh no! He had not been chosen to be part of the English Revision committee of 1881. He did not think like those revisionists! He was a *"boat rocker"*!

Studying at Oxford, he pursued language, daily working with Latin and Greek and mastering the Greek classics such as Aristotle and Herodotus. He also read chapters of the Old Testament daily. He loved the Words of God. When remembering his Bible reading, he said, *"I cannot feel satisfied."* Always, when questions came up about the Words of God, Burgon's trumpet gave a "certain sound." When convinced he was right, he handled every question with courage. He strove to straighten out the *"wrongness"* of his fellows.

Concerning Burgon's diligent defense of God's Words, someone remarked the following:

> *"What a splendid watchdog he is. How loud and furiously he barks when the smallest danger threatens the church or THE FAITH which is entrusted to the church's keeping. It is the business of a watchdog to bark furiously and to even flay at the throats of thieves."*

At his death, Burgon looked at his life's work. He saw the many portfolios of collating and writing he had done to defend THE BOOK. Never having married or had children, his works were his children.

Jeremiah, too, was a "trumpet-blower"! Like Burgon, Jeremiah's message was not always popular, but he had to give it.

So you and I must defend the words of God like Jeremiah and Burgon did. *Do not be afraid of the faces of the opposition.* Don't hold your peace! There is war in the camp! The Words of God are being destroyed in the many *perversions* that have infested our churches today.

STAND FIRM FOR THE RIGHT!
GOD WILL BE YOUR REWARD!

"OH MAN, GREATLY BELOVED, FEAR NOT!"
(Daniel 10:19. Romans 15:4)
PEACE BE UNTO THEE!
"Be strong! Yes, be strong!"
God sent His angel to comfort Daniel with these "Great Words."
TODAY, WE HAVE GOD'S "GREAT WORDS"
IN HIS BOOK, THE BIBLE. (ggs)

Jeremiah 7:6—Jeremiah 10:8
FRANCES HAVERGAL
BECAME A CHRISTIAN

Jeremiah 8:20

"The harvest is past, the summer is ended, and we are not saved."

For many years, I have portrayed the hymn-writer, **FRANCES RIDLEY HAVERGAL.** Perhaps you do not know her by name, but you do know many of her hymns such as *"Take My Life and Let It Be," "I Gave My Life For Thee," "Like a River Glorious,"* and *"Who is on the Lord's Side."*

Frances Havergal lived from 1836-1879. She died at a young age. She was forty-two, and had not been a well woman for much of her life. This was the same period of time that Fanny Crosby lived (1820-1915). Of course, Fanny lived more years than Frances and had a different style of writing. One was more of an aristocrat, well educated, and studious, while the other was a New England Yankee, blind, and homespun. Both of these women loved the Words of God and memorized great portions of Scripture. They knew each other by letters but never met personally. Their knowledge of God's Word manifested itself in their poetry.

Though Frances Havergal was the daughter of a conservative, Bible preaching rector of England's Anglican church, she did not become a Christian until she was about fifteen years of age. One summer, while meditating on Jeremiah 8:20, she feared that she would never become a Christian. The words: *"THE HARVEST IS PAST, THE SUMMER IS ENDED, AND WE ARE NOT SAVED!"* rang in her ears. She knew the evil of her heart and the sinful thoughts of her mind. It was in that season of her life that she said to herself, *"Frances, if you do not become a Christian before the summer is over, you never will be one!"* For her, this was a dreadful conclusion!

It was not Frances' habit to speak to others about spiritual things. When she was a young child, she had the courage to speak to one of her father's clergymen friends. He was a formidable leader in the church. She had heard a sermon on Hell and judgment that had frightened her. So, with as much courage as a child could muster, she spoke to the minister. The *insensitive man* rebuffed her questions, telling her to run along and play. She never spoke to another person about spiritual things for many years.

One afternoon a woman, who was active in her father's church, was with Frances. (As it turned out this woman would later marry her widowed father.) Frances spoke to the woman about her spiritual need. She asked, "Could God forgive my sin?"

Continuing her wondering, she said, *"Could I trust Jesus?"*

The wise woman, sensing the heart need of the young girl asked, *"Would you commit your soul to Him?"* That was a stirring question to Frances. Would she? Could she? Should she?

Quickly FRANCES HAVERGAL ran to her room. She flung herself on her bed. Then got on her knees and prayed. The verse in I Peter 2:24 rang in her ears.

> *"Who his own self bare our sins in his own body on the tree,*
> *that we, being dead to sins, should live unto righteousness:*
> *by whose stripes ye were healed."*

She saw herself in Christ as He bore her sin on Calvary's Tree. That day she trusted Jesus Christ as her Saviour. He who knew no sin was made sin for her.

> *"For he hath made him to be sin for us, who knew no sin;*
> *that we might be made the righteousness of God in him"* (II
> Corinthians 5:21).

Yes, Frances became a Christian before the summer was over! Her fears were past. Her sins were forgiven!

WHAT ABOUT YOU? HAVE YOU RECEIVED JESUS CHRIST INTO YOUR HEART AND LIFE LIKE FRANCES DID SO MANY YEARS AGO?

"BE STRONG, YEA, BE STRONG"
(Daniel 10:19; Romans 15:4)
"Oh man, greatly beloved: Fear not, PEACE unto thee. . ."
God sent His angel to comfort Daniel with these "great words."
TODAY WE HAVE GOD'S "GREAT WORDS" in HIS BOOK,
THE BIBLE. (ggs)

Today's Bible Blessing　　　　　　　　　*August 15*

Jeremiah 10:9—Jeremiah 14:1
A DIRTY GIRDLE & AN OBEDIENT PROPHET

Jeremiah 13:7

"Behold, the girdle was marred: it was profitable for nothing."

Ussher's chronology tells us that Jeremiah's time of prophesying covered a forty-one-year period. That is a long ministry to any country in any language. Jeremiah most likely helped King Josiah during his reign of reform and the reading of the Law to the people. When the king died, Jeremiah and the singers grieved at his death (II Kings 23:1-2; II Chronicles 35:25). They loved him.

Jeremiah was a faithful servant of the Lord. In spite of great opposition, he was faithful to his calling. His assignment was to minister to a people steeped in idolatry. They loved their idols and wicked worship ways. *"Because Thou hast forgotten me (the LORD), and trusted in falsehood"* (Jeremiah 13:25).

Today I am interested in Jeremiah 13. This is the chapter that tells about Jeremiah's "girdle" or waistband. God was helping Jeremiah to understand his ministry. Sometimes a man is so involved in his work that he cannot understand all that is happening to him. Being a prophet was no easy job! People were mean to him more than they were kind. They rejected and made fun of his message.

So the LORD said to Jeremiah, *"Go get a linen girdle."* Put it on. Don't put it in water. It seems, from this verse, that the Prophet was not to wash his waistband at all. JEREMIAH WAS OBEDIENT AND DID AS THE LORD COMMANDED! I admire him for this, don't you? Perhaps he did not understand the significance of this request; yet, he obeyed!

Then after a while, Jeremiah was to go to the shores of the Euphrates River. There he was to dig a hole right by one of the rocks in the area. In that hole he was to bury his cloth sash. After many days—we don't know how many—Jeremiah was to go dig up that girdle from its dirty hiding place.

All this odd behavior was a God-given illustration, especially for Jeremiah's benefit. It pictured the marring of the land of Judah, showing the *unwelcome pride* found in the city of Jerusalem. That city thought it was a city of special gifts and graces. They had a high position among other cities and were well-thought of by many.

The point was that the evil Jewish people imagined they were "something else again." In reality all their religiosity was "good for nothing!" (Jeremiah 13: 10). The LORD mentioned that, as the girdle clings to a man, so will Judah and Israel cleave to Him. At that moment, they were not cleaving or trusting in the LORD God! Someday they would cry out for Him! Soon the whole city would burst as filled wine bottles overexposed to the heat of the day. Someday soon, the whole city, with its idolatrous people, would be battered and bounced back and forth. God will have no pity on their distress. They would be captured by Babylon!

Jeremiah did not want to see his prophecies come true. He begged the LORD'S people to repent. He cried, *"Give glory to the LORD your God, before he cause darkness, and before your feet stumble upon the dark mountains, and, while ye look for light, he turn it into the shadow of death, and make it gross darkness."*

He continued, *"But if ye will not hear it, my soul shall weep in secret places for your pride"* (Jeremiah 13: 16-18). He knew that, if they did not repent, his eyes would weep, and his tears would run down his cheeks in grief.

With all his might, Jeremiah, who is called *"the weeping prophet,"* screamed out to the KING and the QUEEN, *"HUMBLE YOURSELVES! HUMBLE YOUR-SELVES!"* You and I know the answer. With Jeremiah, we must affirm, *"Can the Ethiopian change his skin, or the leopard his spots?"* Judah was accustomed to do evil. THEY COULD NOT DO GOOD! (Jeremiah 13:23).

CAN WE LEARN FROM THIS FRIGHTENING LESSON TO TAKE HEED TO OURSELVES AND GET RIGHT WITH GOD WHILE WE HAVE THE TIME?

"AN EVEN PLACE"
(Psalm 26:12)
"MY FOOT STANDETH IN AN EVEN PLACE!"
If it seems otherwise, it is because I stumble and falter.
His plan for me is perfect–even secure, appointed.
"GOD CAN DO BIG THINGS AS EASILY
AS HE CAN DO SMALL THINGS." (ggs)

Today's Bible Blessing   *August 16*

Jeremiah 14:2—Jeremiah 17:22
HEAL ME, LORD!

Jeremiah 17:18

"Let them not be confounded . . . let me not be dismayed . . ."

Jeremiah said nothing that was recorded during the short, three-month reign of KING JEHOAHAZ. Jeremiah was true to his calling no matter how painful it was for him, a man of a tender heart, to preach out the Words of the LORD! Though he was a gentle soul, he did not flinch to write with a pen of iron. How unlike many of God's servants today!

What does it take for a Christian to stand strong for God? Jeremiah's words were not easy to deliver. His heart was burdened with the heaviness of his message. God's Words filled his thoughts and disrupted his soul. After all, the Words were from the mouth of God! Jeremiah wanted to *"confound"* every ear that heard them. His *hope* was that each person would be totally *"dismayed"* at his message!

The prophet's desire was to *"bring to ruin"* or *"destroy"* his listeners with his words. He tried to bring to shame the hearts of his sin-filled people. Oh, how he wanted them to understand what their sin was doing to them! Today he would have *"damned"* them. He cursed them in an imprecatory way! Yet, in all his fury, Jeremiah did not want to be *"confounded"* himself.

He did not want to be rebuffed to such an extent that he would lose his *"cool"* and run away from his hearers like a scared rabbit. He said, *"Let them be confounded that persecute me, but let not me be confounded!"* (Jeremiah 17: 18). Sometimes mingling with the sinner causes the messenger to yield to the sin of the sinner. It makes him soften his message. Then, the whole testimony of the messenger is marred. That is when Satan gets the victory and the name of the LORD is blasphemed (Romans 2:24; I Timothy 6:1; Titus 2: 5; Revelation 16:21).

"Let THEM be dismayed, but let NOT ME be dismayed . . ." (Jeremiah 17:18). Jeremiah longed that Judah would be overcome with fear and horror. After all, Israel had been carried away captive by Assyria. Judah saw the horror of such captivity. Jeremiah wanted his people to be appalled and intimidated by fear. Yet, he prayed, that in his prophesying, he *himself would* not become frightened and cower in a corner with a closed mouth.

"Heal me, O LORD, and I shall be healed; save me, and I shall be saved: for thou art my praise." This was Jeremiah's prayer. He did not want to fail the LORD. He wanted to be strong in the power and might of his God! (17:14). With mocking words the people would ask, *"Where is the word of the LORD?"* (See verse 15.) But when his words came to their ears, they would not hear. Their minds refused to understand. They preferred the gods of the heathen to the God of Abraham, Isaac, and Jacob.

Comforting himself, Jeremiah reminded the LORD, *"As for me, I have not hastened from being a shepherd."* He said that he had followed God's commands. He did not want the woeful day to come. He declared to God, *"Thou knowest: that which came out of my lips was right before thee"* (Jeremiah 17:16).

ARE YOU LIKE JEREMIAH? Do you have a message of hope to those about you? Yet, your friends look at you *"funny."* They do not understand your burden. You can see the dangers in your friends' lives. Their drift into sin is slowly happening in front of your eyes. You warn them. They do not listen. Soon their lives are ruined because of their sin. Girls become pregnant without marriage. Men fall down drunk on the city streets. The smell of marijuana is in the air. Churches cater to worldly ways and read wrong Bibles from their pulpits. Sin is rampant on every corner. You warn them. No one listens.

You must be careful not to become so discouraged that you give up the *"FIGHT OF FAITH!"* *Do not* bend your standards. Do not lean on the arm of flesh. In such a weakened condition, you too, could succumb to the very sin you are striving to keep out of your friends' lives!

WHEREFORE LET HIM THAT THINKETH HE STANDETH TAKE HEED LEST HE FALL! (I Corinthians 10:12).

"*FAITHFUL TO THE FIGHT*"
(II Timothy 4:7)
Faithful to the fight, Faithful to the Faith,
Faithful to the finish for God.
Faithful to the right, Faithful in His might,
Faithful to the Word of God.
Faithful in the fray, Faithful every day,
Faithful in the fight for THE FAITH.
Faithful to the fight, Faithful to THE FAITH,
Faithful to the finish for God!
(GGS: DEDICATED TO HER SON-IN-LAW, D. A. WAITE)

Today's Bible Blessing   *August 17*
Jeremiah 17:23—Jeremiah 22:10
A BROKEN POT!

Jeremiah 17:23
"They obeyed not, neither inclined their ear . . . that they might not hear."

Jeremiah prophesied under the reign of Jehoiakim (609-597 B.C.). It was a powerful Egyptian kingdom that dominated Judah at the time. Thus, this King Jehoiakim was subservient to Egypt. In contrast, Jeremiah leaned toward the supremacy of the superiority of the Chaldeans. In time, Babylon would conquer Jerusalem. Because of this posture, many considered Jeremiah to be a traitor. Surprising as it seemed, the other prophets and priests lived in a backslidden condition. Because of this, some wanted Jeremiah to be killed as a traitor!

With all this in mind, let us turn to today's Bible reading. Jeremiah gives us a whole discussion on the *SABBATH DAY*. Perhaps you and I should consider the *"day of rest"* with new eyes. It is true we are in the age of grace and we are not under the Law. May I be so bold to ask, *"Are we disregarding the holiness of gathering together with like-minded believers to worship and praise the LORD?"* Or are we *too busy* shopping and picnicking on *THE LORD'S DAY* to remember to sit awhile at the feet of Jesus—like Mary of old—and choose *"that good part"*? (See Luke 10:42.)

It seemed in Jeremiah's time that the Jews were forsaking the sacredness of the Sabbath. They were defiling the DAY that the LORD God had set apart for them to rest (Jeremiah 17:21-22). Notice their defiance in verse twenty-three! THEY OBEYED NOT! If they obeyed—along with some other commands—their Jerusalem would be spared. As usual, they disobeyed! God said, *"I* *will kindle a fire in the gates and it shall devour the palaces of Jerusalem"* (17:27).

When I was a child, my father—who was a good Christian man with strong convictions—had specific rules for Sunday. To some, he was almost a *"legalist."* We did no work that was not necessary on Sunday. That did not include bathing, or cooking, or driving to church; but it did include playing games, or working, or going to the store. He never bought gasoline on Sunday and we never went to the store. In fact, we could not sew a button on a dress or shirt on the LORD'S DAY. *It was not a frivolous day. It was a day of rest and church-going.* For some reason, I was permitted to go for a walk. Though my Dad was strict about the day; his was a far better stance than the baseball and shopping day that Sunday has become now. I feel sorry for those who have no memory when stores were shut on Sundays and women wore hats and gloves to church. WHATEVER HAPPENED TO SETTING ONE DAY A WEEK ASIDE TO DWELL ON THE *"HOLY"*?

In Chapter 18, we are taken into the POTTER'S HOUSE. I don't know what that house looked like. I imagine it was an open place where air could surround the potter as he spun his wheel. If he was a skilled craftsman, he usually made good pots. Occasionally, he would make a mistake. If he caught it in time, he could make something of the clay—perhaps it would not be what it would have been if he had been more careful, but, at least, the pot could be used for something. Sometimes the error was so great, he could do nothing with the marred pot, but throw it away.

Judah was a broken pot! The LORD had molded them. Yet, they sinned. He begged them. Some repented. Not many. Willfully, they turned from God. They *burned incense* to *worthless* things and stumbled from the old paths (Jeremiah 18:15). Not only did they turn to *false gods* and *sacrificed their babies to them—treating* them like non-humans with no feelings—they worshipped Baal and burned their sons on his altars. Their land was called *"the valley of slaughter!"*

Because of their complete disregard for *"THE HOLY,"* the LORD promised, through Jeremiah's voice, that Jerusalem would be a desolate, hissing city. In their heathen desperation, they would eat the flesh of their own children!

For such prophesying, Jeremiah was dragged to the high gate of Benjamin. It was right there by the neglected HOUSE OF THE LORD that his wrists and ankles were jammed into heavy wooden frames called *"stocks."* Few cared that he suffered. Most passing by laughed at him, thinking he was nothing but a ridiculous, eccentric prophet!

"GOD TRIES EVEN THE BEST OF HIS SERVANTS"
(Job 19:27)
Job lost everything, even his friends.
It was difficult.
His brethren and friends failed him,
And forgot him.
We have all had this sorrow.
Only Job's Redeemer loved him.
Job was a good man.
He was a prepared man.
He was under tremendous pressure.
He hated evil.
He believed in prayer and fasting.
He was a "fundamentalist."
(ggs: these notes were taken from a message
delivered by Dr. Arthur Steel.)

Today's Bible Blessing   *August 18*
Jeremiah 22:11—Jeremiah 25:15

A BURNING FIRE!

Jeremiah 23:29

"Is not my word like as a fire? saith the LORD; and like a hammer that breaketh the rock in pieces?"

In yesterday's reading there was a verse that I do not want to skip over. So turn back to Jeremiah 20:9, and *feel the passion* of the prophet as he tells of his ministry. He reminds us that he was going to quit the whole *"prophet"* business. He had been maligned! *"It wasn't worth it!"* were his thoughts. *"I will not make mention of him; nor speak any more in his name!"* He'd had it! BUT!

*"But His word was in mine heart as a burning fire shut up
in my bones, and I was weary with forbearing, and I could
not stay!"*

He could not keep quiet. The LORD'S MESSAGE was so strong within him that he could not be quiet! Even though he suffered depression of sorts from the oppression—sometimes wanting to die (vs. 14-15)—he kept on keeping on.

What an example for you and me. Our lives are not always *peaches and cream;* but we must have a forward look and keep our eyes on the *"prize."* (Philippians 3:13-14).

We see in Jeremiah 22:1 that the LORD told Jeremiah to go down to the king of Judah's house. Thus the prophet did.

363

In my Bible, I have written *"Zedekiah."* So someone, in teaching this passage, must have told me that the king here was ZEDEKIAH. The prophet pushed the king to *"shape up"* and *"do right"* for Judah. If he did not, the whole city would become a desolation. The land would become a wilderness and the cities would be empty. This terribleness would be a result of their unbelief and idolatrous ways. *"Weep not for the dead!"* for they were better off than the living.

Do not weep for Jehoiakim the son of King Josiah. He will be buried like one buries a burro (22:18-19). The disgraced king's son, *Coniah* (JECONIAH), was a despised and broken *"idol."* Coniah would be *"childless"* (22:30)! He would have NO CHILDREN to sit on the throne of David. *This is why the line of the Lord Jesus Christ came through his mother, Mary.* See the Gospel of Luke. Jesus' line did not come through his earthly father, Joseph. See the Gospel of Matthew.

Jeremiah lashed out against the "pastors" (or shepherds) who did not care for the people. They did not feed them *THE TRUTH.* They did not visit them. The sheep were scattered. The message was encouraging because *some day THE RIGHTEOUS BRANCH OF DAVID* would sit on the throne (Zechariah 3:8; 6:12).

> *"And there shall come forth a rod out of the stem of Jesse, and a Branch shall grow out of his roots: And the spirit of the LORD shall rest upon him, the spirit of wisdom and understanding, the spirit of counsel and might, the spirit of knowledge and of the fear of the LORD . . ."* (Isaiah 11:1-2).

We could say that the LORD'S WORD was a *"fire ball,"* or at least, a *"ball of fire."* The LORD asked a question, *"Is not my word like as a fire?"* (See Jeremiah 23:29a.) Yes, some of us have had His Words *burned into* our hearts. The Scriptures have *singed our souls* with conviction. They have *purified* our hearts with their burning.

Then another question was asked. Is not my word, *"like a hammer that breaketh the rock in pieces?"* (See Jeremiah 23:29b.) Sometimes *our willfulness* meets the Words of God and they break up our stubborn ways with heavy conviction. It hits us with such force that our head spins! How good to see ourselves as a nail to be used of God by His *hammering* Words!

Yes, we have experienced the *"fire"* and the *"hammer."* It is good for us to meet the LORD in His Word and let it work in our lives!

LET US NOT BE AFRAID TO LET GOD'S WORD WORK!

"IDLE WORDS"

(Matthew 12:36-37; Proverbs 10:19)
"IN THE MULTITUDE OF WORDS, THERE WANTETH NOT SIN:
BUT HE THAT REFRAINETH HIS LIPS IS WISE."
"Every idle word that men shall speak, they shall give an account."
WHAT IS AN IDLE WORD?
It is one that produces no good effect
and was not intended to do any good.
We all talk too much!
Once we have spoken, we are a servant to that word!
Words are so awesome—
They can be cruel, stern, or beautiful, and comforting.
GOD IS NOT PLEASED WITH IDLE WORDS! (ggs)

Today's Bible Blessing　　　　　　　　*August 19*

Jeremiah 25:16—Jeremiah 28:16

BEWARE OF LYING LIPS

Jeremiah 26:13

"Amend your ways . . . and obey the voice of the LORD your God . . . and the LORD will repent . . ."

The name of *Jehoiachin* has not come up very much in these *"BLESSINGS."* Though he is not in today's readings, I wanted to mention him briefly. Not much is said about this king of Judah. He was the *son of King Jehoiakim*, had a short reign, and was an evil king. He is known for sending a consoling letter of counsel to his family in captivity.

As I have been reading the book of Jeremiah, I've noticed how the narrative does not necessarily follow a time-line. As we read of Jeremiah's life and prophecies, we realize they are not necessarily in chronological order. For me, personally, it makes understanding the book more confusing; but that is how the LORD wanted the prophet's words set forth to us readers.

It is evident in Chapter 26 that Jeremiah gave the WORD OF THE LORD to individuals who did not want to hear it. At peril of his own life, he prophesied. *"Thou shalt surely die!"* (See verse 8.) God gave Jeremiah a message. *"Of a truth the LORD hath sent me unto you to speak all these words . . ."* He delivered the *"words"* in spite of opposition. Some today are not as brave as this prophet. Others today deliver the message they feel God wants them to give, in spite of those about them who object vehemently!

With this opposition staring him in the face, Jeremiah proclaimed:

"Amend your ways and your doings, and obey the voice of the LORD your God, and the LORD will repent him of the evil that he hath pronounced against you" (Jeremiah 26:13).

In verse 16, we observe that the priests were convinced that Jeremiah had spoken words worthy of his death. How out of touch with the truth they were! The princes and the people disagreed, *"This man is not worthy to die: for he hath spoken to us in the name of the LORD our God."* It was then that the elders recalled the prophecy of MICAH THE MORASTHITE. (He prophesied during the reign of GOOD KING HEZEKIAH.) Micah prophesied that ZION would be plowed like a field and JERUSALEM would become heaps! (See 26:18.) King Hezekiah heeded the words of the prophet. The LORD repented of his way. *He believed the prophet and let MICAH live!*

There was another prophet named URIJAH (26:20). He prophesied against Jerusalem as Jeremiah did. King Jehoiakim wanted to kill Urijah, for he rejected his words. The frightened man fled for his life to the land of Egypt. Angry Jehoiakim found him and brought him back to Judah to be killed with a sword.

This was a fearful time for prophets. The rulers did not want to hear the truth. It was too drastic. It spoke of the Judah's soon-captivity. It told of the destruction of Jerusalem. No one wanted to hear! Fortunately, Jeremiah had a friend named AHIKAM. He protected the prophet from death! How good to have a friend in dangerous times!

The LORD instructed Jeremiah to make a wooden collar or "yoke" and put it around his neck. It must have been uncomfortable. It was a *"picture"* of the *"yoke"* that would come to Judah at the hand of KING NEBUCHADNEZZAR of BABYLON. All nations would serve this potentate! *What fearful news!* There would be death by sword, famine. and pestilence. No one wanted to hear it! Jeremiah was accused of lying!

At the start of ZEDEKIAH'S reign, there was a cunning false prophet named HANANIAH of Gibeon. Falsely, he claimed there would be *"peace."* He claimed that the LORD God had broken the *"yoke"* of NEBUCHADNEZZAR. He claimed all would be fine, and JECONIAH, Jehoiakim's son, with all the captives, would be returned to Jerusalem. This was *good news-BUT IT WAS A LIE!* (See verse 28: 15.)

BEWARE OF GOOD NEWS FROM LYING LIPS!

> ### *"NO RESERVE! NO RETREAT!"*
> I do not know where first were written these words,
> but they have been written upon my heart with the mighty pen of
> God. [perhaps *William Borden]
> **"NO RESERVE! ALL FOR HIM EVERY DAY!**
> **NO RETREAT! DRAWING BACK & FALTERING!**
> **NO REGRETS! PRESSING ON, COUNTING THE COST!**
> **TILL I MEET THE KING SOME DAY!"** (by ggs)
> (* the title of a brief biography of William Borden's life/ysw)

Today's Bible Blessing   *August 20*

Jeremiah 28:17—Jeremiah 31:28

THOUGHTS ON PEACE AND PRAYER

Jeremiah 29:13

"Ye shall seek me. and find me, when ye shall search for me with all your heart."

One of the facts that I have discovered in my meditation in the book of Jeremiah is that many, in his day, did not appreciate the work of the weeping prophet. They did not like him because his words were not pleasing to the ears. Because of their scorn for Jeremiah, he was thrown into prison. EBEDMELECH, a royal eunuch, befriended the prophet. Otherwise, Jeremiah would have died. There was an *honored false prophet,* named HANANIAH (594 B.C.) who claimed that the Chaldeans would be destroyed. He said that the Jewish captives would be returned. (Of course, he was wrong.) That's when he grabbed the wooden yoke from Jeremiah's neck. While Jeremiah suffered in jail, Hananiah walked around free.

There was much confusion in the land. Hananiah, by his false words, encouraged KING ZEDEKIAH to fight against NEBUCHADNEZZAR'S army. Often the king, who did not want people to know, would sneak into Jeremiah's prison for counsel. Secretly, he had Jeremiah removed to a more comfortable confinement in the guard house, and saw to it that Jeremiah had a daily loaf of bread. Jeremiah recommended that the Jews yield to the foe and be carried off to Babylon. Even though there may be bloodshed and damage to the city, he said that it would be better in the long run.

It seems that there were three deportations of Judah from Jerusalem to Babylon. The enemy wanted to weaken them completely. It was during the first *"hit"* on the city that people like Daniel, many of the priests, and the important people were taken.

Often, during those years, the city would be surrounded. The remaining people were desperate and hungry. People considered eating their own children, and some did. It was an awful time! Egypt was after Judah, too. Enemies were on every hand. Jeremiah encouraged KING ZEDIKIAH to surrender to Nebuchadnezzar. Instead, the King of Judah tried to escape. That was the beginning of the end for him, in my opinion.

Jeremiah was a letter writer. In Jeremiah 29, we read what he wrote. *It is fascinating!* It is not what we would think he would write. Instead, he told the people—who were taken to Babylon—*"You are going to be there for seventy years!"* He encouraged them to build houses, to plant gardens, to eat fruit, to take wives, to have babies, and *to seek the peace of the city* in which the LORD permitted them to be captives. Also he said, *"Do not be deceived by the prophets that live around you!"* Isn't this good advice for some of us today who find ourselves in a situation that we would rather not be in?

The next verses are precious. I think they have often been lost in the midst of all the powerful prophesying that we see in the book, such as the dreadful ends of people like the lying prophets, ZEDEKIAH and AHAB [not to be confused with kings by the same names]. Both of them were *"roasted in the fire"* (Jeremiah 29:22). That was a kind of death from which the three Hebrew children escaped, if you remember.

NOW TO GET BACK TO THE PRECIOUS WORDS in JEREMIAH 29:11-13.

> *"For I know the thoughts that I think toward you, saith the LORD, thoughts of peace, and not of evil . . . Then shall ye call upon me, and . . . pray unto me, and I WILL HEARKEN. . . And ye shall seek me, and find me, when ye shall search for me with all your heart."*

Things could not have been much worse for the people of God. Here they were in a heathen land—strangers and pilgrims. God's people had forgotten Him on purpose! They did not obey the good prophets! They did not regard the Holy! When they found themselves captured and far from home, they were a backslidden people. Yet, Jeremiah encouraged them to trust the LORD. His thoughts for them were those of *PEACE* and PRAYER. They were in difficulty!

YET, THEY WERE TO SEEK THE LORD WITH ALL THEIR HEARTS AND FIND HIM!

"RUTH"
(Ruth 2:7, 15)
Ruth found her husband among the sheaves!
I wonder, if Orpah had come back with Naomi,
would she have found a husband also?
POOR LOST ORPAH!
It is not enough that a man have barley,
and be a Christian,
His way, and walk, and doctrine
should be according to the Scripture.
Two cannot walk together unless they walk according to Truth!
(ggs: MARRIAGE COUNSEL)

Today's Bible Blessing   *August 21*
Jeremiah 31:29—Jeremiah 34:3
GOD'S CALL IN SPITE OF PEOPLE!
Jeremiah 32:27
"I AM the LORD, the God of all flesh: is there anything too hard for me?"

This is a section in the book of Jeremiah that is definitely not chronological. We'll see this from chapters 30-36. Some of the predications pertain to the present situation with Babylon capturing Judah and making a wreck of the beautiful temple, as well as the city of Jerusalem. All the people who had any talent at all were swooped into NEBUCHADNEZZAR's kingdom. Only those who were thought to be "lesser" people were left.

In thinking about the "lesser" people left in the land, I remembered a church in a small Ohio town where I lived as a young girl. There was a terrific church split. If memory serves me, I believe the rebuffed deacons and trustees determined to starve out the pastor. All the *"important"* people, the ones with money or status in the church and community, fled. To the surprise of everyone, those *"lesser"* people were far from *"nothings."* They were talented men and woman who stepped right into the vacant spots emptied by the *"better"* people. To our surprise, there were musical folk, praying folk, and spiritual folk. God has people of all varieties and stripes, whom He has prepared to fill in the gap when needed. The sad part is that those very people could have been used previously for the edification of the church body, but were never asked. The *"important"* people always took over.

Jeremiah predicted the future. Besides the *"near fulfillment"* of His words, there was a *"far fulfillment"* which reached

369

into the future millennial reign of Christ spoken of in other parts of the Scriptures.

For instance, read Jeremiah 33:15 where, once again, we see the LORD JESUS CHRIST is THE BRANCH OF RIGHTEOUSNESS. Someday He will sit on David's throne!

JEREMIAH 33:15:

"In those days, and at that time, will I cause the Branch of righteousness to grow up unto David; and he shall execute judgment and righteousness in the land."

ZECHARIAH 6:12:

"And speak unto him, saying, Thus speaketh the LORD of hosts, saying, Behold the man whose name is The BRANCH; and he shall grow up out of his place, and he shall build the temple of the LORD. . ."

We see in Chapter 32 that King Zedekiah imprisoned Jeremiah. The reason? He did not like what the prophet said! (See verse 3).

How like some church members today with their pastors. They do not like the message, so they get rid of the pastor. A man spends years preparing for the ministry. He is called to a church. He assumes the church wants him to preach the Words of God. As long as the pastor does not step on the toes of the *"important"* people in the church, all is well. But woe to the pastor who preaches a message that "offends" the moneyed people in the church or the *"church boss"*! Out the pastor goes! Sad! Sad! Sad! But this happens all over the world where pastors are treated as *"nothings"* in the eyes of some church members.

What comfort it must have been to Jeremiah to have the Words of the LORD come to him during such times.

BEHOLD, I AM THE LORD, THE GOD OF ALL FLESH: IS THERE ANY THING TOO HARD FOR ME?

Jeremiah 32:27

"SAY NICE & TRUE THINGS TODAY"
WE SHOULD LOVE WITH A LOVE THAT EXPECTS DAY BY DAY,
THAT RECKONS UPON SCRIPTURE!
Our DEAR ONES are only loaned to us,
and the hour when we must return them to The Lender,
may be even at the door.
What ever kindness you can do should be done today!
SAY NICE AND TRUE THINGS TO YOUR DEAR ONES,
IT HELPS YOU AND THEM. (ggs)

Today's Bible Blessing   *August 22*
Jeremiah 34:4—Jeremiah 37:15
THE BURNING OF BAD NEWS!
Jeremiah 36:2

"Take thee a roll . . . and write therein all the words that I have spoken . . ."

Today, I want us to look at two chapters in Jeremiah. They are different, yet they are similar. They are about two different people, or groups of people. One was obedient to their God, and the promises they made to Him. The others were impudent, and rude to the LORD who loved them, and longed to have them love Him back.

Look with me at Jeremiah 35. I have been interested in these people called the RECHABITES ever since I realized their dedication. Years before Jeremiah ever thought of writing about them, they made a promise to their father, a man named JONADAB, the son of RECHAB, that they, or their sons, would NEVER drink wine. This was some promise! They also promised Rechab's son, their Dad, that they would never build a house, or plant a garden, or have a vineyard. They said they would always dwell in tents. They would always be *strangers*. I suppose that meant *wanderers*. They probably were *shepherds* and led their sheep wherever the pastures were.

Another *"Jeremiah"* is mentioned here in Jeremiah 35:3. He had a son named JAAZANIAH. He was a RECHABITE. All his sons and relatives were brought into the temple area. Guess what happened next? The doorkeeper placed *a large pot of wine* before them. Of all things! Good for the sons of RECHAB! They took a stand and said, *"NO!!"* (Nancy Reagan would have been proud! Remember how she said that was what all of us should say when asked to do drugs?) Because of their obedience to the *"promise"* made years before, the LORD OF HOSTS said, *"JONADAB the son of Rechab shall not want a man to stand before me forever!"* THEY WOULD BE SPARED IN THE SIEGE AGAINST JERUSALEM!

As an aside, several years ago, I read in some paper about a people who are like the RECHABITES of old. There is a tribe of people by that name, somewhere in the Bible land area, that traces their ancestry back to these very people we are reading about in Jeremiah. Still TODAY, THOSE INDIVIDUALS DO NOT DRINK WINE OR SETTLE IN A PERMANENT DWELLING! **How good to hear of a group of people that continue to stand for the things they have been taught down through their generations.** If only more folk today would do so!

Now I want us to look at IMPUDENT KING JEHOIAKIM, the king of Judah (Jeremiah 36), so opposite of the Rechabites! He had no respect for Jeremiah or the Words of the

LORD that came from him. As you recall, the prophet was in prison; yet, the WORDS OF THE LORD came to him there.

BARUCH, a faithful scribe, went to the prison with writing material. Every word of Jeremiah was put on a page. They were words that condemned the KING. As soon as he could, Baruch rushed over to the scribes' chamber where the princes sat, as well as Elishama, the scribe. The words frightened them! What should they do? The prince sent JEHUDI. He wanted Baruch to read them the words, too. They were frightened! There was some discussion about its terrible contents. It was news of the soon-invasion of Judah by NEBUCHADNEZZAR.

It was decided that the KING must hear the dreadful news! They recommended to Baruch, *"You and Jeremiah better go hide!"* When the king, who was warming himself by a fire in his winter house, got wind that Jeremiah had written disturbing news in a *"roll"* (book), he ordered that the man named JEHUDI read it to him. Imagine how frightened the reader was!

As JEHUDI read the roll, the blatant king took his penknife from his pocket, cut one page at a time, and burned each page after it was read. *No one in the room seemed upset over this burning.* Three men wanted such destruction of God's Words stopped! (36:25) Angered over the prophecy, the raging monarch commanded that Baruch and Jeremiah be taken. Their demise was prevented. If you remember, the wise prophet and his scribe had found a safe hiding place.

What insolence! What ignorance! What lack of discernment! The Words of God were not *precious* or *believed* by the ignorant king of Judah. Soon destruction would be at his doorstep. **THEN HE WOULD BELIEVE! BUT IT WILL BE TOO LATE!**

"I WILL KEEP THEE"
(Isaiah 41:13, 18)
*"For I the LORD thy God will hold thy right hand,
saying unto thee, Fear not; I will help thee."*
Things are so hard, but I have the true, fixed promises of God.
1. To hold my right hand.
2. "I will help thee."
So, I PRESS ON–EXPECTING,
RECEIVING MERCIES NEW EVERY MORNING–
UNTIL I SEE HIS FACE!
*"I will open rivers in high places,
and fountains in the midst of the valleys:
I will make the wilderness a pool . . ."*
God can take the blackest desert,
and by His Presence and His Words, make it a beautiful Garden..
NO TRIAL OR TEAR CAN SPOIL THIS LOVELY PLACE!
(ggs)

Today's Bible Blessing   *August 23*
Jeremiah 37:16—Jeremiah 41:17
UP FROM THE PIT OF DESPAIR
Jeremiah 38:9
"My lord . . . these men have done evil . . . to Jeremiah the prophet."

Before we look at today's reading, I want us to review the attacks of Nebuchadnezzar on the city of Jerusalem, as well as Judah's neighboring environs (II Kings 24-25). We see what is called *"the first deportation"* in II KINGS 24:11. At that time, King JEHOIACHIN and his mother were captured, along with the princes, the servants, and the officers to Babylon. Also, all the beautiful treasures of the King's house were taken, as well as the golden vessels from the temple. At that time, *ten thousand captives* were swooped out of Jerusalem to live in Babylon. The only ones left were the poorest of the land.

The second deportation seems to be in II Kings 24:16 (though I am not positive) when seven thousand mighty men, and one thousand craftsman, and smiths, as well as strong men for warriors were taken captive. The final deportation is found in II Kings 25, when the Chaldees built forts around Jerusalem and besieged it. That was King ZEDEKIAH'S eleventh year. There was no food in the city. For fear, I suppose, the strong men fled, as well as the king. His enemies pursued him and dragged him before KING NEBUCHADNEZZAR, who was in Riblah.

There NEBUCHADNEZZAR'S men cruelly killed ZEDEKIAH'S sons before their father's eyes. That was the last thing Zedekiah ever saw, for immediately the Chaldees put out Zedekiah's eyes! If that wasn't bad enough, the king's house was burned down and the walls of Jerusalem were smashed (Jeremiah 39:6-8). Then they took him, as their prisoner, to Babylon. *It was awful!*

The *sad* fact is that if ZEDEKIAH had listened to Jeremiah and not run away, he would have been safe and probably not blinded. As usual, the proud king would not listen to the prophet.

An Ethiopian man named EBEDMELECH was a true friend of Jeremiah. We have noticed on previous occasions that this eunuch had interceded for Jeremiah many times. He cared for the prophet. When men who despised Jeremiah lowered him down into a dungeon to rot, EBEDMELECH took notice.

The ground beneath Jeremiah's feet was mucky mud, damp, and deep. Usually a person thrown down there would have a difficult time remaining upright. There was no food to eat or water to drink. I suppose it was the worst imprisonment that the prophet had ever suffered.

When my husband and I were in Israel many years ago, we were taken to a *"pit."* We were told by the guide that it was the *"pit"* that JEROME was thrown into long ago. There was no way a prisoner could escape from that deep *hole!* If I remember correctly, our guide said that Jerome translated the Scripture there. It is known as the *LATIN VULGATE.*

We all know the account of Daniel in the den of lions. That den was like the one in which Jerome and Jeremiah found themselves. Perhaps it was not wet from a recent rain as Jeremiah's trap was, but it was a *deep pit* from which no one could escape. Hungry lions lived down there. They could jump and dive, but could not escape the depth of that cavity. What a frightening experience for Daniel! The end of his story was *"life,"* very different from the end of the Lord Jesus Christ's imprisonment years later.

Our Holy Land guide told us also, that it was a *"pit"* like the one we saw in Israel where Jesus was put, when He was imprisoned the night before his crucifixion. I am not sure what Bible verse was used—perhaps Psalm *142:7 "Bring my soul out of prison . . ."* I can't remember.

SO JEREMIAH WAS IN THE PIT OF DESPAIR—doomed to die down there! BUT HIS AFRICAN FRIEND, EBEDMELECH, interceded to the King for Jeremiah. He pleaded, *"My lord, these men have done evil to Jeremiah the prophet . . . He will die of hunger, etc, etc."* I believe the king secretly liked Jeremiah. He often sought his advice; but seldom, if ever, took it. *"Take thirty men and get Jeremiah out of that pit before he dies!"* was the king's command.

So the Ethiopian found some old discarded cloth. He told Jeremiah to put those rotten rags under his arm pits. Then Ebedmelech would pull him out. I have an idea that Jeremiah was *thin,* for he was imprisoned many times without food. No matter—he was *freed, though filthy from* the mire, but *happy* to be on firm *dry* ground once again. WHAT AN EXCITING TRUE STORY THAT IS FOUND IN THE BIBLE!

"HIS WORD HEALS"
(Psalm 107:20)
"He sent his word, and healed them . . ."
How often I have said this!
His Word is the only balm on this earth's Gilead.
(If Gilead is on "earth's" side of Jordan)
If there is any comfort or help in our words to others,
it is because we use God's Word in our speech.
Fill your heart and mind with great thoughts!
This you will have, if you continually read
and meditate on the Bible! (ggs)

Today's Bible Blessing   *August 24*
Jeremiah 41:18—Jeremiah 46:14
GEDALIAH, ISHMAEL, & JOHANAN
Jeremiah 42:11

"Be not afraid of the king . . . saith the LORD: for I am with you."

Now we see Jeremiah being freed from his chains by **CAPTAIN NEBUZARADAN** (Jeremiah 39:14). It appeared that the prophet was numbered with Jerusalem's poor, and remained in the land, until he went into Egypt. He had previously found himself a shackled prisoner, for no other reason than that he told the truth! But this time it was different. He was released by Nebuzaradan.

NEBUCHADNEZZAR's captain of the guard recognized that Jeremiah spoke truth concerning the evil that would befall THE CITY OF DAVID. Interestingly, a heathen commander and a wicked ruler could recognize *"true prophecy"* from a *"true prophet."* The Jewish people could not do so! How blind they were to truth!

Freed from his chains, Jeremiah chose to remain with GEDALIAH. He was the man the Babylonian king had set up in Mizpah as Judah's governor. This would have been all well and good, except for a man named ISHMAEL. He had an insidious scheme to murder GEDALIAH. Not believing such a murderous plot, GOVERNOR GEDALIAH encouraged this brazen prospective killer, ISHMAEL, to serve the Chaldeans as all the captives were doing.

Many of the Jews had scattered as NEBUZARADAN captured the city and ravaged their land. When they heard that *"all was well"* (at least allegedly), they returned home from their foreign hiding places. Soon they began to harvest their crops and enjoy its bounty. It was during this time of rejoicing that JOHANAN—and other military men—warned GEDALIAH that a man named ISHMAEL was coming. He was sent by the AMMONITE KING BAALIS to assassinate GOVERNOR GEDALIAH.

Strange as it may seem to us, GEDALIAH did not believe this report. Even a brave, loyal man named JOHANAN suggested secretly to the Governor, *"Let me go and I will slay ISHMAEL, and no man shall know it."* He felt that if the Jews, who had recently returned to the land, got wind that this assassination was near, or that he, Johanan, would slay the culprit, they would scatter again. GEDALIAH forbade the brave warrior from such a killing and said: *"You speak falsely of Ishmael!"*

We learned in Jeremiah 41:1 that ISHMAEL was of *"the seed royal."* He was the son of NETHANIAH. His grandfather was ELISHAMA. As he came into the presence of GOVERNOR GEDALIAH, ISHMAEL grabbed his sword and slew the GOVERNOR!

Witnessing this bloody event were ten men who came with the murderous man. It was swift! It was final! It was over!

Now, no one knew of the assassination! Today there would have been television cameras and eye witness interviews. Hours would be spent viewing the surveillance tapes which would be found in every corner of the castle, but not in the days of Jeremiah. After a couple days, CRAFTY ISHMAEL met some pathetic looking men on the way to the temple. They had offerings and incense with them. Pretending he cared, ISHMAEL wept with the grieving men. Then suddenly, the murdering imposter killed the innocent worshippers. He threw their dead bodies into a nearby pit! What a callous man!

Surprisingly, the assassin spared ten men. I suppose it was for their promised treasury and food supplies. The vile men took the king's daughters, as well as other notables, over toward the Ammonite's country. BRAVE JOHANAN, who wanted to kill ISHMAEL, went after the assassin. Those who had been carried away for the land of the Ammonites were relieved to see him. Though they were rescued, sad to say, Ishmael and eight others escaped.

In chapter 42, JOHANAN consulted with Jeremiah, "Should we flee to Egypt?" "NO!" was the answer! If they went to Egypt, Jeremiah said they would die! If they remained in Judah, God would bless! They did not listen. When would they hear the prophet? **So in time, as Jeremiah said, *"The sword they feared would overtake them in Egypt!"***

"MOSES SHOULD HAVE FOLLOWED THE CLOUD"
He did not need to ask to go through Edom.
The things which God has promised, commanded, or stated,
are not to be prayed for or about. (ggs)

Today's Bible Blessing   *August 25*
Jeremiah 46:15–Jeremiah 49:17
JEREMIAH:
A VALIANT MAN FOR GOD

Jeremiah 46:15a
"Why are thy valiant men swept away . . .?"

As we are nearing the completion of the book of Jeremiah, let us reflect on the prophet himself. What do we think of when Jeremiah's name comes to mind? We think of a man who was called of God. He did not necessarily want to be a prophet. It was thrust upon him by the LORD God. What would his life have been if he had refused *"the call"*? He could have been like all the other

Israelites who were rejecting the true God for idols and imagery of their own minds. His eyes would have been full of adultery, always looking for something better. Instead, Jeremiah had a fire in his bones that he could not put out. He had a message that was like a hammer that broke rocks in pieces.

Often he found himself in prison and/or in chains, hungry and rejected. Some of his scorners would come to him secretly, to hear what the LORD was saying, yet they believed not the prophet. Once, a scornful king burned up Jeremiah's writings. Others listened to his voice. It appears that he never married or had children. His life was a solitary one, befriended by few, but chosen of God, and favored by certain kings.

In today's reading we see the times when "THE WORD OF THE LORD CAME TO JEREMIAH THE PROPHET . . ."

> Against the *Gentiles* (Jeremiah 46:1)
> Against *Egypt* (Jeremiah 46:2)
> Against the *Philistines* and *Gaza* (Jeremiah 47:1)
> Against *Moab* (Jeremiah 48:1)
> Against *the Ammonites* (Jeremiah 49:1)
> Against *Edom* (Jeremiah 49:7)
> Against *Damascus* (Jeremiah 49:23)
> Against *Kedar* (Jeremiah 49:28)
> Against *Elam* [*Persia*] (Jeremiah 49:34)
> Against *Babylon and the Chaldeans* (Jeremiah 50, 51)

One Bible verse comes to mind FOR TODAY. It is Jeremiah 46:15a: "WHY ARE THY VALIANT MEN SWEPT AWAY? In our day, many *"valiant"* men were brave and on fire for God. WHERE ARE THEY? They have fallen by the wayside. Some were snared by the devil into traps of lust and levity. Others were drawn to gold instead of the precious things of God. Others have died young, not knowing what course to take—thus spared from the sin and the humiliation of disobedience.

WHERE ARE THE VALIANT MEN FOR GOD?

"MOTHER DIED TODAY!"
Jennie Elizabeth Castle died today, August 25, 1974.
AGE: 91
HOW I WISHED SHE COULD HAVE ENTERED
HEAVENLY PORTALS WITHOUT DYING!
Her favorite psalms were Psalm 103 and Psalm 121.
She had a "strange" fear, as she grew older,
as her hearing and vision failed.
LORD, MAY I LEARN FROM OBSERVING HER
TO TRUST THEE ABSOLUTELY AS MY LIFE GOES ON.
MAY MY TRUST INCREASE AS MY DAYS DECREASE!
MY MOTHER WAS A WOMAN OF FAITH! (ggs)

Today's Bible Blessing   *August 26*

Jeremiah 49:18–Jeremiah 51:17
BY THE WORD OF HIS POWER!

Jeremiah 51:15

"He hath stretched out the heaven by his understanding."

Look at Jeremiah 51:15-16! See the hand of the MIGHTY CREATOR! Feel his creative power! That *"POWER"* was not known by man until man himself was created out of the dust of the earth.

> *"He hath made the earth by his power, he hath established the world by his wisdom, and hath stretched out the heaven by his understanding. When he uttereth his voice, there is a multitude of waters in the heavens; and he causeth the vapours to ascend from the ends of the earth: he maketh lightnings with rain, and bringeth forth the wind out of his treasures."*

WHEN WAS THE HEAVEN AND THE EARTH *"CREATED"*? Genesis 1:1 tells us they were *"created"* at a certain, specific time. That *time* was *"IN THE BEGINNING"*! Perhaps at that *"time"* called *"IN THE BEGINNING"* was the beginning of *"time"* as you and I know *"time."*

> *"For a thousand years in thy sight are but as yesterday when it is past, and as a watch in the night"* (Psalm 90:4). *"Beloved, be not ignorant of this one thing, that one day is with the Lord as a thousand years, and a thousand years as one day"* (II Peter 3:8).

PICTURE WITH ME *"NOTHING"*! ABSOLUTELY *"NOTHING"*! I don't mean a *blank* space. For if there is a *blank* space, there is something BEFORE and AFTER that *blank* space. We say *"My mind is blank!"* This implies that there are times when our mind is not blank! But with God—prior to Genesis 1:1—there was *"nothing"*! *"NOTHING!"* *"NOTHING!"* You and I cannot picture this.

Yes, there was GOD! His Name in the Genesis account is *ELOHIM.* That is the Name of God which shows that He is *three* Persons–*The Father, The Son,* and *The Holy Spirit.* All three Persons had a part in creating "NOTHING" INTO *"SOMETHING"*! In truth, the Architect of creation is the GREAT CREATOR, Jesus Christ. The word was spoken and GOD CREATED THE HEAVEN AND THE EARTH!

> *"Through faith we understand that the worlds were framed by the word of God, so that things which are seen were not made of things which do appear"* (Hebrews 11:3).

Things that were not seen. That is "NOTHING"! "NOTHING" was made of things which appeared! That was when "NOTHING" became "SOMETHING"!

The best illustration I can think of, for me, is the conception of a child. (It isn't an absolute illustration, but somewhat helpful.) When I was a young bride, I came into our marriage like Mary of old. I had never known a man. Then one day I—who had *"nothing"*—had *"something"!* I was pregnant with our first child. Where did that baby come from? That's where the illustration does not hold up–because there was a seed and a receptor for that seed. But for me, it was like a baby coming from "NOTHING." Now that darling baby boy is an adult man, in fact a grandfather. The wonder of it all! The miracle of birth!

How did the Creator establish the earth? Our verse here, in Jeremiah, tells us that it was established by HIS WISDOM! It was HIS POWER that made the earth. It wasn't a BIG BANG or an off-shoot of a falling star. THE GOD OF *"CREATION"* SPOKE A WORD. *"And God said, Let the waters under the heaven be gathered together unto one place"* (Genesis 1:9). And the earth was made. At the same time, HE STRETCHED OUT THE HEAVENS! Do you know *how* He stretched out the Heavens? He did it by HIS UNDERSTANDING.

WHAT A MIGHTY GOD WE HAVE!

"A CHILD WHO HAS DIED"
A CHILD WHO HAS DIED IS OUR OWN,
JUST AS MUCH IN THE ARMS OF CHRIST,
AS IF HE WERE HERE IN HIS CRADLE.
Our *Audrey is more alive after twenty-five years in Heaven
than she was for twenty years on earth.
For her, it is gain and far better!
I MUST BELIEVE IT! (ggs)

*Audrey was Gertrude's second-born daughter who died of Hodgkin's disease at age twenty.

Today's Bible Blessing   *August 27*

Jeremiah 51:18–Lamentations 1:4
OUT OF PRISON FOR GOOD

Jeremiah 52:31b

"The King . . . lifted up . . . Jehoiachin . . . and brought him forth."

Who was EVILMERODACH? He was the son of the great KING NEBUCHADNEZZAR. You probably remember Nebuchadnezzar. He besieged the Holy City and its land until the Jewish people were weakened. The mighty general took the finest of the land with ease. Judah was like a ripe plum falling off a fruit laden

379

tree into greedy Nebuchadnezzar's hand.

So at NEBUCHADNEZZAR'S death, EVILMERO- DACH became king of the mighty Chaldean empire. His reign was short; only from 562-560 B.C. This king's name is mentioned only twice in the Bible. Look at II Kings 25:27, and Jeremiah 52:31, to see its imprint. His name means *"MAN (or servant) of the god MARDUK or MERODACH."* It is said, by some historians, that KING EVIL-MERODACH was killed by his sister's husband. It appeared that this brother-in-law, whose name was NERIGLISSAR, made himself king in place of the murdered potentate. (This is according to *THE NEW UNGER'S BIBLE DICTIONARY.)*

Before his death, and while he was still king, EVILMERODACH did a very surprising thing. For some reason, he took pity on JEHOIACHIN, who had been in bondage for thirty-seven years. The truth was that JEHOIACHIN was not the only HUMILIATED KING who found himself subservient to the Babylonian rulers. Many others had become a part of Babylon's penal system. But KING EVILMERODACH gave JEHOIACHIN *new life* and *purpose.* The release from prison was surprising, but very welcomed.

COMPASSIONATE EVILMERODACH reached into the dungeon of despair and brought JEHOIACHIN into the light of freedom. Their differences were put behind them. The released king was given fine clothes, as well as daily food at the king's table. For the rest of his natural life, JEHOIACHIN was treated as a guest and not a ruffian. The two kings talked as friends talked. The whole palace could observe that JEHOIACHIN had been promoted. He had a high place in the eyes of all. As the other rulers were pining away, no longer was JEHOIACHIN a prisoner in that dank, dark royal dungeon!

I think of the prison of sin and death into which all of us were born. It was a doomed place, a place of loss and sorrow. Through no fault of our own, we had found ourselves sinners and bound for Hell. *"For all have sinned and come short of the glory of God"* (Romans 3:23). Years before, in Eden's Garden, Adam and Eve disobeyed God. They ate of the forbidden fruit! In so doing, their eyes were opened. They saw themselves naked and sinners.

"Thou shalt not eat!" **(Genesis 2:17).** Oh, it was not that the couple could not eat. It was only that they should not eat the fruit found on the TREE OF THE KNOWLEDGE OF GOOD AND EVIL. There were many trees filled with many fruits and nuts in that Garden Home. BUT ONE TREE WAS FORBIDDEN! Yet, they could not resist tasting of that forbidden fruit. One bite—and their eyes were opened! They were naked! Though they had never heard of *"sin"* before, and did not really know what *"sin"* was, they knew they had sinned.

No one had to tell them they were sinners. They just knew! They hid from God! BUT GOD FOUND THEM. You see, NO ONE CAN HIDE FROM GOD!

This is where the Lord Jesus Christ comes in. He became a man. His conception and birth was unique. God became man! He was sinless. After thirty-three years of living on this EARTH, He permitted Himself to be crucified. It was on a Cross over there near Jerusalem. That was more than 2,000 years ago.

Because JESUS is the sinless Son of God, as well as the sinless Son of man, He was able to take in His body on the cross your sins and my sins. We did not deserve it! He reached down into the HELL-HOLE where we used to live and offered us a new life. He wanted to clothe us sinners in His righteousness! All we have to do is receive Him!

"Who his own self bare our sins in his own body on the tree, that we, being dead to sins, should live unto righteousness . . ." **(I Peter 2:24).**

"THE FIRST MENTION OF THE BOOK"
(Joshua 1:8)
"Joshua was to be guided and governed
wholly by the written WORD,
which was something unexpected and unique.
No man, before Joshua, had received orders from God
to regulate his conduct by the Word of a Book!
JOSHUA and THE BOOK come before us together.
Joshua and all who succeeded him,
must be governed by this BOOK!
God's Words, from its very first appearance as a Book,
occupy the position of unqualified supremacy."
(ggs, from page 38 in GLEANINGS IN JOSHUA, Pink)

Today's Bible Blessing   *August 28*
Lamentations 1:5–Lamentations 3:45
OUR TRICKLING TEARS

Lamentations 3:49
"Mine eye trickleth down, and ceaseth not, without any intermission."

The book of Lamentations is a series of five poems lamenting the decline of Israel. God's heart is broken. Jeremiah reflected that sorrow with his pen. The times were difficult. Israel was the nation from which the promised Messiah was to come. Yet, Israel was in such a state of sin that the LORD God had turned the other way. He permitted the nation to be swallowed up by Babylon. This book is a message of tears and regret, with an occasional glimpse of hope and renewal. It is a poem of poems!

Of interest is how the poems are laid out. In the first two chapters, each verse begins with a new letter of the Hebrew alphabet. It has three parts. In the third chapter, we see the third poem. It devotes three verses to each of the twenty-two letters in the Hebrew alphabet. Dr. Unger's Bible dictionary calls these poems *"dirges."* The dictionary reads: *"In the fourth dirge, one verse composed of two members is distributed to each letter."* (I'm quoting the dictionary because I don't know exactly what it means.) The last *"dirge"* is made up of twenty-two verses. They are not alphabetical.

I suppose the Lamentations that are the most familiar to me are found in Chapter Three, verses 22-23. I'm sure you remember them, too.

"It is of the LORD'S mercies that we are not consumed, because his compassions fail not. They are new every morning: great is thy faithfulness."

As a student at Moody Bible Institute, graduating in 1948, I recall the blessing of singing that moving song, *GREAT IS THY FAITHFULNESS.* Hundreds of voices, both men and women, filled that huge auditorium, declaring that God's *"compassions fail not!"* T. O. Chisholm wrote those beautiful words that we sang to William M. Runyan's melody. We sang all the stanzas. So now, I do not need a hymn book when that song is sung in our church. I know every stanza! I believe in teaching young people many, if not all, the stanzas of some of our majestic hymns. So many songs today are just fluff with little to no spiritual depth to them.

William Culbertson was my president. He served there for years as the spiritual leader of that school. Another man was president when I arrived. I don't know how long he served before my arrival. Only—he died. It was sad. At first it was all *"hush-hush."* As weeks progressed into months, we learned that this beloved man took his own life. Often pain is hard to bear. Sometimes the most noble and gifted—full of spiritual grace and knowledge of God's WORDS—cannot bear the agonies of life.

Another *"lamentation"* I want you to ponder in today's reading is Lamentations 3:49. When I read it today, I thought, *"How true!"* How true it is when grief strikes a soul! *After the first burst of sorrow, our tears flow—not in the early sobs and uncontrolled gushes of shock and grief—but in a slow trickling down the cheeks.* They fall softly! They do not stop! When we talk, they come. When we walk they are there. When we do our daily work, they trickle down our cheeks. They are shameless! It is as if our *"grief"* is melting! We don't want our tears falling onto our tea cups, as we drink our morning tea. We don't want them to come when we see a reminder of *the past* or the loss of *the future.* **YET, THEY COME— *"WITHOUT INTERMISSION!"***

(From the Book, *WITH TEARS IN MY HEART*, by GGS–Pg. 17)
"God gives us tears to wash away the heartache,
To bathe our grief and dim our present loss.
He gives us tears, but promises to dry them,
And tell us WHY we suffered grief and pain."

"ALWAYS, UNTIL THE END"
(Psalm 119:112)
"I have inclined mine heart to perform thy statutes alway,
even unto the end."
INCLINED–HEART
TO PERFORM–STATUES
ALWAYS!
MY PRAYER:
"Dear Lord,   Draw my heart till I continually, absolutely
do what you have commanded all thru my life
in weakness and strength to do always and only Thy will." (ggs)

𝒯*oday's* ℬ*ible* ℬ*lessing*   𝒜*ugust* 29
Lamentations 3:46–Ezekiel 1:20
EZEKIEL'S CALL TO THE MINISTRY
Ezekiel 1:3
"The word of the LORD came expressly unto Ezekiel the priest."

Since childhood we have been taught that there were four major prophets. Their writings were considered *"major"* for they were longer than the smaller writings. It doesn't mean that the *"minor"* prophets were really *"minor;"* it just means that the length of their writings were smaller than the length of the writings by *Isaiah, Jeremiah, Ezekiel*, and *Daniel*.

EZEKIEL was a visionary. He saw into the future, as well as dipping into the past. His writings jump from one subject to another. Often he confuses the reader. Some accounts had passed into history and other accounts foretell that which will come to be. His heart is heavy with *God's Words* smiting his whole being. He must tell it! He must obey it! He must do what the LORD God commands him to do, no matter how difficult or how disturbing.

I am learning about a ruler named NABOPOLASSAR who was a Chaldean, not a true Babylonian, but came to be Babylon's mighty king. He was the father of NEBUCHADNEZZAR who was strong and wise in battle. When his father died suddenly, NEBUCHADNEZZAR was called home to sit on the throne. It had been speculated that if his father had not died, and Nebuchadnezzar had invaded Egypt as he had planned, Babylon would have become as great and as large a kingdom as Assyria. Instead, Nebuchadnezzar came *"home"* and reigned from Babylon—a city he loved. This is evident by his building temples and caring for the kingdom's internal affairs.

First we must realize that Ezekiel, the man, was one of the many captives brought to Babylon by its general. EZEKIEL's name means *"GOD WILL STRENGTHEN."* He was a priest and had been taken captive when JEHOIACHIN was captured five years previously (II Kings 24:12-15). When we first meet EZEKIEL, he is living in Chaldea on the bank of the Chebar River with a group of exiled Jews. It was there that the LORD came *"expressly unto Ezekiel...the son of Buzi"* (Ezekiel 1:3).

In Chapter One we see the famous account of *THE WHEELS.* We can spiritualize them, or we can take them literally. One day Ezekiel looked up in the Northern sky and saw a huge cloud with fire enclosing it. What a frightening sight! As I write this, California is being engulfed with forest fires. I see the red flames covering the land and sky. Houses are burned in minutes. People are running for their lives. What must it have been like for Ezekiel to see this cloud turning to fire—reminiscence of the *pillar of fire* of long ago. There was a whirlwind—a *supernatural whirlwind!*

All of a sudden, out of that confusion of fire and wind, came the color of *"AMBER."* This *"AMBER"* was probably *electrum* which is a natural pale yellow alloy of gold and silver. It gives the appearance of *"brightness and fire"* and is always used to describe *visions* of "divine glory."

Out of this *"electrum"* or *"amber"* appeared four living creatures! Can you imagine the shock EZEKIEL had! How long did he stare at the living creatures before they turned into the appearance of a man, I do not know; but it must have been frightening! What a call to the ministry!

I imagine the whole procedure to be like a giant kaleidoscope. It turned and twisted. Lights of gold and silver reflected in unexplainable brightness! Shapes of animals and faces, wings and feet jumped before his eyes like papier-mâché relief! *"What was happening to me?"* surely was Ezekiel's question.

There were wheels and wheels within wheels. *There was whirling and speed and bluish-green hues beauty!* It went in all directions, like lightning strikes—up and down, forward and backward. The noise of their wings was like the voice of the ALMIGHTY, as rushing waters.

A THRONE! AN APPEARANCE OF A MAN! A RAINBOW! AND THE GLORIOUS LORD!

Today's Bible Blessing   *August 30*
Ezekiel 1:21–Ezekiel 6:6
EZEKIEL'S COMMISSION TO SPEAK
Ezekiel 2:1
"Son of man, stand upon thy feet, and I will speak unto thee"

When we meet Ezekiel today, he is told to stand up on his feet (Ezekiel 2:1). If you recall, he had just heard *the voice of the LORD.* In fact, he had seen *"the appearance of the likeness of the GLORY the LORD!"* Remember the *"wheel"* and the *"wheel"* in the *middle of the "wheel"* (Ezekiel 1:16). The *"spirit of the living creatures was in the wheels"* (vs. 20).

I am reminded of the old Negro spiritual I learned as a child. I may not have the words correct, but it goes something like this:

*"Ezekiel saw a wheel, way up in the middle of the air
And the first wheel run by faith
And the second wheel run by the grace of God
A wheel in a wheel–way in the middle of the air."*

The "SPIRIT" entered into Ezekiel, and stood him on his feet. When we work for the Lord Jesus Christ, we must stand (Ephesians 6:14). We cannot sit! A person can have all his armor on (Ephesians 6:10-18), but if he is not standing, by being physically and mentally prepared for battle, he isn't able to do his job successfully. A soldier could be fully equipped from head to toe with his weapon in his hand; but if he is lackadaisical, he is not prepared. A person in God's army must be standing and ready for spiritual battle. **THE ENEMY IS AT HAND!**

So EZEKIEL was pulled to his feet by the Spirit of God! I don't know if one of the wheels came down and took his hand, pulling him to his feet; or if God took him in His arms, as a father would his child, standing him upright. Whatever, the prophet stood at attention to receive His calling! He was commissioned to prophesy to the children of Israel. They were *rebellious*, stiffnecked, and *impudent* people. It was not an easy assignment!

"BE NOT AFRAID OF THEIR WORDS." **This was the instruction from the LORD God.** *"Speak unto them . . . whether they will hear, or whether they will forbear"* (Ezekiel 3:11). They were a rebellious people.

EZEKIEL WAS WARNED. He should not have been surprised. Being human, he may have had many discouraging times. No one likes his message rejected. No one!

Immediately the prophet was given a book. It is called a "roll" for they did not have hardcover or paper-covered book in those days. *"Eat the roll (scroll)!"* The Bible says that Ezekiel opened his mouth (3:2). I think he opened his mouth in amazement. I know some people who open their mouths wide–as if in a dentist chair–when something remarkable was said. So there he was—opened-mouth EZEKIEL, still a bit shaky from the *"wheel experience"*—standing amazed at God's call in his life. There he was when pieces like writing paper were stuffed into his mouth! He couldn't help it. He ate it!

God commissioned the surprised man, encouraging him to be STEADFAST and UNMOVABLE!

> *Therefore, my beloved brethren, be ye steadfast, unmoveable, always abounding in the work of the Lord, forasmuch as ye know that your labour is not is in vain in the Lord* (I Corinthians 15:58).

This Bible verse in I Corinthians was one of my father's favorite verses. He was a good Christian man, full of *courage* and *determination*. Daddy came from a poor family. Often, as a child, he went to bed hungry. One night he was awakened from his sleep. His father had brought home beans for the family to eat. After his mother cooked them, she awakened her children from a sound sleep to feed them. They were so hungry! I remember when my father told us children that account, he began to cry. I never saw him cry before. His memories were stirred.

This man, my Dad, knew deprivation! He learned to be steadfast in his convictions. He saw the benefits of an unmovable spirit for the right! Let us be like R. O. Sanborn and like Ezekiel! They faced much opposition, as we may be facing, too. BUT THEY STOOD!

FEAR THEM NOT! NEITHER BE DISMAYED AT THEIR LOOKS (Ezekiel 3:9).

Today's Bible Blessing   *August 31*
Ezekiel 6:7–Ezekiel 10:21
EZEKIEL'S VISION
OF A DESECRATED TEMPLE

Ezekiel 8:1

"And it came to pass. . .that the hand of the Lord GOD fell there upon me."

One day, Ezekiel was sitting in his house with some of the elders of Judah. It was on the fifth day of the sixth month (Ezekiel 8:1). That would be the Jewish month *"E'LUL,"* which is comparable to our August/September. It is interesting that E'LUL is right around the time of the year we are in now. The weather during the sixth month is very hot and there is much heat lightning, but little rain. It was the time of reaping (See II Kings 4:18-20). While enjoying himself with his friends, *"the hand of the Lord GOD fell upon him."* I wonder what that was like!

A very strange thing occurred here. EZEKIEL had a vision. Now I don't know if the *"elders"* that sat in front of him saw what Ezekiel saw or not. I tend to believe it was only Ezekiel, but I do not really know.

It was a weird and unbelievable vision. There was *"the appearance of fire."* (The color of *"amber"* is mentioned again.) That means it was not fire, but looked like fire. Remember Moses and the burning bush? Remember the fiery pillar that led Israel from Egypt to the Promised Land? Remember the wheels in chapter one?

EZEKIEL seemed to be looking at the Lord GOD! (Perhaps it was a THEOPHANY or a CHRISTOPHANY.)

Then a form of a hand grabbed him by his hair. He must have had long enough hair to grab. All of a sudden the frightened prophet was in the air! It was like a helicopter ride without the helicopter. There, in Ezekiel's vision, he was dropped right in front of the Northern inner gate. From where he tumbled, he could see the horrible image called *JEALOUSY!* It was there that Israel committed disgusting abominations that should not be practiced anyplace, let alone in the House of the Lord. **But, EZEKIEL was not alone.** Ezekiel 8:4 says *"The glory of the God of Israel was there."* What a comfort for the man to know that he was not alone during this frightening experience.

At the court's door there was a *"hole."* How the Temple had been ignored! Ezekiel crawled in that hole. His eyes could not believe what they were seeing. The beautiful building that David longed for, and, like what we call today a *"crack-house,"* was filled with sinful pictures and practices. Graffiti of hateful beasts, doing hateful things, and idols portraying wicked immoral deeds were painted on the marred walls. **DO YOU GET THE IDEA?**

To make matters worse, EZEKIEL saw seventy of the *"ancient"* men of Israel standing there. There in the middle of the degraded *"spiritual"* leaders was JAAZANIAH. This man was the leader of the seventy elders of Israel. There he was, offering idolatrous worship to a false god. To make matters worse, every elder was waving censers that gave forth thick clouds of incense. It was an unbelievable sight. *"A form of godliness but denying the power thereof . . ."* (II Timothy 3:5). In what a backslidden condition were the priests and Levites in the Land of Promise! How God's heart must have grieved! No wonder He forsook them for a season.

Wherever Ezekiel looked, the sight of sin was worse than the last look. There were several women weeping for Tammuz. (He was an ancient Babylonian deity.) He was the god of pasture, vegetation, flocks, and subterranean water. One of the yearly rites of Tammuz was for a temple priestess to marry the king, in honor of the fertility god.

When EZEKIEL thought things could not get much worse, he was taken into the inner court of the Temple. That was between the porch and the altar. Stunned, he observed twenty-five men facing the EAST worshipping the sun. As we remember, Egyptians were *"sun worshippers."*

Such defilement of the HOUSE OF GOD was more than EZEKIEL could stand. Quickly he organized six men to get their *"slaughter weapon"* and stand by the brasen altar. It was noted that *"the glory of the Lord"* was no longer there. One man was dressed in linen, holding an inkwell. He was supposed to put a mark on the foreheads of those who were sickened at such temple abomination. All the others—men, women, and children—were to be killed. Slaughter would start at the House of God (I Peter 4:17). *"The iniquity of Israel is exceedingly great!"* **God's eye would not spare. God had no pity!**

Today's Bible Blessing   *September 1*
Ezekiel 10:22—Ezekiel 14:8
WOMEN'S DRESS & ACTIONS
Ezekiel 13:22

"Because with lies ye have made the heart of the righteous sad . . ."

Sometimes, it is difficult for the average person, like I am, to follow the writings of Ezekiel. He seems to go back and forth between the past and the future. One minute he is in Chaldea and the next moment, he is in Jerusalem with all of his strange visions. One minute he is superintending the killing of backslidden Judah and the next, he is watching Cherubim winging over Jerusalem in tandem with "wheels within wheels." Often we hear words soaring in praise, and other times, words condemning all sin and degradation.

One time Ezekiel is digging with his bare hands, bringing forth "stuff" as instructed by the Lord GOD. We wonder what the "stuff" was; but we are never told. Now we meet another JAAZANIAH, whose father is a man named AZUR. This son, too, was a leader among the twenty-five apostates, who had been seen by EZEKIEL hypocritically waving incense censors in the temple's filth. This JAAZANIAH had a fellow in "the falling away" in the temple worship. His name was PELATIAH. He died without warning—much to the Prophet's chagrin (Ezekiel 11:1,13). The man fell over dead when Ezekiel was prophesying.

Ezekiel lamented "Ah, Lord God, Wilt thou make full end of the remnant of Israel?" He wondered if there would be anyone left who trusted the true God. There was such an unbelievable "falling away." (To me, it seems to be a foretaste of the "falling away" before the "man of sin" is revealed during the Great Tribulation II Thessalonians 2:3). Perhaps the Lord GOD permitted Ezekiel to have such visions so he could prophesy with greater conviction. What do you think?

We find powerful verses from this Ezekiel's mouth.
"Thus saith the Lord GOD; Woe unto the foolish prophets, that follow their own spirit, and have seen nothing!"
"Likewise, thou son of man, set thy face against the

daughters of thy people, which prophesy out of their own heart; and prophesy thou against them," (Ezekiel 13:3, 17).
HE TAKES A SWIPE AGAINST WOMEN WHO ARE SAYING AND ACTING IN WAYS THAT ARE NOT RIGHT.

We, women, must be careful how we act and look— what we wear, and where we go. People watch Christian women with eagle eyes. Some of us offend others by what we put on, or what we don't put off. Today's styles are very naked. Necklines are extremely low and hemlines are often too short. As my grandmother Sanborn used to say to me when I wore my gym suit around the house, "It doesn't leave much to the imagination." Believe me, in 1945, gym clothes were ample–nothing like the skimpy sports clothes of today. But it was a gym suit.

Ezekiel was concerned with the "pillows" that women were sewing in their armholes. Now this is very foreign to us. I can't imagine a woman sewing a "pillow" to fit under her arm pits, can you? I've heard it said that these "pillows" were used by the temple prostitutes so the ground would be more comfortable in their "work." I don't know.

Others teach that those "pillows" had to do with "magic charms." "Charms" of silver or gold, or precious stones, would attract the eyes of people passing by. "Charms" representing a heathen god—as often earrings did—would signify the religious conviction of the wearer. If you remember in Exodus 33:4-6, we read that the children of Israel were to *"put off"* their *ornaments* when they came near Mt. Horeb. I feel that those *"ornaments"* were false gods just like the earrings that were mentioned in Genesis 35:4. Certainly that conviction would not be for JEHOVAH, the True God.

PERHAPS SOME OF US HAVE FORGOTTEN THAT PEOPLE OBSERVE THE WAY WE DRESS. It tells them by what we wear if we are treating our bodies as the "temple of the Holy Spirit." Little is left to the imagination. Many women today dress like the street walkers dressed in former years. Do you think such "nakedness" is a good testimony to our Lord and Saviour?

Another thing Ezekiel touched upon, when talking to the worldly women of his day, was about LYING. THERE IS NOTHING SO DISAPPOINTING THAN HAVING A FRIEND WHO LIES TO ME. Some say they are "stretching the truth." Others deliberately lie concerning events in their lives. Some are ashamed to be divorced. So they lie about it, thinking no one will know. Others lie about little things. You wonder why they bother to prevaricate. Lying makes the heart of the liar sad, as well as the hearts of those to whom she is lying.

EZEKIEL OBSERVED, "LIES HAVE MADE THE HEART OF THE RIGHTEOUS SAD."

```
"THOU, O LORD"
(Psalm 3: 2-6)
But thou, O LORD, art a shield for me; my glory,
and the lifter up of mine head.
I CRIED–HE HEARD
I SLEPT–FOR HE SUSTAINED ME
I WILL NOT BE AFRAID.
How I needed a "Lifter Up" of my head today.
HE ANOINTED MY HEAD WITH OIL.
(ggs: "Heard this Scripture on morning radio. I was helped.)
```

Today's Bible Blessing   *September 2*

Ezekiel 14:9–Ezekiel 16:62
CARE FOR FOUNDLING ISRAEL

Ezekiel 16:9

"Then washed I thee with water; yea, I throughly washed away thy blood from thee, and I anointed thee with oil."

When God promised Abraham a land he had never seen or been to before, He meant it. So Abraham believed God. He followed Him and founded a family. Isaac was born, then Jacob was born, then his twelve sons.

A nation was born. That nation was Israel. Mr. & Mrs. Abraham, their family and their servants went with GOD. THEY DID NOT KNOW WHERE THEY WERE GOING, BUT GOD KNEW. They followed Him until they got there. They settled and lived in Canaan.

Then the famine came and the nation of Israel ended up in Egypt for over four hundred years. During that time, the people of Israel forgot much of their heritage. They learned to worship idols like the Egyptians, who had myriads of idols for every occasion and need. It is more than likely that some of Israel had worshipped the Sun-god who was dear to the Egyptian people. Yet, some believed in the God of Abraham. Some retained their love for the true God. I believe that Moses' birth parents were believers.

In the passage of time, the Hebrew people went back to Canaan. Being there did not come easy. There were the forty years in the wilderness. Many lessons were learned in their wanderings. Many were born, and just as many died. There were the battles led by Joshua. Conquering their territory was a "must." THE LAND THAT WAS PROMISED TO ABRAHAM HAD TO BE TAKEN ONCE MORE. Those who had been driven out returned while Israel was absent. This was the land and the people EZEKIEL was talking about in Ezekiel 16:3 when he wrote *"Thy father was an AMORITE,* *and thy mother an HITTITE."* That was Israel's heritage.

The land promised to Israel was the land the Jews had lived in under Solomon, as well as the other kings. In Israel's absence, the AMORITES and HITTITES had re-occupied the territory. God commanded that the heathen be pushed away so the Hebrews could claim the land once again. That was the property given to them years ago by God to Abraham.

In today's reading, we see that the Lord GOD is reviewing what He did for Israel. He tells us that He found them like a baby abandoned in an open field. The baby was newborn and neglected. Her naval was not cut probably. She was not washed from her birth fluids. Her pearly newborn covering was dirty and in need of care. No one had bathed or salted the child. It was not "swaddled." People would talk. They did not think Israel was a "proper" child. Israel was worse than an orphan. She was a "foundling." All this did not matter to God—even though she was polluted in blood from the blood of her mother at her delivery. It had never been washed away.

How precious! The Lord GOD found that abandoned babe. He had compassion for the child. He loved her. So, HE REACHED DOWN WITH HIS GREAT ARMS OF LOVE AND SAID, "LIVE" (Ezekiel 16:6).

My heart is touched by this narrative. How God loves Israel. She was a "nothing," and He made her into a "something." Then she betrayed the LORD God who loved her. She worshipped idols in her heart over and over again. In time her secret loves turned into public indecency. She turned from a faithful "wife" to an adulterous "whore." Her appetite had been whetted for sin, and there was no turning back. So the LORD God turned His back on her. He stood by and watched—waiting for repentance and a return to Him.

> *And they shall bear the punishment of their iniquity: the punishment of the prophet shall be even as the punishment of him that seeketh unto him"* (Ezekiel 14:10).

Are you a lost person like baby Israel? Are you lost in a field of self-pity and hopelessness? Do you bear the pain of your sin and rebellious heart? Do you long for God to stoop down and pick you up in His Heavenly Father arms, and say, "I love you"? Take heart. He does. He cares. Jesus Christ came to make it possible for you to have your sins forgiven. He can give you hope like you have never hoped before. Only thing is—you must recognize that you are a sinner and need a Saviour.

"Believe on the Lord Jesus Christ and thou shalt be saved"
(Acts 16:31).

Today's Bible Blessing   *September 3*
Ezekiel 16:63–Ezekiel 20:14
BEWARE OF THAT CERTAIN SOMEONE

Ezekiel 18:24b

"All his righteousness that he hath done shall not be mentioned . . ."

I am in a quandary wondering exactly what I should say today. I am thinking of a Christian who sinned. I do not mean what we call "small sins"–although I know that "sins" is "sin." I am talking about a BIG "sin," a "sin" that mars the Name of Christ in a community. The public sin that causes a stir from the pew to the grocery store.

He who sins so grievously, that not only his testimony for Jesus Christ is marred, but his whole church's name is blackened. The world looks at him in disgust because he cannot practice what he preached. The temptation was too great. And the mighty has fallen. *THE BEAUTY OF ISRAEL IS SLAIN UPON THY HIGH PLACES: HOW ARE THE MIGHTY FALLEN!* (II Samuel 1:19). It is not pleasant to see. It is not happy news to hear.

> *"But when the righteous turneth away from his righteousness, and committeth iniquity, and doeth according to all the abominations that the wicked man doeth, shall he live? All his righteousness that he hath done shall not be mentioned: in his trespass that he hath trespassed, and in his sin that he hath sinned, in them shall he die"* (Ezekiel 18:24).

I do not claim to understand the verses in Ezekiel 18. But, I do understand the public reaction to the awfulness of a Christian drawn into gross sin. The magnitude of the "naughty" draws the eye. The grip of the sensual is stronger than reason. As the pull of steel is drawn to the magnet, Satan comes. And in weakness, under his spell the Christian yields. *"AND NO MARVEL; FOR SATAN HIMSELF IS TRANSFORMED INTO AN ANGEL OF LIGHT"* (II Corinthians 11:14).

Why is it that Satan's baubles are irresistible to the Christian? Could it be that the Christian is walking in his or her own strength? He begins to believe his own press releases. He forgets to *"press forward for the mark"* (Philippians 3:14). He lollygags. He looks around him. He hears the crowd cheering him on. He spies a "special fan" in a short skirt and a low-cut neckline, waving a bright flag with his name on it. She looks at him. His heartstrings sing. That is when he should take stock of himself. That is when he should look at the "mark" ahead of him and the "prize." That is when he should remember his wife and his children and his testimony for Christ.

"I've been doing pretty good," he says to himself. "Look at me, everybody. I am a pastor of a big church. I am on a mission board. I have power more than the average person. I have hundreds of people in my church. I write books. People look to me from all over the world. I must be good."

Soon the self-centered man, puffed up by the flag-waver's praise, begins to believe all the good things said to him by everybody around him, especially her. His wife may tell him the truth. He thinks she is "sour grapes." She begs, "PLEASE STAY HOME WITH ME AND THE CHILDREN." But—he is too busy. He is too heady. Other people need him. They appreciate him more—ESPECIALLY THE ONE WHO HAS THE FLAG WITH HIS NAME ON IT.

Then one sad day, a "certain someone" needs him more than anyone else. She understands him better than any other person. She compliments him in such a way that he is drawn to her. He has to hear her voice when he is away from her too long. He needs her advice. He feels good around her person. Soon this "friendship" grows. There is casual touching of the shoulder or the arm. It leads to a friendly welcoming hug when he has been out of town. Then an occasional fond embrace becomes a daily treat. Before he knows it, he is emotionally drawn to a woman to whom he is not married.

If this attraction is not cut off, there will be sin that can never be forgotten—even though forgiven. It could lead to divorce or even suicide. WOE TO THE ONE WHO CARRIED THE FLAG WITH HER PASTOR'S NAME ON IT! Judgment day is coming! *"For such are false apostles, deceitful workers, transforming themselves into the apostles of Christ"* (II Corinthians 11:13).

(ysw: I wrote this today because of a pastor who recently committed suicide because he could not face his adultery publically.)

"HE MAKETH ME TO LIE DOWN AT NOON"
(Song of Solomon 1:7)
Tell me, you whom I love, where do you feed your sheep?
Where do you let them rest at noon?
WHY SHOULD I TURN ASIDE?
The pressures and heat of my trials
cause me to come to Him and say
"TELL ME WHERE I MAY REST AT NOON?"
"THERE IS A PLACE OF QUIET REST NEAR TO THE HEART OF
GOD."
(Last line quotes Cleland B. McAfee) (ggs)

Today's Bible Blessing   September 4
Ezekiel 20:15—Ezekiel 22:18
KEEP YOURSELVES FROM IDOLS
Ezekiel 20:24b
"They . . . polluted my sabbaths, and their eyes were after their fathers' idols."

As we read today's reading, we get the distinct impression that the LORD, the God of Israel, was thoroughly disgusted with His people. He said that "their eyes were after their fathers' idols." I can feel the disgust in God's voice, can't you? I can sense the hurt in His heart. Here the people whom He loved, the people in whom He had placed all His hopes and future, thumbed their noses at the God who loved Him.

All the LORD, their God, expected was for them to walk in His ways, to keep His sabbaths, to worship Him and not idols, and to be separated from the pagan people living around them. That's all. Evidently, it was too much for Israel to do.

They polluted His Sabbaths. Not only were they to obey the "Seventh Day" rules, but there were other occasions that were called "Sabbaths" on the Jewish calendar, too. What does pollute mean? It means to "defile," to "pollute," to "desecrate," to "profane," to "render unclean." That is what the wicked Israelites did to God's holy days. The wicked did not care what He said or what those days stood for in the community.

It is a fact, that the people in your neighborhood are watching you. If you name the Name of the LORD JESUS as your Saviour, the neighbors are watching. They know if you attend church regularly. They see your car back out of the driveway on Sundays and prayer meeting nights. Believe me; if you break the habit of church going, your neighbors will know that you have backslidden in that department.

Over and over again, in yesterday's and today's readings, we read of the abomination or the loathsome, detestable things the Israelites did. They defiled themselves with the idols of Egypt. It had been many years since their Egyptian bondage; yet they continued to bow before the gods of their captors. The disturbing rituals that went with such worship were theirs. They climbed to the high places up in the groves where no one could see them.

They practiced spiritual adultery, as well as physical fornication, as part of their worship at BAMAH. Carved animals of wood and stone, as well as images of body parts, were a part of their heathen rituals. The evil worship was filthy and contemptible, and they would have it no other way. Of a truth, *THEIR HEART WENT AFTER THEIR IDOLS* (Ezekiel 20:16).

I am reminded of the APOSTLE JOHN'S ADMONITION in his first epistle to us believers. After talking about the love of God in Jesus Christ and after reminding us of the fellowship we have with each other because of Jesus Christ, John wrote very strange words. He said, *"LITTLE CHILDREN, KEEP; YOUR-SELVES FROM IDOLS"* (I John 5:21).

Let us remind ourselves who this man was who made such a request. John was an old man, and well loved by the believers. I am sure he was tired. Perhaps he was weak or ill. I do not know. He had seen it all. More was to come in a few years. Soon he would be swept off to PATMOS ISLAND. There he would have visions and revelations. These are found in the last book of the New Testament.

If you remember, John was well-loved by Jesus. It was John who arrived first to the empty tomb with Peter. But John held back. Perhaps out of respect for his older, slower companion. It was John who stayed at the foot of the cross of his crucified Lord. John witnessed the "agony." He took Jesus' mother home with him and comforted her at the death of her firstborn Son.

So when John tells us to KEEP OURSELVES FROM IDOLS, he must have meant just that. Often preachers teach that anything that takes our thoughts from Jesus is an idol. That may be true. Some point out that the television set could be one, or the internet, or your car, or your home, or even your husband or wife, or child. But I am wondering, in the light of Ezekiel's prophecies, if the APOSTLE JOHN did not mean "real idols" made of wood, stone, or precious metal.

If so, such idol worship is an abomination to God. After all, *"THOU SHALT NOT MAKE UNTO THEE ANY GRAVEN IMAGE, OR ANY LIKENESS OF ANY THING THAT IS IN HEAVEN ABOVE, OR THAT IS IN THE EARTH BENEATH, OR THAT IS IN THE WATER UNDER THE EARTH"* is still in the Bible (Exodus 20:4). I fear we may pass off this second commandment too lightly today. The same God who said: *"POLLUTE YE MY HOLY NAME NO MORE WITH YOUR GIFTS, AND WITH YOUR IDOLS"* (Ezekiel 20:39b) means it as much today as He did in Ezekiel's day.

"YOUR CIRCUMSTANCE"
(Psalm 27:5; Psalm 4:6; Psalm 50:15)
Someone has written:
"HE THAT IS MASTERED BY CHRIST
IS THE MASTER OF EVERY CIRCUMSTANCE"
Does a circumstance press hard against you?
It is shaping you into a vessel of beauty and usefulness for Eternity.
IT IS THE POTTER'S HAND.
DO NOT PUSH IT AWAY.
It is shaping you into a vessel of beauty and usefulness for Eternity.
Your mastery will come, not by arresting its progress,
but by enduring its discipline.
(Copied by ggs. Source unknown.)

Today's Bible Blessing   *September 5*
Ezekiel 22:19—Ezekiel 24:24
FROM SIN TO SADNESS

Ezekiel 24:16
"Behold . . . I take away from thee the desire of thine eyes with a stroke."

It is very evident to me that God hates adultery and fornication. To Him it is the worse sin. The reason I've come to that conclusion is when the LORD explained the waywardness of Israel and Judah, He likened their sin to ADULTERY. Over and over again, we see this sexual sin mentioned in regard to the backslidden condition of His people. THEIR UNSPEAKABLE IDOL WORSHIP WAS LIKENED TO ADULTERY.

Not only did His people profane His Sabbaths, they were idolatrous religiously and physically. They not only sinned with their neighbors' wives, they were sexually familiar with their stepmothers, also. Their priests and princes, who should have been moral leaders, were full of lies (Ezekiel 22: 28). They took usury for greedy gain. Their prophets were like roaring lions, devouring the souls of those they were supposed to be helping. IN HIS WRATH, THE LORD BLEW FIRE ON THEM (22:21). He looked for a man to stand in the gap, to make a hedge of protection for the land. Pathetically, He could find no one (22:30).

I remember a youth pastor. He was successful and charming. One Sunday he preached on this passage. He pleaded for a "man" to stand in the gap. He should have been that man. Instead, he secretly was like the adulterous Israelites. He and the choir leader were committing adultery. WHAT HYPOCRISY!

Next, we come to an allegory about two sisters, AHOLAH, the older, and AHOLIBAH, the younger. God gave them these same names of His cities, SAMARIA, the capital of Northern Israel, and JERUSALEM, the capital of the Southern Judah. They were horrible women. As we read Ezekiel 23, we see they are corrupt women, who have eyes only for sexual deviation. That is all they thought about day and night. Their unrestrained whoredom pictured ISRAEL'S and JUDAH'S debauched condition. No wonder God gave them up for a season to the servitude of Assyria and Babylon. The LORD said, "My mind was alienated from them" (Ezekiel 23:18). He let them be rebuked.

Now we come to a precious, yet sad, portion of Scripture. Here in Ezekiel, Chapter 24, it is revealed to us that EZEKIEL WAS MARRIED. We don't hear much about his wife. We don't know what she looked like or where she came from. What was she like? We will never know. We wonder how she stood the stares and persecution toward her husband as he proclaimed the Truth. We do not know. We can only imagine.

"Son of man," God got the prophet's attention with such a salutation. (He called Ezekiel "Son of Man" ninety-one times in this book.) There was a special "something" between the LORD and the PROPHET. All of a sudden there was bad news. Ezekiel was used to bad news—but not this bad news. *"Son of man, BEHOLD I TAKE AWAY FROM THEE THE DESIRE OF THINE EYES . . ."* (Ezekiel 24:16).

Ezekiel's wife was going to die. What a shock! SHE WAS GOING TO DIE THAT NIGHT. So little warning. Some people suffer long illnesses. They have time to prepare and to settle their affairs. Others have no time. They die suddenly. My father died with no warning; yet, my mother suffered for a short season. Our son died. It was an unexpected moment. He was gone. He was dead. His soul had passed on to GOD'S ETERNAL HOME IN HEAVEN. He had received Jesus Christ as his Saviour. He would say, "I am saved and born-again."

We, who are alive, yearn with the sick ones. We wish we could help their suffering–but we can't. Then our dear one dies suddenly. We are not prepared. We who love and laugh are left and lonely. We are not prepared for death. Never. No matter how long we have to think about it, death is a finality the living know nothing about.

I had never noticed this verse until some thirty years ago. My husband was teaching his Sunday School class. It was a big class of ninety-plus adults. The wife of one of our members had died. It was sudden, unexpected, and sad. Dr. Waite looked out at the grieving husband in the audience in sympathy and kindness, and said,

"God has removed the 'desire of your eyes.'"
IT WAS AN EMOTIONAL MOMENT. I'LL NEVER FORGET IT.

"I WILL KEEP THEE: FEAR NOT"
(Isaiah 41:13)
"For I the LORD thy God will hold thy right hand,
saying unto thee, Fear not; I will help thee."
The Lord gave me this verse when we began to get Beverly ready
for SHEPHERDS HOME & SCHOOL in Wisconsin.
(It was August, 1975)
She is "retarded" and "helpless."
It seemed that this is what the Lord would have us to do.
We are old, and here is a place where they will
care for her when we die.
Beverly stayed ten months. They could not care for her.
We are still learning the reason He allowed us to take her there.
HE WILL HELP ME TO CARE FOR HER.
I TRUST HIM.
Since having her home again,
God has given "peace" about our tomorrows.
They are in His hands & will.
I WILL OBEY. HE WILL HELP.
Perhaps the verse was to tell us that we should keep her home
and He would help. (ggs)

Today's Bible Blessing   *September 6*

Ezekiel 24:25—Ezekiel 28:9
DESTRUCTION OF THE AMMONITES

Ezekiel 25:2

"Son of man, set they face against the AMMONITES, and prophesy"
"Speaking broadly, the purpose of Ezekiel's ministry is to keep before the generation born in exile the national sins which had brought Israel so low (e.g. Ezekiel 14:23); to sustain the faith of the exiles by predictions of national restoration, of the execution of justice upon their oppressors, and of national glory under the Davidic monarchy." (The SCOFIELD REFERENCE BIBLE, 1917 edition, Authorized King James Version)

"And they shall comfort you, when ye see their ways and their doings: and ye shall know that I have not done without cause all that I have done in it, saith the Lord GOD" *(Ezekiel 14:23).*

What was the way that God punished His people? It was from Nebuchadnezzar's triumph over Jerusalem. The Conqueror bided his time. He slowly starved out the people of Judah—eventually surrounding the city and battering it to submission. As you remember, the best of the land were taken to Babylon. Among those captives was Daniel.

Many of the surrounding countries, or people groups, had been tortuous to Israel, too. This did not go without the notice of Israel's God. In today's reading, we see those nations that suffered, along with Jerusalem. They were petrified, pilfered, and persecuted.

The AMMONITES were first mentioned in Ezekiel 25:2. The prophet prophesied at them. They, too, had profaned the Lord God's Sanctuary. They clapped their hands with happiness at every offense they committed against Israel. But God was going to punish them in due time. He promised, "I will deliver thee to the men of the East." Their capital city would be ravished. It would become a stable for camels, and their community would be a resting place for flocks of sheep. For sure—the Ammonites would know that God was the LORD.

Who were these AMMONITES? If you remember, Lot's daughters tricked their father with wine and drunkenness. They both became "with child" on two separate nights with him. This was a shameful thing for them to do. Lot was a stupid man to succumb to such devices. Ammon was a product of that sinful behavior. He was a nomad, and so were all his children. Their language was similar to Hebrew. KING SOLOMON was a bad example when he married Ammonite women. In fact, Rehoboam's mother was one.

If you remember, Ammon came upon many giants in the land. Those tall, frightening people were called ZAMZUMMIMS. God destroyed them, so the Ammonites could live in the land promised to them by God. He protected them, in measure—I think—because of Lot being Abraham's nephew. Israel was forbidden to molest the Ammonites, but often the AMMONITES yoked up with other nations to hurt Israel. Sometime they partnered with Moab, with Amalek, with the Syrians, and with Gebal against Israel and Judah. There was a continual hostility between Israel and Ammon.

They had kings. Their god was MOLECH (MILCOM). Their capital was RABBAH—sometimes called Philadelphia. They had their share of military conflicts. Once they helped the Syrians against SHALMANESER II (854 B.C.). In THE NEW UNGER'S BIBLE DICTIONARY, we learned that, eventually, AMMON was swallowed up by Rome in about 150 A.D. In JUSTIN MARTYR's time, the AMMONITES were numerous. In the days of ORIGEN (about 186-254) they merged with the ARABS.

Yes, the destructions promised to the AMMONITES came to pass as Ezekiel had said (See Ezekiel 25:5, 10; Zephaniah

2:9). Today, there are only ruins—a "perpetual desolation" where once they lived. There are no villages or signs of civilization in their land. "I WILL DESTROY THEE . . ." was God's promise. THOSE WHO TOUCH ISRAEL SHOULD FEAR. Though Judah be disobedient, and need punishing, God Himself will judge those who are not kind to her.

"BEAUTIFUL LIFE"

"It is a beautiful life to grow old gracefully,
To grow every day more and more like Christ.
This is the privilege of age." (Copied)
It is a comforting fact that God has
kept you safe these many years.
That He has kept you from sin, from disease, from accidents.
Or is it an accident?
Looking back from youth to old age,
God has been my Keeper always.
I am in awe.
IT IS A SATISFYING FACT, AND ONE THAT KEEPS ME SINGING
THAT HE MAY COME SOON,
OR IF I LEAVE BEFORE THAT EVENT, HIS WAY IS BEST,
EVEN IN OLD AGE. (ggs)

Today's Bible Blessing   *September 7*

Ezekiel 28:10—Ezekiel 32:4

THE COVERING CHERUB'S DEMOTION

Ezekiel 28:17

"Thine heart was lifted up . . . I will cast thee to the ground"

Today we are going to look at two "ROYALS of Tyrus" mentioned in Ezekiel 28. It is most interesting. One was the mighty king of an earthly nation and the other was a leading cherub in God's Heavenly Realm.

"TYRUS" is the Greek form of TYRE—the ancient Phoenician city which was on the shore of the MEDITERRANEAN SEA. It was twenty miles from SIDON. The city was situated in two parts—some on a well-protected rocky coast; and some on an island about a half mile from shore. People often referred to it as a "crowning city." Isaiah 23:8 tells us that its merchants were princes whose reputations were known all over the world. King David traded with them. The miserable KING AHAB married JEZEBEL, whose father was the king of the ZIDONIANS. Some say she was a daughter of a King of Tyre.

Evidently the good relationship between Israel and Tyre ceased when the TYRIANS and the PHOENICIANS bought Hebrew captives and sold them as slaves to the Greeks and the Edomites. I read that historians know little of the further history of TYRE, from their slave trading days to NEBUCHADNEZZAR'S thirteen-year siege—except what is read in the Bible. Ezekiel 27 & 28 gives much information. The daughters of Cartage hired mercenary soldiers. There was much gold trading from Arabia, as in the time of Solomon. TYRE was wealthy and well-known for its purple dye, made from mollusks, harvested from its shores. EZEKIEL denounced its religious cult of MELCARTH that helped give TYRE the reputation of being a wicked city (Ezekiel 28:1-19).

Now let us notice Ezekiel 28:13 where the mood changes. No longer is Ezekiel talking only about the KING OF TYRE. There are two meanings to his prophecies here. Yes, the king was wealthy, dressed in fine garments, and was powerful; but the prophet's mood changed.

The prophet began talking about THE ANOINTED CHERUB, who was no ordinary being. He was a special "CREATURE" of the Heavenly sort. Why, he walked in the midst of the STONES OF FIRE on the Holy Mountain of God. Not only did that "perfect being" have access to Heaven, but also, he had been in THE GARDEN OF GOD, the place called EDEN.

This "creature" was none other than LUCIFER whom we have come to know as SATAN. Suddenly we are introduced to this beautiful creature—none like any other we have ever seen. His tabrets. His voice. His exquisite sound was like that from the pipes of the most glorious organ. Rare, precious stones were common to his apparel. The brownish red SARDIUS, the olive green TOPAZ, the brilliant DIAMOND, and the turquoise BERYL, all sparkled on his person. The glowing colors of the black & white ONYX, with the brilliance of the blue/green JASPER, dazzled all who looked upon him. The violet blue SAPPHIRE, combined with the green tourmaline EMERALD, with the crystal-deep red CARBUNCLE, made him a showplace of splendor. All about him was the yellow brightness of GOLD. Could there have been any creature more beautiful?

For some reason, the exquisite "CHERUB THAT COVERETH" became overcome with pride. His beauty and power got the better of him. He wanted to be like God, his Creator. His brightness was corrupted. His beauty brought falling pride. Instead of such heights of grandeur, the LORD GOD OF HEAVEN threw the CHERUB out of Heaven. He had defiled God's sanctuaries. He had traded with iniquities. His fall was like lightning striking the sky and piercing all the white clouds with darkness. Fire came from within him and destroyed his beauty. Nothing was left of his glory but ashes.

Today's Bible Blessing   *September 8*
Ezekiel 32:5—Ezekiel 34:25
GRAVES COVERED WITH CLAY
Ezekiel 33:11
"I have no pleasure in the death of the wicked . . ."

The other day, we went to the cemetery where our second-born son is buried. When David first died, I went there almost every month. I suppose it was a once a month visit, because, when he was living, we would visit with him once a month. At first, there was just brown dirt and a small marker on his grave. Then we bought a "foot stone." He is buried in the veteran section of the cemetery. At first, we had business to take care of—such as being sure the stone was level and even. I noticed that grass was growing on his grave. To see the grass there was comforting to me, his mother.

So yesterday, when we were there, it looked all messy and bleak. Besides the new construction in the area—a mausoleum is being built—trees have been cut down. Often, there is huge equipment moving about--trucks, and cranes, and workman. The calm beauty of the grounds has been disturbed since we purchased the plots—one for Dave and two for my husband and me. Yes, the cemetery is being enlarged. People are dying every day. New graves are all about. It is very sad. Just think of all those souls off to Heaven or Hell, depending upon their trust in the Lord Jesus Christ as Saviour. Dave's plot is covered with clay now. It did not used to look that way. It has been disturbed. In the three or four month period that I did not go there—because it was snowy and raining—three new graves have been dug right next to his. The dirt and clay on those graves is yellow and ugly; most unpleasant. The cemetery workers piled the dirt from the new graves all over David's grass, I suppose. His grave looks all barren and dead. It disturbs me. It doesn't bother anyone else. It does me. I am his mother.

403

PRECIOUS IN THE SIGHT OF THE LORD IS THE DEATH OF HIS SAINTS (Psalm 116:15).

Today, as I was reading my Bible, I was struck with the predicted deaths of hundreds and hundreds of men, women, and children. What is the *"word of the Lord"* to Ezekiel here? FOR PHARAOH, king of Egypt—he and his country would be caught in a net (Ezekiel 32:3). His land would be watered with their blood. Other kings and people would fear.

GOD WOULD BRANDISH HIS SWORD (vs. 10). He would use the SWORD OF BABYLON to do God's job. The pomp of Egypt will fall. Her women will wail in grief. The mighty Egyptian will be slain. Ezekiel prophesied that those uncircumcised unbelievers would perish. And they did.

Ezekiel saw the future. He saw ASSHUR, the descendants of SHEM, in graves filled with their dead bodies. Their bodies would decompose at the side of a pit. No one would be left to care. ELAM (or Persia) would have multitudes killed. They, too, would fall into a pit. The Chaldeans would conquer them. That is when Susa will become the capital of Persia. Though, they will fight fiercely, they will die anyhow. MESHECH lived in the mountains south east of the Black Sea. (Many feel this is Moscow.) They are descendants of Noah's son, Japheth. Often MESHECH will partner with TUBAL (Tobalsk) who will settle in the same area. Ezekiel said: *"Though they caused their terror in the land of the living,"* they, too, would be slain by the sword. He said: *"Their iniquities shall be upon their bones"* (Ezekiel 32:26-27).

EDOM, the descendants of ESAU, would be slain by the sword, too. They shall die with the uncircumcised. The ZIDONIANS (Sidonians), whose land extended southward to Mount Carmel, will fall with the others. They will perish like the other countries around them. God said, "I HAVE CAUSED MY TERROR IN THE LAND OF THE LIVING . . ." Yes, the people around Israel, who treated them with disdain, will be judged. Yes, the prophecy came true. Babylon's might and military power conquered them relentlessly.

DEATH IS A GREAT ENEMY. THERE IS NO RESPECT OF PERSONS WHEN THE SWORD FALLS. It behooves you and me to be ready when our name is called. Do you know Jesus Christ as Saviour? Your earthly life may be taken from you, but you can have eternal life through the LORD JESUS CHRIST (John 3:16-20).

Ezekiel 33:11 says: *"As I live, saith the Lord God, I have no pleasure in the death of the wicked, but that the wicked turn from his way; . . . for why will ye die, O house of Israel?"*

"A CHURCH ORDINANCE"
(compiled by ggs)
1. COMMANDED BY CHRIST
2. REVEALED IN THE GOSPELS AS EXPRESSED TRUTH
3. BELIEVED & SET FORTH FOR BELIEVERS AT LARGE
4. PRACTICED BY THE APOSTLES AT LARGE
(foot washing was not mentioned)
A DEFINITION
1. Taught by Jesus
2. Practiced by the Apostles
3. Taught in the Epistles

Today's Bible Blessing   *September 9*
Ezekiel 34:26—Ezekiel 37:27
A CEMETERY FULL OF BONES
Ezekiel 37:3
"Son of man, Can these bones live?

Suddenly "the hand of the Lord" was upon Ezekiel. Remember when this happened earlier his ministry? It was back in chapter 8, when the Lord GOD's hand grabbed the prophet by the hair and dangled him between earth and heaven, to show him that the temple was in a mess. So now, a similar thing was happening. This time, in his vision, Ezekiel was dropped down into a valley. It was no ordinary valley. It was A VALLEY OF DRY BONES (Ezekiel 37). Wow!

Now these bones were extra dry. That means the bones were very old. The flesh had long-gone. Those poor dead people must have died during some kind of unusual tragedy. They had not had a proper burial. So there Ezekiel was with human bones all over the place. It must have been rather "spooky"!

All of a sudden, in that morbid cemetery, the LORD spoke. He asked, *"CAN THESE BONES LIVE?"* What a question to ask the surprised prophet. He must have thought to himself, "Of course not. Whoever heard of bones coming to life?" Then the LORD gave the strangest command. He told Ezekiel to talk to the bones. "Prophesy upon those bones," God commanded. Being an obedient man, Ezekiel did just that. He had become accustomed to odd requests from the LORD. So he spoke to the bones, *"O YE DRY BONES, HEAR THE WORD OF THE LORD."*

All of a sudden, there was a shaking. Before his amazed eyes, Ezekiel watched the bones come together into skeletons. There they were, before him, taking the shapes and forms of men and women and boys and girls. Soon they developed flesh, muscles, and sinews.

405

Yes, they had skin and hair, too. There they were, doing nothing—just lying there, like fallen statues or unused manikins.

Then at the command of the Lord GOD, Ezekiel prophesied to the wind. At Ezekiel's command, in blew the wind. It came from the North, South, East and West. God said, *"Breathe upon these slain, that they may live."* So the wind blew upon all the still bodies. Then the bodies stood up. Not only that, they spoke. How surprised those revived people must have been to be alive again.

Do you know what they said? They did not ask about their loved ones. They did not wonder what the latest news was. They did not ask why they were brought back to life. In fact, they did not ask for food. Instead, they made the statement, *"OUR BONES ARE DRIED, AND OUR HOPE IS LOST. WE ARE CUT OFF FOR OUR PARTS."* What a strange thing to say.

What did all this vision mean? IT WAS A MESSAGE OF HOPE FOR ISRAEL. It really was. The Lord God said that his people, who had been so disobedient to His ways, who had been exceedingly sinful, and idol worshippers, would be revived. They would be like dead people who would come to life—just like the bones.

God explained the two nations would be like two "sticks" becoming one. He said one "stick" would be named JOSEPH (the ten tribes) and another "stick" would be called JUDAH (the two tribes). They would come together and be ONE NATION. It would be like it should have been. They would be taken out of their heathenism that had engulfed them, and serve Him as they were supposed to serve Him. THEY WOULD BE ONE NATION IN ONE LAND WITH ONE KING.

This wonderful time of blessing will be THE MILLENNIUM. Israel will be one. They will dwell in THE LAND. THEY WILL BELIEVE. There will be "showers of blessing" (Ezekiel 34:26). The desert will blossom as the rose.
EVERYONE WILL KNOW THAT THE LORD JEHOVAH IS GOD.

"A LITTLE SLEEP, A LITTLE SLUMBER"
(Proverbs 24:33-34)
Life is ruined and wasted by our own little procrastinating.
ACTUALLY, WE DO NOT REALIZE THAT LIFE IS SHORT,
CONSISTING OF A SHORT YOUTH AND A SHORT OLD AGE.
"We must catch the flying hours and moments on the wing"
WE HAVE ONLY THIS LIFE TO LIVE FOR HIM
AND DO HIS WILL
WE GROW UP. WE BECOME SICK.
WE GROW OLD.
YES.
But we may certainly grow in grace and the knowledge of Him.
(ggs)

Today's Bible Blessing   *September 10*

Ezekiel 37:28—Ezekiel 40:33
THE VALLEY OF HAMONGOG

Ezekiel 39:1b

"Behold, I am against thee, O Gog, the chief prince of Meshech and Tubal."

Today's reading is interesting because we meet some countries that we may not remember seeing before in the Bible. This section is a prophetic section of Scripture that prophecy conference speakers enjoy speaking about. We will just touch on a bit of this today.

Right off the bat, in verse two of chapter thirty-eight, Ezekiel is told to set his face against GOG. Who is GOG? Bible teachers say that GOG is the RUSSIAN PRINCE. How do they come to that conclusion? I think it is because GOG is mentioned as being from a NORTHERN REGION, and is someone that the LORD is against. Next we notice MAGOG—that is a similar word for GOG—which is RUSSIA. See the mention of MESHECH—that is MOSCOW. And TUBAL is another Russian city that is known today as TOBALSK. (The noticeable increase of the Muslim people in our country [the United States of America], and the 9/11 attacks on New York and Washington D.C., as well as the increased Muslim presence in other countries like England and France, to say nothing of the countries where Muslims are prominent all over the world, some Bible teachers are speculating that Gog could be the nations of Islam. I have not heard this preached at this writing, but I have read some print material on this speculation. That is why I am mentioning it here.)

What seems to be happening here, is that the countries are lining up to fight Israel. Remember, at this time, Israel will be united as one nation. Recall the "two sticks" becoming one from yesterday's reading. We learned the significance of this with the *"Valley of Dry Bones Illustration"* to Ezekiel the prophet, in chapter 37. It appears that RUSSIA (or MAGOG) is one of the primary countries in this battle. This battle will become to be known as ARMAGEDDON (Revelation 16:16).

We see mention of other countries, whose names we recognize, such as PERSIA which is IRAN, along with ETHIOPIA and LIBYA. This is found in Ezekiel 38:5. These countries are well prepared for battle like MAGOG will be. They have shields, helmets, armor, bucklers, as well as fine horses for battle. All the warriors will be mighty with the sword. Now I do not know if war at this future time will return to the battle array and weapons of an earlier time in history, or if they will use modern armament that we know of today. It very well may be that the world will have turned itself around and return to the basics used in fighting wars. I do not know.

GERMANY is mentioned in verse 6. It is called GOMER. See the "House of Togarmah." That is thought to be TURKEY. They will come forth out of their home lands in the Northern regions. Everyone will come to battle against the mountains of Jerusalem. All the enemies of God's people will ascend to defenseless Jerusalem like a cloud—as flocks of migrating birds—to attack the city of God. It will be like herds of buffalo trying to overrun that peaceful city. What do they want? These attacking, greedy countries, want the good things--like oil and minerals--hiding in the Dead Sea topography.

Other countries are mentioned in verse 13. See SHEBA. Would that be ETHIOPIA? DEDAN was found on the shores of the Persian Gulf. It could be that these people are descendants of ABRAHAM and KETURAH, and were caravan merchants. (I don't really know.) Some feel "the young lions" are BRITAIN and THE UNITED STATES.

The good news is that the LORD JESUS CHRIST is going to be the commanding general in this battle. He will lead Israel to victory. Every beast, fish, fowl, and man will shake at the presence of POWERFUL JESUS. All the warfare and war room strategies will not defeat General Jesus. The Lord God will say, *"Behold, I AM AGAINST THEE, O GOG, the chief prince of MESHECH AND TUBAL"* (Ezekiel 39). Five-sixths of the population will die. They will fall in the open fields. It will be terrible. The birds will eat their flesh. The beasts of the field will devour the dead. It will take seven months to bury the dead people. Humiliated, Prince Gog will be buried in Israel. The burial place will be named THE VALLEY OF HAMONGOG.

JESUS CHRIST WILL BE VICTORIOUS!

HE WILL BE GLORIFIED!

HE WILL REIGN!

"AI: A TYPE OF THE FLESH:
THE REASON FOR DEFEAT."

(Joshua 7:2)

1. Underestimated it (the nature of the flesh).
2. When we try to overcome in our own strength.
3. When we don't find the course of our defeat,
   and put it away.

THE RESOURCE, PROVIDED BY GOD:

CHRIST DIED IN ORDER THAT THE SIN NATURE

MIGHT BE DEALT WITH.

HE CONDEMNED SIN IN THE FLESH.

VICTORY OVER THE FLESH IS BY THE HOLY SPIRIT,

AND NOT BY OUR OWN RESOURCES. (ggs)

Today's Bible Blessing   September 11
Ezekiel 40:34—Ezekiel 43:24
THE MILLENNIAL TEMPLE AND HOLY GARMENTS

Ezekiel 42:14b

"They shall lay their garments wherein they minister: for they are holy."

Today I am thinking about the garments that the priests of the Old Testament wore as they ministered before the Lord. Notice the interesting procedure the priests followed concerning which garments should be worn where and when. I wonder if we are as careful to dress properly before the Lord.

> *"When the priests enter therein, then shall they not go out of the holy place into the utter court, but there they shall lay their garments wherein they minister; for they are holy, and shall put on other garments, and shall approach to those things which are for the people"* (Ezekiel 42:14).

Before we talk about the dress of the priests, I want us to remember, that Ezekiel is seeing a vision of the future MILLENNIAL TEMPLE. This is not SOLOMON'S TEMPLE or any of the others that were built after his temple was destroyed by the invasion of Nebuchadnezzar's armies. It is not the one built in Ezra and Nehemiah's time, which is known as ZERUBBABEL'S TEMPLE; nor the one that was destroyed after Jesus' death, which was called HEROD'S TEMPLE. THIS ONE WILL BE A NEW TEMPLE. It is a FUTURE TEMPLE that will look back at the work of Jesus Christ at Calvary. Just as the Old Testament Tabernacle—and later at Solomon's Temple, and the one in Ezra's time—the sacrifices look forward to Calvary. THE MILLENNIAL TEMPLE'S SACRIFICES WILL LOOK BACKWARD TO CALVARY. The millennial temple will be a place where redeemed people will look back to the time when Jesus shed His blood for their sins.

TODAY, WE IN THE CHURCH PERIOD WHO ARE BELIEVERS, OBSERVE THE LORD'S SUPPER. Jesus said to do this. He never asked us to remember anything else about Him except His death (not his birth, or his miracles, etc.). So the Saints, during the thousand years of the Lord Jesus Christ's ruling the world, will look back at His death, just as we, in this age of Grace, remember it.

If you think about it, the AGE OF GRACE—or what is called THE CHURCH AGE—is a parenthetical period of time. It is the time period from the CROSS—which occurred over 2,000 years ago—to the RAPTURE—which has not happened yet, and is a future event. When Jesus returns for HIS OWN, and the GREAT TRIBULATION is culminated by the BATTLE OF ARMAGEDDON, a new day will dawn. That new day will be the MILLENNIAL REIGN OF JESUS CHRIST. It is during this time that EZEKIEL'S MILLENNIAL TEMPLE WILL be constructed.

So—when we discuss the clothing of the priests, we are discussing future priests. It seems that they will be related to ZADOK. The priests mentioned in today's passages are called "THE SONS OF ZADOK" (Ezekiel 40:46). In Ezekiel 43:19, they are called "the Levites that are of the seed of Zadok." In our verse today, they are mentioned as "the sons of Zadok." Ezekiel 48:11 sums up these faithful priests by saying, "they are sanctified," and they "kept God's charge." ZADOK and his sons did not "go astray" like many other priests during the captivity that corrupted themselves, as well as the people. (Many Levites were evil, too.) These FUTURE SONS OF ZADOK will be holy men, separated to God for God's work. They will be faithful servants of God—an attribute much needed today.

I don't know if the priest, spoken about in the above verse, was the High Priest or one of his sons. I tend to believe that it must have been the High Priest—but not sure. The place the priest was ministering in was the "holy place"—not the "Holy of Holies." Only the High Priest was permitted in the MOST HOLY PLACE where the Ark of the Covenant was, which was covered by the MERCY SEAT, where the golden Cherubim were.

We should note that they were very careful to keep their special, separated garments away and separate from the inquisitive eyes of the people. Their garments were for God's eyes only. They were careful to be "beautiful" for Him. Today, people seem to have forgotten to present themselves in a pure and "beautiful" dress before their God.

SENSUAL CLOTHING AND ACTIONS SHOULD HAVE NO PLACE IN THE SERVICE OF THE LORD.

"PRAY FOR ONE ANOTHER"

This year (1980), several dear and old friends
died and went to Heaven
to be with the Lord they loved.
Their ages were 85, 90, 92.
I MISS THEM.
I MISS THEIR LETTERS.
I MISS PRAYING FOR THEM.
I MISS THEIR PRAYERS FOR ME.
I did not realize until they left,
how much I was helped by praying for them
and their needs.
INTERCESSORY PRAYER IS A BLESSING. (ggs)

Today's Bible Blessing   *September 12*

Ezekiel 43:25—Ezekiel 47:3
I'LL MEET YOU AT THE EASTERN GATE

Ezekiel 44:1

"Then he brought me back the way of the gate . . . toward the east."

Gates are interesting. They can shut people out and they can welcome others in. I remember as a young girl visiting my girlfriend's Ohio dairy farm. (Believe it or not, I am an Ohio girl.) There was a gate to keep the cattle in and a gate to keep the cattle out. Sometimes they swung easily. Other times, they stuck and would not open. Occasionally a gate was broken. Cows could cross the road without warning. It was dangerous for the cows and dangerous for the cars.

Today I want us to look at a passage of Scripture concerning a gate. It is found in Ezekiel 44:1-3:

"Then he brought me back the way of THE GATE of the outward sanctuary WHICH LOOKETH TOWARD THE EAST; AND IT WAS SHUT. Then said the LORD unto me; This gate shall be shut, it shall not be opened, and no man shall enter in by it; because the LORD, the God of Israel, hath entered in by it, therefore it shall be shut. IT IS FOR THE PRINCE; THE PRINCE, HE SHALL SIT IN IT TO EAT BREAD BEFORE THE LORD; HE SHALL ENTER BY THE WAY OF THE PORCH OF THAT GATE, and shall go out by the way of the same."

I have another friend who is in Heaven now. Her name is Jane. I do not know what her "new name in Glory" is—so I still call her Jane (Revelation 2:17; 3:12). She told her children and grandchildren a most interesting thing. She wanted to meet them in Heaven. Because there will be many people there, she knew it would be crowded so she told them "MEET ME AT THE EASTERN GATE."

Because of Jane, I have become interested in that EASTERN GATE. What happened there and what will happen in the future? My husband, Dr. D. A. Waite, reminded me that when we were in Jerusalem several years ago, we could see the EASTERN GATE from our hotel. It is sometimes called THE BEAUTIFUL GATE, or, at other times, THE POTSHERD GATE because Potters worked near there.

I discussed this gate with my husband. He reminded me of the passage of Scripture in Matthew 21:1-2. It is there that we read that Jesus walked toward Jerusalem. He was coming from the East of Jerusalem from the Mount of Olives. It was about then that He asked two of his disciples to find a colt for him to ride.

As He walked toward the city, He would have had to see the EASTERN GATE. We feel He went through that gate into the city that day. In fact, He may have had the young colt by then, and could have ridden the animal right into Jerusalem by way of that EASTERN GATE. (That's the gate where my friend, Jane, said she would meet her family.) WE CALL THIS DONKEY RIDE, WITH ALL ITS ADULATION, **"THE TRIUMPHAL ENTRY."**

I do remember seeing the EASTERN GATE on the outside of the wall that surrounded the city, when we were on the tour bus. The gate was high on the wall, and was closed. It seemed to be bricked up. Somehow I associate the color "gold" with that Gate. At the time, I wished I could have walked up there on the wall and touched it. My husband reminded me that the EASTERN GATE will not be opened until Jesus comes back to earth again. The third verse of Ezekiel 44 says so, *"HE SHALL ENTER BY THE WAY OF THE PORCH OF THAT GATE AND SHALL GO OUT BY THE WAY OF THE SAME."*

I do not know exactly how Jesus will open that gate. Perhaps He will come in pomp and splendor—for He will be the SUPREME POTENTATE. He will be recognized by all as the King of Kings and LORD of LORDS. How different will be His reception during the Millennium. Or, He may speak the word, as He did at Lazarus' tomb, and the gate will fall down for Him to walk through. I do not know.

If my friend, Jane, is there at that time, she will be wide-eyed with wonder. I hope her grandchildren will be with her to see it all. They will be surprised.

"LET US RUN WITH PATIENCE"
(Hebrews 12:1)
Some days it is very hard to run,
Yet we must, for God has put us in the race.
The objective is to win with His approval.
To be like Him,
To be a faithful witness
as those clouds of witnesses of other years.
WE MUST RUN.
NO TURNING BACK LEST WE STUMBLE.
No glances down to see how rough the way,
BUT LOOKING UNTO JESUS
Who ran the course before us.
The race is hard, but—
LET US ENDURE HARDNESS.
(ggs: written after a personal study in Hebrews 12; 1980)

Ezekiel 47:4–Daniel 2:10
THE DESERT BLOSSOMS
AS THE ROSE

Ezekiel 47:1
"Waters issued out from under the threshold of the house eastward:"

Today as we come to the forty-seventh and forty-eighth chapter of EZEKIEL, we will finish this major book of the Bible. Therefore, we are pleased to meditate on the river that will flow from the MILLENNIAL TEMPLE out to the land east of the city. What an exciting adventure for those who will witness this phenomenon.

Once again, the prophet found himself propelled unto the "door of the house" which we recognize as THE TEMPLE. What Ezekiel beheld was more than he could put into words. READ WITH ME HIS WORDS IN EZEKIEL 47:1.

> *"Afterward he brought me again unto the door of the house; and, behold, waters issued out from under the threshold of the house eastward: for the forefront of the house stood toward the east, and the waters came down from under from the right side of the house, at the south side of the altar."*

What must it have been like to see this "water" as a river coming under the threshold of the House of the LORD? With purpose, it rushed down on the right side of the House as well as the south side of the altar. (I suppose it was the brasen altar.) Did it trickle like a small leaking faucet? Did it flow freely like a stream from a rock next to a busy highway? Or did it pour forth like the river-rush of rain water that runs in rapid motion on the street in front of our house on a stormy day? I do not know.

By this time, the water was rushing by. Ezekiel was speechless. Then "the man with the line in His hand" showed up again. We met this man first in Ezekiel 40:3. Who could forget Him? He appeared to be made of brass. He seemed to be a "measuring man." He stood by the gate holding a measuring reed and line of linen flax in His hand. By the time Ezekiel recognized this unusual man, He had measured whatever He was measuring. There the two of them stood with the water coming to their ankles. There was no doubt about it; this was swift moving water. What was its purpose?

The man kept measuring as the waters rose to their knees. Soon it had rushed to their waists. Still the man of brass kept measuring and measuring. Soon the water was definitely a "river." No longer could they navigate in it. It was a wonder they did not drown. So they had to swim to shore. When they got to the river bank, they saw trees. There were many trees on both sides of the river bank–beautiful healthy trees. What was happening?

Come to find out, this newly formed "river" would flow out to the DEAD SEA—a sea that was six times saltier than the ocean. The ocean's waters would be healed. This transformed sea would be filled with multitudes of fish swimming everywhere. Fishermen would come to fish where there was never any fish before. People will be amazed. Vegetation would flourish where there had been nothing but barren sand. Truthfully the waters would heal the land.

THE DESERT WILL BLOSSOM LIKE THE ROSE (Isaiah 35:1-2).

Let us think back to the "ROCK" in Exodus 17:6. This was another "water" experience. Remember? That was when Moses smote the ROCK in the wilderness, so the CHILDREN OF ISRAEL could have drinking water. It was a miracle. In some ways, it reminds me of Ezekiel's "water" in today's reading. MANY FEEL THAT "ROCK" FOLLOWED MOSES AND HIS BAND ALL THE WAY FROM HOREB TO JORDAN. Otherwise what would I Corinthians 10: 4 mean? *And did all drink the same spiritual drink: for they drank of that spiritual Rock that followed them: and that Rock was Christ.*

COULD EZEKIEL'S "WATER" BE THE SAME "WATER" AS MOSES' "WATER"? WHAT DO YOU THINK?

"MORE TO LEARN"
(Hebrews 12:11)
I thought I had learned all life's lessons,
BUT NO, THERE WAS MORE TO LEARN.
In sickness and in trials, I learned
that which will help me to go on in health.
I SHALL NEVER BE FINISHED LEARNING
THE LESSONS OF GOD.
I have learned that when He teaches His child,
He places His child in a position to learn
and to be exercised by what she has learned. (ggs)

414

Today's Bible Blessing   *September 14*
Daniel 2:11–Daniel 4:17
FOUR HEBREW BOYS
TAKE A STAND

Daniel 2:20

"Blessed be the name of God for ever and ever: for wisdom and might are his."

Now we find ourselves in THE BOOK OF DANIEL. We have ploughed our way through Isaiah, Jeremiah, and Ezekiel with some success and a little wonder. Success, because we read and somewhat understood; wonder, because of the boldness of the prophets and the unbelief of God's people.

Now we must discover THE PROPHET DANIEL'S PROPHESY, and what it means to us Bible-believing Christians. We see that he lived from the time of Nebuchadnezzar's reign to Cyrus' rule. He was a contemporary to Jeremiah, Ezekiel, the high priest Joshua (during the restoration), Ezra, and Zerubbabel. He was handsome, brilliant—sometimes maligned, and other times well thought of. Because there is much narrative in the first few chapters, we will get behind in the story, at first, in our daily pace. But we will catch-up, at the end of the book.

If you recall, the BABYLONIAN KING besieged Jerusalem and all of Judah—besides other countries. He did this three times. With the first wave, he imprisoned KING JEHOIAKIM. With that siege, NEBUCHADNEZZAR took all the talented and exceptional Jews to be his subjects. He used them as slaves to further the delights of his kingdom. Sad to say, I believe many of the men and boys were forced to be eunuchs against their will (Isaiah 39:7).

With this group, the king discerned that some of the young royal people had great potential to help him in the palace. Among those well favored, skillful, and wise, were four intelligent Hebrew "princes." We have come to know them as SHADRACH, MESHACH, ABEDNEGO, and BELTESHAZZAR, better known as DANIEL.

Very soon, upon their arrival in the palace, came the four young men's first test. They took a stand. It would not be the last stand that we read about in the BOOK OF DANIEL. This time, it was about food. Non-kosher food was set before them. They would not eat. So Daniel persuaded the person in charge of him to serve plain beans and lentils instead. Being good Jewish sons, they would not defile themselves with the heathen food. What would we have done?

The man in charge of them was named MELZAR. He happened to be a eunuch, too; and for all we know, could have been a captive-slave from some previous military invasion. With some fear of the king, he permitted the Hebrew boys to eat different food from the others. He gave them ten days, thinking they would become malnourished and weak. Instead, Shadrach, Meshach, Abednego, and Daniel looked better, were stronger, and wiser than any of the others. In fact, after been quizzed by the king, he found they were ten times wiser than all of his kingdom's astrologers and magicians. In time this would be proven true.

One night the king had a dream. It was a disturbing dream. He called all his wise men to his side and asked, "What was my dream and what did my dream mean?" He implored the wise magicians and astrologers, as well as gifted Chaldeans, to tell him. They could not. They were speaking in the Aramaic language which, by the way, is the language in which Daniel 2:4-7:28 is written. The king was desperate. "Why could not his 'wise' men tell him his dream?" In exasperation, he ordered them all killed, even Daniel and his friends.

Bravely, Daniel went immediately before the king, asking the God of Heaven what was the dream and the meaning of it. You better believe, Daniel prayed. All four Hebrews asked mercy of their God to reveal to Daniel the "secret." That night, in a vision, God answered Daniel's prayer. What a wonderful relationship they had. Quickly the "secret" was told to the king. Daniel told Nebuchadnezzar about the "great image" and its meaning. But, not before the young prophet thanked and blessed God.

"BLESSED BE THE NAME OF GOD FOR EVER AND EVER: FOR WISDOM AND MIGHT ARE HIS" (Daniel 2:20).

"STRETCH OUT THE SPEAR THAT IS IN THY HAND"
(Joshua 8:17-26)
"AND DREW NOT HIS HAND BACK"

EACH LEADER MUST STRETCH OUT THE SPEAR TOWARD THE CORRUPTION OF AI IN OUR LAND TODAY.

EXPOSE SIN AND FALSE RELIGION BY STRETCHING OUT THE SHARP SPEAR OF GOD'S HOLY WORD.

COMPROMISE AND NEUTRALISM AMONG THOSE WHO YESTERDAY WERE MEN OF THE FAITH MUST BE POINTED OUT. (ggs)

Today's Bible Blessing *September 15*

Daniel 4:18–Daniel 7:7

GOD'S PROTECTION IN SPITE OF AFFLICTION

Daniel 3:25

"Lo, I see four men . . . and the form of the fourth is like the Son of God."

As I look at Daniel and his friends, I am beginning to see that their life in Babylon was one of continual "testings." Daily before them were "tests" to prove what kind of young men they were. What was the "stuff" of which they were made? Perhaps there were more "tests" than we know. There may have been greater moral "temptations" that were far worse. You say, "How could anything be worse than a fiery furnace or a den of lions?" I don't know.

Often it is the common temptations of life that make a Christian fall. Oh, a Christian man might not yield to a temptress dressed as "a lady of the night"—but a kind Christian woman with "sweet Christian talk" could fell a man who would not otherwise be tempted. A woman might not yield to taking the bright diamond in an exclusive store; but she might slip a fancy stone into her pocket found on a public sink—never reporting it to the "lost & found." A student might not sneak a book of answers under her coat at testing time, but she might look at her classmate's paper and write his answer on her page. It is often the little foxes that spoil the vines (Song of Solomon 2:15).

So it is with interest that we look at Daniel's friends, SHADRACH, MESHACH, and ABEDNEGO, the day the cornets sounded and the strings were plucked. That music was the sign for all to bow down to the IMAGE OF GOLD. There it was, standing in all its golden glory on the PLAINS OF DURA. That was the "god" CONCEITED NEBUCHADNEZZAR had ordained that all should worship. Some think it may have been made in his own likeness. Everyone within earshot heard the music. They knew the command. Every man, woman, and child bowed down with their heads to the ground. Did I say "everyone"? Well, "everyone" but three Jews whom the king had set over of the province of Babylon (Daniel 3:12). WHY, THEY WERE DANIEL'S FRIENDS FROM JERUSALEM.

It is interesting to observe that NEBUCHADNEZZAR himself confronted the men. He asked, "Is it true that you do not serve my god?" Didn't these men know that everyone was to do obeisance to this golden image? Did they not realize that the FIERY FURNACE was the penalty for disobedience? How strange it must have been to look at hundreds and hundreds of people prostrated on the ground. Yet, only three lone men were standing upright, as they had been standing before the music sounded. Those men were men of conviction. Their Babylonian-given names were SHADRACH, MESHACH, and ABEDNEGO.

Immediately the three men were scorned and bound. I can picture ANGRY NEBUCHADNEZZAR watching the process. His contorted face raged as he ordered, "Heat the furnace seven times hotter than before." How long it took to fulfill that command, we do not know. We do not read of any struggle or resistance from the Hebrew men. Soon the time for the "burning" was upon them. Into the crackling flames they were thrown. The sound of the fire was deafening. The guards' hands burned as they opened the dreaded door. Into the flames, they threw their submissive captives. Suddenly, without warning, those angry flames jumped at the guards like a wild animal after its prey. Unexpectedly, the fire consumed the guards like newly ignited gasoline on a bonfire. They dropped on the ground, burned in lumps of cooked flesh. **DEAD.**

With wide eyes, Nebuchadnezzar watched the whole procedure. Somehow, he was able to see into that furnace. To his amazement, he saw four unbound men walking in the fire. How could that be? The fire had been so hot that no one could get near the flames and live. He could not believe his eyes.

Not only were SHADRACH, MESHACH, and ABEDNEGO walking around in the flames, another man was there, too, who looked like the Son of God (Daniel 3:25). IT WAS A CHRISTOPHANY. It was the LORD JESUS CHRIST IN A PRE-INCARNATE BODY. The fire had no "power" over them for Jesus was there. NOR WAS A HAIR SINGED, OR A COAT BURNED, OR THE SMELL OF SMOKE ON THEIR PERSONS.

Of interest: most of the "modern bible versions" say "*a son of the gods*"—instead of the SON OF GOD—thus denying that Christ was in the furnace with the three men, protecting them with His presence and power.

"I WILL UPHOLD THEE"
(Isaiah 41:10)
"I will uphold thee with the right hand of my righteousness."
A SIMPLE STATEMENT.
AN AMAZING PROMISE.
Our God, who upholdeth the world by the word of His power
hath said here in Isaiah 41:10
that HE WILL UPHOLD ME
with the right hand of His Righteousness. (ggs)

Daniel 7:8–Daniel 10:11

INSANITY, FEAR, & FINGERS ON THE WALL

Daniel 4:3

"How great are his signs!" and how mighty are his wonders!"

Hidden in these twelve chapters of Daniel's book are all the emotions one can find in life. We have come to love Daniel whose name means *"God is my judge."* His dedication to the God of his fathers brings nothing but admiration from us. We do not know about his parents. Were they brought as captives to Babylon at the same time that Daniel and his friends were carried there? We do not know. I wonder about his mother, who must have loved her son as all mothers do their sons. Where was she? Did she wonder how he was, where he slept, and what he was eating?

We do know that DANIEL had a rapport with NEBUCHADNEZZAR, ever since he told the king of his first dream. We do not know where the young prophet was when his friends were thrown into the furnace of fire. We are certain that Daniel would not have bowed down to a false god. Was he out of town? Or did the King "overlook" Daniel as he condemned the three? We do not know.

Now we come to a "test"–not for Daniel, but for the king. It was one of the worst types of tests a human being can experience. It had to do with the king's sanity. When a person breaks his arm or needs cancer treatment, his mind can understand the problem; but when a person is mentally ill, his mind is broken and reason goes out the window. It is terrible to watch, but more terrible to experience.

So NEBUCHADNEZZAR had a mental and emotional breakdown. His "reason" left him. It had been predicted by Daniel. The mighty ruler—strong and great—became mentally deranged. His heart was like the heart of a beast. In a confused state, he wandered the fields. Like an animal, he ate grass and became wild eyed. For seven years, the dew of the morning wet his body and the still of the night frightened his soul. His hair grew like bird's feathers down his shoulders and hiding his eyes. His finger nails became long. They curled like bird's claws. This crazed man's spirit tore at his reason. One so mighty had fallen. He was as an insane man in a mental hospital.

Then the change came. He lifted his eyes to HEAVEN and his understanding returned to him. It was then that NEBUCHADNEZZAR praised and honored God who lives forever. He recognized that God had everlasting dominion and that His kingdom was from generation to generation (Daniel 4:34). The recovered ruler declared that GOD was the KING OF HEAVEN, that His works were true, and His judgments right. The recovered ruler declared, "*Those that walk in pride, GOD is able to abase.*" Only a person who has come out of a mental illness can understand what this man went through. In gratitude, He "*blessed the Most High*" (Daniel 4:34). MANY FEEL THAT THIS KING BECAME A TRUE BELIEVER IN DANIEL'S GOD.

Another test. Another king, another fright, another falling apart, another trembling of the knees. His name was BELSHAZZAR, the son of NABONIDUS (539 B.C.), who was probably NEBUCHADNEZZAR'S grandson. There he was in a glorious banquet hall, entertaining friends and drinking from the stolen Jewish Temple's goblets. In their drunkenness, they praised their idol gods formed by the skill of their own hands. ALL OF A SUDDEN A STILLNESS CAME UPON THE HALL. There in front of them were fingers writing on the wall "*THOU ART WEIGHED IN THE BALANCES AND ART FOUND WANTING.*" The silent words screamed at the astonished people.

Daniel was an old man by then. His role in the kingdom had been diminished since Nebuchadnezzar died. The Queen mother remembered Daniel's gift of interpretation. Another test. He interpreted. BELSHAZZAR'S PRIDE HAD LIFTED HIMSELF ABOVE THE GOD OF HEAVEN. Now he would be judged. That night he was killed and DARIUS the Mede wore the crown.
THERE STOOD DANIEL IN THE SCARLET ROBE, HONORED—YET ALONE.

"TELL THEM"
IF YOU LOVE SOMEONE, TELL THEM.
If you miss someone who has been shut in, tell them.
If you are helped by someone, tell them.
If you have been challenged to do better by someone, tell them.
TELLING ENCOURAGES OTHERS.
"*A bell is not a bell unless you ring it.*
A Song is not a song, unless you sing it.
Love in your heart is not love put there to stay
Love is not love unless it is given away"
(Oscar Hammerstein II)
(ggs: every lesson or talk should have an aim.)

Daniel 10:12–Hosea 2:7

PRAYER, CONSISTENCY, & SHINING STARS

Daniel 10:12b

"Fear not, Daniel . . . thy words were heard . . ."

When I was a young girl, from eighth grade until my senior year, my mother would teach us Bible verses at the dinner table. She would quote a verse to us and we would say it after her. Every night until we had learned that verse, we said the Words of God in unison as a family. Then we would learn another one. There were five of us in my family–my father, my mother, and we three sisters. I was the oldest. Mother did not teach us another verse until we knew the first verse perfectly. They became a part of our souls. They became a part of me. I learned many verses in my years of being a Christian, and have forgotten many; but the ones I learned around our supper table, I have never forgotten. One of those verses was:
"And they that be wise shall shine as the brightness of the firmament; and they that turn many to righteousness as the stars for ever and ever" (Daniel 12:3).

Daniel was a man of prayer. Maybe you and I forgot that until today. All his long life, he was consistent in prayer. That cannot be said of all of us. Not only did his friends know it, but also his enemies, too. He did not rush to his God only when in trouble. No. He fellowshipped with HIM "in" and "out" of season (II Timothy 4:2).

In today's reading, we learned that one of his prayers was heard as soon as it was uttered. Yet, it was not answered. (Daniel 10:12-13). For twenty days, after it was prayed, no answer came. This was one of the many "tests" in the prophet's life. For twenty days, Satan interfered with the answer. It is of interest to me, that the CHIEF ARCHANGEL, MICHAEL, contended with the "Interrupter" before the answer came.

Could there ever be such "contention" when we pray? How often we pray—and it is as if the Heavens were made of brass. No answer. No help. No comfort. Yet, there may be "spiritual warfare" on our behalf going on behind the scenes.

We observed Daniel's prayer pattern. It was lived out in his life the day he was pulled from his knees and thrown into the den of lions. You remember that incident. Who could forget it? He was the "first" favorite president in the land (Daniel 6:2). The other leaders were envy-filled. That is when they devised a shrewd plan. They knew how self-centered King DARIUS was. One day, they suggested to him, that a decree should be made, that NO ONE in the land could request anything from anyone, EXCEPT FROM HIM, for thirty days. Being on the conceited side, the king thought that sounded like a fabulous idea. It gave him a sense of power and importance–almost like he was a deity. The document was signed. It was THE LAW OF THE MEDES & PERSIANS. It could not be broken.

Now, it was Daniel's daily custom to pray. Not only did he pray, but he prayed three times a day. Every day. He knelt on his knees facing toward Jerusalem. Perhaps he looked out his open window, wishing he could see his home town--that beautiful city of his boyhood. Of course, he could not, but he could picture it in his mind's eye. It was the place where he learned about the true God from his parents. Now he was an old man. His hope was that "someday," once again, his city would pulse with the feet of believing Hebrews. And "someday," he would see God face to face. In the meantime, he would pray.

All the king's men knew Daniel prayed regularly. They knew his schedule. That is why they had the king make that ridiculous law in the first place. So, those deceitful men watched. Of course they did. Daniel knew of that new law, but that did not stop him from worshipping the true God. This was another "test" in the life of Daniel the prophet. As he knelt in praise and petition, the men pounced upon him. They grabbed him, tied his hands, and dragged him before the king.

What was the king to do? The scheming men reminded the king of his own law. They related that Daniel regarded not the king's decree. The Bible says something interesting about Darius. It says, *"The king . . . was sore displeased with himself"* (Daniel 6:14). The king tried to stop the law. He could not. He could not change what was written. SO, DANIEL FOUND AN UNUSUAL "PRAYER ROOM." GUESS WHERE IT WAS.

IT WAS WITH LIONS AND IN THE PRESENCE OF GOD.

"SONGS IN THE NIGHT"
(Hebrews 3:17-19;Job 35:10)
No man can make "songs in the night" by himself.
Job and Habakkuk sang such a song.
In face of trial and national judgment,
some of the sweetest most beautiful songs of the Christian
have been learned and sung through "tears in the night" alone. (ggs)

Hosea 2:8–Hosea 8:4
HOSEA'S LIFE: AN ILLUSTRATION FOR ALL

Hosea 2:15a
"I will give her . . . the valley of Achor for a door of hope."

Now we come to the book of HOSEA. For me, this book is difficult because of the marriages that the LORD told Hosea to enter. I do not understand why the LORD would tell the man to marry a prostitute. But He did. This union was to illustrate the terrible condition of Israel. This first wife ran back and forth "in & out" of whoredom. He might have married a second wife, though some say he did not. Some teachers teach that these marriages of Hosea were visions and not "real life" (Hosea 1:2; 3:1). They were pictures of the horrid "spiritual adultery" in which Israel found herself. Most Bible teachers that I have heard in the recent years, teach that this was real life.

When we speak of Israel, we speak of the Northern ten tribes–sometimes referred to as either JOSEPH or EPHRAIM. Eventually Israel would be captured by Assyria in about 700 B.C. HOSEA TOLD US THIS IN HIS BOOK. Israel stayed there as captives, at least many of them did, for one hundred and seventy years, give or take a few years.

The LORD longed that His ISRAEL would stay true to Him. He begged Israel to forsake his idols and heathen ways. They brought many wayward religious practices from Egypt. You would think that after all those years that pagan wickedness would have been forgotten. Sin has a way of reproducing itself. It is sad that this wonderful group of people, who had the "presence of the LORD" with them in the cloud in the wilderness, and who experienced many wilderness miracles, could not stay true to their GOD. But they had "wayward" hearts. So many of us today have "wayward" hearts.

This "waywardness" was portrayed by GOMER. She was the wife the LORD told HOSEA to marry. Her name has a strange "ring" to it. It connotes unfaithfulness to me–just the sound of it. She became pregnant immediately after marrying Hosea. It seemed that for a brief period she was faithful to him, not practicing her trade in the beginning of their marriage.

They named the child JEZREEL. His name predicted "THE BLOODSHED OF JEZREEL." It probably had something to do with vengeance on the house of Ahab.

Two more children were born to GOMER and HOSEA. A baby girl came into their lives. They named her LORUHAMAH which means "no mercy." THIS MARRIAGE, TO A SINFUL WOMAN AND

THE CHILDREN SHE BARE TO HOSEA, TOLD A STORY TO THE PEOPLE WHO WATCHED THEM. (People watch us, too. Our lives tell stories also.)

This baby's story was that the LORD would show no mercy whatsoever on Israel, when the Assyrians would swoop down and take her to their land. When it happened, God would turn the other way and let them suffer. It was their punishment for being unfaithful to Him. The BOY LOAMMI came along (Hosea 1:9). His name means "not my people." By this time, the LORD denied being their GOD. He rejected Israel. How very sad.

Someday–that glorious "someday"—Israel will come back to her LORD. He will take the names of BAALIM out of her mouth. There will be a "door of hope" (Hosea 2:15). Praise God. He will betroth her unto Himself in FAITHFULNESS and she will know the LORD (Hosea 2:20). In the meantime, there was much chastening to be felt by Israel in Assyrian bondage.

As I reflect on theses unpleasant verses, I am reminded of the unpleasant marriage situations many have today. Some find themselves married to unsaved mates. If a saved person marries an unsaved person, there will be "religious" differences that will divide the home. Such a division is no small thing. It is sharp like a knife. This union is called "an unequal yoke." Paul warns Christians to avoid such a union (II Corinthians 6:14).

Other unpleasant situations come when one's mate is sexually unfaithful. The precious, exclusive "oneness" that belongs to the couple has been violated. Personal actions have brought a "closeness" to another that was only for the married couple. Sometimes this adultery severs the marriage with no repair. Other times, the marriage survives.

FORGIVENESS REIGNS, AND LIFE GOES ON, BUT IT IS NEVER QUITE THE SAME.

"THE WRITINGS"
(II Thessalonians 2:15)
STAND FAST, AND HOLD THE TRADITIONS (THE WRITINGS).
Other books grow dull and outdated
But the "writings" are ever fresh and timely.
Men's ideas and plans change and pass,
but not so the "writings" which live and abide forever.
Indeed, we cannot stand at all unless we hold to THE BOOK.
ALL THE WRITINGS ARE GIVEN BY "INSPIRATION OF GOD"
(ggs)

Today's Bible Blessing   *September 19*

Hosea 8:5–Hosea 14:2
A PROPHET REJECTED
A PASTOR CRITICIZED

Hosea 11:4

"I drew them with cords . . . with bands of love . . ."

Let us look briefly at HOSEA'S MINISTRY. It spanned about sixty years. *"The WORD of the LORD"* came to him when UZZIAH was king. We remember UZZIAH from Isaiah 6. It was in the year that Uzziah died, that ISAIAH received his "call." I wonder if Hosea and Isaiah ever talked together, and compared prophecies. I really don't know. I just like to imagine it. Also, HOSEA prophesied during the reigns of JOTHAM, AHAZ, and HEZEKIAH. They were kings of the Southern kingdom of JUDAH. This was in the time of JEROBOAM'S reign, and beyond in ISRAEL, the Northern Kingdom. THAT WAS HOSEA'S TERRITORY. Most of his ministry was with the rebellious people of Israel. What an assignment!

HOSEA was a contemporary prophet with AMOS in Israel and MICAH and ISAIAH in JUDAH. It appeared to me that he prophesied "before" and "during" THE CAPTIVITY OF ISRAEL and witnessed the conquering of SAMARIA, its capital city. We do not know for sure if he was carried away to Assyria. He could have been. If so, he may have said to his fellow captives, "I told you so."

Like JEREMIAH, he was a prophet of doom. Not only was his message not received, he had a mixed-up marriage. Wonder how his children turned out with such a mother.

> *I taught Ephraim also to go, taking them by their arms; but they knew not that I healed them. I drew them with cords of a man, with bands of love: and I was to them as they that take off the yoke on their jaws, and I laid meat unto them (Hosea 11:3-4).*

When I read HOSEA 11:3-4, I thought about churches and their pastors. I DON'T THINK THAT THE AVERAGE PARISHIONER REALIZES HOW MUCH HIS PASTOR LOVES HIM. To see a man or woman come into his church makes the pastor glad—especially if it is a small church. HE LOVES THE CHURCH ATTENDER WITH ALL HIS HEART. HE NOURISHES HIM IN THE WORDS OF GOD. HE PRAYS FOR HIM. He visits him when he is sick. He answers his questions concerning the Bible. THE PASTOR YEARNS THAT THE CHURCH PERSON GROW IN GRACE. He spiritually feeds him and tenderly cares for him. If the person has family problems, the pastor draws him to his side. If there is a death in the family, the pastor gives comfort—sometimes beyond his own strength. OFTEN, THE

PASTOR NEGLECTS HIS OWN WIFE AND FAMILY TO CARE FOR HIS "SHEEP"—the church member.

Then one day–an unexpected day–the church member sees a flaw in his pastor or his pastor's wife. (This is the same pastor and wife the church member thought was wonderful a few weeks ago.) He tells a fellow church member about the flaw. They discuss it. They tell another church member. Soon this small "flaw" grows in the mind of "the talkers" until it is no longer a "flaw," it is a GIANT BLEMISH. It is so awful that the talking members cannot put up with it any more. THE SAME PASTOR, WHO MEANT EVERYTHING TO THE CHURCH MEMBER AND HIS FRIENDS, HAS SUDDENLY BECOME *"WEIGHED IN THE BALANCES AND FOUND WANTING"* (Daniel 5:27). All of a sudden, the pastor is "full of wrong."

FROM THEN ON, EVERYTHING THE PASTOR SAYS IS WRONG. The church is a-buzz with criticism. The church members see grievous imperfections in the pastor. THIS WAS THE SAME PASTOR WHO SPENT HIS LIFE TEACHING AND HELPING THE CHURCH MEMBER AND HIS GOSSIPING CHURCH FRIENDS. Nothing that is said, or not said, can help the situation. The church splits, and the disgruntled church members either leave the church or the church votes the pastor out. This man and his wife were the same people whom they said they once loved and whom the people appreciated his caring and praying for them. OFF THE MALIGNED PASTOR WENT, SAD & DISCOURAGED, NEVER TO ENTER THOSE CHURCH DOORS AGAIN.

"THE TRIAL OF OUR FAITH"
(I Peter 1:7)
God has designed us to be a "tried" people.
Trials are a part of our lot;
adorning their season and place in Eternity.
He knows the effect.
TRIALS PASS, BUT HOW WE REACT TO THEM
IS RECORDED IN HEAVEN.
You may think God has passed you by; but let it not be so.
He knows your case thoroughly,
as if you were the only creature He ever made.
(ggs: source unknown)

Today's Bible Blessing   *September 20*
Hosea 14:3–Amos 1:6
LOCUSTS, BLOODSHED, AND DELIVERANCE

Joel 2:32

"Whosoever shall call on the name of the LORD shall be delivered . . ."

Have you ever met a young man–or an older one– whose name was JOEL? I have. It is a good name, a solid name that means "JEHOVAH IS GOD." When his mother would call him for dinner, she would say, "JEHOVAH IS GOD, it is time to eat." Always, every day, in every way, JOEL would be reminded that JEHOVAH is GOD. (The Lord Jesus Christ is the JEHOVAH of the Old Testament)

Joel was a pre-exile prophet to the Southern Kingdom, which was JUDAH. He may have prophesied during the time of KING UZZIAH–around 800 B.C. Because in his writings, he referred often to the priesthood, he could have been a priest. He was a contemporary to HOSEA & AMOS. He knew ELISHA, and maybe ELIJAH. His father's name was PETHUEL.

I wonder what it was like to be a "prophet." I wonder if Joel, as a little boy, knew that he would be one. I do not know. His ministry was that of "warning." It seemed that was what most prophets did. His message was to be told to all people—even the children.

> *"That which the palmerworm hath left hath the locust eaten; and that which the locust hath left hath the cankerworm eaten, and that which the cankerworm hath left that the caterpiller eaten" (Joel 1:4).*

It surely sounded like a terrible famine was in the land. I read that the "palmerworm" and the "locust" are in different stages of the development of the same insect. So, it would mean to me—that this famine, spoken about in Joel 1:4, covered a period of time of a series of disastrous events.

All this talk of insects devouring the land, and calling out the terrible news that the people of Judah would be taken captive, wore on the prophet's soul. Soon prophecies of the future came. The GREAT TRIBULATION would overcome the people.

WAR AND DEATH WOULD BE EVERYWHERE. The armies were desperate for weapons. Their metal plows would be made into swords, and their pruning hooks were pounded into spears (Joel 3: 10). Blood would flow in the streets. This is where we read of the VALLEY OF JEHOSHAPHAT (Joel 3:2), and the terrible treatment of young boys and girls. Then, THE LORD JESUS CHRIST WOULD COME IN POWER AND GREAT GLORY. There will be a battle called ARMAGEDDON. The sun will be turned to darkness and the moon into

427

blood. How frightening! All this will occur before THE TERRIBLE DAY OF THE LORD (Joel 2:31). It will be an awful time of war and death.

IN THE MIDST OF ALL THIS WAR AND BLOODSHED, A WONDERFUL VERSE SHINES OUT FROM THE PAGES OF MY BIBLE. IT IS FOUND IN JOEL 2:32.

> *"And it shall come to pass, that whosoever shall call on the name of the LORD shall be delivered: for in mount Zion and in Jerusalem shall be deliverance, as the LORD hath said, and in the remnant whom the LORD shall call."*

I talked to my husband about this verse. How can the people in the midst of the tribulation be delivered? He said that they might be killed in battle–even so, if they call upon the Lord to redeem their souls, they would be saved. Their bodies might be killed, but they would have EVERLASTING LIFE. How glorious to think that salvation will be offered to those in such a time. Or, it could be that those who run and hide in a place called PETRA, somewhere in EDOM in the mountains of Jerusalem, there the LORD JESUS will come and deliver them. It reminds me of the verse in the New Testament: *"FOR WHOSOEVER SHALL CALL UPON THE NAME OF THE LORD SHALL BE SAVED"* (Romans 10:13).

"ROMANS 8:28"
The great purpose of God toward which
He is bringing every Christian
is not temporary happiness,
but conformity to the image of Jesus Christ.
Did all things work toward that great consummation?
And is He going to bring that about thru prosperity,
thru adversity, thru sickness, thru health,
thru failure, thru success, thru darkness, thru light,
thru joy and thru sorrow?
(ggs: copied from A. C. Dixon)

Today's Bible Blessing   *September 21*

Amos 1:7–Amos 6:6

NO SOUND OF THE WORDS OF GOD ANYWHERE

Amos 8:11

"Not a famine of bread . . . but of hearing the words of the LORD:"

How often we have heard the question, "CAN TWO WALK TOGETHER, EXCEPT THEY BE AGREED?" Or what about the sign we have seen often as we drive down a major highway?

In big, bold letters, it reads "PREPARE TO MEET THY GOD." Did you realize those two startling statements are from the book of AMOS?

Amos was a prophet. We sometimes call him a "minor" prophet. He is so-named by theologians because of the size of his book. It, and other minor prophet's writings, are smaller than the books of Isaiah, Jeremiah, Ezekiel or Daniel; but his words are far from "minor" or inferior. It is interesting to notice that Amos did not attend a prophet school. He had no intention of being a prophet. One day, when he was gathering figs and following his flocks, the LORD spoke to him. I think he must have been surprised, don't you?

Probably Amos looked all around from where that voice was coming. He couldn't see anyone. I'm fairly sure this happened in his hometown of TEKOA. That was near Bethlehem. If you recall, the Lord Jesus Christ was born in the village of Bethlehem.

Has the LORD ever spoken to you? If so, He will use THE BIBLE. Maybe He'll use Amos' words today to help you make an important decision in your life.

Four times in my life, I have had people tell me that a "voice" told them to do something. We don't usually talk about it. Someone may think we are a bit "off." On two of those incidents, a "voice" was heard by family members.

One night, my daughter-in-law was coming on to a busy highway. Her black and white station wagon stalled. Usually it restarted immediately. But this time, she could not get the car moving. She didn't know what to do. Then a "voice" said, "GET OUT OF THE CAR!" As soon as she stepped away from the car—without warning—another car came speeding down the road. Right before her eyes, that car crashed into her station wagon. She could have died.

Another time, someone set the Christmas tree on fire in our son's first floor apartment. He tried, but he could not put the fire out. The "sadistic friend" escaped through the only door. Though the door handle was burning hot, our son turned it. It would not open. Intentionally, the evil man locked that door as he escaped. Our son was trapped. A voice came to him. He said it was the voice of my father, his grandfather.

The voice said, "CLIMB OUT THE BATHROOM WINDOW." It was a very small window. Our son was a good-sized man. Yet, he squeezed his burning body through that window, and fell to the ground. He and his evil friend ran across the street to a pay phone. A man came by who gave them a ride to the hospital. I will always believe that man was an "angel"! He came out of nowhere and left into nowhere. Though David was severely burned, he escaped with his life.

In the time of decision, hearing an audible voice is most unusual. Those who have severe mental illnesses hear voices all the time. Those voices plague them. They will not go away. They haunt the hearer, who longs that the voices would leave. Usually God does not work with an audible voice. Both of my illustrations saved the lives of two people. (I really don't know what to make of it myself.) I hesitated to tell you about them, but this did happen.

GOD SPEAKS TO CHRISTIANS TODAY. HE USES HIS WORDS—THE SCRIPTURES. I have never heard a "voice." In truth, we cannot base a doctrine, or teaching, on "an experience." NOR CAN WE BASE OUR SALVATION ON AN EXPERIENCE. I know a young man who wants an "experience" to "prove" that he was saved. God never dropped fire on his head, or knocked him off a mule. Sadly, that man has turned from the Saviour who bought him with a price at Calvary. The young man has gone back into the world full time. He says he is not "born-again."

Someday, according to Amos 8:11, there will be a great dearth. It will not be for food or water. There will be a lack of the true Words of God in the world. Amos said,

"Behold, the days come, saith the Lord GOD, that I will send a famine in the land, not a famine of bread, nor a thirst for water, but of hearing the words of the LORD."

HOW WOULD YOU FEEL IF YOU NEVER HEARD THE WORDS OF THE LIVING GOD? There may come a time that there won't be a Bible translated from the proper Hebrew, Aramaic, and Greek Words anyplace. So many of the newer versions subtract, add to, or change the words to their own liking.

READ THE KING JAMES BIBLE TODAY & APPRECIATE IT.

"SHALL THE CLAY SAY TO THE POTTER, "WHY"?
"He that is mastered by Christ is the master of any circumstances.
Does the circumstance press hard against you?
It is the Potter's hand.
Do not push it away.
It is shaping you into a vessel of beauty and usefulness for Eternity.
Your mastery will come, not by arresting the progress,
but by enduring its discipline."
(Copied)
(ggs: This quote has been a blessing to me.)

Today's Bible Blessing   *September 22*

Amos 6:7–Jonah 1:11
OBADIAH
A SERVANT OF JEHOVAH

Obadiah 1:13

"Thou shouldest not have entered into the gate of my people"

Theologians use a big word when they classify prophecy. That word is ESCHATOLOGY. It means the unfolding of "future things." Sixteen books of the OLD TESTAMENT are classified as prophetic. Of interest, from one-fourth to one-fifth of the whole Bible are "predictions." With so many words dedicated to the future, we should not neglect them. For my husband and me, PREMILLENNIALISM is the key. We read these words, concerning the Christian's future and the future of the world:

> "The primary division in all prophecy lies between that which is now fulfilled and that which is unfulfilled. This division has never been stabilized, of course. The time word NOW is ever changing. Things that were future yesterday may be fulfilled by tomorrow. No ESCHATOLOGY is complete which concerns itself only with that which is future at a given time. Since all prediction was future at the time it came to be written, a complete ESCHATOLOGY should account for all that is fulfilled and unfulfilled." (Lewis Sperry Chafer, *Systematic Theology*, Vol. 7, page 139)

Today we are going to look at a one-chapter book. There are only FIVE of them in the Bible. OBADIAH stands alone in the Old Testament. PHILEMON, II JOHN, III JOHN, & JUDE, in the New Testament, are one chapter books also. OBADIAH used the term, "THE DAY OF THE LORD" as did other Old Testament prophets. Little to nothing is known about the man. His job was to be FAITHFUL. *"Moreover it is required in stewards, that a man be found faithful"* (I Cor. 4: 2).

The prophet's name means "the servant or worshiper of Jehovah." What a "good name" to carry with a man of God all his life. *"A good name is rather to be chosen than great riches, and loving favour rather than silver and gold"* (Proverbs 22:1). Let us always remember that a man or woman does not have to be famous for God to use him or her. Keep that in mind as you grow in Him.

First of all, OBADIAH, who is called a "minor prophet," had a vision (Obadiah 1:1). Today, the days of such "visions" have passed—though some claim to have them. In this case, the LORD showed OBADIAH the land of EDOM. His whole ministry was against that land. The LORD called them "heathen." The prophet is called to war against that land. Edom was proud. She felt safe, for she lived in the clefts of rocks. She thought she was well-protected.

When God decides to judge a nation or a person, nothing can protect them from such divine judgment.

What does the LORD have for us today in this "one chapter book" which is named after today's prophet, OBADIAH? Read with me what he said in Obadiah 1:13-14:

> *"Thou shouldest not have entered into the gate of my people in the day of their calamity; yea, thou shouldest not have looked on their affliction in the day of their calamity, nor have laid hands on their substance in the day of their calamity; Neither shouldest thou have stood in the crossway, to cut off those of his that did escape; neither shouldest thou have delivered up those of his that did remain in the day of distress."*

Edom interfered with the LORD'S chastening of His people. Because of JUDAH'S waywardness from the true God, the LORD permitted Babylon to capture the Southern Kingdom. This was God's will. Edom stepped into the chastening where she did not belong. Sometimes we do this today when someone we love is being chastened. THE LORD IS NOT PLEASED WITH SUCH INTERFERENCE.

Sometimes, you and I do the same thing. We think we know a situation, and we jump right into the middle of the conflict. Instead of helping, we muddy the waters and hurt many people. *"WHY SHOULDEST THOU MEDDLE TO THINE HURT . . ."* (II CHRONICLES 25:19).
"Meddle not with him that flattereth with his lips" (Proverbs 20:19).
"Meddle not with them that are given to change" (Proverbs 24:21).

"MY GRACE IS SUFFICIENT FOR THEE"
GOD'S GRACE KEEPS ON BEING
SUFFICIENT FOR MY WEAKNESS
ACCORDING TO HIS PROMISE.
1. It is GOD'S GRACE.
2. It is SUFFICIENT ENOUGH.
3. It is FOR ALL CHRISTIANS AND FOR ME.
Paul said that the Lord spoke these words to him
in answer to his prayer.(ggs)

Jonah 1:12–Micah 4:8

JONAH
A COMPLAINING PROPHET

Jonah 1:2; 3:2

"Arise, Go to Nineveh, that great city, and cry against it . . ."

When I think about the man called JONAH, I think of a man who had a mind of his own. It is good to have convictions. It is good to have a purpose; but it is not good to have a contrary will from the will of God. I don't really think of JONAH as a prophet, but he was one (II Kings 14:25). So many contrary happenings are his that it is difficult to picture him as having the "call of God" upon his life. Instead of our thinking of him as the "servant" of the MOST HIGH, we think of him as a disobedient person. Besides that, he was a complainer. Neither of those qualities goes well with the word, prophet, or Christian, for that matter.

So, when God said to JONAH, "GO TO NINEVEH," he went to TARSHISH. When he found himself in a boat in the middle of a storm, he went to sleep. When the crew awakened him, they begged, "PRAY TO YOUR GOD!" Instead of praying, he told his frightened friends, "THROW ME OVERBOARD." That is exactly what they did. All JONAH'S CONTRARINESS CEASED THE MINUTE THE FISH OPENED ITS MOUTH. In went the rebellious man down the throat of that special fish.

Now what was JONAH to do? To be truthful, there was nothing left for him to do but pray. And pray, he did. It was then that JONAH had a private prayer meeting. He certainly had an unusual prayer closet. It was in the belly of a specially prepared fish. Not only could that fish swallow a man, it had a stomach in which the man could live and breathe without drowning for a while. Jonah was in seaweed and sea, coughing and flaying his arms–all the while praying.

It must have been a frightening experience; but JONAH knew exactly what was happening to him and why. That fish took a dive to the bottom of the sea. Picture JONAH hanging on to a rib or two of the fish, praying and crying out to God—and dying at the same time.

Sometimes we wonder how we will die. Where we will be? Will we be alone? Will it be in an airplane? Will we have a stroke? Will it be a disease? BUT WE NEVER DREAM WE WILL DIE IN THE BELLY OF A GREAT FISH. Neither did Jonah. Never in his wildest dreams, did he think he would die in a fish.

Though his body was still in the fish's belly, Jonah's soul was in the depths of HELL and CORRUPTION. From there, he still prayed. HE CRIED OUT, "SALVATION IS OF THE

LORD." Miracle of miracles, the LORD spoke to the fish. God was not done with JONAH yet. The fish obeyed. Sad to say, the fish was more obedient than its passenger. Out on the shore was Jonah's limp body. It flopped around like a rag doll. And in that weakened condition, the LORD repeated his order to the disobedient prophet, "ARISE GO UNTO NINEVEH." God heard his prayer and gave him some further orders.

"So JONAH arose and went unto NINEVEH." It was a large city, full of people whom the LORD loved. There were 120,000 people who did not know their left hand from their right hand. Preachers say they were children—and maybe they were. Sometimes I think that they were uneducated people of all ages that didn't know "left" from "right." They were people who desperately needed holy help and forgiveness.

I must say, JONAH gave his all to preaching and prophesying. By this time, he had a message from God. He cried out, "IN FORTY DAYS, NINEVEH SHALL BE OVERTHROWN." Guess what? The king not only heard it, he heeded it. He repented. The people repented. God spared the city.

Instead of rejoicing, JONAH was up to his old tricks of complaining. He thought people would think he had lied when he said the city would be destroyed. There was not a rejoicing bone in his body. He was so upset and depressed that he sat in a booth outside the city and sulked. He wanted to die. The sun was hot. He complained. Graciously, God made a vine to grow for his protection. A worm ate the gourd. JONAH was angry. He cared more for himself and the gourd than the salvation of NINEVEH's people.

ARE THERE CHRISTIAN SERVANTS TODAY WHO COMPLAIN AS MUCH AS JONAH?
I THINK SO.

"PRAYER"
"INTERCESSION MUST BE PERSISTENT,
not to persuade God, but because of the enemy."
(copied)
Pray without ceasing, God knows Satan's continuous attack. (ggs)

Today's Bible Blessing   *September 24*

Micah 4:9–Nahum 3:2
MICAH'S ELOQUENCE & BETHLEHEM'S BIRTH

Micah 5:2

"But thou Bethlehem . . . though thou be little among the thousands . . ."

Who was MICAH? He was a simple man like AMOS. His message was simple too, and for justice. He was a contemporary of ISAIAH and lived during the reigns of JOTHAM, AHAZ, and HEZEKIAH in JUDAH. Though he lived in JUDAH, he prophesied to SAMARIA. At that time, the kings of Israel were Pekahiah, Pekah, and Hoshea. His native town was a place called MORESHETH. It was a Judean village near GATH which is associated with the Philistines.

MICAH means "WHO IS LIKE THE LORD?" When my husband and I were in Liberia, West Africa, we met the host pastor's children. I wish I could remember how to spell their names—but each name had a meaning. One was "hungry child." It was during an especially trying time in their lives, that this child was born. His name reflected their circumstances at the time. This is true of the names of the prophets we have seen during these "BLESSINGS."

I think of MICAH'S mother and father as they chose his name. How they wanted their son to reflect the LORD. That should be the desire of every Christian parent.

"I am crucified with Christ: nevertheless I live; yet not I, but Christ liveth in me: and the life which I now live in the flesh I live by the faith of the Son of God, who loved me, and gave himself for me" (Galatians 2:20).

I must say that MICAH was an eloquent writer. His words declared the beauty and depths of the heart of the LORD through his prophetic pen. Micah had beauty in his soul. Oft times, it flowed from his person. Read the prophetic word (Micah 5:2) as to the birthplace of the LORD JESUS CHRIST and see what I mean. It is doctrinally altered in the NIV as illustrated in this quotation.

"But thou, Bethlehem Ephratah, though thou be little among the thousands of Judah, yet out of thee shall he come forth unto me that is to be ruler in Israel; whose goings forth ["**origins**" NIV] *have been from of old, from everlasting"* ["**ancient times**" NIV].

This is the prophetic word as to the birthplace of the LORD JESUS CHRIST. It is heretically altered in the NIV.

BETHLEHEM means "THE HOUSE OF BREAD." It was the place where "THE BREAD OF LIFE" was presented to the world wrapped in baby flesh. Such a precious child. He was born of a Virgin and is GOD IN THE FLESH. There was never another birth like

His, and there never will be. As Mary, his mother, held Him to her breast, she was nourishing the ONE who someday would nourish and forgive the world with His salvation from sin.

I've been to BETHLEHEM. I saw the shepherd's field. It is untouched by the commercialism that plagues other historic places in the Holy Land. A shepherd walked by. He was an old man. I imagined what it must have been like, those long ago years, for the shepherds when the angels broke through the night sky with the news of Jesus' birth.

How wonderful that years and years before Mary and Joseph traveled to the city of David, Micah wrote, as only a true prophet could, that the MESSIAH would be born in Bethlehem. He would be THE CHRIST who would be the LAMB of GOD who would take away the sin of the world (John 1:29).

ANOTHER VERSE THAT POETS PEN POEMS ABOUT is MICAH 7:18:

> *"Who is a God like unto thee, that pardoneth iniquity, and passeth by the transgression of the remnant of his heritage? he retaineth not his anger for ever, because he delighteth in mercy."*

What doctrine in this prophecy! Micah asked, "What other god is there that pardons like my GOD?" Remember Israel had slid deep into the slime of idolatry. God had likened her spiritual decline as a man committing adultery against his wife, or a wife being unfaithful to her husband. The idol calves at Dan and Bethel could not pardon. They just stood there silent. Did their gods of wood and stone show any mercy? Are the Israelites able to sense the love of their silent stone deities? NO. There is no response. No forgiveness. No mercy. No love. Just stone silence.

ONLY THE GOD OF ABRAHAM, ISAAC, AND JACOB PARDONS AND FORGIVES.

"FRESH OIL–A NEW STRENGTH"
(Psalm 23:5; Psalm 92:10b; Psalm 92:1)
"Thou anointest my head with oil"
"I shall be anointed with fresh oil."
"It is a good thing to give thanks unto the Lord"
Praise lifts the heart, and takes it from our cares to the Lord.
Praise and praying gives renewed strength.
FRESH OIL: NEW STRENGTH EVERY MORNING.
NEW ZEAL FOR THE SAME TASK.
INDEED, IT IS A GOOD THING
TO GIVE THANKS UNTO THE LORD. (ggs)

Today's Bible Blessing   *September 25*

Nahum 3:3–Zephaniah 1:13
THE GOOD LORD'S STRONG HOLD
Nahum 1:7

"The Lord is good . . . and He knoweth them that trust in Him."

The PROPHET NAHUM had a burden. His LORD put that burden in his life, so he could do nothing else but talk about it, and write about it. Have you ever been burdened by a situation that consumed your life? You thought about it when you awakened in the morning, and you thought about it when you lay down to sleep at night. Nahum was burdened with a message of destruction for the city of NINEVEH. He prophesied in the time of HEZEKIAH, about one hundred and fifty years after JONAH. His book, of only three chapters, is tucked between MICAH and HABAKKUK. It is full of God's wrath for ASSYRIA.

We remember NINEVEH. It was the capital of ASSYRIA. That was the city that repented of her sin after JONAH preached its destruction. But God saw the king's contrition, as well as the people's repentance, and spared that big city for a while. Historians say the city was destroyed a century later as predicted in today's reading. It is said that there is nothing left of it at all.

The chief "god" of Nineveh was the "bull-god." It had a face of a man and the wings of a bird. It reminds us of Romans 1:21-23:

> *Because that, when they knew God, they glorified him not*
> *as God, neither were thankful . . . and changed the glory of*
> *the uncorruptible God into . . . fourfooted beasts . . .*

The following beautiful verse of Scripture (Nahum 1:7) was written by NAHUM. He was a poet. He is called a "minor prophet" by those that teach the BIBLE, but his writings are far from "minor"!

> *"THE LORD IS GOOD, A STRONG HOLD IN THE DAY*
> *OF TROUBLE; AND HE KNOWETH THEM THAT TRUST*
> *IN HIM."*

Yes, the LORD IS GOOD. *"Goodness and mercy"* flows from His great heart. It follows believers all the days of their lives. *"O give thanks unto the LORD; FOR HE IS GOOD: because his mercy endureth for ever"* (Psalm 118:1).

"A STRONGHOLD." What do we think of when we hear the word "stronghold"? I don't know about you, but I think of a fortress of protection during a time of war. I think of something so strong that nothing can penetrate it. Nothing can hurt it. It could be pounded and pierced—but never be destroyed. A STRONG HOLD, as two words, could mean a strong grip on a certain something. A general, like David, took control of Jerusalem. He had a "strong hold." His control showed his authority and strength. No one, nor anything, could take the city from his hand (II Samuel 5:7).

"IN THE DAY OF TROUBLE." The proof of the strength of a bridge is when a heavy train rolls over it. If it passes the "strength test," it will be reliable for future trains of all kinds. The proof of a "strong hold" is in the time of trouble.

Anyone—weak or strong—can claim they will be able to protect a city; but when the armies come, will that "anyone" do the job? When all about me and my dreams are shattered, the LORD, as "MY STRONG HOLD," will never fail. He will hold me up with the strength of his right arm. How do I know this? Because He has passed the test. In times past, when my heart was broken, He has held me strong. In my "DAYS OF TROUBLE," He has been my ROCK and my FORTRESS. He is my "STRONG TOWER" that the righteous run to for safety (Proverbs 18:10).

AND HE KNOWETH THEM THAT TRUST IN HIM. GOD IS OMNISCIENT. That means HE is ALL-KNOWING. We cannot fool Him. Other people may look at us and think, "What a good Christian that person is." But God KNOWS. He knows if we are all pretense. He knows if we are "for real." He knows if we really "trust." He knows our hearts better than we know ourselves. Is all our "holy talk" real? Or are we fooling ourselves?

GOD KNOWS THEM THAT TRUST IN HIM. THAT'S FOR SURE.

"HAVING DONE ALL, STAND."
(Ephesians 6:11, 14)
BETTER DIE WITH A CONVICTION
THAN TO LIVE WITH A COMPROMISE.
"DON'T SAY HOW SHALL I EVER GET OVER THAT MOUNTAIN? Keep to the present little inch that is before you, and accomplish that in the little moment that belongs to it. When you come to the mountain and river, you will come to the strength to cross."
(ggs, copied, source unknown)

Today's Bible Blessing   *September 26*
Zephaniah 1:14–Zechariah 1:8
HABAKKUK: PROPHET, POET, & SONGSTER
Habakkuk 2:4b
"The just shall live by his faith."

It is interesting to me to find that the order of the MINOR PROPHET BOOKS is not necessarily in the order of the history of the people to whom they prophesied. If I were making a Biblical order, I would put them in chronological order; but those who established the canon did not do this. So we find ourselves jumping backward and forward in history to understand HABAKKUK, as well as other prophets.

Now we are in HABAKKUK, a Bible book that most of us are not too familiar with—except for the fourth verse of the second chapter: THE JUST SHALL LIVE BY HIS FAITH. What a verse! Those of us, who are Bible readers, know this verse by heart. Usually, I must admit, we think of this verse as a New Testament verse, except the New Testament excludes the personal pronoun, "his." It was given first, by the Holy Spirit, to the prophet in the time of KING JOSIAH—around the twelfth or thirteen century B.C. That prophet was HABAKKUK.

He wrote: *BEHOLD, HIS SOUL WHICH IS LIFTED UP IS NOT UPRIGHT IN HIM: BUT THE JUST SHALL LIVE BY HIS FAITH.* Even back in Habakkuk's time, as in the days of ABRAHAM, it was not "works" that brought eternal life. It was "FAITH"—the faith in the ETERNAL SON OF GOD, who someday would give His life for man's sin. All the Old Testament people looked forward to the crucifixion of the Messiah. He would shed his blood on Calvary's Cross for the sins of the world "*that whosoever believeth on HIM should not perish, but have everlasting life*" (John 3:16).

The same message was repeated by the APOSTLE PAUL to the Roman Christians when he wrote the following: "*FOR THEREIN IS THE RIGHTEOUSNESS OF GOD REVEALED FROM FAITH TO FAITH: AS IT IS WRITTEN, The just shall live by faith* (Romans 1:17). Again, the same truth theme was restated to the Galatian Christians: "*BUT THAT NO MAN IS JUSTIFIED BY THE LAW IN THE SIGHT OF GOD, IT IS EVIDENT: FOR, The just shall live by faith* (Galatians 3:11). As if to pound it into the head and hearts of the believers, Paul emphasizes the theme for the third time in his written ministry: *Now the just shall live by faith: but if any man draw back, my soul shall have no pleasure in him* (Hebrews 10:38).

Paul's theme was the theme of the Prophet. It was repeated and repeated like a hammer on a nail. Salvation was not of works but of faith. *For by grace are ye saved through faith; and that not of yourselves: it is the gift of God: NOT OF WORKS, LEST ANY MAN SHOULD BOAST* (Ephesians 2:8-9).

HABAKKUK was a poet. Some say that his Psalm in chapter three is one of the most beautiful in the Bible. Who has not heard sermons on Habakkuk 3:2? *O LORD, REVIVE THY WORK IN THE MIDST OF THE YEARS.* Or the beauty of the comforting in verses 17-18:

> "*Although the fig tree shall not blossom, neither shall fruit be in the vines; the labour of the olive shall fail, and the fields shall yield no meat; the flock shall be cut off from the fold, and there shall be no herd in the stalls: Yet I will rejoice in the LORD, I will joy in the God of my salvation.*"

This poet witnessed Nebuchadnezzar's invasion of JUDAH. He saw the first Jewish captives carried away to Babylon. He may have seen Daniel and his "fiery furnace friends" forced-marched to the kings palace. So little is known of this man, except he was a prophet, and well-qualified. He was numbered in the temple choir. In fact, he was a chief singer. (I wonder if he were a bass, tenor, or baritone.) This made him a part of the Levitical family in charge of worship music. He, like Jeremiah and Ezekiel, belonged to the tribe of Levi.

THREE PROPHETS WERE APPOINTED TO SPEAK OF THE JEHOVAH'S JUDGMENT: OBADIAH spoke of the doom of Edom; NAHUM of the doom of Assyria; and HABAKKUK of the doom of Babylon.

"A WORD FITLY SPOKEN"
(Psalm 144:1, Proverbs 25:11)
BLESSED BE THE LORD MY STRENGTH,
WHICH TEACHETH MY HANDS TO WAR,
AND MY FINGERS TO FIGHT.
Sometimes God uses letters and writings
to give forth a militant message!
SOMETIMES ONE WORD CAN GIVE COURAGE TO AN ARMY!
CONSIDER SUCH WORDS AS
EXCELSIOR! VICTORY! HALLELUJAH!
One word may cheer or bless a sad heart.
A word fitly spoken is like apples of gold in pictures of silver.
(ggs)

Today's Bible Blessing   September 27

Zechariah 1:9–Zechariah 7:10
I MUST HAVE GOD

Zephaniah 3:17
"The LORD thy God in the midst of thee is mighty . . ."

What is there to say about this prophet with the strange name of ZEPHANIAH? Who was he? Why did the Holy Spirit move him to write of the impending captivity? He probably wrote during KING JOSIAH'S REIGN and REVIVAL. Remember when HILKIAH, the high priest, found THE BOOK OF THE LAW in the cluttered HOLY TEMPLE? (See II Kings 22:8.) That was during JEREMIAH'S and NAHUM'S prophetic ministries. They too, like ZEPHANIAH, had a pre-revival influence during the reign of KING HEZEKIAH. Though there was an industrious cleansing of THE TEMPLE, as well as a heartfelt turn toward the true God, JUDAH'S heart-change did not endure. But, the LORD God was tender toward the young king. He recognized JOSIAH'S true heart repentance, and did not kindle His wrath against His people until JOSIAH died (II Kings 22:20).

We know little about ZEPHANIAH'S life. That is good, for now we pay more attention to his words than his ways. He was the son of Cushi, whose father was named Gedaliah (Zephaniah 1:1). Some feel today's prophet was the great grandson of HEZEKIAH. ZEPHANIAH WAS A PRE-EXILIC PROPHET. He prophesied around 630 B.C.—prior to the dreadful invasions by Babylon. His name means "JEHOVAH HIDES" or "JEHOVAH PROTECTS."

Now let us look at some of ZEPHANIAH'S beautiful words. Before we do, notice his words of judgment and impending doom toward JUDAH and JERUSALEM. He warns them of "THE DAY OF THE LORD" coming upon them. That will be a day of God's fierce anger. Could it be that the prophet was warning us who live today about the FIERCE ANGER OF ARMAGEDDON that will come upon the ungodly nations in our "*last days*"? (See Zephaniah 1:7, 14) Compare Acts 2:20; I Thessalonians 5:2; & II Peter 3:10.

Now let us look at a beautiful verse of comfort for you and me in this day of political and personal unrest. LET US TAKE THESE WORDS STRAIGHT FROM THE HEART OF GOD TO THE PEN OF THE PROPHET, as if they were written personally to us. HOW WE NEED THEM. They are found in Zephaniah 3:17:

> *"THE LORD THY GOD IN THE MIDST OF THEE IS MIGHTY; HE WILL SAVE, HE WILL REJOICE OVER THEE WITH JOY; HE WILL REST IN HIS LOVE, HE WILL JOY OVER THEE WITH SINGING."*

We need this comfort. We need to feel the beat of the understanding heart of our God. We need to forget the turmoil in our lives—the unkind words of others that pierce our souls. We need to remove ourselves for a brief time from the troubles that plague our lives. We have illnesses and pain. We have sibling squabbles and family feuds. We have financial woes and taxes to pay. We have concerns about our country and the direction it is going. We need comfort and hope from the Scripture.

WE NEED GOD. We need His peace today. Right now, let us run into the arms of our Heavenly Father, for He is THE GOD OF ALL COMFORT and the FATHER OF MERCIES. HE IS OUR NEED.

I MUST HAVE GOD

I couldn't walk this thorny way
with stone beneath and cloud above,
Or meet the struggle of each day without His love.
I must have God.
I couldn't stand the hours at night,
or troubled day with all its length,
Or overlook what others say without His strength
I must have God.
I couldn't share the grief of those,
or comfort one in need of peace,
unless I pray.
(author unknown, ggs—one of ysw's favorites)

Today's Bible Blessing   *September 28*

Zechariah 7:11–Zechariah 12:13

I WILL BE GLORIFIED

Haggai 1:5, 7

"Thus saith the LORD of hosts; Consider your ways."

After the seventy years of Judah's captivity, HAGGAI was given an assignment. He was to minister to the restored remnant that had remained in the land, as well as those who were returning. All of this activity is written about in the books of Ezra and Nehemiah. If you remember, today's prophet, HAGGAI—along with ZECHARIAH and MALACHI—was commissioned by the LORD God to instruct, comfort, exhort, and rebuke God's beleaguered people. Often, being the older prophet, HAGGAI encouraged YOUNGER ZECHARIAH in their endeavor to get the Jews back to JERUSALEM to rebuild the Temple.

IT WAS HAGGAI'S DUTY TO ENCOURAGE AND ADMONISH THE WOULD-BE BUILDERS OF THE TEMPLE. Sometimes it was an easy task, and other times, most difficult. As you know, people are prone to discouragement. God's people were no different. In fact, they seemed to have perfected the job of complaining.

The WORD OF THE LORD came to Haggai when Darius II was the Persian ruler. It was in 520 B.C.—which was Darius' second year as king—during the month of E'LUL (August/September). You remember it was Darias I who had Daniel thrown into the den of lions (Daniel 6).

HAGGAI preached his prophetic messages around 520 B.C. Though HAGGAI may have spoken many other things, the Spirit of God had him only write certain prophecies down on the page.

442

We have them today in the book of HAGGAI.

One of the phrases that is repeated twice in HAGGAI'S writings is "CONSIDER YOUR WAYS." We see this in Haggai 1:5, 7. Because it is twice-repeated, in practically one breath, let us "consider" why.

If you remember, the Jews had started to rebuild the temple. They got discouraged by those around them. The Samaritans frustrated the work. They invoked King ARTAXERXES to stop it. They got lazy. Fifteen years previously, the foundation had been laid. Now they were afraid. It was easier to hide away in their bedrooms. They built their own homes in their own backyard. APPARENTLY, THEY FORGOT THAT THEIR JOB WAS TO REBUILD THE TEMPLE.

How easy it is to become discouraged in the Lord's work. Not only is the task demanding and difficult, other Christians look on and complain. Those who do absolutely nothing, pick on those who do. They gossip and point fingers. All the while they are sitting on their hands doing little, if anything, to make the work a success.

This negligence of not rebuilding of the TEMPLE was wrong. They were to build a HOUSE OF GOD for worship. Everyone who names the NAME of the Lord Jesus Christ should have a place to worship. It does not have to be an expensive edifice, or a church building, for that matter. It can be a grassy hill, a tent, a store front, or even a home like the ones where the early Christians met in the book of Acts. "HOMES" for churches were mentioned in Paul's epistles.

This uncompleted temple, during Haggai's time, was to take the place of the temple that Solomon built. You remember that one. The LORD promised KING DAVID that his son would build a House for God after his death. It was that exquisite edifice that was sorely destroyed by NEBUCHADNEZZAR'S army.

Look at VERSE SEVEN. Again HAGGAI gives the LORD'S WORDS. "CONSIDER YOUR WAYS." The LORD of hosts was talking to the whole group of Jews who had put down their tools and had gone home afraid of their own shadows.

When the plural, "your," is used in the KING JAMES BIBLE, the audience is addressed as a group. (While the singular pronouns are "thee," "thou," & "thine," the plural pronouns in the King James Bible are "ye," "you," & "your.")

What did GOD say? Look at Haggai 1:8. *"Go up to the mountain, and bring wood, and build the house; and I will take pleasure in it, and I will be glorified, saith the LORD."* In other words, GET UP OUT OF YOUR CHAIRS AND GET TO WORK.

Then the Lord gave a "message" saying, "I AM WITH YOU."

"ALL FOR HIM"
LIFE IS LIKE A COIN.
You may spend it as you wish. You may spend it only once.
If we are a Christian, our highest privilege,
and that which gives the greatest eternal results,
is to "spend" our life for the Lord Jesus.
The interest compounds far past our life-span.
LIVE FOR HIM.
GIVE FOR HIM.
WITNESS FOR HIM.
SPEAK FOR HIM.
AND PERHAPS—DIE FOR HIM.
(ggs)

Today's Bible Blessing   *September 29*
Zechariah 12:14–Malachi 4:6
MY LORD AND MY GOD
Zechariah 13:6
"What are these wounds in thine hands?"

Zechariah is an exciting book of fourteen chapters. It is two chapters longer than the book of Daniel; yet Daniel was a major prophet and Zechariah was a minor one. I wonder why?

ZECHARIAH'S PROPHECY was in Darius' second year just like Haggai's was. The rebuilding of the Temple was very important to the LORD God. This was Zechariah's plea. Sadly, the house of God had been reduced to ashes. Though the Jews had started to rebuild, they had become indifferent to the cause.

Do you know where it is prophesied that Jesus would be sold for thirty pieces of silver? It is right here in ZECHARIAH 11:12-13. Yes, the betrayer took thirty pieces of silver. The love of money is the root of all evil (I Timothy 6:10). There he stood with "blood money" in his hands. He cast it down on the temple floor.

> *"So they weighed for my price thirty pieces of silver. And the LORD said unto me, Cast it unto the potter: a goodly price that I was prised (appraised) at of them. And I took the thirty pieces of silver, and cast them to the potter in the house of the LORD"* (Zechariah 11:12-13).

Judas Iscariot went out and hanged himself. Apparently, after he hanged himself, his body fell to the ground as described in Acts 1:18: *"Now this man purchased a field with the reward of iniquity; and falling headlong, he burst asunder in the midst, and all his bowels gushed out."* He passed into eternity's blackness.

Back at the temple, the chief priest scooped up the money. Immediately, they purchased the field where Judas' body dropped. It was the field where potters made pots for the villagers. From then—and 'til now—that place of death is called *"the potter's field."*

LET US LOOK AT ANOTHER PROPHECY ABOUT OUR SAVIOUR in Zechariah 13:6. *And one shall say unto him, What are these wounds in thine hands? Then he shall answer, Those with which I was wounded in the house of my friends.*

What a prophecy! It is here that the method of the crucifixion of the Lord Jesus Christ is predicted. His hands would be pierced (Psalm 22:16). Those hands that created the universe would have nails pounded into them. Where? On a cross. People would stare at Him. They would gawk at his naked body. They would see the blood drops fall to the ground from the nail wounds. That day, at Calvary, Jesus Christ suffered and died for my sins and yours.

Some of the modern versions translate this verse in a perverse way. Instead of *"What are these wounds in thine hands?"* as the King James Bible says, the NEW KING JAMES VERSION and the NEW AMERICAN STANDARD VERSION say "What are these wounds between your arms?" The NEW INTERNATIONAL VERSION says "What are these wounds on your body?" THIS DISCREPANCY IS DUE TO THE WRONG INTERPRETATION OF THE HEBREW TEXT.

WHAT DID THOMAS SAY IN JOHN 20:25? He said, *"Except I shall see in his hands the print of the nails, and put my finger into the print of the nails, and thrust my hand into his side, I will not believe."* Thomas knew Jesus' hands had been pierced as Zechariah had predicted. Yet, the new translators are denying it.

Recently a doctor told me a true story. A patient had a dreadful condition. Only a blood transfusion could help her. The small hospital had an insufficient blood supply. Because the doctor had the blood type that could be used for any person, he made a decision. Swiftly, he lay down next to his patient. Then he put his arm out toward the dying woman. Soon the doctor's blood was transferred into the patient's arm. The healthy blood of the doctor became the lifesaving blood of the patient's. That doctor not only cared for the patient, but also, he gave his blood to save the patient's life.

When I heard this true story, I thought how Jesus shed His blood to save my soul. He hung on the cross. He stretched his arms out toward me. He shed His holy, sinless blood for me to cleanse the sin-sicknesses of my dying soul.

No wonder, when Thomas saw the nail holes in our Saviour's hands, he cried out,
"MY LORD AND MY GOD."

445

Today's Bible Blessing September 30
Matthew 1:1–Matthew 4:20
TRUTH: A NECESSARY ATTRIBUTE
Malachi 3:10
"Prove me now herewith, saith the LORD of hosts . . ."

AS WE READ THE BOOK OF MALACHI, WE ARE STRUCK WITH THE BEAUTY OF THE COMPOSITION, AND HIS USE OF WORDS. MALACHI WAS A "WORDSMITH"! *"For the prophecy came not in old time by the will of man: but holy men of God spake as they were moved by the Holy Ghost"* (II Peter 1:21). Malachi spoke after HAGGAI'S and ZECHARIAH'S prophecies ceased. For some reason, Nehemiah was not there.

Nothing much is known about the personal life of MALACHI, except his name means "MY MESSENGER." And he was. MALACHI proclaimed hard sayings. One hundred years had passed since those who heard him had returned from their seventy-year Chaldean captivity. A Persian governor was their ruler. The TEMPLE had been rebuilt. The worship of the LORD God was a ritual with little-to-no-meaning to many. Their sacrifices were poor and their incense was offered to anybody and to anything.

We should realize that after Malachi put down his pen, no more prophetic words were spoken until the birth of the LORD JESUS CHRIST (Matthew 2:1-2). That time is known as the 400 silent years.

MALACHI SPOKE FOR TRUTH, AGAINST DIVORCE, AND ENCOURAGED TITHING. TRUTH IS A NECESSARY ATTRIBUTE FOR THE BELIEVER (Matthew 19:18). The Old Testament priests were to have the *"law of truth"* in their mouths (Malachi 2:6). The born-again believer is in a "royal priesthood," too (I Peter 2:9). **Today in this "post modernism" age, people practice their own "truth."** Even those who name the Name of Christ "lie," and say it is "truth." Their "truth" may not be your "truth." Someone can tell a lie with a straight face—because it is her "truth." It may be as false as a counterfeit bill, but she says it is true–even if it isn't. *Thou shalt not bear false witness against thy neighbor* (Exodus 20:16) is still in the Bible.

The LORD hates divorce (Malachi 2:14-17). Have you ever wondered why? It behooves us to see "divorce" from God's eyes. I believe God's distaste for "putting away" is because Israel, in the Old Testament, was His "wife." Israel had committed "spiritual" adultery" with other gods over and over again. GOD HATED IT.

In the New Testament, "saved people" are the "BRIDE OF CHRIST." A marriage between a man and a woman is a picture of the union that Jesus Christ had with His "bride" (Ephesians 5:22-33). That "oneness" can never be broken. A Christian cannot lose his or her salvation. When there is a divorce, the "holy union" is broken. The perfect picture of Jesus Christ and His Bride is marred. Did you ever realize that your marriage pictures the spiritual union the believer has with the Lord Jesus Christ? When a divorce occurs, that "picture" is marred. GOD HATES DIVORCE.

WILL A MAN ROB GOD? That surprising question was asked to those who "claim" to love God (Malachi 3:8). What pretense some have, as to their love for HIM. As long as it does not touch our pocket books, we love Him. We would not take a gun and point it at God, demanding money from his treasury. Yet, God says we have done so. How? In tithes and offerings.

It is amazing to me, how some church goers can attend church regularly and never put anything in the offering box. Yet, they enjoy the services. They ask for special prayer. They share their lives with the pastor and fellow-members. In lean times, they ask for "help." Their car is broken, or their rent is due. Yet, when God blesses them financially, they are irregular in "giving."

In truth, they are robbing God. If He was displeased with the Israelites lack of "giving" in MALACHI'S time, how much more is He displeased with us today in this "age of grace"? GOD CHALLENGES US TO PROVE HIM. He promises to "OPEN THE WINDOWS OF HEAVEN WITH UNEXPLAINED BLESSINGS."

THE TRUTH IS, GOD LOVES A CHEERFUL GIVER (II Corinthians 9:7). **ARE YOU ONE?**

"GOD FOR ME"
(Job 23:6, II Corinthians 12:9)
Will He plead against me? No, He will put strength in me.
God is for us in all He allows.
Whatever He allows is all right—always.
What strength is needed for what He allows,
HE PROVIDES.
The Lessons we must learn in our problems and trials is that
HIS GRACE IS SUFFICIENT.
In trials don't ask, "WHY?"
Ask 'WHAT ARE YOU DOING, LORD?" (ggs)

Today's Bible Blessing   *October 1*

Matthew 4:21–Matthew 6:32
WHAT AM I SUPPOSED TO DO?
Matthew 1:20b

"Fear not to take unto thee Mary thy wife . . . "

> *"Now the birth of Jesus Christ was on this wise: When as his mother Mary was espoused to Joseph, before they came together, she was found with child of the Holy Ghost. Then Joseph her husband, being a just man, and not willing to make her a publick example, was minded to put her away privily. But while he thought on these things, behold, the angel of the Lord appeared unto him in a dream, saying, Joseph, thou son of David, fear not to take unto thee Mary thy wife: for that which is conceived in her is of the Holy Ghost. And she shall bring forth a son, and thou shalt call his name JESUS: for he shall save his people from their sins"* (Matthew 1:16-22).

Though God is the author of the first book of the New Testament, a man named Matthew was the writer of the book. He was a tax collector and hated by many. It is interesting to me that a disliked man such as Matthew was used of the Holy Spirit to pen the words describing the birth of the Lord Jesus Christ. Though he was a Jew, he worked for Caesar's government as—what we would call it today—an Internal Revenue agent. Just think, the Holy Spirit came upon a converted tax collector to write down the historical account of Mary and Joseph's pre-nuptial encounter with an angel!

Though an angel named Gabriel informed Mary that she was to be the mother of the Messiah, to be perfectly honest, it was only to Joseph, in Matthew's narrative, who had an angel speak to him on the matter. It was in a dream that THE CARPENTER heard the news (**Matthew 1:20**). We do not read of *Mary's fright* until we come to Luke 1:26-38. Yes, she was frightened! As for Joseph, a godly man, instead of being frightened, HE WAS COMFORTED!

WHAT AN EXCITING *"TIME"* WAS THIS *"FULLNESS OF TIME"*!

> *"BUT WHEN THE FULNESS OF THE TIME WAS COME, GOD SENT FORTH HIS SON, MADE OF A WOMAN, MADE UNDER THE LAW, TO REDEEM THEM THAT WERE UNDER THE LAW, THAT WE MIGHT RECEIVE"* THE ADOPTION OF SONS (Galatians 4:2).

Can you imagine the consternation that was Joseph's, when Mary whispered shyly into his ear, "I am with child." *"The shame of it all!"* was what the young carpenter thought. It brought confusion to his mind! He knew he was not the father, for he had been very careful with Mary. *"How could she do this to me?"* His face was probably hot with embarrassment. How could he have been so blind? Why had he not seen Mary's faults and failures! Had her sweet nature deceived him?

His inner question was, *"What am I supposed to do?"* The law said that she should be stoned! Yet, he cared for Mary. How could he expose her to such ridicule and to such an awful public death? He could not help himself for caring. She was so darling. She was so sweet. She had appeared to be a devoted believer in the LORD God! How could he have been so wrong?

That night–the night that the Angel came to him– Joseph could not sleep. When he finally fell into slumber, his sleep was fitful. He would awaken. He would sleep. He would awaken. He would sleep! Finally, utterly exhausted, he fell into an apparent dream (Matthew 1:20). Always, subconsciously, and without wanting to, he thought of Mary and her baby! *"Who was the father?"* His dreams were fitful. He may have thought, *"Wait until I get my hands on that scoundrel for what he did to my espoused wife!"*

THEN THE ANGEL CAME TO HIM IN A DREAM! Joseph *believed* the angel. He could have sloughed it off as his imagination! Instead, he believed *THE ANGEL OF THE LORD!* Often, when God used an *"ANGEL"* to instruct a person, the person would become frightened. Joseph had no fright of the angel. Instead, he was relieved! Now, he had no fear to take Mary as his lawful wife! He rejoiced to have an explanation of Mary's condition. Joseph believed the angel so EXPLICITLY that he named the boy Jesus (Matthew 1:21). The prophet Isaiah called him "GOD WITH US"–EMMANUEL! (Matthew 1:23; Isaiah 7:14).

THIS ACCOUNT COMFORTS US WHEN WE HAVE UNEXPLAINABLE DISTRESSES!

"WITHIN YOUR CIRCUMSTANCES"
ARE YOU IN DIFFICULT CIRCUMSTANCES?
Are you bowed down trying to live a falsetto above them?
Or are you weighed down beneath their burden?
OR ARE YOU LIVING IN SUBMISSION
TO WHAT HE HAS ALLOWED
AND LIVING IN PEACE
WITH YOUR GOD-ALLOWED CIRCUMSTANCES?
NOT <u>ABOVE</u>. NOT <u>BENEATH</u>. BUT <u>WITHIN</u>.
WITHIN IS WHERE GOD WILL MANIFEST HIMSELF TO YOU
and strengthen and comfort! (ggs)

Matthew 6:33–Matthew 9:20
CONSIDER THYSELF!

Matthew 7:1-3
"Judge not, that ye be not judged. "

How many times have we heard Matthew 7:1 quoted to try to stop someone from pointing out a flaw in another? *"Judge not!"* is thrown at us. Somehow those words are supposed to stop all criticism of another whether justified or not. An action is seen, or a word is spoken; and if an observer declares it is not the right thing to say or do, the *"holier than thou"* person will get a certain look on her face, as she quotes *"JUDGE NOT THAT YE BE NOT JUDGED!"* The person condemned stands there helpless with that Bible verse lingering in her ears.

> *"Judge not, that ye be not judged. For with what judgment ye judge, ye shall be judged: and with what measure ye mete, it shall be measured to you again. And why beholdest thou the mote that is in thy brother's eye, but considerest not the beam that is in thine own eye?"* (See Matthew 7:1:3.)

Strange as it may be *"JUDGE NOT"* is not used when someone is praising another person. An observer could watch a kind action or a good report given concerning another. That same observer may tell a friend about it in an approving manner. When done, the same *"holier than thou"* woman does not get that look on her approving face and declare, *"JUDGE NOT!"* Isn't *"praise"* of an idea or an action "judging"? Jesus said, *"Judge not according to the appearance, but JUDGE RIGHTEOUS JUDGMENT* (John 7:24). In other words, *"Go ahead and 'judge,"* but be sure you are right on the subject!"

Remember who the speaker is in today's passage. It is the LORD JESUS CHRIST Himself! We can review many of His *"judgments"* that He made as He walked this earthly path. In this same chapter in today's reading, Jesus calls a person a *"hypocrite"* who judges another when the *"hypocrite"* himself has MANY or MORE of the SAME FLAWS as the one he is judging (Matthew 7:3). Also in verse six, Jesus told His listeners not to give holy things to *"dogs,"* or *unsaved people.*

In verses nine & ten, Jesus is *"judging"* by asking would a man give his son bread instead of a stone, or would he give his son fish to eat instead of a snake. Later, in verses Matthew 7: 13 & 14, He observes that few go into the *"narrow gate,"* while many walk through the *"wide gate"* on to Hell's boardwalk. Then, in verse fifteen, Jesus declares that *"false"* prophets are not true prophets at all, but are really greedy wolves dressed in beautiful clothing.

Later as Jesus continues His *"judging,"* He notices that good trees bear *"good"* fruit, and that *"bad"* trees do not! (vs. 17) Jesus judges that not everyone who says, *"Lord, Lord,"* will enter The Kingdom of Heaven–only those who do the will of His Father in Heaven (vs. 21). I wonder what the self-righteous woman mentioned above, with the wizened-up face, would say to Jesus if she had been in the same room with Him that day! I can hear her now, pursing up her saccharine smiling lips and saying, *"JUDGE NOT THAT YE BE NOT JUDGED!"*

True, Jesus instructs us to look at ourselves before we start correcting and judging others! Often we forget to do this, it is true. But He does not tell us to walk life's journey with absolutely no discernment whatsoever, like robots without a thought in our heads. The Apostle Paul extorted Christians to judge many times in his letters to them. One time he told the worldly Corinthians to judge *"all things"* (I Corinthians 2:15).

The apostle told the "spiritual believers" in Galatia to judge all things. Yet, they were to live in such a godly way that they should not be judged by any one. *"For who hath known the mind of the Lord, that he may instruct him? But we have the mind of Christ"* (I Corinthians 2:16).

> *"Brethren if a man be overtaken in a fault, ye which are*
> *spiritual, restore such an one in the spirit of meekness;*
> *considering thyself lest thou also be tempted."*
> (Galatians 6:1)

BEFORE JUDGING OTHERS, WE SHOULD POINT OUR FINGERS AT OURSELVES FIRST!

"FAITH IS SUBSTANCE"
FAITH IS NOT A BLIND AND CARELESS ASSENT
TO MATTERS OF LIFE.
FAITH is not a state of mental suspense
with a hope that things may "turn out" to be as the Bible says.
FAITH is the firm persuasion that what God says is so!
Such FAITH makes a Christian independent
of the world in which she is.
It is quite a different world in which the man of FAITH LIVES.
(ggs)

Matthew 9:21–Matthew 11:25
ORDINARY MEN WITH EXTRAORDINARY GIFTS

Matthew 10:1

"He gave them power against unclean spirits . . ."

Today, as we read Matthew 10, we observe that Jesus is choosing his twelve apostles. They were men who helped Jesus establish Christianity in this world. They carried out His wishes after His death, and loved Him as Saviour and LORD! They were willing to die for Him. Before we discover who they are, let us consider their CALL! See MATTHEW 9:37-38:

> *"Then saith he unto his disciples, The harvest truly is plenteous, but the labourers are few; Pray ye therefore the Lord of the harvest, that he will send forth labourers into his harvest."*

Jesus was visiting all the cities and villages. It says in MATTHEW 9:1 that he came to His "own" city. Was His "own" town a place called Nazareth? Anyhow, He healed the man with the palsy and forgave his sins there, too. We're told He knew the thoughts of His critics.

Around this time, JESUS commanded MATTHEW, the author of our book in today's reading, to *"follow"* Him. There is something *"compelling"* in the *"call"* of Jesus! When Jesus calls a person, that person follows (Matthew 9:9). Some people today are questioning whether a person is "called." They say the "need" is the "call." What do you think?

As Jesus was teaching and healing, He was moved with compassion at the needs of the multitudes. They were like a field of wheat ready to be harvested with no one to do the work! He implored those hearing Him that they would pray that THE LORD OF THE HARVEST would send help! *Who is this LORD?* He must be the Heavenly Father!

HELP WAS ON THE WAY!

The LORD OF THE HARVEST answered the prayers of Jesus and those in the multitude who prayed that day! I suppose Matthew was one of them. Immediately, we discover that Jesus called twelve disciples! Twelve were all that Jesus needed. He could have called hundreds; but he only needed twelve. Numbers are not important to Jesus! He needs *faithfulness. Crowds are fickle!* Recently, my husband and I have been criticized because we have a "little" church. We meet in our house like the early Christians did in the New Testament. It is comforting to realize that Jesus chose a "small" group to work with and for Him. Usually, in a large group, there are only a few who do the work!

Let me list the "LABOURERS" who have come to be known as "APOSTLES" or *"sent ones"*! They were *ordinary* men to whom Jesus gave *extraordinary* gifts; and they died *unordinary* deaths. Their *"gifts"* included healing diseases and casting out unclean spirits. The ailments that plagued people in Jesus' day are the same afflictions that people have today.

These *"APOSTLE-LABOURERS"* **preached, too!** Their message was that the Kingdom of Heaven was at hand (Matthew 10:7). Surprisingly, they would have power to raise the dead! If they and their ministry were not received by others, they were to *"keep on keeping on."* THEY WERE ORDINARY MEN WITH AN EXTRA-ORDINARY *"CALL"*!

So, it is similar for you and me today, if we are born-again. We, who are *"ordinary,"* must *"keep on keeping on"* with our *"ordinary"* life and let God—if it pleases Him—to do an *"extra-ordinary"* work of grace in and through us!

In today's reading, we read of the first days of ministry of those *"HARVESTERS"* **called the twelve apostles.** Sometimes they were bold! Sometimes they were cowards! How like some of us! All but one fulfilled his *"call,"* no matter the price to themselves or their families!

"Tradition" **records of the ends of their lives!**
PETER—crucified upside down,
ANDREW—crucified,
JAMES THE GREAT—beheaded,
JOHN—died as an old man,
PHILIP—crucified & stoned,
BARTHOLOMEW—flayed, crucified,
THOMAS–speared,
MATTHEW–stoncd,
JAMES THE LESS–stoned,
THADDAEUS–arrows or javelin,
SIMON the ZEALOT–sawn in half,
JUDAS ISCARIOT–suicide.
HONOR THEIR MEMORIES TODAY!

"IT WILL PASS"
"A trial comes—it will pass.
In a few days or months or years, we shall have forgotten it.
But: The way we meet that trial
Our inner attitude toward it belongs to the things that are eternal."
"ALL THAT GRIEVES US IS BUT FOR A MOMENT.
All that pleases is but for a moment.
Only the eternal is important"
(ggs quotes AMY CARMICHAEL)

Today's Bible Blessing   *October 4*

Matthew 11:26—Matthew 13:30
FOR SELF OR THE SOUL

Matthew 13:5

"Some fell upon stony places, where they had not much earth . . ."

Every time I read Matthew 13:5, I think of a certain woman. The day she came to our church, she had a *"fear"* she would die. Her whole body shook from sobbing! Her shoulders moved up and down with crying. Her face was contorted with grief! She had no husband! Probably, she was in her late forties. I can't remember her name. She had a *"fright"* in her life! Her *"fear"* was real! She thought she had aids! You see, a few months ago, she had been with a man romancing. She really did not know the man. Another friend suggested that he had AIDS! She was scared to death!

This woman was a mother. She had a son. He was her whole life—except when she was committing fornication with strangers. *Her son was in cancer remission.* He looked like he should be in *"middle-school."* Only he did not go to school. Since his illness, she was home-schooling him. Mostly he played video games. He knew nothing about the Bible! She loved him dearly, but not dearly enough to be sexually pure or to teach him God's WORDS! She feared she would die and leave him all alone. He had no other relative but his mother.

I never have met a woman quite like her before. She did not know how to behave in church! She would bring candy and pass it around during the service, as if she were at a ball game. She would burst out with an unrelated comment during the preaching service. She would enter the church room boisterously with loud words—even though the service had started. Pastor Waite and I tried to help her. She needed the LORD!

She kept telling us that a certain pastor, in the past, told her that she was like the *"seed"* that fell on the stony ground! She knew some TRUTH! She was like a house on a poor foundation. We tried to help her. I tried to make her face reality—not only concerning her alleged condition, but also, that her son could decompensate from his remission. Having had a young sister die of cancer, a husband who had cancer years ago and having a long childhood disease myself, as well as a son with a mental illness, I knew the reality of deadly diseases! She would hear nothing of it! Her head was in the sand, as far as from a possible remission was concerned. The *"comfort"* and *"hope"* of the Scriptures meant nothing to her!

Matthew 13:4-6:

"And when he sowed, some seeds fell by the way side, and the fowls came and devoured them up: Some fell upon stony places, where they had not much earth: and forthwith they sprung up, because they had no deepness of earth:

And when the sun was up, they were scorched; and because they had no root, they withered away."

In a few weeks, her blood test was found to be "normal." Her concern for herself and an impending death as well as the possibility of abandoning her son flew out the window. What did she need with church and praying believers? Her need for us was no more! She returned hundreds of dollars-worth of books and Bibles, leaving them on our doorstep. She said she was never coming back again. She scorned me on the telephone and told me that I lived in an *"IVORY TOWER"* with not a problem in my life! **The preacher that told her she was like the "seed" that fell on stony ground was right!**

NO TIME FOR GOD? WHAT FOOLS WE ARE
TO CLUTTER UP OUR LIVES WITH COMMON THINGS
AND LEAVE WITHOUT HEART'S GATE
THE LORD OF LIFE AND LIFE ITSELF–OUR GOD!
(Norman L. Trott)

"HELP US O LORD!
(II Chronicles 14:11; Psalm 57:1; Psalm 3:3)
Help us, O Lord, for we rest in Thee!
God can do big things as easily as He can do the small things.
In the shadow of Thy wings will I make my refuge.
Thou, O Lord are a shield . . . and a lifter up of my head.
He knows when I need a shield from the enemy's dart
and when my head and heart droop. (ggs)

𝒯oday's 𝐵ible 𝐵lessing   𝒪ctober 5
Matthew 13:31–Matthew 15:21
JESUS THE NAZARENE

Matthew 13:57
"A prophet is not without honour, save in his own country . . . and house."

When I went to Bible school many years ago, our **GOSPEL OF MATTHEW BIBLE TEACHER had us students learn what was in every chapter of the book of Matthew.** At that time I was able to give you a bird's eye view of this portion of God's Words with ease. Though I have forgotten much, I have always remembered that Matthew 13 was the chapter devoted to Jesus' parables. As you may remember, *a "parable" is an earthly story with a "heavenly" meaning.*

People in His home town were amazed at Jesus' teaching! They looked at each other in disbelief! *"IS NOT THIS THE*

455

CARPENTER'S SON?" they asked. Isn't He Mary's son? Aren't His brothers James, Joses, Simon, and Judas? He had sisters, too! Mary and Joseph had many children!

Of course, Jesus was NOT born of Joseph! He was the oldest in the family. The oldest child has many responsibilities that the later-born children do not have. Sometimes, it doesn't seem fair, but that is how it is. I was the oldest, too. I am sure Jesus was a very good brother, as well as an excellent carpenter. Alas, His hometown friends thought Jesus' birth was a scandal. The truth was His birth was *a "virgin birth."* Probably, they disbelieved that whole story about His birth, the angels, the shepherds, and the wise men. Later, we read in John 8:41 that some compared their birth to His. They ridiculed Him! They said, *"We be not born of fornication!"*

It is in this Bible passage that we read insightful words: *"A PROPHET IS NOT WITHOUT HONOUR SAVE (except) IN HIS OWN COUNTRY AND IN HIS OWN HOUSE"* (Matthew 13:57). Because of this, Jesus did few mighty works in His home town! Think of the blessings that were missed! Is this true of you and me? HAVE WE BECOME SO *"USED"* TO THE BIBLE THAT WE HAVE FORGOTTEN ITS *"PRESERVATION"*? Even some have forgotten that our Authorized Version translation came from the original *"God-breathed"* HEBREW, ARAMAIC, AND GREEK WORDS. Shame on us! We forget to read and be blessed by those Words.

LET US LOOK AT THE EARTHLY *HOMETOWN* OF OUR SAVIOUR, THE LORD JESUS CHRIST.

The village of NAZARETH is located ten miles from the plain of ESDRAELON. It lies in a basin. So one cannot see its surroundings until one climbs to the edge. Then the view is magnificent! Twenty battlefields are remembered there. Barak's & Gideon's victories! Saul's & Josiah's defeats! Naboth's vineyards were there! Jehu's revenge of Jezebel was there! Mt. Carmel can be seen! That is where fire came down on Elijah's altar! To the east is Jordan's valley & to the west is the Great Sea. Today the city is called *en-NAZIRA.*

DO NOT CONFUSE THE TERM *"NAZARITE"* WITH A "NAZARENE." LET US MAKE IT CLEAR THAT THOSE WHO CAME FROM NAZARETH WERE REFERRED TO AS NAZARENES! A NAZARITE was either a man or woman, who took a special vow not to drink of the fruit of the vine. They let their hair grow for a specific period of time. When they cut it, they offered their hair as a sacrifice to the LORD God. Samson was a NAZARITE from birth and before. I think John the Baptist may have been one—not sure. Nazarites had certain restrictions placed upon them during the time of their vows— like touching a dead body. Some were NAZARITES for life. Some, only for a certain self-imposed period of time. JESUS WAS NOT A NAZARITE!

Jesus grew up in this Galilean town of Nazareth. As an older person, He taught in its synagogue (Matthew 13:54). The village of Nazareth was not well thought of. The *uncultured citizens* had an *odd dialect*. Perhaps Jesus had the same accent. It was an irreligious town—known for its immorality. (Perhaps that is why Mary was received in the community.) We could judge that NAZARETH was no more corrupt than some of our cities and towns today.

Remember Nathaniel? Prior to his introduction to Jesus, Nathaniel asked, in John 1:46: *"Can there any good thing come out of Nazareth?"* Philip ignored his question. Instead, He said, *"COME AND SEE!"*

THAT'S WHAT I SAY TO YOU TODAY.
IF YOU HAVE NEVER MET THE SAVIOUR,
"COME AND SEE!"

"COME UP TO THE PALM TREES"
(Song of Solomon 7:8)
"Earth has no words which can set forth the holy calm
of a soul who is leaning on Jesus."
The nearest place to the gates of Heaven is the Throne of Grace.
Much alone there, you will have much assurance.
Sit thou under the shadow of Jesus.
Come up to the *palm tree and take hold of the branches
(*The palm tree is a type of Jesus.) (ggs)

Today's Bible Blessing   October 6
Matthew 15:22–Matthew 18:12
A TROUBLED MOTHER OF FAITH
Matthew 15:25
"Then came she and worshipped him, saying, Lord, help me."

One day Jesus came to the rocky coastal town of Tyre and the nearby older city of Sidon. Interestingly enough, Tyre was a wealthy place—larger than Jerusalem. Their most celebrated product was the *purple dye* that came from mollusks harvested from the nearby shores.

The mother was from Canaan. Probably she didn't live in either Tyre or Sidon. I think she came from her region expressly to see Jesus. She had a good reason! Her daughter was troubled with *evil spirits*! She knew how Jesus had helped many infirm people—even those with evil spirits. Her *mother-hope* was that He would heal her child! WHEN A MOTHER HAS A SICK CHILD, NO MATTER HOW OLD OR YOUNG THAT CHILD IS, EVERY FIBER OF HER BEING YEARNS FOR HER CHILD! To see her suffer without a cause, to see her frightened at her condition, and to see the pain in her eyes is more than she can bear. *I know.* Who with such a sick *"child"* would not move heaven and earth for her to see Jesus?

Do you wonder about the land of Canaan? We remember that place as we read the Old Testament. This land took in all of Palestine west of the Jordan River. I'm sure you remember the man for whom Canaan was named. He was Ham, son of Noah. After the worldwide flood, followed by Babel's Tower, the people scattered. Did you know that Ham's descendants were of the darker race? This is very interesting to me because I never pictured this distraught mother of Matthew 15:21-28 as being of the darker people, until now. I think she was, don't you?

You may recall that the Canaanites were wicked in their religious practices. Their god of *"thunder"* prevailed with the ungodly worship of Baal, as well as sinful obeisance to three sex goddesses. This was the religious background of the distraught mother. She crossed her line of *"faith"* to see Jesus. Many people today have fears to try a *different religion.* When the need was so great in the heart of the lost sinner, this mother stepped across her familiar line of belief to see Jesus. Psalm 34:38 says: "O TASTE AND SEE THAT THE LORD IS GOOD!"

"My daughter is grievously vexed with a devil," she cried to Jesus. Strange as it may seem, He answered her not a word! Really, his disciples had HAD IT with her! They probably wondered what this kind of woman was doing near the Master! They said, *"Send her away!"* Jesus' Words rebuked! He did not send her away. My, were they surprised!

Then the woman came closer to Jesus. *She worshipped Him.* How does one *"worship"* the LORD out on the street? I don't know exactly. All I know is in her heart, she loved Him. In her manner, she reverenced Him. And in her body language, she bowed to Him in prayer.

Then Jesus made a strange statement. At least it is strange to us; but it was not to the woman. She understood. He said that it was not proper to give good food to a *dog.* She replied, *"Yes, but the dogs are permitted to lick up the crumbs from the floor under the table."* In truth, Jesus was not talking about literal *"dogs."* He was speaking of her as an *outcast* to the Jewish people. She knew what He meant. She let Him know that any little thing He could do to help her daughter would be appreciated. It did not have to be much. Just a small blessing! She knew the smallest deed from the Saviour was better than a large act from a mere mortal. As the saying goes, and it is true, *"little is much when God is in it!"*

Dear Jesus! He looked at her and said, *"O woman, great is thy faith: be it unto thee even as thou wilt!"* It just took a word from the Son of Man! It just took the faith of a daughter of Ham! The Bible says in Matthew 15:28: *And her daughter was made whole from that very hour!*

Another verse in today's reading is found in Matthew 18:11: FOR THE SON OF MAN IS COME TO SAVE THAT

WHICH WAS LOST! Jesus proved his mission with the woman of Canaan. If anyone was "lost," she was!

Did you know that this verse is missing in the NEW INTERNATIONAL VERSION? As well as other versions, too!

> *"TRUST"*
> The future is not yet ours.
> Perhaps it will never be.
> If it comes, it may come wholly different
> from what we have foreseen.
> Let us shut our eyes then to that which God has hidden from us
> and keeps in reserve in the treasuries of His own counsels.
> Let us worship without seeing.
> Let us be silent.
> Let us abide in peace and trust.
> (Francois Fenelon, ggs)

Today's Bible Blessing   *October 7*

Matthew 18:13–Matthew 20:32
FORGIVENESS IS THE KEY

Matthew 18:21

"How oft shall my brother sin against me, and I forgive him?"

We are going to look into a subject that is often controversial and difficult. It is the subject of *FORGIVENESS!* Peter asks Jesus *our* question in Matthew 18:21: *"HOW OFT SHALL MY BROTHER SIN AGAINST ME, AND I FORGIVE HIM?"* Thinking himself most magnanimous he suggested *seven* times! To Peter's surprise, and without hesitation, Jesus answered, *"FOUR HUNDRED NINETY TIMES!"*

Then Jesus gave an illustration of His "seventy-times-seven forgiveness formula." There was a king's servant who owed the ruler about ten million dollars. He could not pay it! He was frantic! Out of the kindness of his heart, the king forgave his servant the entire debt! WHAT FORGIVENESS!

Then a fellow-servant owed $17.00 to the "forgiven" servant! Instead of remembering the forgiveness granted him by the king, the servant threw his fellow-servant into prison! When the king heard of such unforgiveness, he had the ungrateful servant thrown into prison, too. Then Jesus looked at Peter and said, in Matthew 18:35: *"So likewise shall my heavenly Father do also unto you, if ye from your hearts forgive not everyone his brother their trespasses."* WHAT A MOUTHFUL TO *SWALLOW!*

Later, when Jesus was in Judea, the Pharisees decided to *test* Him. They thought the *"divorce & remarriage"* controversy would be a good trap. They questioned, *"Is it lawful for a man to divorce his wife for every cause?"* What a controversial question! Immediately Jesus asked them if they had read Moses' law. (Read the passage again and see Jesus' answer *"except for fornication."*) My purpose today is to discuss FORGIVENESS!

The *root* of couples getting *divorced* is that ONE OR BOTH OF THEM WILL NOT *"FORGIVE."* Often times, one partner wants a *"new"* experience with a *"new"* person. On the other hand, sometimes neither one will let himself or herself be forgiven! Marriage is the hardest alliance of any partnership ever thought of or conceived! Staying married takes the skill of a brilliant craftsman. Marriage is work! Let's face it! No matter what people say, TWO SEPARATE PEOPLE ARE TWO SEPARATE PEOPLE. It takes years of *"living"* for two people to get the *"hang"* of what they promised in their marriage vows when they agreed *"in honor preferring one another."*

Because the truth is that each mate is thinking wrongly. He thinks that it is "in honor, you prefer me first, what I think, and what I say first!" Instead the attitude should be, "I will honor you, and I will prefer you and your opinions and words above mine." Because this is almost impossible, JESUS SAID FOR CHRISTIANS TO FORGIVE SEVENTY TIMES SEVEN!

It is when couples will not forgive *"Jesus' way"* that unforgiveness and bitterness get a foothold in every area of their lives. Then, often, they find themselves in the divorce court! They are exactly like the king's servant who would not forgive his fellow-servant!

Previously Jesus had answered Peter's question about *"forgiveness"* (Matthew 18:15-20). He explained how people who are a part of a church fellowship with disagreements should behave. He said that if a Christian does or says something wrong against you, go to that Christian, and tell the person what is bothering you. The offending person may be completely unaware that you are offended!

Jesus did not say go tell your OTHER church friends that you have been offended! When that happens, Jesus' *"formula for forgiveness"* breaks down! The conversation should be between two people only! Then Jesus said that IF you are not heard by that one person, then, and only then, do you tell *one or two* other persons. You take that one or two *other* persons to the offender and see if things can be worked out. If that fails to bring forgiveness, then take the matter before the church. In my opinion, this should be avoided as much as possible. Church splits often happened after the third step. If the offender does not listen, treat him or her as a wicked tax collector!

Jesus did not mean for Christians to be running to each other over small matters that the Christian cannot get over on his own between himself and his Lord. A Christian should have a *"forgiving heart attitude!"* He should not be ready to fight over every matter. This is how *"church splits"* come. *"Mountains are made out of molehills!"*

FORGIVENESS BEGINS IN THE HEART.
RENEWED FELLOWSHIP SHOULD BE THE GOAL!

"ABANDON YOURSELF
TO HIS CARE & GUIDANCE,
AS A SHEEP IN THE CARE OF A SHEPHERD"
Trust Him utterly.
No matter that you may seem to yourself
to be in the very midst of a desert,
with nothing green about you inwardly or outwardly,
and you may think you will have to make a long journey
before you can get into green pastures.
"And the LORD shall guide thee continually,
and satisfy thy soul in drought, and make fat thy bones:
and thou shalt be like a watered garden,
and like a spring of water, whose waters fail not." (Isaiah 58:11)
Our shepherd will turn that very place where you are
into green pastures, for He has power to make the desert rejoice
and blossom as a rose.
(ggs: from H. W. Smith's DAILY STRENGTH BOOK, page 195)

Today's Bible Blessing   *October 8*

Matthew 20:33—Matthew 22:37
THE SON OF DAVID & A DONKEY
Matthew 21:2

"Ye shall find an ass tied, and a colt . . . bring them to me."

What do we know about the writer of this book? We know his name is Matthew and he was an apostle. Even though Matthew was Jewish and the son of a man named ALPHAEUS, he was not well liked by his own Jewish people. Why? He was a tax collector! Another name for his profession was a PUBLICAN! Often he was called LEVI, having been named after his grandfather (Luke 5:27). His home was in CAPERNAUM near LAKE GENNESARET. Many of the residents were fishermen. The Romans set up a customhouse there which was Matthew's place of business.

It was while he was sitting at his tax table that Jesus saw him, inviting him to FOLLOW Him. Maybe he knew Jesus previously, I don't know. Maybe he had watched Jesus minister and heal the sick. Because of this, Matthew's heart must have leaned toward the Saviour, for he immediately left his work and followed

Jesus. I wonder what the bystanders thought when they saw their hated tax man stand up, leave his money and important records in his office, and follow Jesus. Who is this Jesus Who could call this businessman using only two words—*"FOLLOW ME"*?

As we read about Jesus in the gospels, we are struck with the fact that He is a compassionate man! Two blind men begged Him to heal them! Wouldn't you beg Jesus to heal you if you were blind? They had heard of His miracles. They did not want to be left out of the *"great healing"* from the compassionate Jesus! Notice Matthew 20:31b: *"Have mercy on us, O Lord, thou Son of David!"* Notice several things about that declaration. They knew He was a man of *"mercy!"* *"MERCY"* IS NOT GETTING SOMETHING YOU DO DESERVE!

Those sightless men knew they did not deserve His healing, but they asked anyhow. That is how it is with us sometimes. We know we do not deserve a blessing in a certain area, yet, we ask. We pray and hope that God will grant our petition. The blind men called Him *"Lord."* Though they could not see Him, they knew He was *"over"* them in authority. He was more authoritative than they. He was like their *"Master."* He was their *"Lord"*! Notice— they called Him *"Son of David."* Who told them that He was of the line of David? Was it His kingly manner? Was it His composure in crowds? Was it His kindness and compassion? All I know is that Jesus touched their eyes and they saw immediately! What a miracle!

In Chapter 21, we see that Jesus, and those walking with him, were approaching Jerusalem. Probably they could see the *Golden Gate* looming ahead of them. Soon they would walk through that archway to meet the multitude. He asked two of his disciples to go into a village and find a burro for him to ride. It wasn't that Jesus could not walk. It wasn't that Jesus was too tired that He wanted a donkey to ride.

It was because Jesus knew that He should enter Jerusalem with the pomp of a KING, and with the command presence of a potentate. He had prophecies to fulfill. Had not Zechariah 9:9 directed this moment?

> *"Rejoice greatly, O daughter of Zion; shout, O daughter of Jerusalem: behold, thy King cometh unto thee: he is just, and having salvation; lowly, and riding upon an ass, and upon a colt the foal of an ass."*

What must it have been like that day for the donkey and the young colt? One of my sons used to tell me that if he had been with Jesus that day, he would have wanted to be the *donkey* to carry the Saviour on his back. The crowds cheered! The donkey kept walking. Garments and branches were spread on the ground. Its hooves walked on them carefully.

Children called out in their young childish voices, *"HOSANNA! HOSANNA!"* Why, they called Jesus *"the Son of*

David!" Yes, He came in the Name of the Lord! They cried out, "HOSANNA IN THE HIGHEST!" The question was asked, *"WHO IS THIS?"* And if the donkey could have talked, like Baalim's burro, he would have answered with ☫ all the people. **"THIS IS JESUS THE PROPHET OF NAZARETH OF GALILEE!"**

"PRAYER & PRAISE"
BREVITY!
Wordy prayers are windy prayers!
BE DEFINITE!
"Nothing can dispel the Spirit of gloom from a Christian
than the cultivation of gratitude and praise.
This will cheer and encourage fellow Christians." (copied)
"Lord, Thou knowest all things;"
even this precious truth comforts and leads us to trust Him more.
(John 21:15-18)
(ggs)

𝒯𝑜𝑑𝑎𝑦'𝑠 𝓑𝑖𝑏𝑙𝑒 𝓑𝑙𝑒𝑠𝑠𝑖𝑛𝑔   𝒪𝑐𝑡𝑜𝑏𝑒𝑟 9

Matthew 22:38—Matthew 24:37
HYPOCRITES TO THE CORE?

Matthew 23:28

"Within ye are full of hypocrisy and iniquity."

One of the things that we can say about Jesus is that He was forthright in His speech! Except, of course, when He talked in parables. Then His words could not be understood clearly by those around Him. One reason was that often His hearers refused to understand because of the hardness of their hearts; but for those who wanted to know what the Master was saying, His words were crystal clear and meaningful after He explained them.

So in today's reading in Matthew 23:13-29, we catch a glimpse of our LORD'S anguish and despair with the scribes and Pharisees of His day. They were the religious Jewish leaders. They should have known who He was! *"WOE,"* He said to them over and over again. In fact, He uttered such verbal grief at least eight times in this passage! It is a wonder that those proud men stood there and took it.

Jesus called them "HYPOCRITES" *(vs. 13, 14, 15, 23, 25, 27, 29)*, *"BLIND GUIDES"* (vs. 16, 24), *"FOOLS,"* and *"BLIND"* (vs. 19, 26). They *"appear righteous"* (vs. 28). Their forefathers killed the prophets (vs. 31, 34). He said they were *"serpents"* and a *"generation of vipers"* (vs. 33)! CAN YOU BELIEVE SUCH HOLY BOLDNESS?

The *"scribes"* in this passage were *"lawyers."* They were experts in, as well as teachers of, the Mosaic law. Recall the *"lawyer"* who asked Jesus which commandment was greatest in Matthew 22:35-36. According to *The New Unger's Bible Dictionary*, the *Pharisees* were given their name by those who observed their ways, calling them *"separatists."* That seems to be the meaning of the word, *"Pharisee."*

The Pharisees were very particular about separating themselves from uncleanness—not only from the heathen but from certain unclean Israelites! They called themselves *Haberim* (*associates*). THEY ASSOCIATED THEMSELVES WITH THE LAW AND AGAINST HELLENISM! The Hellenists were the Jews (and others) who spoke the Greek language and observed some of the Greek customs, but were not Greeks by birth.

LET US LOOK AT JESUS' EIGHT WOES TO THE PHARISEES & SCRIBES!

- They closed the KINGDOM OF HEAVEN; didn't go in themselves, kept others out (vs. 13).
- They took advantage of *widows*, and made long pretentious prayers (vs. 14).
- They went around the world to convert a proselyte, yet *both* are on the way to Hell! (See verse 15.)
- They esteemed gold and gifts (the material things) above the spiritual things. The temple was the house of God and the altar was the place of giving to God (vs. 16-22).
- They tithed their insignificant herbs (*mint, anise, & cumin*); but neglected to show *judgment, mercy, & faith* to others. They strained at a gnat and swallowed a camel (vs. 23-24).
- They cleaned the cup's outside, but ignored that within the cup—*extortion and excess* (vs. 25).
- They were as whited tombs—beautiful on the outside, but full of dead men's bones and corruption (vs. 27).
- They built memorial tombs for dead prophets; yet they will persecute, kill, and crucify the living prophets (vs. 29-35).

HAVE YOU NOTICED HOW STRONG JESUS WAS IN CONDEMNING THE PHARISEES AND SCRIBES? THEY WERE HYPOCRITES TO THE CORE!

He did not mince words! Some people would say that He was not *"loving"* at all. Yes, they were correct. The truth was, as he pronounced His WOES, He did not sound like *"love"* or even "compassion!"

Jesus' words and attitude, when speaking to them, were *"frightening!"* words—as well as *"rude"* ones! Jesus had *"had it"* with these men! They were all show! *It was "me, me, me"!* They wanted the best synagogue seats! They wanted to be called

"*Rabbi*" so people would notice them! They exalted themselves and knew nothing of "*humility.*" Sometimes harshness is necessary, even with those we love. (WARNING: DON'T OVERDO IT!) It is evident that Jesus cared for them. He cried over them in Matthew 23:37:

"HOW OFTEN WOULD I HAVE GATHERED THY CHILDREN TOGETHER, EVEN AS A HEN GATHERETH HER CHICKENS UNDER HER WINGS, AND YE WOULD NOT."

WE SHOULD EXAMINE OURSELVES TO SEE HOW SINCERE WE REALLY ARE!

"TIME IS SHORT"
(Romans 8:29)
Does it seem that in these later years,
God is dealing with us more sternly?
If so, it is because our time is short,
and there is not much time to rub off the rough edges
to transform us into the image of His Son.
HE MAY COME TODAY
OR HE MAY LET US SLEEP IN DEATH.
THEN, IT WILL BE TOO LATE TO TRANSFORM US!
Pleasing time is now! (ggs)

Today's Bible Blessing   *October 10*
Matthew 24:38–Matthew 26:25
A CONSPIRACY FOR DEATH

Matthew 26:4
"That they might take Jesus by subtilty and kill him"

Why was it that the chief priests and the scribes conspired together to kill Jesus? (See Matthew 26:3.) What exactly had Jesus done or said to cause such a desire for Him to be dead? What made Judas Iscariot, one of Jesus' twelve apostles, decide to deliver Him unto them? As I think about it, it is rather a mystery to me! I wonder if the speeches that Jesus had made on the Mount of Olives are to blame for such hatred? What do you think? (See Matthew 24 & 25.)

What had He said to bring on such contempt? For one thing—Jesus said the Temple would be destroyed. That would make any Jew angry! He said many would come saying they were "*CHRIST*" when they were not. He must have been speaking of the signs of the times before the second phase of the *SECOND COMING OF CHRIST.* That would be when "*NATION SHALL RISE AGAINST NATION.*" Jesus said that would be *the beginning of "sorrows"* (Matthew 24:8). Then Jesus commented on DANIEL'S PROPHECIES and *THE ABOMINATION OF DESOLATION* (Matthew 24:15).

At that time there would be false Christs, false prophets, and the GREAT TRIBULATION would erupt! That would be when He—the SON OF MAN—would come in the clouds with power and great glory! No one will know, said Jesus, when that day will come. Only His Father in Heaven knows.

SAYING THAT GOD WAS HIS FATHER ANGERED THE JEWS! It would be as *THE DAYS OF NOAH* when the Son of Man comes! All this preaching about the future was too much for the CHIEF PRIESTS and THE SCRIBES! Even CAIAPHAS, the HIGH PRIEST got into the act! Evidently, it was too much for JUDAS ISCARIOT, too!

WHAT IT WAS THAT TURNED PERFECTLY NORMAL RELIGIOUS LEADERS INTO UNREASONABLE MURDER-ERS, I AM NOT SURE; BUT ALL THREE GROUPS WANTED JESUS' LIFE TERMINATED!

Jesus knew all of this conspiracy! He knew every-thing, for He is *"God incarnate."* He permitted a woman to pour precious ointment on his head. He accepted that adulation! Judas Iscariot thought it a waste. Jesus said she was preparing His body for burial. The meaning of His prophetic statement went over their heads. They were oblivious to the fact that they would soon become a part of the most dramatic event in history.

Soon the HOLY SON OF GOD would be sacrificed for the sins of the world! All they could think of were financial matters. Do not condemn them! We are the same! SOMETIMES MONEY MATTERS CONSUME OUR THOUGHTS! *"How will we pay this bill and that debt?"* All the while, God is about to do a good work in us for our future benefit!

The disciples questioned Jesus. They wondered where He would want to keep the Passover. He said there would be a man in the city who would welcome them into His house for the FEAST. All twelve of them sat down to eat at the table. Probably they had the regular Passover meal. It was the same kind of Passover food that had been eaten in Moses' day.

After eating, Jesus made a startling statement. He said, *"One of you shall betray me!"* This was a surprise! Who would do such a thing? One man knew. Pretending, he said with the others, *"Master, is it I?"* He knew it was he! Had not he, Judas, been paid *thirty pieces of silver* to identify Jesus for death?

As the meal came to an end, Jesus predicted His death: *"It is written, I will smite the shepherd and the sheep of the flock shall be scattered abroad"* (Matthew 26:31).

Peter objected to such talk. Peter claimed he would never stumble because of Jesus. But Jesus contradicted him and said, *"This night before the cock crow, thou shalt deny me thrice."*

IN TIME, PETER WOULD REMEMBER JESUS' WORDS. SOON THE SAVIOUR WOULD FULFILL THEM.

466

"OBEY GOD! OBEY HIS WORDS"

As a young woman, I was impressed by a great evangelist's teaching. He taught that a woman should obey her husband no matter what he commanded. Also the evangelist said that children were to obey their parents, even if it was contrary to God and their conscience.

By God's grace, my husband never required anything of me or the children contrary to Scripture. Years later, I found I had been following a man's teaching and had not read the Bible itself.

Every woman and child stands naked before God, to obey Him. A husband and father is not an intermediator. Women are to submit to their husbands, and the children to their fathers as long as they do not contradict God's Words.

THE ORDER IS GOD FIRST!

(ggs)

Today's Bible Blessing　　　　　　　　　　*October 11*

Matthew 26:26–Matthew 27:35
LORD IS IT I?

Matthew 26:24

"Woe unto that man by whom the Son of man is betrayed!"

JESUS AND THE TWELVE HAD JUST OBSERVED THE PASSOVER IN THE HOUSE OF AN UNNAMED FRIEND. *It had been a traumatic time for all of them.* Jesus spoke of His body being broken for them at Calvary. HE WOULD BE THE PASSOVER LAMB. I am not sure the disciples understood.

Judas Iscariot was there! Perhaps he understood more than any of the others. He knew the chief priests and elders were after Jesus. In fact, Judas had made plans to betray Jesus that very night. It was to JUDAS that thirty pieces of silver had been given. No doubt Judas had that silver in his money bag at his side, too. He could hear it jingle as he walked. Every time he changed his position, he could sense the silver coins rub up against each other. It was *"blood money."*

So when Judas asked, *"Master, (not "Lord") is it I?"* Jesus declared, "ONE OF YOU SHALL BETRAY ME." Both Jesus and Judas knew the answer. Once again Jesus reiterated in Matthew 26:24:

"THE SON OF MAN GOETH AS IT IS WRITTEN OF HIM: BUT WOE UNTO THAT MAN BY WHOM THE SON OF MAN IS BETRAYED! IT HAD BEEN GOOD FOR THAT MAN IF HE HAD NOT BEEN BORN!"

I have been to GETHSEMANE. At least it was the place where many feel that Jesus prayed the night He was betrayed. I REMEMBER THE OLIVE TREES. We were told that those trees were the same trees that were in the garden during Christ's time. Now they weren't the *exact trees*, but they were *"relatives"* of the roots and off-shoots of those early olives of Jesus' day. *We learned that olive trees live to be hundreds of years old.* I REMEMBER THE OLIVE PRESS. How fitting that Jesus, who would be emotionally pressed beyond measure, would pray near that press. He, too, would be pressed & wounded!

In my mind's eye, I could picture Jesus kneeling, at the foot of one of those gnarled trees, praying to His Father in Heaven. As droplets of blood fell like perspiration from His brow He prayed, *"Not as I will, but as thou wilt."* Ahead of Him was death! GETHSEMANE COMMENCED HIS AGONY!

HIS WOULD BE NO ORDINARY DEATH! Besides the cruelty of a crucifixion—all its suffering and humiliation—JESUS WOULD BE MADE SIN! No one ever had done that before—or could have done that. *The sin of the world would be upon Him!* For this *"death"* was the *"death"* of the *SON OF GOD* Who had been made flesh to die for the sin of the whole world! He was born to die for you and me—our *"Substitute"*!

PRAYER TIME WAS OVER! Betrayal was coming! Preparing for the worst, Jesus announced in verse 46: *"HE IS AT HAND THAT DOTH BETRAY ME!"* AS JESUS WAS SPEAKING, A MULTI-TUDE OF MEN, CARRYING TORCHES AND STAFFS, PUSHED THEIR WAY INTO THE GARDEN! Soldiers with spears and staves came closer to Jesus. It was a dreadful sight!

Stepping out from this angry mob came JUDAS ISCARIOT! With a *devilish* look in his eyes, Judas walked right up to Jesus. Sarcastically, he spoke: *"HAIL MASTER!"* It was then that he kissed Him. That was his signal to the soldiers for action! Even though it was night, they knew they had the right man!

I think of men and woman today who say they are followers of the Lord Jesus Christ. They claim to have received Him as personal Saviour. They make *a pretense* of loving Jesus. They read *His Words* often. They attend church regularly. They donate money to its financial needs. Yet, *one day*—in a *time of temptation*—greater than they can endure—THEY BETRAY JESUS! Are you numbered among them?

The crowd thinks their sin is right. It is not! They steal! They lie! They curse God with their mouths! They commit adultery! They *think* their actions are fine! It *"feels"* good! Blinded by Satan's lie, he deceives them! YES, THEY ENJOY THEIR *"THIRTY PIECES OF SILVER"*! Then one day—after the *euphoria of the sin* passes—they awake. TOO LATE THE DEED WAS DONE! THE SIN HAD BEEN COMMITTED! Throwing the *"silver* coins" on the floor of the

temple cannot make it right. The betrayal kiss will not go away! REMORSE FOLLOWS! YES, REPENTANCE CAN BRING FORGIVE-NESS; BUT IT CAN NEVER REMOVE THE SCAR OF PAST SIN! **GOD FORGIVES AND FORGETS; BUT PEOPLE REMEMBER! HE THAT THINKETH HE STANDETH, TAKE HEED!** (I Corinthians 10:12)

"A PRICELESS WOMAN"
(Proverbs 31:25-26)
"Strength and honor are her clothing."
Rejoicing is her stance.
Do I present such a person as the woman of Proverbs 31?
"She openeth her mouth with wisdom,
and in her tongue is the law of kindness." (ggs)

Today's Bible Blessing   *October 12*
Matthew 27:36–Mark 1:34
THE KING OF THE JEWS

Matthew 27:42
"He saved others; himself he cannot save!"

There they were—the soldiers—sitting on the ground watching Jesus die on the cross. How many other crucifixions had they seen? Death on the cross was common to these men. They had become calloused and indifferent to such suffering. There were others being crucified that day. In fact, two more hung there—one on each side of the man called *"JESUS, THE KING OF THE JEWS."* In fact, He had a sign posted above His head. It read so in Greek, Latin, and Hebrew! Yes, this person was more distinct from any other they had ever crucified. And they had crucified many.

It was true that Pilate, the Roman governor, found nothing wrong with the man. It was true that He was a bit different! He said almost nothing in His defense. Yet, He did agree that He was the *"KING OF THE JEWS"*! That was strange—as Israel had not had a king for hundreds of years.

When it came to this Jesus, the soldiers observed that the *Jews were most radical.* They had released a *notorious prisoner* so they could crucify this Jesus! They were angry with Jesus because He said He was the equal with God. Also, He called Himself the *MESSIAH!* The Jews considered that blasphemy! Even Pilate's wife could not sleep because of this man. Pilate's wife suffered many things in a dream because of this (Matthew 27:19). Pilate washed his hands, declaring himself *innocent* of the blood of Jesus (Matthew 27:24).

469

That day, the soldiers noticed more than the usual amount of jeering from people passing by this One who called Himself *THE KING OF THE JEWS.* People sneered! They jeered! They wagged their heads and pointed their fingers at Him. In Matthew 27:40 they called out, saying: *"If thou be the Son of God, come down from the cross!"* Odd—but the chief priests, with the scribes and elders, came by. That was unusual! They, too, taunted Him, scorning that He said He could destroy the temple and rebuild it in three days (vs. 40). They mocked (vs. 42): *"He saved others; himself he cannot save!"* It was quite a scene!

The soldiers remembered the relentless beatings that were given Jesus. That was prior to his being nailed to the cross. Some of their fellow-solders stripped Him naked. That was in the governor's hall. There was laughter and vulgar man-talk directed at Jesus! In fact, a band of soldiers gathered around Him jeering. Mockingly, they called Him *"THE KING OF THE JEWS!"*

They threw a scarlet robe over Jesus' shoulders. It could have been Pilate's! They wove sharp thorns into a crown for His head. They bowed in pretense, feigning royal reverence. They spit on Him. They pounded Jesus on the head using a hollow reed. Every blow forced the thorn-crown deeper into His skull and brow. *"It was barbaric!"*

At the sixth hour of their watch, the soldiers were extremely frightened! All about them was *darkness,* as if it were night! But it wasn't! Three hours later, in the midst of the darkness, Jesus cried loudly, *"MY GOD, MY GOD WHY HAST THOU FORSAKEN ME?"* The soldiers were frightened! Never had they experienced such anguish! In sympathy, someone ran to Jesus' cross, offering Him a sponge of vinegar to drink. Others just watched, speculating, *"Let's see if God will rescue Him!"*

It was then, that Jesus cried out! His voice was loud! It was strong! Matthew does not record what Jesus said, but Dr. Luke does. In Luke 23:46, Jesus cried out: *"FATHER, INTO THY HANDS I COMMEND MY SPIRIT!"* At that moment the veil in THE TEMPLE, which hung between the Holy Place and the Holy of Holies, tore in two. It ripped from the top to the bottom. At the same time there was an earthquake! Everything shook wildly! Rocks violently split in two! It was frightening!

More frightening, than the earthquake, was that the graves opened after resurrection of the Lord Jesus Christ. Out from those yawning graves, bodies of the dead saints came to life. Those *once-dead people* walked around Jerusalem alive and well in rotting grave clothes! People recognized them! Those that had been dead for years talked and walked. Some who had just died the night before probably kissed their loved ones. All this was unexplainable to the soldiers! It was one of the most fearful days in their lives!

The Centurion and the one hundred soldiers under his command feared greatly. In Matthew 27:54c, the only conclusion they could come to, and it was the right one, was **"TRULY THIS WAS THE SON OF GOD!"**

"OCTOBER 7, 1979"
(Psalm 91:11)
Today we wrecked our Dodge Motor Home.
It was a total loss. Value: $20,000!
We were able to walk out of it alive, after an instantaneous skid
and a turn-over into a water-filled ditch.
GOD MUST HAVE SOMETHING FOR US TO DO IN OUR OLDER
YEARS TO HAVE SPARED OUR LIVES.
Thank you Lord for the assurance that all was well with my soul,
as I knew I was facing death,
seeing the crash coming! (ggs)

Today's Bible Blessing   *October 13*

Mark 1:35–Mark 4:11
THE CALL OF GOD!

Mark 1:7
"There cometh one mightier than I after me . . ."

Now we find ourselves in the gospel of Mark. Perhaps you would be interested to know that the first three gospels in the New Testament, MATTHEW, MARK, & LUKE, are called *THE SYNOPTIC GOSPELS.* Each writer of these gospels has written about Jesus Christ in one broad view of their life with Him. John, in his gospel, reveals Jesus from a different viewpoint. As you may remember, while the gospel of Matthew shows us the Lord Jesus Christ as the *"Messiah of Israel,"* the gospel of Mark lets us see Him as a *"Servant."*

The writer of this gospel was John Mark. He was the son of a woman named Mary who was the sister of BARNABAS. His mother had a house in Jerusalem (Acts 12:12). We don't know his father's name. Perhaps he had died. They were Jewish. Perhaps their church met in their home, for often they had prayer meetings there. Probably the Apostle Peter introduced Mark to Jesus Christ, for he calls Mark *"his son"* (I Peter 13:13).

Young Mark accompanied the Apostle Paul and his Uncle Barnabas on a missionary journey (Acts 12:25, 13:5); but he left them in PERGA to go back home to Jerusalem. THIS DISPLEASED PAUL! So when Barnabas assumed Mark would go on Paul's second missionary journey, Paul put his foot down and said, *"No!"* There was such a division between the two older men that they never went on a *"mission trip"* together again.

In time, young John Mark mellowed. Later, Paul spoke kindly of Mark—sometimes referring to him as *"Marcus"* (Colossians 4:10; Philemon 24). During Paul's second Roman imprisonment, he asked Timothy to bring Mark with him. Paul wanted to see him. In fact, Paul wrote that Mark was profitable to him. It is encouraging for you and for me to observe how Mark matured in life and in his spiritual walk. Now Mark could be used of the Lord. Perhaps his youthful selfishness and restlessness had gotten in the way of his usefulness in the past. In fact, his growth in grace had developed to such an extent that the Holy Spirit used him to pen this gospel.

The GOSPEL OF MARK begins with a reminder that God sent a *"messenger"* to cry out, *"Prepare ye the way of the Lord, make His paths straight."* That *forth-teller* was *JOHN THE BAPTIST* whom we will see, was really the last of the Old Testament prophets. He did *"preach the baptism of repentance for the remission of sins"* (Mark 1:4).

A few years ago, when we were in Israel, my husband and I saw the Jordan River. It was not a large swelling body of water, but, at the time, a quiet small stream. Jesus was baptized by John the Baptist there. That was a time of identification for Jesus with the Holy Spirit and His Heavenly Father. That day, as John lifted Jesus out of the water, THE HEAVENS OPENED! We read, in Mark 1:10-11: the HOLY SPIRIT descended, like *a dove,* from that open space. *He rested on Jesus.* SUDDENLY *A VOICE* CAME FROM THE FATHER! It said, *"THOU ART MY BELOVED SON, IN WHOM I AM WELL PLEASED!"*

I do not know if everyone saw that *"dove-like"* descent of the Holy Spirit that day; or if anyone, but Jesus and John, heard the voice of God! But, I do know THAT WAS THE DAY THAT JESUS BEGAN HIS EARTHY MINISTRY! IT WAS A CONFIRMATION FROM HEAVEN! TO THE WORLD THAT *JESUS WAS THE SON OF GOD!*

Because Jesus was baptized in the Jordan River, many tourists wanted to be baptized there, too. In fact, there is a special place for *"baptisms"* where visitors can go down into the Jordan and be immersed. This seems strange to us as *"baptism"* and *"water"* have nothing to do with *"salvation."* All the water in the world will not *"save"* a person's soul.

***"Baptism"* is a sign that a person, who has accepted Jesus Christ, wants to be identified with Him.** It is a picture that a believer has identified himself or herself with Christ's death, burial, and resurrection. The Bible says in Romans 6:4:

> *"Therefore we are buried with him by baptism into death: that like as Christ was raised up from the dead by the glory of the Father, even so we also should walk in newness of life."*

WHAT A REMARKABLE BEGINNING!
JOHN BAPTIZING JESUS AND JESUS' MINISTRY BEGINS!

"BE YE SEPARATE"
(Ephesians 3:19)

"Too much association with the world hinders our spiritual life because it tends to bring us under the influence of the visible and temporal." (ANDREW MURRAY)

We have for our hearts the invisible and the Eternal.

We see the "unseen," and know that "which passeth knowledge."

(ggs)

Today's Bible Blessing　　　　　　　　　　*October 14*

Mark 4:12–Mark 6:12
COME OUT,
THOU UNCLEAN SPIRIT!

Mark 4:37

"There arose a great storm of wind, and the waves beat into the ship."

Today's reading really touched my heart! It brought tears to my eyes. I could feel them swelling within me. They were a different kind of tears! They did not come in sobs of distress or in streams of sorrow. Yet, they encompassed me! They welled up within my heart and surfaced in my eyes. *They hurt my inner soul!* They were not of *"pain"* or *"self-pity."* They did not require a handkerchief or a wipe of the hand; they just rested in my eyes and would not come out!

We read in Mark 4:37: *And there arose a great storm of wind, and the waves beat into the ship so that it was now full!* Jesus had a full day of teaching and healing. He was tired. He and his friends embarked into a boat. There were other little boats in Galilee that day too. Being tired, Jesus fell asleep in the stern of the boat. How very human was the Son of God!

Suddenly a storm rocked the boat. Storms come up suddenly on the Galilee. The Bible says that the storm beat so strongly on the little craft that the waves overwhelmed the vessel. They rolled into the boat and it began to fill it up with the sea. The Bible says *"it was "full."* Probably the disciples bailed out the water as fast as they could. They were used to the sea—but this storm was an unusual one! Frightened, they awakened Jesus. They asked, *"MASTER, CAREST THOU NOT THAT WE PERISH?"* Jesus opened His eyes. Took command. Rebuked the wind. And spoke, *"PEACE BE STILL!"*

I can't help but reflect on the storms that rocked our little boat called "life"! One minute, we were happy like children at a picnic. Life seemed good and rewarding. Then *suddenly* a storm of untold magnitude hit our boat of "life," and we feared! We did not understand what was happening to us! All that was good turned bad! All that was *hope* dumped *care* and *sickness* into our laps! We bailed out the bad and prayed to God, as we had in the past; but the wind blew harder and the waves rose higher! Our hearts feared! Our eyes saw danger! Our days were long and filled with pain and despair! IT WAS THEN THAT WE CRIED OUT IN GRIEF! *"MASTER, CAREST THOU NOT?"*

Now look at chapter 5. Here we see Jesus disembarking from the little boat. Immediately meeting him was a *frightening* man. He had seen Jesus from afar. He had watched the boat docking at the shore. He wanted help! He knew he needed it! How he needed Jesus! He was a *crazy* man, full of evil spirits, living among the tombs and sepulchers. He roamed the burial grounds night and day, making odd sounds, seeing things that were not there, hearing voices that no one heard, and cutting himself with stones. Many were afraid of him. Others tried to restrain him. It was impossible. His super-human strength came from his madness!

This mad man ran to Jesus. He fell to the ground in worship! Then he cried out the oddest words, *"WHAT HAVE I TO DO WITH THEE, JESUS, THOU SON OF THE MOST HIGH GOD?"* Those contrary words came from the *"unclean spirits."* Those *"spirits"* had taken hold of his being. They were not the man's words! How many years had those *"evil spirits"* taken command of the man's mind and body? Sometimes *"they"* came with such force and anger that *"they"* tore the man's person with anguish. Other times, he was calm and peaceful—almost normal—for a few moments. It was his illness! He never knew what he would say or do next! The evil spirits in the man screamed out at Jesus! *"I adjure thee by God; that thou torment me not!"* IT WAS A RAUCOUS SOUND!

But Jesus, who reads the heart knew those words were not the man's words. They came from his mouth; but they were words of the *"evil one"*! Jesus read the wild man's heart! It was then that Jesus spoke to the *Legion* that had possessed the helpless man for years (Mark 5:8). The Lord said: *"COME OUT OF THE MAN, THOU UNCLEAN SPIRIT!"* It was as if once again, Jesus had rebuked *"the wind"* and said to the *"sea, "PEACE BE STILL!"*

I know what it is like to have someone dear to me possessed by an illness that overtakes the mind; that turned him into someone he wasn't. When I read about this poor man who lived in a grave yard, who was tortured by evil spirits, tears came to me—and the hurt, that I thought was passed, returned! I remembered how I had prayed for my dear one, and longed that Jesus would heal him and say *"PEACE!"* to his troubled life! But the *"evil"* never left, until he died!

"GOD IS FAITHFUL"
(I Corinthians 10:13)

GOD IS FAITHFUL TO MAKE A WAY OF ESCAPE!

AN "ESCAPE" NOT FROM TRIALS,

BUT A WAY TO BEAR THE TRIAL!

The WAY He provides to escape may be varied.

To me, the Word of God, to which I fled, was my escape.

Reading it and realizing it was by inspiration in the originals,

and for my learning, and comfort, was more real than my trial.

HE COMFORTED BY HIS WORDS!

There hath no temptation taken you but such as is common to man: but God is faithful, who will not suffer you to be tempted above that ye are able; but will WITH THE TEMPTATION ALSO MAKE A WAY TO ESCAPE, that ye may be able to bear it.

NOTE THE WORD "ALSO"!!

The temptation or trial is from Him!

And WITH THE TRIAL, God ALSO makes a way of escape!

HE WANTS US TO BE ABLE TO BEAR IT! (ggs)

Today's Bible Blessing   *October 15*

Mark 6:13–Mark 8:4
HER NAME WAS HERODIAS!

Mark 6:18

"It is not lawful for thee to have thy brother's wife"

In the sixth chapter of the gospel of Mark, we find one of the greatest *"flashbacks"* in Biblical history! You see, KING HEROD had heard about JESUS! From what he had been told, this man, JESUS, sounded very much like JOHN THE BAPTIST. Because the king knew (Mark 6:16) that John the Baptist had died, he thought, *"Surely "THE BAPTIST" must have risen from the dead!"*

The thought that there had been such a resurrection disturbed the already disturbed ruler. Herod knew John was dead, for he, himself, had him beheaded! Had not he seen John's bloody head on a royal platter?

Yet, this Herod seemed to have had a tender conscience of some sort. As we read today's passage from Mark 6:13-32, we see a king who wanted to do right but did wrong! How like many of us! We find ourselves in the same spiritual dilemma. The APOSTLE PAUL knew well this inner struggle. He put it succinctly in Romans 7: 19-21:

"For the good that I would I do not: but the evil which I would not, that I do. Now if I do that I would not, it is no

475

more I that do it, but sin that dwelleth in me. I find then a law, that, when I would do good, evil is present with me."

There was gross adultery in the palace! Everyone knew it. This Herod had lusted after his brother Philip's wife—so he took her. She was a powerful, ruling force in the court! Her name was HERODIAS. What Herodias wanted, Herodias got!

JOHN THE BAPTIST DID NOT FEAR HERODIAS! He was a just man! He preached against this sin in the highest house of the land! *"It is not lawful for thee to have thy brother's wife!"* he said to HEROD! John pointed his accusing finger right to the king's face. What a shock for the king to have someone speak the truth with candor! Strange as it may seem King Herod respected The Baptist!

But—*"HERODIAS had a quarrel against him!"* (Mark 6:19) *"How dare this crude wilderness prophet tell me that I should not have married my Herod!"* she might have grumbled. You see, marrying Herod was the best political move she had ever made! In revenge, she forced her adulterer husband to throw John into prison. This he did to pacify her anger. Days went into months and Herodias stewed, stirring her belligerence to greater heights. *"I'll get even with that man if it is the last thing I do."* she may have promised herself. Some of us are the same way. We have experienced a wrong, we remember it, and we hold it in abeyance waiting for our turn to get even. So it was with this ruling woman. She bided her time for revenge!

THE OCCASION WAS HEROD'S BIRTHDAY! There was a feast. Many Galilean nobles were there! There was entertainment! Herodias' DAUGHTER danced before the king! She was beautiful. I think Herod was more than pleased! We often hear of the *"dance of the seven veils."* If I remember, this is the dance associated with this beautiful young woman. With apparent passions aroused, he verbally erupted, *"Whatsoever thou shalt ask of me, I will give it thee, unto the half of my kingdom!"* What a foolish promise from a foolish king! He did not know the depth of degradation that his scheming wife would go!

"THE HEAD OF JOHN THE BAPTIST!" was the evil reply! The daughter rushed from her mother's glee to the side of the regretful King. *"GIVE ME THE HEAD OF JOHN THE BAPTIST!"* the dancer asked (Mark 6:25-28). Immediately, an executioner beheaded John! With one swipe of a sword, the man who had said, *"BEHOLD THE LAMB OF GOD WHICH TAKETH AWAY THE SIN OF THE WORLD!"* (See John 1:29.) was decapitated!

Today's Bible Blessing   *October 16*

Mark 8:5–Mark 10:1
A COMPASSIONATE DAY!

Mark 8:2

"I have compassion on the multitude . . ."

Jesus seems to have been a traveling evangelist! Often he walked the dusty roads. Once He rode a donkey. Many times He sailed in a boat to the next preaching station (vs. 10, 13). No matter where He was, He ministered to the people as in Matthew 20:28: *"the Son of man came not to be ministered unto, but to minister, and to give his life a ransom for many!"*

This is how a Christian should be. She should be a continual witness to the grace of God that brought salvation to her life! (See Titus 2:11.) She should be thinking about others and not herself all the time! One who names the Name of Christ should care about other's needs, not demand that others care about hers! Jesus preached, He healed, and He fed the hungry.

Being the compassionate God-Man, Jesus saw needs. Sometimes Jesus saw the needs of people before the people themselves knew there was a need. For instance in Mark 8:2, Jesus said, *"I HAVE COMPASSION ON THE MULTITUDE."* They had not discovered the problem yet. I am so glad that he had compassion on me when He gave His life a ransom for me, and I, as a little girl, trusted Jesus as my sin-bearer and Saviour. Why do you think that there was more compassion than usual that day on the hillside?

True—it was time for Jesus to leave the multitude and go to His next preaching station. But He would not go! Why do you think that hundreds of human beings followed Jesus and stayed with Him so long that day? They were so enthralled that they would forget to eat? They were mesmerized by HIM! They had never seen a Man like him before! The people had come from great distances to be a part of it all. The crowd had been with Him for three days. They came in droves without the aid of "Facebook" or "twitter." It could be they brought food for a day or two—but not three days! Perhaps they had bedrolls with them for night-sleeping. Maybe they had skins of water for drinking. I don't know. I do know that they were out of food when we come here to this part of the story! Jesus said so! JESUS CARED! He would not send them home hungry!

Come to find out, the disciples still had seven loaves of bread with them, as well as a few small fish! Don't you wonder how they kept those fish from spoiling out there in the hot sun, or maybe they had gone to the sea and caught more fish for their own lunch! The bread was probably the dark, coarse, round, flat loaf made from barley with a bit of millet, spelt, beans, and lentils in the mix. But their remaining food could not feed so many!

When my husband and I were in the Holy Land, we were served fish at a certain place near the Sea of Galilee. The people called it *"Peter's fish."* I remember well. It was full of bones. We had to be very careful when eating it.

I asked myself a question: *"What made hundreds of human beings follow Jesus and stay with Jesus so long that they would forget to eat?"* I concluded it was His miracles! Some may have listened to His message! Yes. Others may have come just to see the *"show."* I don't know. Did the multitude understand that Jesus was the *"LIVING BREAD"* that came down from Heaven? (See John 6:51.) Some did, perhaps. I am not sure. All I know is that the people ate the food and were filled.

Now they could return home without fainting on the way. After all the four thousand people were fed, there were seven baskets of bread left over. Always God has *blessings* for us that are *full and running over* (Luke 6:38). That is, if we look for the extra blessings. This *"feeding"* was reminiscent of the previous feeding of the five thousand (Mark 8:9) that we read about in John 6:9-13.

Then Jesus encountered the Pharisees in Dalma-nutha. These men who carefully observed the written Jewish law demanded a sign! No doubt they had heard of the four thousand being fed. In BETHSAIDA, a blind man was healed. In Caesarea, Philippi, Peter made his remarkable declaration to Jesus: *"THOU ART THE MESSIAH!"* (Mark 8:29), but later spoiled it all by denying Him. There's that THREE DAYS again! It was after THREE DAYS that Jesus multiplied the seven loaves and few fish. IN THREE DAYS, AFTER HIS DEATH, JESUS SAID HE WOULD RISE FROM THE DEAD! PETER WOULD HAVE NONE OF THAT!

> **"TRUSTING IS BELIEVING"**
> (Psalm 28:7)
> *The LORD is my strength and my shield;*
> *my heart trusted in him, and I am helped:*
> *therefore my heart greatly rejoiceth;*
> *and with my song will I praise him.*
> TRUSTING DOES HELP,
> Indeed, there is no other help or protection!
> TRUSTING IS BELIEVING WHAT GOD SAID!
> There will be no rejoicing if there is no trust,
> and certainly no songs of praise!
> REJOICING COMES FROM TRUSTING
> AND BELIEVING WHAT GOD HAS PROMISED! (ggs)

Today's Bible Blessing   *October 17*

Mark 10:2–Mark 12:1

A PATTERN FOR A GOOD MARRIAGE!

Mark 10:11

"Whosoever shall put away his wife, and marry another, committeth adultery . . ."

The Pharisees were trying to trip up Jesus with a trick question. The question was *"IS IT LAWFUL FOR A MAN TO PUT AWAY (divorce) HIS WIFE?"* (See verse 2.) Now Jesus knew that Moses permitted divorce for certain conditions. The Lord Jesus Christ was not ignorant of the Law. The Lord knew it was permitted because of the hardness of men's heart (Matthew 19:8). But that was not God's intent at creation!

This was Jesus' answer to the Pharisees' question as found in Mark 10:11-12:

> *"Whosoever shall put away his wife, and marry another, committeth adultery against her. And if a woman shall put away her husband, and be married to another, she committeth adultery."*

Yes, Jesus went back to the BOOK OF BEGINNINGS, Genesis, showing His contenders that God created the first marriage with a man and a wife being united as one flesh for life. This *"life"* sentence, so to speak, is the very reason great care should be taken when choosing a life's mate. Because of Adam and Eve, we have a pattern. That pattern is *"the leaving and cleaving"* principle. A man is to leave his father and mother and cleave (or cling) to his wife. They are glued together!

A person's length of life can be very long. If you marry someone you cannot stand, you will be in that unpleasant union for life! I suppose that is one of the reasons that people divorce. They just can't stand the person they married. Sometimes the very attribute that drew the couple together is the thing that disturbs them most after being married. Their ideas clash. Their personality differences irk! They do not want to do the things the other person does. And they definitely don't want to be a mailman's wife, a furnace-fixer's wife, a lawn-man's wife, a teacher's wife, or a pastor's wife! etc., etc., etc. That which was cute and endearing in courtship has become an agitation to the highest degree!

I am eighty-four at this writing (I was born in 1927). That means that when I was twenty years of age–as I was becoming engaged to be married, I had to have the wisdom of the ages to choose a man with whom I could live for the rest of my life! The same for my husband. We both were Christians. He loved the Lord, and so did I. But the blending of our two lives was not easy!

My husband has said in these later years of our marriage, that he did not know how to be a husband. I could agree with that! I suppose it could be said the same for me that I did not know how to be a wife. And he could agree with that. A bride and a groom have a big dose of *"me, me, me"* when they start housekeeping. Everything went his way in the past—and the same for me. I tried to be submissive. The more I tried the less he thought I was. It was a most confusing time for me and not *"apple pie"* for him. But we both learned to adjust to one another and to remain in love.

So far, with Dr. Waite and me, it has been almost sixty-three years of marriage (married in August, 1948). We have five children born to us. I will confess we did not have the wisdom to know what we were doing when we chose each other. Yet, we both had an ideal–a goal, as well as a BOOK to guide us. In spite of our ignorance, God has given us good mates! A good marriage is a work in progress like a painting! It is very difficult!

I have not always been happy. Neither has my husband. Learning to live as *"one"* is difficult. We had to **learn** to be happy together. It was not easy for either of us. We chose each other when we were barely out of high school. He was in college and I was in Bible school! We knew very little about the *"in's and out's"* of living.

The only pattern of marriage that we had was from our parents and grandparents. We had good families. There were no divorces! They were people whom we could emulate in our marriage. We attended a fundamental Bible-believing church with excellent Bible teaching. Our Pastor agreed with Jesus when He said, *"Whosoever shall put away his wife, and marry another, committeth adultery against her. And if a woman shall put away her husband, and be married to another, she committeth adultery."* IF IT WAS

GOOD ENOUGH FOR JESUS, IT WAS GOOD ENOUGH FOR US!

> ### *"Set up the standard toward Zion"*
> (Jeremiah 4:6)
> All our life, our whole purpose should be
> to please the Lord.
> In life or death never detour!
> No deviation! No regret! No retreat!
> LET US GO ON!
> His face will greet us at the end of our course. (ysw)

Today's Bible Blessing   *October 18*

Mark 12:2–Mark 14:5
MY FRIEND ROSE

Mark 12:11

"This was the Lord's doing, and it is marvellous in our eyes!"

As I read my Bible, certain Scripture verses remind me of certain people. Today is one of those days! See MARK 12:11! *THIS WAS THE LORD'S DOING, AND IT IS MARVELLOUS IN OUR EYES!*

I remember the first time I saw my friend, Rose. She was with her family in the back of the church. There she stood with her family—her parents, her sister, a small brother, and a darling little girl with curly hair named Esther. Rose was the oldest child in that family. She looked to be about my age. I couldn't wait to meet her! Rose Marie and I became close friends. It was a friendship like that of David and Jonathan!

Her story started in a big church in Cleveland, Ohio. A woman in that church had a burden for girls! So, she started a sewing class with two goals. One was to teach the young women to sew. The other was to win them to Jesus Christ as personal Saviour.

I do not know how much sewing those young women learned that year; but I do know that the *"seed"* of the *"patience"* and *"comfort"* of the Scriptures gave *"hope"* to two girls' hearts one day! *ETERNAL LIFE* WAS THEIRS AS THEY TRUSTED JESUS CHRIST, AND HIM ALONE. The gospel seed was planted deep in their souls! Bless the memory of that woman who cared! The needle and thread was not important any more as the Words of God were memorized and explained.

"THIS WAS THE LORD'S DOING, AND IT IS MARVELLOUS IN OUR EYES!"

"Not by works of righteousness which we have done, but according to His mercy He saved us, by the washing of regeneration, and renewing of the Holy Ghost; which He

481

shed on us abundantly through Jesus Christ our Saviour, that being justified by His grace, we should be made heirs according to the hope of eternal life" (Titus 3:5-7).

Rose, with her sister, Betty, were missionaries to their family. They went home to their mother and father and told them about the *"unsearchable riches"* they had found in Jesus Christ. They told their Catholic parents that all the praying and penance they had been doing would NOT get them to Heaven. They explained that Jesus paid it all when He died on the cross years ago. Yes, the Lord Jesus Christ had died to forgive their parents' sins too.

SOON THE PARENTS WERE SAVED! They saw that all their labor and works to gain entrance into Heaven had been in vain. It was *"faith"* and *"faith"* alone in all that Jesus had done at Calvary that could take away their sin. Yes, Rose and Betty's parents became real *"Christians"* like those talked about in the book of Acts (Acts 11:26b).

What God did in that family is remarkable! He took two devoutly religious, Slavic immigrants and redeemed their souls! He gave them a love for the Words of God. After their salvation, their daily thoughts were of Jesus. Their love for Him constrained them to tell others of His wonderful salvation! Hundreds of gospel tracts were passed out wherever crowds gathered. Ballparks found this family evangelizing! They knew what religious blindness was. For once they were blind. Now they could see! (See John 9:25)

No wonder Rose grew up with the love of Jesus in her heart. WE BECAME FRIENDS! We sang together, prayed together, went to Bible School together, and stood by each other as we were married. We were in each other's weddings. It was at Bible school that Rose met her husband, a man of God. Missionary service was their goal! So off they went to the mission field!

Soon, her husband was involved in Christian education and seminary studies for the national Christians in the Philippines. MY DEAR FRIEND, ROSE WEISS DURHAM, WORKED BY HIS SIDE. They had three children. Every prayer letter was titled *"DURHAM DOINGS"* taken from our verse today, Mark 12:11.

THEN ONE SAD DAY, MY DEAR, DEAR FRIEND DIED! Cancer had raised its ugly head! WITH NO MERCY, it GRABBED HER! God took her HOME to be with HIM, and left those who loved her, alone and lonely! **In today's reading, the husbandman's son was killed by those who cared less about the Father.** In time, *"the stone (Jesus) that the builders rejected"* became important (Mark 12:10). So with my dear friend's life. It was a *"seed"* planted for tomorrow's harvesting.

HER LIFE WAS MARVELOUS IN MY EYES!

*"THE PRICE OF UNDERSTANDING SYMPATHY
IS PERSONAL EXPERIENCE!"*
(II Corinthians 1:4)
*Who comforteth us in all our tribulation,
that we may be able to comfort them which are in any trouble,
by the comfort wherewith we ourselves are comforted of God.*
The comfort wherewith He has comforted us
is precious and may be shared.
To have someone comfort you that has had the same trial
is like a balm.
To have that someone be a Christian who has gone through
the fiery trial himself or herself,
somehow helps us take up our cross for one more day. (ggs)

Today's Bible Blessing   *October 19*
Mark 14:6–Mark 15:18
THE NIGHT PETER CURSED GOD'S NAME

Mark 14:72
"Before the cock crow twice, thou shalt deny me thrice!"

Where was Peter when the high priest asked Jesus, *"Answerest thou nothing?"* (See Mark 14:60.) What was Peter doing when that same priest ripped off Jesus' clothes? What was Peter doing when Jesus stood there naked and exposed before the jeering crowd? Where was he? Where? Why wasn't Peter close by Jesus to help Him and see those who hated Him? Why wasn't he there to see those who spit on Him? Or to see those who covered his face with a bag, demanding Jesus to prophesy who it was who hit him?

I'll tell you where he was. He was away from the court action. He was nowhere near Jesus. He did not hear the sentence of death! The Bible says that Peter was *"beneath in the palace"* (Mark 14:66). His eyes did not see the harm that was being done to the One Peter claimed to love. Why, only a few hours previously, Peter had declared to Jesus face to face that He was THE MESSIAH, THE CHRIST! (Mark 8:29b) Where was all that bold talk when Jesus needed him the most?

It was a chilly night. Peter was cold. He found a fire and was warming himself over the hot embers. My, it felt good! He had made himself *"at home"* among the gawking crowd. A young girl saw him rubbing his hands together over the flame. In spite of herself, she kept staring at him. *"He looks familiar,"* she thought. Personally, I think she struck up a conversation with Peter just to check out his accent. I think they talked awhile, for the Bible records a statement that seems to belong to an earlier sentence or two. She continued, *"And thou also wast with Jesus of Nazareth!"*

All of a sudden, Peter became talkative! He denied the young girl's statement! With as much conviction as he could muster, Peter blurted out, *"I KNOW NOT, NEITHER UNDERSTAND WHAT THOU SAYEST!"* In other words, he said that he did not know what the young woman was talking about! As she walked away, one could hear a rooster crowing.

I must say that this "maid" was persistent, for she returned to the fire and to Peter. She, too, was chilly. As she warmed her hands with the others, she glibly commented about Peter to those about her, *"THIS MAN IS ONE OF THEM!"*

"Why was she always talking about me?" **Peter was befuddled!** It was then that Peter denied her truth again! This pest of a girl was getting under his skin. Why did she persist on saying he was *"one of them"* who had been with Jesus? Peter did not know this girl. What business was it of hers to interfere in his life? She was too much!

By this time, those gathered around the fire looked at Peter more intently. They had nothing else to do! In fact, they were beginning to believe the maid! Again they studied Peter. Finally one of them said to Peter, *"SURELY THOU ART ONE OF THEM: FOR THOU ART A GALILAEAN, AND THY SPEECH AGREETH THERETO."* In other words, *"HEY YOU ARE ONE OF THEM! You talk like Jesus and like all those men from Galilee who follow Him!"* (If you remember, those from Galilee had a different kind of accent than those from other parts of the Holy Land.)

Well, PETER HAD HAD IT! He was sick of these people trying to *"out"* him and linking him with Jesus! *"Who do they think they are anyhow? Why can't they let me alone?"* To prove he was independent from the *"criminal, Jesus,"* he denied Him! He used self-demeaning words like other sinners did. Not only that, he *"denied with an oath"* (Matthew 26:72) that he knew the Lord Jesus Christ. IT WAS AGAINST THE LAW OF MOSES TO DO SO! How awful! How sinful! How uncouth! He cried out in a loud voice so all could hear, *"I KNOW NOT HIS MAN OF WHOM YE SPEAK!"* Yes, everyone heard! Also everyone heard the GALILAEAN accent that betrayed the very curse words Peter was mouthing!

THEN THE ROOSTER CROWED AGAIN! Oh, OH! Embarrassed Peter remembered Jesus' Words, *"Before the cock crow twice, thou shalt deny me thrice!"*

IT WAS THEN THAT PETER WEPT!
HOW COULD HE HAVE BEEN SO ASHAMED OF JESUS,
WHOM HE HAD CALLED THE CHRIST? (See Matthew 16:16.)

> ### *"GLAD WE ARE HIS!"*
> (Nehemiah 8:10)
> *Lord: neither be ye sorry;*
> *for the joy of the LORD is your strength.*
> Perhaps we cannot be happy, happy all the time;
> but we can be glad,
> GLAD WE ARE HIS.
> Glad for the privilege of service each new year and each day. (ggs)

Today's Bible Blessing   *October 20*

Mark 15:19–Luke 1:36
A PLACE OF DEATH & A PLACE OF LIFE

Mark 15:47
"And Mary Magdalene and Mary . . . beheld where he was laid."

THE WRITTEN WORD

It is the contention of some that the last twelve verses of the Gospel of Mark are bogus—not really Scripture. THIS CONTROVERSY POINTS OUT THE PROBLEM THAT THE TWO OPPOSING GREEK TEXTS BRING TO US! The *TEXTUS RECEPTUS*, which was always the Greek Text that underlies the New Testament for centuries, contains these last twelve verses. THIS IS THE GREEK TEXT WHICH UNDERLIES THE KING JAMES BIBLE! All these Textus Receptus Manuscripts were used as Scripture for 1,500 years. Any other manuscripts were rejected until a man named Tischendorf found a rejected copy of the *SINAI MANUSCRIPT* in St. Catherine's monastery's library in Egypt's desert.

That *Vatican manuscript* was unused and dormant for years, gathering dust in the Vatican library in Rome. Then two men, named BISHOP WESTCOTT and PROFESSOR HORT, used that *spurious Greek Manuscript* to change the New Testament! It is the use of *spurious Greek manuscripts*, along with the translation method of DYNAMIC EQUIVALENCE that has brought about the deluge of new Bibles that are confusing the Christian world today!

Because of these *spurious* Greek manuscripts, doubt has been placed on the last twelve verses of Mark. When the manuscripts were copied, the scribes must have been instructed to skip these verses as they copied the Scriptures. That is why there are manuscripts minus Mark 16:9-20 today. Of great interest to me, is that anyone can see the *empty spaces* in the Sinaiticus manuscripts where the verses, which belong there, could have been written.

After the same amount of blank space is seen, one notices that the GOSPEL OF LUKE begins. The other *spurious* manuscript has an interesting phenomenon. Though the space is filled, the letters are elongated so that the space between, where verses 9-20 should be found, is filled with Greek letters. This makes what would be an *"empty space,"* at the start of the GOSPEL OF LUKE, commence where it would normally begin in the manuscript!

THE LIVING WORD

NOW, let us meditate on the DEATH and RESURRECTION of our Lord and Saviour. Pilate marveled that Jesus had died so quickly (Mark 15:44). Others, who were crucified, took longer for their life to ebb from their tortured bodies. It was customary for the soldiers to break the legs of the crucified to hasten death. Jesus died differently. HE DISMISSED HIS *"SPIRIT!"* Only God can do that! This is remarkable! By His own will, he died. Normal people cannot just *"die"*! They may die suddenly, without warning; but they cannot just *"think **die**"* at a particular instant and *"die"*! JESUS COULD DO THIS BECAUSE HE WAS THE CREATOR OF LIFE ITSELF! As GOD THE SON, at the creation of the world, He breathed into Adam *"the breath of life."* (Genesis 2:7) That was when man became a living soul!

Mary Magdalene, Salome, and other women watched Jesus die. I have never seen a person die, have you? Our second-born son died suddenly in a hospital emergency room. My husband and I, and his sister, rushed to see him. But he had *"gone"* already. We saw him just as the emergency people left him! It seemed rather cruel to me. I saw our son's body lying there with lifesaving emergency equipment still in place. His body was there for anyone to see–but no one cared to see him, except the undertaker. There he was, dead!

Perhaps those Bible women had that strange emotion when they saw Jesus dead. His body had become burdened with the heavy weight of His demise; yet it was still on the cross. The nails still in his hands pulled at His lifeless hands from the weight of His body. His eyes open and blank looked but could not see.

A man named Joseph took Jesus' body and laid it in his own unused tomb. As I am writing this, I remembered that a man named Joseph from Nazareth was there at Jesus birth; and here, at His death, was another man named Joseph. This Joseph of Arimathaea wrapped the dead Jesus with fine linen, and then rolled a heavy stone to cover the tomb's opening. That stone would keep prying eyes from the lifeless corpse of the Saviour (Mark 15:43-47).

My husband and I saw the Garden of death. It was near GETHSEMANE. Looking down from that place of tears, we could see Gordon's Calvary where some feel Jesus was crucified. Strange as it may seem to you, today it is a bus station.

Within that borrowed tomb, Jesus' body lay lifeless for three days and three nights. It was *THE PLACE* where Mary Magdalene and Joses' mother saw Him dead (Mark 15:47). Perhaps there was some kind of committal words said as Jesus was laid on that slab within the barren tomb. We are not told.

I wonder what energy was generated in *THE PLACE* where death was conquered and life exploded! Soon it would be *THE PLACE* where an angel sat, dressed in white.

In Mark 16:6, THE ANGEL WOULD SAY *"HE IS NOT HERE: BEHOLD THE PLACE WHERE THEY LAID HIM!"*

"THE LAW OF THE MANNA"
The law of the manna still holds true.
Every day we need a time of such communion with our Father.
THAT WHICH IS HEAVENLY CANNOT REMAIN GOOD
VERY LONG ON EARTH, BUT MUST,
DAY BY DAY, BE RENEWED AFRESH FROM HEAVEN.
(ggs, quoted from ANDREW MURRAY)

Today's Bible Blessing   *October 21*

Luke 1:37–Luke 2:41

SIX PEOPLE & TWO BABIES USED OF GOD!

Luke 1:6

"And they were both righteous before God, walking in all the commandments . . ."

As I read yesterday's and today's readings, I am struck with the men and woman who believed God! Look first at ELISABETH and ZACHARIAS, husband and wife, with no children (Luke 1:5-7). Both were *righteous* before God. They were *blameless*! They kept the ordinances of Zacharias' priesthood. They kept all the commandments to a "T"! Why, PRIEST ZACHARIAS was so close to THE ALMIGHTY that an angel spoke directly to him. Old BARREN ELISABETH, of all things, would soon have a son named JOHN! ZACHARIAS' only fault: HE DID NOT BELIEVE THE ANGEL! So, God struck him speechless for nine months! In spite of his unbelief, old, tired, Elisabeth became pregnant with BABY JOHN.

Next, we are introduced to another couple who believed God! Their names were MARY and JOSEPH! They too, though younger, were devout godly people! An Angel came to Mary! It was a birth announcement! *"THOU ART HIGHLY FAVOURED,"* the angel said. We know from Matthew's gospel that

JOSEPH was a *"just"* man! Then THE ANGEL said strange and unfamiliar words to her, in Luke 1:28: *"The Lord is with thee: blessed art thou among women!"* Such surprising news was spoken that day! Mary, who knew no man, would conceive and bare a son. He would be *THE SON OF THE HIGHEST* whose Name was JESUS! (Jesus means Saviour.) He would save His people from their sin!

In time, Joseph and Mary would marry; but, when we first meet them, they are only *"espoused."* An *"espousal"* is a legal binding promise between a man and a woman who have been *promised* to each other for a *future* marriage union. Joseph was called Mary's *"husband."* Mary was called Joseph's *"wife."* (Matthew 1:19-20). A *"dowry"* (money & gifts) is passed from the intended groom to the intended bride's family to seal the promise. Legal papers are signed. It is, as if, they were actually married; but do not come together as *"man & wife"* until after the wedding ceremony.

I read that a young woman who is *"espoused"* is taken to live at her intended husband's house or the house of her husband's father. (Am not sure this is true in all cases.) There is no sexual union until an actual marriage ceremony. I personally believe that is the reason that Mary was with Joseph when they both went to pay their taxes in Bethlehem. An *"espousal"* is different than our engagements. To break this *"espousal"* promise, one had to go to law. Such a promise was only broken when there had been *fornication* on the part of the woman.

Now we meet two other *devout* people. Their names are SIMEON and ANNA. They are not married. I surmise they knew each other well for they spent much time in the Temple. PIOUS, ELDERLY SIMEON lived in Jerusalem (Luke 2:25-27). Somehow the Holy Spirit revealed to this reverent man that he would not die until he saw the Lord's Christ. By this time, BABY JESUS had been born. His mother, Mary, and her *espoused husband*, Joseph, brought the baby to Jerusalem for religious reasons. Who do they meet in the temple but spirit-filled Simeon! He took *the baby* in his arms and blessed Him saying, *"Behold, this Child is set for the fall and rising again of many in Israel . . ."* (Luke 2:34).

When I was a new mother, I brought my firstborn son to see my grandfather. GRANDPA BARKER WAS A SICK & DYING MAN! I can see him now, sitting in a straight chair, holding my newborn son in his arms. He looked down at my baby and pronounced Simeon's words, *"Lord, now lettest thou thy servant depart in peace, according to thy word: for mine eyes have seen thy salvation . . ."* (Luke 2:29-30).

THEN THERE WAS ANNA! One hundred and seven years old!–that's how old she was. Widowed for eighty years! Since the death of her husband, her life was devoted to *"fasting & prayer."* She never left the Temple! That day, when Simeon blessed the child, Anna walked by. She stopped and spake of Him as the Redeemer! (See Luke 2:36-38.)

These six devout people, and two babies named before
they were born, were chosen for chosen tasks!
HOW THEY WERE USED OF GOD!

> *"PEACE"*
> (John 14:27; Phil. 4:7)
> Peace is God's gift to those who leave it all to Him.
> *"My peace I leave with you."*
> Pray, and His peace will garrison your heart. (ggs)

Today's Bible Blessing   *October 22*

Luke 2:42–Luke 4:36
HIS FATHER'S BUSINESS

Luke 4:22

"Gracious words which proceeded out of His mouth!"

When my husband and I were in Jerusalem many
years ago, our guide told us that boy children stayed with
their mothers when they came to Jerusalem's wailing wall.
That is, they stayed with their mothers *until* they were twelve years old.
After they had their bar-mitzvah, *at the age of twelve*, they accompanied their fathers at THE WALL! It was impressive! Near the wall,
where the Jewish men rocked back-and-forth, men prayed, as well as
the teenage boys. After putting a small, rolled-up piece of prayer-paper
into a wall's tiny crack, they prayed. They wept. They chanted! I have
been told that Jews today, at THE WALL, are praying for the
MESSIAH to come. Of course, He has come already; but they do not
recognize that the One they crucified, so many years ago, is HE of
Whom the prophets spoke!

In Jesus' day, the wall around Jerusalem was intact.
When we were there, and even today, only a small portion of the wall is
left standing. I recall *festive people* nearby playing instruments of
praise, in celebration of recently bar-mitzvahed boys. Those lads
would have been twelve years old, just like Jesus was in today's
reading. The boys were dressed in brilliance—probably it was the
prayer shawls that I remember. Big scrolls with *holy words* were
carried by specially appointed men. That day, over to my left shoulder,
higher above where I was standing and behind the men, the women
stood with their children by their sides watching!

In Luke 2:42, we read that Mary and Joseph attended
a feast in Jerusalem every year. Jesus went with them that
particular year. Maybe He went every year. I don't know. It was a
time of joy and gladness! I do not know if it was the *FEAST OF
PASSOVER* & UNLEAVENED BREAD, or *THE FEAST OF WEEKS*

(Pentecost), or *THE DAY OF ATONEMENT*, or *THE FEAST OF BOOTHS* (Tabernacles)—but JESUS WAS THERE! Meeting together yearly for these feasts was required by the LORD God! It was what Jews did. They remembered Him. Every feast had a special meaning. Trumpets were blown. Memories were stirred!

Perhaps with his new twelve-year mindset, Jesus walked freely into the Temple. He found Himself in the section where Scriptural discussions and teachings of the LAW commenced. It was then that He sat down to listen to the brilliant TEMPLE TEACHERS! Jesus was there, too, day and night, for three days, answering difficult theological questions. I don't know where He slept, do you? Probably on a pallet out under the stars. The *"doctors"* were astonished at His understanding. How unusual for a twelve-year-old boy!

In the meantime, Mary and Joseph were plodding along toward Nazareth, their home. Probably, Joseph was busy with the luggage as he talked with the other male travelers. There was always *"men talk"* and plans for their homeward journey. Mary, busy with the children—as well as chatting with her friends—noticed that Jesus was not with her. She assumed He was with Joseph. After all, He was twelve! I think she may have been pleased that He was with his *"father"* and the men. It was good for Jesus to be with men! Soon Jesus would shoulder more responsibilities in the carpenter shop. The more Jesus handled the work, the more money would come in for bills and food—and maybe goods for new curtains, too.

THE TRUTH WAS JESUS HAD TO DO HIS HEAVENLY FATHER'S BUSINESS! (See Luke 2:49.)

In manhood, Jesus was an educated man! (See Luke 4:16.) Right there in Nazareth where *The Carpenter Shop* was, Jesus taught in the synagogue. He read from the Hebrew scrolls (Isaiah 61:1), explaining that *the Spirit of the Lord was upon Him.* When finished, He would roll up the scroll. Yes, all eyes were fastened on Him. Sitting down, He said, *"THIS DAY IS THIS SCRIPTURE FULFILLED IN YOUR EARS."*

All wondered. How did He know so much? They knew He was Joseph's son! (Joseph was Jesus' earthly father.) They could not help but wonder how Jesus could speak with such *"GRACIOUS WORDS"* (Luke 4:22).

"IS THERE UNRIGHTEOUSNESS WITH GOD?"
(Romans 9:14)
In our trials and testings, in our particular circumstances,
the Spirit of God asks a question,
"Is there unrighteousness with God?
GOD FORBID!"
We shall not say "why"!
Hath not the Potter power over the clay? (ggs)

490

Today's Bible Blessing   *October 23*
Luke 4:37–Luke 6:38
JESUS THE PREACHER-TEACHER
Luke 5:4
"Launch out into the deep, and let down your nets . . ."

Luke was the human writer of the body of work that is known as THE GOSPEL ACCORDING TO LUKE. Many say it is some of the most beautiful writing of Scripture—at least in the New Testament. Luke also wrote the book of Acts, and traveled much with the Apostle Paul. He was a medical doctor. Because, in today's world, the medical profession has advanced so since the New Testament times, we cannot help but wonder what kind of medicine was practiced back in A.D. 63 & 68!

Many people feel that Luke was a Greek and they give their reasons, while others say he was of Jewish heritage. They say his skillful use of the correct Greek marks him as a Jew of the *"dispersion."* According to the 1917 edition of *The Scofield Reference Bible, "Tradition says that Luke was a Jew of Antioch, as Paul was of Tarsus."* If this be true, that would make the entire Bible—both New Testament and Old Testament--written by the Jews. *The New Unger's Bible Dictionary* feels that Luke was a Greek because Paul did not reckon him *"who are from the circumcision"* (Colossians 4:11, 14).

Luke presents the Lord Jesus Christ as the SON OF MAN! He traces Jesus' genealogy (Luke 3:23-38) back to ADAM, through NATHAN (King David's son) up to Mary! Luke presents Jesus with a clear, clean kingly line! We are told the key verse of this gospel is Luke 19:10: *"For the Son of man is come to seek and to save that which was lost!"* Dr. Luke takes us, with Jesus, from Galilee to Jerusalem, and shows us the crucifixion, resurrection, and ascension of this "SON OF MAN"*!*

It is true. Jesus was becoming a very famous Man! Word of His miracles, as well as His outstanding teaching, were noised about to all! (See Luke 4:37.) He taught in the synagogues of CAPERNAUM. People were astonished as His doctrine! *His words were powerful!* No matter how He tried to get away for some rest, the people followed Him. Even when he fled to a deserted spot, they found Him. He told them, *"I must preach the kingdom of God to other cities also . . ."* This must mean that He walked by foot all over doing His work. He had a strong constitution and a heart-dedication for His work!

It is so interesting to me that Jesus preached! I don't usually think of Him as a *"preacher,"* do you? He preached in the synagogues of Galilee! He declared in Luke 4:43: *"I MUST PREACH THE KINGDOM OF GOD TO OTHER CITIES ALSO."* He must have had a powerful voice to be heard by those crowds of people in the open air. They flocked to His side for His messages. I wish I could have heard one of His sermons. He preached on the land. He preached by the sea. Often He used a boat for his pulpit!

Once, after preaching, He encouraged Peter to launch out into the sea to do some fishing. Peter reminded the Lord that he and his companions had fished all night and caught absolutely nothing! **But Simon Peter said** *"Nevertheless at thy word, I will let down the net."* I personally think that Peter was humoring Jesus. But guess what? Lo and behold! THE NET BECAME SO FULL OF FISH THAT IT BROKE!

What was different about that fishing trip? I am not sure—except for two facts!
Fact #1–JESUS WAS THERE!
Fact #2–PETER LAUNCHED OUT INTO THE DEEP!

Could it be that we are just like Peter? Could it be that we just go through the motions? We do what is required! We mend our nets! We get into our boats. We row out to a good spot. We throw out our nets. We would never think of doing our work in a different way! **We just sit there in the boat waiting for something to happen.** We wait for the fish to come to us! When they don't, we are not surprised! We did not expect any fish anyhow!

The truth is we have lost our zeal for Christ. Fishing has become *"ho-hum"* to us. We don't care if we ever get any fish! We have become complacent! Who ever heard of *"launching out"* in the dcep anyhow?

WHY NOT TRY IT!

"FEAR"
A NOISE IN THE DARK IS MUCH MORE FRIGHTENING THAN VISIBLE DANGER.
Imaginations concerning the unknown are far worse than facts. Many times, the uncertainty of what lies ahead is a harder trial than the pressure of some present ill or adversity that is already upon us.
LET US BE CONTENT TO SEE GOD IN THE UNKNOWN AND SEEK NOT TO KNOW
WHAT IS KNOWN BEST ONLY TO HIM.
WHATEVER THE UNKNOWN IS, GOD IS IN IT.
That should be enough for the Christian to know.
(ggs gleaned this from "I WILL TRUST" by Oliver Green)

Luke 6:39–Luke 8:24
THE HUMBLED CENTURION

Luke 7:9d
"I have not found so great faith, no, not in Israel"

Now, in Luke, chapter seven, we meet a *"certain centurion"* (Luke 7:2). He was a powerful military man in the Roman legion, being the captain of sixty companies of one hundred men. He was accustomed to men obeying his every command. Perhaps you remember CORNELIUS in Acts 10:1. He was a centurion, too, of the Italian band.

This centurion, about whom Dr. Luke was talking, had a trusted servant! The Bible says that this servant was *"dear"* unto his master. Much to the centurion's chagrin, *his man-servant was nigh unto death!* When the military leader heard about Jesus, his ears pricked up. Immediately, He sent an errand boy over to the Jewish elders, commanding them to urge Jesus to heal his servant! Imagine!—thinking of *"ordering"* around the One who created the universe! Think about it! This *powerful man*, who was used to being obeyed, expected the One who came to give His life for his ransom, to obey his commands!

Dr. Luke tells us that they obeyed the centurion *"instantly!"* Under normal circumstances, the elders probably would have had nothing to do with Jesus. After all, this was important! The Centurion had done many philanthropic deeds for the nation! Why, he had donated funds to build their new synagogue! It is rather humorous, to me, to see some of the very Elders, who later would want to kill Jesus, beg Him to heal this wealthy man's servant. It is plain to see that their concern was more for the monetary than the healing!

Before we go on, let us think about this "servant." Why was he so loved by his master? In those days, many trusted men (and women & children) were slaves. Some became slaves to pay off a debt. Others chose to remain as slaves because their wives and children were slaves in a certain household. At one time, the whole nation of Israel were slaves in Egypt. You and I have an image of *"slavery"* from the *"slaves"* that we are told about in our country before the civil war. True, that was one kind of servitude or slavery, but all *"slavery"* was not like some of us picture it. I do not say that "slavery" is good. Hagar was Sarah's "slave." Naaman's wife's child-slave encouraged him to obey the prophet. Yet, the Apostle Paul considered himself a *"slave"* to Jesus Christ.

I think of DANIEL in the Old Testament. He, with all the most intelligent and gifted people of Jerusalem, were taken captive. They became *"slaves"* of NEBUCHADNEZZAR in Babylon. Daniel and his friends were well thought of and valuable to that country. In fact,

Daniel, as an older and wise man—a slave—became one of the trusted presidents of the land under DARIUS and CYRUS (Daniel 6:28).

Think also of Joseph, who was sold into slavery by his brothers. Soon he became Potiphar's *"servant,"* winding up in prison through no fault of his own. Eventually this *"Hebrew slave"* became a powerful ruler of Egypt directly under the MIGHTY PHARAOH!

We learn from this passage that the "servants," whom Paul instructed to obey their masters (Colossians 3:22), **were not only *"valuable,"* but *"loved."*** They were like trusted members of the family. They were *"in charge"* of the house which included the finances. Yes, they were *"slaves,"* but not like we picture them. Often these *"servants"* owned property. In fact, some of the famous, philosophers of history were *"slaves."*

As Jesus and the elders were approaching the centurion's house, word came that the centurion had second thoughts. He felt too unworthy to have Jesus come into his house. No doubt it was a pretentious house full of beautiful furniture and baubles. Suddenly it was not good enough for Jesus! He may have said: *"Why don't you just say the 'word,' and my servant shall be healed!"*

What an about face! This bossy man, who previously practically ordered Jesus to heal, had a change of heart. Instead, of demanding *"healing,"* he accepted Jesus as his superior! It is amazing the change in the centurion as he contemplated Jesus for who He was!

Jesus was amazed! He had not seen such faith in all Israel!

"I WILL NOT BE AFRAID"
(Psalm 57:1; Psalm 3:3)
*"In the shadow of Thy wings will I make my refuge,
until these calamities be overpast."*
ALL COMFORT IN PRESENT CALAMITIES
IS TO BE HAD BY NEARNESS TO GOD!
*"But thou, O LORD, art a shield for me;
my glory, and the lifter up of mine head."*
I WILL NOT BE AFRAID! (ggs)

Luke 8:25–Luke 9:53

JESUS' CARE FOR CHILDREN

Luke 9:48a

"Whosoever shall receive this child in my name receiveth me"

Today, let us notice Jesus' compassion on peoples' children. For instance, look at Luke 8:42-49. Here we see a father with great concern for his dying daughter. She was twelve! She was his *"only daughter"*—perhaps his only child. Picture the sorrow and fright beating in that parent's heart. The grieving father's name was JAIRUS! He was an important man, for he was a ruler of the *synagogue.*

A SYNAGOGUE was a place of *"prayer"* and *"public discussion."* In post exilic times, it was a building for the *"reading of the law"* and *"public instruction."* It was a place to read the Scriptures on the Sabbath day. It was a common *"gathering"* for Sabbath instruction. Such *"assemblies"* began in Ezekiel's day when folk met in his house during the Babylonian captivity (Ezekiel 8:1, 20:1). A *"ruler"* of the Synagogue, like JAIRUS, was in charge of its business. His job was to choose the person to pray, read the Scriptures, and preach each Sabbath.

Perhaps, because of the demand of the crowd, Jesus did not get to the side of the girl immediately (Luke 8:49). *SHE DIED!* This is the way with death. It has an appointed time. It comes and is seldom welcomed. JAIRUS' heart was breaking! I do not know if he had other children, but one thing I do know is that one child cannot take the place of another child! Some people say to a mother of many, after one of her children has died, *"Well, you have other children!"* As if it doesn't matter so much that one of hers has died for she had many children. This is not true. So Jesus went to the bedside of that still and lifeless child, and said, *"MAID ARISE!"* She, who was dead, got out of bed. She was no longer dead! In fact she was hungry!

Immediately after the surprising visit from MOSES and ELIJAH on the MOUNT OF TRANSFIGURATION with three of Jesus' disciples, He went back to work as usual (Luke 9:35-37). Throngs of people greeted him. There, among the crowd, was a *"disturbed father.* His only child, a son, had been overtaken by an *"evil spirit."* I do not know how old this son was. The poor boy was possessed by a power greater than he. This *"thing"* made him say evil and disturbing words. It threw him on the ground, injuring his body. The father was beside himself! The feeling of helplessness and dismay blanketed his heart! The father had hoped the disciples could help. They could not!

"BRING YOUR SON HERE!" were Jesus' words to the distraught father.** Have you ever had a son or daughter ill with an unspeakable *"demon"* controlling his being? Have you ever fallen to your knees begging God to heal that child? If not, you have no idea the comfort this particular father felt that day when Jesus said the words, *"Bring your son here!"* Yes, Jesus cared for that boy! Not only that, He cared for the father. At the immediate *"healing"* of the man's son, all *"the years of his agony"* melted from the father's soul. His dear son was made whole. How?—by the Word of the Saviour!

Now look at Luke 9:46-48. There was an argument among the disciples. The subject was *"which one of them was the greatest?"* How selfish! To settle this self-centered discussion, Jesus took a child from the group of people around him. Perhaps it was one of the disciples' children, I do not know. Jesus said that whoever received one of these little ones in His name received Jesus. Also, He declared that whoever received Jesus received His Father. It seems to me that Jesus changed the subject.

I remember many years ago, my family and I *"happened"* to come into the presence of a famous Christian man. It was unexpected. As the man passed by, he stopped walking and placed his hands upon our son David's head. The man blessed him! Whenever I read this Bible passage, I think of that day. That man was Bob Jones, Sr. (I recognized him from seeing his pictures.) In some respect, Luke 9:47-48 came to life for me! So when I recall what Jesus said about the child here in the gospel of Luke, the verse comes to life for me. What a day for that Bible-recorded-child!

That was the day when Jesus said, *"Whosoever shall receive this child in my name receiveth me."*

"THE WORD OF GOD ABIDETH FOREVER"
The Bible is the only book that will last for all eternity.
Everything you get from it here you will have for the ages to come in eternity.
It will be explained and understood perfectly and enjoyed forever.
Someone has said Heaven would be a great continuous Bible class.
(ggs)

Luke 9:54–Luke 11:34
INSTRUCTIONS FOR CITY-WIDE VISITATION

Luke 10:1

". . . the Lord appointed other seventy also, and sent them two and two . . ."

As I read Luke 10:1-37, I am interested in the Lord's **appointment of SEVENTY MEN to go into every city and place.** These "seventy" were to help with the plenteous harvest of souls living all around them. Now, I have made an assumption here that these *"seventy"* are *"men"*! They very well could have been woman, but I don't think so. In Jesus' day, it would seem that men would be traveling with him, doing His home missionary work. They would be the *"door to door"* evangelists or teachers that Jesus wanted. What do you think?

Not that women did not follow Jesus. They did. They ministered to Him. Once I made a study of the women who went with Jesus and took care of him—probably doing the cooking and clothes washing, etc. But, in this instance, I really feel that *"THE SEVENTY"* were men!

WHY SEVENTY?   Let's reflect on this question. We know that *"seven"* is thought, not only to be the *"perfect number,"* but also, the *"heavenly number."* So, we could say that *"seventy"* would be *"seven"* ten times *"perfection"*! Then we remember that in Moses time, he chose, by the commandment of the LORD God, *"seventy elders"* out from the people. It was upon them that the Spirit rested (Numbers 11:16, 24). These men, not only prophesied, but they assisted Moses in his work.

Another writer says that the Jews believed that the human race was made up of "seventy" people. Fourteen were descended from JAPHETH, thirty from HAM, and twenty-six from SHEM (Genesis 10). These were Noah's sons, as you know. [*Godet Commentary on Genesis*] **THIRTY-SEVEN VERSES ARE DEDICATED TO INSTRUCTIONS FOR THE SEVENTY!**

After pointing out that LABORERS were needed to reap the vast HARVEST OF PEOPLE, Jesus sent them into that HARVEST! He called his disciples "LAMBS" and the people to be "harvested," *"WOLVES"*! How would you have liked that assignment?

These workers were not to pack a suitcase for such mission work! They were to go two by two, and not be cumbered with luggage. As they approached a house, they were to say, *"PEACE BE UPON YOUR HOUSE!"* Who could turn away such a greeting? If they were invited to eat at the house, they were not to refuse the food, but enjoy the hospitality for *"the labourer is worthy of his hire."*

Then Jesus told His *"SEVENTY"* a strange thing. He said, *"Go not from house to house!"* Evidently, they were not to canvass the whole neighborhood. I wonder why! It is so different from the *"house to house"* visitation churches do today.

These "SEVENTY" were to go to various cities. Perhaps that is why they did not go to every house. If they were well-received in a city, they were to stay and eat. While there, they were to heal the sick and tell them, "THE KINGDOM OF GOD IS COMING NIGH UNTO YOU!" It seems they were preaching the *"gospel of the Kingdom."* At that time, Jesus' message was that He was THE KING and would be setting up His kingdom soon. As it turned out, we know that the Jews did not accept Him as King and would reject and crucify Him; but Jesus was giving them the opportunity to accept him as their King then. This seemed to be the message that *"THE SEVENTY"* gave to all who would listen.

Jesus gave good advice to these men when it came to "rejection"! It would be good for us to take heed, too. SO MANY ARE REJECTED TODAY AND DO NOT KNOW HOW TO HANDLE IT. Jesus recommended that if they were not well-received in a city, that they get out of that city and wipe the dust from the streets off their feet. But, before leaving, remind those ungrateful people that the Kingdom of God had come very close to them, and they rejected it!

Jesus taught that it would be better for Sodom, Tyre, and Sidon in the day of judgment than for Chorazin, Bethsaida, and Capernaum. So it is today, many so-called good cities have rejected Christ and seem not to care.

JESUS SAID THAT THOU WHO DESPISE GOD'S SERVANTS DESPISE HIM!
HOW SAD!

"A CHILD IN GOD'S HANDS"
(Psalm 138:3)
"In the day when I cried thou answeredst me,
and strengthenedst me with strength in my soul."
A CHILD IN GOD'S HANDS
IS BETTER THAN A CHILD IN YOUR HAND,
IF THAT IS THE WAY GOD WANTS IT."
(ggs heard this. The source is unknown.)

Luke 11:35–Luke 13:6
WOULD I RATHER HAVE JESUS?

Luke 12:15
"Take heed, and beware of covetousness."

This is the Bible verse I have on a small card in my kitchen. It is by the light switch. Every time I flicked on the switch, my eyes would read that verse. It was a verse for me to contemplate. It is an easy one to agree with–especially when a person has just enough money for her daily bread. When one has more money, it is a verse with a different meaning. We don't have to pray for daily bread, we have it already.

Then one day, we had a financial loss! I will not go into the whole thing; but once again, I had to examine my heart! Suddenly the *"abundance"* had shrunk to *"less abundance."* I asked myself, *"DID MY LIFE CONSIST OF THE ABUNDANCE OF THE THINGS WHICH I POSSESSED?"*

> *"And He said unto them, Take heed, and beware of covetousness: for a man's life consisteth not in the abundance of things which he possesseth"* (Luke 12:15).

When my husband and I were married, BOB ROGERS, our dear friend, sang at our wedding. BOB was like a *"brother"* to us. He sang George Beverly Shea's song, *"I'd Rather Have Jesus."* You remember the words, don't you? They go something like this: *"I'd rather have Jesus than silver or gold. I'd rather have Jesus than riches untold."*

The singer was expressing the bride's and groom's dedication to the Lord Jesus Christ. The words declared my husband-to-be and I would rather have Jesus than anything—even to being a King or Queen of a vast domain, etc. etc. With his beautiful tenor voice, Bob was telling all those in the church that *Donald A. Waite* and *Yvonne Gertrude Sanborn* had dedicated their marriage and their lives to the Lord Jesus Christ, to be used of Him in any way He wanted to use them.

When one is young, one does not know the depth of such a promise. Money was not our goal in life! Serving Jesus was! My husband, with no job, and I, his bride, were on our way to Seminary in Dallas, Texas. I was the one with a *"promised job"* at the seminary library. Commenting on his son and our early marriage, my financially successful father-in-law was heard to say "FROM PENNIES TO PEANUTS IN ONE GENERATION!"

Then one day, in the recent past, the Lord blessed us with "silver and gold." Oh, we were not the ROCKEFELLERS, but suddenly, we did not have to scrimp as we had all our married life. I will admit it was very nice! It was fun to go to a store and buy without worrying how we would pay for the product!

Then another day–just as suddenly–the financial climate of our country changed, and we were made to be more careful with our funds. IT WAS A SHOCK! I had become accustomed to the freedoms that extra money brought. I could have a radio program. I could give hilariously to THE BIBLE FOR TODAY. I could give gifts to our children. I could help those in need. It had been the happiest financial freedom I had ever had. But that HILARITY was soon-over!

It was then that I took myself aside and gave myself a good talking to. "Vonnie," I said, "Did you really mean it when you got married and told your Heavenly Father, that you'd rather have Jesus than anything?" I continued questioning myself. *Did I really mean it when I sang, through the soloist, on our wedding day that I'd rather have Jesus than be as well-off and popular as a Queen?* I remember that day and its vows and promises very well. It was not that long ago.

Once again I had to find out if my heart was right with God when it came to financial matters. I discovered—Yes! I meant it in 1948, in that little church out in an Ohio field; a field that is now a part the Cleveland airport. Yes! I meant it then, and I meant it that recent day, too, as I contemplated once more the same question, *"Would I rather have Jesus than silver or gold?"*

We were grateful for the abundance that God gave us in the past, and we are grateful to the measure of financial security we have today. Yes, it is less than it was. My husband and I know that money–even though it is nice to have–is a fleeting pleasure. It can go with the wind on a stormy day, or it can stay like a faithful dog watching our every move.

Jesus said "CONSIDER THE RAVENS!" and "CONSIDER THE LILIES!" He told his disciples, *"Therefore . . . take no thought for your life, what ye shall eat . . ."* (Luke 12:22-23).
YET, WE DO!

"THE DISPOSITION OF THE HEART"
(Revelation 20:6)
Every trial is a temptation,
for it serves to make manifest the prevailing disposition of the heart
whether it be holy or unholy.
In the sympathy of our Lord Jesus Christ,
we find a sustaining power.
He sympathizes with me and that makes me strong.
To know He cares, and knows my frame, is like a balm
(ggs)

Luke 13:7–Luke 15:21
HUMILITY IN ACTION!

Luke 14:11

"He that humbleth himself shall be exalted!"

"Several years ago, this verse was acted out in my own life. I remember it, as if it were yesterday. A friend of mine invited me to go to some kind of dinner function at a church in the Philadelphia area. I can't remember if it was only for women or not. It was in honor of a famous Bible teacher. He was the banquet's guest speaker for the evening. Sitting with him at the head table was his wife.

Strange as it may seem, I had forgotten that she could be there. You see, I knew her from my husband's seminary days. At the time, she was married to a different husband. So, my association with her was in a different setting. Her first husband had died suddenly years ago. The speaker's first wife had died, too, leaving him with several children. Now my friend became the wife of this famous man, and had mothered his children, as well as her own.

There she was--up at the head table! I would have liked to have rushed up and greeted her, but it did seem a bit presumptuous. I thought to myself, *"I'll say hello when the whole affair is over!"* It was good to see her—even from a distance. I had not seen her since seminary days. She'd moved "up" in the theological world because of her famous husband!

As I was waiting for the dinner to begin, someone came to me and whispered in my ear, *"The speaker's wife wants you to come sit with her at the head table!"* I was flabbergasted! To be picked out of the crowd and summoned to the *head table* was something else again! It was an honor! She had recognized me from afar! Needless to say, I excused myself from my friend and sat as a *"guest"* at the banquet.

"For whosoever exalteth himself shall be abased; and he that humbleth himself shall be exalted" (Luke 14:11).

Remember when Jesus told a parable about a similar situation. He said when we are invited to a wedding, we should not choose the best seat in which to sit. We should choose a *"humble place."* We would be embarrassed if we sat in the more *"honorable"* seat; and then be asked to move because the guest of honor was to sit there. Everyone would notice how presumptuous we had been! Jesus recommended that we should always find a lowly place. If the host wanted us to sit in the best seat, he would bring us to a *"higher"* chair. Jesus was teaching "humility." Learning to be *"humble"* is a gift from God. We read in James 1:9-10:

"Let the brother of low degree rejoice in that he is exalted: But the rich, in that he is made low: because as the flower of the grass he shall pass away."

One of my favorite Scripture passages is found in I Peter 5:5-7. It gets to the core of a Christian woman's being. She is encouraged to clothe herself in HUMILITY! This not only means to dress like a godly woman, but also connotes a humble attitude. The first step is *"respect"* for others. A person dressed in *"humility"* would never run to the best seat or disrespect an elder. God will give *"grace"* to those of a humble mind. If you and I humble ourselves, circumstances will not humiliate us. We must wait for God's timing in due time! HE WILL EXALT!

Once, my husband and I, as reporters for THE BIBLE FOR TODAY, attended a large "evangelical" gathering. While there, I witnessed an unbelievable illustration of humility! It was in Switzerland! A CHRISTIAN PHILOSOPHER named FRANCES SCHAEFER, entered silently into the huge auditorium. He was to be the next speaker. There was no chair for him on the platform. What did he do? Without a word or any pretense, he sat down on the main floor and waited. At the time, I did not know who he was. I wondered who that little man with the goatee, sitting on the floor, was. Talk about someone who took the lowly seat! **I SAW *"HUMILITY"* IN ACTION THAT DAY!**

MAYBE MORE OF US SHOULD SIT ON THE FLOOR!

"THE DAY OF LIFE"
(Genesis 1:5)
"YOUTH TO OLD AGE IS ALL PART OF THE DAY OF LIFE."
There is a beauty, both in the sunrise and the sunset.
Sing of it, as if glorifying the Lord. Consider thy service"
under all changes.
(ggs quotes <u>Morning & Evening</u>)

Today's Bible Blessing　　　　　　　　　*October 29*
Luke 15:22–Luke 18:6
A CERTAIN MAN HAD TWO SONS!
Luke 15:24
"This my son was . . . lost, and is found."

Often in the best of families, there is sibling rivalry. I am not sure if this was the reason in Luke 15:11-32, that *SON #2* wanted to leave home. All I know is that, after he persuaded his father to give him his inheritance, he left home! Perhaps *SON #2* felt *"lesser"* because he had a *disability* which made him *different"* from his accomplished brother. *I don't know. But I do know that SON #1 had a* *"green thumb,"* and was *"gifted"* in animal husbandry. Their father could count on him!

Whatever the cause of the restlessness in his soul, SON #2 had the wander lust. He desired to escape the home-front and to flee to the great beyond. He marched to the beat of a different drummer. There was a whole world *"out there"* that he was missing! There were people and pleasures he wanted for his own. He was tired of the sameness of his boyhood home, the strictness of his father, and the *"gloating"* of his only brother. He'd *"had it"* with the *"house rules"*!

We read in Luke 15:11 that a "certain man" had two sons. Notice this was a real family, a real father who actually had two sons! When Jesus gave life illustrations of real people, He made it clear to all of us by using the word, "certain." This father was an actual man in an actual life circumstance. Jesus wanted us to learn from this true account from this father/son relationship! Here, we are introduced to a real family with real problems. This is an account that touches our lives.

No sooner had the father turned over SON #2's inheritance to him, that the boy left home. The son was excited! Finally he was on his own! He could make his own decisions! No longer was he stuck to the humdrum life on the farm!

Off he went to the big city with all of its people and excitement. Little did he know the *pitfalls* before him. The lights of the metropolis mesmerized him! Soon he became a captive of sin! His money attracted the *unseemly!* Sin's allure dazzled! Ungodly companions enticed him! *"Ladies of the night"* seduced him! Life was an unstoppable merry-go-round. THAT IS—UNTIL HIS MONEY GAVE OUT!

Meanwhile back on the farm, his father's heart was breaking Where was his son? What was he doing? Why had he been unhappy at home? As usual, the father and the older boy worked the farm. They plowed! They planted! They harvested! Winter was long! Spring came! Summer followed! Then came autumn! Every day–all throughout the day–the father watched for the return of his wayward son. The older son observed such yearning. At sunrise, the father gazed to the East for a sign of the boy's return. At noon, there was a place at the table for his son. At night, his last look lingered for a sight of the young man's return.

There is no mention of the mother. Yet, she may have been there. At night when sleep was difficult, she thought of her boy. Where was he? Had he fallen among thieves? Was he cold? Was he ill? Was he in the hands of a wicked woman? She dreamed frightening nightmares of him on the sinful streets–hungry and in despair!

I, too, know the anguish of this mother. My SON #2 walked out of our house one rainy night. He walked into the darkness, away from the strictness of our home, away from the protection of his father into the bleakness of an unknown life. He took no coat, no money, no plan! The sickening feeling in a mother's heart is unexplainable to those who do not know. A boy–GONE! If only! If only! If only! The *emptiness* from the loss of a lost son cannot be explained!

After days of not knowing and hours of not hearing, the telephone rang. It was a call from middle America. A voice said, *"Are you looking for a boy?"* Money was wired! A ticket was purchased! My Son #2 boarded a bus! Like the prodigal son, our son said to himself, *"How many of my father's servants have food, and I perish with hunger?"*

His Dad took the train to the big city bus station. He went to meet his PRODIGAL. They missed each other. Looking out the window, I, his mother, saw our son. He did not stop at our door. Quickly, I ran down the street calling his name. He came toward me. I hugged him. I kissed him. His father arrived and said, ***"For this my son . . . was lost, and is found"*** (Luke 15:24).

"GOD'S WAY IS THE RIGHT WAY"
(Psalm 107:7; Psalm 138:8)
THE LORD WILL PERFECT THAT WHICH CONCERNETH ME.
GOD ALWAYS LEADS IN THE RIGHT WAY,
ALWAYS HAS! ALWAYS WILL!.
"And He led them forth by the right way,
that they might go to a city of habitation." (ggs)

Today's Bible Blessing   *October 30*
Luke 18:7–Luke 19:48
ANSWERED PRAYER ACCORDING TO THE NEED
Luke 18:14b
"He that humbleth himself shall be exalted."

I've come to the conclusion that Jesus was a *"people person"*! After all, He came to earth to *"seek and to save that which was lost!"* (See Luke 19:10.)   Luke 18 commences with Jesus instructing that people should always pray rather than faint. *"Faint"* here means to lose hope. What an encouragement to us today with all our problems! He examples *"prayer"* in interesting ways. The first example of praying was with the troubled, wronged widow that a judge heard and helped.

The next example of proper praying was his story about two "prayers." One was the bragging publican who prayed fancy prayers of self-importance and self-diagnosed purity. The other was the repentant tax collector who prayed privately— away from the ears of others—telling God he was a sinner. Concerning this kind of praying, Jesus comments, *"for every one that exalteth himself shall be abased; and he that humbleth himself shall be exalted"* (Luke 18:14).

Continuing teaching, Jesus holds a baby in his arms. He holds an *"infant"* (vs. 15) close to His heart! In fact, many *"infants"* were there. Nothing pleases a mother more than to have another enjoy her children. The disciples were disturbed. These babies were taking up Jesus' time. Instead, Jesus used the little ones to continue his instruction on *"prayer"* (vs. 15-16). Jesus insisted, *"SUFFER [permit] THE LITTLE CHILDREN TO COME UNTO ME!"* In so doing, He explained that the Kingdom of God was made up of such *"children."* Jesus taught that anyone who came to Him must do so with childlike faith.

Listening in to the above conversation was a certain ruler. (He was a real person.) He asked Jesus, *"Good Master, what shall I do to inherit eternal life?"* First of all *"eternal life"* cannot be "inherited," but Jesus ignored that. (The man only knew how to make conversation in financial terms.) Jesus questioned, *"Why callest thou me good?"* Immediately, Jesus answered his own question, *"None is good except God!"* Then the conceited man boasted that he had kept all the commandments from his youth. *What a lie!* No one could keep all the commandments but Jesus. So, Jesus suggested, *"Sell all you have and distribute it to the poor; then follow me."* Surprise! Surprise! The rich man could not do that! Though nothing is said about *"prayer,"* in this passage, it is plain to see that no man, in such a poor spiritual condition, could pray with faith for anything! HIS TRUST WAS NOT IN JESUS, BUT IN HIS RICHES!

After instructing His apostles about His soon-coming death and resurrection, they came near to Jericho. (Jericho is a beautiful place—something like an oasis in the desert.) On the way to that refreshing city, a blind man was begging. When the *sightless pauper* was told that Jesus had arrived, the blind one called out, *"Jesus, thou son of David, have mercy on me."* It was a *prayer* for compassion and release from his terrible condition. I do not know how the blind man knew Jesus was close. Perhaps everyone did. Calling Jesus the *"son of David"* showed us readers, that the poor man recognized Jesus as THE KING! Without any hesitation, Jesus answered that prayer! The blind man received his sight!

Now we come to the man named ZACCHAEUS. He is the only one in this study whose name is known. Though he was small in stature, the man had great power, for he was a hated tax collector. He'd heard of Jesus. Now I don't know what he had heard, but it was interesting enough that the CHIEF PUBLICAN ran ahead of the crowd. Being a short man, he climbed up into a tree to see. He wanted a good view of the Master. (This event happened on the other side of Jericho.) When Jesus, with the following crowd, got to ZACCHAEUS' perch, Jesus glanced up and said, *"Come on down, ZACCHAEUS. Hurry up. I'm going to your house today!"* I wonder what Zacchaeus thought, but more than that, I wonder what the crowd thought! They considered ZACCHAEUS a *"sinner,"* for he stole from them. Immediately, Zacchaeus was convicted of his sin. In repentance, he said he'd give half of his goods to the poor, as well as repay what he had stolen fourfold. This was a case of *answered prayer* for Zacchaeus' need! Jesus said, *"This day "salvation is come to your house!"*

From this brief meditation on "prayer," we realize that "praying" comes in all forms and ways, according to the heart need.

"LIFE'S RACE"
My feelings are too small to know God.
I must know Him through His written Word!
SHORT IS LIFE'S RACE,
STERN IS GOD'S PACE,
BUT HE IS THE PRIZE BEFORE MY EYES.
PRESS ON! PRESS ON! (ggs)

Today's Bible Blessing   *October 31*

Luke 20:1–Luke 21:38
OUT OF HER POVERTY, SHE GAVE ALL

Luke 21:4b
"Of her penury hath cast in all the living that she had!"

WHILE IN THE TEMPLE, JESUS OBSERVED PEOPLE CONTRIBUTING TO THE TEMPLE TREASURY! Today let us meditate on some *"giving"* people. Contributing to the expenses of God's work is a good thing! Everyone who attends church today should take a page out of this true account of *"giving"* to the work of the Lord. The Apostle Paul, spoke of this, when he said, *"Let the elders that rule well be counted worthy of double honour, especially they who labour in the word and doctrine"* (I Timothy 5:17). It is encouraging to observe that people in JESUS' TIME were faithful givers. EVEN TODAY, CHURCHES, MISSIONARIES, AND PASTORS MUST BE SUPPORTED BY THOSE TO WHOM THEY TEACH & PREACH.

In the Temple that day, there were two distinct classes of "givers." Jesus was there and noticed a group of men by the treasury box. Others noticed them, too. Probably everyone saw their *"giving"* attitude. Jesus said they were "RICH MEN!" (See Luke 21:1-4.) Even if Jesus were not *"all knowing,"* anyone can tell a rich man by the way he dresses. Usually both men and woman dress their best when going into the Lord's house. It is only in recent years that church attendees are showing their disrespect for *"the holy"* by their lowered dress standards. In the relaxed attitudes that prevail in today's mega-church mentality, people pride themselves that they have a *"come as you are"* dress code.

The term *"rich"* is relative. What a *"street person"* or a *"bag-lady"* would think *"rich"* meant, would be far different from what a billionaire would consider to be the meaning of the word. Let's go with the definition of *"having more than enough material possessions, owning much money, property, and wealth."*

The "rich" men in today's reading have never been introduced by name. We are curious! Have we met them before? All we know is that they walked into THE TEMPLE and "cast" some "gifts" into the treasury box. We know this to be true because the Bible says so.

Could the men have been some of the *"rich men"* Jesus told us about previously? Let's see: There was the *"rich man"* who could barely get into the Kingdom of God (Matthew 19:23). Jesus assured that it was possible, but difficult. Maybe he was there. Or was "rich" JOSEPH OF ARIMATHAEA present? He placed Jesus' dead body in his own tomb after the crucifixion (Matthew 27:57). Or, could one of them have been the *"rich man"* who built bigger barns (Luke 12:16) and died of greed? Maybe one was the *"rich man,"* dressed in purple, who ended up in Hell (Luke 16:19). Or *could one of them have been "RICH ZACCHAEUS"* (Luke 19:2), whom Jesus forgave? Maybe another one was the *"rich young ruler"* who loved Jesus, but loved his money more (Luke 18:23). Or could it have been the *"rich man,"* who asked his steward for an accounting of his stewardship? Had he been in the temple that day? (See Luke 16:1.)

Now let us give our attention to the woman in this story. We are told she was a *"poor widow."* The death of her husband had been difficult, as all deaths are. Still she grieved his loss. Her dress betrayed her *"widowhood."* Her cloak was dark. It was worn. Everyone could tell she was poor. Perhaps she knew *OLD WIDOW ANNA,* (Luke 2:36). This particular widow paused until the men had ceased their contribution display. Stealthily, she came quietly to the treasury box, hoping no one would notice. It may have been difficult for her to walk. She may have used a cane. Yet, though poor, she worshipped JEHOVAH from the depth of her soul. JESUS SAW HER. He saw her heart. Her contributions, compared to the rich man's were not much, *only two mites*! IT WAS ALL SHE HAD! *Out of her poverty, she gave her all!* While the rich men had much, they did not give out of their *"abundance."* Think about that!

> ## *"WHAT IS THE PRESENT TIME?"*
> (Romans 8:18)
> *"For I reckon that the sufferings of this present time*
> *are not worthy to be compared with the glory*
> *which shall be revealed in us."*
> "THIS PRESENT TIME" IS THE TIME WE CALL LIFE,
> DURING WHICH WE LAUGH AND CRY. (ggs)

Today's Bible Blessing   *November 1*

Luke 22:1–Luke 23:14
THE DAY CHRIST DIED

Luke 23:27
"There followed him a great company of people . . . which bewailed and lamented him."

The events during the last hours of our Lord Jesus Christ's earthly life moved swiftly! The very reason He was born was coming to pass! The swiftness of the moment was breathtaking! From the time Jesus and *"THE THREE"* were in the Garden, the clock's hands moved forward with momentous rapidity. Soon Judas, the betrayer, was there kissing his Master on the cheek. The soldiers hastened to Jesus, pulling and pushing Him in all directions and arresting Him. The charges were false!

While the trial was in progress, Peter was warming his hands at the fire of the faithless, pretending to be one of them, as he denied the Lord. Roosters were crowing and confusion reigned. It was then that Jesus turned from his accusers and *"looked"* at Peter. Such a *"look"* Peter had never seen! It penetrated his soul. Peter's denial was certain. It brought tears of repentance. But it was too late! Unkind words cannot be taken back. Tears cannot remove betrayal!

"Prophesy who hit you!" **the** soldiers mocked Jesus! They blasphemed his holy Name—not realizing who He was! The chief priest and the two-faced elders led Jesus before the Sanhedrin, a deciding council. The question of the day was *"ART THOU THE MESSIAH?"* Without hesitation, Jesus replied, *"I AM."* In so doing, He was telling them that He was the GREAT *"I AM"* of Abraham, Isaac, and Jacob! BUT, THEY DID NOT COMPREHEND!

The Bible says that "multitudes" were there! That was in Pilate's hall! They said Jesus perverted the people and the nation. They said He forbad paying tribute to Caesar. They lied! They claimed Jesus stirred up the people with His teaching. Pilate found no fault in Him! The Jews gnashed their teeth. Their fists pounded the air!

Off Jesus was sent to HEROD'S COURT. Though questioned, Jesus said nothing. The priest and scribes vehemently accused Him! The men of war treated Him as a "NOTHING," throwing a gorgeous robe around his shoulders. After careful examination, Herod, like Pilate, found no fault in Him. *"Nothing worthy of death"* was the conclusion!

Because of their hatred of Jesus, the Jews begged for the release of MURDERER BARABBAS that day! If you remember, one prisoner was allowed to be released at such a time. From then on, the only words from their mouth concerning Jesus was, *"CRUCIFY HIM!"* Those words will fill the air forever! They will deny it, but deep inside, they know they were said.

Jesus was being beaten and chastened. The blows weakened His strength! A man named Simon—from out of the country—was pulled from the crowd to help Jesus carry THE CROSS. Great crowds followed him as he trudged to Calvary. Women wailed! Many lamented!

Upon Jesus' arrival to the execution hill, two others were there ahead of Him. They, too, were to be crucified. They were thieves and sinners. Jesus was not! They would die, hanging next to Him. IT WAS TERRIBLE! Nails! Ropes! Ill-treatment! Vinegar! Spit! Slaps! Taunts! The tree-made-cross was hoisted upright. The pounding into the ground jarred Jesus' body. His hands and feet were nailed! Tears and rips were in His skin! His arms pulled! His body mangled! Pain! Punishment! Darkness! Lightning! Time! Anguish! Sin! Sadness! All this, and more, was poured on and into His Holy soul. THAT WAS THE DAY JESUS WAS MADE *"SIN"* FOR YOU AND ME (II Corinthians 5:21)!

AND THE PEOPLE SMOTE THEIR BREASTS IN UNBELIEF AND GRIEF!

"DEATH IS NOT FAILURE"
(Psalm 30:5b)
DEATH IS NOT FAILURE FOR THE BELIEVER.
IT IS THE DOOR TO HEAVEN!
Life is so short that no man can afford to lose a day!
God knows as much about tomorrow as He did about yesterday!
"Weeping may endure for a night, but joy cometh in the morning"
(ggs)

Luke 23:15–Luke 24:43
AND THEY REMEMBERED HIS WORDS

Luke 24:34

"The Lord is risen indeed!"

The cross was empty–that place of Roman execution, that place where sin was placed on the Lamb of God! Yet, most who watched did not comprehend the *atoning miracle* that happened that day! Those standing at the cross did not hear the ripping of the TEMPLE'S HOLY VEIL from top to bottom. They did not understand the darkness that blanketed their day as Jesus died. Nor were they able to digest Jesus' Words when He cried out with a loud voice, *"FATHER, INTO THY HANDS I COMMEND MY SPIRIT!"* All they knew was empty loneliness. A *"righteous man"* had died! (See Luke 23:47.)

Joseph of Arimathaea, a counselor and a just man, had taken the dead body, wrapped it, and laid it in his own tomb. What an act of devotion to Jesus, the crucified! Those women, who had ministered to Jesus in life, continued their ministry to Him in death. Love does not stop for a precious one just because the breath of life is emptied. Love is an intangible thing, a bonding of soul to soul and spirit to spirit. That is why, when one of ours dies, we still love her or him. Love is a gift that God has given to humans to warm their lives.

So those GALILAEAN women, who daily ministered to Jesus, hurried to the sepulcher. It was early morning. In fact, it was Sunday, the FIRST DAY of the week. In their hands were spices to grace the body of their *dead loved One*. To their amazement, the stone that closed the tomb had been rolled away. Had there been foul play? Could not the hatred of Jesus cease after death? Perplexed, but undaunted, they walked into the tomb. JESUS' BODY WAS GONE! Before they could speak, two *"men"* in shining garments appeared! Their *"brightness"* blinded the women's view! They were frightened! Then the *"men"* spoke, questioning, *'WHY SEEK YE THE LIVING AMONG THE DEAD?"*

It was then that Jesus' words were remembered. He had said that He would rise from the dead three days after His crucifixion. They dropped their spices, and ran to tell the apostles the *good news*. But the apostles did not believe them. The men thought the women's *"grief"* caused them to *"see"* things that were not there.

My husband and I have been to EMMAUS. It is six miles from Jerusalem. We entered a small church there in a country setting. It was a beautiful place—simple—blue skies and sunshine crowning the day. The call of a rooster warmed our ears. Inside, on the front wall of that chapel was a large painting. We saw an artist's conception of the *"two"* who walked with the risen Christ that day on the way to the very Emmaus where Dr. Waite and I stood. We came there with a bus load of touring people. I remember it well!

Much to our surprise, painted on that wall, were a husband and wife. The artist had been constrained to put his view of THE TWO on canvas! I liked his thought. He said it was a man and his wife walking together. *Love of a husband and wife is a special gift from God!* The years united in wedlock bring a couple either closer or further apart—depending on the will of the married. The couple in this portrait were together when Jesus overtook them on the road. It was to them that He taught the Scriptures concerning Himself. *Their grief over His recent death blinded their weeping eyes.* Grief has a way of doing whatever it wants to a person.

Inviting Jesus for a bit of food was a beautiful thing. The couple welcomed the resurrected Christ into their home. Many words of comfort and encouragement can be given over a cup of tea. It was then, as Jesus broke the bread, that the nail prints on His hands could be seen. It was then that the man and his wife saw Jesus for Who He was and what He did.

TRULY HE WAS THE RESURRECTED LORD!
(Luke 24:31)

"THINK OF THE GAIN!"
(Romans 8:23)
"We ourselves groan within ourselves, waiting for the adoption, to wit, the redemption of our body."
It has pleased the Lord to take your dear One.
It has also pleased the Lord to leave you here alone.
DON'T THINK OF THE PARTING! THINK OF THE MEETING!
DON'T THINK OF THE LOSS! THINK OF THE GAIN!
(ggs)

Today's Bible Blessing 　　　　　　　　　*November 3*
Luke 24:44–John 2:24
THE WORD WAS MADE FLESH
John 1:1
"In the beginning was the Word . . . and the Word was God!"
　　Once, when I was a teenage girl, I gave a testimony out on the BEREA TRIANGLE. Instead of a *"square,"* our town had a "TRIANGLE." Pastor Nika was our young pastor—fresh from Bible school—eager to serve the Lord in our town. Because he was interested in the *"lost souls"* of our town, the Pastor began *"street meetings"* every

Friday night during good weather. Berea was a college town, close to the big city of Cleveland, and it still is a wonderful place in which to grow up!

Our church purchased a sound system which sent our voices thither and yon. There were green benches on the TRI-ANGLE. Occasionally someone would sit down on one and listen. Cars stopped at the light. Their windows were always opened. So, they could hear us. No one had air conditioned cars in those days! In fact, no one had air conditioned houses or stores, for that matter. The year had to be before 1945—for that was the year I graduated from Berea High School. They were the WORLD WAR II years. Soon there would be rationing of sugar and shoes and gasoline. If not already.

One Friday night a young man, in his early twenties, sat on one of those benches. He was discouraged. Recently his father had been put in jail. I do not remember the crime. One night he sat on one of those green benches. It was during our street meeting. He heard the gospel for the first time in his life. Oh, how he needed the SAVIOUR! Soon he realized that he was a sinner, and he needed to be "born-again" & "saved." He received Jesus into His heart and life. What a happy day for him!

> *"But as many as received him, to them gave he power to become the sons of God, even to them that believe on his name"* (John 1:12).

From then on the young man, who had accepted Jesus Christ, became a part of the street meetings. He gave his testimony how Christ saved him, and he brought his trumpet to sound forth our music. It was good. He grew in the Lord and the Word of God!

Getting back to the time I gave a testimony out on the Berea Triangle. I was telling whoever was listening about the "WORD OF GOD." I mentioned Hebrews 4:12 how the "Bible" was *"quick and powerful"* and sharper than a *"two edged"* sword. Then I quoted John 1:1. (It's in today's Bible reading.) I said that the "WORD OF GOD," in the verse, was the Bible. I WAS WRONG! In my ignorance, I said that THE BIBLE was *"in the beginning,"* and that it was *"with God,"* and that it *"was God"*! Then I sat down—not knowing any difference!

Later, Pastor Nika took me aside and said, "Yvonne, the "WORD OF GOD" in that passage, referred to Jesus Christ." Oops! I was mortified that I'd said a wrong thing! Soon I learned how Jesus Christ was *"THE LOGOS."* HE IS "THE LIVING WORD," THE REVELATOR!

From *"IN THE BEGINNING,"* it was His job always to reveal the WORDS of the OLD TESTAMENT, as well as those in the NEW TESTAMENT! The "LOGOS" (JESUS) *"reveals all things."* All the *"Words"* of Scripture are in His care! *"For ever, O LORD, thy word is settled in heaven"* (Psalm 119:89).

John 1:14 explains to us "Jesus" as "THE LIVING WORD"!!

"And THE WORD was made flesh, and dwelt among us, (and we beheld His glory, the glory as of the ONLY BEGOTTEN OF THE FATHER,) full of grace and truth!"

Getting back to the young man who was saved at the street meeting; He drew a picture of me. It was beautiful! He gave me handpicked violets. He would bring his trumpet to my house and we'd do music together. He wanted to marry me. I said, "NO!" In one week, he was engaged to another girl. In time, I married Dr. D. A. Waite. He never drew a picture of me or picked wild violets; but he did play the saxophone; and I love him—that's for sure!

And—we've been married, as of this August, **sixty-three years!**

"LOT LOST EVERYTHING BECAUSE HE LOST HIS SEPARATION!"
(II Corinthians 6:17; Genesis 19:29-30)

He lost:

> His property,
> His wife,
> His daughters,
> His sons-in-law,
> His reputation!

NO ONE WANTS TO EMULATE LOT,
AND CERTAINLY NOT LOT'S WIFE!
"Wherefore come out from among them, and be ye separate, saith the Lord, and touch not the unclean thing; and I will receive you . . ." (ggs)

Today's Bible Blessing   *November 4*

John 2:25–John 4:48
NICODEMUS QUESTIONS

John 3:16

"For God so loved the world, that He gave His only begotten Son."

The Apostle John finished the second chapter of his Gospel with these words: *"FOR HE (JESUS) KNEW WHAT WAS IN MAN!"* So, when we meet Jesus, discussing the *"new birth"* with NICODEMUS, we see this *"all knowing"* attribute of the Son of God in action.

NICODEMUS, the PHARISEE, whose name meant *"VICTOR OVER THE PEOPLE,"* was a ruler of the Jews. He was an influential member of the Sanhedrin. This Nicodemus was one of the three richest men of Jerusalem. Some say he was *NICODEMUS BEN GORION*, historian JOSEPHUS' brother.

NICODEMUS was a curious man. He had heard of RABBI JESUS and all that He had done. He had heard of His preaching and healing. In fact, this Jewish ruler plainly said, *"We know that thou art a teacher come from God!"* NICODEMUS did not need convincing, for no one *"not from God"* could do such miracles!

Concerned and curious, NICODEMUS lost no time. It was night and dark outside. He could not stay too long. Probably he had worked all day and needed to get home to his family. So, this inquisitive man got right down to the subject that was on his mind. He asked Jesus, *"HOW CAN A MAN BE BORN WHEN HE IS OLD?"* Jesus was the one who had brought up the subject, explaining that no one could *see* the Kingdom of God without being *"born-again."*

This *"born-again"* language was new to Nicodemus! Jesus' response was mysterious. The learned Pharisee was trying to understand the concept. Was a person to go back in time and become a baby in his mother's womb? Listening carefully, the questioner heard that one must, not only be born *"of water,"* in a regular birth for an earthly life, but also, a person had to be *"born of the Spirit"* to an heavenly birth to receive *"eternal life."*

Then Jesus talked about the *"wind."* It blows things around. For instance think of a *"tornado."* A person cannot touch that "tornado," but can see the damage it has done. So it is with being *"born of the Spirit."* A person cannot "see" the Holy Spirit, but when one is *"born of the Spirit,"* one knows it!

Jesus questioned *why* NICODEMUS, as a MASTER IN ISRAEL, did not understand these things. JESUS reviewed the familiar account of Moses, the pole, and the brasen serpent! Probably Nicodemus knew this account since childhood. Hundreds of Israelites out in the wilderness had been bitten by poisonous snakes. What was Moses to do? God instructed Moses to put a brass serpent on a high pole, so everyone in the camp could see it. The cure from that deadly snake bite was to "LOOK" at the brasen serpent on the pole! Therefore, the sick people had no excuse not to be healed. Hundreds looked. Hundreds lived. Yet, some were stubborn in their unbelief, and would not look. They died a painful death in their unbelief!

It was then that NICODEMUS heard strange words. That night, he was told that Jesus Himself, was to be lifted up on a *"pole,"* exactly like the brass serpent in Moses' day. Why? *"THAT WHOSOEVER BELIEVETH IN HIM SHOULD NOT PERISH, BUT HAVE ETERNAL LIFE!"* What a statement!

Then NICODEMUS was privileged to be the first to hear the most beautiful words ever spoken. They are *holy Words.* They came from the mouth of Jesus one dark Jerusalem night. Children have learned them all over the world. Adults have spoken them in reverent belief! I learned them as a young person from the mouth of my Mother. I will never forget them! Listen, as NICODEMUS did, and weep!

"For God so loved the world, that he gave his only begotten Son, that whosoever believeth in him should not perish, but have everlasting life. For God sent not his Son into the world to condemn the world; but that the world through him might be saved. He that believeth on him is not condemned: but he that believeth not is condemned already, because he hath not believed in the name of the only begotten Son of God" (John 3:16-18).

ARE YOU LIKE NICODEMUS OF OLD? Do you wonder how you can be "born-again? You and this learned man of old are not the only ones with such a question. ALL YOU NEED TO KNOW TO HAVE ETERNAL LIFE IS WHAT JESUS TOLD NICODEMUS ONE DARK NIGHT LONG AGO.

JESUS ANSWERED HIM IN JOHN 3:3-7:
"Verily, verily, I say unto thee, EXCEPT A MAN BE BORN-AGAIN, HE CANNOT SEE THE KINGDOM OF GOD!"

Then Nicodemus asked Jesus another question:
"HOW CAN A MAN BE BORN WHEN HE IS OLD? Can he enter the second time into his mother's womb, and be born?

Jesus answered,
"Verily, verily, I say unto thee, EXCEPT A MAN BE BORN OF WATER (human birth) AND OF THE SPIRIT (spiritual birth), HE CANNOT ENTER INTO THE KINGDOM OF GOD. That which is born of the flesh is flesh; and that which is born of the Spirit is spirit."

**"MARVEL NOT THAT I SAID UNTO THEE,
YE MUST BE BORN-AGAIN!"
WHY NOT RECEIVE JESUS TODAY?**

JESUS, THE SON OF GOD, CAME TO EARTH TO FREE YOU FROM THE CONDEMNATION THAT HANGS OVER YOUR SOUL AND SPIRIT which came upon all men because of Adams' sin. That condemnation is unforgiveness from God and an eternal sentence to Hell as a destination (Matthew 23:33). That *"condemnation"* is physical death. And after death the judgment (Romans 6:18; Revelation 1:18). None of us can escape it unless we receive the Lord Jesus Christ! (See Romans 10:9-10.)

ACKNOWLEDGE that you are a sinner. Agree with God that nothing you can do, say, or any works, can make a way to the forgiveness of your sins, to a Holy God, or to a Heavenly Home.

"For by grace are ye saved through faith; AND THAT NOT OF YOURSELVES: it is the GIFT of God: NOT OF WORKS, lest any man should boast" (Ephesians 2:8-9).

LOOK TO JESUS!
"Behold the Lamb of God, which taketh away the sin of the world" (John 1:29b).

ACCEPT JESUS AS YOUR SIN-BEARER AND REDEEMER FROM THAT SIN!
"For He hath made Him to be sin FOR US, who knew

no sin; *THAT WE MIGHT BE MADE THE RIGHTEOUSNESS OF GOD IN HIM"* (I Corinthians 5:21).

"But God commendeth his love toward us, in that, while we were yet sinners, Christ died for us" (Romans 5:8).

ONLY RECEIVING JESUS CHRIST AS YOUR OWN PERSONAL SAVIOUR AND PERSONAL SIN BEARER CAN BRING YOU FORGIVENESS OF YOUR SIN AND ETERNAL LIFE.

The Bible says in John 1:12 the following:

"But as many as received him, to them gave he power to become the sons of God, even to them that believe on his name. . ."

ISN'T IT ABOUT TIME THAT YOU BECAME A CHRISTIAN BY RECEIVING JESUS CHRIST AS YOUR SAVIOUR?

"Believe on the Lord Jesus Christ, and thou shalt be saved. . ." (Acts 16:31).

"A LONELY JOURNEY"

I took a lonely journey
Into the Valley of Pain;
And each time from this place of anguish,
As I came forth again and again,
I held in my hand a child's hand
And started a small new life
Out on the Roadway of Living
And into the Highway of Strife. (ggs)

The author gave birth to three daughters
Beverly's birth was extremely difficult
It was during the birthing process that Beverly's brain was damaged causing
her to be retarded—not able to talk, etc., all of her life.

𝒯*oday's* ℬ*ible* ℬ*lessing*   𝒩*ovember* 5

John 4:49–John 6:32
THE DIFFERENCE WAS JESUS!

John 5:8

"Jesus saith unto him, Rise, take up thy bed, and walk."

Presently we are reading the GOSPEL OF JOHN. It would be well, if we considered the writer of this work. His name is JOHN. It means *"THE LORD IS GRACIOUS"*! Often, he was referred to as *"the other disciple"* or the one *"whom Jesus loved."* In time, he became the Master's most beloved apostle. Tradition says he was thrown into boiling oil, but survived that punishment. If I remember correctly, he was the only apostle who died a natural death. He was around the age of ninety.

This remarkable man spent his last days as an outcast, doing hard labor on a *rocky* and *bleak* island called PATMOS. It was a fifty-mile square piece of ground—a place where criminals did their *"time."* John was sentenced there by the DOMITIAN and the Roman government. While a prisoner, slaving daily in the island's mines, John wrote *THE BOOK OF THE REVELATION OF JESUS CHRIST* about A.D. 96. John penned *THE GOSPEL OF JOHN* around A.D. 85-90 and the three epistles bearing his name in A.D. 90.

I believe his mother's name was Mary, though some say it was Salome. (See Matthew 27:56; Mark 15:40.) She may have been John's aunt. It is assumed that John came from a family of means because he was aquatinted with CAIAPHAS, the high priest (John 18:15). Because of this, his mother was free from financial care to help Jesus during much of His three-years of public preaching. Besides ministering to Jesus in life, she grieved for Him at Calvary, and helped discover His empty tomb on Resurrection Sunday!

John and his brother, James, were called "THE SONS OF THUNDER," not because they were in a motorcycle gang, but because their father, Zebedee was a boisterous man. The family business was *"fishing,"* and they often partnered with Simon Peter on the Sea of Galilee. Prior to following Jesus, John's heart was prepared, as he may have been a disciple of John the Baptist.

LOOK WITH ME AT JOHN 5:1-27, AND SEE A CRIPPLED MAN.

He had an *"infirmity"* for thirty-eight years. Think how long that is. I was thirty-eight years old when our youngest son was born. I'd lived a full life—sick as a child, the oldest of three. At first I was a city girl who moved to a country town, lived in a Cleveland, Ohio suburb, attended Bible school after high school, married, etc. etc. I had lived a whole life by then.

But this "certain" helplessly weak man lay on a mat all those years. I KNOW WHAT IT WAS LIKE TO LIVE IN A BED! But my time was only three years. My bed became my world. All I knew was found within the square corners of my sheets! So that mat became this man's world, too.

We read of a "pool" (John 5:2). It was no ordinary one. At *"certain"* times of the year, after an "ANGEL" came and stirred the waters, it would bubble up with healing power. Whoever stepped *first* into that moving pool was healed! The helpless man was too disabled to move. All those years, he hoped someone would care enough for his plight, pick him up, and dip him into the pool. No one came. Instead, another hurt person would be healed.

We have heard of *"healing waters"*—even in our country. I remember a well-known president, of earlier years, who often went to the soothing pools of Warm Springs, Georgia, for such relief. A paralyzed young man I knew as a girl, traveled, at great expense and discomfort to Lourdes, seeking healing. Neither was healed. The difference between those healing streams and the *"pool"* called *"BETHESDA"* was Jesus!

Jesus saw the man! He listened to his plight. Immediately He *spoke* a command to the crippled man: *"RISE, TAKE UP THY BED, AND WALK!"* It is of interest also that Jesus gave another command. He said, *"Sin no more, lest a worse thing come unto thee."* These words make us realize that the man's infirmity must have come upon him because of his sin. So often, our health problems are a result of our own failures and waywardness. By the way, the healing was done on THE SABBATH, and the watching Jews did not approve!

Before we leave this passage, we note that parts of John 5:3 and all of John 5:4 are not in any of the critical Greek Texts which underlie most of the modern bibles people read today!

"PRESSED DOWN WITH CARE"

(I Thessalonians 5:18; Job 23:6; II Corinthians 12:9)
Today, I have a sweet and wonderful peace
which I should have had yesterday.
The "everything" seemed against me,
and I am pressed down with care.
I know the LORD is for me!
I know He pleads my cause.
I know He cares.
WILL HE PLEAD WITH ME WITH HIS GREAT POWER?
NO! BUT HE WOULD PUT HIS "STRENGTH" IN ME!
(A helpful pastor gave me this verse. It has stayed with me all these years.)
(ggs)

Today's Bible Blessing　　　　　*November 6*

John 6:33–John 7:46
JESUS IS THE BREAD OF LIFE!

John 6:35

"Jesus said . . . He that cometh to me shall never hunger . . ."

As we read the GOSPEL OF JOHN, we see Jesus with different eyes. He is portrayed as the *SON OF GOD*. Remember, Matthew showed us Jesus as the *King*; Mark gave us Jesus as the *Servant*, while Dr. Luke opened our eyes to Him as the *Son of Man*. Now we see Him as **THE WORD**, who became *"flesh,"* and dwelt among us (John 1:14).

In John, chapter six, we read a startling statement. Jesus taught in verse thirty-two that HE WAS *THE TRUE BREAD*

FROM HEAVEN! What did He mean by that? Well, first of all, the Jewish people were well acquainted with the account of the *MANNA* that was found every morning during the *"wilderness wanderings"!* Never need the people of God go to bed hungry! Never should they wonder if they would have food for tomorrow! They were nourished by food supplied from Heaven. Every morning, except the Sabbath morning, there was sufficient sustenance for that day, and double food for Saturday!

When Jesus preached that He was the TRUE BREAD, he reflected on the *"manna"* of years ago. The Jews had experienced the faithfulness of the LORD God for forty years! He explained that He, Jesus, was THE BREAD OF GOD from Heaven that would give LIFE to the world!

> *"I am the bread of life: he that cometh to me shall never*
> *hunger; and he that believeth on me shall never thirst. . ."*
> (John 6:35).

Suddenly, in the middle of the discussion on "Jesus being THE BREAD OF LIFE," Jesus interrupted Himself with a deep theological discourse. It concerned the equality of His "FATHER" with HIMSELF. This raised the ire of those listening in that CAPERNAUM synagogue!

Christ preached the following:

> *"All that the Father giveth me shall come to me; and him*
> *that cometh to me I will in no wise cast out. For I came*
> *down from heaven, not to do mine own will, but the will of*
> *him that sent me"* (John 6:37-38).

After being rejected by Nazareth, Jesus adopted CAPERNAUM as His home base. That is why He was found preaching there so often. Several years ago, my husband and I visited CAPERNAUM by the Sea. It was an area filled with *"ruins"* from former civilizations.

Remember, how Jesus had said, *"If the works done in CAPERNAUM had been done in Sodom, they would have repented"* (Matthew 11:23). Well, His predictions that it would be destroyed came true. CAPERNAUM BECAME COMPLETE RUBBLE! After its collapse, the city was unknown. Years later, two German archaeologists (1905) and some Franciscan monks (1926) discovered the site. It was then that the ruins of a synagogue were discovered. It had been rebuilt over the original site of the synagogue that had been constructed by the centurion in Luke 7. Remember it was his servant who had been healed by Jesus.

Jesus proclaimed that it was the will of God that everyone who saw the Son should believe and have *everlasting life.* This promise of *"everlasting life"* and *"resurrection"* was combined with the fact that *no one can come to THE FATHER, except THE FATHER draw him* (John 6:44). This teaching, combined with Jesus' words to Philip and Andrew in John 12:32, is profound teaching.

Jesus belabored the point with great emphasis. *"HE THAT BELIEVETH **ON ME** HATH EVERLASTING LIFE!"* (See John 6:47.) No other *"WAY"* or *"PERSON"* could bring such *"LIFE"*! It is such an important truth which is revealed in this verse! ONLY BELIEF ON JESUS CHRIST CAN BRING EVERLASTING LIFE!

Do you realize that THE NEW INTERNATIONAL VERSION, THE NEW AMERICAN STANDARD VERSION, the ENGLISH STANDARD VERSION, THE NEW KING JAMES VERSION IN THE <u>FOOTNOTES</u> (of the Study Edition), and almost every other modern version do not have the important words, "ON ME" in this verse?

We know that

*"Neither is there salvation in any other: **for there is none other name** under heaven given among men, whereby we must be saved"* (Acts 4:12).

When the modern versions follow the wrong Greek Texts, by omitting reference to Jesus, they are committing a grievous error. What a relief it is to know that we, who use the King James Bible, have the *"assurance"* that words and verses are not removed or added to our Bible.

So when Jesus said, *"I AM THAT BREAD OF LIFE,"* there is no doubt!

JESUS IS THE ONE WE MUST TRUST!

"IN OUR HEARTACHES"
(Joshua 2:18, 21; 6:17)
Each time the Children of Israel
marched around the walls of Jericho,
they saw the scarlet thread from Rahab's window.
It was an evidence of her faith in the Promise.
In our heartaches, let us remember.
Gideon's men did not weep over one broken pitcher,
but rejoiced that the lamp blazed forth more.
**SOMETIMES WE ARE UNAWARE OF THE FLAME,
BUT OTHERS SEE IT.** (ggs)

John 7:47–John 9:19
THE DAY NO STONES WERE THROWN!

John 8:11

"Neither do I condemn thee: go and sin no more!"

In yesterday's reading, we read an insightful verse. It was John 7:24. Jesus warned the murmuring ones, *"Judge not according to the appearance, but judge righteous judgment!"*

Today, we come to an important—yet controversial—portion of Scripture! It is found in John 7:53-8:11! It is the portion commonly called *"THE WOMAN TAKEN IN ADULTERY."* This passage is not only of interest because Jesus handled the question of *"marriage unfaithfulness,"* but also, it is a passage of Scripture that many feel is not in the Bible. Why? Because these twelve verses are not found in the *Vatican* and *Sinai* manuscripts. For some reason modern scholarship holds those codices to be a *"sanctum sanctorum."* They, along with other Greek texts, are the Greek foundational texts used in most of the modern bible versions today.

THE GOOD NEWS IS THAT THE GREEK TEXT THAT UNDERLIES THE KING JAMES BIBLE HAS THESE VERSES WITHIN ITS PAGES. That Greek text is called *THE TEXTUS RECEPTUS or TRADITIONAL TEXT*! It is the text which was used to translate THE KING JAMES BIBLE!

After spending time on the Mount of Olives, Jesus entered THE TEMPLE. It is interesting how much time our LORD spent in THE TEMPLE. He was eager to teach or to confront for the TRUTH!

The scribes must have seen Jesus. So, they stopped their writing momentarily, and with the Pharisees, practically dragged an *embarrassed woman* with them to sit down where Jesus was seated. They did not care much about the woman, nor what was going to happen to her. Their main motive was to catch Jesus in some infraction of THE LAW OF MOSES. It seemed, as in the past, they were trying to catch Jesus in some legal kind of *faux pas.*

The first words from their lips were surprising! *"Master, this woman was taken in adultery, in the very act!"* How they found her *"in the very act"* is always a wonder. Who was the guilty man with whom she had been with at the time? Could it have been one of them? If not where was he? They pushed her to Jesus. She sat there looking at the ground.

Knowing that the law commanded *"stoning"* for adultery, the gleeful men tested Jesus. They knew the punishment for *"adultery"* was stoning. What would Jesus say?

Perhaps they were planning the punishment in their minds as they attempted to trip-up the Teacher! Strange as it may seem to you and me, Jesus appeared to ignore the men and took little notice of the woman. In fact, those nearby thought He had not heard a word the excited men had said to Him. Then, without pretense, Jesus stooped down on the ground. He began to make movements with his finger on the dirt at the woman's feet.

The men would not be deterred! In spite of Jesus' ignoring them, the scribes and Pharisees kept jeering over and over again, *"MOSES IN THE LAW COMMANDED US, THAT SUCH SHOULD BE STONED: BUT WHAT SAYEST THOU?"* Standing up, Jesus looked each man in the eye and stated, *"He that is without sin among you, let him first cast a stone at her!"* The accusers did not expect such a statement! What was Jesus doing? In their minds *she* was the guilty one–*not they*!

To the surprise of the squirming men, Jesus stooped down again and wrote on the dirt once more. What He wrote we do not know! Conviction burned in the souls of the accusers! Each knew his own heart! Beginning with the oldest man to the youngest youth, they left. Jesus continued writing on the ground. The guilty woman trembled, paralyzed in fear. It was then that Jesus stood to his full stature. He asked, *"Where are those thine accusers? Hath no man condemned thee?"* Her answer was brief. She said, *"No man, Lord!"* Jesus looked in the eyes of this sinner, and said, *"Neither do I condemn thee."* But that was not all He said. **He commanded her, *"GO AND SIN NO MORE!"***

SO IT IS, WHEN OUR SINS ARE FORGIVEN,
WE SHOULD FORSAKE SUCH BEHAVIOR
AND NEVER DO IT AGAIN!

"HELP OTHERS WITH SCRIPTURE"
(Isaiah 35:4)
**"SAY TO THEM THAT ARE OF A FEARFUL HEART,
BE STRONG, FEAR NOT:**
"Behold, your God will come . . . he will come and save you."
**"COMMIT THY WORKS UNTO THE LORD,
AND THY THOUGHTS SHALL BE ESTABLISHED"**
(ggs)

Today's Bible Blessing   *November 8*

John 9:20–John 11:21
UNDER THE PROTECTIVE ROD!

John 10:9

"I am the door: by me if any man enter in, he shall be saved."

When my husband chose the "800" telephone number for our *BIBLE FOR TODAY MINISTRY*, he decided that 1-800-JOHN 10:9 was a good configuration of numbers (1-800-564-6109) for people to punch into their telephones to call us.

Whenever we tell people to order materials from us, we say for them to CALL 1-800-JOHN 10:9, hoping that the actual Bible verse will be recalled and remembered in their minds.

"I am the door: by me if any man enter in, he shall be saved, and shall go in and out, and find pasture."

I must admit that saying our *"800"* number has become so familiar that I have forgotten to think of the words behind that reference. I say this to my shame! How could I forget the beautiful relationship that a shepherd has with his sheep?

In John, chapter ten, Jesus is teaching that He is not only THE SHEPHERD, but also, HE IS THE DOOR. This is an interesting comparison, illustrating how Jesus, as THE SHEPHERD, looks at the Christian as *His "sheep."*

Compare John 10:11.

"I am the good shepherd: the good shepherd giveth his life for the sheep" (John 10:11);

with John 10:9

"I am the door: by me if any man enter in, he shall be saved, and shall go in and out, and find pasture" (John 10:9).

In order for us to understand, in some measure how Jesus is the believer's shepherd, we must understand what it means to be one. From what I have read, being a *"shepherd"* is hard work. It is not an artist's conception of a romantic leisurely occupation, situated in a green pastoral setting.

Instead, a man who becomes an Eastern shepherd, either by choice, inheritance, or need, finds himself in a never-ending occupation of watching and waiting. It is a job full of hardships and danger. He finds himself in extreme temperatures—either hot or cold. His food is simple, like that of John the Baptist—either pods from the carob tree, or sycamore figs, or locusts and wild honey. It was not unusual for him to meet up with a lion or bear as the young psalmist David did. Nor was it uncommon for his beard to be frosted or his person to shiver, or for him to be so warm, he can barely breathe.

His day was consumed with his sheep. They were his chief concern day and night! Early in the morning, he led his sheep out from the sheep fold where they had slept together. He had been with them all night, lying in the doorway. In fact, he was the door! Nothing could touch the sheep with the shepherd there. Any robber or wild animal would have to touch the shepherd first, before they could harm his sheep. They slept in peace for their shepherd cared! When he called them, they knew his voice. If another man spoke, they would not respond. The sheep were never thirsty for the shepherd led them where there was water. There was a special relationship peculiar to the sheep and their shepherd.

Every night, the shepherd would bring his sheep back to the fold. It could be a fenced-in place, or cave. As each one walked into the place of safety, the shepherd held his rod out and each sheep walked under it. The shepherd examined each sheep with his eyes to observe if they were all right and if any were missing. With a motion of his hand, the sheep would pass under the rod and find their resting place. They were safe, for their shepherd was with them—watching and protecting the flock!

So it is with our HEAVENLY SHEPHERD! He cares for us, who are saved! We are *"THE SHEEP"* of *"His pasture."* His *"care"* is more than any earthly shepherd's care known to man. Jesus said, *"I LAY DOWN MY LIFE FOR THE SHEEP!"* (See verse 15.)

This He did at Calvary! Jesus saw our great need! Our sins were draining our life away. We needed *"forgiveness"* and *"remission."* As our GOOD SHEPHERD, He laid down His life for us that we might have eternal life!

There is something "special" about the "Christian Sheep"! He or she was given to THE SHEPHERD by the HEAVENLY FATHER. Once a sheep—a person who is "born-again"—receives Jesus Christ as personal Saviour, he or she is in the "HAND" of the Shepherd. Then that "HAND" is secured in the HEAVENLY FATHER'S HAND."

We read a glorious truth about this "HAND" in John 10:29. *No man is able to pluck the believer out of the FATHER'S HAND.* Why? Because Jesus said, *"I AND MY FATHER ARE ONE!"*

ARE YOU ONE OF THE GREAT SHEPHERD'S SHEEP?

"A STRONG TOWER"
(Proverbs 18:10; Psalm 61:3)
This has been a long and helpful verse to me.
In other years, perhaps, my comfort was in the words,
"STRONG TOWER"!
Today, I find my blessing in the Name of the Lord Jesus.
None other Name is so dear.
None other Name gives such blessing and hope. (ggs)

John 11:22–John 12:49
THEN JESUS CAME!

John 12:3

"Mary anointed the feet of Jesus, and wiped his feet with her hair."

There was a man, in a certain Bethany household, who became famous. His name was Lazarus. His notoriety was not because he had done an evil deed, or that he had performed a noble act. His fame was for a most unusual reason. He had died. Many men had died in Bethany, but Lazarus was different! He came back to life four days later! He had been entombed and mourned for, and his friends were grieving. His sisters, who loved him, pined over the loss! Their house was empty. The absence of their brother's voice was deafening! No longer were his footsteps heard at the door. *"Why had not Jesus come?"* The question haunted them.

Then Jesus came. Why He chose to delay His coming until after the death was not understood, but it was a fact! When Jesus arrived, the grieving sisters walked Jesus to the tomb. There was sadness in the air. The girls were crying, as well as the town's people. Jesus wept, too! This family was special to the Saviour. When He came to the tomb, He asked that the stone be rolled away. Then Jesus did a very odd thing! He called the dead man by name! (See John 11:43.)

Then happened the most frightening event that anyone in Bethany had ever witnessed. LAZARUS APPEARED! Struggling to walk, because of his grave clothes, the dead man came out of the tomb! Immediately, Lazarus became as popular as Jesus. Everyone, including strangers, came near the man who had been dead, and gawked at him. The news of this miracle, and the attention it brought, disturbed the chief priests in Jerusalem. They consulted with others to put Lazarus to death! (See John 12:10.)

Often we read in the Bible about BETHANY, the hometown of Lazarus and his sisters. Sometimes it is called *BETHABARA*. That was the area, beyond the Jordan River, where John the Baptist ministered and baptized (John 1:28). It was located on the eastern slopes of THE MOUNT OF OLIVES—almost two miles from the City OF JERUSALEM. It was a LONELY PLACE, a welcoming area, where invalids gathered. Often it was called *"THE HOUSE OF MISERY"*!

Could it be that LAZARUS, prior to his death and resurrection, had a lifelong infirmity? Could he have been paralyzed from some congenital birth injury—perhaps cerebral palsy? Could it be that is why he and his sisters lived together? If Unger's dictionary is correct, there was more than one disabled person in the village. This could explain why the three siblings never married and lived in the one house together. The girls were there to care for their brother. It is true, Lazarus could have been married, as well as the sisters, but there is no mention of a wife or husbands in any of the passages where their names are written. Because Jesus spent many hours with this family, I "imagine" that, if Lazarus had a *lingering, chronic illness*, Jesus would have healed him. I think, in this case, the death was sudden. Remember Sister Martha's words, *"Lord, if thou hadst been here, my brother had not died . . ."* (John 11:21). This was John, chapter eleven!

Now in chapter twelve, we read that there were six days before the Passover! Jesus was on His way to Jerusalem with His disciples. HIS DEATH WAS NEAR! So, He stopped to see his friends at Lazarus' house in Bethany. Judas was there too (John 12:4-7). They had been invited to a special banquet. Because of the excitement over Lazarus, the other guests forgot that the *"honored"* one was Jesus. At the time, crowds followed Lazarus—more than they did Jesus—at least in Bethany.

It was then Mary, the younger sister, went to the back of the couch where Jesus lay at the dining table. (In those days, guests lay down to eat with their faces by their plates and their feet behind them.) Mary kneeled down at Jesus' feet. No one seemed to notice! She opened a fragrant box of ointment, and anointed Jesus' feet. The room was filled with the sweet odor of perfume!

Unpinning her long, virgin hair, she wiped her Master's feet with her *"glory"* (I Corinthians 11:15). SHE HAD PREPARED HIM FOR HIS SOON-BURIAL! A TRUE ACT OF DEVOTION.

"RIGHT WORDS"
(Job 6:24-25; Proverbs 25:11; Ephesians 4:15; Colossians 4:6; Proverbs 31:26; Psalm 19:14)
"How forcible are right words!"
"A word fitly spoken is like apples of gold in pictures of silver."
"Speaking the truth in love."
"Let your speech be alway with grace, seasoned with salt. . ."
"In her tongue is the law of kindness."
"Let the words of my mouth, and the meditation of my heart,"
go together! (ggs)

Today's Bible Blessing   *November 10*

John 12:50–John 15:16
FOOT WASHING THEN AND NOW?
John 13:16
"The servant is not greater than his Lord . . ."

Events moved swiftly that day. Jesus and His disciples–including the TRAITOR–found themselves in a large room with majestic arches and pillars gracing its decor. It would be their last meal together.

I remember distinctly, when we were in Israel, being in that *"upper room."* It was a large, pretentious place. We were told by our guide that it was the authentic room where Jesus brake the bread and served the wine. Not sure how they know. It was from that room that Judas, who was bent on betraying Him, left Jesus.

After the resurrection, Jesus would appear twice to His disciples in that room. Many say that it was in that very room, on *THE DAY OF PENTECOST*, that the Holy Spirit filled the house! (See Acts 2: 1-4.)

Like a servant, Jesus wrapped a towel around his waist, took a basin of water and washed the disciples' feet. This was a normal practice in the homes of that day. People wore loose sandals. The ground was dusty. Their feet were dirty. It was nothing for a servant to do this as the guest arrived. It was the hospitable thing to do. The eating posture in those days was that of lying on a couch. The guests leaned on one side of their body and ate with the opposite hand. When I was a child I ate this way all the time from my sick bed. So I know it is possible to enjoy one's meal in such a position. Only I was on my back.

Why did Jesus do the work of a lowly domestic? He was teaching the disciples, as well as you and me, to be *"lowly."* We should not resist the less important work that the Lord requires of us. Jesus as the *"meek and lowly in heart"* was teaching *"humility"* that day.

> *"Verily, verily, I say unto you, The servant is not greater than his lord; neither he that is sent greater than he that sent him"* (John 13:16).

Also, He was fulfilling the prophecy found in Psalm 41:9:

> *"Yea, mine own familiar friend, in whom I trusted, which did eat of my bread, hath lifted up his heel against me."*

There is no record that the other *"eleven"* objected to such kindness–but Peter did! He complained, *"Thou shalt never wash my feet!"*

In those days, homes did not have private bathrooms. The community had a *"bath house"*! That is where the men went to bathe. I suppose the women had their bath houses also. I am not sure.

When we were in West Africa, the women had them. It was a private place where they could throw pails of water on themselves as they bathed. The little children would be bathed out in the open. I remember how clean the Africans kept themselves—washing often, and cooling themselves from the heat.

No doubt, the men in this account had been to the bath house. They were clean—all but their feet! Peter understood what Jesus was saying when Jesus said, *"If I wash thee not, thou hast no part with me."* Changeable Peter demanded Jesus wash his hands and head also. A complete bath was not necessary. *"He that is washed needeth not save to wash his feet, but is clean. . ."* was Jesus' retort (John 13:10).

> *"Verily, verily, I say unto you, The servant is not greater than his lord; neither he that is sent greater than he that sent him"* (John 13:16).

It was then that Jesus stated that one of them was "unclean." That was Judas! No one else knew it. I wonder what Judas was thinking when Jesus washed his feet, including his heels!

Before the night was over, Jesus spoke the most comforting words: *"LET NOT YOUR HEART BE TROUBLED: YE BELIEVE IN GOD, BELIEVE ALSO IN ME"* (John 14:1).

QUESTION: IS "FOOT WASHING" TO BE OBSERVED TODAY? The criteria for any church *"ordinance"* to be observed today was taught to us by our late pastor, CARL ELGENA.

He said for an *"ordinance,"* to be observed in our churches today, it had to have been used by the LORD JESUS in His ministry on earth! Also, it had to be practiced by the early church, and IT MUST BE TAUGHT IN THE EPISTLES!

"ACQUAINTED WITH ALL MY WAYS"

(Psalm 139; Ezekiel 11:5; Job 23:10; Psalm 113:14; Proverbs 15:3; Psalm 34:1; I Peter 3:12)

"I know the things that come into your mind, every one of them."
"BUT HE KNOWETH THE WAY THAT I TAKE:
WHEN HE HATH TRIED ME, I SHALL COME FORTH AS GOLD."
"For he knoweth our frame; he remembereth that we are dust."
"THE EYES OF THE LORD ARE IN EVERY PLACE. . ."
"THE EYES OF THE LORD ARE OVER THE RIGHTEOUS . . ."
"For the eyes of the Lord are over the righteous,
and his ears are open unto their prayers:
but the face of the Lord is against them that do evil."
(ggs)

Today's Bible Blessing   *November 11*

John 15:17–John 18:16
DEITY HAS SPOKEN!

John 18:6

"They went backward, and fell on the ground"

When Jesus answered those who came to arrest Him, He revealed His deity with the words, *"I AM!"* Boldly He asserted, *"I AM* HE!" With those words, all his offenders fell backward. *DEITY HAD SPOKEN!* (See John 18:5-8.)

From the time of ABRAHAM, God revealed Himself as the great "I AM." This is His Name! "I AM" is *THE ALMIGHTY GOD* who walked before Abram saying, *"Fear not, Abram: 'I AM'' thy shield, and thy exceeding great reward"* (Genesis 15:1). When Isaac was in Beersheba, the LORD appeared and said, *"I AM the God of Abraham thy father: fear not, for 'I AM' with thee, and will bless thee"* (See Genesis 28:13.) When Jacob dreamed of a ladder that went from earth to Heaven, God said, *"I AM the LORD God of Abraham thy father, and the God of Isaac . . . behold, 'I AM' with thee"* (Genesis 28:13-15.)

Remember the day "I AM" revealed Himself to MOSES? A bush burned with fire, but was not consumed. Frightened, Moses stood still! He heard the voice of God saying. *"I AM THAT I AM!"* And God said, *"Thus shalt thou say unto the children of Israel, 'I AM' hath sent me unto you"* (Exodus 3:14).

So, when we meet the LORD JESUS CHRIST in the Gospel of John, we meet GOD IN FLESH. Often He spoke of Himself at the "I AM." Few understood that He was God in flesh! He clarified His deity and power with such statements as: *"I AM THE BREAD OF LIFE: he that cometh to me shall not hunger, and he that believeth on me shall never thirst"* (John 6:35). He was the better *"bread"* from Heaven–better than the manna in Moses' day.

Jesus is the "I AM"*—the light of the world!* (See John 8:12.) A person who follows Him will not walk in darkness. Just think; a Christian does not have to be in the gloom of sin! In John 10:9, Jesus introduced us to Himself as "THE *DOOR*"! When He said, *"I AM the door: by me if any man enter in, he shall be saved."* He gave us the *"secret"* to the passage way to Heaven. Unless a person receives Jesus Christ as personal Saviour, that person cannot pass from *"death"* to *"life."* He cannot enter Heaven apart from *"THE DOOR."*

It's a fact! There are bad shepherds. They do not care for the sheep. Jesus said, "I AM the good shepherd!" How do we know this? Because—*"The good shepherd giveth his life for the sheep"* (John 10:11). Because Jesus died for us sinners and rose again, we see that He has resurrection power. When he said, *"I AM the resurrection, and the life: he that believeth in me, though he were dead* (spiritually dead), *yet shall he live; and whosoever liveth and believeth on me shall never die"* (John 11:24-25).

In John 14:2, Jesus spoke of HEAVEN. It is a comforting passage for those of us who have loved ones in Heaven. He speaks of the *"mansions"* that He is preparing for those who love Him. This is like a *"map"* to Heaven. He said, *"I AM THE WAY." He is the HOLY* "global positioning system" that points us to ETERNAL LIFE and our HEAVENLY HOME!

In this day of *"postmodernist lying,"* **it is comforting to know JESUS, the "I AM,"** *IS THE TRUTH!* Combined with *"THE WAY"* and *"THE TRUTH,"* **JESUS, the "I AM" is** *"THE LIFE"!* Concluding this startling revelation, Jesus makes a dogmatic statement: *"No man cometh unto the Father, but by me!"* (See John 14:6.)

In conclusion, Jesus startled the disciples by saying "I AM *the vine, ye are the branches!"* (See John 15:5.) In other words, He informed His disciples and us, that He is the main life-source of our Christian life! Without His life flowing through us, we, as believers, would have no life at all. WE MUST STAY WITH HIM FOR OUR LIFE SUPPORT!

Before we leave this precious truth that Jesus is the great *"I AM,"* **a reality presented to us throughout the Old and New Testaments, LET US BE WARNED!** Some are attributing the *"I AM"* to themselves–the "god" within them. Those that teach this heresy align themselves with THE NEW AGE MOVEMENT. Often, this teaching is called *"COSMIC HUMANISM"* which says man is god! Many famous people, seen on television all the time, believe that world peace cannot come except by *"God"* and our "higher self"! (This *"God"* they speak of is a *"god"* of their own making, not *THE HOLY GOD* of Scripture!!) It is most deceiving.

So when these false teachers encourage you and me to discover our *"higher self,"* **the hairs should stand up on the back of our neck!** When we hear the words, *"I AM,"* or the "I AM PRESENCE," or similar phrases like *"the 'god' within us,"* or *"the 'Christ' within us"* or *"the 'spirit' within us,"* our ears should prick up with spiritual discernment! Run from that person's teaching. Stop following him or her! (See John 7:24.) As my husband often says, *"LEARN TO DISCERN!"*

> *"Judge not according to the appearance, but judge righteous judgment."*

NO ONE IS THE GREAT "I AM" BUT JEHOVAH GOD, THE SAVIOUR OF THE WORLD! A person, no matter how *"good"* and dedicated to a cause, is not the *"I AM"*! Nor are you, no matter your good intentions. **IT IS BLASPHEMOUS TO CALL ONESELF OR ANOTHER** *THE "I AM!"*

> ### *"THAT YE MAY BE ABLE TO BEAR IT"*
> (Deuteronomy 1:30; I Corinthians 10:13)
> *"THE LORD YOUR GOD WHICH GOETH BEFORE YOU,*
> *HE SHALL FIGHT FOR YOU. . ."*
> IN ALL THE PROBLEMS OF LIFE, HE GOETH BEFORE.
> HE WILL NOT ALLOW ONE THING IN OUR PATH
> THAT WILL BE TOO GREAT TO BEAR.
> *"There hath no temptation taken you*
> *but such as is common to man:*
> *but God is faithful,*
> *who will not suffer you to be tempted above that ye are able;*
> *but will with the temptation also make a way to escape,*
> *that ye may be able to bear it."* (ggs)

Today's Bible Blessing   *November 12*

John 18:17–John 20:20
YOU ARE NEVER FORGOTTEN!

John 20:13

"Because they have taken away my Lord, and I know not where . . ."

"And they say unto her, WOMAN, WHY WEEPEST THOU? She saith unto them, Because they have taken away my Lord, and I know not where they have laid him" (John 20:13).

Tragedy had struck Mary Magdalene. Her LORD, the One who had set her free from the demons that had ripped her soul, had died. His death was ignominious! She, and the other women, watched the inhuman cruelty of the Roman soldiers. They beat His body and a sword pierced His side! The Jews were not a whit better. They demanded that Jesus be executed! Though Pilate found no fault in the Saviour, to pacify them, Jesus was cursed and crucified!

Tears flowed. Hearts were broken. Emotions were damaged. Jesus was dead! Death is the *"final call"* for all who are born. As a hiker's steady footfall on the Appalachian Trail, death marches on. Some finish their course at an old age; and others die in the prime of their earthly life. No matter. Death comes! It leaves behind tears and weeping. Even though the one who passes has given testimony to his or her *"salvation,"* DEATH plows on.

Mary was bereft of the One who had given her a new life's purpose. Sorrow upon sorrow! She had come to minister to the dead body of Jesus. He had been buried so quickly. The proper preparation had been hurried. She would perfume His lifeless form with spices and sweet-smelling ointments. She would remember Him with tears and yearnings. BUT! Sorrow upon sorrow! His body had been stolen! What was she to do? She ran to tell Peter and the others,

"They have taken away the Lord out of the sepulchre, and we know not where they have laid him" (John 20:2b).

From a distance, she watched John outrun Peter to the tomb. She saw Peter dash into the cave. She could not detect what made them leave the grave so suddenly. Soon she would know. Yes, it was empty, save for the grave clothes and the head covering folded neatly in place. Mary stooped. She looked. Sitting in the place where the corpse should have lain, were two angels. It was then they asked her, *"WHY WEEPEST THOU?"* The messengers from Heaven knew that Jesus was resurrected and alive. They had joy! But Mary did not know. Her grief was real. Her hurt was deep. Often, we do not know God's future plans!

Today, I must go to a *"viewing"* **of a young man—only forty-nine.** I knew him as a child. Occasionally, our paths would cross. He became a husband, a father, a preacher, and a precious servant of God. An illness consumed his body, but not his soul. His obituary said, *"He wanted nothing more than to show God's love to others through his life."* This, TIMOTHY P. SCHIEBER did to me, and I will miss him!

"THRU DEATH—NO LONG PERIOD—THEN HOME"
We, who know Jesus Christ as Saviour, are not far from "home"!
A MOMENT WILL BRING US THERE!
THERE IS NO LONG PERIOD BETWEEN
THE INSTANT OF DEATH
AND THE GLORIES OF ETERNITY!
Death is not banishment!
It is a return from exile,
A going home to many mansions!
Death is not going out, it is entering in!
The first face we will behold is JESUS,
Whom our eyes have longed to see. (ggs)

Today's Bible Blessing　　　　　　　　　　　*November 13*

John 20:21—Acts 2:24
EIGHT DAYS LATER

John 20:28
"Thomas. . .said unto him, My Lord and my God."

Before we finish our time in the Gospel of John, we should know that many feel that John 20:30-31 is the pivotal verse in this gospel.

"And many other signs truly did Jesus in the presence of his disciples, which are not written in this book: But these are written, that ye might believe that Jesus is the Christ, the

Son of God; and that believing ye might have life through his name."

Whenever Bible teachers teach the book, they always say *"These are written, that ye might believe that Jesus is the Christ, the Son of God; and that believing ye might have life through his name."* The book of John was written so the reader would realize that Jesus is the Son of God. This heart-knowledge was difficult for many when He was on earth. Even the disciples had to come to the realization it was true. Peter declared, *"Thou art the Christ, the Son of the living God!"* (See Matthew 16:16.) Martha agreed, *"Yea, Lord: I believe that thou art the Christ, the Son of God, which should come into the world"* (John 11:27).

Thomas was slow in believing that Jesus was the resurrected Messiah! He had been absent that evening, after the resurrection, when Jesus stood in the midst of the other disciples. If I recall, they were in the same room where they last broke bread together. That was Sunday, the very day that Jesus rose from the dead. They had been at His death! How disturbed they had become when His body was missing!

HOW GOOD IT WAS TO HEAR OF MARY MAGDALENE'S NEWS! She had actually seen the RISEN LORD! THEN JESUS APPEARED WITHOUT WARNING TO THEM THAT NIGHT! Remember how He calmed their fears? He showed them His wounded hands and side! He granted them *"peace"* in the midst of much confusion! Then, He commissioned *His disciples. They were to GO!"* as His Father had sent Him! (See John 20:21.) How were they to do that?

Next we read of an unusual event. Jesus *"breathed"* on those gathered in that room. He said, *"RECEIVE YE THE HOLY GHOST!"* (See verse 22.) I had forgotten this event myself. Remember with me that Pentecost had not happened! (See Acts 2:1.) YET, JESUS WAS GIVING THEM IMMEDIATE *"HOLY SPIRIT LEADING"* TO TEACH AND HELP THOSE ABOUT THEM. This *"coming and going"* of the Holy Spirit was no new event in the Old Testament. Immediately, I think of Samson, don't you? The *Spirit* came and went with him, as with King Saul and others. Though Jesus Christ had died and was resurrected, the church was not formed yet. It would come at Pentecost. Until Calvary, the Jewish people were living under the Old Testament law.

As soon as the people in the community would learn of Christ's resurrection, there would be questions. It would be the talk of the city. Jesus gave His disciples a commission to teach about what had happened at Calvary. They were to instruct the inquiring people, who wanted their sins forgiven that Jesus paid it all on the cross at Calvary (vs. 23). No longer would they need to make sacrifices for their sins in the Temple. JESUS WAS THE "SIN SACRIFICE." All they had to do was acknowledge they were sinners, and genuinely receive Jesus as their Saviour.

Eight days after the resurrection, He met with his disciples again in that same room. It was the Sunday after Jesus was raised from the dead. It is interesting to notice that from then on, Christians met together on Sundays and not on Saturdays. No longer were they under the Jewish Sabbath law! They were no longer under the Law of Moses!

THAT SUNDAY THOMAS WAS THERE! Previously, he had said, *"Except I put my fingers into the print of the nails in his hands and thrust my hand into His side, I will not believe!"* Even though the doors were closed, Jesus had appeared again, as he had the previous week. It was then that Jesus challenged Thomas to have FAITH. It was then that Thomas joined Peter's and Martha's former exclamations concerning who Jesus was and exclaimed: *"MY LORD AND MY GOD!"* (See John 20:28; Matthew 16:16; John 11:27.)
THOMAS BELIEVED. DO YOU?

"WHY QUIT?"
"Though hot the fight, why quit the field?
Why must I either fly or yield,
Since Jesus is my shield?"
When creature's comforts fade and die,
worldlings may weep, but why should I?
Jesus still lives, and still is nigh."
(ggs seems to be quoting John Newton here)

Today's Bible Blessing   *November 14*
Acts 2:25–Acts 4:37
MEANWHILE–BACK IN JERUSALEM
Acts 1:8
"Ye shall receive power . . . and . . . be witnesses unto me."
Now we come to the exciting book called THE ACTS OF THE APOSTLES. Once again we are treated to the writing of Dr. Luke. Remember him? He was the writer of the book of Luke. That's the gospel that bears his name. We will talk of the history, etc. of the book of Acts another day.

As you remember, Jesus had died, was buried, and rose from the dead. This miraculous event was the talk of the town. It should be noted that He did not immediately leave the earth for Heaven. Oh No! Jesus was with his disciples and others for forty days! People saw Him. They could testify that He, who had been dead, was alive again! There was no getting around this fact!

Jesus used those forty days to teach His followers many things pertaining to the KINGDOM OF GOD. If we had time, we could contemplate the many "forties" in the Bible—such as "forty days" and "forty nights" of rain, and Jesus' "forty days" in the wilderness, etc. This personal teaching must have been thrilling! Finally His disciples were understanding all that Jesus had previously taught!

He commanded his followers to stay in Jerusalem. The reason was that the HOLY GHOST was coming soon. This should not have been a surprise, for—if you remember—Jesus taught them, prior to His death, about *THE COMFORTER'S* coming (John 14:26). Of course, they, being Jews, were eager to know when *THE KINGDOM OF GOD* would be established. In a way, He said that it was none of their business! But, He did tell them that when THE HOLY SPIRIT would come upon them, they would have *"POWER"*!! That *"POWER"* would turn them into *bold witnesses* as far away as Samaria and to the ends of the earth!

Immediately after that statement, to everyone's surprise, Jesus *"was taken up into the clouds"*! It was the strangest thing! One minute, He was there talking with them, and the next minute, He was gone! Immediately, two men in white clothes told them that *"someday"* Jesus would come back again the same way He left!

After that we find them back in Jerusalem in the UPPER ROOM again—all eleven of them with some others who followed Jesus. They prayed together there. Then Peter preached to them. There were about 120 people in attendance, including Jesus' mother. Peter reminded them of JUDAS' betrayal, as well as his horrible suicide. For some reason, the remaining disciples decided they would elect a replacement for the deceased man. Instead of waiting for the HOLY SPIRIT to come and lead them, they voted on two men. Matthias was one of them. He was chosen to be an apostle. He was elected by a *"chance."* Very strange indeed! (Many feel Paul was the one chosen by Christ and Matthias chosen by man!)

In CHAPTER TWO, the *"DAY OF PENTECOST"* was *"upon"* them! A very odd thing happened that day. The event was most startling! All of a sudden, there was a *"SOUND"* like *"rushing wind."* *It* filled the house! It swished about their heads, swirled by their feet, and hovered where they sat. People did not understand what was happening! Then "FIERY TONGUES" landed on all of them! I'm not sure if this event happened to the same people we found in chapter one, or not. I think so. If so, there were one-hundred-and-twenty people there! What was happening? It was the *"promised"* Holy Spirit!

Never in their lives had those people seen anything like it. It was the *"power of the Highest"* preparing them to be *"THE WITNESSES"* Jesus said they should be! Why, people were preaching the gospel in languages they did not know! Peter assured the others, who were not a part of this, that they were not drunken. Many who heard about this "anointing" were completely confused and confounded. Joel, the prophet, had written of such an event! (See Joel 2:29.) It was partially fulfilled that day!

As he preached, Peter emphasized *"that whosoever shall call on the Name of the Lord shall be saved."* Whether he realized it or not, Peter was beginning his missionary outreach right there in Jerusalem that day!

WHERE IS YOUR MISSIONARY OUTREACH TODAY?

"SURELY THE HARDNESS OF GOD IS SOFTER THAN THE KINDNESS OF MEN."
(I Chronicles 21)
Compare DAVID'S CHASTISEMENT for numbering the people, instead of trusting God (at Satan's instruction).
David accepted God's punishment.
He said he would rather trust in the hand of God. (ggs)

Today's Bible Blessing   *November 15*

Acts 5:1–Acts 7:29
VOLUNTARY GIVING IS GOOD

Acts 4:20
"We cannot but speak the things which we have seen and heard."

Today, we are introduced to a series of people whose lives were important enough for the Spirit of God to record what happened to them. It is interesting that Peter and John went to the Solomon's Porch section of the Temple to pray and to preach (Acts 3:1). We meet them there about three o'clock in the afternoon. Who should they see, begging at the gate of the temple, but a man who had been lame since birth. The physically challenged man asked the disciples for financial help.

Instead, Peter gave him a small sermon! He said, *"Silver and gold have I none; but such as I have, give I thee."* (Notice the beautiful poetical cadence found in the King James Bible!) I don't know what the crippled man expected, but he was healed! Peter took the man's hand and said, *"in the name of Jesus Christ of Nazareth rise up and walk!"* The Bible says that *"IMMEDIATELY HIS FEET AND ANKLE BONES RECEIVED STRENGTH!"* All the people around praised God! What an afternoon that was!

As Peter was finishing his sermon, the priest and other TEMPLE leaders approached John and him. Unexpectedly, those temple officials grabbed them and threw them in jail overnight. *"By what power have you healed that man?"* was the question posed to them. What could those leaders say against the healing of the *formerly* crippled man who was standing before them? The disciple's answer infuriated them. They charged them: *"DO NOT SPEAK OR TEACH AT ALL IN THE NAME OF JESUS!"* (See Acts 4:18.) Forthrightly, the disciples replied, *"WE CANNOT BUT SPEAK THE THINGS WHICH WE HAVE SEEN AND HEARD!"* They could do nothing else but obey God rather than men! (See Acts 4:19-21.)

After hearing of Jesus' resurrection and the *great grace* bestowed on the disciples, the multitudes believed! As the new converts' hearts were warmed by the love of Christ, they gave abundantly to the disciples for the benefit of others in need. Even BARNABAS, a Levite from Cyprus, sold his property and laid the proceeds at the apostles' feet. In time, this *"SON OF CONSOLATION"* would become a valuable asset to Paul's future ministry (Acts 4:36-37).

Because voluntary "giving" of one's possessions and funds was practiced in the new Christian community, a man and wife named ANANIAS and SAPPHIRA wanted to be a part of the action. In reality, they wanted the *"praise"* that came with such contributions. So, they sold *"a possession."* We are not certain what that *"possession"* was; but it must have been worth a pretty penny. Pretending to give ALL the money, the couple marched right up to the apostles and put their money gift at their feet. In reality, they conspired together to keep back *"part of the price"*! It must be remembered that no one told them to sell their *"possession."* And if they sold it, no one told them that they had to contribute the entire amount of the sale to the Apostles for a philanthropic cause.

Soon Ananias brought the money to the Apostles. Peter, being filled with the Holy Spirit, sensed the truth! He questioned, *"Why hath Satan filled thine heart to lie to the Holy Ghost, and to keep back part of the price of the land?"* Ananias had lied to God! Peter knew the scheme! *"Why hast thou conceived this thing in thine heart?"* When the deceiver heard those words, he fell over and died! (See Acts 5:5.)

Three hours later, SAPPHIRA, *pretending* great spirituality, waltzed in to Peter. Peter inquired, *"TELL ME WHETHER YE SOLD THE LAND FOR SO MUCH?"* She lied, as had her husband! Peter excoriated the woman, for she and her husband had conspired together *"to tempt* [test] *the Spirit of the Lord!"* She was caught in her lie! *FEAR STRUCK HER HEART!* Like her husband, she fell dead on the ground! Great apprehension came upon the church.

TRUTH IS VERY IMPORTANT TO BE MAINTAINED IN A CHRISTIAN'S LIFE. JESUS DECLARED, "I AM THE TRUTH. . .!" (See John 14:6.)

A Christian person should wrap the core of her being with truth (Ephesians 6:14a). She should be known as a "truth-teller." One lie can affect her entire church, as well as her family, and herself!

TRUTH is the bedrock foundation between one individual to another. It is the *"core"* that tells another who we are. The people of the devil's world lie in wait to lie and deceive. A born-again person must put away such cunning craftiness with *FAITH* as her shield! (See Ephesians 6:16.)

"*Wherefore lay apart all filthiness and superfluity of naughtiness, and receive with meekness the engrafted word, which is able to save your souls. But be ye doers of the word, and not hearers only, deceiving your own selves*" (James 1:21-22).

YES, SPEAK THE TRUTH IN LOVE, BUT SPEAK THE TRUTH! (See Ephesians 4:15a.)

"THE LORD TRIETH THE RIGHTEOUS"
(Psalm 11:5)
"You never would have possessed
the precious faith which now supports you,
if the trial of your faith had not been like unto fire.
You are a tree, that never would have rooted so well,
if the wind had not rocked you to and fro,
and made you take firm hold upon the precious truth
of the covenant (promises) of faith."
(from Spurgeon's M&E–
"This excerpt encouraged me often as I read it"—ggs)

Today's Bible Blessing   *November 16*

Acts 7:30—Acts 9:15
PREACHING WITH BOLDNESS & POWER

Acts 6:3
"Look ye out . . . seven men of honest report, full of the Holy Ghost."
WE ARE NOW INTRODUCED TO STEPHEN. He was one of the seven honest deacons, full of the Holy Spirit, chosen to serve in the Jerusalem Church. Though he and his fellow deacons were chosen to relieve the apostles of menial tasks, Stephen, as it turned out, was a mighty preacher.

Because Stephen was a spiritual man, performing miracles and wonders, he made enemies among many who did not believe in Jesus. Unbelievers bribed *lying witnesses* to file *false charges* against Stephen. They dragged him before the council. The members saw Stephen's face change before their eyes. It looked like the face of an angel (Acts 6:15). I am not sure what an angel looks like, but I am sure it does not look like those we see on Christmas cards. Angels were messengers—and often the message was not pleasant. Stephen's truthful message was not well-received by the dignitaries.

Deacon Stephen preached with holy boldness and power. He spoke of Abraham, of Joseph, of Jacob, of Moses, and of Solomon! He told details concerning Moses that we would not have known if it were not for this sermon. The Jews were angry. They gnashed their teeth. They could not bear hearing such words! Then, Stephen looked Heavenward. He saw Jesus standing on the right hand of God! The unbelievers, as a group, ran at Stephen. They grabbed him and threw him out of the city. Then they stoned him! As he was dying, he kneeled down and prayed, *"Lord Jesus, receive my spirit!"*

Before Stephen expired, he loudly cried, "Lord, lay not this sin to their charge!" A young man stood nearby watching the event. Stephen's clothes had been thrown at that man's feet! His name was Saul. He was from Tarsus. Later, he would be known to all the world as the Apostle Paul.

NOW LET US LOOK AT ANOTHER DEACON. HIS NAME WAS PHILIP. He was not the Philip whom Jesus called to be His disciple (Matthew 10:3), nor was he the Philip of Bethsaida, who found Nathanael (John 1:48). He was the Philip who preached Christ in Samaria, a city which was about thirty-five miles north of Jerusalem (Acts 8:5). He, like Stephen, must have been a marvelous preacher. If you remember, a *sorcerer* got saved under Philip's preaching. After the difficulties with that man, Philip was instructed by the Angel of the Lord to travel about eighty miles to Gaza. (Today we know about the Gaza Strip.)

In the meantime, there was a man, who had spent some time on business in Jerusalem. He was returning home to Ethiopia. He was an *extraordinary person* of great authority. In fact, he was the treasurer of the Ethiopian QUEEN CANDACE. It very well could be that he was a *"servant-slave"* like Daniel and Joseph were in the Old Testament. Riding in his chariot, from worshipping in the Holy City, the eunuch was reading from a scroll of the prophet Isaiah. He was reading from Isaiah 53:7-8, which tells how the Messiah was led like a dumb lamb to the laughter, how Jesus opened not His mouth, and His life was taken from the earth (Acts 8:31-32). THE READER WAS CONFUSED!

It was then that the Spirit of God brought Philip to the man's chariot. Philip explained the passage to the inquisitive man. THE TREASURER WAS RIPE FOR SALVATION! As soon as he was *"saved,"* he got out of his chariot. Because there was water nearby, he asked to be baptized. Philip said to the new believer, *"If thou believest with all thine heart, thou mayest"* (Acts 8:37a).

Did you know that the entire verse found in Acts 8:37 is missing from most, if not all, of the modern versions? YET, IT IS IN *THE KING JAMES BIBLE* BECAUSE THE GREEK TEXT

(The TEXTUS RECEPTUS GREEK TEXT) HAS THOSE WORDS IN IT!

Because there was nothing to hinder the baptism, Philip and the eunuch went down into the water. The new convert was immersed. Both men left that day—happy in the Lord. Off he went to Ethiopia; and the Spirit of the Lord took Philip to AZOTUS for more preaching! **WHAT A DAY THAT WAS FOR THE LORD!**

"DO NOT BE AFRAID OF THE FUTURE"
If you are a Christian, the future is your friend.
THE FUTURE IS BRIGHT WITH THE PROMISES OF GOD!
Worry & fear are not from the Lord, but are from "the enemy."
Regardless of external circumstances,
the Christian's ultimate future is radiant, beautiful and inviting,
as we look forward to meeting our Saviour!
IF YOU ARE WORRYING, YOU ARE NOT TRUSTING. (ggs)

Today's Bible Blessing   *November 17*

Acts 9:16—Acts 11:10
FLEEING TO JUDEA & SAMARIA

Acts 8:1

"There was a persecution against the church . . . and they were scattered."

Before proceeding into the life of the Apostle Paul, let us consider some rudimentary facts concerning the book of Acts. Some of us may recall a special doctor in our lives. I remember when our son's doctor died. That physician was the only one our son had ever had. For sixteen years he had known him—and he was *"gone"*! The loss was great, for he was loved. I imagine that Dr. Luke was that kind of a man, as he was often referred to as the *"beloved physician."* He traveled with Paul, caring for his needs.

Do you remember the "young" man who watched the stoning of Stephen? Do you recall that the murderers, bothered by their clothes, laid them at the feet of a young man named SAUL? Without their outer garments, they could "stone" Stephen with greater ease? Do you remember? If someone would have told SAUL that someday he would be a *"Christian,"* Saul would have laughed in immediate denial! For SAUL was an enemy of the *"CROSS OF CHRIST."* It was no accident that he was at Stephen's stoning. Oh no!

At the time, persecution was strong against the Jerusalem church. In desperation, the Christians fled to all the regions of Judea and Samaria—except for the apostles (Acts 8:1). (That was when Deacon Philip escaped to the city of Samaria.) The Bible says that this SAUL made havoc of the church! We read of the persecution of the people, and the destruction of homes and meeting places. Even today we see the killing of Christians and the pilfering of churches in heathen, religious countries. It was the same in Jerusalem in Dr. Luke's day.

Christianity was contrary to the LAW OF MOSES. The memory of *"THAT JESUS"* and His resurrection had to be obliterated—lest it grow more than it had already grown. SAUL WAS COMMITTED TO DESTROYING THE CHRISTIANS! He invaded houses without warning. He violently thrust men into prisons. He carried screaming women to the dungeons. He killed many! THERE ARE NOT WORDS ENOUGH TO TELL OF SAUL OF TARSUS' HATRED OF THE PEOPLE OF *"THE WAY."*

Because Christianity was growing far away from its home base—even into DAMASCUS two hundred miles from Jerusalem—Paul, the Christian bounty-hunter had to stop it! He breathed out threatening and slaughtering vibes against the disciples! With such indignation, he asked and received certified papers from the High Priest. They gave Saul official permission to incarcerate those of *"THE WAY"*—both male and female. He would bind them and bring them captive to Jerusalem. This was *THE PLAN*.

But God had other plans. He saw potential in this Saul. He saw a man whose life would be changed for Jesus Christ. The LORD looked ahead, past the murders and persecution, and viewed educated Saul—gifted in languages and the law. He saw a special *"witness"* for Him. God saw the future person who would reveal the *"hidden mystery."* Future generations would call that *mystery* by the name of *"THE CHURCH"* or *"THE BRIDE OF CHRIST."* But let us not get ahead of the story.

An unusual thing happened to Saul on the road to Damascus. Without warning, as sudden as a blink of the eye, a LIGHT FROM HEAVEN beamed about and around Saul. No doubt he was petrified! The beam was so bright—so startling—that it knocked Saul to the ground! It was like lightning, only more powerful. With the astounding surprise, and with such sudden power, Saul was completely consumed with weakness and fright! He was powerless to move! A voice spoke. It was as clear as any voice Saul had ever heard.

The *"VOICE"* spoke directly to his ear and said,
"SAUL, SAUL, WHY PERSECUTEST THOU ME?"

"A PREPARED REST"
(Matthew 11:28)
"BRING YOUR HEAVY BURDEN AND LAY IT DOWN
BESIDE THE LOVING KINDNESS
AND TENDER MERCY OF GOD!"
(COPIED)
WHAT A WONDERFUL INVITATION TO COME
WHEN WEARY AND HEAVY LADEN!
WE ARE POOR COMPANY TO OTHERS WHEN IN DISTRESS,
BUT NOT TO HIM!
Jesus notes our burden and has His rest prepared for us;
BUT WE MUST "COME"! (ggs)

Today's Bible Blessing   *November 18*
Acts 11:11—Acts 13:41
ANSWERS IN AN UNEXPECTED WAY

Acts 10:34
"Of a truth I perceive that God is no respecter of persons."
Whenever we are in a Bible class studying the BOOK OF ACTS, we learn there are two divisions in the book. Chapters 1-12 catch us up on Peter's life after the resurrection of the Saviour. We are amazed at Peter's spiritual leadership! It was to the Jews. It is with bated breath that we watch the miracles Peter is privileged to perform. Because of the believer's persecutions, the churches grew. Christians were scattered from Jerusalem to Judea, Galilee, and Samaria (Acts 9:31).

Then we are taught about the life of Paul from chapters 13-28. He is turned from a persecutor of Christ to a proclaimer of the *"mystery"* of THE CHURCH. Paul would minister to the Gentiles!

The men, Peter and Paul, were completely different. One was a fisherman—successful in his business, aggressive and compulsive. A man with a tender heart. The other was a learned man, dedicated to the things of Moses' law, as well as the works added to that law. When Jesus blinded Paul on the Damascus Road, his eyes beheld Christ for the first time as *"the Son of God"* and his *"Saviour."* But, both had changed lives!

Peter ministered to various people. For instance, in LYDDA, he met AENEAS, a man with severe palsy. He healed him! This resulted in all the people in the area turning to the Lord.

Ten miles from there was Joppa. Joppa was the place where everyone was in mourning. TABITHA HAD DIED! I imagine this woman had been a woman of inner beauty and poise. Her love for others shined as a jewel in a setting of compassion and care. Her blessing and love had been sewn into every garment she made. That is why everyone was upset because TABITHA had died. I wonder how her mother felt as she looked at her dead child lying there so still. The grief was great! There is a special tie that binds a mother and her daughter. The daughter is a little piece of the mother who lives on. I have a daughter whose grace and manner blesses my heart. Every time I see her I think, *"How beautiful and kind she is!* WHAT MUST TABITHA'S MOTHER HAVE THOUGHT! No one wants to outlive her child!

JOY! IN THE MIDST OF SUCH GRIEF, PETER RAISED TABITHA FROM THE DEAD! AND MANY IN JOPPA BELIEVED!

Next, we are introduced to a centurion named CORNELIUS. He was from CAESAREA. At the time, Peter was in Joppa, sixty miles away. Though devout, CORNELIUS was not a Jew. Soon Peter would minister to him. Before this was comfortable for Peter to do, God had to deal with Peter's heart. (Some of us know how that is.) While praying, Peter had a *"vision."* It was about twelve noon! PETER WAS HUNGRY! He fell into a trance and saw a sheet, like a big screen, coming down from heaven. It had *unclean* animals, birds, and creeping things pictured on it! A *"voice"* told him, *"Rise, Peter, kill, and eat."* Peter refused, saying he had never eaten anything unclean!

It was then *"the voice"* admonished, *"WHAT GOD HATH CLEANSED THAT CALL NOT THOU COMMON!"* Soon Peter understood what that *"vision"* meant. Three men had come to see him there in Joppa. They took Peter with them back to CAESAREA to meet CORNELIUS. When the powerful centurion saw the Apostle, he fell down at Peter's feet to worship him.

Peter commanded "Stand up: I myself also am a man!" Peter refused such adoration! (It should be noted, he did not want *"worship"* of any kind given to him—not even the kissing of his ring.) SOON CORNELIUS RECEIVED JESUS CHRIST AS SAVIOUR! Peter pronounced: *"OF A TRUTH I PERCEIVE THAT GOD IS NO RESPECTER OF PERSONS!"* (See Acts 10:34.) This was a much needed lesson for Peter to learn—and for us, too.

A sad fact! James, the brother of the beloved disciple, John, had been killed at the hand of pompous Herod. That king sent sixteen soldiers to apprehend Peter. Such an imprisonment would win the king *brownie points* with the Jews.

Meanwhile, back at John Mark's mother's house, a prayer meeting was being held! Christians were praying for Peter's release! It was then, back at the jail, that a bright light shined. An ANGEL nudged Peter, waking him, saying, *"ARISE!"* His chains fell to the floor. As if in a dream, Peter followed the ANGEL. The iron gates squeaked open. The Lord delivered Peter from the hand of Herod!

Peter made his way to the house where his friends were praying for him. He knocked on the door. A young girl saw him at the gate. Her name was RHODA. The astonished girl told the praying people that Peter was there. They thought she was seeing things! Instead of welcoming Peter, they kept on praying.

HOW LIKE SOME OF US!
WE DON'T ALWAYS RECOGNIZE ANSWERED PRAYER.
SOMETIMES THE ANSWER COMES
IN A MOST UNEXPECTED WAY!

"PUT ON THE WHOLE ARMOUR!"
(Proverbs 3:26; Ephesians 6:14-18)
"THE LORD SHALL BE THY CONFIDENCE,
AND SHALL KEEP THY FOOT FROM BEING TAKEN."
HAVE YOU HAD SOME LOSS IN A BATTLE TODAY?
Check and see what part of the armour you did not put on today.
Satan is here with his wiles.
We must put on God's armour if we are to withstand. (ggs)

Today's Bible Blessing   *November 19*

Acts 13:42–Acts 16:6
PAUL TURNED TO THE GENTILES

Acts 13:49
"The word of the Lord was published throughout all the region."

The book of Acts was written about A.D. 63 and was addressed to a distinguished gentleman named THEOPHILUS. It is an account of the early life of the church, its foundation, the coming of the Holy Spirit, and the accounts of Peter's and Paul's ministries. It is interesting to note the church—its growth, and its progress—as the Christians were led by the Spirit of God in those formative, early years.

I do not think that many of us realize the great difficulty the Apostle Paul had to be a missionary for Jesus Christ. Their mode of transportation was either by foot, or sail boat—perhaps a donkey, camel, or ox cart. There were no cars, trains, or planes in those days. We must remember that in Paul's day there was no swift means of communication as we have it today in this century.

There were no radios, televisions, e-mails, YouTube, texts or tweets, with reporters speeding the events of the day to every part of the world. Paul wrote letters, carried by friends to destinations far away. It took weeks or months for news to reach the ears of those for whom it was intended. Not only that–it was difficult to preach the gospel to people who had no idea what was being talked about.

So, for Paul to stand on *"foreign soil"* and proclaim the unsearchable riches of Christ was much different than it is today. He and Barnabas were commissioned by the church in ANTIOCH to be missionaries. The two of them, along with John Mark, arrived at PAPHOS where Paul, filled with the Holy Spirit, rebuked the SORCERER ELYMAS with blindness! (See Acts 13:8.) When they came to PERGA in PAMPHYLIA, John Mark left them for Jerusalem, 100 miles from ANTIOCH in PISIDIA. (This is a different "ANTIOCH" than the one in Acts 13:2.) The two went to the local synagogue on the Sabbath day.

When Paul and his partner Barnabas (in today's reading) *"waxed bold,"* telling the Jews and religious proselytes the gospel, their message was rejected. In fact, the missionaries were cursed! Therefore, Paul turned to the Gentiles who received the message gladly. In Acts 13:48, "ordain" means *"agreed with."* But the *"honorable"* women, stirred up the town against the two missionaries, making their life miserable. So Paul and Barnabas left the area. (Many church splits are brought on by gossipy, cantankerous women!)

Later, while in ICONIUM, Paul's preaching caused a terrible division! The Jews stirred up the populous against him. So, they left town! He and BARNABAS ended up in LYSTRA in the region of DERBE in LYCAONIA. It was there that Paul healed a man who had been disabled since birth. The man *jumped up* and walked. It was then that the people *jumped* to the conclusion that the men were *gods!* They surmised, of all things, that BARNABAS was JUPITER and PAUL was MERCURY! The *"PRIEST OF JUPITER"* came. He began to prepare an animal sacrifice to them. Mortified, Paul cried out, *"We are men of like passions as you!"* What heathen these people were! They needed Jesus Christ!

Great contention hit LYSTRA! That was the theological climate in which Paul and Barnabas found themselves. Many Gentiles believed Paul's message. The Jews did not! A mob came! Jews from ANTIOCH and ICONIUM had stirred up LYSTRA. They hated Paul's message! THEY STONED PAUL! I don't know where BARNABAS was. He may have watched in horror and fear! IT WAS A DELIBERATE ACT OF DEFIANCE AGAINST THE WORDS OF GOD FROM THE MOUTH OF PAUL!

Paul died that day! His corpse was dragged out of town. In unbelief, the grieving Christians looked at his lifeless body. Much to their amazement, Paul opened his eyes! He stood up! He and his friends walked to the city. (What did the Jews think when they saw him?) The next day, he and BARNABAS went off to DERBE to work!

From that day on, Paul's vision of Heaven was brighter, for He, himself, had been *"caught up into Paradise!"*
HE HEARD SUCH "UNSPEAKABLE WORDS" THAT HE DID NOT DARE REPEAT THEM!
(II Corinthians 12:4)

"YE ARE CHRIST'S, AND CHRIST IS GOD'S"
(I Corinthians 3:23)
When pleasures charm, say, "I am Christ's!"
When tempted to loiter, rise to the work and say,
"NO, I AM CHRIST'S, I CANNOT STAY"
When tempted to sin, reply,
"I cannot do this great wickedness, for I am Christ's!"
(ggs quotes Spurgeon)

Today's Bible Blessing   *November 20*
Acts 16:7—Acts 18:18
THE MACEDONIAN VISION

Acts 16:31
"Believe on the Lord Jesus Christ, and thou shalt be saved."

When Paul, on the Damascus Road, uttered the words, *"WHO ART THOU, LORD?"* he had no idea what lay ahead of him. That's the way it is when one consecrates her life to the Lord, she does not know what is ahead of her. She just knows that Jesus is THE WAY, and she follows Him.

The day when the Lord struck Saul temporarily blind, was the day his life was changed! One of the *"changes"* was Saul's call to the mission field. Jesus Christ commanded him to minister to the Gentiles! Another change was a change in name from Saul to Paul. This new path was all new territory for Paul, the Roman citizen and *"Pharisee among the Pharisees"*!

Today we observe Paul, with his new missionary companion, Silas, establishing churches. *Establishing churches* does not mean building church buildings. I think it means bringing people to the Lord Jesus Christ as Saviour, baptizing them, and encouraging them to meet together to meditate on the Words of God with a pastor/teacher as the leader. Often, from this group, an assembly or *"church"* is formed. Before passing on to his next missionary outreach, Paul taught the new converts the doctrines that he, himself, had learned during those three years with Jesus Christ on the backside of the desert.

PAUL

Paul and Silas wanted to go to BITHYNIA in Asia Minor; but the Holy Spirit gave no liberty to do so. So on to TROAS they went! While there, Paul had a *"vision."* In the time of the early church, God spoke to some of His servants in *"visions."* This is not how He speaks to people today. Now Christians have the *written Words of God* for such direction. Christians have the New Testament. Paul and Silas did not have it. In his vision, there before Paul's eyes, a Macedonian man was begging Paul to come and help him! Without a doubt, it was God's *call* to Paul to preach the gospel there! Immediately he and Silas hopped aboard a boat to help that man!

Before they knew it, they were in the chief city of PHILIPPI on the SABBATH DAY. They found themselves by the river, with a gathering of *"devout women"* worshipping God. Of interest, there was no synagogue in Philippi. In order to have a synagogue, there had to be at least ten men and there were not enough Jewish men to form a synagogue at that time. That is why the women met by the riverside.

LYDIA was one of the women praying by the riverside. Upon hearing the gospel, she received Jesus as Saviour and was baptized. Her heart had been prepared to receive the gospel and the Saviour. Those in her household were saved also. What a glorious time! She was an affluent business person, dealing with *"purple dye"* that wealthy customers purchased to dye their clothing. With much grace, she opened her home to the missionaries and other Christians. More people should be given to hospitality today. Our lives become so busy, that we forget the social graces of hospitality and charity toward one another.

Soon a young, demon-possessed girl followed the two missionaries, causing quite a commotion wherever they went. Finally Paul *cast out* the evil spirit from the girl. This made her master angry. Now he could not get money for her predictions. Her healing caused him a financial loss. To get even, the master caught Paul and Silas and took them to the rulers in the marketplace. The officials agreed that Paul and Silas were causing confusion in the neighborhood. Soon the authorities tore the missionaries' clothes off of them and beat them with many stripes. After that, Paul and Silas were thrown into the dungeon.

It was then that God's servants found themselves in the inner ward of the prison! What a shock! But the men made the best of a bad situation. Though their feet were in stocks, they sang praises and prayed to God. It was midnight! All the other prisoners heard them singing. They were amazed. The jailer heard them, too.

All of a sudden, without warning, the earth shook! The prison's foundations were shaken! The jail doors flew open! The shackles fell off every prisoner! The jail keeper woke up! He saw the confusion! Certainly the prisoners had escaped! Instead, Paul called out, *"We are all here!"* The honesty of Paul and Silas, combined with their previous behavior that night, overwhelmed the jailer!

He cried out, "WHAT MUST I DO TO BE SAVED?" PAUL'S ANSWER WAS, *"BELIEVE ON THE LORD JESUS CHRIST AND THOU SHALT BE SAVED!"*

"IT'S A FACT"
(Proverbs 22:6; Hebrews 11:26)
"Train up a child in the way he should go:
and when he is old, he will not depart from it."
Pharaoh's daughter said, "TAKE THIS CHILD,
AND NURSE IT FOR ME."
Moses mother knew some things Pharaoh's daughter did not.
She knew to train up a child, and when he was old,
he would not depart.
This is not so much a promise, as a fact!
Because of what his mother taught him, Moses knew the difference.
He esteemed the reproach of Christ greater riches,
than the treasures in Egypt. (ggs)

𝒯𝑜𝑑𝑎𝑦'𝑠 𝐵𝑖𝑏𝑙𝑒 𝐵𝑙𝑒𝑠𝑠𝑖𝑛𝑔   𝒩𝑜𝑣𝑒𝑚𝑏𝑒𝑟 21

Acts 18:19—Acts 20:35
THE SECRET TO JOY!

Acts 20:24
"But none of these things move me . . . so that I may finish my course."

> *"BUT NONE OF THESE THINGS MOVE ME, NEITHER COUNT I MY LIFE DEAR UNTO MYSELF, SO THAT I MIGHT FINISH MY COURSE WITH JOY, AND THE MINISTRY, WHICH I HAVE RECEIVED OF THE LORD JESUS, TO TESTIFY THE GOSPEL OF THE GRACE OF GOD"* (Acts 20:24).

What a beautiful verse! It is the heart-testimony of a seasoned missionary who had given his all to Jesus. WHAT WERE THE *"THINGS"* WHICH DID NOT BOTHER PAUL ANYMORE? Why were they so *"insignificant"* that his own life was not important to him? What was this *"COURSE"* he was determined to *"finish"*? Where did he find his *"JOY"*? How did he, in the midst of persecution, continue to *"TESTIFY"* to *"THE GOSPEL OF THE GRACE OF GOD"*? When you and I know the answer to these questions, we will discover the "SECRET" to Paul's victorious life—no matter the circumstances.

In chapter 18 of Acts, we meet AQUILA and his wife, PRISCILLA. At the time, Paul had come from ATHENS to the wicked city of CORINTH. Christian work is most difficult. People are fickle and needy. Weary and worn from the battle scars of Christian service, Paul was glad to stay with friends for a season. There is nothing like good friends where one can be herself or himself, where every fault and frailty is not measured against perfection. Those kinds of friends are few and far between.

BOTH PAUL AND THIS COUPLE WERE SKILLED TENT MAKERS! I have read that all Jewish boys were taught a trade of some kind, even if they went on to higher education. Many men, who want to serve the Lord, must work outside their Christian work in order to support their families. My husband did this for years. We often refer to those Christian workers as *"tent makers."* Being a *"tent maker"* was a good thing for Paul, as, it seemed, he had little-to-nothing financially to keep him out of the poor house. So, the three of them made tents together. Those tents were not little camping tents that we have seen Boy Scouts use. They were large, heavy tents used by people who lived out in the wilderness.

Soon Silas and Timothy caught up with Paul at Corinth. They arrived from MACEDONIA. The three of them witnessed to the Jews in the synagogue. They told that Jesus was THE CHRIST. This infuriated the Jews. Paul shook his garments and said, *"Your blood be upon your own heads!"* Then he declared that he would preach to the Gentiles!

Soon Paul visited a religious man named Justus. His home was near the synagogue. Of interest, the chief ruler of the synagogue–a man named CRISPUS–believed on the Lord! This brought much consternation to the Jews! Yet, many Corinthians believed and were baptized because of CRISPUS' testimony. To calm his fears, the Lord spoke to Paul in a vision saying, *"BE NOT AFRAID, BUT SPEAK AND HOLD NOT THY PEACE FOR I AM WITH THEE!"* God assured Paul that He had many people in that city!

All at once, the Jews revolted as a group! They brought Paul to DEPUTY GALLIO and his judgment seat! They declared that Paul taught people to worship God contrary to THE LAW! GALLIO determined that the Jews were just quibbling about words! They had no real case against the Apostle! Then the Greeks took SOSTHENES, the believing chief ruler, whom we read about in Acts 18:17 & I Corinthians 1:1, and beat him mercilessly. After staying a good while in Corinth, PAUL, with PRISCILLA and AQUILA, sailed to SYRIA. I'm glad he had such faithful friends, aren't you?

During his last imprisonment—with death staring him in the face—Paul wrote to TIMOTHY. HE ENCOURAGED HIS SON *"in the faith"* TO PREACH THE WORD! Timothy was to teach doctrine and reprove, rebuke, & exhort! He was to *"endure"* afflictions, as Paul had endured. He was to be an evangelist, as Paul had been an evangelist. This was no easy assignment!

Because Paul had done these things, at the end of his life, the apostle could declare,

"I HAVE FINISHED MY COURSE WITH JOY!"
CAN YOU?

"FEAR IN THE NIGHT"
(Song of Solomon 3:8)
"They all hold swords, being expert in war:
every man hath his sword upon his thigh
because of fear in the night."
These words picture those who "preach the Word,"
and are ready for the defense of The Faith!
FEAR IN THE NIGHT IS THE ENEMY! (ggs)

Today's Bible Blessing   *November 22*

Acts 20:36—Acts 23:13
PAUL'S MIXED MESSAGE

Acts 21:14b
"The will of the Lord be done"

For some reason, Paul, the apostle called out of *"due time,"* had made a *"vow"* (I Corinthians 15:8). We know this from Acts 18:18 and it is confirmed in our thinking from today's reading in Acts 21:23. WHY HE DID THIS, WE ARE NOT CERTAIN. What that *"vow"* was and what it was not, we do not know. He said that he took this *"vow"* in CENCHREA. Cenchrea is the eastern harbor of Corinth. It is where Paul established a church, and was eight miles from Corinth. That area is mentioned for us again in Romans 16:1, in connection with a woman named PHEBE, and her work at the church in CENCHREA. She is the first person remembered by Paul to the Romans in his letter to them. After that, he asked those reading his epistle to say "hello" to Priscilla and Aquila. If you remember, they were his friends and helpers in the ministry as well as fellow tent-makers.

Why he made this vow in the first place, we do not know. Could it have been PHEBE'S influence in his life, or Priscilla's and Aquila's? We do know that he was convinced that he had to go to Jerusalem for the feast because of this *"vow."*

It is difficult to believe that this Paul, who taught the believers so much about the grace of God vs. Moses' law, would entangle himself with keeping any part of the law. Later, he would write to the Roman Christians that *"CHRIST IS THE END OF THE LAW FOR RIGHTEOUSNESS TO EVERY ONE THAT BELIEVETH!"* (See Romans 10:4.)

Later to the Christians in Colosse he wrote:
"Beware lest any man spoil you . . . after the tradition of

550

men . . . and not after Christ . . ." "LET NO MAN THEREFORE JUDGE YOU IN MEAT, OR IN DRINK, OR IN RESPECT OF AN HOLY DAY, OR OF THE NEW MOON, OR OF THE SABBATH DAYS . . ." (Colossians 2:14-18).

Could it be that Paul had taken the vow of a Nazarite? It's not clear in the Bible, but if so, that *"vow"* was a vow that a person would *"separate themselves to vow a vow of the Nazarite."* The person who would *"vow,"* would also not drink wine or strong drink—not even vinegar, or eat fresh grapes, or raisins. The person would NOT cut his or her hair; or if a man, he would let his beard grow without trimming it until the *"vow"* was over. When the *"vow"* was over, the person would go to the priest in the temple, offer his or her offering, shave his or her head at the door of the temple, and put the hair in the fire with his or her peace offering (Numbers 6:1-27).

After what seemed to me to be a complicated sea journey to and from various ports, Paul ended up in CAESAREA BY THE SEA at the Evangelist Philip's house. While there, PROPHET AGABUS showed up to warn Paul not to go to Jerusalem. This prophet took Paul's belt-like sash and bound his own hands and feet with it. The prophet's odd actions were supposed to illustrate to Paul that if he goes to Jerusalem to keep that vow, the Jews there would bind Paul as the prophet had bound himself with the sash. THEN THEY WOULD DELIVER PAUL TO THE GENTILE AUTHORITIES!

All of Paul's friends urged him NOT to go to Jerusalem! PAUL WOULD NOT LISTEN! He insisted on going and said that he was willing, not only to be bound, but also, to die at Jerusalem for the Name of Jesus! When they realized they could not stop Paul, the people said, *"The will of the Lord be done!"*

So Paul and four other men, who had vowed a *"vow"* and had purified themselves and shaved their heads, attempting to *"keep the law"* (Acts 21:24), entered the Temple. This was exasperating to the Jews who saw all this! They grabbed Paul, explaining that he was the man who taught against Moses law! Evidently, the men Paul brought into the temple were not Jews. The charge, whether true or false, was that in the past, Paul brought Greeks into the Temple, thus polluting it! (See Acts 21:28.)

From then on, Paul found himself judged and imprisoned. Soon he was thrown into a Roman dungeon and persecuted, but found mercy from the Lord. It was in this terrible confinement that he wrote epistles to the churches that he had founded.

Perhaps, if he had not been there in the dungeon, we would never have had the letters to Ephesus, Philippi, and Colosse for us to read today!

551

"MEDITATE DAY & NIGHT"
(Joshua 1:8)
This command was given to Joshua as he began to lead Israel.
Meditation was to enable him to be prosperous and successful.
LORD, TEACH ME TO MEDIATE ON THY WORD,
THE THINGS I READ AND LEARN,
TO THINK ON THEM OVER AND OVER AGAIN,
TO HOLD THEM TO MY HEART
AS THE VERY BREATH OF GOD! (ggs)

Today's Bible Blessing   *November 23*
Acts 23:14—Acts 26:10
IMPRISONED BY THE SEA
Acts 26:6
"I stand and am judged for the hope of the promise made of God . . ."

To keep up with Paul makes me breathless. How about you? Pure born, well-educated, and a persecutor of Christians, this man's life made a one hundred and eighty degree turn. Now he was the one being persecuted. In the past, he was the devout Jew who beat and jailed Christians. Now it was just the opposite. This son of a Pharisee defended himself before the high priest. Soon they learned that Paul was a Roman citizen! Fearing Paul would be torn in pieces, soldiers forced him into a castle for protection. In the midst of such fright, the Lord stood by Paul saying, *"BE OF GOOD CHEER!"* (See Acts 23:11.)

Even Paul's nephew pled his uncle's cause. The news was that forty men had pledged they would not eat until Paul was killed (Acts 23:12). At nine o'clock that night, two hundred soldiers brought Paul, under the cover of darkness, unto GOVERNOR FELIX at CAESAREA, thus rescuing the apostle, the Roman citizen.

An orator named TERTULLUS accused Paul before ANANIAS, the high priest. Felix was involved. It was said that Paul was a seditionist; a ringleader of the sect of the Nazarenes, as well as a profaner of the temple. Though those charges were false, many Jews lied that those words were true. Paul said it had been twelve days since he was in the temple and he made no disputations while there. He declared that the charges could not be proven. Paul said, *"I have a conscience void of offence toward God, and toward men."*

It was then that Paul told FELIX about his faith in Jesus Christ, explaining what Christ had done for him. Though Felix did not believe in Jesus Christ, he was under such conviction that he *"trembled"* in fear (Acts 24:25).

I remember a revival meeting that I attended as a child. It was in an Ohio country town. The evangelist preached Christ crucified, buried, and resurrected. It was powerful preaching! Some accepted Jesus as Saviour. Others did not.

I remember someone, under such conviction, who grabbed the pew in front of him with shaking hands and whited knuckles. The Spirit of God had moved upon that person with such conviction that he had perspiration on his forehead. Yet, he hung on to that pew in front of him, and never went down the aisle to accept Christ. As far as I know, that man is lost today—perhaps even in Hell. Felix heard the gospel that day and refused Christ for fear of people making fun of him.

FESTUS was the successor of FELIX. No sooner had he been appointed governor of Judea by Emperor Nero that he had to tend to the Apostle Paul controversy. He felt Paul would be safer remaining in CAESAREA BY THE SEA. It was about eighty miles from Jerusalem.

I remember being there. I recall the ruins of the 200-foot-wide jetty that Herod built.

For two years, Paul was imprisoned there. It was in Caesarea that he testified before AGRIPPA and other notables. One day Paul, the prisoner, was summoned before FESTUS. He wanted to favor the Jews. Paul appealed to Caesar. Some believe, if he had not appealed to Caesar, he would have gone free.

Paul was not disobedient to the heavenly vision that Jesus gave him while back on that Damascus Road. Imprisoned and punished, hungry and tired, he suffered for Jesus like few have ever suffered since or before. If Paul had not been imprisoned, we would not have the letters that he wrote from his prison cell.

OFTEN GOD USES OUR GREATEST AFFLICTIONS FOR HIS GREATER GLORY.

"A GARDEN ENCLOSED"
(Song of Solomon 4:12)
It has come to me lately as I have had trials
Which have kept me from attending church services,
to teach or sing there,
that it is not necessary at all that I ever get loosed
from what keeps me *shut in.*
Right now I am more important *shut in*
Than having freedom which he has not given me in these years.
The Lord wants me here enclosed.
The people in church do not need me, or may not miss me;
But my Lord observes me closely
As he walks in my garden
inspecting the fruit of the Valley. (ggs/1978)

Acts 26:11—Acts 28:20
AT THE MERCY OF CONTRARY WINDS

Acts 27:15

"When the ship was caught, and could not bear . . . we let her drive."

Now we come to the end of Paul's life and imprisonments. Just because he praised the Lord and wrote victorious words to the churches, did not mean that Paul did not suffer physically and emotionally. He had the emotional pain of any man!

Chapter twenty-six gives us Paul's address before KING AGRIPPA. This seemed to take place in CAESAREA, but I am not positive. Caesarea was where kings lived! Paul was safer there than in Jerusalem where the Jews wanted to kill him. It was before HEROD AGRIPPA (I think the second) that Paul said, *"O King Agrippa, I was not disobedient unto the heavenly vision."*

Paul's defense of his ministry and his explanation of Jesus Christ's great salvation, caused KING AGRIPPA to confess, *"ALMOST THOU PERSUADEST ME TO BE A CHRISTIAN!"* How interesting! Paul's witness was so compelling that both FESTUS and AGRIPPA got the message, yet rejected Christ! How like so many others today who do the same. They hear and understand, but reject!

Because Paul appealed to Caesar, there was nothing for the officials to do but to send Paul to Rome. Now there were no airplanes or large ships in those days. But, there were sturdy sail boats. Paul, a prisoner, found himself with other prisoners, under the watch of JULIUS, the centurion of Augustus' band. For some reason, he trusted Paul, and gave him liberty to visit friends.

They sailed close to Cyprus at the mercy of the contrary winds. They took them over the SEA OF CILICIA and PAMPHYLIA, coming to LYCIA. While there, JULIUS found a ship, which they boarded, heading for ITALY. Again, *at the mercy of the winds*, they missed CRETE—sailing toward SALMONE, landing at THE FAIR HAVENS near LASEA. Because it was not commodious to winter there, they moved on. (The Day of Atonement was upon them, but they were on dangerous seas.) Paul told those in charge that there would be a *violent tempest* and *danger* to their lives, as well as the cargo, but they would not die!

The centurion believed the experienced ship's captain rather than Prisoner Paul. They sailed toward PHENICE, and THE HAVEN OF CRETE, planning to dock there. Paul thought that was a good idea. But without warning, a tempestuous storm came up! There was nothing to do but *go with the wind!* It was a swift sail—

554

frightening, yet challenging.

It reminded me of the sudden storms in our lives where there is nothing to do but "go with the wind"–so to speak. This is what we Christians must do in the unexpected stormy trials of life!

With difficulty, the crew navigated away from Clauda Island, avoiding the quicksand. In great fright, they threw the ship's tackling overboard to lighten the load. Because of the tempest, the skies were dark for days! So long without food, Paul spoke up, reminding them he had advised them not to leave Crete. He encouraged, "BE OF GOOD CHEER! No man will lose his life in this storm!" An angel had come to Paul in the night encouraging him that he would stand before Caesar!

After fourteen storm-tossed nights, the captain ordered that four anchors be dropped. Paul advised staying with the ship, but the sailor relaxed the ropes and let the ship turn where it wanted. PAUL ENCOURAGED THEM TO EAT. They had been fourteen days without food. The 276 people on board would live! Soon they hoisted the mainsail, heading into the wind and toward the shore. Suddenly they ran aground. The ship fell apart in the violent waves! Though some wanted Julius to kill the prisoners–he would not, to spare Paul's life. The swimmers–prisoners as well as free men—swam toward shore. They grabbed boards from the broken ship or swam on their own. Soon, the weary men found themselves beached on MELITA ISLAND. **Barbarians greeted them with open arms!**

"GOD'S CONSTANT DEALINGS"
THE LIFE OF A BELIEVER IS A SERIES OF MIRACLES
WROUGHT BY THE MIGHTY HAND OF GOD!
God takes a common thing
and by His constant dealing
transforms a cinder into a beautiful gem
for all the world to be amazed.
(ggs—copied in part)

Today's Bible Blessing   *November 25*
Acts 28:21–Romans 3:14
PAUL'S IMPETUS FOR SERVING
Romans 1:16
"I am not ashamed of the gospel of Christ . . . the power of God . . ."

We last left Paul and the other ship-wrecked survivors washed to shore on the Island of Melita. Wet and harried from the sea and tired and torn from fighting the tempestuous waves with only a board or a plank between them and death, they were greeted by barbarians. By a bonfire, Paul was bitten by a poisonous viper. For sure the islanders thought he was being punished by the gods as a murderer! Soon they had a mind change, for Paul did not fall down dead. Then they said he was a god!

The island's chief was a man named PUBLIUS, whose father was dying. Paul saw the man, laid his hands on him, and the man was healed! All the sick on the island flocked to Paul's side for healing. It was a wonderful three-month period for the citizens of Melita!

Again the traveling, the tensions, and the journey to other mission fields lay ahead of the Apostle, who was still a prisoner. A centurion was his constant guard! Off he and the other prisoners sailed, on an Alexandrian ship. There were people there who needed Jesus. They stopped at places with names such as SYRACUSE and RHEGIUM. What joy! At PUTEOLI they found fellow Christians. Then off they sailed toward ROME!

Though the other prisoners were transferred over to the captain of the guards there in Rome, Paul lived by himself with a soldier guarding him day and night! You can be sure that he took advantage of those one-on-one evangelism opportunities.

Soon Paul called together the Jewish leaders who had heard nothing whatsoever about Paul's coming to Rome. He told the Jewish leaders that he was imprisoned because he spoke of the HOPE OF ISRAEL! The leaders were ignorant of the charges. On following days, Paul spoke to them about Jesus. Some believed! Some did not!

Paul lived under *"house arrest"* in his own house for two years. Even though he was under constant guard, he was free to *"teach freely"* about Jesus Christ. It was a remarkable turn of events!

NOW WE WILL TURN TO THE EPISTLE TO THE ROMANS

As I have tried to follow the Apostle Paul, in the book of Acts, through his conversion and his call to the ministry, I have been amazed at the stamina this man had. I am convinced THE IMPETUS that kept him going was from the time he was stoned (Acts 14:19), and left for dead! HE PERSONALLY SAW HEAVEN! It was that *heavenly vision,* in my opinion, that kept him going and going and going. That *beauty* and *perfection* that he experienced, before he came back to life, was the *energizing motive* that gave him strength for each day—in spite of great trials and tribulation. He kept going on *"for the Prize of the high calling of God"* (Philippians 3:14), because he had seen THE GLORY BEYOND, and knew all the suffering of this world was worth it all when he would return to Heaven to be with Christ which was *"far better."* You and I *"say" "which is far better"*–but we have never experienced it. *BUT*

PAUL KNEW FROM EXPERIENCE THAT HEAVEN WAS "FAR BETTER"*!* (See Philippians 1:23.)

Let's look at Romans 1:16. This is a verse that I have known since childhood. It's beautiful in word, as well as meaningful in exposition. Paul said that he was not ashamed of the gospel of Christ! (The modern versions have removed the Name "of Christ" from their bibles, but it is in the *King James Bible* where it belongs!) WHAT A WONDERFUL *"GOOD NEWS"* THAT *"GOSPEL"* IS! Paul told us later, in I Corinthians 15:1-4, that the GOSPEL was the DEATH, BURIAL, and RESURRECTION OF CHRIST. Paul knew the POWER of that gospel. It had changed his life! You, too, know what Jesus has done for you, if you are born-again. He took you and me, as sinful children of Adam, and *"empowered"* us with Himself when we were saved! THAT SALVATION IS LIKE *"SPIRITUAL DYNAMITE"* TO US WHO HAVE BELIEVED!

"I HAVE CALLED THEE"
(Isaiah 43:1-3)
WHEN THOU PASSETH THRU THE WATERS,
I WILL BE WITH THEE. (difficult things: deep)
AND THRU THE RIVERS, (more difficult: deeper)
THEY SHALL NOT OVERFLOW THEE. (very difficult: deepest)
WHEN THOU WALKEST THROUGH THE FIRE,
(hot scorching trials: intense)
THOU SHALT NOT BE BURNED. (intense)
NOTICE THE DEGREES OF TRIAL
waters: passeth
rivers : passeth
fire: walkest
(ggs)

Today's Bible Blessing   *November 26*

Romans 3:15–Romans 6:23
IT IS CALLED ETERNAL LIFE!

Romans 3:23
"For all have sinned and come short of the glory of God! "

The Apostle Paul was a very interesting man! We remember his intense hatred for Christians before his conversion. Now, we see him as a devoted follower of the LORD JESUS CHRIST. His zeal for Christ was as intense for Jesus as it was against Him. Often, his love for his own Jewish people got him into trouble. Always, he wanted to go to ROME to tell the Romans the *"unsearchable riches of Christ."* (Perhaps it was because he was a Roman citizen.) His name

"PAUL," which means *"little,"* was his Roman name. (Saul was his Jewish name.) We remember him in Ephesus when he said the Holy Spirit gave him a purpose, not only to go to MACEDONIA, ACHAIA, and JERUSALEM, but also to go to ROME. In fact, he declared, *"I MUST ALSO SEE ROME!"* (See Acts 19:21.) His determination was great! Little did he realize that this desire would come by way of imprisonment!

In the *colophon* at the end of Paul's Roman letter, it tells us that the epistle was written by Paul to the Romans from Corinth. Of interest, it was delivered by PHEBE, a worker in the church there in CENCHREA. If you remember, CENCHREA was the eastern harbor of Corinth, eight miles away. Paul sailed with Priscilla and Aquila from this harbor in Acts 18:18. (That's where he shaved his head.)

In today's Bible reading, we have Romans 3:23 and Romans 6: 23. (Technically, Romans 6:23 is in tomorrow's reading.) Both verses end in *"23,"* which is a good memory hint. Often when talking to an "unsaved" person, we try to bring them to the realization that she or he is a sinner using Romans 3:23: *"For all have sinned, and come short of the glory of God."* A person must realize they are sinners; otherwise, that person has no need of a Saviour.

Now that I am older, I use a wheelchair in the large airports. Going from one concourse to another, or even walking to a faraway gate, can wear me out! Some older or infirm folk are too proud to do this; but they pay for this *"pride"* by becoming worn out physically before they arrive at their destination. If you don't know—airports can be difficult with all the security measures, prior to boarding. I make *"friends"* with the people who push my chair from one destination to another. Sometimes the walk is very long. I use this time to talk about Jesus.

I'll never forget this one young man. I WAS EXPLAINING TO HIM THAT ALL HAVE SINNED. I told him about Adam's sin that was passed on to the human race. I told him that the Bible said that he had fallen short of God's righteous standard! I told him that he needed a SAVIOUR, or he would go to HELL! It was then that he told me in all sincerity, *"I AM NOT A SINNER!"* I got up from my wheelchair and looked at him in the eye and said, *"Let me look at you!"* I declared, *"You are the only person in the whole world who is not a sinner!"* He looked at me with ignorant confidence. Stunned, I replied, *"I guess you do not need a Saviour, for Jesus only died for sinners!"* And I sat down!

Now we come to our second verse: *"FOR THE WAGES OF SIN IS DEATH!. . ."* Down deep in every human's soul is a seed called *"DEATH."* It was planted there by the first man named Adam. It comes with the fact that we have been born into the world. All our lives we are living with this *"death"* stalking us. Some day we will die! That is a fact! The surprising thing is that life pays *"wages."* The *"wages"* is **DEATH!** Everyone who dies outside of Jesus Christ receives that *"wage"*! WHY? It is because of ORIGINAL SIN!

The good news is that there is a *"GIFT"* from God that can erase those awful wages. The "GIFT" was PAID FOR by Jesus Christ on CALVARY. Jesus took your and my *"WAGES"* in His body—cancelling out our sin. He was made a SIN OFFERING for us! (See I Peter 2:24.) ALL WE HAVE TO DO IS ACCEPT HIS *"GIFT."* **IT IS CALLED *"ETERNAL LIFE"*!**

"WHEN MY HEART IS OVERWHELMED"
(Psalm 61:2)
"When my heart is overwhelmed and my spirit wonders, "WHY?"
Lead me to the Rock that is higher than I.
GOD IS GREATER THAN MY HEART!
(ggs)

Today's Bible Blessing   *November 27*

Romans 7:1–Romans 9:22
PURPOSED AFTER THE COUNCIL OF HIS OWN WILL

Romans 8:28
"And we know that all things work together for good . . . "
ROMANS 8:26-27

> *"Likewise the Spirit also helpeth our infirmities: for we know not what we should pray for as we ought: but the Spirit itself maketh intercession for us with groanings which cannot be uttered. And he that searcheth the hearts knoweth what is the mind of the Spirit, because he maketh intercession for the saints according to the will of God."*

HOW MANY TIMES HAVE YOU BEEN SO DISTRAUGHT THAT YOU CANNOT PRAY? I don't mean you *"can't"*–I mean that words will not come out of your mouth with any coherent meaning to your own ears. Yet, you are praying fervently! IT IS YOUR VERY SPIRIT AND SOUL *MOANING IN GRIEF OF SORROW* TO YOUR HEAVENLY FATHER! At such times, you know that God is very near to you, *"tenderly caring"* with a *"listening ear."*

There have been times in my life that I've fallen to my knees with such "want." I reached out to God with no words, only sounds of grief and hurt. In AGONY OF SOUL, I have cried out to God! The words I spoke were not words at all. They were sorrow in sound! Disappointment in distress. And UNBELIEF WRAPPED IN FRAIL TISSUE-PAPER THOUGHTS!

It was then that I realized that the Holy Spirit was filling in the blanks of my unbelief with words that I could not utter. My heart was crying out to God with *"unintelligent sounds"* and *"inner screams of grief."* I did not understand what was going on in my life. I did not know where to turn for help, but to GOD! Who but He would understand my thoughts? Who but He would sift my words of unbelief and doubt to understandable heart-cries? It was then that I learned that THE SPIRIT was helping my *"infirmities"* with groanings which I COULD NOT UTTER.

It is the same SPIRIT Who raised Jesus from the dead Who dwells within the believer. Paul tells us this in Romans 8:11. How can that be? *"He that raised up Christ from the dead shall also quicken your mortal bodies by his Spirit that dwelleth in you."* How can that be? The same *"power"* that brought Jesus' dead body to life, is the same "Spirit" Who teaches me how to pray. He is THE THIRD PERSON OF THE TRINITY! It is He Who makes intercession for me with *"groanings"* that have no meaning to anyone but my Father in Heaven and me!

ROMANS 8:28:

> *"AND WE KNOW THAT ALL THINGS WORK TOGETHER FOR GOOD TO THEM THAT LOVE GOD, TO THEM WHO ARE THE CALLED ACCORDING TO HIS PURPOSE."*

When my sister, Audrey, died at age twenty, it did something to my parents' inner-being. She had suffered so with Hodgkin's disease. There was no cure then. That was 1952. About thirty-plus-years later, my husband suffered from the same disease. She died. He did not.

People would quote Romans 8:28 to my mother so often that she thought she would scream if one more person said to her, *"All things work together for good. . ."* What did those BIBLE QUOTING PEOPLE, who never had a daughter die, know? Later my mother wrote concerning this verse the following:

> *"This was a "hard saying" to me during her tragic sickness—much quoted with little understanding by those who quoted it. It was only after the Spirit of God led me further into the verse that I saw HIS PURPOSE as the important thing in it all, not my understanding of it; and I rested in Him, who purposed it after the council of HIS OWN WILL—not ours."* (Quote from Gertrude G. Sanborn)

"I HEAR THE BELLS!   I HEAR THE BELLS!
(AUDREY JUNE SANBORN DIED NOVEMBER 30, 1952)
**As though it were yesterday,
I see her dear sick frame.
The agony dulled by a powerful drug.**
She did not know I spent myself, watching and caring.
"I HEAR THE BELLS BEHIND ME," SHE SAID,
AS SHE SLIPPED FROM OUR ARMS
INTO THE EVERLASTING ARMS!
Such music in Heaven!
BELLS, HARPS, TRUMPETS, AND SINGING!
When our DEAR ONE was taken by THE ANGEL
in an instant to be with Him for evermore!
SHE HEARD THE BELLS OF HEAVEN RING
WHEN SHE PASSED OVER!
Here, Pain!
There, Glory!
(ggs)

Today's Bible Blessing   *November 28*

Romans 9:23–Romans 12:18
O GOD, USE ME TODAY!

Romans 12:1-2

"Present your bodies a living sacrifice unto God."

It's true, verses of Scripture bring memories! God has used them in our lives to support us, to challenge us, and to encourage us for *'today's living'*–as well as for tomorrow's. It's also true, we have no guarantee for tomorrow, and our *"today"* is only the present moment. I remember a dear woman, upon awaking, reaching for her Bible. She began to read God's Words for her new day. AS SHE WAS READING, THE LORD TOOK HER *"HOME"* TO HIMSELF! *Her "today" was only a few hours that day!*

Today, let's think about ROMANS 12:1-2. Most Christians know this verse by heart. Often the verse has struck a chord in their lives. I know it has in mine. I was saved when I was ten. I remember well the day I was saved, as well as the day I raised my hand in church to proclaim it to the world. My *"world"* then was a country church in a small Ohio town.

My heart was tender toward the LORD! I wanted Him to use me for whatever He wanted of me. I had a different childhood from many, being a sick child for at least three years. I WAS SO THANKFUL I COULD WALK AND BE A PART OF MY FAMILY, as well as a part of the community. THEN TO TOP IT OFF–I HAD RECEIVED JESUS CHRIST AS MY PERSONAL SAVIOUR! As the Apostle Paul, I presented my "self" to Jesus on the altar of consecration for Him to use however He wanted.

That was a BIG STEP for a young girl in her early teens. I meant every word of it—A LIVING SACRIFICE! Holy! ACCEPTABLE TO GOD! Like TRUSTING ISAAC climbing MOUNT MORIAH, I put my hand in Jesus' hand and climbed life's mountain. *"Please, Lord, use me!"* was my dedication. *"Help me not to be conformed to this world! Transform my mind to be Thy mind!"* I did not know my future, but I was willing to go anywhere. It even meant that if the Lord did not want me to marry, I was willing. Yet, I wanted to be married. In all this dedication, in spite of my shyness with boys, God had a husband for me. He gave me a man of God–not perfect, as I am not perfect–but one who had dedicated himself to *"prove what is that good, and acceptable, and perfect will of God."*

God used ROMANS 12:1-2 in Dr. Waite's life, too. I am sure as a young Christian; he offered his life on the altar of God's will, too. I remember his telling me of a certain rededication of that life. It was when he was fifty-six years old. We had taken our youngest son to college in Northern Florida. On the way back from there, we stopped to see our daughter in Virginia. While there, she looked at her father's neck and asked, ***"Dad, what is that 'lump' on your neck?"*** **That discovery was the beginning of a difficult fight with a cancer called Hodgkin's disease!** For me, it was like *déjà vu* all over again. For me, it was a diagnosis of "death"! Thirty years or so previously, my beautiful sister, Audrey, had died of that same cancer. At the time there was no cure! She was twenty!

My husband's fight with cancer began! He heard of some non-invasive treatment for Hodgkin's in another state. I believe it was NEVADA. Reno–to be exact. While there, as was his custom, he attended a Baptist church. The preacher knew him. He asked my husband to preach. It was from Romans 12:1-2 that he expounded the text. It was to those people, as a stranger, that he poured out his heart's rededication to the LORD. I wish I had the notes to that sermon before me. He explained the text. He told the meaning of those fifty-nine words! As he preached, he spoke of his present life and his new dedication of that life to his Saviour and Lord.

Frances Havergal, the great Christian poetess and hymn writer composed her "CONSECRATION HYMN" with ROMANS 12:1-2 in mind. She had to give up certain desires in her life for a full consecration to God!–her hands, her feet, her voice, her silver and her gold. **What are you and I holding back *"today"* from such a dedication, to let God use us *"TODAY"* for His service?**

562

"A TEACHER OF GOOD THINGS"
To grow every day more and more like Christ—
this is the privilege of aging.
It is a beautiful thing to grow old gracefully,
to manifest more of the Lord Jesus from day to day.
We've learned more.
We've been through more.
We've had more.
We've seen more.
YET HITHERTO, HE HAS HELPED US!
We should be exemplary,
showing the blessings of following God, as dear children—
TEACHERS OF GOOD THINGS!
(ggs)

Today's Bible Blessing   *November 29*

Romans 12:19–Romans 16:13
PATIENCE & EXPERIENCE BRING HOPE

Romans 15:4

"Whatsoever things were written . . . were written for our learning."

One of the verses that I have known most of my life is
ROMANS 15:4. In truth, it takes in the whole of Scripture, especially
the Old Testament.

*"FOR WHATSOEVER THINGS WERE WRITTEN
AFORETIME WERE WRITTEN FOR OUR LEARNING,
THAT WE THROUGH PATIENCE AND COMFORT OF THE
SCRIPTURES MIGHT HAVE HOPE!"*

**This is a verse of admonition and warning, as well as a
verse of recall and reminiscence.** We human beings are slow
learners—even we who name the Name of Christ! Mistakes are made!
Often we do not profit from them. Marriage blunders leave some of us
in a union that plagues us our whole life. That which endeared us to
our mate, bothers us as the years go on. Relationships with others are
difficult—not only because the other persons are peculiar, but because
we are not congenial and are selfish. So, we are like the people we read
about in the Bible. They were real people with real problems making
some of the real blunders that you and I make. Perhaps, as we read
about their lives, we can learn what not to do.

**Paul writes to the Christians at Rome—whom he had
never met—that all that was written down by Moses and the
prophets, as well as people like David and Job, were written**

down for you and me to observe and learn. Why?—that we might learn from their mistakes, that we might get acquainted with patience, that we might be comforted in our trials and tribulations, that we might observe how to live when a precious loved one dies—and most of all—THAT WE WOULD HAVE *"HOPE"*!

> *"And hope maketh not ashamed; because the love of God is shed abroad in our hearts by the Holy Ghost which is given unto us"* (Romans 5:5).

WHAT IS THAT "HOPE" that is ours, as we reflect on people like Eve and her "small talk" with the serpent? Or women like Sarah who laughed when she was told she would have a child in her old age? Or Noah's wife as she endured Noah and his boat building, or her daughters-in-law who married into a different kind of family. WHAT IS THAT HOPE that is given to us Christians as we read of Hagar's time with Abraham as he walked not *"by faith?"* What lessons are "of HOPE" as we watch Lot's wife disobey God, turning back and dying, because of her unbelief; or her daughters and their sin with their drunken father, causing an embarrassment for all—even to our present years? What of the tears shed at Sarah's tomb, after the great lady passed from this world? What of Keturah—married to Abraham after Sarah's death—always loved less than the first wife? What courage we can learn from Rebekah who left the familiar to marry a husband she had never seen, or with her weariness in her dealing with "the daughters of Heth" who found her sons desirable for marriage (Genesis 27:46; 28:8)!

What is THAT HOPE we find in the lives of women like Rachel who could not have children, or in Leah who loved with no return—bearing many children? Or in Bilhah or Zilpah—just servants—used for childbearing with no tender love. Or Dinah's shame in Succoth, or Tamar's playing a prostitute to have a child, or Asenath, a daughter of On, who married Joseph for political reasons, or Jochebed, or Miriam, or Bathsheba who tempted the king with her indiscretions.

The answer is found in Romans 5: We should *GLORY IN TRIBULATION* because trials teach us PATIENCE which gives us EXPERIENCE; and it is the experience which teaches us that there is HOPE!

Our HEAVENLY FATHER has given us HOPE by the resurrection of Jesus Christ (I Peter 1:3). That HOPE is beyond description. It is full of faith! In times of discouragement may we remember that *"HOPE MEANS SOMETHING FUTURE—BUT ASSURED!"* It gives *"comfort"* & *"patience"*! JUST REMEMBER!

"MEDITATE MUCH ON HEAVEN"
Meditate much on Heaven.
It will help thee to press on
and forget the toil of the way.
We shall be going to our Father's House
—where Jesus is—
to that Royal City which has foundations.
(ggs)

Today's Bible Blessing   *November 30*

Romans 16:14–I Corinthians 4:2
THEY VOWED TO STARVE
THE PREACHER OUT!

I Corinthians 1:10
"That there be no divisions among you."

As I look into Paul's letter to the church in Corinth, I am reminded that this church was a typical church. Why do I say that? Because there were many church problems within the assembly. Every sin that churches have today was there in Corinth.

Right *away in I Corinthians 1:10,* Paul calls for UNITY. He wrote "*that you all speak the same thing, and that there be no divisions among you . . .*" He gave a similar plea to the Roman Church in Romans 16:17, "*Mark them which cause divisions and offences contrary to the doctrine.*"

I remember my first church split. Maybe I was in seventh grade. It was in a Baptist church in a small Ohio town. That was the church where I was baptized when I was ten years old. We lived close to the church. A sportsman could have thrown a ball from our front door to the church's door.

As in many Baptist churches, there are certain families that *"run"* the church! A new preacher came to our tiny town of three hundred. It was smack dab in the middle of many dairy farms. After the *"honeymoon"* was over, reality set in. The *"church bosses"* were still *"church bosses."*

My father was the Sunday School superintendent. We were the *"city folks."* We put in indoor plumbing and had pasteurized milk delivered to our door. You can imagine the "talk" when we did not have the local dairy deliver unpasteurized milk to us. (*I had become very ill, as a small child from unpasteurized milk!*) The *"church split"* was over *THE GOSPEL HERALD.* It was a good periodical for which the church subscribed for every member. I remember my mother daily reading it as she ate her lunch.

The Pastor and my Dad thought it would be wiser for each family to subscribe to the magazine instead of the church paying for each subscription. Remember these were the depression days. I think the preacher's salary was five dollars a week–or something like that. We could buy a pound of hamburger for twenty-five cents. A loaf of bread was about ten cents. My sick uncle, recovering from TB, rented a large, old farmhouse for $5 a month in Oberlin.

Well—there was a church split! The more affluent families, who had been running the church, got huffy and left. They had vowed to *"starve the preacher out!"* Only the *"followers,"* who had been assigned to the *"lesser"* church jobs, remained. Much to the surprise of everyone, within that remnant, were talented people. There were musicians, and teachers, and financial contributors! What a lesson for my future life of *"church splits."* There are always people who can be used of God, who never had the opportunity to serve Him because others had hogged the show!

I have seen other such "divisions" of which Paul warned. In our little church near the Cleveland airport, while the pastor was absent, my grandfather called a church meeting. I was sixteen and not permitted to be in there. I'm not sure what happened, but Grandpa was dismissed from the membership because of it. There were divisions in our family over this. In fact, my aunt favored the pastor's position, and my parents, my grandfather's. Though we stayed in the church, it was a very sticky situation. Years later, the pastor apologized to my grandfather—but much damage had been done!

Fresh out of the Navy chaplaincy, my husband moved us to Massachusetts where he pastored a prominent church in Newton. Much to the surprise of the deacons, Pastor Waite followed the Bible and the church constitution. Whoever heard of doing that? The deacons had been calling the shots. One Sunday morning, during an announcement, the church leaders stormed the platform. There was a mini-riot! That was back in 1961, when such things were not "in vogue" as now. The police were called. Needless to say that was one of the kinds of divisions about which Paul had warned Corinth! Sad to say, I could tell of other *"divisions"* and *"splits"*–but I'm running out of time and paper.

"A MIND STAYED ON HIM"
(Isaiah 26:3)
"WILT KEEP HIM IN PERFECT PEACE,
MIND STAYED;
BECAUSE HE TRUSTED IN THEE."
(Read without italics)
(ggs)
GOD WILL STAY THE MIND, IF WE TRUST IN HIM!
**We are learning lessons here, which in eternity
shall be displayed as fruit for us.**
(Copied)

Today's Bible Blessing   *December 1*

I Corinthians 4:3–I Corinthians 7:34
A MARRIAGE SECRET

I Corinthians 7:5

"Defraud ye not one the other except it be with consent for a time.

Corinth was an ancient Grecian city of culture in North East Peloponnesus, a wealthy trade headquarters between East and West, and a graceful, elaborate artistic community. Perhaps you have seen the tall *"Corinthian"* pillars built today which are patterned after its architecture. If I recall from previous study, it was a wicked city with all sorts of vice and debauchery. The Christians in the Corinthian church had been saved out of a very sinful lifestyle. Paul had his hands full teaching the *"Christian"* way to live. As we read this letter, we can see how they were prone to backslide often.

Paul wrote his Corinthian friends about the **sanctifying of their bodies.** In I Corinthians 6:19, he told them that their bodies were *"temples."* They had never heard anything like this before. He reminded them that they had led sinful lives before their conversions. He reflected on their past. Some were fornicators, idolaters, adulterers, male prostitutes, and abusers of themselves with mankind. Some had been thieves, greedy, drunkards, revilers, and extortioners (vs. 9-10). What a motley crowd of sinners found all in one place! But, Paul did not want his friends to dwell on their past sins. He encouraged them, *"Some of you were such sinners!–but YOU ARE WASHED IN THE PRECIOUS BLOOD OF CHRIST!"* What miracles of grace were these people of God!

As Paul explained that their bodies were **"TEMPLES OF THE HOLY SPIRIT,"** the Corinthian Christians caught a glimpse of their wonderful standing in Christ Jesus. Because they were bought by Christ's blood at Calvary, they should glorify God in their bodies and in their spirits. The truth was that since they were *"bought,"* their bodies did not belong to themselves any more. They belonged to God!

I remember a young woman in one of my *"Husband Loving Lesson"* classes. She told how she and her husband lived together before they were married. They didn't have a clue that it was wrong! When they got saved they continued living together. Soon the pastor told them that it was sinful. They should cease this activity, separate, and get legally married. When they realized that it was wrong, and that the Bible taught them they were *"living in fornication,"* they followed the Word of God and got legally married. Now they have a God-blessed union! Their lifestyle had been exactly like the unsaved Corinthians' lifestyle. So many couples today see nothing wrong with *"shacking up."* Their conscience is seared with a hot iron! It has to be trained by the Words of God.

I Corinthians 7 is an extremely important chapter of God's Word which teaches married couples not to defraud one another in their most intimate times together. It is very important for married people to read, understand, and practice verses 3-5. The husband's body is not his own; it belongs to his wife. And the wife's body is not hers; it belongs to her husband. If married people would only recognize the exclusive right one's mate has to the other mate's body, there would be no adultery!

As I write, there is a scandal brewing about a well-loved golfer. He has a beautiful wife and family; yet it is coming out in the news that he has been unfaithful to his wife. It appears, if the reports are true, that he is like the proverbial sailor with a girl in every port. **Paul teaches that there should be no long delays of many days between intimacies.** He taught them to DEFRAUD NOT ONE THE OTHER, except by mutual agreement. Then the *"time-out"* should be short that Satan tempt them not (I Corinthians 7:5). We should be mindful of such marriage education too! IT'S A MARRIAGE SECRET!

"DRAW THE SWORD & USE IT!"
(I John 4:4)
We conquer through Christ
Greater is He that is in you
than he that is in the world!
RESIST THE DEVIL!
Draw the sword & use it!
The Sword is the Word of God.
It is not merely two edged, it is all edged.
THE WORD IS FINAL AND SUFFICIENT!
IT IS THE VERY BREATH OF GOD!
(ggs/ Perryman, page 24)

Today's Bible Blessing   *December 2*

I Corinthians 7:35–I Corinthians 11:7
HER NAME WAS BEVERLY

I Corinthians 10:13

"God is faithful, who will not suffer you to be tempted above that ye are able."

The Bible verse I have chosen to think about today is I CORINTHIANS 10:13! It is the verse that my mother claimed as her own, in regard to accepting and caring for my brain damaged sister. HER NAME WAS BEVERLY! She was seven years younger than I. We loved her—my mother, father, sister and I. I remember Mother making a basinet from a wicker clothes basket for our baby. Carefully she lined it with fabric, putting some kind of mattress in the bottom, and fixed a bow to the handle. That was Beverly's bed until she outgrew it. What a precious baby was our baby!

I do not remember Mother "great with child"–to use a Bible phrase. Life was all new for me on *"the outside."* Walking and running was an exciting experience for me! I remember the day I learned to skip with two feet. Up until then I only could skip with one. It was a thrilling experience. I ran home and said, *"Mother, I can skip!"* She was happy, too! I remember when I learned to roller skate–all of this was on Wager Avenue in Lakewood, Ohio. Aunt Norma had given me a *"Mickey Mouse"* watch for Christmas. I loved that watch. One day I learned to roller skate. I was thrilled! Only one day, I forgot to take it off before I went skating. I fell down. My watch broke! I cried and cried!

I do remember visiting my mother in the hospital after my younger sister was born. She had been moved from a ward into a private room. As a little girl, I did not realize the significance of such a move. I remember I ran to her bedside. I think I was wearing my red-sailor-dress that Grandma Barker had made me. (Grandma Barker sewed to help Grandpa earn money in those depression days.) My mother said, *"Vonnie, you aren't supposed to be here!"* In those days, children were not to visit in the hospitals.

Later, at home, my mother read in the local paper that many of the women, who had been in that hospital ward with her, had died. Some of the babies had died, too. They all had staph infection–unbeknownst to my mother. That's why my mother had been moved. Her life was spared and so was her baby's!

When Beverly was born, she had an extremely difficult birth. Her face was black and blue. Little did we know that Beverly had suffered irreparable brain injury during her birth. I remember what a darling baby she was. How cute she looked in that little basket-bed that Mother had made especially for her. She was a good baby. She cried very little. Later, Mother was told that was a sign that Beverly had a problem. But no one told my mother—not even the doctors and nurses in that hospital. I am sure they knew. Beverly would have a very different life! That difference would change my mother's life forever. And—that change would affect mine, too.

For years, my mother thought Beverly was just a slower child from my sister and me. One day, in another town with another doctor, my mother learned *the heart breaking news* that something was wrong with our little sister. I remember hearing my mother praying in her room, begging God to heal her little girl. Those were heartbreaking days! Then one day, mother realized that God was not going to heal her little child. Instead, He was going to help my mother live and care for such a child. **The** *"BEVERLY TEST"* **was not easy.** Mother came to realize that God was a *"FAITHFUL GOD!"* He would not permit her to be tested above what she and Daddy were able. Combined with this heartbreaking loss, God would give her *"a way to escape"*! This *"escape"* would help her to be *"able to bear"* the trial (I Corinthians 10:13). All the rest of my mother's life, until she died at eighty-three, I watched my mother run to the Words of God for endurance, help, and comfort as she cared for my retarded sister. NOW IN HEAVEN, BEVERLY CAN COME TO MOTHER AND THANK HER FOR THOSE YEARS OF CARING!

"WITHIN THE CIRCUMSTANCES"
Where am I living? Not "above" my circumstances!
This is only mental.
Though surely not "beneath" for this is carnal weakness!
But "within" whatever God allows—
those trying things which He allows,
those sorrows, those losses, those wearinesses—
right there *"within."*
This is *"where"* I live.
THIS IS WHERE I CAN AND SHOULD LIVE – A RADIANT AND
FRUITFUL LIFE – AND SHOW FORTH HIS PRAISES!
He, in the form of THE FORTH, is with us,
as He was with Daniel in the Den of Lions.
LIVING WITHIN our daily circumstances! (ggs)

I Corinthians 11:8–I Corinthians 14:15
Is Hair a Heresy?

I Corinthians 11:9

"Neither was the man created for the woman; but the woman for man."

I think it is very interesting that I Corinthians 11:9 has such a prominent place in the midst of various doctrinal truths in this epistle. Paul told the Christians in worldly Corinth that *"there must be also heresies among you!"* He wrote that the need for *"heresies"* was so the truth would be made manifest! That reminds me of the way a person can tell a true five dollar bill from a counterfeit. *"How?"* you ask. By being very, very familiar with the real five dollar bill!

First of all let's answer the question: *"WHAT ARE HERESIES?"* The English definition of the word is found in the footnotes of **THE DEFINED KING JAMES BIBLE.** Heresies are *"teachings or opinions that differ with established religious beliefs."* In other words, some men or women, who have their own ideas on a certain religious subject and who teach it as truth, are teaching *"heresies"*! In so doing, they come to have followers who cling together in that false teaching and cause dissension and divisions within the church body as a whole by doing so.

First of all Paul exhorts, through his letter, that the Christians should continue to follow him because he follows Christ. He praises them for doing so. He encourages them to keep the traditions that he set up for them to follow. Some people think that all *"traditions"* are wrong. That is not true. It is true that there are some bad *"traditions,"* but it is also true that there are some good *"traditions."* They should not be discarded.

So with interest, we notice what were some of the *"divisions"* in this early church. From reading I Corinthians 11:3, it seemed that the women were not being submissive to their husbands. So Paul reminded the women that their husbands are their "heads." In other words, the women were to report or acquiesce to their husbands, and their husbands were to report to Christ.

Then Paul keeps talking about the man's *"head."* He said that when a man prays he dishonors his *"head"* if his head is *"covered"* (vs. 4). What is this *"covered"*? Which "head" is this? I think Paul is talking about the actual physical *"head"* of the man—not Christ. (I may be wrong.) Could the *"covering"* be the man's hair?

Now Paul calls attention to the woman's head. He says the opposite about the woman. If she prays with an *"uncovered head,"* she dishonors her *"head."* Now which *"head"* is this? Is it her literal "head"–or is it her husband as her "head"? (Remembering that his "head" is Christ.) And what is this "covering"? Is it the same kind of "covering" that the man should not have?

The conclusion is that it is a shame for woman to have her head shaven or have a short haircut–i.e. "shorn." The first question that is asked is "HOW SHORT?" The reason a man should not have long hair is because he is in the image of God. WOMEN SHOULD HAVE LONG HAIR BECAUSE THEY ARE THE GLORY OF MAN. All of this seems to revert back to the creation of man and woman made from man's rib. Now I am thinking that in verses 5-6 it is actual hair and **not** a scarf or a hat.

Because of the emotional attachment of the woman to the man and the man to the woman—as well as the sign of the man's authority over the woman—the woman should have longer hair than the man. (But what about the unmarried woman? Who is her head? Can she cut her hair?) The reason given in verse 7 is not only that the woman is the "glory" of man; but also, that the woman's long hair shows her "power" by willing submissiveness to the man.

So, could it be said that the woman who wears shorn hair and says she is submissive to the man, is fooling no one but herself? If so, in reality, she is nothing but a counterfeit five dollar bill!

"BE SOBER, WATCH"
Because your adversary, the Devil, as a roaring lion,
goeth about seeking whom he may swallow up.
Whom resist, firm in THE FAITH,
being accomplished in your brotherhood
which is in the world.
Your triumph is guaranteed because God holds the world
in the hallow of His hand.
He is before you, behind you, above you, beneath you,
and best of all, in you.
GREATER IS HE THAT IS IN YOU
THAN HE THAT IS IN THE WORLD!
(ggs)

Today's Bible Blessing   *December 4*
I Corinthians 14:16–I Corinthians 16:3
MY FATHER: A GOD-MADE MAN
I Corinthians 15:58

"Be ye stedfast, unmoveable, always abounding in the work of the Lord."

Every time I read I Corinthians 15:58, I think of my father. This was one of his favorite Bible verses. Another verse that I associate with my dad is Joshua 1: 8:

"THIS BOOK OF THE LAW SHALL NOT DEPART OUT OF THY MOUTH; BUT THOU SHALT MEDITATE THEREIN DAY AND NIGHT, THAT THOU MAYEST OBSERVE TO DO ACCORDING TO ALL THAT IS WRITTEN THEREIN: FOR THEN THOU SHALT MAKE THY WAY PROSPEROUS, AND THEN THOU SHALT HAVE GOOD SUCCESS."

Daddy used to refer to himself as a "self-made" man. Some people criticize men who speak of themselves this way. They say that *"self-made"* is of the flesh, and that only God can make a man who has nothing and is a *"nobody"* into something. Yes, that is true; but if a man does not yield himself to the Lord and refuses to do anything at all about his pitiful plight, he has let himself be a *"failure"* of a man.

My father was a man of the Words of God. I don't mean that he was always studying and quoting Scripture–though he knew his Bible. He was a *"doer of the word,"* as another of his motivating verses advised: *"BE YE DOERS OF THE WORD, AND NOT HEARERS ONLY"* (James 1:22).

I remember my dad telling of the poverty that he knew as a child. One time my father told me how he and his siblings went to bed hungry. In the night, my grandfather came home with some "beans" for his children's growling stomachs. My grandmother cooked the beans and awakened the family to eat. That was the first time I saw my father cry.

The other time I saw him cry was at my sister's funeral. Audrey was his follower. As a little girl, wherever Daddy went, Audrey was right behind him. She watched him work in the garden. (He had big gardens and prize-winning yards.) She helped him wash the car. She followed him to church. He loved her and bought her a car. It was always called "Audrey's car"–even after she died!

When Audrey died of Hodgkin's disease at age twenty, Daddy felt helpless. The protecting father who never let her go hungry, who watched over her purity, and could answer all her earthly problems from algebra to associations, from finances to friends, could not keep her free from pain and death. He was there when she died. Her last words were *"I hear the bells behind me!"* The golden bells of Heaven were chiming her arrival. HE CRIED!

My father, who had nothing, worked every day of his life so he could have something. One of his aims was to provide for my youngest brain-damaged sister. He saved his money so Beverly would have financial help after he died. This he did—with great bounty! Daddy loved Beverly!

In the early years, Daddy was a Fuller Brush salesman! He went house to house, knocking on doors. The housewives knew him, trusted him, and purchased cleaning products & mops & brooms from him. In those days, women did not work outside the home. Sometimes I would go with him to deliver his merchandise. He knew where everyone lived and never got lost.

My father loved my mother! He loved my sisters and me. Most of all he loved the Lord Jesus. He put Him first in his life. No matter where we lived, or where we visited, R. O. Sanborn was always in church—never traveling on Sundays—always respecting THE LORD'S DAY. Often when visiting a church, the pastor would presume my father was a preacher, and asked him to preach. He gave *"hilariously"* to the Lord's work, and was instrumental in Cleveland's Baptist Bible Institute becoming Cedarville College. You guessed it! **MY DAD WAS A GOD-MADE MAN!** His motivation came from I Corinthians 15:58! HE WAS *"STEDFAST, UNMOVEABLE, AND ALWAYS ABOUNDING IN THE WORK OF THE LORD!"*

"REMEMBER"
(Psalm 77)
DURING A TIME OF PHYSICAL DISTRESS AND PAIN, PSALM 77 WAS REAL TO ME!

Verse 1— I cried unto the Lord & He gave ear to me.
Verse 2— In the day of my trouble, I sought the Lord.
　　　　(My soul refused to be comforted "until.")
Verse 3— I remembered God!
　　　　(I was so troubled that I complained.)
Verse 6— I called to remembrance my former songs in the night.
　　　　(My spirit made diligent search & I remembered
　　　　how great & good He had been in the past.)
Verse 10— I remembered His years at the Right Hand of God.
Verse 11— I remembered His works and wonders.
Verse 12— I meditated and talked of His doings. His way for me
　　　　was in the Sanctuary.
I REMEMBER, & I PRAISE & TRUST! (ggs)

Today's Bible Blessing   *December 5*

I Corinthians 16:4–II Corinthians 4:6
YOU KNOW THAT I KNOW
YOUR SORROW

II Corinthians 1:3

"Blessed be . . . the Father of mercies, and the God of all comfort."

"BLESSED BE GOD, EVEN THE FATHER OF OUR LORD JESUS CHRIST, THE FATHER OF MERCIES, AND THE GOD OF ALL COMFORT; WHO COMFORTETH US IN ALL OUR TRIBULATION, THAT WE MAY BE ABLE TO COMFORT THEM WHICH ARE IN ANY TROUBLE, BY THE COMFORT WHEREWITH WE OURSELVES ARE COMFORTED OF GOD" (II Corinthians 1: 3-4).

When I portray blind FANNY CROSBY, the great lady of gospel songs, I tell the true account of her grief in the loss of her baby. Many do not know that she was married to ALEXANDER VAN ALSTYNE; a blind musician, whom she met while teaching at the New York Institution for the Blind. They had a flat or an apartment in Brooklyn where Van–that's what she called him–taught music, and she composed some of her gospel songs and hymns. They were married for forty-four years. She often said in reflecting on the years of her marriage, in *THE TRIBUTE TO FANNY CROSBY*, *"Some of them were longer than others."*

Fanny said, "I knew the joy of holding a baby in my arms; but the angels came and took my baby to the Throne of God; and left me alone and barren." It is a touching scene. Fanny's heart was broken. She never forgot the loss of that child. Little more is known about that baby. We do not know if the little one was a boy or a girl. All we know is that it affected Fanny Crosby greatly.

One thing we do know is that it was in a time like that, as well as in other times of sorrow, that Fanny Crosby, the author of *BLESSED ASSURANCE* and *TO GOD BE THE GLORY*, learned of *"THE COMFORT OF GOD!"* It was then that the *FATHER OF MERCIES* and *THE GOD OF ALL COMFORT* came to her, as a mother hen would gather her chicks under her wing, and said, *"There, there, Fanny, I love you!"*

I too—like you—have had sorrow. I know the loss of precious ones in death, as well as the disappointments of life and the shock of an illness. When such hurts have overcome me with no earthly place to flee, I have found *"comfort"* in the arms of Jesus! No one else understands! No one else really cares! I've had a soft loneliness that cannot be explained and experienced the gentle hand of God on my arm with His consolation.

At first the pain is so great that the *"COMFORT OF GOD"* cannot be felt in its fullness. But soon, as the days creep into months and years, I–like the Apostle Paul–have discovered that *"as the sufferings of Christ God abound in me, so my consolation also aboundeth by Christ."* I do not want to pretend that I have no feeling of loss or emptiness at times; nor that I do not wish some heartaches had not come my way. For if I did, it would not be true.

I have discovered the truth in what Paul has written when he said *"WHETHER WE BE AFFLICTED, IT IS FOR YOUR CONSOLATION AND SALVATION, which is effectual in the enduring of the same sufferings which we also suffer: or whether we be comforted, it is for your consolation and salvation"* (See verse 6.) It may surprise you to discover that there were times when Paul was so depressed that he wished he were dead! He said he was *"pressed out of measure, above strength insomuch that we despaired even of life."*

It is because I have suffered loss, disappointment, and death, that I can understand your heart's sorrow. It is an understanding, permitted in my life, from God's hand. Because God has comforted me, I can comfort you! In fact, I do not have to say a word–I just have to stand by your side, and you know that I know the sorrow that you feel. This is the balm God gives us who have suffered, to help others that are presently in trouble and pain. IT IS A *"CONSOLATION"* FROM THE FATHER'S HAND!

"PRESENT WITH THE LORD IN AN INSTANT"
A DEAR ONE DIED TODAY (11/28/1977).
HOW WE LOVED AND MISS HIM ALREADY!

He was our brother, Clayton Van Sanborn. When he drew his last breath, all the trumpets sounded on the other side, and he was present with the Lord! He was delivered and released from the poor racked and weak body that on earth housed his soul!

WE, WHO REMAIN, STANDING HERE GAZING, AS IT WERE, ARE SEPARATED FROM HEAVEN. Earth is poorer because Heaven is richer. Our tears magnify faith's vision of the glorious wonders of Heaven that our brother now enjoys.

BUT WE MISS HIM! (ggs)

II Corinthians 4:7–II Corinthians 8:19
THE REFRESHING FRIENDSHIP OF TITUS

II Corinthians 7:6

"Nevertheless God . . . comforted us by the coming of Titus."

FRIENDSHIP

Oh, the comfort–the inexpressible comfort
Of feeling safe with a person,
Having neither to weigh thoughts,
Nor measure words–but pouring them
All right out –just as they are—
Chaff and grain together—
Certain that a faithful hand will
Take and sift them—
Keep what is worth keeping—
And with the breath of kindness
Blow the rest away.
(Dinah Craik)

II Corinthians is a favorite book of mine. I recall reading it slowly during a difficult time in my life. Every verse and phrase I pondered. I had been extremely tired from the cares of life–partly because of some lack in my body chemistry and partially from the strain that was mine from the weight of sorrow I carried because of our mentally ill son. So, to read of Paul and his human frailties and needs, as well as the soothing words of his counsel to the Corinthian Christians, it comforted my soul.

At the time, I would write to those whom the Lord laid on my heart. I would prop myself up in bed with my Bible; and as a verse of II Corinthians spoke to my heart, I would write to a friend. One of those friends was a young man suffering from AIDS. He was the son of a man whom I had known almost all of my life. The boy had strayed severely from *"the straight and narrow"*–only to return ill and dying to his father's house. I wrote him weekly. I thought to myself *"I wish someone would write to my son with concern and comfort."*

It is difficult for us, who live in this twenty-first century, to comprehend the traveling difficulties that were Paul's as he traveled here and there preaching the gospel. His *"call"* was always upon him, and his *"care"* for the churches he had established, was constantly on his heart and in his prayers.

Though he was with people often, I perceived that he was a lonely man. He writes in II Corinthians 7:6 of the *"comfort"* he found when young Pastor Titus visited him. Paul spoke of God's *"comfort"* to them that were *"cast down."* I think that, at times, Paul was overwhelmed with his missionary responsibilities. THAT WAS WHEN TITUS STOPPED BY! When the Apostle wrote the Corinthian Christians, he thanked them for their *"refreshing"* friendship and encouragement to Titus. It comforted him. Paul was no different than you and me. He enjoyed hearing the news about those he loved.

I remember a time when a woman came to help me clean my house. I had been seriously ill and in the hospital. In my weakness, I made a mistake. I talked with her as a *"friend."* She was a regular attendee in our church. I told her about a personal concern I had that affected me. Much to my surprise, she turned this *"concern of mine"* into an inward anxiety within her. In a day or two, she not only turned against me, but poisoned the minds of other women in our church. All I had done was treat her like a *"friend"* instead of a *"client."* How many times I had listened to her problems! But she could not handle hearing one of mine.

"A GARDEN INCLOSED"
(Song of Solomon 4:12)
A GARDEN INCLOSED!
A SPRING SHUT UP!
A FOUNTAIN SEALED!
We are a garden where things grow, inclosed to Him!
A spring shut up to a particular use.
A fountain sealed for His service alone.
IN OUR DAILY LIVES, HE HAS SET US,
SHUT UP TO HIM ALONE. (ggs)
(This is what God permitted in Gertrude Sanborn's life as she cared for her mentally challenged daughter for over sixty years.

Today's Bible Blessing   *December 7*
II Corinthians 8:20–II Corinthians 12:15
ARE YOU A CHEERFUL GIVER?
II Corinthians 9:8
"God is able to make all grace abound toward you . . ."

Let's begin with the subject of *"ministering to the saints"* (II Corinthians 8:4, 9:1). What exactly does this mean? First, we must realize that every person who has received Jesus Christ as Saviour is considered a *"SAINT"* in the eyes of God. A person does not have to perform a miracle and have his name brought before a church group to be *"sainted."* NO! He or she is a *"saint"* by the <u>fact</u> of the *"new birth."*

In this chapter, Paul is speaking of the giving of *"money gifts"* to further the gospel, as well as helping those Christians in financial need. Previously in I Corinthians 16:1-2, the *"Saints"* had been told, in Paul's first letter, that the church people were to bring their contributions to the church where it would be kept for Paul. So, when Paul arrived, the money gifts would be there for Paul's missionary work.

If this were done weekly, there would be no embarrassment when the time came to give to Paul in person. Look at Paul's exact words back then: *"Now concerning the collection for the saints, as I have given order to the churches of Galatia, EVEN SO DO YE. Upon the first day of the week let every one of you lay by him in store, as God hath prospered him, that there be no gatherings when I come."*

Now in this letter some time later; Paul brought up the subject of Christian giving again. I am not sure if it was because the Christians were not giving, or that he wanted to emphasize what *"grace"* it was for a believer to contribute to the work of the Lord. Whatever it was, Paul thought it *"necessary to exhort"* them that they would *"make up beforehand"* their *"bounty."* His reason was that the *"bounty"* or money offerings would be *"ready."* He affirmed it was not because of "covetousness" on his part, or anyone else's part. IT WAS THE DUTY OF THE CHURCH PEOPLE TO GIVE!

As a person who was taught since childhood to give an offering to the church out of her twenty-five-cents weekly allowance, I cannot understand some church members—or attendees—who fail to see that it is their *"spiritual"* service to God to contribute to the church where they attend.

In the Old Testament, God's people were taught to tithe. A tithe is a tenth of our "bounty." In the New Testament, Christians were taught that a tenth was just the beginning. It was very plain in the Old Testament that the offerings or funds or substance was what the priests and Levites used to live on. It is the same today. The expenses of the church must be met by the loyal contributions of the church people. GOD BLESSES THOSE WHO GIVE TO HIS WORK. Paul continued in II Corinthians 9:6: *"HE WHICH SOWETH SPARINGLY SHALL REAP ALSO SPARINGLY; AND HE WHICH SOWETH BOUTIFULLY SHALL REAP ALSO BOUNTIFULLY."*

Now no one puts a gun to the head of a church attendee forcing him to give. It should behoove a person, who sits in church, listening to the preaching and enjoying the singing of the hymns and gospel songs, to purpose in his heart to give. This giving should not be done *"grudgingly, or of necessity"* but cheerfully! Why? BECAUSE GOD LOVETH A CHEERFUL GIVER! That's the motivation!

Our church doesn't take up an offering. WE HAVE A BOX AT THE DOOR. The Lord supplies the needs of our church for its missionary giving and *extraordinary giving* in other areas. One thing really puzzles me! SOME PEOPLE GIVE! SOME DO NOT GIVE! Some who ask for help seldom give. Others, who have great needs, give. It is a mystery.

"And God is able to make all grace abound toward you; that ye, always having all sufficiency in all things, may abound to every good work." Who would have thought that this verse was talking about church offerings? Yes, GOD LOVES A CHEERFUL GIVER. ARE YOU ONE?

"TRUST YE IN THE LORD FOREVER"
(Isaiah 26:4; I Peter 5:7)
"For in the Lord Jehovah is everlasting strength."
Just to leave in His dear Hands little things
We cannot understand.
All that stings—
Just to let Him take the care sorely pressing;
Finding all we let Him bear
Changed to blessings.
(ggs/ Frances Ridley Havergal)

Today's Bible Blessing   *December 8*
II Corinthians 12:16–Galatians 3:21
BEWITCHED CHRISTIANS FALLING INTO SIN
II Corinthians 12:20a
"I fear, lest, when I come, I shall not find you such as I would . . ."

As Paul closed his second letter to the believers in Corinth, he confided to them his fear. I can sympathize with him. Sometimes in families there are differences. Siblings have issues left over from childhood which surface at family gatherings. A time that should be happy and delightful for the parents may turn topsy-turvy and become a day of tainted memories and bad words. He wrote of his fear in II Corinthians 12:20. He was afraid, when he would visit, instead of their being as he would have wanted, he would discover the debating of differences, as well as envying and wrath, and strife and malicious slandering—as well as whisperings and arrogance, accompanied with much condemnation.

Besides these outer sins, his concern was great over their sexual promiscuity (vs. 21). This is why he exhorted the whole church, *"Examine yourselves, whether ye be in the faith; prove your own selves. Know ye not your own selves, how that Jesus Christ is in you, except ye be reprobates?"* (See II Corinthians 13:5.) (The pronouns that begin with **"Y"** are the plural pronouns, which in the King James Bible, refer to more than one.) Paul was speaking to the whole church. What a worldly mess of Christians!

NOW LET US TURN TO THE LETTER TO THE GALATIAN CHURCHES

The Galatians—or the Gauls—were thought of as barbarians by many. Coming from Asia Minor, they devoured the land, claiming it for their own, demanding tribute, and hired themselves out to whomever as mercenaries. Soon the land became a Roman province under Augustus, ranging from the borders of Asia and Bithynia to Iconium, Lystra, and Derbe, as well as cities in Lycaonia.

Paul identified himself as an "apostle" as he greeted the Galatian churches warmly with *"grace"* and *"peace"*! If I recall, *"grace"* is the Grecian greeting and *"peace"*—the Jewish *"shalom"*! This greeting does not come from Paul; it came from God the Father and the Lord Jesus Christ. This is interesting indeed. It shows to me that his letter was truly *"inspired of God,"* as Paul wrote these words, just as much as the prophet's Words were *"inspired"* and *"God-breathed."* Paul wrote in Greek and the Old Testament prophets in Hebrew with a small part in Aramaic.

In speaking of Jesus Christ, Paul identified Him as the One *who gave Himself for their sins* for the express reason that the Galatian Christians and Paul (as well as you and me), might be delivered from this present evil world (Galatians 1:4). WHAT A MOUTHFUL! This victorious lifestyle is possible only as the believer is crucified with Christ, forgetting themselves and their foolishness, to return to A LIFE OF FAITH; and stop frustrating the *"grace of God"* by returning to the Mosaic Law (Galatians 2: 20-21).

Paul knew the Galatian Christians were not living as they should. They had succumbed to *"another gospel."* He asked them, *"HOW COULD THIS HAPPEN?"* That's a question we could ask ourselves today. As we look around in our churches, we see so many *"another gospels."* There is a wave of Pentecostalism sweeping many churches today. Tongues-speaking and carrying-ons that glorify the flesh and not the Spirit. That's another *"gospel!"* Most modern Bible versions are based on the Gnostic Critical Greek Text. Over 8,000 Greek differences are found between the New Testament Words of the King James Version and the modern *"alien bibles."* In these 8,000 differences, there are more than **356 doctrinal passages involved**. I'd call that "ANOTHER GOSPEL," wouldn't you? **Paul, in this letter, told the Galatian Christians they were wrong!** That took Holy boldness! He did this to Peter who began to slip back into his old ways (Galatians 2:11). THERE IS A TIME THAT A BELIEVER SHOULD REBUKE A *"BEWITCHED"* CHRISTIAN WHO IS STUMBLING INTO SIN! (See Galatians 6:1.) IT IS NOT EASY TO DO, AND IT IS NOT EASY TO WATCH!

"MORE TO CONQUER, MORE TO LEARN"
TODAY IS MY SEVENTIETH BIRTHDAY!
(December 5th)
I THINK IT IS THE MOST EXCITING ONE
SINCE I WAS SWEET SIXTEEN.
I AM AMAZED THAT GOD HAS PRIVILEGED
ME TO LIVE THESE MANY YEARS.
I THANK HIM!
There is much more that I need to do
before I see Him face to face.
So much to read from His Word!
So much to glean from other men's writings and readings.
So many people to help.
So much to tell and write
May I not be like a Solomon or Hezekiah or others
and grow weak spiritually as I grow old. (ggs)

Today's Bible Blessing   *December 9*

Galatians 3:22–Ephesians 1:3

ISAAC & ISHMAEL ALL OVER AGAIN

Galatians 4:16

"Am I . . . become your enemy because I tell you the truth?"

This was the penetrating question that Paul posed to the churches in Galatia. But they turned their ears from his mouth. They did not want to hear the Apostle tell them that they were *mixing* GRACE with the LAW. They would not recognize their failures of *"returning to the weak and beggarly elements"* of the Law. They appeared to Paul to want to be in bondage again. How could that be? They were observing—of all things—days, and months, and times, and years.

It not only broke Paul's heart, it made him very angry! He challenged them! *"You who want to be under the Law again—listen to what that Law says!"* was his declaration. They were foolish people wanting to forsake the grace of Jesus Christ for Moses' binding commandments.

It was then that Paul reviewed for them concerning Abraham and his two sons—Isaac and Ishmael. One son was the *"promised seed,"* born of Sarah. She was an old woman—a miracle conception, gestation, and birth. His name was Isaac. HE WAS A CHILD OF FAITH! The other was born of human reasoning—a disobedient thought, a fleshly conception. Her name was Hagar. She was an Egyptian girl–young and fertile. The child's name was Ishmael–a son of the unbelief.

Each woman represented a covenant–a testimony, a promise. Hagar was a reminder of the LAW given on Mount Sinai. It spoke of bondage and deep servitude. While Sarah, bearing Isaac, spoke of freedom and obedience. Isaac was the child of God's promise–the beginning of a countless "seed"—more than the sand of the sea and the stars lacing the heavens. The Messiah was descended from him!

The fact was that Hagar's future grandchildren would persecute Sarah's. Sad to say, Paul's words are true today. We see it in the rivalry and prospect of wars and conflicts in the Middle East. We read about it in the papers every day (Galatians 4:29).

Paul reminded his Galatians converts how they used to know Jesus Christ in liberty and freedom. They used to be free from the laws and rules they now sought to maintain their salvation. Instead of being *"free"* in the *grace* in which they had been called, they had turned to the weak and beggarly elements of observances. They used to know the freedom of Christ–but they had tied their own spiritual hands with Moses' law and their ritual rules. Paul questioned them, *"Why oh WHY do you desire to be in bondage again?"* He was baffled. They had returned to observing *"days,"* and *"months,"* and *"times,"* and *"years"* (4:10). He was at a loss to know what to do, except to teach them all over again. But–would they listen?

The solution to the whole "law" versus "grace" problem was to do exactly as Sarah had done in her day. It is the only thing to do when sin enters the home. *"Cast out the bondwoman and her son!"* Otherwise, the son of the bondwoman would be an heir with the son of the freewoman. It was as simple as that! The Galatian Christians, whether they wanted to believe it or not, were not the children of the bondwoman. They were the children of the free woman! Paul's major fear was that he had labored among them in vain. All that missionary effort gone down the drain because the Judaizers had infiltrated the church! How often today a false doctrine will gain a foothold in a church that used to be strong and bold for the truth. How soon the climate of churches change with the charismatic, forty days of promises seeker-friendly approach in churches today. BE CAREFUL THAT WE ARE NOT OVERTAKEN IN A FAULT! It is so easy to do (Galatians 6:1).

"MY TIMES–HIS HANDS"
(Psalm 31:15)
So often we have to drop our little plans
and our human maneuvering
to look up and realize that HE IS GOD! –absolutely!
Going along in confidence of the flesh,
we are stopped by His mighty Hand.
Stopped by tragedy, by loss, by betrayal,
and made to realize what a small thing is OUR TIMES,
REGULATED BY HIS GREAT HAND. (ggs)

Today's Bible Blessing   *December 10*

Ephesians 1:4–Ephesians 4:23
OUR INCESSANT TURNING IN GOD'S HAND

Ephesians 2:10
"For we are his workmanship, created in Christ Jesus unto good works . . ."

We read that Paul spent more than two years as a missionary in Ephesus (Acts 19:8, 10). Ephesus was on a major trade route and was the center for the worship of Diana. Her temple was one of the Seven Wonders of the World. When Paul preached there, this ancient, prosperous city was part of the province of Asia and the residence of the Roman governor. Ephesus came into the Roman Empire in 133 B.C. Paul wrote his letter to the church there in A.D. 64. It was possibly the first of Paul's letters that we have. It was written from prison.

Many Jews who lived in Ephesus were influenced by Christianity. It was at the church in Ephesus that Timothy pastored. A historian wrote that the APOSTLE JOHN spent his last years there, opposing the doctrines of NESTORIUS. Paul, too, opposed the city's idolatry and shrine worship, as well as the practice of magic. In fact, his opposition produced dreadful riots!

Once again Paul addresses the Christians in the Church of Ephesus as "SAINTS" (Ephesians 1:1). By now you realize that all who have received Jesus Christ as Saviour are *"SAINTS."* A *"SAINT"* is a regular *"saved"* person, who is called out from other unsaved people, to be set apart for God! That is a holy calling! Being a *"called out"* believer is an awesome responsibility. If only all of us Christians would take that *"calling"* seriously!

Our attitude and life behavior, as Christians, should be a product of our Christian walk with the Lord. A believer is *a "workmanship."* (See Ephesians 2:10.) We are a work of God, the master craftsman. He started with a rotten sinner, born into Adam's race, and He conformed us into the image of His dear son (Romans 8:29), for His purpose (Romans 8:28), whom He is making a *"work of art."* Or, as Paul calls us, a *"WORKMANSHIP"*!

"FOR WE ARE HIS WORKMANSHIP, CREATED IN CHRIST JESUS UNTO GOOD WORKS, WHICH GOD HATH BEFORE ORDAINED THAT WE SHOULD WALK IN THEM."

Recently I watched a man do what he called "WOOD TURNING." HE took a small block of maple wood. Turning it on a lathe, he placed that block of wood right on that whirling sharp instrument. It did an amazing thing. It cut and carved, and shaped and sawed. The man turned that wood in this and that direction. As he worked, chips from the wood fell to the floor. Often the man stopped the machine and held up the wood to see what it looked like. It didn't look like anything to me. But the man knew what he was doing.

The lathe kept turning. The chips kept falling. The drill kept drilling. The whining machine sounded loud to my ears. It was incessant! Soon, before my eyes, a shape came to be. What was it? The noise stopped and the man held up the wood. It was no longer a useless block of wood. It was a small spinning top, just right to fit in a boy's pocket. The man gave it to me. I have it on my dresser. When I look at it, I think to myself, *"That top is my friend's "workmanship!"*

So it is with God's children. He turns us this way and that—sometimes upside down or right side up. He tests with trials. He tempts us with people. He tries us with circumstances. Sometimes we think we cannot take another moment of such attention. Soon the dross of our lives falls to our *"Craftsman's"* feet. He keeps swirling us around in the confusion of life. He keeps cutting and pruning the dead branches of sin and selfishness from our sides. In time, we will feel Him hold us up to the Light of His Words and say, ***"THIS IS MY "WORKMANSHIP" CREATED IN CHRIST JESUS UNTO GOOD WORKS!"***

"MY STRONG TOWER"
(Psalm 61:3; Proverbs 18:10)
FOR THOU HAST BEEN A SHELTER FOR ME,
AND A STRONG TOWER FROM THE ENEMY.
The Name of the LORD is a strong tower:
the righteous runneth into it, and is safe.
HOW PRECIOUS!! HIS NAME! HIMSELF!
My Strong Tower!
I flee from my care and weariness
to this Marvelous Rest! (ggs)

Today's Bible Blessing   *December 11*
Ephesians 4:24–Philippians 1:20
A CHALLENGE TO KINDNESS IN OUR CENTURY

Ephesians 4:32

"Be ye kind one to another, tenderhearted, forgiving one another"

"AND BE YE KIND ONE TO ANOTHER, TENDER-HEARTED, FORGIVING ONE ANOTHER, EVEN AS GOD FOR CHRIST'S SAKE HATH FORGIVEN YOU."

What wonderful words of exhortation we are reading today from the pen of the Apostle Paul. KINDNESS IS A GOLDEN JEWEL! If one wears it with distinction, all who come by will be blessed. If one does not wear this virtue, it will show like an open sore upon the face. The dictionary defines the word as affection, beneficence, tenderness, goodness, generosity, and good will. The virtuous woman has *"the law of kindness is in her tongue"* (Proverbs 31:26). *"The desire of a man is his kindness . . ."* (Proverbs 19:22). In affliction the Psalmist recognized the *kindness* of God (Psalm 119:76).

Paul not only instructed the Ephesian Christians to be kind, he wrote the same message to the Christians in Colosse also. I take it that he unearthed the fact that many in those churches were unkind. Otherwise, why would he write them to:

"PUT ON . . . KINDNESS . . . LONGSUFFERING; FORBEARING ONE ANOTHER, AND FORGIVING ONE ANOTHER . . . AND ABOVE ALL . . . PUT ON CHARITY"
(Colossians 3:12-14).

I think there was an undertow of unkindness in the Ephesus church. In fact, I think it began in the homes. Notice— after Paul spoke of *"KINDNESS"* to one another, he brought up the *sins* of the flesh versus the *fruit* of the spirit. Evidently, such a contrast was among the membership. One of his recommendations for KINDNESS was singing of *"psalms and hymns and spiritual songs"* (Ephesians 5:19). Those unkind Christians needed a melody in their hearts that would effuse kindnesses toward one another.

Personally, I think there was much unkindness in the homes of those early church members. It's the same today. Otherwise, why did Paul give marriage instructions to them? The husbands were not loving their wives as they should, and the wives were not being submissive to their husbands as was proper. It was a two-way street! Sometimes we are the harshest, rudest, and most resentful to those we love the most. Our tempers flare up at the least criticism. Our tongues fire off rockets of ill-mannered words. Willa Cather, a twentieth century author, wrote: *"I want nothing from you but to get away from your uncivil tongue!"* We forget about *"tenderheartedness"* and *"forgiveness"*!

Where does the redeemed sinner find *"God's kindness"*? He finds it in the love of God, when the Saviour appears. *"It is not by works of righteousness which we have done, but according to his mercy he saved us . . ."* (Titus 3:4-5). WHAT KINDNESS!

God said that the hills may be moved but HIS KINDNESS shall not depart from His own (Isaiah 54:8). Both the prophets, Joel and Jonah, tell us that God is *"slow to anger, and of GREAT KINDNESS"* (Joel 2:13; Jonah 4:2).

When Paul and his shipmates came to Melita, they were welcomed with *"kindness."* When Paul was beaten, the Holy Spirit ministered to him with great *"kindness."* This is what Abraham's servant received when Rebekah brought water from the well to him and his camels. *"Kindness"* was manifested by Rahab when she hid the Jewish spies away from the prying eyes of her countrymen. *"Kindness"* was done by Ruth to Boaz when she favored him above the younger workers in the field. *"Kindness"* was Jonathan's action toward his friend, David, by sparing his life; and *KINDNESS* was returned by a promise to care for Jonathan's seed. Esther obtained *"kindness"* from Hegai, the women's keeper. Should we, who love Jesus, be less kind than those Bible people who lived in another time and place?

"PUT ON THE WHOLE ARMOUR!"
(Ephesians 6:10)
ARE YOU HAVING PROBLEMS?
Are you failing in the battles of life?
Check and see if you have on the whole armour.
In your battle with Satan,
put on each piece of armour. (ggs)

Today's Bible Blessing   *December 12*
Philippians 1:21–Colossians 1:2
A POSSIBLE CHURCH SPLIT
Philippians 4:13
"I can do all things through Christ which strengtheneth me."

Philippi was named after a King Philip—whoever he was. It was a town of gold mines and fertile soil. That productive land was the battlefield on which Mark Antony fought—somewhere around 42 B.C. The city was on the main road to Asia, making it strategically important. The Philippi in which Paul witnessed for Christ was a Roman colony, founded by Augustus. Many feel that it was on Paul's second missionary journey that he and Silas were in prison.

Christians enjoy reading this Pauline letter, written from prison around A.D. 64. Many feel that the Philippians were happy and rejoicing people. I always wondered, if this were true, why Paul had to tell them to rejoice so often. Usually happy, contented people do not have to be reminded to be so.

It is difficult to choose one or two verses to think about in this book of four chapters. There are so many truths and exhortations to apply to our lives today. How good it was for the early Christians to think about them. We, too, must meditate on Paul's being torn between living or dying (Philippians 1:23). Paul, having been caught up into THE THIRD HEAVEN, after being left for dead (II Corinthian 12:2), gave him a special impetus for dying and going Home to be with Christ.

Most of us do not have that vision—so we hang on to our life and its last breath. Paul knew better. He realized that to stay alive in the flesh was better for the Christian to whom he was writing. He knew that his being alive brought joy in faith and rejoicing in Jesus Christ for his friends. It is true, for many of us who love a Bible teacher and desire for him to remain, feel it is best for us that the teacher remains in the Land of the Living. But God is in charge of such *"living and dying."*

Paul encouraged these Christians to be "of one mind." See Philippians 1:27—*"stand fast in one spirit, with one mind striving* (or struggling*) together for the faith of the gospel"*; Philippians 2:2—*"be likeminded, having the same love, being of one accord, of one mind."* I THINK THERE MUST HAVE BEEN A DISAGREEMENT OF SOME SORT IN THE CHURCH! There must have been various opinions on a matter. See how Paul encouraged the church people to *"LET THIS MIND BE IN YOU, WHICH WAS ALSO IN CHRIST JESUS."* It seems to me that PRIDE must have been raising its ugly head in that community for Paul to have to remind them of the humility of Jesus Christ.

The apostle does call out by name two strong, contentious women. Their names were EUODIAS and SYNTYCHE. Perhaps they were leaders of two factions in the church. If they could be *"friends"* again, and if they could be of the same mind, it would help the Christians in Philippi to rejoice! He reminded them that their names are written in the BOOK OF LIFE (4:2-3)! THEY SHOULD ACT LIKE REJOICING BELIEVERS INSTEAD OF CAUSING TWO FACTIONS IN THE CHURCH.

He encouraged those women, as well as the whole congregation, to stop worrying, to pray with thanksgiving, stop being jealous, to expect the peace of God, and to keep their hearts and minds in Christ Jesus. They should think of good, honest, and true things instead of *"stinking thinking;"* and follow

Paul as an example. HE WAS IN PRISON REJOICING, WHY COULDN'T THEY?

Paul wanted them to realize that anything was possible in their church. They did not have to have a split or a division. He told them that He could do all things through Christ which strengthened him. If Paul could do this in a stinking, wet, dank, rat-infested dungeon, why couldn't they? (4:13)

"HEAVEN"
WE ARE NOT FAR FROM HOME,
A MOMENT FROM BEING THERE!
Let us determine not to waste one moment in murmuring,
or useless activities, or crying for that which we may not have.
LET US LIVE, AS THOUGH THIS WERE OUR LAST MOMENT.
THIS WOULD BE PLEASING TO GOD!
(ggs)

Today's Bible Blessing   *December 13*
Colossians 1:3–Colossians 4:11
VON AND DON
ARE COMPLETE IN HIM

Colossians 1:17b
". . . and by him all things consist . . ."

It is interesting to discover that the Apostle Paul did not start the Colosse church. In fact, he had never been to Colosse at all when he penned his epistle. Colosse was a prosperous town of some commercial importance in Phrygia, twelve miles from Laodicea and about sixty miles east of Ephesus. The other day, in our church's Bible discussion, mention was made of a kind of healing salve that was manufactured there.

It is thought, by some, that the church was founded by EPAPHRAS (Colossians 1:7; 4:12). The problem of *"Judaic-Gnosticism"* had hit this church, and Epaphras, as well as other men of the church, were overwhelmed by it. They visited Paul in the Roman prison for advice. Legalism, combined with reducing Christ to a lesser god, had hit the church! Paul wrote his letter to straighten out the misguided Christians there. This doctrinal confusion shows us that churches and Christians are no different in our times than in Paul's day. False doctrines seep into churches easily. That is why we must be on constant alert to such deception. This background helps us readers to understand the reasons for some of the strong teachings found in this book of the Bible.

Though there are many subjects and verses of importance discovered on the pages of this book, I want to talk about two that have influenced my life. As you may or may not know, I graduated from Moody Bible Institute before my husband and I were married in 1948. As I write that date down for you, it seems so long ago–and it was. (We are now in another century.) Yet, for me–as I go back in my memory–sitting in the large lecture hall in one of the school's old, original buildings–it seems like almost yesterday.

The teacher for the book of Colossians was MR. FITZWATER. I thought he was a very old man at the time. Maybe he was–but for a young girl in her late teens and early twenties, any man with white hair and bushy eyebrows seemed *"old."* He was tall, and authoritative with a loud growling voice that commanded attention. We were studying Colossians 1:16-17: *"For by him were all things created, that are in heaven, and that are in earth, visible and invisible, whether they be thrones, or dominions, or principalities, or powers: all things were created by him, and for him: AND HE IS BEFORE ALL THINGS, AND BY HIM ALL THINGS CONSIST!"*

Dr. Fitzwater must have been teaching about the eternality of Jesus Christ, and how He is the CREATOR of the whole earth and universe. I remember his bellowing out this truth as if it were yesterday. With his long pointing finger, he pointed to the posts in that old room that held up the ceiling that kept the room intact. As he pointed at the pillars, he cried out words something like this: *"JESUS CHRIST IS HOLDING UP THIS ROOM TODAY!"* Then he reflected on the moon and stars fixed in the Heavens. He shouted, *"JESUS CHRIST IS HOLDING THE STARS AND MOON IN PLACE!"* We learned that the spinning earth kept its orbit because Jesus Christ keeps it there. You and I do not spin out into space, because the omnipotent Lord Jesus Christ is holding our feet to this earth. Otherwise we would spin off into space, unbound from the God-given gravity that keeps our feet on *Terra Firma*.

When my husband and I were engaged, he was a student at the University of Michigan. I was in Chicago. He sent me a little round metal thing he made from a vending machine. It said *"Von and Don are complete in Him!"* (See Colossians 2:10a.) Being a new Christian since high school days, Jesus was precious to my husband-to-be, as He was to me. That gift and this verse have been a seal of our love and His love in our hearts all these years! No wonder I'm glad Paul wrote to the Christians in Colosse!

> ## "KINDNESS AS A RULE OF LIFE"
> (Proverbs 31:26b)
> *IN HER TONGUE IS THE LAW OF KINDNESS!*
> Let this law govern my way in my life before the family and others.
> Let it control my speaking, and let me grieve
> when I break this Heavenly Law.
> (ggs)

Today's Bible Blessing   *December 14*

Colossians 4:12–I Thessalonians 5:18

THE HOPE WHICH REPLACES SORROW

I Thessalonians 4:18

"Wherefore comfort one another with these words."

The city of THESSALONICA was located on the road that joined Rome with the whole region north of the Aegean Sea. The church was founded during Paul's second missionary journey. It was a vital link to many places where the gospel could be preached. Commercially, the city was on par with Corinth and Ephesus. It was in the Jewish synagogue that Paul preached, making many converts to Jesus Christ. Churches were planted. Paul purposed to reach the empire through the cities.

This may have been Paul's earliest epistle. Pastor Timothy went there to encourage the persecuted believers. Paul wrote from Corinth. Later he ministered in Berea and Athens. As I read this book, I am struck with the Thessalonian Christians' faith, their labor of love, and patience of hope in the Lord Jesus Christ (I Thessalonians 1:3). Paul was blessed by remembering them, often thanking God for them in prayer!

Sometimes you and I become so busy that we forget to thank God for our Christian friends. Just today, I told a young preacher that I would be praying for him. Though he is familiar with the Korean language, he is not familiar enough to pray extemporaneously. His Korean wife will write his prayer out phonetically for him. He will have to practice so it sounds smooth and true.

I told him that I would pray for him. He objected and said, *"You don't have to pray for me. Just pray for the sick people."* He thought to pray for him was not needful, as it was a small thing. I told him I did not think it a trivial matter for which to pray. I said *"This is something your mother would have prayed for concerning you."* THEN HE UNDERSTOOD! (His mother had died a few years ago.) PAUL PRAYED FOR THE CHRISTIANS—NOT BECAUSE THEY

WERE SICK OR IN NEED, BUT BECAUSE HE LOVED THEM! **Paul advised the Christians to imitate Silas, Timothy, and him, as examples in the LORD** (I Thessalonians 1:6). Though they experienced much affliction, the new Christians received THE WORD with *"Holy Spirit joy"*! When the Macedonians and Achaians heard that the Thessalonians, not only followed the LORD and His WORDS; but also they were waiting for Jesus to return, they became very excited! The excitement was so great that it caused a big stir in their cities (1:9-10)!

Paul instructed the Christians who had been waiting for Jesus to return, not to sorrow that their loved ones had already died before He returned. Paul encouraged with HOPE! He gave them comfort (4:18)! He assured them that those who had already died would not be held back when the rapture of the Saints occurred! It was then that Paul explained the procedure.

Jesus Himself would come down from Heaven! There would be clouds. What kind of clouds we are not told! As He descends, He will be shouting a command! It will be awesome! His voice will be *"authoritative"* like that of an ARCHANGEL! At the same time, a LOUD TRUMPET will sound! It will be a *"special trumpet call"* only for the DEAD IN CHRIST!! Their dead ears will come to life! THEY WILL COME OUT OF THEIR GRAVES! It will happen first before anything else. I do not know how this will be; but Paul said it would happen, and he has been right on everything else he has said.

UP WILL COME THE BODIES OF THE "BORN-AGAIN" SAINTS WHO HAD DIED IN THE TIME OF GRACE since Jesus died, rose, and ascended up to Heaven. The dead people's ashes, who had been cremated to save money, will collect themselves and become a body again. No matter where those ashes were scattered, if the dead person were a Christian, the ashes will be a body again! THE DEAD IN CHRIST WILL RISE UP! **Then BELIEVERS, WHO ARE STILL LIVING, will be caught up TOGETHER WITH THE RISEN DEAD ONES TO MEET THEIR COMMANDER, THE LORD JESUS CHRIST, IN THE CLOUDS!**

"COUNT ALL MY STEPS"
(Job 31:4)
DOTH NOT HE SEE MY WAYS, AND COUNT ALL MY STEPS?
Is not His eye upon the sparrow and does He not note its fall?
There is not one little hurt, not one "slight,"
or undeserved rebuke, or misery,
but our Father notes it.
He notes the sparrow's fall.
He knows our downsitting and uprisings.
The God with whom we have to do is omniscient.
(ggs)

Today's Bible Blessing   *December 15*

I Thessalonians 5:19–I Timothy 2:9
TWO FEARS IN THE THESSALONIAN CHURCH

II Thessalonians 3:6

"Withdraw yourselves from every brother that walketh disorderly."

> *"And that we may be delivered from unreasonable and wicked men: for all men have not faith. But the Lord is faithful, who shall stablish you, and keep you from evil"* (II Thessalonians 3:2-3).

How very true–all men do not have FAITH! There are human beings who walk around in complete *"unbelief."* They do not believe in God–not alone the redemptive work of Jesus Christ on the Cross of Calvary. BELIEF or TRUST in God is the rudiment of FAITH. Without God there is no need of *"faith"* or any ONE in Whom to have *"FAITH"*! Samuel Davies said it all when he penned, *"WHO IS A PARD'NING GOD LIKE THEE? OR WHO HAS GRACE SO RICH AND FREE?"*

Paul commanded the Thessalonian believers to withdraw from disorderly brothers and sisters (II Thessalonians 3:6). It was such an imperative need for the Christians to be separated from corrupted BELIEVERS that Paul warned them *"in the Name of the Lord Jesus Christ."* He had the same warning to the Corinthian Christians when he commanded,

> *"Be not deceived: evil communications corrupt good manners! Awake to righteousness and sin not; for some have not the knowledge of God: I speak this to your shame"* (I Corinthians 15:58).

Evidently the Thessalonian church had suffered severe persecution. They had the idea that *THE DAY OF THE LORD JESUS CHRIST* was at hand. They thought they were living in the end times because their suffering was so great. Paul instructed them to NOT be deceived. The beginning of THAT *"DAY"* SHOULD NOT COME EXCEPT THERE COME A FALLING AWAY FIRST! The *"man of sin"* had to be revealed first. He would show himself to be *"GOD"*! THEY WERE COMFORTED BY PAUL THAT THEY WERE NOT LIVING IN *"THAT DAY"*!

From a fast look at I & II Thessalonians, we see that those Christians had a few fears. One was that the Lord would return and their loved ones would not be raptured; and second that the *"Man of Sin"* would be revealed. They thought they were living in the *"last days"*! Paul calmed both of these delusions.

TODAY'S READING GOES INTO THE BOOK OF I TIMOTHY.

Young Timothy was a convert of the Apostle Paul. He looked to Paul as a *"father,"* and Paul saw him as a *"son."* There is a special affection that a person has for his or her *"spiritual children"* or *"spiritual father."* His biological father was a Greek; but his mother was a Jewess. Though mixed marriages were unlawful, frequently, there were such marriages in the late Jewish history. When I was a child, many Jews did not intermarry, any more than other races intermarried. Timothy's Jewish mother and grandmother trained him in the Scriptures. So Timothy was ripe for the gospel when Paul came along.

Years ago, I had two large Bible Clubs in our homes. One was in the Miami, Florida, area and another in Corpus Christi, Texas. My clubs had as many as fifty-plus children in them! We sang Bible songs and told Bible stories. It was wonderful! Children loved to come. Many accepted Christ.

I remember one girl. She was the DAUGHTER of a Marine major. (My husband was a Navy Chaplain overseas at the time.) Her last name was Rose, but I cannot remember her first name. When someone asked her if she was *"saved,"* she said, "YES!" The person asked her how she knew it. Her reply was, *"Mrs. Waite said I was!"* Of course, that was the wrong answer.

I have always been disturbed over this answer because it is not what I said that verified her salvation. It was whether or not she had accepted Jesus Christ as her Saviour. We moved from that place and I never saw that girl again. She would be a grown woman in her sixties by now. I wonder if she ever was really *"born-again."*

"VICTORY THRU HIM"
For by thee I have run through a troop;
and by my God have I leaped over a wall.
BY THEE –HIS ENABLEMENT!
I have been through a troop,
I have been enabled to do battle
with all life's oppressive defeats and circumstances.
AND BY MY GOD–
because He has enabled me,
I have been victorious and have overcome.
I can do all things through Christ that strengtheneth me.
(ggs)

Today's Bible Blessing   *December 16*
I Timothy 2:10–II Timothy 1:2
NOT A NOVICE LEST HE FALL
I Timothy 3:6

"Not a novice, lest being lifted up with pride he fall into condemnation"

I have seen several pastors–some of them mine–who have failed miserably in fulfilling Paul's ministry standards found in I TIMOTHY 3:1-7. These men were good men. Most of them were fine expositors of the Words of God and led exemplary lives–*at least in public.* But something went wrong!

I am thinking of pastors I've known. Two are divorced by their wives–wrecking their ministries; and the other committed adultery, ruining his own ministry. One of the pastors, because of a correct Biblical stand, was *"kicked out"* by the church bosses. Now he teaches school someplace. One pastor moved on to another church–perhaps because of the uncomfortable church situation. Another was pressured to retire after twenty-four years. (Seemed like the church could have put up with him for one more year.) Another successful pastor felt the pressure to resign. I think the deacons wanted a younger more glamorous man in the pulpit. That young, glamorous man became an adulterer! I observed a *"Purpose Driven"* pastor ruin a church, kicking out the founding members and faithful contributors for new *"seeker-friendly"* methods. The church faltered miserably! I saw another prosperous church, full of people, dwindle down to a shadow of its former self. Why? They changed the Bible and brought in *"new songs"* and *"new methods"* to bring in the young people. After the damage was done, the pastor left, a sick and dying man. Now the church is a skeleton of its former self! Yet, another pastor, who built his ministry from the ground up–including the people and the building, controlled everything, including the finances. He died with his boots on, turning his work over to his son!

Paul wrote in I Timothy 5:22: *"LAY HANDS SUDDENLY ON NO MAN!"* I am beginning to think that when the word *"elder"* is used, in regard to the pastor/bishop/ELDER, it means just what it says: *"ELDER"*! The dictionary explains that *AN "ELDER" IS AN OLDER PERSON WITH SOME AUTHORITY OR DIGNITY IN A TRIBE OR COMMUNITY."* (I am not sure how "old" is "older"!)

"Let the ELDERS that rule well be counted worthy of double honour, especially they who labour in the word and doctrine" (I Timothy 5:17). Though this passage is speaking of financially paying the pastor well–and that is good–THE PASTOR SHOULD BE A MAN WITH SOME *"AGE"* TO HIM! MANY MEN

595

JUMP INTO THE PASTORATE IMMEDIATELY AFTER GRADUATING FROM BIBLE COLLEGE OR SEMINARY. Their experience in life and marriage, to say nothing of the ministry, is next to nothing! They have had practical Christian training in school—maybe a summer internship—but LITTLE TO NO LIFE EXPERIENCE!

Some have no children or are starting their families. They know NOTHING of raising children or being proper husbands. Their wives are still adjusting to married life. Both are selfish. They rule their wives with an iron hand, hurting their psyches—thinking it is Scriptural. They have never seen a person die or know where to stand when the casket is put into the hearse. They have never helped an old man walk across the street or watched him try to pick up the morning paper. They have never seen a mother mourn when she puts her son in the cold grave. Yet, these inexperienced YOUNG MEN begin *"ruling"* a church as if they are top army generals—and *appear* to know nothing about humility.

After being a Christian for more than seventy years, I've concluded that a pastor should be an "elder"—not a "novice" (I Timothy 3:6)! By then his marriage would have had time to ripen to a *"good thing"* or fall away. His children will be older and be seen to be walking, or not walking with the Lord. His people-skills will have sharpened or shown up to be lacking. True, he may not be a "barn burner" or a builder of a super aggressive church; but he will have proven to be *"blameless,"* the husband of one wife, and an *"elder that ruleth well his household"* (3:4). Yes, his walk with the Lord will be evident! HE WILL HAVE A *"GOOD REPORT!" (See* I Timothy 3:7.) Who could ask for more?

"JOY COMETH IN THE MORNING"
(Psalm 30:5b; Philippians 4:4)
REJOICE IN THE LORD
AND AGAIN I SAY REJOICE!
The joy He gives keeps our hearts singing,
and it strengthens us for our daily tasks.
JOY IS THE FRUIT OF THE SPIRIT!
(ggs)

Today's Bible Blessing   *December 17*
II Timothy 1:3–Titus 1:5
PAUL MARTYRED FOR JESUS
II Timothy 4:6
"I am now ready to be offered . . . the time of my departure is at hand."

As I read today's reading, I was struck with the comparison of Paul to Timothy. Paul wrote of himself as *"Paul, the aged"* (Philemon 9) and of Timothy as "young," *"DO NOT ALLOW ANYONE TO DESPISE THY YOUTH!"* (See I Timothy 4:12.) Probably, the young pastor was in his early forties at the time. One man was tired, weak, and looking forward to being with Christ–yet victorious in spirit. The other was in his prime, desiring to serve the Lord, no matter the cost—not realizing the full price he would have to pay.

We read Paul's command to his son in the faith, to "continue thou in the things which thou hast learned and hast been assured of, knowing of whom thou hast learned them. . ." (II Timothy 3:14). We know that it was his mother and grandmother that taught Timothy the Scriptures from a child. Those Old Testament Hebrew *"Scriptures"* were what is called, **"THE TANACH."** Jesus HIMSELF referred to this "threefold division of the Hebrew canon" when he spoke to THE TWO on the Emmaus Road in Luke 24:44. *"These are the words which I spake unto you . . . which were written in the law of Moses, and in the prophets, and in the psalms, concerning me."*

"T"	=	TORAH	=	THE LAW
"NA"	=	NAVI'IM	=	THE PROPHETS
"CH"	=	CHETHUVIM	=	THE WRITINGS

Paul's message for Pastor Timothy was summarized in the charge that he gave to *him* to *"preach the word"* that he had learned as a child, compounded with what Paul had been teaching him as an adult. The foundation of both of their ministries was built on the *"God-breathed"* Scriptures which *"HOLY MEN of God spake as they were moved by the Holy Ghost"* (II Peter 1:21).

> *"Nevertheless the foundation of God standeth sure, having this seal, The Lord knoweth them that are his. And, Let everyone that nameth the name of Christ depart from iniquity"* (II Timothy 2:19).

Compare what Paul said of himself, when he wrote of his years of ministry, *"I am now ready to be offered, and the time of my departure is at hand . . ."* (II Timothy 4:6).

There was no denying it! The Apostle felt it in his bones! His *"time"* was nigh! In fact, he was passing the "torch" to

Timothy, as he affirmed, *"I have fought a good fight, I have finished my course, I have kept the faith!"* (See II Timothy 4:7)

How many of us can claim that our job is finished? Perhaps we should gather up all the loose ends of our lives and get our *"houses in order"* too. Our *"courses"* may be closer to the finish-line than what we know. On the one hand, Paul is sad. HE IS LONELY! He misses his friends–especially Timothy whom he loved dearly, begging him, *"Do thy diligence to come shortly unto me."* (II Timothy 4:9). The incarcerated man was cold! He needed his cloke! He had left it long ago with Carpus at Troas.

Demas, who had traveled with him, had forsaken him. Luke was near him. Mark was there too. (He had matured and changed his fickle ways.) Paul had sent Tychicus to Ephesus to minister there. He longed for his books–always the student! Most of all he wanted the Scriptures–his *"parchment"* scrolls of animal skins.

His end was near. He knew it! He'd been in prison a long time. His bones were tired. He was treated like a common criminal. He shivered with the chill! Illnesses had come with his confinement–*always* chained to a guard. This was his second imprisonment–so different from the first. He waited for his final trial. DAILY HE LOOKED FOR HIS PHYSICAL RELEASE! INSTEAD, HE WAS DECAPITATED—MARTYRED FOR JESUS CHRIST. That was the summer of A.D. 67 or 68.

"UNANSWERED PRAYER BUT SUFFICIENT GRACE"
(II Corinthians 12:8-9)
Paul cried out to the Lord three times.
"Take it away!"
"Take it away!"
"Take it away!"
GOD HEARD.
1. Paul was spiritual and on praying ground.
2. Paul believed God, BUT
He left it there.
THE OBJECT OF DIVINE LOVE WAS TO TAKE AWAY
THE REBELLION
AND GIVE SUBMISSION. (ggs)

Today's Bible Blessing　　　　　　　　　*December 18*

Titus 1:6–Hebrews 2:6
THE DAY A SLAVE & MASTER BECAME BROTHERS

Titus 1:15

"Unto the pure all things are pure . . . unto the defiled . . . is nothing pure."

Let us look at two men with whom Paul corresponded. They are TITUS and PHILEMON. In my opinion, they are as different as night and day! ONE WAS A PASTOR, AND THE OTHER MAY HAVE BEEN A BUSINESS MAN AND/OR A BISHOP IN THE CHURCH OF COLOSSE; BUT FOR SURE—A CHRISTIAN SLAVE OWNER. One was poor and the other had money. One traveled everywhere, preaching and teaching the gospel of grace. The other stayed put in his own back yard, managing his business and attending to his church responsibilities.

Titus pastored a church in Crete. Crete was a small island one hundred-fifty miles long. Mount Ida's view was a breathtaking sight every morning as Titus ate breakfast. As a prisoner, Paul had sailed along the Southern coast of that island on the way to Rome.

Several years ago, when my husband and I were flying to Israel, we flew over an island. It may have been Crete! I looked out the window while some Palestinian men explained it all to me. The Cretian men were known for their excellence in sailing, as well as archery. SADLY, THE ISLANDERS HAD A POOR REPUTATION! They were liars, lazy, gluttonous, and crude.

Paul's affection for TITUS, his son in THE FAITH, was like that for a natural son. Paul held Titus in such high regard that he often bragged about him. It was in CRETE that Titus pastored a church. Once when Paul arrived at Corinth, he was saddened because his young friend was not there. Perhaps wrongfully, Paul had boasted about Titus' work and character. No one is perfect! For some reason the Galatian Christians, who had fallen back under the law, persuaded Titus, an uncircumcised Greek, to be circumcised. Perhaps it was because he was such a compassionate man, that he went along with that Old Testament ritual. I really don't know—but it was wrong!

There are many favorite Bible verses in this letter. For instance: *"Unto the pure all things are pure: but unto them that are defiled and unbelieving is nothing pure; but even their mind and conscience is defiled"* (Titus 1:15). WHAT AN APPROPRIATE TEACHING FOR THE CORRUPT CRETIANS! I can't help but notice the wise exhortation for the older women of the church. They were to behave as it becometh *"holiness,"*—not false accusers, given to wine— BUT TO TEACH GOOD THINGS (2:3)! With such a loose moral and lying background, such words were certainly needful! Women should set the moral standards!

The young men were to be a pattern of good works with sound speech—not swearing as had been their custom! The servants, who were trusted slaves, were to be faithful and truthful. NO MORE LYING! They were to obey the law and manifest the kindness and love of God toward others. It was not of their *"goodness"* or *"good works"* that Jesus had saved them! (See Titus 3:5.) BECAUSE THEY BELIEVED IN GOD, THEY SHOULD STRIVE TO DO GOOD WORKS! This "life-change" would prove they were Christians!

NOW LET US TURN OUR ATTENTION TO PHILEMON. In those days a *"servant"* or *"slave"* had a different connotation than for us who remember the Civil War slaves. I am told that the *"slaves"'* in Bible times were well-loved and cared for. Many of them were captives from the bounty of war. Others became slaves because they owed money to someone and couldn't pay. They became part of the family and were trusted. Whatever the relationship that ONESIMUS had with his owner, he spoiled it by stealing from him and running away. It seems that Paul became acquainted with the run-away in prison.

I would say that ONESIMUS did something illegal to put him in jail with Paul. That is why Paul was able to lead the man to Jesus Christ. He became a Christian! Paul would have enjoyed keeping him near, but honesty demanded ONESIMUS return to his rightful owner. Now that relationship was more than *"slave"* and *"master;"* it had become *"brothers in Christ."* **Wish we could have been in their HOUSE CHURCH that first Lord's Day when Philemon and Onesimus broke bread together, don't you?**

"IN EVERYTHING, PRAISE"
(Psalm 33:1; 147:1)
PRAISE IS COMELY, BUT PRAISE IS COSTLY.
It is called in Psalms 116:17, *"the Sacrifice of Thanksgiving."*
In Hosea 14:2, it is *"the calves of our lips."*
In Hebrews 13:15, it is *"the fruit of our lips."*
PRAISE LIFTS OUR EYES FROM THE BURDEN
TO THE LORD JESUS.
When you *"praise,"* it keeps your heart worshipping.
You cannot murmur when you praise.
(ggs)

Today's Bible Blessing   *December 19*

Hebrews 2:7–Hebrews 7:5
A CHALLENGE FOR PERSONAL HOLINESS

Hebrews 4:12

"The word of God is quick, and powerful, and sharper than any two edged sword . . . a discerner of the thoughts and intents of the heart.

This letter to the Hebrew Christians, wherever they would be, is a masterpiece of literary excellence! It reviews Israel's history with pride and expounds the Christian's *"hope"* and *"calling"* in the things of Christ. Within its pages is a recognition of the Lord Jesus Christ's *"sonship"* and *"eternality"* (Hebrews 1:8*)*, as well as a challenge for personal holiness. It is a pocket-size-letter for the Hebrew Christians—as well as the Gentile Christians—for review of their early heritage and present standing with Christ.

READ THE SALUTATION OF THE WRITER! Feel the majesty of the APOSTLE PAUL'S WORDS! He is teaching that the prophets' *"inspired"* words were written down on parchments for our learning (Hebrews 1:1-2).

> *"God, who at sundry times and in divers manners spake in time past unto the fathers by the prophets, hath in these last days spoken unto us by his Son, whom he hath appointed heir of all things, by whom also he made the worlds . . ."*

Paul spoke of the original Hebrew and Aramaic words that the Old Testament writers wrote, not the translation of words written today into many languages for our reading. Even as Paul wrote, his written words were ONE TIME *"breathed out," "God-breathed,"* and *"inspired by God."* What a comfort to know that Paul was not confused! Rest assured, we have an accurate, faithful, and true *translation* of those original Hebrew, Aramaic, and Greek Words in our King James Bible!

Paul's question in Hebrews 2:3 is pertinent, "HOW SHALL WE ESCAPE, IF WE NEGLECT SO GREAT SALVATION?" People rush around carrying out their *"world view"* for themselves. They have no thought of Jesus who was made a little lower than the angels. He suffered death for them so they would not have to taste the *"death"* of the separation from God in eternity (Hebrews 2:9). What a Saviour!

God—through Jesus Christ—has made it possible for man or woman to be free from the *"bondage"* of the FEAR OF DEATH (Hebrews 2:15). What an interesting statement. So many are afraid to die—even Christians. I do not judge them, as I have not yet been in the *"dying process"* of gasping for breath or in intense dying pain. I, as well as you, are in the *"lineup"* for *"death."* It's a fact!

I am not being "morbid." I'm just speaking the truth. When Adam was made from the dust of the ground, he had no *"death"* in him. If he had never disobeyed God (sinned), he would never have died. The world would be entirely different place. No death! No sickness! No wars! Sadly, the fact is that ADAM DID EAT OF THE FORBIDDEN FRUIT AND DEATH CAME! The arrival of *"death"* (because of his sin) into his being changed the whole complexion of our lives. Now—because of Adam—all have sinned!

This is why Jesus was made "sin," in order to take away your sin and mine. Of course, we must individually recognize that we are sinners and need a Saviour. Not only is Jesus our High Priest, but He is also our sacrifice (Hebrews 2:14-18). WHAT AN EXCEPTIONAL DEMONSTRATION OF GOD'S LOVE SHOWERED ON YOU AND ME. Paul warned against having an *"evil heart"* of unbelief (3:12) or hardening the heart as the Israelites did in the wilderness (3:8; 4:7). Rest is provided for the people of God! SALVATION! HEAVEN!

We have a workbook called THE WORD OF GOD (Hebrews 4:12)! It tells us of Jesus, of Heaven, and how to live in a *"crooked"* and *"perverse"* generation. It is *"quick"* and *"powerful"*! It enables the believer to be ALIVE and STRONG in all of life's situations.

I remember when my mother taught me this verse as my family sat around our kitchen table. It is planted deep within my heart! Now, because of Jesus and HIS WORDS, I can come boldly to the THRONE OF GRACE and find *"mercy"* and *"grace"* in time of need (Hebrews 4:16). HOW ABOUT YOU?

"I HAVE LEARNED IN WHATSOEVER STATE I AM, THEREWITH TO BE CONTENT!"
(Philippians 4:11)
We wonder how long it took this great apostle
to learn to be content.
Contentment is not our natural inclination.
Discontent, murmurings, and covetousness are as natural to man
as weeds are to soil.
WE MUST LEARN TO BE CONTENT!
We learn through God's discipline and training.
CONTENTMENT IS ONE OF THE FLOWERS OF HEAVEN,
IT MUST BE CULTIVATED.
It must be learned in every "state" (place or condition) we are in.
Sometimes we think we have it learned,
and a new "state" or situation comes,
and we must learn more perfectly.
The new nature alone cannot produce this lovely grace.
SUBMISSION IS THE KEY! (ggs)

Today's Bible Blessing   *December 20*

Hebrews 7:6—Hebrews 10:22
THE INCARNATE SON SPEAKS

Hebrews 10:7

"Then said I, Lo, I come to do thy will, O God!"

WHO WAS ORIGEN?

I must say that I was very surprised to read in THE NEW UNGER'S DICTIONARY that many scholars believed that Paul (or whoever they attest to being the writer of Hebrews) used the SEPTUAGINT for his Old Testament quotations. I must have been sleeping during those classes when this was taught. I know that the DEAN BURGON SOCIETY has had speeches on this too. *UNGER'S* says that all the O.T. quotations were from the LXX except Hebrews 10:30.

My husband, Dr. D. A. Waite, told me that he does not believe that the Septuagint was in existence in the Old Testament period. It was composed in the time of ORIGEN (around 225 A.D.). It is found in ORIGEN'S fifth column of his six-column work called *The Hexapla*. This fifth column contains the Old Testament translated into Greek. (As you know, the O.T. was written mostly in Hebrew.) From what I understand, it is true that **only a few** O.T. books were translated from Hebrew into Greek B.C. Dr. Waite says he will agree to that. LET ME RESTATE: ALL OF THE OLD TESTAMENT BOOKS WERE NOT TRANSLATED INTO GREEK UNTIL ORIGEN'S TIME!

WHO WAS ORIGEN? *In my opinion, he was an awful man!* **He was one of the leading GNOSTICS of his day.** He allegorized the Bible. He said Jesus was a created being. He denied a literal Hell. He denied Jesus' physical resurrection. He believed in the pre-existence of the human soul. He believed in baptismal regeneration, taught transubstantiation, alleged that Satan was paid a ransom by Christ's death, and accepted the Apocrypha. Besides all that, he mutilated himself which probably affected his mental faculties. WHO COULD BELIEVE ANYTHING HE SAID OR WROTE?

JESUS' BEAUTIFUL WORDS TO HIS FATHER

Now let's turn to the beautiful words of God to the Hebrew Christians from the pen of Paul the Apostle. How well I remember the Sunday morning that a visiting preacher spoke from Hebrews 10:5-9a. He spoke of the *"incarnation"* of Jesus Christ. HE WHO WAS WITH THE FATHER FROM THE BEGINNING WAS SENT ON A SPECIAL MISSIONARY JOURNEY TO EARTH FROM HEAVEN. He, who never had been limited by time or space—not alone a body, became a *"man"* to become a *"human sacrifice."* Jesus did this for you and me!

We recoil at the thought of a *"human sacrifice."* And well we should! It is *"inhuman"* and *"pagan."* Yet the LORD told Abraham, His faithful servant, to do it! Remember how Abraham had to face this prospect? God commanded him to take Isaac up on Mount Moriah to sacrifice him to God (Genesis 22:2). Of course, we know that God provided a ram instead–thus saving Isaac's life. This is a picture of the Lord Jesus Christ Who died as our Substitute as the *"lamb of God which taketh away the sin of the world"* (John 1:29b).

I CAN PICTURE THE LORD JESUS CHRIST AS THE HOLY CHILD IN A MANGER, LOOKING UP AT HIS FATHER AND SPEAKING THESE WORDS:

"SACRIFICE AND OFFERING THOU WOULDEST NOT, BUT A BODY HAST THOU PREPARED ME" (See Hebrews 10:5b.) Continuing His praise, JESUS proclaimed:

> *"In burnt offerings and sacrifices for sin thou hast had no pleasure. Then said I, Lo, I come (in the volume of the book it is written of me,) to do thy will, O God. Above when he said, Sacrifice and offering and burnt offerings and offering for sin thou wouldest not, neither hadst pleasure therein; which are offered by the law; Then said he, Lo, I come to do thy will, O God"* (Hebrews 10:6-9a).

"THE COUNSEL OF HIS OWN WILL"
(Ephesians 1:11)
God worketh ALL THINGS after the counsel of HIS own will.
It may seem that God is not doing His will
in bringing things to pass in our lives.
BUT GOD'S WAYS ARE NOT MAN'S WAYS.
And our all-wise loving Father is accomplishing His will. (ggs)

Today's Bible Blessing   *December 21*

Hebrews 10:23—Hebrews 12:29
BELIEVING IN THAT WHICH WAS NOT SEEN

Hebrew 11: 1
"Faith is the substance of things hoped for, the evidence of things not seen."

Now we come to the great HALL OF FAITH chapter! Men and women of *"faith"* are mentioned. The Holy Spirit, through Paul's pen, skims off the cream of their lives and jots down the highlights for us.

Paul tells of CREATION, and the framing of the worlds by God's spoken Word! What power in each of His syllables. We meet **ABEL**, the good brother, who died because of his goodness. ENOCH, Methuselah's father, walked with God! He had such a testimony that God swept him Heavenward with no deathbed experience! **NOAH** heeded God's warning! In fear, he built an ark to save his family from an unspeakable flood. Then, we read of ABRAHAM who blindly followed the LORD to an unknown place and to unknown people who had unknown problems! As a wanderer, He lived in a tent with Sarah. He and his son and grandsons were heirs of the same *"promise."* Would you and I have been as obedient?

Then there was Sarah (vs. 11)! What a *"holy"* woman! I have learned much from her. I learned *"submission"* from her in I Peter 3:5-6—how to dress, and how to trust God in the impossible. The FAITH she had to give birth to her child was remarkable! Oh, to have more women of FAITH in our day! All her *"seed,"* as well as that of other believing women, died IN FAITH (vs. 13)! They believed in what they could not see. These Old Testament believing couples were seeking a country and a city that had never been seen; yet they believed it to be.

Yes, Abraham was tested often. Sometimes he failed; but not the time when he took his son, ISAAC, up the mountain to *"sacrifice"* him. God had requested it. It was a picture of Jesus' crucifixion and resurrection. Because of Abraham's faith, God received this *"sacrifice"* as if Abraham had done it (vs. 19). Later, ISAAC blessed his sons, JACOB and ESAU, concerning future events in their lives. Later JOSEPH was blessed by JACOB's FAITH when he believed that his bones would be returned and buried in the Canaan Land someday. WHAT MEN OF FAITH!

Then there was Moses! His parents saw him as a *"special"* child. In spite of the king's edict to kill all boy babies, Moses' parents protected their child from death by devising a plan. They put their baby in the area of the Nile River where Egypt's royal princess bathed.

After years of proper training in Egypt's royal palace, MOSES realized it was not for him. BY FAITH, he aligned himself with the people of his birth. He moved to where his Hebrew parents lived. Somehow, he had knowledge concerning the future Messiah—perhaps his birth-mother told him. With full awareness of what his choice would mean, Moses chose the *"reproach of Christ"* which was *"greater than the riches of Egypt!"* (See verse 26.) He forsook Egypt! He kept the Passover! He passed through the Red Sea! HE BECAME A LEADER OF THE FAITH!

Then Paul reminded us of the WALLS OF JERICHO, and how they fell in SEVEN DAYS (vs. 30)! Who would have believed what FAITH could do? Peaceful RAHAB was a woman of FAITH too! Who would have thought? Then our attention is drawn to GIDEON, and BARAK, and SAMSON, and JEPHTHAE, DAVID, and SAMUEL. We remember their daring actions and their FAITH!

We notice people like DANIEL who "stopped the mouths of lions" (vs. 33). Torture fires were extinguished! Sword's slashed! Some escaped! THE WEAK BECAME STRONG IN BATTLE! Surprised women welcomed their resurrected dead! Others were tortured! Crowds mocked! Many wandered the desert dressed in goat skins. Others fled to the mountains and hid in caves. Others were stoned! Some were sawn asunder. MOCKINGS! SCOURGINGS! IMPRISONMENTS!

Paul memorialized these faithful people. THE WORLD WAS NOT WORTHY of them! Now we, who are born-again, have a *"better thing."* THE PROMISED SEED CAME AND IS THE SAVIOUR OF MEN!

"TRIUMPH IN CONFLICT"
(II Corinthians 2:14)
YOU WILL NOT ALWAYS BE ABLE TO SMILE,
BUT YOU WILL ALWAYS BE ABLE TO TRIUMPH
IN CHRIST!
"Triumph" presupposes conflict!
And "conflict" you will have sometime,
SOMEWHERE! (ggs/ copied)

Today's Bible Blessing   *December 22*

Hebrews 13:1–James 3:8
A DOER OF THE WORD

James 1:5
"If any of you lack wisdom, let him ask of God . . . "

"But be ye doers of the word, and not hearers only, deceiving your own selves. For if any be a hearer of the word, and not a doer, he is like unto a man beholding his natural face in a glass: For he beholdeth himself, and goeth his way, and straightway forgetteth what manner of man he was" (James 1:22-24).

Whenever I read or hear this verse, I think of my father, R. O. Sanborn. HE WAS A DOER OF THE WORD! I've written you about him before. He loved the Lord Jesus and His Words as much as any man I know. He read his Bible. He prayed. He supported his church with gifts and offerings, and he was a *"separatist."* I am not sure there are many men like him left in this sinful world.

I remember that he would not marry my mother until she got saved. He said, *"I have something to ask you, Gertrude, but not until you do something."* He would not tell her what the "something" was. It was that she must receive Jesus Christ as her Saviour. He did not tell her what it was, lest she would say she was *"born-again"* just to marry him.

My father did not believe in an *"unequal"* yoke in marriage or in business, for that matter, as taught in II Corinthians 6:14-17. Sadly, there are couples who want so desperately to marry that they have allowed themselves to *"fall in love"* with an unsaved person and even marry him or her. My father would not do that. So, my mother became a Christian and married my father. She was eighteen. He was nineteen. They were married sixty-five years, if I remember correctly.

Eight weeks after my mother died, Daddy went home to be with Jesus! He had lost a leg to a blood clot the last few years of his life. Mother said that he never complained about this condition. I remember her crying as she reflected on this sad, unexpected event in his life. My father kept on working in spite of it. In fact, he had just returned to his wheelchair from his riding mower when he died. He was 84! The neighbor who found him said that Daddy had a peaceful look on his face. Much different, he told me, from the *"horror"* he had seen on his own father's face when he died. I was comforted by this.

I believe the AUTHOR of this *"general"* EPISTLE OF JAMES was JAMES, Jesus' half-brother. He was one of Mary's and Joseph's many children. James was written around A.D. 62, not to a church, but to Jewish Christians scattered abroad. Definitely, whether we are Jewish or not, the book was written for you and me, if we are *"saved."* These five chapters are considered to be one of the first epistles, if not the first, written to the Jewish believers who were scattered all over the Roman Empire. What a needed message!

Christians were confusing themselves by thinking that *"works"* were not necessary in their Christlike walk. Swiftly, he puts a stop to such wrong thinking! He tells them to *"count it all joy"* (James 1:2) when we have *"testings"* in our Christian walk. This is normal! We must get used to it. Many virtues are reaped from such testings. He recommends letting *"patience"* work itself *"perfectly"* in our lives! Later, the Apostle Peter will remind us to add to *knowledge temperance*; and to *temperance patience*; and to *patience godliness . . .* (II Peter 1:6). James instructed that we, in our confused lives, should seek *"wisdom"* from God who gives it liberally (James 1:5-6).

I think that my father had this wisdom. He only went to the ninth grade in school; yet he knew more than many college men. HE WALKED IN FAITH (vs.6). He was not *"double-minded"* or *"unstable"* in his ways. James wisely wrote: "BLESSED IS THE MAN THAT ENDURETH TEMPTATION: FOR WHEN HE IS TRIED, HE SHALL RECEIVE THE CROWN OF LIFE, WHICH THE LORD HATH PROMISED TO THEM THAT LOVE HIM" (vs. 12). That kind of a man is a *"DOER OF THE WORD"* like my Dad! ARE YOU A *"DOER"* TOO?

```
┌─────────────────────────────────────────────────┐
│              "A PRAYER LESSON LEARNED"            │
│                   (Romans 8:26)                   │
│             What a wonderful lesson I learned     │
│             in the time of weakness and incapacity.│
│      TRYING TO PRAY AND NOT BEING ABLE TO THINK!  │
│        Grieved that those for whom I was interceding│
│               would not be mentioned to GOD.      │
│      Then the Spirit of God spoke to my heart by Romans 8:26.│
│          He knew my longings and my infirmities.  │
│               He carried them in my behalf,       │
│     And in grace, gave me consciousness of His work│
│  of intercession for me and for those I prayed for when I was well.│
│                      (ggs)                        │
└─────────────────────────────────────────────────┘
```

Today's Bible Blessing   December 23

James 3:9–I Peter 2:14
RULES FOR A HAPPY MARRIAGE

1 Peter 3:8

"Finally, be ye all of one mind, having compassion one of another, love as brethren, be pitiful, be courteous:"

As I look at Peter's letter, memories of certain passages come to mind. I remember teaching *"Husband-Loving Lessons"* to many women in several different classes in homes and churches. The truth of I Peter 3:1-9 still rings in my ears! As Jesus Christ was subject to the Father's will, so is a wife to be in subjection to her own husband in areas that do not contradict the Scripture. He who reviled not or threatened in suffering was and is the example for a married woman's relationship to her husband. Often this is a difficult lesson to learn, especially if the husband is not as Christ who loved the Church by giving His life for her.

It is the Christian wife's privilege to live in such a manner that if her husband is not a born-again Christian, he will see Christ in her. It is her hope that he will want to know the Saviour who has changed his wife to be the loving women she has become. It behooves those of us who are Christians already to live in *"like manner."* I fear many of us do not do this. I say this to our shame.

The Christian wife is to adorn herself in a "meek and quiet" spirit. She is not to rely on immodest clothing, precious jewels, or the latest styles to make herself the Christian woman she was meant to be. Sarah of old is the example-wife (I Peter 3:6). Even though she did not understand all that was going on in her life, Sarah respected Abraham and did not become paralyzed with all he did as he followed the True God. Soon His FAITH became her faith. This was shown to be true with the birth of Isaac in her old age.

Husbands are not overlooked in this passage either. They are to live with their wives *"according to knowledge"* (I Peter 3:7-9). What exactly does that mean? I think it may mean that the husband should learn that *"women"* are a different kind of people than *"men."* Yes, there is much *"learning"* that a new husband much learn in order to be a good husband. I think that is why the young men in the Old Testament were not to go to war during their first year of marriage.

> *"When a man hath taken a new wife, he shall not go out to war, neither shall he be charged with any business: but he shall be free at home one year, and shall cheer up his wife which he hath taken"* (Deuteronomy 24:5).

Notice the husband is to *"cheer up"* his wife. Nothing is said about the wife *"cheering up"* her husband. In other words, the husband is supposed to do everything in his power to make his wife happy during that first, fundamental, basic year of the marriage! So many life-long marriage problems could be avoided if in the new marriage, the husband would be concerned with *"cheering up"* his wife, and not the other way around.

Often because the new husband thinks he must establish himself as the *"head of the house,"* he harms their early marriage with *"ruling"*! Thus the man disregards the young wife's feelings by *"bossing"* her around. He must always remember that God made her to be the *"weaker"* vessel. She had left everything to be with the man of her dreams when suddenly he has become this *"cruel"* potentate, instead of the wooing suitor of their pre-marriage days. Dwelling with a wife *"according to knowledge"* is a big assignment! The happiness and contentment of the marriage depends on that first year!

A married couple should be "like-minded"—or as Peter puts it *"of one mind."* The marriage license does not end *"compassion"* or *"courteousness"* for one another! (I Peter 3:8) Some married people treat strangers better than their own mates. A Christian couple should never forget they are *"brothers and sisters"* in Christ. They should not render evil for evil or be bitter or abusive toward one another. There should be no deceit or defrauding in a Christian marriage. If so, how can their prayers ever be answered?

"THE GREATEST OF THESE IS LOVE"
(I Corinthians 13)
**Love is the greatest in that it remains
when HOPE and FAITH are fulfilled and realized.**
HOPE REALIZED!
FAITH BECOMES SIGHT!
LOVE CONTINUES!
(ggs)

Today's Bible Blessing   *December 24*

I Peter 2:15–II Peter 1:20
THE ANTIDOTE TO SATAN'S ATTACKS

I Peter 5:6
"Humble yourselves therefore under the mighty hand of God . . ."

> *"Be sober, be vigilant; because your adversary the devil, as a roaring lion, walketh about, seeking whom he may devour: Whom resist stedfast in the faith . . ."*
> (I Peter 5:8-9).

This verse, as well as the preceding verses, could be considered *to be "my verses."* Not that they are not for others to ponder and apply to their own lives; but they became *"mine"* after one of the most horrendous *"testings"* in my life. Have you had such a "testing"?

It was during this period of time that I realized that what was happening to me was an attack of the Devil! It seemed to me that Satan was invading my life with such force that it was as if an earthquake had shaken me! I felt completely at a loss! What was I to do?

Have you ever seen a cat watching his prey? Quietly the cat sees his victim. He watches patiently. Then at the exact time when the prey is least expecting, the cat pounces on it. He catches it in his claws. The victim cannot get away. If the cat is hungry, he kills and eats the poor thing. Sometimes the feline is not hungry; he just wants to play with his victim. Yes, Satan is like that cat. He is seeking whom he may devour!

For all you know, that "roaring lion" is stalking your marriage. He crouches, waiting to pounce. Being a professional "trickster," Satan is patient. He waits. He crouches in the bushes of your life. Being observant, he sees your disappointments. He finds the weakest area of your personality. It is then—as a dreaded lion—that he pounces. *"Where did he come from?"* you wonder. He is hurting you. He is tearing you apart. He's got you! Then the sound of Satan's *"roaring"* is heard in your ears! It is too late!

You did not know he was watching. As you struggle in his paws, you are dazed. *"How did this happen?"* you keep asking yourself. Perhaps that was how Eve felt that day in Eden when she ate of the forbidden fruit (Genesis 3:6). She saw the *"desired tree."* It was good for food and pleasant to the eyes. Satan had deceived her with his words and handsome ways. She didn't know it until it was too late!

Then there was God's servant Job. How many years had Satan *"watched"* that *"just"* and *"righteous"* man? Yes, God permitted

Satan to pounce upon His servant, even asking the Tempter, *"Hast thou considered my servant Job?"* (See Job 1:8.) The *"testings"* of Job touched every facet of his life–from his pocket book to his possessions, his business, his home—even to the deaths of almost all the people he loved and for whom he cared. Job, in his lifetime, may never have known he had been hit by Satan's wiles!

Peter, himself, had experienced the power of the Evil One in his own life. As he warmed himself by the fire of those who despised Jesus, he denied his Lord with the very mouth that declared he never would do so. From his lips came Peter's denial *"I know not the man of whom ye speak!"* (See Mark 14:54, 71-72.) For those who could hear, the "roar" of the lion sounded. Peter wept! He knew he had been in the paw of that wicked beast.

What is the deterrent for such Satanic attacks in the believer's life? How can we prevent our foolish yielding to the *perverted word* as Eve did, or to the *destroying pride* like Peter, or even to the *hidden assaults* of the Evil One behind our backs? It is a proven fact that none of us is impervious to the Devil's devices. He hates the Christian woman to walk in the Light. He wants nothing more than to destroy her Christian testimony.

I think the preceding verses in today's Bible reading hold the answer. *"Humility"* and *"casting one's care"* on Christ is *THE ANTIDOTE TO SATAN'S ATTACKS* in our lives. It sounds easy but because we are human, it is most difficult to follow.

Read it:
". . . Be clothed with humility: for God resisteth the proud, and giveth grace to the humble. Humble yourselves therefore under the mighty hand of God, that he may exalt you in due time: Casting all your care upon him; for he careth for you" (I Peter 5:5b-7).

IT IS WHEN WE THINK WE ARE *"SOMEBODY"* THAT GOD "RESISTS" OUR PRIDE TO PROVE TO US THAT TRULY *WE ARE* "NOBODY"!

"SICKNESS CAN BE A BLESSING"
(Psalm 91:3)
SURELY HE SHALL "DELIVER" THEE
FROM THE SNARE OF THE FOWLER (Satan),
AND FROM THE NOISOME PESTILENCE!
It may not seem to be "deliverance," but consider these:
ALL WERE DELIVERED
1. Daniel—Den of lions
2. Three Hebrews—Fiery furnace
3. Joseph–Potiphar's wife
4. Children of Israel—slavery, Sinai, & Egypt
5. Peter
6. Paul
Sometimes the sick bed
is really a protection against Satan.
A great theologian wrote that most of his great works
were written as he sat at the bedside of his sick wife. (ggs)

Today's Bible Blessing   *December 25*

I Peter 1:21—I John 3:6
HOW TIMES HAVE CHANGED!

I John 2:15
"Love not the world, neither the things that are in the world . . ."

Isn't it interesting how some Bible verses bring back memories? As I read today's reading and come to I John 2:15-17, I think of my father. I've written about him before in these devotionals. I remember when he gave me my first leather-bound Bible. He wrote two Bible verse references in the fly leaf. One of them was found in ECCLESIASTES 12:1 (*"Remember now thy Creator in the days of thy youth . . ."*) and the other one was this one in I John 2:15-17:

> *"Love not the world, neither the things that are in the world. If any man love the world, the love of the Father is not in him. For all that is in the world, the lust of the flesh, and the lust of the eyes, and the pride of life, is not of the Father, but is of the world. And the world passeth away, and the lust thereof: but he that doeth the will of God abideth for ever."*

I don't remember exactly how old I was; but I suppose I was in my early teens–perhaps thirteen, maybe eleven or twelve. I was thrilled to have a *"real"* Bible–not that the hard-covered ones were not real Bibles! Of course, it was the King James Version as no one who loved the Lord Jesus, that I knew, used any other version. That was long before the perversions were popular among Bible-believing Christians. It was even before the much-condemned REVISED STANDARD VERSION hit the press.

In those early "depression" and "post-depression" years, money was hard to come by. In those days, my father was a door-to-door salesman. He worked hard and long to feed his family. He never stood in a bread line. I do not say that to condemn those that did, but I say it to help you understand how hard my father worked to support his family. Sometimes he traded his products for goods such as eggs, etc. In fact, that is how we got our first piano. Daddy traded mops and brooms and furniture polish for it. I took my first piano lessons on that bartered piano! I tell you all this because as I am writing to you, I am realizing that my *"leather"* Bible must have been a sacrifice for my family to purchase.

I remember when my great Uncle George, who had moved to our little Ohio town, needed money. My parents gave him their last quarter. I remember how I wanted to go to summer Bible camp. My parents sacrificed their last thirteen dollars to pay my way there. Of course, I did not know of any of this financial sacrifice at the time, as they never told me until later.

Getting back to our verse. In those early days of my Christian life, preachers preached hard on sin and taught the Bible. Many sermons were preached on the *"second coming"* of Jesus Christ! We, who loved the Lord Jesus, did not want to be *doing* or *saying* anything that would not please Jesus when he suddenly returned to snatch away those who had accepted Him as Lord and Saviour. We did not want to be ashamed at His coming! Many accepted Jesus Christ as Saviour at such preaching. They did not want to be left behind!

Christian girls did not want to be found looking un-Christlike in risqué clothing or painted faces when Jesus came. We wanted to be ready! Non-worldliness in behavior, as well as dress, was important to show that we loved the Lord Jesus. GOOD CHRISTIANS DID NOT DO CERTAIN THINGS OR LOOK CERTAIN WAYS, OR GO TO CERTAIN PLACES. *"For all that is in the world . . . is not of the Father."* A Christian looked and acted differently than those who did not know Christ. The impetus to live a separated life to Jesus and away from the world was that *"the world passeth away . . . but he that doeth the will of God abideth for ever."* HOW TIMES HAVE CHANGED! But has God?

"CONFORMITY TO CHRIST"
(Romans 8:28)
**"THE GREAT PURPOSE OF GOD
TOWARD WHICH HE IS BRINGING EVERY CHRISTIAN
IS NOT A TEMPORARY HAPPINESS.**
BUT IT IS A CONFORMITY TO THE IMAGE OF JESUS CHRIST.
FOR ALL THINGS ARE WORKING
TOWARD THAT GREAT CONSUMMATION!"
Also, His purpose is that Christ shall be preeminent
in a great family—not just a few.
(ggs quoting from an unknown source.)

Today's Bible Blessing   *December 26*
I John 3:7–III John 1:13
LEARNING TO WALK IN TRUTH
II John 4

"I rejoiced greatly that I have found of thy children walking in truth,"

I remember well when our firstborn son learned to walk. We were living in a small twenty-six-foot trailer behind Dallas Seminary. That was back in the olden days when there was only one main building and one dormitory on the whole campus. Because there was not enough housing for many of the married students, a place was provided behind those buildings for house trailers for married students.

As I look back at it, we lived in primitive conditions. We had no bathrooms in the trailers. The water from the kitchen sink drain splashed on the ground. We had to walk to the bathroom. At first we walked on wooden boards. Then cement ones were made. I think my husband helped lay those sidewalks. We students' wives had a common wash house. It was there we scrubbed our babies' diapers by hand and used the same stationary tubs to bathe them in—only with clean water.

Those were good days! Many who became famous Bible teachers were our neighbors. You would be surprised if I told you who they were.

It was on those narrow walks that our little son learned to walk. I used to hold him by his hand as he ventured out into the *"big"* world. He held his hand high meeting mine. We walked all over the area. One day, I let go of his hand. He did not realize it. There he was walking all by himself, not knowing he did not have my hand. There he was, with his arm held high above his head and his hand out, as if he were holding on to mine. He was walking all alone.

He didn't even know it. He was a big boy now!

Our little boy was a good boy. He was obedient. Obedience does not come naturally. At an early age he learned to obey. I had boundaries for him. He was not permitted to go past a certain area on the sidewalks. He never did.

Later, during those seminary days, we had another little boy. He, too, learned to walk. I was happy he could do so, as he'd had a serious illness and was polio-paralyzed for a while. I loved him dearly, as I did our firstborn. For both of these boys, we had the same boundaries. Only little boy number two did not keep them. I had to watch him like a hawk or he would dash away from our trailer on to unknown paths and lurking dangers.

So, I can relate to the APOSTLE JOHN as he thought about the *"elect lady"* and her children (II John 1, 4). I rejoiced that these children, not only could walk, but they could walk *"in truth"*! She had taught her children to walk *in the truth* that John and the other apostles had taught. This mother not only received the teaching, but she passed it on.

Many mothers do not pass on THE TRUTH to their children. They drink it all in. They go to church meetings and fill notebooks with the preacher's points and Scriptural nuggets, but do not convey this truth to their own children. Other mothers make it their primary business to teach their children about the Lord Jesus Christ and His Words. Their goal in life is to have Christian children who love the Lord and who are testimonies for the Truth.

Now I realize some teach, and they may be correct, that the "elect lady" is the local church. And the *"children"* of the *"elect lady"* are the members of that local assembly. No matter, the Apostle was very pleased that those *"children"* were walking in TRUTH.

This *"walking in truth"* is paramount in this progressive, *"post-modern"* age where people, even some Christians, think nothing of lying and acting as if their lies were true. When, indeed, they are prevaricating with a full face of pretended innocence.

"TELL ME WHERE THOU FEEDEST"
(Song of Solomon 1:7)
"Tell me, where O thou whom my soul loveth,
where thou feedest thy flock,
where thou makest thy flock to rest at noon . . ."
Why should I be as one that turns aside?
I am self-examining.
Where ever the Shepherd stands, there I,
as His sheep, may lie down and rest at noon.
I need not be as one who turns aside.
The food He gives to His flock is for me also.
I am one of His lambs.
"There is a place of quiet rest near to the heart of God."
(ggs)

Today's Bible Blessing   *December 27*

3 John 1:14–Revelation 3:11

DEEDS JOHN WOULD REMEMBER

3 John 9

"DIOTREPHES . . . receiveth us not."

Today we have read from the pen of the Apostle John. It is his third epistle. As you probably know, he was the disciple whom Jesus loved (John 13:23). It seemed that as a young man, John was special to Jesus. Perhaps, it was because John was like an apprentice to the Saviour. In fact, he was the only one who stood at the foot of the cross on that cruel crucifixion day. The other disciples scattered in fear. If you remember, it was to John that Jesus entrusted His mother. John lived a long life–longer than any other of the apostles. In those last years, he was ostracized to the island of Patmos, and probably imprisoned. In fact, it was there that he wrote his last work. **It seemed that John called himself "the elder."** The year was A.D. 95 or so. People may have thought him old as they looked at him, but he was far from "OLD" in spirit and determination. He is an encouragement to all who have longevity. Still God had a work for John to do. Do you think that fellow Christians made fun of him and of his age? Perhaps. The truth is that John wrote his controversial and most studied work as a senior citizen. It is called THE REVELATION OF JESUS CHRIST.

It was in this letter that John wrote to GAIUS. It was a personal letter full of personal remarks. The recipient of this letter seemed to have been a man of some means. He had been a charitable man. He had supplied the financial needs of his fellow church members.

It seemed he supported the church's missionary projects (vs. 5-7). Sadly, it appeared that Gaius may have had a financial loss, for John hoped that Gaius would prosper again (vs. 2).

John wished also that Gaius' health would improve (vs. 2). What kind of sickness Gaius had, we do not know. It is evident that he was a sick man. His illness may have come from a virus or a bacterial infection, cancer, or congestive heart failure. We do not know. We do know that John wished that his friend's body was as healthy as his soul!

It appeared that in the past, Gaius had some influence in the leadership of that small church. In verse nine, we picked up that the little assembly of believers, where Gaius worshipped, had some kind of internal strife. We are not sure of all the details of what it was; but it was severe enough for John to mention it in a letter. It seemed, even in the early days of the church, there were church fights and splits.

Previously, John had written the church itself and his letter was not received (vs. 9a). Evidently in the past, one of the church leaders named DIOTREPHES, did not want John or those who traveled with him to visit the church (vs. 9c). I suppose, if John had come to speak to Gaius' church, everyone would have gathered around John. They would have listened to his every word. They would have fussed over John and given him gifts like churches do for the guest speakers. DIOTREPHES would have felt ignored. He would not have been the preeminent person there that day. That humiliation would have been too much for Diotrephes to handle; so he forbade John to come.

In the letter, John said that someday he would visit the church. When he would come, he predicted, *"I WILL REMEMBER!"* Yes, John would remember Diotrephes! He would remember the man who wanted to be the preeminent person in the church. Yes, John would remember Diotrephes' prating about. John would remember the proud boasting. He would remember the man's controlling attitude. Yes, John would remember the malicious words! Yes, John would remember Diotrephes!

Who could forget? The discontentment! The evil! The uncharitable attitude the proud man had against his fellow-believers. John would remember that jealous Diotrephes would not permit certain Christians to join the church fellowship lest he lose some power and prestige. When it came to church affairs, where Diotrephes was concerned, it was his way or the highway. The Apostle John would have none of that!

John wrote: *"Follow not that which is evil, but that which is good. He that doeth good is of God: but he that doeth evil hath not seen God."*

In stark contrast, John mentions DEMETRIUS in his letter to Gaius. Every report he had of this man was good! DEMETRIUS WAS A MAN OF TRUTH IN CONTRAST TO THE

MALICIOUS DIOTREPHES. John confirmed that his record was true as far as DEMETRIUS and DIOTREPHES' were concerned.

There was much more John wanted to say to Gaius, but some things are best unsaid. He ends his letter with the anticipation that *"someday"* they would talk face to face. I wonder if that *"someday"* ever came.

"USE YOUR MIND"
(Ephesians 4:23; Colossians 3:16; Romans 12:2)
Your brain has been redeemed as much as your heart.
BE RENEWED IN THE SPIRIT OF YOUR MIND!
That ye put off concerning the former conversation the old man, which is corrupt according to the deceitful lusts . . . Let the word of Christ dwell in you richly in all wisdom . . . And whatsoever ye do in word or deed, do all in the name of the Lord Jesus . . . And be not conformed to this world: but be ye transformed by the renewing of your mind, that ye may prove what is that good, and acceptable, and perfect, will of God.
UNDERSTAND WHAT THE WILL OF THE LORD IS!
(ggs)

Today's Bible Blessing   *December 28*
Revelation 3:12–Revelation 9:3
THOUGH YE ONCE KNEW
Jude 5a
"I will therefore put you in remembrance . . ."

JUDE! WHAT an epistle! **Written by James' brother, who very well could have been the half-brother of Jesus Himself**—thus making Jude a half-brother of Jesus, too. This Jude does not mince words! He gets right down to business in his writing.

His first intent, when picking up his pen, was to write a friendly compassionate letter of encouragement con-cerning the *"salvation"* that he shared with the "sanctified" (Jude 1). I don't know exactly to whom he was writing. It really doesn't matter, does it? We do know it was written to *"born-again"* Christians who had been *called to serve* their Saviour. Some say Jude was written in A.D. 66, and others hold to A.D. 75-80. No matter the date, Jude's message was one of warning and witness.

You know how it is. Sometimes you determine that you are going to be positive and use honeycombed words when writing, but a present situation is so overwhelming and hurtful, that you just have to talk about it to your friends. This is what I think happened to Jude as he began to write. He was disturbed! I can't say that I blame him!

618

Within the church or group of Christians to whom Jude was writing, certain men had crept into their fellowship. At first, because of their *deception*, they had been accepted. It turned out these men were *lewd individuals* whose minds were in the gutter, and who, eventually, defiled the Lord Jesus Christ with their lifestyle. What a muddled mess in the middle of good believers!

Jude compared these intruders to those Israelites in the wilderness who did not believe. Remember? They marched out of Egypt with Moses, miraculously crossed the Red Sea, and came right up to entering Canaan Land and stopped! Why? It was because of a false report. They did not believe that the LORD God, who had brought them that far, would protect them against the giants looming before them (Jude 5).

Jude refreshed the memories of his correspondents concerning the fallen angels. Others were punished for using *great swelling words* (vs. 16). Their willful rebellion had doomed them to *"everlasting chains"* and *"darkness"* until their great judgment day (vs. 6). He reviewed the complete destruction of Sodom and Gomorrah because of their sinful sexual pursuits (Jude 7).

Other rebellious people viewed with contempt those in authority. They thought nothing of belittling and chastising their leaders (vs. 8). Jude says the Lord would rebuke them as He did the Sodomites in Abraham's time. What a terrible group of ungodly criticizers who had crept into James' fellowship!

Jude's words penetrated his readers' hearts! How could Jude say such things against those people who had become James' friends? I am sure it was not easy for Jude–but it had to be said! He screamed out on the page,

"THEY HAVE GONE THE WAY OF CAIN!"

"THEY HAVE RUN AFTER BALAAM IN GREED!"

"THEY WILL PERISH LIKE HINDERING KORAH!"

These people thought they were so right when they were so wrong! Why did Jude call them brute beasts? Why? Because they spoke evil concerning things they knew not of! Like foaming waves, they splashed their relentless shame upon all nearby.

Those very people, who seemed *so nice*, were like "spots" in the Christian's charity feasts. In other words, all that the Christians had done by giving to missions, feeding the poor, building a church building, being kind and forgiving to others, preaching THE GOSPEL, as well as and reading and memorizing the Scriptures, etc., etc., was like a GIGANTIC FLAW on a beautiful piece of cloth. Those intruders were like beautiful clouds in the sky with no rain. They were like barren, old dried up trees ready for winter.

Perhaps you know someone like those murmurers who grumbled out lies, using swelling and arrogant words. They claimed to have new *"truth,"* a new *"doctrine"*–undiscovered until they found it! Perhaps you know someone, who with tickling words—in their books and in speeches—has persuaded you and your beguiling friends to slide into her false doctrine. BEWARE! **TAKE HEED TO JUDE'S WARNING!** *"There will be mockers . . . who shall walk after their own ungodly lusts."* **REMEMBER & BEWARE!** (See Jude 5.)

"HE THAT HATH THE SON HATH LIFE"
(I John 5:12)
Brother Clayton Sanborn has been in heaven one month today.
We miss him. He died November 28, 1977.
Even while he was in death's throes,
Struggling as a moth to leave his cocoon,
He was alive!
He slipped out of grave clothes into the Presence of the Lord.
He never died.
His eternal life began when he received Christ and was saved.
HE THAT HATH THE SON HATH LIFE!

~~~

FOR US LOSS!
FOR YOU, BROTHER, GAIN!
(ggs)

Today's Bible Blessing   *December 29*
Revelation 9:4–Revelation 14:3
WHAT KIND OF CHURCH IS MINE?
Revelation 1:11
"What thou seest write in a book, and send it unto the seven churches which are in Asia . . ."

Now we come to the book of THE REVELATION OF JESUS CHRIST. Who would have thought that I would attempt to write something from this difficult book of the Bible? I say it is difficult because it has many prophetic passages that, after much thought, are not understood. The book is full of the *"past,"* the *"present,"* and the *"future";* therefore, it affects all of us today.

The author of these amazing words was Jesus' most beloved disciple, the APOSTLE JOHN. The year was A.D. 96. The place was a prison island called *Patmos.* John penned his words in his very late years as an esteemed senior citizen. Such an endeavor is an encouragement to those of us who have come into our eightieth and ninetieth years of life. Some have written that John was a circuit preacher, of a sort, who ministered to the seven churches mentioned in Revelation 1:11.

THE EPHESUS CHURCH had good qualities, but was full of a group of Christians who had lost their *first love* for the Lord Jesus. THIS IS A SAD SPIRITUAL CONDITION MANY CHRISTIANS FIND THEMSELVES IN TODAY. But when a church has lost its *"first love,"* what good is it?

THE SMYRNA CHURCH was a persecuted church. Many of her members were imprisoned and put to death. To them was promised the *"crown of life"* (Revelation 2:10).

THE PERGAMOS CHURCH was a bold, brave assembly situated in the midst of Satan's territory; yet she corrupted herself with heathen intermarriages, as well as ecclesiastical pride and divisions between the clergy and the congregation. Such behavior is prominent today in our churches.

THE THYATIRA CHURCH was a church full of love and good works; yet she let a false preacher/teacher lead them–**a woman named Jezebel**. By her womanly wiles, she influenced the whole assembly, seducing them by her self-made false doctrines which came from the depths of Satan himself. Her teachings ruined the church, and stole the hearts of the pastor and people, giving them a bad name forever (2:20-23).

THE SARDIS CHURCH was a church of good works–yet full of false piety and spiritual dead wood. This condition was so severe that their members' names were in danger of being blotted out of the *Book of Life*. The good news was that some had not defiled themselves and were worthy, overcoming the evil about them. So, by the example of this church, we learn that it is possible for believers to stand true for the truth to the end.

THE PHILADELPHIA CHURCH had works known to John and the Lord Jesus Christ. Because they kept His *Patient Word*, the Lord Jesus Christ kept them true, as they were tested and tried. He promised that group of *"overcoming"* believers that He would give them a special crown when He comes.

THE LAODICEAN CHURCH was a congregation blinded by its own self-importance. In reality, their good works were insipid to God. They made the Lord Jesus Christ nauseated. Because they had material things and money, the church thought they were something special. When in reality, they were sick and puny, poor and naked, as well as wretched and miserable. In truth they were a spiritual, self-deceived mess.

As I look at these Bible-believing, supposedly Christ-centered churches of John's time, I wonder about our Bible-preaching churches in our century–the ones that you and I attend. What kind of spiritual temperature do they have? Can we honestly say that we, as believers in the amazing atonement provided for us at Calvary, still have that fiery *"first love"* for Him as we did when we were first saved? Do we remember when our testimony was so strong that it offended others, causing us to be persecuted for His name's sake, as the Smyrna believers were in John's day?

How many "unequal" yoke marriages do we find in our churches–not only with unbelievers, but divorces and remarriages becoming the vogue, corrupting the purity of Christ's body of believers? Christians are no different from the world with their adultery, divorces, lying etc. Where is the victory among church members today who are provoked to good works by Christ-like love?

Do the men of our churches sit back and allow our women to rise within our congregations to the status of a JEZEBEL, letting the women teach and unscripturally rule because the men are too lazy to study and lead as Christian gentlemen should do? Do we church people become smug in our doctrines and music thinking we are *"it,"* as far as churches go, with no fear of being cast aside as SARDIS almost was?

How few PHILADELPHIA churches are found where the body of believers, as a whole, are *"overcomers"* **and whose works throw open the door for Jesus Christ**–a door which cannot be shut, always welcoming those who pass by. Or is our church full of *"self-importance,"* money, and counting our numbers. Are we proud of our beautiful building and new carpet? Do we joy in our attendance and outward show when all the while the Saviour is kept in the background as man is glorified in the pulpit and in the choir?

TODAY'S CONTEMPLATION HAS GIVEN ME MUCH TO THINK ABOUT. HOW ABOUT YOU?

"ALWAYS WITH US"
(Isaiah 7:14: IMMANUEL)
This was a precious truth to me in my daily reading of
Spurgeon's Morning & Evening (12/25/77)
Of all things that can set the heart to burning,
there is nothing like the presence of Jesus.
He promised in Matthew 28:20 to be with us.
"JUST A GLIMPSE OF HIM SETS THE HEART BURNING.
Even the smell of the aloes and myrrh
causes the sick and faint to grow strong.
Only moments leaning on His breast
and we are cold no longer."
HIS PRESENCE WILL BE MOST REALIZED
BY THOSE WHO ARE MOST LIKE HIM.
HE WILL REVEAL HIMSELF TO OUR EARNEST PRAYER
AND SUFFER HIMSELF TO BE DETAINED BY OUR
ENTREATIES AND TEARS.
(Spurgeon seems to be quoted and then ggs writes.)

Today's Bible Blessing   *December 30*

Revelation 14:4–Revelation 18:22

COMFORT FOR THE ACHING HEART

Revelation 14:13

"Blessed are the dead which die in the Lord . . . that they may rest from their labours; and their works do follow them."

Once again we find ourselves in the Bible book that is called REVELATION. To many of us, it is a *"mystery"* book with many picturesque ideas and images.

Today we discover that JESUS is called a LAMB. Remember previously, the author, the APOSTLE JOHN, called Jesus THE LAMB OF GOD. We read about this in the gospel of John, chapter one and verse twenty-nine.

Now we see Jesus is standing on Mount Zion with hundreds of men! (See Revelation 14:1-3.) These men have the Heavenly Father's Name written in their foreheads! I do not know in what form *His Name* is written there, but it is written. It may have been with indelible ink, never to fade, or could have been on some microchip that appeared on a computer screen. I do not know. Yet, I do know that these men were brave, righteous, fearless men! Collectively, they are called *"THE ONE HUNDRED AND FORTY-FOUR THOUSAND"* (Revelation 14:3).

Surprisingly these individuals were one-hundred-and-forty-four-thousand redeemed, singing, men who had never been with woman—guiltless and faultless! (See 14:4-5.) I wonder, could that many virgin men be found in our day? Yet, I am reminded of discouraged Elijah who, in his day, thought he was the only prophet who had never bowed his knee to Baal. All along, there were seven thousand good folks who had not succumbed to such evil worship (I Kings 19:18). I read in Revelation 14:5 that those redeemed ones stood before the throne of God.

There are many flying angels mentioned in the two chapters—14 & 15. One has the *everlasting gospel.* They cry out, *"Fear God, and give glory to him, for the hour of his judgment is come . . ."* (vs. 6). A second angel cried out, *"Babylon is fallen."* The third angel declared loudly, *"If any man worship the beast . . . and receive his mark, . . . the same shall drink of the wine of the wrath of God."* (That condemned person will be tormented with fire and brimstone in the presence of the Lamb and holy angels.) **Then a voice from Heaven is heard.** Is it THE FATHER'S VOICE, an angel's, or that of the LAMB? I do not know at this point (vs. 13a). What this *"voice"* speaks is a *"word of comfort"* for grieving loved ones. *"BLESSED ARE THE DEAD WHICH DIE IN THE LORD!"*

How the grieving need comfort! Only those who have lost a loved one know the need. Others say such peripheral things. Even Christians who *think* they are *"comforting,"* go on and on about the glories of Heaven for the Christian who has passed. While we, who stand with empty arms, endure their words and ache with the loss.

Now, as we continue to read, we discover that the *"Comforter"* in this verse is the *SPIRIT OF GOD*! Of course, we should have known! Didn't Jesus tell His disciples He would send Him (John 15:26; John 16:7)? The Spirit's holy comfort was that the ones who have died *"in the Lord"* would REST! Oh, how the dying needed rest!

I remember when my mother died. She had worked almost all of Beverly's life caring for my brain damaged sister—at least fifty-five years. The pressures of caring for Beverly were a part of Gertrude Sanborn's life. When God took Mother *"Home"*, Mother was *"safe"* in the arms of Jesus—*resting from her labors.* What a wonderful rest for her! It comforted me in her death.

I remember being glad that Mother could *rest* from her labor. Preceding her death, she suffered strokes, etc. Today this verse makes an arresting statement to you and me. *"AND THEIR WORKS DO FOLLOW THEM!"* These are words of true comfort! Paul writes about such comfort in II Corinthians 1:3-4. **How grateful we are to let the Spirit of God wash our aching hearts!**

"AWESOME WORDS"
"GLADLY, I CLOSE THIS FESTIVE DAY.
GRASPING THE ALTAR'S HALLOWED HORN,
MY SLIPS AND FAULTS ARE WASHED AWAY.
THE LAMB HAS ALL MY TRESPASS BORN."
This verse was sent to me by a friend.
It continues to bless me, even many years later.
The above was typed on a slip of paper enclosed in a letter.
Just a few words on a page, but they comfort and bless me
each time I read them.
WHAT A BEAUTIFUL VEHICLE OF THOUGHT ARE WORDS.
AWESOME THAT GOD ENTRUSTED THIS GIFT TO US.
(ggs)

Today's Bible Blessing   *December 31*
Revelation 18:23–Revelation 22:21
NO TEARS OR PAIN THERE

Revelation 21:4
"God shall wipe away all tears from their eyes; and there shall be no more death, neither sorrow, nor crying, {nor} pain."

It has not been my intent in looking at this book to do an *"in depth"* study of all the mysteries found within the pages of the book of Revelation. It would take me a year, in itself, to explain this and that. Then my explanations could be wrong and you and I would be left unfulfilled in our understanding of what the book was really saying. Sometimes I wonder if anyone—even the most profound prophetic preachers—really knows what God has hidden for us within the Apostle John's words. Some day it will be revealed to us. Personally, I choose to leave all the *hidden meanings* of the book to the time when the Lord Jesus Himself will either explain them to me or the fulfillments will be acted out in real life in their time.

The Apostle John saw THE HOLY CITY coming down from Heaven (Revelation 21:2). It was that beautiful city with a gold-paved street and jeweled gates that we read about (vs. 10-14, 18-21). There has never been a city like it, nor will there be another. Some say the NEW JERUSALEM will hover over the earth, I suppose, like a space ship of some sort.

One very important aspect of this *"city"* is that there will be no sorrow within its walls. How do I know this? Because John tells us that GOD SHALL WIPE AWAY ALL TEARS FROM THE EYES OF THOSE WHO LIVE THERE (vs. 4). Think of it!—especially you who live in constant pain. There will be no pain there! No need for aspirin or Tylenol. No need for heating pads or special chairs or orthopedic shoes. NO PAIN!

Another "no-no" in this NEW JERUSALEM is *NO DEATH*! Can we mortals understand a place where death will be gone and never heard of? Always on this earth, we experience *"death"* in some form or another. Even a seed dies to produce fruit. I saw a dead bird in our yard the other day and thought how God knew of its death—for not a sparrow falls that He is not aware (Luke 12:6).

Once I heard someone postulate that we, who die *"in the Lord,"* may arrive to Heaven with *"tears"*–but God will take his big handkerchief and wipe them away. I do not know if this be true or not, but I do believe this verse where it says there will be NO MORE *death, sorrow, crying, or pain!* All those conditions are conditions of earth. They are the result of Adam's sin. Jesus has promised, *"I make all things new!"* Nothing will be the same in that glorious NEW JERUSALEM. All new! Life as we know it here on planet earth will be a vague memory, if not completely forgotten. Life there will be so new and different that you and I—as *earthlings*—have no vocabulary to explain it today as mere mortals.

Another amazing attribute of this new city is there will be no street lights or electric lights, not alone oil lamps or candles! In fact, there will be no light bills to pay at all. Why? For there will be no need for artificial lighting of any kind for JESUS CHRIST, who is *"THE LIGHT,"* will be *"THE LIGHT"* in that city (Revelation 21:23). I think it will be that ever-burning, constant shining SHEKINAH GLORY OF GOD. (Remember Moses and the *burning bush?*)

RETHINK WHAT THE APOSTLE JOHN, THE SAME PENMAN OF REVELATION, WROTE CONCERNING JESUS IN JOHN1:4-9:

> *"In him was life; and the life was **THE LIGHT** of men. And **THE LIGHT** shineth in darkness; and the darkness comprehended it not. There was a man sent from God, whose name was John. The same came for a witness, to bear witness of **THE LIGHT**, that all men through him might believe. He was not **THAT LIGHT**, but was sent to bear witness of **THAT LIGHT**. That was **THE TRUE LIGHT**, which lighteth every man that cometh into the world."*

I am reflecting on Jesus' own words in John 8:12, when He proclaimed: *"I am **THE LIGHT** of the world: he that followeth me shall not walk in darkness, but shall have **THE LIGHT** of life."* Do not His words take on a whole new meaning as we think of Him as THE LIGHT in the New Jerusalem?

"THE PEACEABLE FRUIT OF RIGHTEOUSNESS"
(Hebrews 12)

The year is drawing to a close,
and my mind races back along memory path,
I SEE HOW HE HATH KEPT ME CLOSE TO HIM
and drawn me by invisible bands
to lean closer to Him through tears and fears—
their failure and losses.
HOW HARD SOME DAYS SEEMED.
YET, IN THE LIGHT OF TODAY,
I CANNOT SEEM TO REMEMBER THEIR STING!
TODAY I AM REAPING
THE *"PEACEABLE FRUIT,"*
WHICH HE HAS NURTURED AND CULTIVATED
IN ME ALL THIS YEAR! (ggs)

INDEX

boldness, 27, 112, 117, 341, 415,
539, 581
bones, 33, 141, 165, 236, 241,
244, 323, 363, 377, 404, 405,
406, 461, 464, 478, 597, 598,
605
born-again, 27, 61, 95, 96, 104,
113, 248, 253, 275, 284, 305,
321, 341, 398, 430, 446, 453,
512, 514, 515, 524, 557, 594,
607, 608, 618
brasen, 33, 51, 170, 218, 388, 413,
514
brasen serpent, 33, 170, 514
brass, 32, 33, 151, 175, 190, 413,
421, 514
breakdown, 419
break-downs, 317
breath, 1, 17, 61, 80, 177, 234,
263, 289, 314, 322, 343, 443,
486, 510, 542, 576, 577, 588,
599, 601
bride, 8, 10, 93, 127, 299, 323,
379, 447, 480, 488, 499
Burgon, 354, 355
calamities, 135, 494
Caleb, 56, 67, 69, 92-94, 97, 99,
100, 102, 153, 176
Calvary, 27, 31, 36, 37, 211, 273,
338, 344, 347, 357, 409, 430,
439, 445, 467, 482, 486, 509,
517, 524, 533, 568, 593, 622
camp, 29, 30, 38, 39, 41, 42, 49,
55, 57, 64, 67, 69, 71, 80, 81,
83, 103, 141, 161, 340, 355,
514, 613
camping, 69, 70, 549
Canada, 53
cannibalism, 83, 84
Capernaum, 498
careful, 2, 7, 90, 94, 102, 104,
105, 195, 239, 313, 333, 338,
360, 362, 390, 409, 410, 448,
478, 500, 509
Cedarville College, 574
chaplain, 52, 128, 180, 337

Chaplain Waite, 128
cherubim, 27, 147
Chicago, 302, 303, 352, 590
Christ Jesus, 103, 231, 567, 584,
588
Christophany, 11
cigarettes, 85
circumstances, 18, 43, 82, 86, 92,
123, 144, 153, 159, 163, 188,
190, 200, 209, 213, 220, 264,
280, 295, 299, 344, 430, 435,
490, 493, 540, 548, 570, 585,
594
Clayton Van Sanborn, 576
Cleveland, 298, 481, 500, 512,
517, 566, 574
cloud, 52, 53, 70, 147, 156, 247,
272, 343, 384, 408, 423, 442
Collingswood, 26, 53, 259, 337
colophon, 558
compromise, 98, 107, 150
concubine, 4, 153, 181
confidence, 103, 130, 335, 336,
558, 584
confusion, 3, 9, 53, 82, 103, 135,
143, 218, 270, 283, 334, 367,
384, 448, 508, 533, 547, 585,
589
Corpus Christi, Texas, 52, 594
corruption, 172, 233, 239, 350,
464
counsel, 39, 47, 90, 109, 126, 183,
248, 262, 270, 272, 297, 308,
314, 364, 365, 367, 577, 604
courage, 57, 71, 165, 188, 199,
200, 253, 255, 341, 355, 356,
386, 564
covenant, 73, 109, 137, 183, 187,
215, 221, 239, 240, 281, 538,
583
creation, 245, 248, 328, 331, 378,
479, 486, 572
creator, 330
cremation, 167
Crete, 555, 599

ABOUT THE AUTHOR

Her Experiences. Saved since childhood, Yvonne has years of walking with the Lord Jesus Christ on the "narrow way" in the good and bad times of daily Christian living. She has written,

"I desired from girlhood to go where God wanted me to go. One thing was certain, 'staying with the stuff,'—being a mother and wife, was my life's work!"

She looks at life through the eyes of a mature, godly woman, having experienced personal, physical, emotional, and spiritual battles. Many of her private, personal crises and convictions are reflected on the printed page—as well as heard devotionally from a speaker's platform. These personal feelings and experiences contribute to making the portrayals of FANNY CROSBY and FRANCES HAVERGAL "real" to her audience.

Her Education. Mrs. Waite and her husband graduated from Berea High School in 1945. In 1948, she graduated from the Moody Bible Institute, the same year Dr. Waite received his baccalaureate degree from the University of Michigan. In 1996, she was given an honorary Doctor of Humanities degree by the Great Plains Baptist Divinity School in Sioux Falls, South Dakota. Even though she is a graduate of the Moody Bible Institute, along with other studies, Yvonne feels that her greatest educational enrichment has been that of being married to her husband. Dr. and Mrs. Waite became husband and wife in 1948. Her husband's knowledge and wisdom has influenced her life through his teaching and godly insights. Also the early training and example of her parents in a Bible-believing home taught invaluable lessons. Now that she is the mother of adult children, she has found satisfaction in their wisdom and Biblical leadership, too, as well as the invaluable lessons learned from their spouses.

Her Husband. The Waites were married on August 27, 1948, in a small independent Baptist church then bordering the Cleveland Hopkins International Airport near Berea, Ohio. Dr. Waite graduated from the University of Michigan with a B.A. in Classical Greek and Latin; from the Dallas Theological seminary with a Th.M. and Th.D. in New Testament Greek and Bible; from the Southern Methodist University with an M. A. in Speech; and from Purdue University with a Ph.D. in Public Address. He is the founder and director of **THE BIBLE FOR TODAY, INC.,** as well as being the president of **THE DEAN BURGON SOCIETY** since its founding in 1978. One of her husband's books is the well-received *DEFENDING THE KING JAMES BIBLE* **(BFT #1594-P @ $12.00 + $7.00 S&H)**. This was the first of many, other books defending the King James Bible and its underlying Hebrew, Aramaic, and Greek Words that he has written.

Her Writing. Since January, 1974, Mrs. Waite had penned a column in the *BIBLE FOR TODAY NEWSREPORT,* called "FROM THE TENT DOOR" until it ceased publication. Through this column she was able to speak to women about issues of the day, Scriptural truths, and "women things." Years ago Yvonne was published in the REGULAR BAPTIST PRESS, adult Sunday School take-home papers; and recently in a church-sponsored digest. She said, "It was fun while it lasted!" Since June of 1986, she has authored a monthly newsletter called *The BFT UPDATE* which is sent out around the world into **BFT-LAND**. She chats about places, people, convictions, books, articles, and tracts that Dr. Waite has written, as well as the Bible teaching meetings where Dr. Waite preaches.

Her Variety. The Waites are the parents of five adult children (four sons and one daughter) and have eight grandchildren and eleven great grandchildren as of this writing. Their second-born son, David, went Home to be with the Lord April, 2008. He is greatly missed. Yvonne has followed her husband where he has followed the Lord as a student's wife, a Navy chaplain's wife, a pastor's wife, a teacher's wife, and the wife of the writer, editor, radio speaker & publisher of *THE BIBLE FOR TODAY NEWSREPORT, and* its daily & weekly radio broadcasts.

She has supported her as he founded and led the Dean Burgon Society for over three decades.

Her Travel. As a couple, Dr. and Mrs. Waite have traveled to Liberia, Sierra Leone, Ivory Coast in West Africa, to Singapore, Japan, Taiwan, Korea, to Switzerland, France, Holland, England, Northern Ireland, to Israel, Jordan, Egypt, Japan, Taiwan, and Hawaii, as well as dozens of other states in the United States and into several provinces of Canada.

Her Ministries. Mrs. Waite has taught the Bible to a whole age-spectrum—from nursery through adolescents to adult women's classes. In years past, she taught Bible clubs of forty or fifty children in her home as well as leading two Junior-church choirs. It has been her privilege to speak at women's meetings, mother and daughter banquets, Bible classes, etc. As of 2010, Mrs. Waite has presented "A TRIBUTE TO FANNY CROSBY" more than 300 times as well as scores of Frances Havergal presentations. Her readers may know her through the *Bible For Today Update*, a letter which is sent monthly to contributors to the BFT ministry. Her radio program, *Just For Women*, is heard by many, not only by radio, but also around the world by means of the Internet. For many years, she was the Bible For Today's videographer and has made hundreds of videos of her husband's teaching and that of others also.

Her Blending. It has been said of Yvonne Waite's portrayal of Fanny Crosby in "THE TRIBUTE TO FANNY CROSBY" that it is as if the "First Lady of Gospel Songs" were in the very room. Her blending together of the two personalities— that of the sightless song writer and that of the actress—results in a dramatic presentation which captures the hearts of the people.

Her Presentations. In 1978, at the invitation of her church's music director, Yvonne studied, wrote, and caught the joyful spirit of blind Frances Jane Crosby. Also in May of 1986, she researched the life of the devotional, English poet and hymnist, the frail Frances Ridley Havergal—one of Fanny Crosby's contemporaries. "THE PORTRAIT OF FRANCES HAVERGAL" has been also well received. Complimenting Mrs. Waite's unique monologues, in both presentations, is the professional narration of her husband, Pastor D. A. Waite, Th.D., Ph.D.

Her Compositions. Her "HUSBAND LOVING LESSONS" covers more than 287 pages, and gives practical application from God's marriage manual, the Bible. Her work was a result of teaching women in her local area the subject of marriage. Recently Mrs. Waite has written *My Daily Bible Blessings From My Daily Bible Reading.* It teaches, comforts, and reflects on life for the Biblical education and edification for all women and their children.

Another study written for women by Mrs. Waite is "FOR AND ABOUT WOMEN" which is a manual of four in-depth, original studies about Sarah, Hannah, Lydia, and Mary Magdalene. Her play called "THE EVE OF CHRISTMAS" is a drama bringing Adam and Eve back to our present century, searching for the Christ-child amidst the commercialism of Christmas. It was presented to a large Christian High School in Maryland, and to a large Bible-believing Church in New Jersey, with convicting impact.

Another Bible study, in written form, is called "THINGS CALLED LOVE," which covers in 56 pages—three chapters of original writing—a Biblical definition of what love is and what love is not. *"REFLECTIONS OF A DAUGHTER"* is a gracious tribute to Yvonne's mother, Gertrude Sanborn, which tells of the first days after her mother's death; and continues into the example, consecration, and purity taught by her mother which was spiritually planted in Yvonne's life and grounded into the life of Yvonne's daughter.

Two other booklets are available. The first is entitled "WITHIN THE BORDERS OF OUR LIVES" (Psalm 16:6) It tells about how the times, trials, and temptations of a woman's life are revealed as her "pleasant places." The second booklet is called "MARRIAGE DEFRAUDING AND OTHER MATTERS ESPECIALLY FOR WOMEN" is a series of published articles concerning marriage and the proper deportment for a Christian woman. There is also a "STUDY ON RUTH" which was given in West Africa as well as Singapore. (All of the above and other Bible & devotional subjects are available upon request from the **BFT**.) BOTH of the portrayals are not only in audio-tape form but are on video, as well as other talks by Mrs. Waite which may be ordered from the **BIBLE FOR TODAY.**

Her Impact. Teaching women the verities of their Faith has been Yvonne's pleasure. Her series titled "HUSBAND-LOVING LESSONS" has awakened many a married woman "to walk within her house with a perfect heart." (Psalm 101:2b) Her talk on "THOSE PESKY 'THEE'S' AND `THOU'S'" is well received. She was the first person to reveal in print the homosexuality of one of the NIV language consultants, not only by writing and speaking about Virginia Mollenkott, but also interviewing her personally. This was before this lesbian was officially "out of the closet"!

Her Assessment. It has been said of Yvonne Waite's writing that it shows the curiosity of a child, the frankness of an adolescent, the humor of a comedienne, the sarcasm of a philosopher, the truth of a prophet, the wisdom of a sage, and the beauty of a poet. The thrust of her ministry is to be herself with no pretense, to be the genuine person and use the personality which God has given her—not a copycat of anyone. When God asked her, as He did Moses many years ago, "What is that in thine hand?" (Exodus 4:2), Yvonne desired to use what she found there for God's glory. Thus, in emptying her hand into His, Yvonne Sanborn Waite has found a pen. Thus it became her duty, with beauty, to use that discovery and penetrate hearts with words to thousands all over the world!

According to the Scripture, Mrs. Waite, born in 1927, feels that she is in the "bonus" years of her life (Psalm 90:10), and her desire is to serve the Lord Jesus Christ in every way He leads before she *"flies away"* to Heaven.

"Casting all your care upon Him, for He careth for you."

(1 Peter 5:7)

Other Selected Materials Available To Order—You Can Order Them By Name Or Number At: BFT@BibleForToday.org, Or By Phoning 856-854-4453 Or 1-800-John 3:16 (564-6316)

Special Books & Materials
By Yvonne S. Waite
If you need the audio cassettes converted to a CD, please let us know.

Husband-Loving Lessons (BFT #3488 @ $20.00 + $7.00 S&H)

My Daily Bible Blessings (BFT #4009 @ $30.00 + $7.00 S&H)

With Tears In My Heart (BFT #3196 @ $25.00 + $7.00 S&H)

Reflections of a Daughter (BFT #1949-P @ 2.00 + $1.00 S&H)

Within the Borders of Our Lives (BFT #2998 @ $2.00 + $1.00 S&H)

Marriage Defrauding & Other Matters Especially For Women (BFT #2868 $2.00 + $1.00 S&H)

The Day David Died (Compiled by his mother) (BFT #DWW @ $3.00 + $2.00 S&H)

Just For Women Radio Messages see the following LINK:
http://www.sermonaudio.com/search.asp?SpeakerOnly=true&currSection=sermonsspeaker&Keyword=Yvonne%5eSanborn%5eWaite,%5eD.Hum.

Various BFT UPDATES see the following LINK:
http://www.biblefortoday.org/idx_Pages/idx_news_updates.htm

Yvonne S. Waite's Materials With Bible For Today (BFT) Numbers

Mrs. Waite's papers, articles, booklets, audio and video messages: All these can be ordered by number on the Web Page (www.BibleForToday.org) or by phoning with your credit card (**856-854-4452 or 1-800-John 3:16 (564-6316)**). **Please add Shipping and Handling with your order**. On this list, sometimes there are items with the same number. But notice, there are articles with pages, there are scripts, there are audio cassettes, and there are video cassettes (VCR).

Cassettes ##0316--0934

0316 Cassette @ $4.00 *Sara--Where Are You?* By Yvonne S. Waite

0412 Cassette @ $4.00 *God's Liberated Woman* By Yvonne S. Waite

0463 163pp. @ $16.00 *Husband-Loving Lessons* By Yvonne S. Waite

0513 Cassette @ $4.00 *Mother's Day Melodies* By Yvonne S. Waite

0608 Cassette @ $4.00 *Tribute To Fanny Crosby (A Dramatic/Musical Play)* By Yvonne S. Waite

0608BROCH 2pp. @ $2.00 *Tribute To Fanny Crosby, A (Brochure for the Tribute)* By Yvonne S. Waite

0608SCR 30pp. @ $3.00 *Tribute To Fanny Crosby, A (Script for #608 Tape)* Yvonne S. Waite

0608VCR @ $15.00 *Tribute To Fanny Crosby (A Dramatic/Musical Play)* By Yvonne S. Waite

0623 5pp. @ $2.00 *Mandates For Marriage--68 Hints For Women* By Yvonne S. Waite

0635 Cassette @ $4.00 *Marriage As A Ministry* By Yvonne S. Waite

0683 22pp. @ $3.00 *The Eve Of Christmas (Script For Dramatic Play)* By Yvonne S. Waite

0684 Cassette @ $4.00 *The Eve Of Christmas* (Cassette To Go With #683) By Yvonne S. Waite

0697 Cassette @ $4.00 *Interview With Pro-Lesbian Virginia Mollenkott* By Yvonne S. Waite

0721 70pp. @ $7.00 *For And About Women Waite* By Yvonne S. Waite

0806 Cassette @ $4.00 *The King's Daughters* By Yvonne S. Waite

0815 Cassette @ $4.00 *Two Miracles For Magdala* By Yvonne S. Waite

0934 Cassette @ $4.00 *Numbering Our Days As Women* By Yvonne S. Waite

Cassettes ##1079--1850

1079 Cassette @ $4.00 *Zacharias, Mary, & The Angel & Studying The Bible* By Yvonne S. Waite

1177 Cassette @ $4.00 *Memories Of 60 Years Of Marriage--Sanborn's 60th* By Yvonne S. Waite

1202 Cassette @ $4.00 *What Happens During Cremation? Interview* By Yvonne S. Waite

1231 Cassette @ $4.00 *Women Who Influenced Moses* By Yvonne S. Waite

1249/1-7, 7 Cassettes @ $21.00 *Husband-Loving Lessons On Tape (For Wives)* By Yvonne S. Waite

1286 23pp. @ $2.00 *Ordained Adulterers & Other Marriage Topics-Tent Door* By Yvonne S. Waite

1313 Cassettes @ $4.00 *Focusing On Friends* By Yvonne S. Waite

1341/P 56pp + Cassette @ $7.00 *Things Called Love--3 Talks To Women* By Yvonne S. Waite

1341/1-2 Cassette @ $7.00 *Things Called Love--3 Talks To Women* By Yvonne S. Waite

1341VCR @ $15.00 *Things Called Love--3 Talks To Women* By Yvonne S. Waite

1377 Cassette @ $4.00 Single, Sexual, & Sanctified--A Talk For Women By Yvonne S. Waite

1377-P 134pp. @ $13.00 *Single, Sexual, & Sanctified--A Talk For Women* By Yvonne S. Waite

1378 Cassette @ $4.00 *Some Things Called Love--Three Talks To Women* By Yvonne S. Waite

1403/1-3, 3 Cassettes @ $9.00 *Dean Burgon Society '86 Women's Meeting* By Yvonne S. Waite and others.

1417/SCPT 26pp. @ $2.50 Take *My Life--A Portrait Of Frances Ridley Havergal* By Yvonne S. Waite

1417TP Cassette @ $4.00 *Take My Life--A Portrait Of Frances Ridley Havergal* By Yvonne S. Waite

1417VCR @ $15.00 *Take My Life--A Portrait Of Frances Ridley Havergal* By Yvonne S. Waite

1434/1-4, 4 Cassettes @ $12.00 *Husband-Loving Lessons (4 Cassettes)--For Women* By Yvonne S. Waite

1447 Cassette +6pp. @ *$5.00 Music Of Easter (Cassette + Original Script)* By Yvonne S. Waite

1739/6 Cassette @ $4.00 *New KJV--A Danger To Our Children & Devotions* By Yvonne S. Waite

1745V-W VCR $15.00 *Ruth--Important Lessons For Liberian Women (8/89)* By Yvonne S. Waite

1751/1-3, 3 Cassettes @ $9.00 *Sarah's Significance--Talks To The Women Of Liberia* By Yvonne S. Waite

1751VCR @ $15.00 *Sarah's Significance--Talks To Liberian Women (8/89)* By Yvonne S. Waite

1848/7 Cassette @ $4.00 *Daughter's Reflections On Her Mother-- Gertrude G. Sanborn* By Yvonne S. Waite

1848/VCR @ $15.00 *Daughter's Reflections On Her Mother--Gertrude G. Sanborn* By Yvonne Waite

1848/2 Cassette @ $4.00 *Take My Life--A Portrait Of Frances Ridley Havergal* By Yvonne S. Waite

1848-P 14pp. @ $2.00 *Reflections of a Daughter--A Tribute to Gertrude Sanborn Waite* By Yvonne S. Waite

1850/6-P 7pp. @ $2.00 *How "Ye" And "Thee" Help Me--A Worksheet* By Yvonne S. Waite

1850/6 Cassette @ $4.00 *How "Ye" And "Thee" Help Me--Pesky Thee's & Thou's* By Yvonne S. Waite

Cassettes ##2002--2500

2002/6 Cassette @ $4.00 *Dean Burgon Society '91 Women's Meeting* By Yvonne S. Waite

2045 Cassette @ $4.00 *Conversation About Fanny Crosby--An Interview* By Yvonne S. Waite

2101 12pp. @ $2.00+C925 *Independent Baptist Fellowship Report—*

1991 By Yvonne S. Waite

2104TP Cassette @ $4.00 *Israel Trip With Dr. & Mrs. Waite (8/92)-- Sound Track* By Yvonne S. Waite & Dr. D. A. Waite

2104VCR @ $15.00 *Israel Trip With Dr. & Mrs. Waite (8/92)* By Yvonne S. Waite & Dr. D. A. Waite

2182/6 Cassette @ $4.00 *Dr. Logsdon's Change From NASV & Devotional Talks* By Yvonne S. Waite and others.

2271 23pp @ $3.00 Ruth—*A Model For Lovely Ladies (For the Women of Singapore)* By Yvonne S. Waite

2273/1-2 Cassette @ $4.00 *Ruth--A Model For Lovely Ladies--Studies For Women* By Yvonne S. Waite

2273VCR @ $15.00 *Ruth--A Model For Lovely Ladies--Studies For Women* By Yvonne S. Waite

2319 15pp. @ $2.00 *Lesbian Mollenkott (On NIV Committee) Out of Closet* By Yvonne S. Waite

2410/1-3, 3 Cassettes @ $9.00 *Ruth--A Model for Lovely Ladies (In Sierra Leone, W. Africa)* By Yvonne S. Waite

2410-P 14pp. @ $2.00 *Ruth—A Model for Lovely Ladies (For the women in Singapore)*

2490/8 Cassette @ $4.00 *Lesbian Virginia Mollenkott Exposed & the NIV* By Yvonne S. Waite

2491 Cassette @ $4.00 *Lesbian Virginia Mollenkott--Her Lesbianism & Part in the NIV* By Yvonne S. Waite

Cassettes ##2500--3342

2500 Cassette @ $4.00 *Beautiful Thee's & Thou's vs. the Version Changes* By Yvonne S. Waite

2508 12pp. @ $2.00 *As I Saw It--IBFNA'94 Report* By Yvonne S. Waite

2584/1-2, 2 Cassettes @ $7.00 *Ninety-Four Favorite Hymns for Pastor Joah in Liberia* By Yvonne S. Waite & Dick Carroll

2617 6pp. @ $2.00 *Especially for Women--"Impious Irreverence"* By Yvonne S. Waite

2673/1-2, 2 Cassettes @ $7.00 *Husband-Loving Lessons to Women in Indiana* By Yvonne S. Waite

2673VCR @ $15.00 *Marriage--Two Cars in One Garage--for Women* By Yvonne S. Waite

2728 Cassette @ $4.00 *Portrait of Frances Havergal--at Williamsport, PA* By Yvonne S. Waite

2748 Cassette @ $4.00 *The Lines of My Life--Advice for Kansas BBF Ministers' Wives* By Yvonne S. Waite

2802 Cassette @ $4.00 *The Borders of our Lives & the Pleasant Places* By Yvonne S. Waite

2839 12pp. @ $2.00 *Who Was Dean John William Burgon?* By Yvonne S. Waite

2892 Cassette @ $4.00 *King James 21 & Dr. Ted Letis Analyzed for DBS Women* By Yvonne S. Waite

2892-P 122pp. @ $12.00 *King James 21 & Dr. Ted Letis Analyzed for DBS Women* By Yvonne S. Waite

2918 Cassette @ $4.00 *Oprah Winfrey Into Spiritism?--Disturbing Quotes* By Yvonne S. Waite 2931 7pp. @ $2.00 *Oprah, Into Spiritism?--Remembering Your Spirit* By Yvonne Sanborn Waite

2932VCR @ $15.00 *Husband-Loving Lessons--Marriage Submission, Sex, & Scripture* By Yvonne S. Waite

2939 6pp. @ $2.00 *Killers at Columbine High* By Yvonne S. Waite

2949 19pp. @ $2.00 *Don't Tell Me You're Changing to the New King James?* By Yvonne S. Waite

2961/1 Cassette @ $4.00 *Lessons From Sarah* By Yvonne S. Waite

2986 Cassette @ $4.00 *Duties of Wives: Respect your Husbands & Be Friends Together* By Yvonne S. Waite

2998 44pp. @ $2.00 *Within the Borders of Our Lives--Our Pleasant Places (Psalm 16:6),* By Yvonne S. Waite

3342 22pp. @ $3.00 *A Woman's Heart--The Secret To A Happy Home* By Yvonne S. Waite

Yvonne S. Waite's Materials Without BFT Numbers

November, 1983 6pp @ $1.50 *An Ode To Virgil Henry Waite* By Yvonne S. Waite

February, 1985 2pp @ $1.50 *What Is A Friend?* By Yvonne S. Waite

July, 1987 2pp @ $1.50 *Words Often Used In Textual Talk* By Yvonne S. Waite

July, 1993 14pp @ $2.00 *Write On My Heart Every Word* How Fanny Crosby Used the King James Bible In Her Hymns 14 pp @ $2.00 By Yvonne S. Waite

November, 1996 12pp @ $2.00 *From My House To Yours— Thanksgiving Thoughts* 12pp. @ $2.00 By Yvonne S. Waite January, 1989

July, 1998 92 pp @ $10.00 *Critique of the KJ-21 Bible—A Comparative Word Study* By Yvonne S. Waite

Undated 2pp @ $1.50 *Major Westcott and Hort Changes In The Textus Receptus* By Yvonne S. Waite

Undated 3pp @ $1.50 *My Caution and Concerns For The Single Woman* By Yvonne S. Waite

A Few Select Books
By Pastor D. A. Waite, Th.D., Ph.D.

Question & Answer Books ##1-4 $14.00 each + $7.00 S&H

    #1 BFT #3309 @ $14.00 + $7.00 S&H

    #2 BFT #3473 @ $14.00 + $7.00 S&H

    #3 BFT #3482 @ $14.00 + $7.00 S&H

    #4 BFT #3494 @ $14.00 + $7.00 S&H

The Superior Foundation of the King James Bible (BFT #3384 @ $10.00 + $7.00 S&H)
Defending the King James Bible (BFT #1594 @ $12.00 + $7.00 S&H)
Foes of the King James Bible Refuted (BFT #2777 @ $10.00 + $7.00 S&H)
Preaching Verse By Verse Books by Pastor D. A. Waite, Th.D., Ph.D.

1. *1 Peter–Preaching Verse By Verse* (BFT #2945 @ $14.00 + $7.00 S&H)
2. *Galatians--Preaching Verse By Verse* (BFT #2955 @ $14.00 + $7.00 S&H)
3. *Ephesians--Preaching Verse By Verse* (BFT #2973 @ $14.00 + $7.00 S&H)
4. *Philippians--Preaching Verse By Verse* (BFT #2977 @ $14.00 + $7.00 S&H)
5. *Colossians* & Philemon--*Preaching Verse By Verse* (BFT #2988 @ $14.00 + $7.00 S&H
6. *Romans--Preaching Verse By Verse* (BFT #2906 @ $25.00 + $7.00 S&H)
7. *1 Timothy--Preaching Verse By Verse* (BFT #3085 @ $14.00 + $7.00 S&H)
8. *2 Timothy--Preaching Verse By Verse* (BFT #3105 @ $14.00 + $7.00 S&H)

CPSIA information can be obtained
at www.ICGtesting.com
Printed in the USA
FFOW02n1342030114
2916FF